# PUBLICATIONS

## OF THE
### STATE DEPARTMENT OF ARCHIVES AND HISTORY

# THE PAPERS OF
# WILLIAM ALEXANDER GRAHAM

# The Papers of
# William Alexander Graham

———

Edited by

J. G. DE ROULHAC HAMILTON

———

VOLUME THREE

1845-1850

RALEIGH

STATE DEPARTMENT OF ARCHIVES AND HISTORY

1960

iii

# CONTENTS

v

# PREFACE

This is the third volume in a series of approximately seven volumes containing the Papers of William Alexander Graham. The first volume was published in 1957, and the second was published in 1959. Other volumes will follow this one.

Dr. J. G. de Roulhac Hamilton, professor emeritus of the Department of History of the University of North Carolina, has edited three other series for publication by this Department. He also has material ready for the printer which will be published by the Department as soon as funds become available.

William A. Graham was a Whig in politics. He served in the North Carolina General Assembly, as Governor, United States Senator, Secretary of the Navy, and Confederate State Senator. The material in this volume covers the period when he served as Governor of the State.

October 1, 1960                    D. L. CORBITT, *Head*
Raleigh, N. C.                     Division of Publications

# LIST OF LETTERS

## Letters Written by William A. Graham Printed in this Volume

| Place | Date | Written to |
|---|---|---|
| Raleigh | Feb. 6, 1845 | Miss Mary W. Burke |
| Raleigh | Feb. 8, 1845 | François Xavier Martin |
| Raleigh | Feb. 8, 1845 | David L. Swain |
| Raleigh | April 13, 1845 | James W. Bryan |
| Raleigh | April 16, 1845 | Samuel S. Phelps |
| Raleigh | May 5, 1845 | James W. Bryan |
| Raleigh | June 9, 1845 | James W. Bryan |
| Raleigh | July 2, 1845 | David L. Swain |
| Raleigh | July 31, 1845 | David L. Swain |
| Raleigh | Aug. 8, 1845 | David L. Swain |
| Raleigh | Aug. 26, 1845 | David L. Swain |
| Raleigh | Sept. 2, 1845 | David L. Swain |
| Raleigh | Oct. 4, 1845 | Messrs. Gales & Seaton |
| Raleigh | Oct. 22, 1845 | Edward W. Johnston |
| Raleigh | Nov. 22, 1845 | William H. Foote |
| Raleigh | Jan. 17, 1846 | Cherokee County Committee |
| Raleigh | Jan. 24, 1846 | James W. Bryan |
| Raleigh | Feb. 23, 1846 | James W. Bryan |
| Raleigh | April 19, 1846 | James W. Bryan |
| Waynesville | July 4, 1846 | Michael Francis |
| Raleigh | Aug. 9, 1846 | James W. Bryan |
| Raleigh | Dec. 1, 1846 | James W. Bryan |
| Raleigh | March 20, 1847 | John A. Fagg |
| Raleigh | March 27, 1847 | Daniel Webster |
| Raleigh | March 27, 1847 | David L. Swain |
| Raleigh | May 4, 1847 | James W. Bryan |
| | June 21, 1847 | Robert Nash Ogden |
| Hillsboro | Oct. 10, 1847 | James Graham |
| Raleigh | Jan. 11, 1848 | James W. Bryan |
| Raleigh | April 5, 1848 | James Graham |
| Raleigh | June 9, 1848 | James Graham |
| Raleigh | July 13, 1848 | James W. Bryan |
| Raleigh | Nov. 9, [1848] | James W. Bryan |
| Raleigh | Dec. 5, 1848 | James W. Bryan |
| Hillsboro | Jan. 13, 1849 | Hillsboro Committee |
| Hillsboro | Aug. 13, 1849 | Washington C. Kerr |
| | | Henry Hardie |
| | | Samuel E. Whitfield |
| Hillsboro | Aug. 26, 1849 | James W. Bryan |
| Hillsboro | March 24, 1850 | James Graham |
| Greensborough | July 19, 1850 | James Graham |
| Hillsboro | July 24, 1850 | James Graham |
| Hillsborough | July 25, 1850 | Millard Fillmore |
| Washington [D. C.] | Aug. 13, 1850 | Susan Washington Graham |
| Washington [D. C.] | Aug. 20, 1850 | Susan Washington Graham |
| Washington [D. C.] | Aug. 25, 1850 | James Graham |
| [Washington, D. C.] | Aug. 28, 1850 | Daniel Webster |
| Washington [D. C.] | Sept. 25, 1850 | James W. Bryan |
| Washington [D. C.] | Oct. 1, 1850 | James W. Bryan |
| Washington [D. C.] | Oct. 17, 1850 | Susan Washington Graham |
| [Washington, D. C.] | Oct. 29, 1850 | George C. Read |
| Washington [D. C.] | Dec. 21, 1850 | C. N. Stetson |

# Letters Written to William A. Graham Printed in this Volume

| Place | Date | Written by |
|---|---|---|
| Boston | Jan. 8, 1845 | Daniel Webster |
| Memphis, Tennessee | Jan. 10, 1845 | James Seawell |
| Chapel Hill | Jan. 17, 1845 | David L. Swain |
| At Mrs. White's | Jan. 24, 1845 | David L. Swain |
| New Orleans, Louisiana | Jan. 24, 1845 | Edmund Pendleton Gaines |
| Chapel Hill | Jan. 31, 1845 | David L. Swain |
| Washington [D. C.] | Feb. 5, 1845 | Kenneth Rayner |
| [Washington, D. C.] | Feb. 10, 1845 | Daniel M. Barringer |
| Agency Office | Feb. 12, 1845 | Jacob Siler |
| New Orleans [Louisiana] | March 20, 1845 | James Graham |
| Columbus, Mississippi | March 20, 1845 | Richard T. Brownrigg |
| New Orleans [Louisiana] | March 29, 1845 | François Xavier Martin |
| Middlebury, Vermont | April 2, 1845 | Samuel S. Phelps |
| Nauvoo, Illinois | April 25, 1845 | Brigham Young |
| Hillsborough | May 5, 1845 | John W. Norwood |
| Marion, Alabama | May 12, 1845 | Mary W. Burke |
| Chapel Hill | June 9, 1845 | David L. Swain |
| Newbern | June 16, 1845 | James W. Bryan |
| Chapel Hill | July 12, 1845 | David L. Swain |
| Greensboro | July 17, 1845 | Ralph Gorrell |
| Pleasant Hill, Kentucky | Aug. 9, 1845 | G. R. Runyon and David French |
| Rutherfordton | Aug. 19, 1845 | James Graham |
| Chapel Hill | Aug. 22, 1845 | David L. Swain |
| Waxsaw Settlement | Aug. 27, 1845 | Samuel H. Walkup |
| Chapel Hill | Aug. 28, 1845 | Elisha Mitchell |
| Washington [D. C.] | Oct. 11, 1845 | Edward W. Johnston |
| Greensboro | Oct. 15, 1845 | John M. Morehead |
| Concord | Oct. 22, 1845 | James W. Osborne |
| Raleigh | Oct. 30, 1845 | William Henry Foote |
| Chapel Hill | Oct. 28, 1845 | David L. Swain |
| Marion, McDowell County | Nov. 4, 1845 | John Gray Bynum |
| Abrams Plains [N. C.] | Nov. 7, 1845 | James W. Downey |
| Romney, Virginia | Nov. 19, 1845 | William H. Foote |
| Charlotte | Dec. 9, 1845 | James W. Osborne |
| Washington [D. C.] | Dec. 18, 1845 | James Graham |
| Washington | Jan. 4, 1846 | James Graham |
| Chapel Hill | Jan. 6, 1846 | David L. Swain |
| Agency Office for the collection of Cherokee County | Jan. 7, 1846 | Jacob Siler |
| Plymouth | Jan. 8, 1846 | Hezekiah G. Spruill |
| Washington [D. C.] | Jan. 15, 1846 | John D. Hawkins |
| [Washington, D. C.] | Feb. 2, 1846 | James Graham |
| Newbern | Feb. 8, 1846 | James W. Bryan |
| [Washington, D. C.] | Feb. 20, 1846 | James Graham |
| [Washington, D. C.] | March 13, 1846 | James Graham |
| Oxford | March 29, 1846 | Robert B. Gilliam |
| Tuskegee, Alabama | March 30, 1846 | Theodore W. Brevard |
| [Washington, D. C.] | April 7, 1846 | James Graham |
| Edenton | April 9, 1846 | Augustus Moore |
| [Washington, D.C.] | April 18, 1846 | James Graham |
| Newbern | May 9, 1846 | James W. Bryan |
| Wilmington | May 17, 1846 | Alexander MacRae |
| Rossville, Cherokee County | May 23, 1846 | N. G. Harrell |
| New Orleans | May 26, 1846 | James A. King |
| Lincolnton | May 28, 1846 | John Gray Bynum |
| Oxford | May 28, 1846 | Robert B. Gilliam |
| Washington [D. C.] | June 3, 1846 | Edward Stanly |

| | | |
|---|---|---|
| Asheville | June 11, 1846 | Nicholas W. Woodfin |
| Milton | June 15, 1846 | Charles N. B. Evans |
| Asheville | June 20, 1846 | Burgess S. Gaither |
| Raleigh | July 10, 1846 | Charles L. Hinton |
| [Washington, D. C.] | July 29, 1846 | James Graham |
| Greensboro | Aug. 8, 1846 | John A. Gilmer |
| Palmyra | Aug. 8, 1846 | Samuel F. Patterson |
| Newbern | Aug. 9, 1846 | James W. Bryan |
| Murphy | Aug. 11, 1846 | Felix Axley |
| Tuskeegee [Alabama] | Aug. 18, 1846 | Theodore W. Brevard |
| Charlotte | Aug. 30, 1846 | James W. Osborne |
| Rutherfordton | Sept. 15, 1846 | James Graham |
| New York | Nov. 16, 1846 | Benson J. Lossing |
| [Washington, D. C.] | Nov. 16, 1846 | William L. Marcy |
| Romney [Virginia] | Nov. 17, 1846 | William Henry Foote |
| Washington [D. C.] | Nov. 18, 1846 | George Talcott |
| Raleigh | Nov. 19, 1846 | Gaston H. Wilder |
| Elizabeth City | Nov. 20, 1846 | J. Q. Perkins |
| Wilmington | Nov. 23, 1846 | Louis H. Marsteller |
| Dockery's Store | Nov. 23, 1846 | Alfred Dockery |
| Raleigh | Nov. 23, 1846 | Andrew Joyner |
| Yale College | Dec. 11, 1846 | Denison Olmsted |
| [Washington, D. C.] | Dec. 18, 1846 | Daniel M. Barringer |
| Goldsboro | Dec. 20, 1846 | S. A. Andrews |
| Washington [D. C.] | Jan. 2, 1847 | William B. Lloyd |
| Washington [D. C.] | Jan. 10, 1847 | James Graham |
| [Washington, D. C.] | Jan. 14, 1847 | George E. Badger |
| Washington [D. C.] | Jan. 17, 1847 | James Graham |
| [Washington, D. C.] | Jan. 18, 1847 | Alfred Dockery |
| Hillsboro | Jan. 22, 1847 | Hugh Waddell |
| Greensboro | Jan. 23, 1847 | John A. Gilmer |
| [Washington, D. C.] | Jan. 26, 1847 | Daniel M. Barringer |
| Greensboro | Jan. 27, 1847 | John A. Gilmer |
| Washington [D. C.] | Jan. 31, 1847 | James Graham |
| Wilmington | Feb. 3, 1847 | Shepard K. Nash |
| Oxford | Feb. 10, 1847 | Robert B. Gilliam |
| Washington [D. C.] | Feb. 28, 1847 | James Graham |
| Washington [D. C.] | March 30, 1847 | Daniel Webster |
| Chapel Hill | April 7, 1847 | David L. Swain |
| Fayetteville | April 9, 1847 | E. L. Winslow |
| Chapel Hill | April 20, 1847 | David L. Swain |
| Chapel Hill | April 23, 1847 | David L. Swain |
| Washington [D. C.] | April 24, 1847 | Daniel Webster |
| Kinston | April 30, 1847 | J. C. Washington |
| Fayetteville | May 3, 1847 | John McRae |
| Rutherfordton | May 10, 1847 | James Graham |
| Cottage Home | June 3, 1847 | William W. Morrison |
| Annapolis [Maryland] | June 15, 1847 | James Iredell Waddell |
| Greenville, S. C. | June 18, 1847 | David Reinhardt |
| Cottage Home | July 2, 1847 | Robert Hall Morrison |
| New Orleans | July 8, 1847 | Robert Nash Ogden |
| Brookland [Alabama] | July 28, 1847 | Sophia G. Witherspoon |
| Oxford | Dec. 13, 1847 | Calvin H. Wiley |
| Fayetteville | Dec. 14, 1847 | Edward J. Hale |
| Charlotte | Jan. 7, 1848 | William Johnston |
| Hillsboro | Feb. 26, 1848 | John M. Morehead |
| Mount Sterling | March 5, 1848 | Joseph Allison |
| Sattillo, Mexico | March 6, 1848 | Patrick M. Henry |
| Asheboro | April 8, 1848 | Jonathan Worth |
| Mecklenburg [Tennessee] | April 8, 1848 | James G. M. Ramsey |
| Washington [D. C.] | May, 10, 1848 | Augustine H. Shepperd |
| Chapel Hill | May 13, 1848 | David L. Swain |
| Salisbury | May 17, 1848 | James Madison Leach |

| | | |
|---|---|---|
| Rutherfordton | May 19, 1848 | James Graham |
| Newbern | June 1, 1848 | James W. Bryan |
| Oxford | July 8, 1848 | Robert B. Gilliam |
| [Washington, D. C.] | July 13, 1848 | George E. Badger |
| Granville County | July 17, 1848 | Robert B. Gilliam |
| Greensboro | July 17, 1848 | John M. Morehead |
| Newbern | July 18, 1848 | James W. Bryan |
| Memphis [Tennessee] | July 27, 1848 | George Cavallor Graham |
| Raleigh | July 7, [Aug. 7,] 1848 | William W. Morrison |
| Raleigh | Aug. 8, 1848 | Charles L. Hinton |
| Raleigh | Aug. 14, 1848 | William W. Morrison |
| Raleigh | Aug. 22, 1848 | William W. Morrison |
| Brookland [Alabama] | Oct. 4, 1848 | John R. Witherspoon |
| Wadesboro | Oct. 11, 1848 | James W. Osborne |
| Snow Camp | Oct. 19, 1848 | John Stafford |
| Hillsboro | Nov. 19, 1848 | Hugh Waddell |
| Earhart Place | Nov. 22, 1848 | James Graham |
| Chapel Hill | Nov. 28, 1848 | William H. Battle |
| Wilmington | Dec. 1, 1848 | William E. Anderson |
| [Hillsboro] | Dec. 10, 1848 | Hugh Waddell |
| Cottage Home | Dec. 18, 1848 | Robert Hall Morrison |
| Leaksville | Jan. 5, 1849 | Patrick M. Henry |
| Hillsboro | Jan 12, 1849 | Hillsboro Committee |
| | | Stephen Moore |
| | | Jno. W. Norwood |
| | | Pride Jones |
| | | H. K. Nash |
| | | P. B. Ruffin |
| Raleigh | Jan. 18, 1849 | Giles Mebane |
| Raleigh | Jan. 26, 1849 | Hugh Waddell |
| Raleigh | Jan. 26, 1849 | Charles L. Hinton |
| Leaksville | Jan. 27, 1849 | Patrick M. Henry |
| Charlotte | Feb. 17, 1849 | James W. Osborne |
| St. Augustine [Florida] | Feb. 19, 1849 | George Washington |
| Leaksville | Feb. 24, 1849 | Patrick M. Henry |
| Charlotte | March 20, 1849 | James W. Osborne |
| Fayetteville | April 23, 1849 | Edward J. Hale |
| Chapel Hill | May 11, 1849 | William Mercer Green |
| Raleigh | May 24, 1849 | Charles L. Hinton |
| Norfolk | May 26, 1849 | William Ward |
| Washington [D. C.] | June 1, 1849 | Robert T. Paine |
| Washington [D. C.] | June 6, 1849 | Robert T. Paine |
| [Chapel Hill] | July 29, 1849 | Washington C. Kerr |
| | | Henry Hardie |
| | | Samuel Whitfield |
| Memphis, Tennessee | June 7, 1849 | James Graham |
| Mobile [Alabama] | June 13, 1849 | Richard Lee Fearn |
| Washington [D. C.] | June 14, 1849 | Robert T. Paine |
| [Hillsboro] | July 19, 1849 | Cadwallader Jones |
| St. Augustine [Florida] | July 30, 1849 | George Washington |
| Charlotte | Aug. 1, 1849 | James Graham |
| Chapel Hill | Sept. 10, 1849 | David L. Swain |
| Wake Forest College, Forestville | Sept. 13, 1849 | John B. White |
| Hillsboro | Nov. 11, 1849 | James F. Waddell |
| Fayetteville | Feb. 8, 1850 | Edward J. Hale |
| Ouchiata County, Arkanas | March 20, 1850 | Joseph Montrose Graham |
| [Washington, D. C.] | April 2, 1850 | Edward Stanly |
| Earhart Place | April 21, 1850 | James Graham |
| Alamance | May 1, 1850 | John Newlin |
| Chapel Hill | May 15, 1850 | John M. Morehead |
| Chapel Hill | May 15, 1850 | David L. Swain |
| Chapel Hill | June 20, 1850 | Samuel Field Phillips |

| | | |
|---|---|---|
| [Washington, D. C.] | July 11, 1850 | Augustine H. Shepperd |
| Raleigh | July 14, 1850 | Charles L. Hinton |
| Washington [D. C.] | July 16, 1850 | Augustine H. Shepperd |
| Raleigh | July 17, 1850 | Charles L. Hinton |
| Raleigh | July 18, 1850 | Charles L. Hinton |
| Raleigh | July 20, 1850 | Charles L. Hinton |
| [Washington, D. C.] | July 22, 1850 | Augustine H. Shepperd |
| [Washington, D. C.] | July 22, 1850 | Augustine H. Shepperd |
| | July 22, 1850 | Millard Fillmore |
| Charlotte | July 22, 1850 | James W. Osborne |
| Raleigh | July 24, 1850 | Charles L. Hinton |
| Hillsboro | July 28, 1850 | Hugh Waddell |
| Goldsboro | July 30, 1850 | W. F. S. Alston |
| Washington [D. C.] | Aug. 2, 1850 | Thomas Corwin |
| | Aug. 3, 1850 | Daniel Webster |
| Washington, Pennsylvania | Aug. 3, 1850 | William B. Rose |
| Washington [D. C.] | Aug. 4, 1850 | William Robinson |
| Pittsboro | Aug. 4, 1850 | Maurice Q. Waddell |
| Washington [D. C.] | Aug. 5, 1850 | Friederick Schmidt |
| Arkansas City, Arkansas | Aug. 6, 1850 | J. W. Clay |
| Warrenton Springs, Virginia | Aug. 6, 1850 | William Smith |
| | Aug. 7, 1850 | Millard Fillmore |
| Tuscaloosa [Alabama] | Aug. 7, 1850 | Rufus Haywood |
| Oxford | Aug. 8, 1850 | Robert B. Gilliam |
| Morganton | Aug. 8, [1850] | Frederick Nash |
| Norfolk, Virginia | Aug. 9, 1850 | Joseph F. Battley |
| Earhart Place | Aug. 10, 1850 | James Graham |
| Jefferson Barracks | Aug. 13, 1850 | Richard C. Gatlin |
| Port Tobacco, Maryland | Aug. 18, 1850 | Daniel Jenifer |
| Columbus, Mississippi | Aug. 20, 1850 | Oscar T. Keeler |
| Princeton, Arkansas | Aug. 20, 1850 | P. K. Rounsaville |
| New York | Aug. 21, 1850 | Silas E. Burrows |
| | Aug. 21, 1850 | Winfield Scott |
| Washington [D. C.] | Aug. 22, 1850 | Daniel Webster |
| Raleigh | Aug. 22, 1850 | Charles L. Hinton |
| Nashville, Tennessee | Aug. 24, 1850 | B. R. McKennie & Company |
| Chapel Hill | Aug. 27, 1850 | Elisha Mitchell |
| Washington [D. C.] | Aug. 27, 1850 | John S. Gallaher |
| [Washington, D. C.] | Aug. 28, [1850] | Daniel Webster |
| Hillsboro | Aug. 29, 1850 | William W. Kirkland |
| Chapel Hill | Aug. 30, 1850 | David L. Swain |
| [Washington, D. C.] | Aug. 30, 1850 | Daniel Webster |
| Selma, Alabama | Aug. 31, 1850 | William Seawell |
| [Washington, D. C.] | Sept. 2, 1850 | Daniel C. Goddard |
| [Washington, D. C.] | Sept. 2, 1850 | Daniel Webster |
| Washington [D. C.] | Sept. 3, 1850 | Daniel Webster |
| Wheatlands | Sept. 5, 1850 | James Buchanan |
| Jacksonport [Arkansas] | Sept. 8, 1850 | Joseph Graham Witherspoon |
| Yancyville, Caswell County | Sept. 11, 1850 | James Reid |
| Hillsborough | Sept. 13, 1850 | John Cameron |
| Raleigh | Sept. 16, 1850 | Richard Hines |
| Wilmington | Sept. 18, 1850 | William A. Wright |
| Wilmington | Sept. 18, 1850 | James H. Dickson |
| Columbia, South Carolina | Sept. 20, 1850 | Francis Lieber |
| Halifax | Sept. 20, 1850 | William L. Long |
| Wilmington | Sept. 22, 1850 | Joseph Togno |
| Raleigh | Sept. 23, 1850 | Charles L. Hinton |
| Oxford | Sept. 24, 1850 | Robert B. Gilliam |
| Washington [D. C.] | Sept. 26, 1850 | William D. Porter |
| [Washington, D. C.] | Sept. 26, 1850 | John Macpherson Berrien |
| Washington [D. C.] | Sept. 26, 1850 | David L. Yulee |

| | | |
|---|---|---|
| Cottage Home | Oct. 1, 1850 | Robert Hall Morrison |
| Columbus, Mississippi | Oct. 3, 1850 | Oscar T. Keeler |
| Washington [D. C.] | Oct. 6, 1850 | George S. Bryan |
| Washington [D. C.] | Oct. 7, 1850 | Matthew F. Maury |
| [Washington, D. C.] | Oct. 8, 1850 | Matthew F. Maury |
| Washington [D. C.] | Oct. 9, 1850 | Millard Fillmore |
| Columbia, South Carolina | Oct. 10, 1850 | Francis Lieber |
| Earhart Place | Oct. 13, 1850 | James Graham |
| Raleigh | Oct. 14, 1850 | Richard Hines |
| Washington [D. C.] | Oct. 15, 1850 | Millard Fillmore |
| Oxford | Oct. 15, 1850 | Robert B. Gilliam and James T. Littlejohn |
| Cooperstown | Oct. 16, 1850 | James Fenimore Cooper |
| Windsor | Oct. 18, 1850 | David Outlaw |
| Halifax | Oct. 19, 1850 | William L. Long |
| Saint Louis [Missouri] | Oct. 19, 1850 | F. Knox |
| Charlotte | Oct. 19, 1850 | James W. Osborne |
| Edenton | Oct. 20, 1850 | Robert T. Paine |
| Raleigh | Oct. 21, 1850 | Kenneth Rayner |
| Greensboro | Oct. 24, 1850 | Hugh Waddell |
| Annapolis [Maryland] | Oct. 26, 1850 | C. K. Stribling |
| Redwood [Virginia] | Oct. 27, 1850 | John Strother Pendleton |
| Earhart Place | Oct. 28, 1850 | James Graham |
| Boston [Massachusetts] | Oct. 29, 1850 | "Boston" |
| Lincolnton | Oct. 29, 1850 | Haywood W. Guion |
| | Nov., 1850 | Hugh Waddell |
| New York | Nov. 1, 1850 | Edmund Coskery Bittinger |
| Norfolk [Virginia] | Nov. 5, 1850 | Francis P. Mallory |
| Haw River | Nov. 7, 1850 | William K. Ruffin |
| New York | Nov. 7, 1850 | James W. Simonton |
| Little Bay, Arkansas | Nov. 9, 1850 | Joseph M. Graham |
| Boston [Massachusetts] | Nov. 13, 1850 | Daniel Webster |
| Lincolnton | Nov. 14, 1850 | Haywood W. Guion |
| Oxford | Nov. 21, 1850 | Robert B. Gilliam |
| Philadelphia [Pennsylvania] | Nov. 25, 1850 | James E. Harvey |
| Raleigh | Nov. 29, [1850] | Thomas J. Lemay & Son |
| Sommerville | Dec. 2, 1850 | James P. McRee |
| Raleigh | Dec. 6, 1850 | Charles L. Hinton |
| Raleigh | Dec. 9, 1850 | William Hogan Jones |
| Trenton, New Jersey | Dec. 11, 1850 | Dorothea L. Dix |
| University of Alabama | Dec. 11, 1850 | Basil Manly |
| Washington [D. C.] | Dec. 12, 1850 | Nathan K. Hall |
| Tuscaloosa [Alabama] | Dec. 12, 1850 | Rufus Haywood |
| Marshall, Texas | Dec. 13, 1850 | Edward G. Benners |
| | Dec. 17, 1850 | Edward Stanly |
| Raleigh | Dec. 18, 1850 | Bartholomew F. Moore |
| St. Paul, Minnesota | Dec. 19, 1850 | C. K. Smith |
| Washington [D. C.] | Dec. 23, 1850 | Jackson Morton |
| Hillsboro | Dec. 24, 1850 | Edmund Strudwick |
| Hillsborough | Dec. 27, 1850 | John W. Norwood |
| Hillsboro | Dec. 28, 1850 | William W. Kirkland |
| Greensboro | Dec. 28, 1850 | John M. Morehead |

# Speeches and Other Writings of William A. Graham
## Printed in this Volume

## Miscellaneous Letters Printed in this Volume

## Miscellaneous Documents and Items Printed in this Volume

# SYMBOLS USED TO DESIGNATE DEPOSITORIES OF GRAHAM PAPERS

A.              North Carolina Department of Archives and History

U.              The Southern Historical Collection of the University of North Carolina

U. Bryan Mss.  The Southern Historical Collection of the University of North Carolina

U. Swain Mss.  The Southern Historical Collection of the University of North Carolina

G. P.           Governors' Papers, North Carolina Department of Archives and History

G. L. B.        Governors' Letter Books, North Carolina Department of Archives and History

## Notes on Murphey's
## Historical Writings and Materials[1]

### 1845

---

### History of North Carolina.

---

It seems to have been the author's design to introduce the History of the Colony and State of North Carolina, by a cursory review of the great events, which, since the revival of learning in the fifteenth century, have changed the intellectual character and moral condition of nations. This was conceived necessary to enable the reader to understand the character of the colonists, and the structure, policy, and tendency of that government which they and their posterity have reared. This portion, and this only, of the contemplated work appears to have been partially completed. A manuscript of twenty-five or thirty pages, in the well known, neat, and beautiful hand of the author, is found to contain a brief but glowing sketch of the revival of letters, and science, the effects of their cultivation upon the arts and improvements of men, and of the progress of personal freedom, and civil, political, and religious liberty in all those countries of Europe, from which our own was settled. In this discourse it is asserted, that the principal improvements in Ethical science for the last hundred and fifty years, have been made by the Courts of Justice. "It may be said with confidence (says the author) that the Chancellors, and a few of the Common Law Judges of England, having Lord Mansfield at their head, the Chancellors of France, the Judges of the Supreme Court of the United States, the Chancellors of New York, and a few others, have contributed more to the development and illustration of the principles of Ethics and their proper application to the business and affairs of life, than all the other learned men of the world." Having thus given us a general acquaintance with the

---

[1] Hoyt, W. H., ed., *The Papers of Archibald J. Murphey,* from which the following note is also quoted:
"From the original MS in the possession of Major William A. Graham, commissioner of agriculture. It was probably prepared in 1845 for Gov. Swain's use. Gov. Graham wrote Gov. Swain, July 2nd, 1845, (letter in the possession of the University of N. C.) 'I had expected to see the Murphey papers on a recent visit to Hillsboro,' but Mr. Kirkland, who had charge of them, was absent on his canvass for the clerkship.' "

actual state of the European world at the period when our History commenced, the author appears to have intended to furnish a full and complete narrative from thence downward to the present time. A skeleton of the Colonial History is found among the manuscripts, in which it is divided into Epochs, beginning A. D. 1583.

The 1st.   From the first patent granted to Sir Walter Raleigh, 1584, to his death in 1600.

2nd.   From A. D. 1600 to 1663.

3rd.   From A. D. 1663 to 1712.

4th.   From 1712 to the abolition of the proprietary Government, 1729.

5th.   From the establishment of the regal Government, 1729, to the death of Governor Dobbs, 1765.

6th.   From the latter period to the establishment of Independence.

On the first and second of these periods it is believed that but little new matter had been procured. Whatever accounts may exist besides those already published of the voyages of the agents of Sir Walter Raleigh, and of their attempts to establish a colony on Roanoke Island and its vicinity, are probably locked up in the office of the board of trade and plantations in England. This is no doubt equally true of the history of the province, from the abandonment of the settlement on Roanoke Island in 1587, to the grant of the charter to the eight Lords proprietors by Charles 2nd. Indeed, with the exception of a small settlement in Currituck, a colony of Quakers, (who emigrated originally from England to Virginia, and thence, to avoid the persecutions of that Colony, to the Albemarle) in the Counties of Perquimons and Pasquotank, and a small colony from Massachusetts on old Town creek of Clarendon River, there seem to have been in Carolina, previously to the year 1663, no other inhabitants than its native beasts and savages. It was much desired by the author that the office of the board of trade and plantations in London, should be searched for information on the foregoing, as well as subsequent parts of our colonial history, and he once presented a memorial to the Legislature, praying its aid to accomplish that end. Leave was granted by that body to raise, by means of a Lottery, such a sum of money as was supposed to be sufficient to defray the expense of an agent to Europe, and of publishing the contemplated History when finished. But this scheme, for causes unnecessary to be related, wholly failed.

After the Grant to the Lords Proprietors in 1663, Sir William Berkely, then Governor of Virginia, was instructed to organize a Government in Carolina—which was done in the following year, and Drummond appointed Governor. Ever since this period, there has existed in some form or other, an organized Government in the province. A Gen'l Assembly was first convened 1667. Lord Ashley was appointed by the L'ds Proprietors to prepare a form of Government for the Colonies. He engaged the services of the celebrated Philosopher, Mr. Lock, who framed a complicated theoretical system, which was adopted 1669.

County of Clarendon, on Old Town creek, established 1665 by a colony from Barbadoes. Sir John Yeamans, Gov'r. Gov'r Drummond died. Succeeded by Sam'l Stephens. Stephens dies, 1669. Insurrection. President and council seized, and put in prison. Imbecile Government. Many good men leave the Province. Seth Sothel, assignee of L'd Clarendon is appointed Gov'r. A tyrant, takes bribes, and oppresses the people. He is seized by the people, to be sent to England for trial. At his request, he is tried by the Gen'l Assembly, and ordered to resign, and leave the colony. Evil effects of this anarchy. The Population, both in the Northern colony of Albemarle, and southern of Port Royale, consisted of high churchmen, sectarians, and profligate adventurers. Locke's Gov'r't too aristocratic, and abolished. Dissensions of High churchmen and dissenters allayed in the southern Colony by Gov'r Archdale, a Quaker. Soon revived after his death. Church of England established. Refusal to naturalize Hugonots. Indian tribes and changes in their condition. Scarcity of money 1711, Hides, deer skins, tallow, etc., made legal tender in paym't of quit rents. Printing presses forbidden. Laws read at Court house. Heavy tax to support Clergy. Episcopalians supported by wealth and aristocracy. Dissenters common people. 1707 Hugonots settle on Trent. Germans from Heidelburg 1709. Lewis Michele and Christopher De Graffenreid. De Graffenreid and Lawson taken by Indians. The latter put to death. Massacre of whites by Indians 1711.

The 4th. Period commences with the war with the Indians, which was brought to a close by defeat of the Tuskaroras 1713. They emigrate to the North. Death of Gov'r Hyde. Presidency of Thos. Pollock. 1715 is the first year of our statute book. Emission by Gen'l Assembly of £8000, in Bills of credit. (Chas. Eden, Gov'r, arrives 1714.) Declare common Law in force. Legislation assumes form and system. Gov'r Eden dies 1722. Pollock, President, dies in 6 months. Succeeded by Wm. Reed, Pres't, who governs until the arrival of Gov'r Burrington, 1723. Until 1722 Courts of Justice sat in private houses. Gen'l Assembly then fixed court houses. Weakness of Gov'r Burrington. Removed, and Sir Rich'd Everard appointed. Boundary with Va. run 60 miles.

Crown purchases for £17,500, 7/8 of the province. Lord Carteret retains his part. £40,000 emitted in bills of credit 1729.

5th.    Prosperity of the Colony, promoted by the establishment of regal Government. Sir R'd Everard removed and Burrington appointed. Weak and foolish. Gabriel Johnston appointed Gov'r 1734. Continues 19 years. The colony prospers under him beyond any former period. Injured, however, by a new emission of bills of credit.

After 1715 the Assembly met at Edenton until 1738, when they met at Newbern. In 1741 they met at Wilmington, after which met sometimes at one of the towns and sometimes at another. Many new counties erected and wholesome Laws enacted this session.

A revisal of the Laws made 1746 by act of assembly. Called Swan's revisal. All laws therein confirmed 1749. Earl Granville same as L'd Carteret. Line between him and the crown begun 1743. Extended to west side of Saxapahaw river 1746, afterward further west. Line with So. Ca. run 1737. Quarrel between the assembly and council, and the representatives reduced from 5 to 2 for each county. Henry McCullock appointed surveyor, etc. Population increases rapidly. Presbyterians and Moravians in the middle and western counties. History of each.

Highland colony under Neil McNeil settled in Cumberland in 1749. Gov'r Johnston dies 1752. Succeeded by Nat'l Rice, Pres't. Dies in short time. Matth. Rowan, Pres't of council, administers Gov't. 1754 act passed to encourage James Davis to set up and carry on the business of printer in the province. Arthur Dobbs appointed Gov'r 1754. Catawba and Cherokee Indians. Hugh Waddell appointed to treat with them. French war. Braddock. Upon his defeat, the Cherokees harrass our frontiers. Major Waddell sent out with Gen'l Forbes against Indians of the northwest, who are defeated. War with the Cherokees by No. and So. Carolina. Peace concluded 1761. In the same year, parties of men penetrated the western wilderness to hunt and gave names to rivers, mountains, etc., which they yet retain.

The History of the contests between the prerogative of the crown and the freedom of the citizen during this period, is interesting. The former, believing that too much liberty was enjoyed by the colony, for the safety and policy of his Government, assails their privileges, first by reducing the number of members of assembly from 5 to 2 in each county. The next attempt was to claim for the king the right of creating counties, and in 1754 he accordingly repealed the Laws by which 13 counties and 5 boroughs had been formed, intending to erect new counties and boroughs thereafter, by his charter, according to his pleasure. Property in the corporate boroughs reverted by this repeal to the original grantors. Creates great indignation, and the Gov'r, Dobbs, consents to a Law re-establishing the counties, "saving the prerogatives of the crown." Charters taken out by the counties and made a source of profit to Government. The assembly ask that the Judges shall be commissioned during good behavior. The Gen'l Assembly appoint an agent to reside in London, and solicit the affairs of the province. In 1760 the assembly in committee of the whole, pass resolutions censuring the Governor, and transmit copies to their agent in London.

1762 Assembly met at Wilmington, and recriminations pass between them and Gov'r. He desires to turn out the printer; they direct the Treasurer not to pay any money upon an order of the Gov'r and council.

Great frauds were practised by the land officers of Lord Granville, extortions, etc. Office shut 1765. Quarrel between Gov'r Dobbs and the Assembly continues. He dies 1765. Succeeded by Wm. Tryon, who had come out 1764 as Lieut. Gov'r. *Proc* money. Episcopal Church provided for. Glebe lands purchased, and salaries for ministers, etc., but the middle, northern, and Western counties being settled by dissenters, they refused to execute the Laws for the benefit of the church establishment. Gov'r Tryon is liberal towards dissenters.

The 6th. period contains a history of much interest. (Tho' here the author's manuscript ends). It commences with the attempts on the part of the British Parliament to subject the colonies to their power by laying taxes on sugar, Indigo, and other articles not produced in the colony, under pretence that they should be appropriated to Colonial defence. It embraces the rebellion called "the *Regulation*," etc.

There is a review of European History from Cabot to Raleigh 1494 to 1568, written out, also a succinct account of the foremost powerful Indian Tribes of N. C., i.e., the Cherokees, Catawbas, Sauras, and Tuskarorahs.

*Inaugural Address.*[2]

January 1, 1845

Senators and Gentlemen of the House of Commons:

In presenting myself before you to take the oaths required for my qualification as Chief Magistrate of the State, I gladly embrace the occasion to express to our common constituents my deep and abiding sense of gratitude for their confidence and approbation, as manifested in the election which calls me hither. If, by diligence, faithfullness, and impartiality to the high trust I am about to assume; if, by a constant observance of those great maxims of liberty and justice that are embodied in the Constitution, which I shall swear to support: if by a consultation of our history and a deference to those precepts and examples which are deemed most excellent in past times, I can gather that wisdom which my own deficient faculties are unable to supply, I may hope to render to my countrymen some, although it may be an inadequate, return for this mark of their favorable consideration.

A philosophic observer of our Institutions has attributed as a defect to the State Governments, that they do not comprehend objects of sufficient interest to human ambition. Although the fact be otherwise, yet it is much to be apprehended that there is a tendency in the affairs of the Federal Government, extending as it does over so vast a territory, and so many millions of inhabitants, identified in recollection with the proudest events of our history—with its power to make war and peace, and being constantly surrounded with the pomp and circumstance of warlike preparation by land and sea—with its large revenue and expenditures—its numerous officers and their superior compensations above those of the States—it power to regulate commerce, to conduct our foreign intercourse, and to administer the code of nations, with the great and concentrated powers and patronage of the executive—that there is a tendency in the affairs of that government, with these attributes for admiration and attraction, to

---

[2] From the *Hillsborough Recorder,* January 9th, 1845.

engross too much of the attention which is bestowed by our citizens on public affairs. That these important concerns of the Nation should be objects of constant observation and active vigilance, is to be expected and desired. But that they should be so, to the exclusion of those more immediate interests which "come home to our business and bosoms," our homes and firesides, and which are wisely retained under State jurisdiction, is a misfortune to be deprecated.

If we glory in the name of American citizens, it should be with feelings akin to filial affection and gratitude, that we remember we are *North Carolinians!* And that the preservation and prosperity of our system and its ability to secure the permanent and habitual attachment of the people, depend quite as much, nay, much more upon an enlightened policy and a correct administration in the State Governments than in that of the Union.

In omitting, therefore, to occupy this occasion with more than a passing notice of matters which concern the action of the general government, I am actuated by the belief that other topics are more appropriate, and, moreover, that for recent opportunities, my opinions on national affairs are not unknown.

Let it suffice then, to say that the line of partition between State and Federal powers should be kept distinctly marked; and while those yielded by the States should be liberally exercised for the general good, those retained should be carefully watched over and preserved—that I regard the liberty and union of these United States as inseparable, and that it is the duty of those entrusted with authority, as well as of all good citizens, "indignantly to frown upon the first dawning of every attempt to alienate any portion of our country from the rest, or to enfeeble the sacred ties which link together its various parts."

But for the cultivation of that harmony so essential to unity, we must bear in mind, that it is necessary not only that the course of the general government should be characterized by justice, wisdom, and a large patriotism; but that the several States shall keep the covenants of the Constitution as undertaken by them, not merely in letter, but in spirit, and in good faith. Certain parts of that instrument require duties to be performed or omitted by the State governments or some department thereof, without however providing penal sanctions for the failure, relying only upon the comity, the sense of right, and the official oaths of public servants for their observance.

Yet it is obvious that a non-compliance on the part of a State in these articles, is as injurious to the rest of the confederacy as can be any usurpation by the Federal government. The constitution having stipulated that Congress shall have power to "establish a uniform rule of naturalization"; that Congress, having exerted the power, by prescribing a previous residence in our own country of five years, and a declaration of an intention to become a citizen, in some Court of Record, at least two years before any foreigner shall be naturalized, it is manifest that any State which undertakes to confer the right of citizenship on aliens with a shorter residence and upon other terms than those declared in the Acts of Congress, commits an infraction on the Constitution injurious to the other States. And if they are enumerated in the census of her population, so as to give her a greater number in the apportionment of Representatives, and admitted to the right of suffrage in elections affecting the Union, she acquires importance and power beyond her due, and by means unauthorized by the Constitution. Yet regulations for the naturalization of foreigners after a residence of but six months, or other period less than that required by the Acts of Congress, have been introduced in several of the States and are believed to have already had an important influence in great national results.

So also the Constitution in express terms provides that criminals fleeing from justice in one State to another, and that persons held to labor escaping into other States shall be delivered up on proper demand to be carried to the places whence they fled. Nevertheless, instances have occurred of refusal by State authorities to make such delivery, because the state of servitude alleged in the particular case did not exist in the State where the demand was made; or because the crime charged was not regarded as an offence there. No difference can be perceived whether the crime be treason against a State, larceny of a slave, or other property, or whether the person demanded be a slave or apprentice, a ward, or infant child, the obligation under the Constitution to deliver up, in any and every of these cases is alike imperative and unavoidable.

I have thus particularly pointed out these breaches of our constitutional duty in other States, because the Judiciary of this State have uniformly held that the right of naturalization could only be acquired under the laws of the United States. The executive has never failed to deliver up on proper demand and due proof of identity any fugitive criminal or person held to service; and your predecessors in the General Assembly have aided the requirements of the Constitution, for the surrender of criminals by statutory enactment.

Another source of disturbance to the harmony of the Union from failure in duty by the State government rises from the toleration within their limits by particular States, of organized societies, or combinations of individuals having for their object the subversion of the government or particular institutions of other States. If it be a matter of boast in the Federal government, that it has made similar combinations against foreign powers punishable as crimes in courts of justice, it would seem to be demanded by the duties of good neighborhood, to say nothing of closer ties, that such interference in the affairs of sister States should be prohibited by each member of the confederacy. And if particular frames of government or organizations of society existing in any other States at the formation of the Constitution and recognized and guaranteed by it, are to be warred upon by the inhabitants of other States, no matter from what motive of faction or fanaticism, or with whatever hopes of driving them to a greater ideal, perfection of liberty, or humanity, the consequences cannot but be most disastrous to the general peace and happiness.

It is now near seventy years since the organization of the government of the State of North Carolina. Never in her colonial condition, enjoying the sunshine of royal favor and participating in but a limited degree of the patronage and honors of the General Government which has succeeded to the principal powers from which patronage flows, possessing a soil upon the average not above the medium grade of fertility, but yielding fruitful returns to patient toil in our generally salubrious climate—excluded by the nature of a sea coast from any enlarged share in the commerce of the world; her people have been enured to self-reliance, industry, economy, and, for the most part, to competence, but moderation in fortune.

The natural fruits of this situation have been personal independence, unostentatious self-respect, habits in general of morality, obedience to the laws, fidelity to engagements public and private, frugality in expenditures, and loyalty to the government, which is at once the offspring of the will and a type of simple manners, and honest and manly character of the citizens.

Our Constitution both in its original and amended features exhibits a government affording every essential right of freedom, yet sufficiently conservative to give to it permanence and energy in administration. Nowhere can we find a better practical illustration of liberty secured by law. Our statuatory enactments embodied in a volume of but little more than six hundred octavo pages, in which are comprehended every Act of the legislation, effecting the citizens in general from the earliest English statutes until within a few years past, attest how well the simplicity and plainness of the fundamental law have been followed in the general legislation. In fulfilment of the requirements of the Constitution a Judiciary system was early put in operation, which being matured from time to time as experience suggested improvement, will compare favorably with the best system of other States. Under its administration by officers in the main of a high degree of ability, learning and purity of character, our standard of professional eminence has been uniformly elevated, justice has been executed, and truth maintained in such a manner that in no part of the world have life, liberty and property, been more secure than within the borders of our venerated State.

More than half a century ago our University was established, which has gradually increased and diffused its lights not only in our own but in others of the States, until it now justly ranks among the first of the seminaries for education in the Union. Other institutions on private foundation furnish opportunities for literary, scientific, and religious instruction in various parts of the State, and within a few years past the long deferred duty enjoined by the Constitution of providing a system of Common Schools for the instruction of all our youth, has been undertaken with earnestness and vigor. May it prosper until we shall realize the desire of the Roman Emperor who "would have every citizen so learned that a portion of the republic might be committed to his charge."

While such is the happy situation of our government, and such some of its more fortunate results, we cannot delude ourselves with the belief, that our advancement and prosperity and wealth has equalled that of most of our sister States, or that the task of those honored with the confidence of the people of North Carolina, and entrusted with their delegated power, is one of ease or indolence. Such has been the flow of emigration that our population has not yet doubled its number at the first federal census in 1790. Its general increase, however, during the decennial period until the last, was at the average rate of about 80,000 souls in each ten years. But during the period from 1830 to 1840, owing to the temptations to removal, from the action of the General Government, both in relation to the currency and the extinction of the Indian title to public land, the increase was only about 20,000 souls. Notwithstanding, however, the augmentation of the population from 393,000 in 1790 to 755,000 in 1840, and the consequent increase of production and consumption of articles of commerce, the imports and exports of the seaports in our own limits, as shown by the table of commerce of the Treasury of the United States, are no greater at the latter than at the former period. The Inlets on our coast have undergone no change for the better; but few of our rivers have improved in navigation, though all have obstructions and that extended tract of country lying between this capital and the Blue Ridge and northwest of the river Cape Fear, comprehending more than one-third of our whole territory, population, and taxable wealth, enjoys but little better facilities of transportation than when it was traversed by the baggage wagons of hostile armies in the midst of the Revolution. Those beneficent establishments, the products of modern humanity and science in which cures are administered to minds diseased "the dumb are almost made to speak and the blind to receive their sight," have as yet no foundation among us, and although a common school system has been commenced, a surprisingly large part of our people are yet destitute of the first rudiments of education. Our earth abounding, as it is believed, beyond any other region of no greater extent in the precious and useful metals, in materials for manufacturing and for building, and a thousand other desirable objects, is not half explored. Our agriculture though attracting more intelligence than formerly is yet greatly in need of improvement; and our capabilities for manufacturing are but beginning to be understood.

It is most obvious that to meliorate our condition in any or all of the particulars alluded to, pecuniary means are indispensable. In common with the greater portion of our constituents, I have looked for years to a distribution of the proceeds of the sales of the public land as a source from which we were to derive the supplies necessary for objects so desirable. If in this hope we shall be doomed to disappointment, those among us who prefer a different disposition of that fund, but who yet concur in the enlightened policy of diffusing education and improving our situation in every practical method, will be expected to bring forward some other scheme of finance to effect ends so important. Whatever system may be adopted, no time should be lost in putting into energetic operation such measures as may be best calculated to add to public and private wealth.

Our country must be made to hold out the hope and expectation of acquiring the means of comfortable livlihood and of reasonable accumulation, or its population cannot be expected to remain, nor its resources to increase. While labor is the only true foundation of national wealth, it may be much aided in its efforts by the kind and upholding hand of Government.

No State is more diversified in its field of labor or its varieties of marketable productions than our own. The great majority of the people being engaged in Agriculture there are far more than a superficial observer would imagine, who are, with perhaps greater profits employed in the forests and fisheries, mines, manufacturies, and mechanic arts. Our agriculture again, such is the variety of soil and climate, comprehends every great staple cultivated in the Union except Sugar and Hemp. It is difficult to say in the present state of statistical information, which of our chief exports of Cotton, Tobacco, Rice, Wheat, and Flour, or Indian Corn, is of the greatest value. While that of Cotton would seem to be the greatest, we must remember that fully one-third of the domestic supply of that article is manufactured at our own mills, and finds a market chiefly at home in this manufactured state. These varieties of occupation and production, creating apparently diverse interests, may be made to contribute to mutual accomodation, to multiply the bonds of fraternal feeling, if government will but open communication between different sections and give to the producer a cheap and easy mode of transportation to market, or shall encourage new employments by means of which the production shall find a market nearer home.

In view of the great deficiency of facilities for transportation, under which we labor in the larger portion of the State, and extended system of internal improvement, or a more general devotion of industry to mining and manufacturing would seem to be indispensable. If we cannot, without too great a loss of profits, send our staples to existing markets, we must endeavor to bring a market nearer to them. This is most obviously our interest, especially since in raising them out of revenue necessary for the

Federal Government, the practice of laying discriminating duties for the protection of manufactures and other pursuits of domestic industry, seems to be a settled part of our National policy. Unfamiliar with the details of our affairs, it will hardly be expected that I shall at present attempt any recommendation of specific measures to your consideration. This would indeed be presumptuous, after the lucid and interesting review of them in a message of my distinguished predecessor at the opening of your present Session. I cannot, however, forbear to impress upon the Legislature my deep conviction of the importance of his recommendation to undertake without delay an Agricultural and Geological Survey of the State, with particular reference to the discovery of means to improve our soil and cultivation.

In whatever we produce, we have millions of competitors throughout the world. And unless we avail ourselves of all the natural resources we possess, in addition to the lights of science, the skill of experience and application of industry, we shall be left behind in the great race of increasing profits by cheapening production.

In contemplating the important interests which require the care of government, it is a consolation to me to know that by the wise distribution of powers, the Executive in the general discharge of its duties, but moves in the rear of the Legislature, endeavoring to carry out their wise determinations, by such means as they have committed to its hands.

Whatever in our respective spheres we may find demanding our attention, I trust no pledge is necessary on my part, nor exhortation to you on yours, that the public engagements of the State shall be observed scrupulously and faithfully. In our past history, we have gained a high character for the virtues of honesty and fidelity; thus far our escutcheon is unstained—the public faith has been kept, the public honor inviolate. And whatever destiny may await us in the future, let us fervently unite our invocations to that good Providence, who has so signally upheld and preserved us heretofore, that our beloved North Carolina may still be permitted to "walk in her integrity," the object of our loyalty and pride as she is the home of our hearts and affections.

*From Daniel Webster.*                                    U.

Boston,

Jan. 8th, 1845

I hope I am indebted to you for a copy of your address to the Legislature of North Carolina, which has come to hand this morning.

I have read it with much interest, not only on account of its being the production of a Gentleman for whom I have much sincere regard, but also for its own ability and merits. The tone which it holds in regard to the relations between the State Governments, & the General Government, is just, proper, dignified and constitutional; & the views it presents on questions of internal policy, the development of resources, the improvement of markets, & the general advancement of industry and wealth, are such as belong to the age, & are important to our Country, in all its parts.

I congratulate you, my Dear Sir, most sincerely on this auspicious commencement of your administration; & pray you to be assured, that no one entertains more cordial wishes, that the course of your public life may continue to redound to the good of the State, & of the Country; and to the further advancement of your own reputation.


*From James Seawell.*                                     A.

Memphis, Tennessee.,

January 10th., 1845.

I am requested by Henry Patillo, Esq'r., of this place, to solicit for him the appointment of "Commissioner of Affidavits" for North Carolina. Mr. P. is a gentleman of unquestionable respectability, a lawyer of fair standing in his profession, and esteemed for his moral worth, and would doubtless fill the situation with satisfaction to the public, and credit to himself. Should there be no other applicant whom you would prefer, I should be gratified to see Mr. P. obtain the office.

We have nothing in the shape of news in the great valley of the West. *Politically*, we Whigs are as dead as a skined Coon, whilst the *locos* are yet unable to account for the real cause of their success. Indeed it would seem that the result of the late Presidential election was involved in some inexplicable mystery, such as presents to my mind the commencement of a revolution in the political history of our Confederacy that cannot fail to change the theory, if not the future destinary of the American States.

As to my own feelings upon the aspect of our affairs, as they now stand. I am without a hope for the future, the causes that have been made to operate upon the public mind by the leaders of the dominant party in the late canvas, admonishes me to expect in the prospective something much worse than what can be seen at the present. We have seen in the public mind a disposition to *barter* away the National welfare, and to hazard the stability of the Union for an imaginary boon in the wilds of Texas. Now, I have no objection to the annexation of Texas, if effected upon rational grounds, and as becomes an enlightened people. But when we see *principles* sacrificed, and the National prosperity abandoned, to subserve the advancement of political aspirants, it is indeed alarming.

We are now without a rallying point. Like ancient Troy, we have fallen by the stratagem of a Wooden horse, the particulars of which is described by Virgel. It matters not whether the people be ruined by becoming dupes to Superstition, or to misplaced confidence; the American States being duped by a Texan *Pony,*—the Trojans by their superstition to a wooden figure resembling a horse. What is the difference?

I learnt from a gentleman a few days since, who had recently passed through Columbia, the town in which the President elect resides, that the Village was, and had been for several weeks past, crowded to overflowing by the Colonel's *particular friends,* collected from all parts of the Union to present their gratulations, etc. But at the same time it was understood, that they were, to a man, applicants for office. My informant added that they "appeared to take a compound of odd genius."

The new Pres't spends what time his visitors allows him to be from home at the *Hermitage.* The hatchet between the old Gen'l and J. C. Calhoun being buried, the latter will doubtless be in the confidence of the Colonel, and in all probability occupy in the new Cabinet the place he now fills in Mr. Tyler's. Query in that event, whose adm'n will the next be?

On looking back I fear I have written you a long letter. I fear I am intruding upon your patience, but not without assurances of my profound respect, high regard, and best wishes, etc.

*From David L. Swain.*                                    **A.**

Chapel Hill,

Jan. 17th., 1845.

I am gratified to perceive from the captions of the Resolutions, as contained in the Star of Wednesday, that the Legislature has made provision for completing the series of Letter Books in the Executive department, and collecting the proceedings of the various town, county, and district Committees organized under the Articles of American Association adopted by the Continental Congress of 1774; and of the several Councils of Safety established by our own Legislature.

I suppose that a good deal of copying will be required, and that proper remuneration for such services has been authorized. Our young friend, James G. Scott [3] writes a fair hand, and, under your supervision, would probably perform the service well. Neither he nor his friends are aware of this suggestion, or indeed that such services are required.

Your familiarity with our revolutionary history is so great, that you will, in the discharge of that duty imposed by the Resolution, need very little assistance from others. Should you feel any disposition, however, to lessen your labours by dividing them, or desire a conference on difficult questions that may present themselves in the progress of the work, you will at all times find me to [be] disposed to participate in it *con amore.*

Judge Battle and myself have agreed to visit Raleigh on Wednesday next, if the weather should be favourable, unless we should hear in the mean time that you will be absent.

*From David L. Swain.*                                    **U.**

At Mrs. White's,

Jan. 24th, 1845.

I have for you the order book mentioned last night. You will find on examination that it was first kept by some one under the

---

[3]James Graham Scott (1826-1884), of Hillsboro, a graduate of the university, who settled in Onslow County, and represented it in the lower house of the legislature, 1870, in the senate, 1872, and in the convention of 1875.

command of Sir Henry Clinton, who was subsequently under the command of Gen'l Leslie, when the latter proceeded via Portsmouth, Va. to reinforce Lord Cornwallis in So. C. After the junction of the two armies at Winnsboro, S. C. Lord Cornwallis was Comm. in Chief, and from that time it gives all the orders issued by him. It, of course, contains nothing with reference to his Lordship's first invasion of the province in Sep. 1780.

The limitation to $500. of expenses to be incurred in collecting and recording documents will not, I apprehend, admit of any provision for James G. Scott, of the nature suggested in my letter from Chapel Hill.

He knows nothing of my suggestion, and is therefore doomed to no disappointment.

*From Edmund Pendleton Gaines.*[4]          A.

New Orleans, Louisiana.,

January 24th., 1845.

I do myself the honor to enclose herewith for your perusal and acceptance, a copy of my official report of the 24th. of September, 1844, to the civil and military authorities of the War Department, reiterating my views of previous dates regarding the defenceless condition of our Sea Port Towns—more especially this city, and that of New York, and the consequent necessity of a radical change in our system of National defence.

Neither of these great and growing cities can be assaulted by fifty such Steam Ships of War as those referred to in the enclosed report, without jeoparding the lives and property of most of the inhabitants of both sexes and all ages. Nor can these two magnificent commercial emporiums be taken by surprise or sacked by such an Enemy without giving a tremendous shock to near twenty millions of the good people of the Union; nor without a loss of

---

[4] Edmund Pendleton Gaines (1777-1849), a native of Virginia, whose family moved to North Carolina, (now Tennessee) after the Revolution. He joined the army during the Indian troubles in 1797, surveyed the road from Nashville to Natchez, and, later, made the arrest of Aaron Burr. He studied law, and began practice, but the War of 1812 brought him back to the army. He served later with Jackson, against the Creeks and Seminoles. He was promoted to brigadier (brevet major) general. In his violent enmity towards Scott, he compared him to Benedict Arnold, and Scott, officially, said he was insane. He was always at outs with the War Department. Of reprimands he wrote: "I carelessly submit to them, as they seem to be a source of pleasure to the War Department, and certainly inflict no injury on me."

money and property amounting to hundreds of millions of dollars more than the cost of all the means of defence necessary—not only to secure New York and New Orleans from any well grounded apprehension of assault, but sufficient to render *them* and most of the other Sea port towns referred to, comparatively *impregnable in War,* and by means so essentially applicable to inland purposes of commerce, as to give them perpetual value for these purposes *in Peace & in War.*

As in a War against any great maritime power *we must* calculate on the entire abandonment of all commerce upon the "high Seas" until our floating force shall be so much augmented as—first, to aid in the protection of our principal Sea Port towns—and secondly, to be able to cope with the Steam Ships of War opposed to us. In this case our Steam Boat and Rail Road facilities will be all important to our inland commerce, as the most durable ligaments of union to all the States—while men aced as we are with the incendiary votaries of premature abolitionism that would forever destroy the fair prospects which the African population have of acquiring for themselves, and in due time giving to their miserable Savage brethren of Africa that *rational freedom & universal civilization* which they can never obtain otherwise than by patiently waiting and cheerfully working with us in giving security to our Sea port towns, and increasing our means of defence and National strength until we shall be able, in the face of all Europe and Asia to place these people upon their own quarter of the Globe, practically learned in all the useful arts, and afford them *protection* in completing the great object of their final independence, which an over-ruling Providence appears to have designed in their forced migration to this land of Liberty, and their preparatory term of servitude here; in which I am convinced that their condition is in every respect better than that of most of the labouring classes of the civilized world. We shall thus give Civilization and self-government to Africa. We shall commence this glorious work before the middle of the coming century—when our white population will amount to more than two hundred millions.

I cannot but persuade myself that my views upon this subject will be found to be plain, matter-of-fact views. They have been irresistably forced upon my mind, somewhat disciplined as I am in these matters by experience, and by carefully observing, as in duty bound to observe, the unexampled revolution which Steam power applied to Ships and vessels of every description and to Railroads has produced in the Art of War.

I address myself to you, and through you to the General Assembly of the Sovereign and patriotic State, over which you preside, under a strong impression that the time is not far distant, if it has not already arrived, when the subject of our *Harbour defences* against Fleets propelled by Steam power will no longer be suffered to rest upon the theories of military writers of the last Century, ignorant of the possibility of Fleets or Armies ever being moved by Steam, against wind and tide, at the rate of one mile in a month, whilst we have all seen for a quarter of a century past, that men and merchandize have been, and consequently that Armies and Navies will be propelled by Steam power against wind and tide at the rate of three hundred miles in one day by land and water.

If I am correct in these views I cannot but persuade myself that the system of defence which I propose, or that other and better system which I cordially invite and challenge, will be carried into effect, regardless of such devices as *Submarine Torpedoes* by which the thoughless and the weak are made to believe that New York and New Orleans and other vital points of approach are to be defended by *Magnetic wire workers*—without any considerable outlay of money, and without the moral and physical effort which every effective system of defence known to History has required; and regardless of our unfortunate system of Great Forts, such as those at Old Point Comfort, and New Port, Rhode Island, and those recommended at the dry Tortugas, without the cooperation of the Floating force which I have recommended. Great Forts such as no invading foe headed by men of experience would ever think of approaching, until they had taken and sacked all our Sea port towns approachable by fleets propelled by Steam power.

Give us the means of defence which I propose, or that better system which I invite, and, in connection with our Rail roads from the Central and Western States to the principal Sea port towns of the East and South, give us Dr. Morse's *Magnetic Telegraph* by which the Commanding General at New Orleans or New York can in less than one hour announce to the Governors of every State in the Union the approach of a hostile Fleet, whereby from one to ten thousand Regiments of brave Volunteers may, in a few hours be put in march at the rate of three hundred miles a day, prepared to meet and beat the invading foe;—give us these means of defence and we shall speedily achieve the great moral triumph hitherto unknown to man; the moral triumph of a system for repelling invasion in war, *by inventions and discoveries applicable alike to Peace and War,*—The discoveries and inventions of our own citizens. Otherwise our Sea port towns must be left at the mercy of Pirates—or at the mercy of a Nation of land and Naval robbers in War but little better than Pirates.

You have the proud satisfaction of enjoying the success with which the inherent *military mind* of your ever vigilant State has provided for the defence of your principal Sea Port towns *by land.* When your Rail roads from your interior and mountain districts—planned as most of your Rail roads have been, and for the most part constructed as they ought to be for Military, as well as commercial and other civil purposes, are completed, you will want nothing to give security to your most exposed Sea Port towns but three small Martello Towers near the entrance of each of your principal inlets, with three such War Steamers as those which I have recommended to be made of Oak and Iron—*principally of Iron*—having Engines of great power, to enable your fine Volunteer Batallions, with your Steam Boat officers and men, to cooperate with the U. S. troops, and occasional Naval force to render your most vital Points of approach invulnerable in War, and prosperous and happy, as I pray you may ever be, in Peace and in War. When your Rail roads are completed from your Sea Board to the mountains which separate you from Tennessee, the whole of your Sea port towns may confidently calculate upon the effective cooperation of from fifty to one hundred thousand of the Sharp Shooters of the Western States within twenty four hours after their concentration upon your Western border—armed and amply supplied with everything necessary and proper to their Health and comfort—and to render them *"Inflexible in faith, and Invincible in arms."*

I am, dear Sir, with very great respect and esteem,

Your friend,
Major General U. S. Army.
Commanding the Western Division.

*From David L. Swain.*                                    **A.**

Chapel Hill,

January 31st., 1845.

Your note by Mr. Morehead was rec'd yesterday evening. That the Trustees residing in Raleigh should desire the Asylum to be located there, and at the first suggestion should over-estimate its importance to the political metropolis, is very natural. But that they should support for a moment that *female* mutes would be safer there than here, seems to one who knows both places as I do, strange enough. I regret the decision, and am surprized by the reason assigned for it.

With respect to the blind, I more than doubt the propriety of attempting to do anything with the State, unless the cooperation of S. C. and Georgia can be obtained. The Perkins Asylum for the Blind is the only institution of that kind in New England, and was established and is supported at great expense. Col. Perkins[5] alone, is said to have contributed $100,000. Liberal movements in N. C. are too frequently sudden and spasmodic. When we do begin, we begin in a hurry, and in other instances than the Rail Road, repent at leisure. Dice deliberum—cito face, is a maxim, memorised at School, to be reversed in the subsequent conduct of our affairs.

I have just concluded a long letter to Mr. Sparks on the subject of our revolutionary history, and finding myself still under high pressure, have determined to invade your domain. You will find enclosed a memorandum in the hand-writing of Gov. Caswell, showing very clearly where his papers ought to be—where they actually are, is, I suspect, by no means so certain. Some of them are doubtless dispersed in various localities in the public offices, others may have been carried to New Orleans by Judge Martin. Our college friend, Doct. Geo. S. Bettner can ascertain the fact, and, armed with the authority given you by the Resolution of the Gen. A. may be able to reclaim and return them. A part may possibly be found among Judge Murphy's collections. A few very interesting letters, I am informed by our friend, J. H. Bryan,

---

[5] Thomas Handasyd Perkins (1764-1854), of Boston, a merchant, and ardent Federalist, a backer of the Hartford Convention, who served eight terms in the state senate, and six in the lower house. A philanthropist, he was deeply interested in relief of the blind, and the Perkins Institute was named for him, in appreciation of his gift of a house. He, himself, became blind for a time, but recovered his sight.

Esq., were shewn to him last summer by Lucius J. Polk,[6] Esq., these the latter gentleman promised to send to me for the Hist. Soc. of the Univ. but has not done so. The best mode to obtain them would probably be thro' Mr. Rainer. Mr. B. or C. J. Ruffin, both of whom saw them, can probably give more definite information.

Gov. Nash's papers, which must be intensely interesting, if not among Judge M's collection were probably appropriated by F. X. Martin, with whom an official correspondence ought to be opened forthwith. I have made two ineffectual attempts to extract a letter from him. Like my drunken French Prof. Burgevin,[7] one of Napoleon's Captains, when I directed him to retire from a Senior examination, you may enquire, "Is it a request or a command? if it is a command I obey,—if it is a request I will not go."

Gov. Burke's papers are all in my possession in good order. Like the collections of Gov. Caswell and Gov. Nash I suppose you have a right to consider them as public documents, public property, and to take them wherever you find them. If J. G. Scott should be engaged as copyist, it will perhaps promote his convenience to copy Gov. B's papers here. Any assistance I can give in the character of editor is freely tendered.

Some papers it may be proper to purchase now; others may be reserved for the consideration of the next General Assembly. I am anxious to have an opportunity afforded me to examine and ascertain the extent and value of Judge Murphey's collection. The depository of them (Mr. John Kirkland) if requested to do so by you, would probably be willing to send them down, and allow me to examine them at leisure. It is not probable that any one will purchase them, without knowing what they are.

Have you any knowledge of the Mecklenburg *Female* Declaration? I have sent to Mr. Sparks[8] and enclose to you a paragraph in relation to it.

---

[6] Lucius Junius Polk (1802-1870), a son of Colonel William Polk, of Raleigh, a graduate of the university. He moved to Tennessee in 1823, and settled in Maury County.

[7] A. Burgevin was a Frenchman, who was for a short time professor at the university.

[8] Jared Sparks.

*From Kenneth Rayner.*                    A.

Ho. Reps.,

Washington,

Feby. 5th, 1845.

\*   \*   \*   \*   \*

I had a bad time in reaching here, having been detained one day in Gaston, and another in Richmond—owing to the failure of the cars to make the connection at those two places.

Benton is this morning speaking upon a substitute offered by him for the resolutions in regard to Texas, that passed our House.

It seems to be generally understood that the resolutions of our House cannot pass the Senate, and I do not think any *other* project can pass our House. So we now begin to have hopes, that this outrageous measure may not succeed after all.

You see the Oregon occupation bill has passed our House by a very large majority; and if it passes the Senate, I think we shall soon find that we have not Mexico to deal with. This measure will share the same fate as Texas. The passage of one is dependant on the passage of the other. It seems to have been arranged that they shall progress *pari passu*.

We have winter at last in good earnest.


*To Miss Mary W. Burke.*[9]                A.

Executive Office,

Raleigh,

Feb. 6th., 1845.

To Miss Mary Burke,
    Marion, Ala.

Our General Assembly at its last session has made it my duty to collect and have transcribed for preservation, the correspondence, and other official documents pertaining to the administrations of

---

[9] From Governors' Letter Books, 36:24.

Gov's Caswell, Nash [10] and Burke.[11] No portion of the Letter Books of any one of them being now to be found in this office. As their administrations comprehended the entire period of the War of the Revolution, the defect is probably to be accounted for by the invasion of the enemy, and the necessity for frequent removals of the public Archives, to avoid capture by them. It is, however, by far the most entertaining part of our history, which I am happy in believing is beginning to excite the curiosity of many literary men in our country, both without and within the State.

Gov. Swain, the President of our University, whose researches upon this subject have been quite extensive, informs me that he has borrowed from Dr. Webb, certain Manuscripts of your Father, left with the Dr. by you, which are in a good state of preservation, and will sustain the character of the author for ability, patriotism, and scholarship. And my purpose in now addressing you, is respectfully to ask as a favor to the State, that you will transfer to it all the papers of your Father of a public nature, to be arranged and deposited in this office for preservation.

There has now [been] found among the papers of the late Mrs. Watters[12] of Hillsboro, a bound manuscript Book, purporting to be the order Book of the British Commanders in 1780, 81, first at New York, 2nd. at Portsmouth, Va., 3d. in South & North Carolina, embracing the invasion of the latter State by Lord Cornwallis, & terminating on Deep river after the battle of Guilford C. H. Will you be good enough to say in your reply whether you know any thing of its history?

I gladly embrace the opportunity to express my gratitude for numberless acts of hospitality & kindness during your residence

---

[10] Abner Nash (1740 ca.-1786), a native of Virginia, who came to North Carolina in 1763. He represented Halifax in the assembly, 1764-1765, 1770-1771, was a delegate from New Bern to all five provincial congresses, a member of the council of safety, speaker of the first house of commons, speaker of the senate, 1779, governor, 1780-1781, and member of congress of the Confederation, 1782-1786.

[11] Thomas Burke (1747-1783), a native of Galway, Ireland, a physician, came as a youth to America, and began practice in Virginia. He studied law, practiced a short time in Norfolk, and settled in Hillsboro. He was a member of all the provincial congresses except the first, and of the continental congress, 1776-1781. He was elected governor in 1781, and soon afterwards was captured by Tory raiders, and taken to Charleston. He was placed on parole, but received no protection from the British, and after he had been shot at, he gave notice of his intention, and escaped. He was bitterly criticized for this by many American officers. He resumed his office, declined to be considered for re-election, and died not long after his term ended.

[12] Mrs. Joseph Watters, of Wilmington and Hillsboro. The house Graham lived in was known as the Watters place.

in Hillsboro', and assurances of the high respect & esteem with which

I am Your friend & Ob't Servant,
Will. A. Graham

*To François Xavier Martin.*[13]    A., G.L.B.

Raleigh, N. C.

February 8th., 1845.

Sir:

The General Assembly of North Carolina at the last session have made it my duty to collect the Memorials of the Revolutionary History of the State, and especially, if possible, the correspondence of Governors Caswell, Nash & Burke. Presuming that your researches when engaged in writing the History of the State put you in possession of many of the letters of these early Governors, as well as other Documents of great interest to our people. I have to request, as a special favor, to North Carolina, that you will be kind enough to communicate to me any of our public documents of the description desired, which may be under your controll, or that you will inform me as early as your convenience will permit, where copies of them may be procured. The public offices here afford but scanty information in relation to some of the most important periods of the Revolution. And a General desire exists among the more intelligent part of our population to have access to the material collected by you, with a view to complete your History of North Carolina.

In the hope that you will not disappoint our wishes in this respect, and that I may hear from you in relation thereto, at your earliest leisure,

I am, Dear Sir,
With high respect,
Your ob't Servant,

W. A. Graham

---

[13] From Governors' Letter Books, 36:22.

*To David L. Swain.*          U. Swain Mss.

Raleigh,

Feby. 8th, 1845.

I do not remember to have heard any thing of the declaration of Independence by the ladies of Mecklenburg, tho' I have from infancy heard hundreds of tales of their patriotism and sacrifices in the cause of the Country.

The Mem. of Gov. Caswell's papers sent by you seems to have been made at the close of his second administration, the letter Books of which are here, and I do not despair of being able to find the whole budget unless they were destroyed in the burning of the Capitol. Except during his own time, I don't think Secr. Hill very familiar with the files of his office, and I do not know any one that I can send there, to make the proper searches untill I can command suff'c't leisure myself. He has furnished me with the Council Book of Govr. Caswell's 2nd. administration, ending with the proceedings against the Franklin rebellion. A Journal of a Council at Johnston C. H. Decr. 1776. And the proceedings of the "Board of War" from Sept. 14th. 1780 till Feby. 1781. The last is a document of exceeding interest. I presume you have not met with it, as it is not mentioned in Gov. Morehead's Message, nor in any of our conversations on this subject.

The Gen'l Assembly seems to have established a Board of three persons, called a Board of War, who appear to have had the control of Military operations in that most critical period, when invasion was threatened on both sides of the State, and came with fearful ravages on one. Gov. Nash was present at Hillsborough at the beginning of their Session, but soon left. They occasionally correspond with him & desire him to be in nearer vicinity & finally he quarrels with them for a disposition to dictate to him, and questions the power of the Gen'l A. to confer on them the powers they are exercising. I infer that he was mortified from the first with the erection of the Board, (and with good reason, as he could not be rightfully superseded as Commander in Chief by the Gen Ass.) and hence his departure, first to Granville & subsequently to New Bern, when the enemy were all over our Western border. The Journal shews copies of all letters written by the Board, but not of those received, the entries being "Rec'd a letter from Gen'l Davidson etc. filed No. 1 etc." I have the Secretary now searching for those files, if found we shall have the history of L'd Cornwallis' two invasions written by the actors on our side.

The most curious matter in this Journal is the astonishing fact that the Gen'l Assembly of N. C. appointed Col. Smallwood [14] of Maryland a Major Gen'l of Militia and required Sumner, Davidson, etc to obey him. Caswell, then a Maj. Gen'l for some reason not explained was not then in the field. Sumner would not submit to the overslow, and quit the service & went home from Mecklenburg, the enemy being then near—as did also many other continental officers. The Board have daily intercourse with Gates, who was there more than two months, and shews them a Protection issued by Govr. Josiah Martin from Charlotte, to some Tory who had gone there, & informs them he is issuing many.

Morgan accompanied Smallwood from Hillsboro' and very probably bore a N. C. Commission also. Gov. Rutledge[15] of S. C. and others are there as refugees. And on letters being afterwards received for him they are sent to the house of Mr. Hooper at Wilmington, where he had gone. Another evidence that Hooper was then in association with Whigs. This is altogether the most interesting document I have found as yet. It shews good judgment in making provision for the immense army then expected, high courage and public spirit, and a generous humanity to the non-combatants among the tories. Just contempt is expressed for the Virginia Militia under Stevens—who rendezvoosed there also.

---

[14] William Smallwood (1732-1792), of Maryland, who rose from colonel to major general in the Revolution, a highly unpleasant officer, who threatened to resign when von Steuben was placed over him. His appointment to command North Carolina troops was bitterly resented in the state. He seems to have been essentially a drill-master, and had the reputation of being ready to sacrifice his men. He was governor of Maryland, 1785-1787.

[15] John Rutledge (1730-1800), of South Carolina, studied law in Charleston, and at the Middle Temple in London. He was a member of the commons, 1760, attorney general pro tem., 1764-1765, delegate to the Stamp Act congress, 1765, to the continental congress, 1774-1776, president of South Carolina, 1776-1778, governor, 1779-1782, member of the congress of the Confederation, 1782-1783, delegate to the Federal convention of 1787, and the resulting South Carolina convention of 1788. He was associate justice of the supreme court, 1789-1791, resigning to become chief justice of South Carolina. Washington appointed him chief justice of the United States in 1795, but a Federalist senate rejected him, because of his opposition to the Jay Treaty.

Comm'rs are John Penn,[16] Alex'r Martin,[17] Orandotes Davis.[18]

I have written to F. X. Martin, also to Miss Burke requesting all papers in possession or under control of either. Desiring to begin at the beginning I shall defer the commencement of copying untill I see what papers of Gov. Caswell can be obtained. Though if you think we may properly undertake Gov. Burke's before hearing from his daughter, I will send Mr. Scott a Book, & let him set out under your direction, of which I shall be happy to avail myself.

The old Order Book, sent me by you, is I presume, the copy of the Adjdt. of some of the Regiments, and probably found its deposit at Hillsboro', thro' Fanning[19] (who is said in it to have been at Portsmouth) or some other loyalist.

P. S. Since writing this, the Sec. of State has handed me several of the bundles of Gov. Caswell's letters, labelled as stated in the mem. you sent me, and they will no doubt be all found, they embrace 77, 78, etc.

---

[16] John Penn (1740-1788), of Granville County, a native of Virginia, who had few educational advantages until he studied law under his uncle, Edward Pendleton. He then moved to North Carolina, and, unceasingly industrious, became a careful and successful lawyer. He was a delegate to the provincial congress of 1775, of the continental congress, 1775-1780, and a signer of the Declaration of Independence. He was a member of the state board of war, 1780-1781.

[17] Alexander Martin (1740-1807), of Guilford, a native of Virginia, a graduate of Princeton, who then settled in North Carolina. He was a successful lawyer, and was whipped by the Regulators. He was a member of the assembly, 1774-1775, lieutenant colonel of the second North Carolina Continental Regiment. Accused of cowardice at Germantown, he was acquitted, and resigned, entering upon one of the most remarkable political careers in the history of the state. He was a member of the board of war, state senator, 1779-1782, 1785, 1787-1788, and speaker always, except the first session, and as such, he was acting governor during Burke's imprisonment. He was governor, 1782-1784, 1789-1792, delegate of the Federal convention, and United States senator, 1793-1799. He voted for the Alien and Sedition Acts, which probably retired him.

[18] Oroondates Davis, of Halifax, served in the state senate, 1778-1781, and was a member of the board of war throughout its existence.

[19] Edmund Fanning (1739-1818), a native of New York, a graduate of Yale, settled at Hillsboro, and became a lawyer, with a large and lucrative practice, which he supplemented by holding numerous offices, and charging illegal fees. He sat in the assembly, 1762, 1766-1768, 1770-1771. He was poisonously hated by the masses of that whole region, and Frank Nash, while defending him, characterized him as "a gentleman carpet-bagger," adding that he respected no rights of the masses that conflicted with his interest. He was brutally beaten by the Regulators, who also burned his home and all his possessions. He went to New York in 1771, was colonel of a Tory regiment during the Revolution, and later was lieutenant governor of Prince Edward Island for nineteen years. He became a British major general in 1793, and general in 1808.

*From Daniel M. Barringer.*                        A.

Ho. of Reps.,

Feby. 10th, 1845

Your letter has been sent to the Editors of the Express, New York. Texas, I mean the resolutions & Bill of the House, will be rejected in the Senate. Benton, and is also supposed Tappan, Allen, Dix,[20] Niles,[21] & Fairfield [22] will oppose it.

I think nothing final will be done on the Texas question this Sess. Oregon is likely to involve us in some trouble with England, more so than any question that has been agitated here for the last 30 years. Much will depend on the action of the Senate. There has been a wild and reckless spirit in the legislation of the House on this subject, in the midst of its negotiation elsewhere, without a parallel in our history.

I am glad to learn that our Whig friends in N. C. are resolved to keep their flag to the breeze. We shall need all their aid and energy to maintain our ground under the disheartening results of the late election. The Locos will make, as I am well assured, a desperate united & determined effort to carry our State next Summer—& thus lay the foundation for future success. The Whigs must be wide awake. Our majority is clear, if we can bring them to the polls. This will be the difficulty, & I trust we shall be able to surmount it.

I have not received the Resolutions passed by the Legislature on the subject of the Branch Mint. Please send me a copy.

---

[20] John Adams Dix (1798-1879), a native of New Hampshire, was at fourteen an officer in the War of 1812, and he rose to the rank of major. Remaining in the army, he studied law, and resigning later, settled in New York. He was a sturdy Democrat, and was made adjutant general in 1830. He was later secretary of state, and *ex officio* superintendent of public schools, which he greatly improved. He was United States senator, 1854-1859, and becoming a free soiler, opposed the admission of California unless slavery was prohibited. A man of great ability, character, and attractiveness, he was hampered in his Democratic politics by his well-known anti-slavery opinions. He was serving as a railroad president when Buchanan made him secretary of the treasury. Lincoln made him a major general, and he commanded the department of the east during the war. He was minister to France, 1866-1869, and governor, 1872-1874.

[21] John Milton Niles (1787-1856), of Connecticut, lawyer and editor, Whig United States senator, 1835-1839, postmaster general, 1840-1841, and again senator, 1843-1849.

[22] John Fairfield (1797-1847), of Maine, a native of New York, graduate of Bowdoin College, a lawyer, was a Democratic member of congress, 1835-1838, governor, 1839-1843, and United States senator, 1843-1847.

*From Jacob Siler.*                                    A.

Agency Office,

February 12th, 1845.

Your Excellency is probably aware that in my report to the Treasurer under date of August last, I mentioned the circumstance of divers persons having applied to this agency for permission to work the unsold Cherokee lands in search of Gold, and other minerals, and that such applications had been made in the absence of any authority on the part of this agency to grant permission. The object of this paragraph was to solicit attention to this (as I regarded it) undefined subject.

The Act of 1840–41 entitled an act "to authorise the Governor to appoint an Agent in the County of Macon or Cherokee," does require the Agent to gard and protect the General interest of the State in connection with the lands, whether sold or unsold, and report to the Treasurer the condition of the debtors, etc. I am informed that at this time there is quite a number of the citizens of Cherokee County all most insane on the subject of silver mines.

I am told there are some and perhaps many who calculate on laying their locations and obtaining a jury to set apart 3000 acres, the enterer professing that his object is to build iron works.

There are some, however, who doubt the lawfulness and even the expediency of such a course, but at the same time are exceedingly anxious to have permission to make a fair test of their discoveries, and at the same time be protected from the intrusion of others.

You are therefore respectfully requested to say whether or no this Agency has any such power. Any direction that your Excellency may see proper to give will be promptly obeyed by your faithful servant.

REVOLUTIONARY HISTORY
OF
NORTH CAROLINA.[23]

EXECUTIVE OFFICE, )
March 1st, 1845. )

The undersigned most respectfully invites public notice to the following Resolution, adopted by the General Assembly at its last Session, viz:

---

[23] From Executive Document No. 8, *Executive Documents, Printed for the General Assembly of North Carolina, at the Session of 1844-1845.*

*Resolved,* That His Excellency, the Governor, be, and is hereby authorized and empowered to collect, if possible, such papers as may be necessary to complete the series of Letter Books, and have them copied and arranged under his supervision; and to obtain, as far as practicable, either the original or copies of the proceedings of the several Town, County and District Committees, organized in the Province, in compliance with the recommendation of the Continental Congress of 1774, for the purpose of carrying into effect the Articles of American Association; and the proceedings of the various Committees and Council of Safety, subsequently convened under the authority of the Provincial Legislature.

It will be observed, that the Resolution requires the collection of two classes of Documents:

*1st.* The correspondence of the Executive Department, from the adoption of the Constitution in 1776, till the latter part of the year 1784, when it was first made the duty of the Governor, by Act of the General Assembly, to keep a Letter Book for the purpose of recording all important Letters. The period embraces the entire administration of the three first Governors, viz. Caswell, Nash and Burke. The correspondence of Governor Burke exists, as I am informed, in a good state of preservation, and can be readily obtained. A part of that of Governor Caswell has been found in the Department of State, since the adjournment of the Legislature, corresponding in the number of the packages, and in other particulars with a memorandum left by him, of his public papers, stated to have been deposited in that Office. And the residue, it is believed, are also there. Of the papers of Governor Nash, none have as yet been discovered, except letters written to him by the Board of War of the State, which held its session first in Hillsboro', and subsequently at Halifax, from the 14th. of September, 1780, until the 30th. of January, 1781, copies of which are recorded on the Journal of the Board, preserved in the Department of State. Frequent entries also appear on that Journal, of letters, said to have been received from him, and numbered and filed, but not copied. As his death occurred but a few years after his administration, and during the early childhood of his only surviving son, this gentleman, in reply to enquiries from me, is unable to give any information respecting them. If yet in existence, and not among the mass of old documents in the Capitol, they may most probably be found in the

Town of New Berne, the residence of the author during the time he held the office of Governor.

*2d.* The second class of Documents, relates to the period which preceded the organization of the State Government under the Constitution, from 1774 to December 1776. A large manuscript bound volume, in the Office of the Secretary of State, contains the Journals of:

1st. A Provincial Convention or Congress at New Berne, on the 5th. of August, 1774, at which were appointed the first delegates to the Continental Congress in the following month.

2d. A similar Convention at the same place, 3d. of April, 1775.

3d. A Congress at Hillsboro', 20th. of August, 1775.

4th. A Provincial Council at Johnston Court House, 18th. October, 1775.

5th. A Provincial Council at Johnston Court House, 18th. December, 1775.

6th. A Provincial Council at New Berne, 28th. of February, 1776.

7th. A Congress at Halifax, 4th. of April, 1776.

8th. A Council of Safety at Wilmington, 5th. June, 1776.

9th. The Journal of the Congress or Convention at Halifax, 12th. November, 1776, which formed the Constitution, is in a separate volume. The Provincial Congresses or Conventions, and in their recess, the Provincial Councils, exercised all the general powers of Government, Legislative, Judicial and Executive, from the dissolution of the Royal Government until the present organization. But besides these depositories of sovereign powers of the State, there were Town, County and District Committees, in the several sections, who exercised a local jurisdiction "in compliance with the recommendation of the first Continental Congress, for the purpose of carrying into effect the articles of American Association. The memorials of the proceedings of those Committees, can be obtained only in the districts where they acted. And the object of this publication is to request those, having control of any such papers as are comprehended in the above mentioned Resolution, to comply with the patriotic desire of the Legislature, in forwarding them to this Office, to be arranged and preserved for public inspection. Or at least to grant a temporary use of them, for the purpose of examination and making copies. After which, if desired, they will be returned. Gentlemen in the different Counties, where such memorials exist, who have leisure and take an interest in such investigations, are particularly solicited to lend their aid in seconding the efforts of the Government, to rescue from oblivion these honorable testimonials of our Revolutionary History. The assistance of the Newspaper press, is also invoked, by copying this article.

WILLIAM A. GRAHAM.

*From James Graham.*                                    U.

New Orleans,

March 20th, 1845.

\*    \*    \*    \*    \*

At Mobile I called to see Judge Goldthwaite and his family. He is well situated in the outer part of the City on *Twenty Acres* of Land tastefully cultivated in gardens, fruits, flowers, and vines. I saw at his house Mary, Louisa and Alfred, children of Sister Sophia. Mary is grown and very pretty.

I expect to be at home early in May, perhaps sooner; I will return by Nashville, Knoxville, and Asheville.

The political atmosphere here is very tranquil, no person seems to know or care any thing about the administration of the Government. The new Cabinet is *gaul and wormwood* to the Calhoun clique, but acceptable to the Van Buren portion of the party.

The annexation of Texas is quite popular here with all parties. [P. S.] The line of Turnpike Road, for which a Survey is directed to be made from Raleigh and Fayetteville to the Western part of the State, ought, I presume, to pass through Chatham and cross the Yadkin about the Narrows, thence along a fine Ridge to Beatie's Ford. The Fayetteville Road should unite about the Narrows.

I doubt the propriety of a Turnpike Road for so great a distance, but think a good public Road on that line, (turnpiked in short bad places) would answer just as well, and save two thirds of the expense, and be much more acceptable to the people. A Turnpike Road would not pay for the construction at present.

Still, the survey must be made, in pursuance of the Act of Assembly, and my remarks are only intended [to] ask you to consider the propriety of having the survey and estimates made with a double aspect, one for a *Regular* Turnpike, as directed and another for a good public Road upon which public money should be only appropriated to make and improve very bad places, while the statute labor of the counties could very well make the Road on clay soil and hard, firm Ridges, which are Nature's best Turnpikes.

These are only suggestions to you.

*From Richard T. Brownrigg.*[24]    U.

Columbus,

Mississippi.

March 20th. 1845.

Your letter of 7th. Feb. I receved in due course of Mails, and I would have answered it sooner if I could have seen Mr. Jo Sewell Jones. Yesterday I had an interview and shewed him your letter, after reading it attentively, he said he had none of his papers in Mississippi, that the papers alluded to by you, were in North Carolina with a large number of others, and many *confidential letters* in the same Trunks. He said this in answer to my request that he would permit some friend in whom he could confide to Examine the Trunks for the papers. He further said that there was no one whom he could permit to look into those confidential letters, etc.

He did not appear unwilling to surrender the papers you requested; but I see no way at present for you to obtain them, unless he should return to N. C. and I do not think he has any intention at present of doing so. He resides with his father in law, Mr. James Gordon about 15 miles from Columbus and is but seldom in Town. Mr. Gordon is a very worthy gentleman, and *might* have some influence with him but I doubt whether he will consent for the Trunks to be examined, and did not inform me where they were.

Permit me through you, to present my best Respects to Dr. Baker,[25] Mr. Boylan, & to Judge Cameron, and accept the same

[24] Richard T. Brownrigg (b. 1793), of Mississippi, a native of Edenton, a student at the university in 1808, who served in the commons in 1816, and in the state senate, 1818, 1822, 1831. He later moved to Mississippi.

[25] Probably Dr. Simmons Jones Baker, of Martin County, a student at the university, 1821-1825, and long a trustee., M.D. of Edinburgh, and a distinguished physician, an extensive planter, who served in the commons, 1814-1815, and in the state senate, 1816-1818.

for yourself. I wish my adopted State was as correct in Politicks and Morals as the Old North State. With many wishes for your health and happiness

P. S. Remember me affectionately to Mr. Iredell and family

*From François Xavier Martin.*[26]     A., G.L.B.

New Orleans,

March 29th., 1845.

I received the letter you favoured me with, asking the communication of the memorials of the Revolutionary History of the State of North Carolina, and specially relative to the correspondence of Governors Caswell, Nash and Burke, which can be in my possession.

The History of North Carolina I wrote, finish precisely at the period of time in which the revolution began. Documents relative to that time have been collected by me, and it is with regret that I find us not able to sadisfy you, as I would have been desirous to do.

I am with respect, Sir,

Your obedient Servant.

*From Samuel S. Phelps.*[27]     A.

Middlebury, Vermont.,

April 2nd., 1845.

The object of this communication, when disclosed, will I trust supercede the necessity of any apology for troubling you.

Upon the occasion of my selection to the Senate in October last, sundry charges were made against me by my personal enemies in regard to my course in the Senate, which demand some notice at my hands. A communication in writing was made to the Whig Convention while deliberating upon the subject of a candidate for the Senate, from which I make the following extracts, presuming that the writer has reference to the passage of the tariff bill on the 27th. Aug't, 1842, and to the occurrences of that day. He

---

[26] From Governors' Letter Books, 36:132.

[27] Samuel Shethar Phelps (1793-1855), of Vermont, a native of Connecticut, a graduate of Yale, soldier in the War of 1812. He was a judge of the state supreme court, 1831-1838, and United States senator, 1839-1851, 1853-1854.

says, "I was informed (by whom I cannot remember) that he [Mr. Phelps] [28] had been offended at some supposed slight, or want of attention [on the part of some Senators,] and used opprobrious language in regard to them, and *declared with oaths that he would not vote on the bill,* and I understood in the course of the day *that several Senators had made ineffectual efforts to soothe him."* The writer further states that he "repaired to the Senate Chamber and found that Mr. P. was not in his seat, and enquired of the doorkeeper at the southern entrance where Mr. P. was, who informed me that he was in a small ante room just at the entrance, with Mr. Conrad of Louisiana, who I understand *was endeavouring to persuade him to vote."*

He then goes on to state that when the question was propounded I was absent from my seat, was sent for and after coming in, refused to vote until my name had been called three times.

Now, Sir, I have thought it my duty to call the attention of my associates in the Senate to these statements, with a view to my own vindication. I have communicated with every Senator who voted for the bill, and every Whig then in the Senate, except yourself, not one of whom has any recollection of such accurrences.

Will you do me the favour to give me your recollection, if you have any in relation to these statements, and more especially whether you have any knowledge of the "opprobrious language" the declaration that I "would not vote on the bill," of my absence when the question was put, or anything unusual in giving my vote at last—and in general what my course was in reference to that measure.

You will perceive, and I trust appreciate, my motives in this appeal to you. Although vindicated to some extent by a re-election to that important trust, yet I desire to clear myself altogether from these imputations, and the proper witnesses are my associates in the Senate.

Your early answer is desired, and will be duly appreciated by your friend and late associate,

P. S. Please return this (or if not, preserve it) that the tenor of this inquiry may hereafter be compared, if necessary, with the answer.

---

[28] Brackets appear in original.

*To James W. Bryan.*                    U. Bryan Mss.

Raleigh,

April 13th, 1845.

\* \* \* \* \*

You perceive that we have not removed yet. Susan spent last week with me at the Govt House, where I have been staying as a watch over the public property, for two or three months, it being in imminent danger from Rogues and Rats. We have been painting and refitting parts of the establishment, which, in its best plight, is a wretched concern—and have gotten George to undertake to purchase furniture for us in New York, to the amount of the appropriation of the Legislature. This has not yet come to hand. We calculate on being here *cum omnibus copiis* by the last of this month. I have been meditating a journey to Mecklenburg in the mean time, occasioned by the death of Dr. Alexander, my brother-in-law, and the singular situation of his widow as to her rights in his estate, which, tho' ample, is limited by his Father's will, at least the realty, to his children, and deprives her of dower except in Alabama. I have not yet determined to go. That section of Country has been dreadfully afflicted recently with putrid sore throat combined with Erisypelas, which has prevailed as an Epidemic from Guilford West. There have been a few cases of it here, and one death. A Dr. Jeffreys, occupying Genl. Daniel's old office near this House.

I have not made a minute search for the correspondence of Gov. Caswell since my publication in regard to the memorials of our History, but have no doubt it will be all found, according to his mem. of public papers which Gov. Swain sent me. If Mr. Hubbard [29] designs to write his Biography, he ought to spend a month or two here examining the public records, as the work should embrace the entire history of the State, for a period of about 20 years. Some of the letters you recently published are inexplicable without reference to the documents in the office of the Secretary of State. For example, he says the Genl Assembly

---

[29] The Rev. Fordyce Mitchell Hubbard (1809-1888), a native of Massachusetts, graduate of Williams College, and tutor there. He studied law, but became an Episcopal minister. He came to North Carolina as rector of Christ Church, New Bern, in 1842, became head of a church school in Raleigh in 1847, and was professor at the university, 1849-1868. At its closing, he taught at St. John's School, Manlius, N. Y. He returned to Raleigh in 1881. He was an editor for a time, and was the author of the sketch of William R. Davie, in Sparks; *American Biography.*

Feby. 1781, had explained the appointment of Smallwood &c. This refers to the extraordinary fact that after Gates' defeat in Aug. 1780 and retreat to Hillsboro', that the Genl Assembly appointed Smallwood of Maryland a Maj. Genl. of N. C. Militia, *overslaughing* Caswell, Sumner &c, which gave so much offence (justly, according to all Military rule and pride) that although the enemy were in Charlotte, Genl. Sumner[30] and other Continental officers left the army beyond the Yadkin, and returned home. This appears from the Journal of the Board of War—a body also created by the Genl. Assembly to supersede the Governor in his Constitutional right to command the Military force of the State, and which probably induced Gov. Nash to resign his office.

I hope you and Mrs. B. will make us a visit this summer, and please say to Mr. Hubbard that I will be happy to afford him every facility in my power for the execution of his proposed work, should he find a visit to the seat of Government desirable in the execution of his plan.

A Loco meeting here yesterday recommended Jas. Sheperd as their Candidate for Congress. It is considered a triumph by him, over all the party leaders in Wake. The matter is yet to go before a district Convention, a week or two hence.

\* \* \* \*

Caldwell is a highly acceptable Judge to the bar and public. There is a review being published in the Norfolk Beacon of Judge Ruffin's opinion in the State vs Rives,[31] which is quite clever, and Mr. Iredell supposes it to be by Tazewell.[32]

---

[30] Jethro Sumner (1733-1785), a native of Virginia, who, after service in Virginia troops, 1758-1761, moved to Bute (now Warren) County, N. C. He was sheriff in 1772, a member of the provincial congress, 1775, and, entering the Revolutionary War as a major of militia, saw active service as a colonel, and then brigadier general in the continental army.

[31] 27 N. C., 297.

[32] Littleton Waller Tazewell (1774-1860), of Virginia, a graduate of William & Mary, who studied law under George Wythe, and practiced, first at Williamsburg and later in Norfolk. He was a member of the house of delegates, 1798-1800, a Republican member of congress, 1800-1801, and again in the delegates, 1804-1806, 1816-1817, United States senator, 1824-1832, delegate to the convention of 1829, and governor, 1836. In general a follower of Jefferson, he opposed the Embargo and Non-Intercourse Acts, preferring war with Great Britain. He was an opponent of Nullification, but was equally opposed to any coercion.

*To Samuel S. Phelps.*[33]          A., G.L.B.

Raleigh, N. Carolina,

April the 16th., 1845.

Dear Sir—

Your letter of the 2d. Inst. was sent to my residence at Hillsboro', and did not reach me untill to day. You state that a communication was addressed to the Whig Convention of Vermont when about to select a candidate for the Senate in October last, charging, in substance, that when the Tariff Bill of 1842 was under consideration in the Senate of the United States, you declared with oaths that you would not vote for the Bill, that much effort was used to procure your suport to it, that you were absent when the question was put, on the passage of the Bill, & that, after being sent for and called in, you refused to vote untill your name had been called three times: and ask for my recollection as to the truth or falsehood of these several charges. In reply I have to state that I remember nothing going to substantiate any one of them. I know that many Senators (at least several) who finally voted for the Bill, had determined when it came from the house not to vote for it, because the provision for the distribution of the land proceeds had been abandoned, and that they ultimately yielded their objections and did vote for it. But I have no remembrance of your being one of them. As to hesitation when called by the Secretary to vote, the only instance remaining in my remembrance is that of one of the Senators from Maine, who did not vote untill after the call had ceased, tho' present, and who then went to the Secretary's desk, and ascertaining by counting up the yeas and nays that his vote was required to pass the Bill, voted in its favor.

I shall at all times be pleased to hear of your health and prosperity, and with the kindest remembrance,

Your friend & servant,

William A. Graham.

Hon. Samuel S. Phelps.
Senator U. S.

---

[33] From Governors' Letter Books, 36:143.

*From Brigham Young.*[34]                                    A.

Nauvoo, Illinois,

April 25th, 1845.

Suffer us, Sir, in behalf of a disfranchised and long afflicted people to prefer a few suggestions for your serious consideration, in hope of a friendly and unequivocal response, at as early a period as may suit your convenience, and the extreme urgency of the case seems to demand.

It is not our present design to detail the multiplied and aggravated wrongs that we have received in the midst of a nation that gave us birth. Some of us have long been loyal citizens of the State over which you have the honor to preside; while others claim citizenship in each of the States of this great confederacy. We say we are a disfranchised people. We are privately told by the highest authorities of this State, that it is neither prudent nor safe for us to vote at the polls; still we have continued to maintain our right to vote, until the blood of our best men has been shed, both in Missouri and Illinois, with impunity.

You are doubtless somewhat familiar with the history of our extermination from the State of Missouri, wherein scores of our brethren were massacred, hundreds died through want, and sickness occasioned by their unparalleled sufferings; some millions of our property were confiscated or destroyed, and some fifteen thousand souls fled for their lives to the then peaceful and hospitable shores of Illinois; and that the State of Illinois granted to us a charter, *for the term of perpetual succession* under whose provisions private rights have become invested, and the largest city in the State has grown up, numbering about 20,000 inhabitants.

But, Sir, the startling attitude recently assumed by the State of Illinois forbids us to think that her designs are any less vindictive than those of Missouri. She has already used the Military of the State, with the Executive at their head, to coerce and surrender up our best men to unparalleled murder, and that too under the most sacred pledges of protection and safety.

---

[34] Brigham Young (1801-1877), a native of Vermont, the second president of the Mormon Church, and colonizer of Utah, who probably prevented the dissolution of the church after Joseph Smith's murder by his powers of leadership, and his genius for colonization. Ruthless and domineering as a leader, he was benevolent and kindly in private life.

As a salvo for such unearthly perfidy & guilt, she told us, through her highest Executive officer, that the laws should be magnified, and the murderers be brought to justice; but the blood of her innocent victims had not been wholly wiped from the floor of the awful arena, where the citizens of a sovereign State pounced upon two defenceless servants of God, our Prophet and our Patriarch, before the Senate of that State rescued one of the indicted actors in that mournful tragedy from the Sheriff of Hancock County, and gave him an honorable seat in her Hall of Legislation. And all others who were indicted by the Grand Jury of Hancock County, for the murder of Generals Joseph & Hyrum Smith, are suffered to roam at large, watching for further prey.

To crown the climax of these bloody deeds, the State has repealed all those chartered rights by which we might have defended ourselves, lawfully, against aggressors. If we defend ourselves hereafter against violence, whether it comes under the shadow of law or otherwise, (for we have reason to expect it both ways,) we shall then be charged with treason and suffer the penalty. And if we continue passive and nonresistant, we must expect to perish, for our enemies have sworn it.

And here, Sir, permit us to state, that Gen. Joseph Smith, during his short life, was arraigned at the bar of his Country about fifty times, charged with criminal offences, but was acquitted every time by his Country, his enemies, or rather his religious opponents, almost invariably being his judges; and we further testify, that as a people, we are lawabiding, peaceable and without crime, and we challenge the world to prove the contrary; and while other less cities in Illinois have had special Courts instituted to try their criminals, we have been stript of every source of arraigning marauders and murderers who are prowling around to destroy us, except the common magistracy.

With these facts before you, Sir, will you write to us without delay, as a father & friend, and advise us what to do? We are, many of us, citizens of your State, & all members of the same great confederacy. Our fathers, nay, some of *us*, have fought and bled for our Country, and we love her Constitution dearly.

In the name of Israel's God, and by virtue of multiplied ties of country and kindred, we ask your friendly interposition in our favor.

Will it be to much for us to ask you to convene a special session of your State Legislature, and furnish us an asylum, where we can enjoy our rights of conscience and religion, unmolested?

Or will you, in a special message to that body, when convened, recommend a remonstrance against such unhallowed acts of oppression and expatriation as this people have continued to receive from the States of Missouri & Illinois?

Or, will you favor us by your personal influence, & by your official rank?

Or, will you express your views concerning what is called the *"Great Western Measure"* of colonizing the Latter Day Saints in Oregon. The Northwestern Territory, or some location remote from the States, where the hand of oppression shall not crush every noble principle, & extinguish every patriotic feeling?

And now, Hon. Sir, having reached out our imploring hands to you with deep solemnity we would importune with you, as a father, a friend, a patriot and statesman; by the Constitution of American liberty; by the blood of our fathers who have fought for the independence of this republic; by the blood of the martyrs, which has been shed in our midst; by the wailing of the widows and orphans; by our murdered fathers and mothers, brothers and sisters, wives and children; by the dread of immediate destruction from secret combinations now forming for our overthrow; and by every endearing tie that binds man to man, and renders life bearable; and that too, for aught we know, for the last time, that you will lend your immediate aid to quell the violence of mobocracy, and exert your influence to establish us, as a people, in our civil and religious rights, where we now are, or in some part of the United States, or at some place remote therefrom, where we may colonize in peace and safety, as soon as circumstances will permit.

We sincerely hope that your future prompt measures towards us will be dictated by the best feelings that dwell in the bosom of humanity—and the blessings of a grateful people, & of many, ready to perish, shall come upon you.

We are, Sir,
With great respect,
Your most obed't Servt's

Committee in behalf
of the Church of Jesus
Christ, of *Latter Day
Saints,* at Nauvoo, Ill.
BRIGHAM YOUNG, President
WILLARD RICHARDS,[35] Clerk of the
Quorum of the Twelve

N. K. WHITNEY[36]
GEORGE MILLER[37]
Trustees of the
Church of Jesus
Christ of Latter
Day Saints

P.S. As many of our communications, postmarked "Nauvoo," have failed of their destination, and as the mails around us have been intercepted by our enemies, we shall send this to some distant office, by the hand of a special messenger.

*From John W. Norwood.* U.

Hillsborough,

May 5th, 1845.

You have heard that the Caldwell Institute[38] is to be removed from Greensborough. Yanceyville, Oxford, Hillsborough, and perhaps Rockingham Springs will make proposals. Oxford will offer by far the largest sum of money & Yanceyville is the favourite at present, decidedly.

---

[35] Dr. Willard Richards (1804-1854), a native of Massachusetts, an early convert to Mormonism. He was made a bishop in 1837, went to Utah with Brigham Young in 1847, was secretary of state of Deseret, 1849-1851, editor of the *Deseret News,* and the first postmaster of Salt Lake City. He wrote profusely, and with ability, and was one of the influential leaders of the community.

[36] Newel Kimball Whitney (1795-1850), a native of Vermont, a soldier in the War of 1812, who became one of the first bishops. He was presiding bishop in 1844. "Blessed by the Prophet," he became Joseph Smith's private secretary. He went to Utah in 1848.

[37] George Miller was one of the early bishops, and was very influential while the Mormons were at Nauvoo. He handled the construction of the temple and other buildings there, and was a regent of the projected university. He apparently never reached Utah. He was bent upon a Mormon move to Texas, and angered Young, who pronounced his views "wild and visionary."

[38] Caldwell Institute, at Greensboro, was founded by the Orange Presbytery, and succeeded well. Because of danger from epidemics, it was moved in 1845 to Orange County, and located in the country outside of Hillsboro. The Rev. Alexander Wilson, a teacher famous in North Carolina, was at the head of it, with the Rev. Silas Lindsley as his assistant.

Yet I am confident we can have it if we know our own interest. We must raise about $3000. in money besides the contemplated improvements to the Academy, which the Town will pay for.

The Trustees owe $1800. and must have a house for the President. We are to have a meeting of the Trustees at Yanceyville on the 15th. to receive proposals & *recommend* a location to Presbytery, which meets at Cross Roads on the 11th. June.

My object in writing this hasty note is to ask you how much you will give—3 an[nual] instalments. Please write to Dr. Long,[39] as we wish to have every thing done this week. There is no opposition.

We had a Town Meeting Saturday—all right.

*To James W. Bryan.*          U. Bryan Mss.

Raleigh,

May 5th, 1845.

*  *  *  *  *

I will go to Hillsboro' for my family the last of this week, and we will all come down about the middle of the next. We have delayed the removal longer than we intended on account of the whooping cough among our children, and some domestic arrangements.

There has been quite a hubbub here for a few days past, owing to a statement of Dr. Stith that "black tongue" prevailed epidemically in the City. The Register and Star, and it is said, the other faculty deny it, while Stith's publication appears editorially in the Standard. It is a sort of "cock and bull" story, the amount of which is, that many who thought they had only bad colds or hysterics, have had the real *atra lingua*. Though the market people are said to have been scared out, and there has been quite a scarcity of supplies.

You have probably seen in the National Intelligencer a notice of the death of our Classmate, the Revd. E. D. Sims,[40] professor in the University of Alabama. Mr. Badger, who returned a day or two since from Northampton Court informs me that Cherry was dangerously ill at the C. H. having been attacked there with pneumonia. He tho't the probabilities against his recovery.

---

[39] Dr. Osmond Long.

[40] Edward Dromgoole Sims (1805-1845), a native of Virginia, Methodist minister, graduate of the university, professor in Randolph Macon College, student at the University of Halle, professor at the University of Alabama.

You have seen in the papers, I presume, the account of the death of Geo. E. Spruill of Warren. He had previously lost some 8 or 10 negroes with the same disease.

\* \* \* \* \*

The frost and drought in Orange have greatly injured the crop of wheat, and there had been no rain of consequence when I left, for nearly eight weeks. Here, there have been copious showers, and the vegetation has quite recovered from the frost, except what was killed dead.

My friend Mr. Bennehan left here a day or two since, accompanied by Judge Cameron to consult the physicians at Philadelphia as to his health. He is threatened with dropsy in the chest, and is evidently very seriously affected.

The School for the Deaf and Dumb opened on the first inst. tho' but few Counties have attended to the Law; and we shall put in operation a school for the blind, as soon as applications are made for a sufficient number of pupils.

Will you come up to Commencement? You see by the Register that an extraordinary bill of fare is in preparation.

*From Mary W. Burke.*[41]　　　　A., G.L.B.

Marion, Ala.,

May the 12th., 1845.

To His Excellency
William A. Graham:

I have been duly honored with your Excellency's communication. In compliance with your solicitations, made in obedience to a resolution of your last General Assembly.

I have directed my friend, Dr. Webb, of Hillsboro', to place at your disposal the correspondence and other official documents pertaining to the administration of my father, Gov. Burke, now in his possession.

It has been nearly twenty years since I examined any of those papers, and it is much to be feared that time has so dimmed many of the documents, that much of that interesting portion of the history of our venerable Commonwealth will be lost, which would have given additional brightness to the page on which is recorded

---

[41] From Governors' Letter Books, 36:201.

the worth of those Revolutionary Sires long since taken to the bosom of their and thine God.

It would perhaps not be inappropriate that I should say to your Excellency, that many years ago the Honorable Chief Justice Ruffin remarked to me that he had seen some official letters of my father (I think) "in the office of Raleigh," which gave him a high estimation of Gov. Burke's "talents as a business man;" it is possible he can refer you to some official letters of his, not in my possession.

I sincerely regret that I am unable to give your Excellency any information in relation to the bound manuscript book found among the papers of the late Mrs. Watters, of Hillsboro', as enquired of in your letter, but suppose it to have come to her possession through Gen. Clarke.

Feeling the most anxious solicitude in whatever pertains to the Revolutionary History of my native State, I trust that, under the favorable auspices of your Excellency, every thing which will tend to elevate & elucidate the character and motives of her sons, who from a love of liberty & a religious devotion to their Country and her course, & spent their lives and their fortunes in her defence, will be brought to light to their honor and renown.

Accept my sincere thanks for the kind terms in which your solicitation has been proferred, and be pleased to receive the highest assurances of regard and esteem with which I am, your Excellency's

Friend & obedient servant,<br>Mary W. Burke

Gov. Graham.


*To James W. Bryan.*    U. Bryan Mss.

Raleigh,

June 9th, 1845.

* * * * *

We were all, that is all Raleigh, at the Commencement at Chapel Hill last week. The assemblage was greater than I had ever witnessed there before, and there were some new exercises, as the papers will inform you. The occasion passed off well, and the Institution is in a highly flourishing condition. Mangum,

J. Y. Mason[42] & Prest. Polk were made L. L. Ds. Dr. Hawks was proposed for the same distinction, and has no doubt more of the learning implied in the degree than all of them put together, but it was deemed proper to postpone the matter untill his difficulties in his Church [43] should become settled.

Mr. Hubbard has been searching records with diligence and will, I hope, give us some interesting accounts of early times and characters.

*From David L. Swain.*          A.

Chapel Hill,

June 9th., 1845.

Since your departure I have rec'd from Doct. Webb a box of papers scarcely less in magnitude than the one sent you a short time since, which I, at that time, supposed contained all Gov. Burke's papers.

I have as yet given but a very cursory examination to the second series, but have found some of great historical value. Among them is autograph of John Adams, of 8 pages, presenting his views with respect to the form of government best calculated to secure the happiness of the people. It was furnished at the request of Gov. Burke, and is without date, but is probably older than any of our State Constitutions. There are several interesting letters from Gov. Johnston, and one written in 1777, presenting unfavorable auguries of our new State Constitution, which had just gone into operation, and a severe critique on the first legislative body organized under it, which was then in session.

The more I consider the subject, the clearer are my convictions, that nothing should be recorded untill the collections are as complete as it may be possible to make them. "Every thing throws light upon every thing." If the Murphy papers cannot be obtained, the mere knowledge of what they consist, might enable you to edit the volumes to be prepared under your direction, in a much more satisfactory manner.

---

[42] John Young Mason (1799-1859), of Virginia, a graduate of the university, a lawyer, served four years (1823-1831), in each house of the legislature, was a Democratic member of congress, 1831-1837, Federal district judge, 1837-1844, secretary of the navy, 1844-1845, 1846-1849, attorney general, 1845-1846, minister to France, 1854-1859.

[43] Francis L. Hawks, while rector of St. Thomas' in New York City, established at Flushing St. Thomas' School for Boys, which failed with great financial loss. He was severely criticized, and resigned as rector, and removed to Mississippi.

*From James W. Bryan.*                                      U.

Newbern,

June 16th, 1845.

\* \* \* \* \*

We hear certain strange rumors of scandal here, respecting
certain of the *Élite* of your City. I know not how to credit them.
Our *Élite* have taken desperate colds attending the concerts of
the Orphans, and I am glad nothing worse has happened to them,
as they are so much better off in that respect than those of the
Capitol.

Poor Dr. Hawks, the publication of his Doctorate in the Nat.
Int. will just have the effect to give him an unenviable notoriety
again; he has the luck of it. He comes so near the attainment of
high honors that he reminds me of the Exclamation in Horace of
*Eheu fugaces!*

All join me in love to you all.

*To David L. Swain.*          U. Swain Mss.

Ex. Office,

Raleigh,

July 2nd., 1845.

I did not reply to your last letter, relative to the completion of
the Executive Letter Books, etc., because I presumed that you
would have visited Raleigh by this time. Having spoken to Mr.
Scott to make the copies, and obtained his consent to do so, I feel
solicitous on his account, that the work should be commenced, as
it may prevent him from embarking in other business.

I will be glad to have your aid in editing the Letter Books,
especially those of Gov. Burke, which you have recently examined.
I had expected to see the Murphey papers on a recent visit to
Hillsboro', but Mr. Kirkland, who had charge of them, was absent
on his canvass for the clerkship.

Please let me know, at your earliest leisure, whether you can
render the assistance desired, and how soon, in your opinion, the
transcribing may commence. I presume the Resolution of the
Gen'l Assembly requires the copying, only, of the Letters written
and received by the early Governors in their official characters.

This will abbreviate the work to be copied, though, under the other branch of the Resolution, the whole of their correspondence should be arranged and preserved.

*From David L. Swain.*[44]     A.

Chapel Hill,

July 12th., 1845.

1.—Georgius Washington, L. L. D. Harv. 1776, et Yale 1781, et Brown 1790, et Phil. et Wash. Exercituum Amer. Foed Imperator, A. A. et S. P. A. Soc. Rerum—pub. Foed Praeses.

2.—Johannes Adams. Mr. L. L. D. Harv. 1781, et Dart. 1782, et Yale 1788, et Brown 1797. Mass. Reip. Cur. Sup. Jurid. Pavic.— A. A. Praeses, S. H. et S. P. A. S. apud Bat. Rerup. et Gall. et Brit. Aul. Legat.—Rerum—pub. Vice Praeses et Praeses.

3.—Thomas Jefferson, Gulielm et Mar. L. L. D. et Yale, 1786, et Harv. 1787, et Brown, 1787, et Neo. Caes. 1791.—A. A. Socius.— S. P. A. Praeses—Reip. Virg. Gub.—apud Aul. Gal. Legatus—Rerum—pub. Foed. Secret. Polit.—et Vice Praeses et Praeses.

4.—Jacobus Madison, L. L. D. Neo. Caes. Rerum—pub. Foed. Amer. Praeses.

5.—Jacobus Monroe, Gulielm et Mar. L. L. D. et Harv. 1817 et Dart. 1817 et Neo. Caes. 1822. Reip. Virg. Gub.—apud Aul. Gall. et Brit. Legat.—Rerum—pub. Foed. Senat.—et Secret Polit. et Milet et Praeses.

6.—Johannes-Quincy Adams, Mr. L. L. D. Harv. 1822 et Neo. Caes. 1806. Rhet et Orat. Prof. Boylston.—A. A. Praes.—S. H. et S. P. A. Socius:—apud Remp. Bat. et Pruss et Bat. Aul. Legat.— Rerum—pub. Foed. Senat. et Secret. Polit. et Praeses.

7.—Andreas Jackson, L. L. D. Harv. 1833.—Rerum—pub. Foed. Senator et Praeses.

8.—Martin Van-Buren, L. L. D. Rutg. 1829.—Reip. Nov. Ebov. Gub.—Rerum—pub. Foed. Senator et Secret. Polit.—Vice Praeses et Praeses.

10.—Johannes Tyler. Gulielm et Mar. L. L. D. 184- Reip. Virg. Gub.—et Rerum—pub. Foed. Senator—et Vice-Praeses, et Praeses.

11.—Jacobus-Knox-Polk, Mr. L. L. D. Univ. Car. Septent. Reip. Tenn. Gub. et—Rerum—pub. Foed. Praeses.

---

[44] Printed as written, punctuation being impossible.

My dear Sir;

The two preceeding pages exhibit facts and involve principles which at present seem to be more frequently and freely discussed in your community, than accurately known, or clearly comprehended.

Of 11 Presidents, 7 graduated at American Colleges. 2, Gen'l Washington and Mr. Jefferson have received the degree of L.L.D. from 5 Colleges. 2, John Adams and Mr. Monroe from 4. John-Quincy Adams from 2, and all the others from one, with the exception of Gen'l Harrison, who is not known to have been thus distinguished. No College Commencement occurred during that brief period that intervened between his inauguration and death. No Western College, so far as my knowledge extends, has published any triennial catalogue. It is probable, but not certain, that his premature decease deprived him of a distinction won, and worn, by all our other Presidents.

Gen'l Washington, Gen'l Jackson, Mr. Van-Buren, and Gen'l Harrison, did not receive collegiate educations. Of the remaining seven, 3 graduated at William and Mary, 2 at Harvard, 1 at Princeton, and 1 here. I send a copy of the annexed catalogue to Mr. Badger, and leave you to dispose of yours in manner you choose.

Should occasion offer, it may be well to shew it to the members of the Ex. Com. & others, of the Board of Trustees.

*From Ralph Gorrell.*                                A.

Greensboro',

July 17th., 1845.

At the time the Caldwell Institute went into operation at this place, there was in existence a Society called the Adelphian Society, which was composed of the boys in Mr. Lindsly's School, then in operation, and some of the boys of the town. They held regular meetings, and had a small library attached to their Society. When the Institute was established here, Mr. Lindsly was appointed one of the teachers, and his School was merged in the institute, and the Adelphian Society went on in connexion with the institute, as it had done before with Mr. Lindsly's academy, and was composed of the boys who came to school from time to time as regular students at the institute, and such other persons as they chose to admit as Honorary members. Some short time after the operations of the institute commenced, another Society was formed which was called the Hermian Society.

These two societies in the course of the nine years during which the institute was in operation here, had both been very prosperous, and had formed large and respectable collections of valuable books, a considerable portion of which were donations from the citizens of our town and contributions made by them to assist the boys in buying books.

After the resolution of Presbytery at Danville to remove the institute from this place, and the organization of the school here, the Hermian Society held a meeting and resolved that they would not follow the institute, but would remain with their society in connexion with the school here. Some few members of the Adelphian Society (only three or four it is said) held a meeting, and resolved to follow the institute wherever it might go. I have not been able to see the constitution of the society, but am told by its provisions no meeting could be held in vacation, and that a majority of the regular members was necessary to constitute a regular meeting and in order to have a majority, eighteen were necessary. Upon the day on which the meeting of Presbytery was held at the Cross roads, to determine upon the final location of the institute, Robert Dick, who had been during the whole of this time of his being a student of the institute, a regular member of the Adelphian Society, went into the library to get a book, and found in it two of Doctor Wilson's sons, another of the members, and a negro man belonging to Doct. Wilson, with a number of boxes for the purpose of packing up the books at the library. Dick had the key of the Hall, and the others had effected an entrance by means of another key. From the remonstrances of Dick, they desisted in packing up the books. But the news soon spread over the town, and produced a considerable excitement among the members of the society here, who are opposed to the removal and the Honorary members, who claim a large interest in the books on account of donations and contributions by them made. This excitement was by no means allayed when it was understood that Doct. W. had told some of the boys that the books must be secretly and speedily removed, and when it was believed the contemplated packing up was done under his directions. Under this state of things, the trustees of our school have caused locks to be put on the doors, and have kept the keys in their possession, not with the purpose of seizing on the books permanently, or detaining them here, but in order to wait 'till a more quiet state of affairs would be produced, and 'till the school at Hillsboro' would go into operation, when the matter could probably be satisfactorily settled.

A portion of the members of the Adelphian Society at Hillsboro' have recently held a meeting, in which they resolved to transfer the property of the society to that place. A portion of the same society here have held a meeting in which they resolved that the library and furniture shall remain, but at the same time proposing to divide upon such terms as they deem equitable. Our trustees on Wednesday last held a meeting at which they have determined to hold possession of the library no longer, as the purpose for which they took possession has been accomplished.

Now, Sir, the question is, to whom do these library [books] belong? Are they not derelict, and therefore the property of the University. I am the attorney for the University in this County, but have never felt myself authorized, without instructions, to seize the books for the use of the Trustees, but at the same time I think the matter of that importance that requires them to be distinctly informed of the state of affairs in relation to these libraries.

I have therefore taken the liberty to address this communication to you as the President of the Board of Trustees, with the request that you bring the matter to their attention, and that I may be instructed what course to pursue, if any action is by them deemed necessary.

The matter will require a speedy action, as it is probable the boys may soon come to some adjustment of the matter.

*To David L. Swain.*          U. Swain Mss.

Raleigh,

July 31st., 1845.

The Executive Committee of the Board of Trustees of the University, have had under consideration a letter from Hugh Waddell, esq., written at the request of a "Major" or "Professor" Roberts, teacher of fencing, Boxing, etc., and asking permission for the latter to teach these arts to the students at Chapel Hill. The letter also states, that application had been made to you for this liberty, by Mr. R., and that you had referred him to the Board of Trustees.

I have been authorized by the Committee to say, in reply to Mr. Waddell, that they have no objection to Mr. R's "undertaking to teach his art of defence, (fencing, boxing, etc.) to such students of the University as choose to patronize him, provided that it be done in hours of leisure among the students, and shall in no manner interfere with the studies or policy of the College. His instructions must therefore be subject to the supervision of the Faculty, and liable to be suspended whenever they may conflict with the proper business and order of the Institution." I have thought proper to apprize you directly, of this proceeding of the Ex. Committee, to the end, that if Mr. Roberts shall present himself, you can inform him of the College regulations, and require him [to] conduct his instructions accordingly.

The Literary Board have been thwarted in commencing a school here for the Blind, by reason of the Abolition feeling which seems to mingle in all benevolent enterprizes at the North. I have been obliged to reject a teacher highly recommended by Dr. Howe in other respects, because of a spirit of propagandism on this subject. Dr. Howe now offers to come here in October, and spend two or three months in setting up the school, and giving instruction to any person we may employ for the purpose, as a teacher for the blind. And, it being an art easily learned, (as he says) by any well educated person, we now desire to employ a young man having aptitude for the task, whom we will place under Dr. H. while here, or, if need be, send for a few months to the Perkins Institute, to qualify himself for a tutor. You will readily perceive that we wish a young man of energy, and some knowledge of the world, as well as education. Can the faculty recommend such an one among the recent graduates, or teachers in the State? We can afford a salary of $500. & Board, at the outset, and may be expected to increase that, if the school shall prosper. I would be glad to have an early reply, as I shall make similar inquiries in other quarters.

*To David L. Swain.*     U. Swain Mss.

Executive Office,

Raleigh,

Aug. 8th, 1845.

Circumstances have prevented a call of the Executive Committee, upon the subject of your last letter, but I have conversed with Maj. Hinton & Mr. Bryan, who concur with me in saying that the former communication of the Committee is not to be understood as implying anything imperative in favor of Mr. Roberts.

Being informed that he was referred to the Trustees for the permission desired by him, they declared that no objection was entertained by them, to the students receiving instruction, at their option, in the arts he professed to teach. But the policy of the College was to be in no manner relaxed, nor its usual course of study interrupted.

His *morale* was not considered by the Committee. I had read his recommendations and stated to them, that they consisted of letters and testimonials from persons professing to have been his pupils, of no one of whom had I any knowledge. I presume, however, that if he is, as you are informed, a London prizefighter, there can be no hesitation on the part of any one, in saying that he is no fit instructor for the young gentlemen of the University.

As to the exercise of the Bowie-Knife, if it be the weapon attached to the Pistol, and used on Board our ships of War, it may be unobjectionable. But if it applies to the concealed weapon worn about the person, it is not an useful or ornamental accomplishment, in civilized society, either for War or peace and should not be allowed.

On the whole, the Faculty who have the opportunity of personal interview, will be expected to exercise a sound discretion over the whole matter, keeping in view the intimations already given by the Committee.

*From G. R. Runyon[45] and David French.*          A.

Pleasant Hill, Mercer County, Ky.,

Aug. 9th., 1845.

Accompanying this letter, are two copies of the second part of a Book, written by a member of the United Society called Shakers, at New Lebanon, Columbia County, State of New York. This Book was written by divine inspiration, and printed by the Society agreeable to the command of the Almighty. And this second part contains the testimonies alluded to in part first, page 218.

And we are requested by the Lord God of Heaven & Earth, to present two copies to the government of North Carolina. Accordingly, two copies of the first part were forwarded to your predecessor January 12th., 1844; and if they have not been delivered to you, we hereby authorize & respectfully request you to procure them, as it is the intention of the donors that the Books should be for the use of the Governors of the State, only in their official capacity.

We do not feel it our province to judge of the work and designs of our Heavenly Father, in this matter, nor do we consider ourselves responsible for the same, but we feel under the most solemn obligations to obey his command, which has been made known to us, by the inspiration of his Holy Angel, with that degree of evidence that we cannot doubt.

We therefore hope, that we shall not be considered as intruding upon the government, by our conscientious fulfilment of the duty thus requested of us. We are aware that the manner in which the Book was written in the name of inspiration from the Almighty, is not according to the generally received opinions, and present sense and ideas of mankind, but we solemnly testify that it was not directed by any natural wisdom.

And, although evidence of this cannot so satisfactorily appear to those who are unacquainted with the manner in which it was revealed; yet, to us, there was sufficient evidence given, by which we are fully convinced it could proceed from no other source, than from the infinite wisdom of the Creator of Heaven and

---

[45] G. R. Runyon is the only one of the persons named who has been identified. He was a signer of the church covenant of 1814 in Mercer County, Kentucky. The Shakers came in 1805 to Pleasant Hill, (better known as Shakertown), Mercer County, Kentucky. The book was published in 1843. Philemon Stewart, "duly commanded by the Lord," went to the "Holy Mount" on "Holy Sinai's Plain," and received "in flames of fire" the "Rolland Book."

Earth. Therefore, as dependent beings on his power and goodness, we feel it our duty humbly to receive his word, and bear witness of the same before all men, and we hope it will be kindly received, seriously read, and conscientiously considered, by all into whose hands it may come.

We sincerely desire that the Book may not be cast aside as the effects of a highly wrought state of phrenzy and fanaticism, which has a tendency to cast obscurity over true revelation, but these things we leave to be manifested by the fruits.

Yet, we would respectfully suggest that the well known character of the Society, for honesty, integrity, and uprightness, which has been established for sixty years past, is a guarantee to every reasonable mind against the supposition that this work originated from any other source than herein declared.

We present the Book, as performing a conscientious duty, without the least expectation or desire of any compensation otherwise than the good we hope it may do our fellow mortals.

With this short address, we fervently desire and pray, that it may be productive of good to all who receive it with the like good will, with which we send it forth.

The Society to which we belong is in a secluded and humble position in life, we have, therefore, omitted the fashionable style of address, as it might not, in some respects, be compatible with the plainness of our profession, we hope that, whatever may be found objectionable in that line, on our part, may be excused.

With all due respect, we remain, sincerely, your friends and well wishers.

G. R. Runyon,
David French.

In behalf of the Society.

Note 1st.—The words written on the first leaf of the first part of the Book, are commanded so to be done by the mighty Angel, who hath directed this work from the beginning.

Note 2nd. If any correspondence by letters, respecting the Book, is desired, the writers may address the undersigned; excepting their object is to reprint the Book; and in that case, it will be most proper to address the persons whose names are mentioned in a Note at the close of the first part of the Book; i.e. Richard Bushnell and Frederic W. Evans.

P.S. You will please acknowledge the receipt of this, and inform us whether you have the first part, or are likely to obtain it.

Direct, Shawnee Run Post Office, Mercer County, Kentucky.

G. R. R.

D. F.

August 15th., 1845.

*The National Intelligencer*[46]

*and*

*The Revolutionary Legends of North Carolina.*

I.                                                         A.

To the Editor of the Union—

The National Intelligencer of Aug. 1st. under the head of "Revolutionary Legends," contains an editorial critique upon an article in the "Union" of July 11th. entitled "Sketches of the Revolutionary War, in North Carolina," to notice a part of which I must request a brief space in your paper. The individual now addressing you, had no agency in the preparation of these sketches, nor any knowledge that such a publication had been made, or was intended, untill within a day or two before the appearance of the Intelligencer's remarks upon it. It may be proper further to add, that although a subscriber and constant reader of the National Intelligencer, he is not that subscriber who desired a republication of these sketches in its columns. Nor does he take any exception to its declaration, that they are devoid of interest. But feeling a natural concern in the fame of the person, who is the principal subject of the first of the sketches, and with whose services & sufferings at the darkest period of the War in the South the Intelligencer is pleased to trifle—very much to the amusement at least of the editors—he is constrained to interpose, not merely to assert the truth of history, but to repel such gross and causeless injustice.

These sketches purport to be narratives derived from a matron eighty-five years of age, now living in the vicinity of Charlotte in Mecklenburg County, who is denominated by the writer "Aunt

---

[46] From a copy, in Graham's writing, in the Graham papers. The letter was published in the *Union* of August 20, 1845.

Suzy," [47] & whose family name appears to be Alexander. And it may be remembered by your readers that one of them refers to the refuge (as is alleged) of the family of Genl. Jackson, (then in his boyhood) at the house of this old lady's father about the time of the British invasion of North Carolina; and the other, to the succor and relief afforded by herself & her mother to Joseph Graham, an officer who had fought under Col. Davie in the defence of Charlotte, on the 26th. of September, 1780; who had been badly wounded in the retreat, and who came bleeding and disabled to their dwelling on the evening of the same day. This individual is described in the editorial remarks prefixed to the "sketches" as the father of the present governor of that state, and is readily recognized by every one, in the least familiar with the traditions of the section of country, where these events happened, as the late General Joseph Graham, then of Mecklenburg, but for the last few years preceding his death (in 1836) an inhabitant of the adjoining county of Lincoln.

The Intelligencer denounces these stories as entirely fabulous, so far as they concern Jackson, because contradicted by history: and if not *impossible* as they relate to Graham, altogether incapable of having their truth ascertained since history had not deigned to notice him at all. The editors then proceed in vein of very great merriment to consign him to oblivion, loaded with such a weight of ridicule as practised pens are enabled to educe from the familiar contraction of his name in which the old matron indulges herself—her description of his dress—and from the appli-

---

[47] The article on "Aunt Suzy" first appeared in the *Washington Union*, July 11th., 1845. It was reprinted in the *National Intelligencer*, August 1st, 1845, with a blundering, supposedly witty, but rather stupid introduction, written, as it later developed, by Edward Johnston, one of the staff. There was nothing in the original story at all discreditable to General Joseph Graham, and, for that matter, nothing of the kind in Johnston's introduction, but the attempted witty comment evidently outraged Governor Graham's devotion to his father. The reference to Joseph Graham follows:

"With these [referring to anecdotes of the Jacksons]—equally uninstructive—are mixed some adventures of one Jo. Graham, who appears to have escaped the pursuit of Tarleton's dragoons when they chased Col. Davie's men from Charlotte.

\* \* \* \* \*

Now history, we saw, afforded no means of clearing up the facts concerning Jo. Graham, inasmuch as that negligent muse, Clio, has never given herself the slightest thought of rescuing the deeds, and even the 'red coat and white small clothes' of the puissant Jo. from unmerited oblivion. They say—at least Horace says—that she was quite in the habit of treating great men so, before Agamemnon's day.

'Viscere fortes ante Agamemnona
Multi: sed omnes illacry mobiles
Urgentur, ignotique longa
Nocte, carent quia vate sacro.'

As to Jo. Graham, therefore, we had no hope of making the muse and the midwife correct and check each other's fables."

cation of epithets or sarcasm. And being *classiques* they conclude this strain with a derisive application of the hackney verse of Horace

Vixere fortes ante Agamemnona
Multi: etc—

Possibly it may turn out, that the brave men who lived before Agamemnon had this advantage over their successors in 1780— that if they have been doomed to sleep unknown in the long night of ages for want of the *sacer vates* (the truthful author) to record their deeds, they have been at least exempted from the persecutions of the buffoons of literature, who beyond the narrow circle in which they choose to minister as the dispensers of fame, will not suffer a violet to spring from the grave of a hero, without plucking it up and casting it in mockery away.

All this is done, as the critique declares, according to the most approved "rules of historical criticism" "with great zeal for truth," and after a professed examination of the entire history of that period. Indeed it was to have been presumed in common charity, that such a course of derision & insult, would hardly have been indulged by those professing deliberately to give information to the public, without having had recourse to the best sources of information and finding them to justify it. "Its *truth* (say the editors) there was no ascertaining; but, at least, we thought we might be able to satisfy ourselves of the *possibility*, though not the reality of the facts; so we considered, consulted, and remembered." But they could find no trace of such a character in history.

Now, after all this, those who have read the remarks of the editors, will readily agree, that, if some such person as "Jo. Graham" did in fact exist, he was never in greater danger of annihilation, from the sabres of Tarleton's dragoons, than is his memory from the sneers of the critics of the National Intelligencer. How much they "considered & remembered" on this matter there is no ascertaining; nor is it very apparent how either process would have helped them to facts which, it is very evident, were never within their knowledge, though with their pretensions on the subject, they should have been. But they also "consulted," in search of the truth. Pray with whom? Certainly with no one having the slightest acquaintance with the traditions of the Revolution in Western North Carolina. The gallant defence of Charlotte by Davie, with but few more than two hundred men, against the approach of the whole British army—his driving back their columns of horse in three several charges which they made, and keeping them at bay untill Cornwallis advanced in person to his cavalry, reproached them with cowardice and by reinforcements of overpowering numbers at last compelled our troops to retire from the unequal contest—are remembered by the people of that region with a pride bordering on enthusiasm. And the part borne by Graham in that action, at the head of the volunteers of Mecklenburg—his command of the reserve covering the retreat, his being wounded and left for dead about four miles from the village, on the Salisbury road, are as familiarly known to the whole people of the western section of the State, as the defeat of Ferguson at Kings Mountain, or the fall of Davidson at the passage of the Catawba. It may be safely said that they are more generally known. The event occurred at his own home—in defence of that village in which five years before, while quite a youth, he had witnessed the declaration of Independence by the people of Mecklenburg—in a county which he often afterwards represented in the Legislature of the State, and in both of the Conventions which deliberated on the adoption of the Federal Constitution by North Carolina—in a vicinity where he ever after resided throughout a long life, and wore the scars of those wounds received there—and among a people whose militia he commanded in the capacity of brigadier general in 1814, when they cooperated with General Jackson in the subjugation of the Creek Indians. It is to be regretted, for the sake of peace to his ashes, that some portion of his public services had not brought him to the notice of the editors of the "National Intelligencer."

It may be asking too much of those who discourse so flippantly of muses and poets as these reviewers do, to "consult" muster rolls and records for evidences of the reality of one, whom they are determined to consider as a mere *nom du guerre*. But what historian have they "consulted," who furnishes a decent excuse for the mockery with which they have treated his memory? Is there any who professes to give details of the action at Charlotte in which the name of Graham is not mentioned? "Lee's Memoirs of the War in the South," written by a distinguished officer, who joined the Southern service soon after the affair at Charlotte, and, with this identical "unknown" of the reviewers, served in many a well-fought field in the winter and spring of 1781, contain this statement in substance: "On the approach of Cornwallis towards Charlotte, Genl. Sumner, who had been encamped at Providence, retired on the nearest road to Salisbury, leaving Col. Davie, strengthened by a few volunteers under Major Graham to observe the movements of the enemy.

\* \* \* \* \*

Davie, relying on the firmness of the troops determined to give them (the British) an earnest of the spirit of the country into which they had entered. — — — — — —

"His infantry, also dismounted, with Graham's volunteers, were advanced eighty yards in front, on each side of the street, covered with the enclosures of the village."

\* \* \* \* \*

"Lieutenant Locke & five privates were killed, and Major Graham & twelve wounded."

The account is too long to be copied here at length, but will well repay perusal by those taking interest in the subject. It will show that the "midwife," though professing no familiarity with the muse, is far better sustained by her than the National Intelligencer, which presumptuously affects to speak in her name. The mistake of the venerable old dame, in the rank held by Graham at that time, goes but to corroborate the general testimony of one who had known him in every grade from a sergeant to the head of a battalion.

Your present correspondent never saw Mrs. Alexander and knows nothing of her habits of life, which are detailed with some minuteness in connexion with these sketches of the Revolution, though from his earliest recollection he has heard of her kind ministerings to the wounded officers who sought her aid on the 26th. of September, 1780, and has been taught to cherish for her a hereditary gratitude, and affection. He well remembers that in September, 1836, about a month before the death of General Graham on the anniversary of the invasion of Charlotte, he recurred to the circumstances in which he had been on that day fifty six years preceding, and acknowledged the hospitality and good offices of these benevolent and patriotic females in terms altogether confirmatory of that portion of the narrative of the sketches.

I have no information concerning the authenticity of the account in relation to the visit of the Jackson family to the house of her father, but perceive no good reason why it should be doubted. Her accuracy as to what she herself saw, in the part of the story already considered, entitles her to be fairly treated as concerns the residue. There is surely nothing in the condition of things at that time to render it improbable, much less *impossible*, as the reviewers suppose. The people of Waxhaw and Mecklenburg in those days of dread and trial, were united in the strongest bonds of patriotic sympathy and good neighborhood. They were not more than a day's journey apart; and it would have been no difficult undertaking, on any occasion of alarm, for Mrs. Jackson to have sought protection under the hospitable roof of Mr. Alexander, in the manner related by his daughter. Her being at variance with the dates of events in Kendall's Life of Jackson, cannot be regarded as at all decisive against her credibility. Time is very often not material in determining the actual occurrence of events. There was no occasion for fleeing "farther and faster" into Guilford then, as the reviewers suppose. They seem not to be aware that Lord Cornwallis proceeded no farther than Charlotte at that time; but that, upon hearing of the defeat of Ferguson, he decamped from Charlotte in the night, after a stay there of fifteen or twenty days, and retreated to Camden; and that he did not again invade North Carolina until late in December following. It is no very violent conjecture, therefore, to suppose that Mrs. J. may have lingered in Mecklenburg a few weeks, before going to Guilford. This, however, is mere suggestion. I go not into any dispute upon *that*. I have been forced reluctantly to ask the indulgence of your columns, to repel an unprovoked attack upon one whose military reputation is cherished with some pride by his countrymen, and whose character is esteemed a richer legacy than any inheritance he has left to his children. That done, my end is accomplished.[48]

---

[48] The *National Intelligencer* of August 29th., 1845, published a letter from J. H. Gibbon, superintendent of the Charlotte mint, dated August 9th., 1845, stating that he had sent to the *Union* a copy of the article, and attested the accuracy of Aunt Suzy, and had sent a copy to the *Intelligencer*. The latter commented, "our displeased but still courteous opponent . . . ought certainly not to be surprised, if under the travestie of Jo. Graham, we could not, without any other indication of his identity as the father of the highly respected Governor of North Carolina. The figure he makes in the narrative was a little too strange to beget in us the suspicion who was meant."

*From James Graham.*                                    U.

Rutherfordton,

August 19th, 1845.

\*    \*    \*    \*    \*

I reached this village on the 9th. day of July on a lame horse.
I was strongly solicited to be a Candidate for Congress on my road
home by my old Whig friends. On Monday after my return, it
being a public sale day, and a large number of people assembled,
I was very strongly urged to run for Congress, and indeed told
by my old Whig friends they intended to run me at any rate,
they said, they never did vote for Clingman; and since his voting
with the North against the South they never would.

I still declined, saying I had not time to do myself, or my
friends, justice; but the people said I could be elected notwithstanding *that great disadvantage,* because there was a deep and
abiding dissatisfaction among the people with regard to Clingman's course. After strong and general solicitations in Rutherford,
I said I would go to Burke Court next day, and see and ask the
opinion of some of my Whig friends there what they would advise
me to do at so late a period. They advised me to run, and I
became a Candidate on the 17th. day of the month, (July), and
from that day to this, I have been assailed in the most bitter and
violent manner. I only addressed the people in a public speech in
Burke, Caldwell, McDowell, and Rutherford, still *I am elected
by a majority of 326 votes,* having every disadvantage to encounter.

There were Committees, justices, and Deputies at Morganton,
Asheville, and Rutherfordton, out actively against me.

I objected to Clingman's votes on Dromgoole's 2d. Resolution,[49]
and his votes on the 21st. or 25 Rule.

I also told him as he had declared with me four years ago that
he was for the annexation of Texas, he ought in my opinion to
have voted for Milton Brown's Resolutions,[50] or have presented,

---

[49] On January 2nd, 1845, George Coke Dromgoole (1797-1847), of Virginia, presented a bill in the house for the admission of Texas, after a Texas convention
should have adopted a suitable constitution. On January 21, he presented "sundry
amendments," not published in the *Congressional Globe.* He was a lawyer, who,
after quite extended service in both houses of the legislature, and membership in
the convention of 1829, was a Democratic member of congress, 1835-1841, 1843-1847.
[50] The resolutions introduced by Milton Brown, of Tennessee, provided for the
annexation and admission of Texas, on terms closely resembling those finally
adopted.

himself, some other and better scheme to procure annexation. I told the people I was uniformly opposed to the terms and conditions in Tyler's Treaty,[51] Ingersoll's Resolutions,[52] and all other propositions I had seen presented to Congress for annexation; *until I saw the terms and conditions* proposed in Milton Brown's Resolutions, and they met my approbation, and I could not see how any one who lived in the South and was for any annexation at all, could present better terms and conditions. I said further, I considered Walker's Amendment [53] in the Senate no advantage to Brown's Resolution; but, if the fact was [as] I understood it was; that Walker's amendment was offered *solely* for the purpose to reconcile and secure two or three Senators without which Brown's Resolutions could not pass the Senate, then I would have voted for Walker's amendment, rather than loose Brown's Resolutions altogether.

I stated further, that I considered Walker's amendment and Archer's Resolutions[54] as substantially the same.

Whether annexation should be accomplished by Treaty or Resolution, I prefered the last mode to the first, though I admitted, since the annexation of Louisiana and Florida, it might be done either way.

The Whigs in Tennessee are almost unanimously in favor of annexation according to the terms and conditions in Brown's Resolutions, and there is a deep and general regret there that Brown and Foster[55] did not vote for Walker's amendment—and if Foster looses his election it will be owing to that vote. I expressed myself in favor of Brown's Resolutions, in this place, the

---

[51] Tyler's treaty was, of course, the one submitted to the senate in 1844, and rejected by it.

[52] On January 2nd, 1845, Charles Jared Ingersoll (1782-1853), of Pennsylvania, as chairman of the foreign relations committee, reported resolutions to the House, providing for the admission of Texas, on certain conditions, practically identical with those included in the resolutions introduced in the senate by George McDuffie.

[53] Robert J. Walker was largely responsible for the recognition of the independence of Texas in 1837. He was influential with Tyler in the whole question of annexation. Also he had been active behind the scenes in securing the nomination of Polk. He drafted the final compromise resolutions, which were finally adopted.

[54] William S. Archer, who was chairman of the senate committee on foreign relations, introduced a resolution opposing the annexation of Texas, and its admission as a state by the proposed joint resolution.

[55] Ephraim Foster (1794-1854), of Tennessee, a native of Kentucky, graduate of Cumberland College (later University of Nashville), secretary to Jackson in the Creek War, member of the legislature for several terms, and twice unanimously elected speaker. He became a Whig in 1836, and was United States senator, 1838-1839, but resigned rather than obey legislative instructions. He was elected later, and voted against the admission of Texas, which probably caused his defeat for governor in 1845.

very day the Intelligencer brought them here last Feb. Court
to different persons.

\* \* \* \*

*From David L. Swain.*                                    U.

Chapel Hill,

Aug. 22nd, 1845.

Mr. Scott has recorded Gov. Burke's correspondence from 1774
to 1780. I have this morning arranged the papers for the month of
June, 1780, and find more difficulty in performing the task satisfactorily than I had anticipated. I cannot ascertain from any
papers here the precise day of his entrance upon or retirement
from, the office of Chief Magistrate. A rough and rather imperfect
copy of what I suppose to have been his first Message to the General Assembly, bears date of 29th. June. He was a voluminous
writer, and his Messages went much more into detail than those
of his immediate predecessors or successors. It is very desirable,
I think, that these shall be accurately recorded, and I must beg
you therefore to have the files of the House for 1780-81 carefully
examined, and the original Messages transmitted to me. It is not
improbable that other important papers may be found with them.
Mr. S. will be able to proceed little further until I hear from you.
One or more quires of copies of the Governor's letters, besides
those shewn to you, is either lost, or remains in Hillsborough. I
must have thorough search made for the manuscript there.

Do you expect to be in attendance on our next Superior Court?
Please inform me, and if you do, it is not improbable that I will
meet you there. It will serve my convenience more effectually,
however, if you will make Chapel Hill a stage in your way, and
spend a night at least at my house. This much I think I have a
right to insist upon, as a duty to the public, aside from private
obligations.

I believe you have in the State Library the Letters of John
Adams to his Wife in 2 Vols. By turning to page 273 of the 1st.
Vol. (in the Appendix) you will find an interesting history of
all the circumstances connected with the autograph letter from
Mr. A. found among Gov. Burke's papers. The following is an
extract, p. 275. "Thus much for the printed pamphlet. Now for
the unprinted letter. Some time in the ensuing Spring [1776]

the Legislature of their State instructing them to apply to me for the delegates from North-Carolina called upon me with a vote of advice concerning a form of government to be instituted in that State. I blushed to be sure, to find that my name had reached so far as North-Carolina, and still more at such an unexpected honor from so respectable an assembly. Overwhelmed, however, as I was at that period, night and day, with business in Congress and on Committees, I found moments to write a letter, perhaps as long as that to Mr. Wythe, and containing nearly the same outlines. In what points the two letters agree or differ I know not, for I kept no copy and have never seen or heard of it since, till your volume revived the recollection of it."

Is it not strange that this Resolution of our Assembly was never heard of in N. C. in our day, and that our first knowledge should be derived from Massachusetts, more than 60 years after the occurrence of one of the most interesting events in the history of the State and the Union. I suppose that it will prove to have been the first legislative action in relation to a form of Constitutional government, here or elsewhere. But where is the Resolution itself? I cannot find it in any journal here. Do have proper search made for it, and inform me of the result.

I am very much pleased with the deportment and apparent diligence of our young men during the present session. Our present number in actual attendance is 155,—30 Seniors, 42 Juniors, 48 Sophomores, 32 Freshmen, & 3 irregulars. Among the applicants for admission were young men from 8 Colleges. We have a pretty fair opportunity offered us, in the examination of these representatives of different sections of Country, for comparing the modes and testing the accuracy of instruction from Connecticut to Alabama.

*　*　*　*

If you placed my latest letter on file, some weeks since, you may inclose in it the accompanying copy of a letter from Gen'l Washington to President Styles,[56] tending to prove, (as the lawyers

---

[56] Ezra Stiles (1727-1795), a native of Connecticut, graduate of Yale, and tutor there, 1749-1755. He became a Congregational minister, but retired because of religious doubts, and studied law, only to return to the ministry, in which he was noted for eloquence, and liberality of opinion rare in that day. He was sought by other denominations, but was pastor at Newport for many years. He was deeply interested in science, was a friend of Franklin, and a member of the American Philosophical Society. He was one of the founders of Brown University, was an ardent patriot in the Revolution, and became president of Yale in 1778. After he was forty, he learned Arabic, Syriac, Armenian, and French. He was one of the most versatile Americans of his day.

phrase it) that the great man was not so entirely superior to humanity as to be wholly regardless of the highest literary honors. It will afford you, moreover, ready means of comparison of the style of the first and last President, if, (as I suppose) you have a missive from the latter on the same subject now before you.

I have heard nothing from Professor Roberts, since the date of your last letter, and conjecture, that supposing that "scope and verge enough" was not allowed him, he decides not *to accept your terms*, in all which he has the hearty concurrence of the Faculty.

A call to the field from one of Napoleon's Captains (the late Professor Burgevin) some years since, has produced a decided disposition upon my part to *fight shy* of all foreign Professors.

*To David L. Swain.*      U. Swain Mss.

Executive Office,

Raleigh,

Aug. 26th, 1845.

I have readily found the Inaugural in other Messages of Govr. Burke at the Session of the Gen'l Assembly at Wake C. H. in June 1781. The ceremony of inauguration you will perceive is the same that was observed at the installation of Gov. Caswell. What has become of the old sword of State is a matter worthy of curious inquiry.

You will preceive that Burke was elected Governor on the 25th. of June 1781, and installed either the next, or the second day following. The inaugural, I believe, is without date, but other Messages bear date the 27th. The files of this Session & that of 1780, shed a much more favorable light on the character of Gov. Nash, than any documents I have yet seen. He served as a member of the Senate untill the 26th. of April 1780, when he was elected Gov. and a Committee was appointed "to confer on him the honors of Government." He continued in this office untill Burke's election, as before stated. In his Message at the opening of this Session, he states that he had acted one year under an election, & two months "by an act of Assembly," says that the office is one of very limited powers by the true reading of the Constitution, but that the Gen'l Assembly had interfered with it, in various ways of restriction, though principally by the creation of a Board of War. And that though ready to have taken the field in person, after this Board was dissolved, he was again superseded by their conferring on Major Gen'l Caswell the Supreme Command of the Military forces. He declines a reelection in his first Message, but is put in nomination with Johnston, Williams, Ashe, etc., and writes a letter to the Speakers of both Houses to withdraw. A vote of thanks followed, from both branches, for his "patriotic, able, etc. administration." So that he did not resign; and left office in good credit, apparently, at least. I have not yet ascertained how Caswell held office as Gov. for three years, and from Decr. '79 to 26th. of April 1780 besides, and Nash for two months more than a year. And it may be questioned whether either was constitutional, if by act of Assembly making a request to that effect, since an annual election was required.

I will examine the files of 1782 for further Messages of Burke, and will also search for the resolution of request to John Adams for his views of a form of Government. It most probably sprung from the Congress at Halifax in April 1776. Though it will perhaps turn out to have been an informal and private request, of which no record was made on the Journal.

\* \* \* \* \*

You are mistaken in supposing that I have any epistle from the President of the U. S. in acknowledgement of his doctorate. Perhaps he relies on a Trustee, who figured lately in the Raleigh Register, to make his acknowledgements.

Your letter supposes that Burke was elected Gov. in 1780. You may therefore find other letters which should be inserted before his messages which begin in June 1781.

I have felt compelled to address an article to "the Union" of 20th. of Aug. (I believe it is) on the subject of the action at Charlotte, in consequence of an extraordinary article in the National Intelligencer of a previous date.

\* \* \* \* \*

I have just rec'd a magnificent edition of the "Exploring Expedition" for the use of the State Library.

*From Samuel H. Walkup.*[57]     A.

Waxsaw Settlement, N. C.,

Aug. 27th., 1845.

Hon. Sir,

I trust you will pardon my liberty in addressing you when you learn my motives. An act of the Legislature has, I *believe*, made it your duty to inquire into & collect all that portion of the history of N. C. which has been neglected & which might affect her high standing and her glory. This duty, or any other duty, I know, no one would more earnestly pursue than yourself, either officially or in your private character. It is to endeavour to establish a fact, very immaterial in the opinion of some, & truly of very small consequence to N. C. any way, that induces me now to trouble you with this epistle, & viz., to produce very strong evidence of the birth place of Gen. A. Jackson being in this County of Union & State of N. C.

It is true we are resisted by the current of public opinion, founded upon the several biographies, written by his authority & direction in this particular. But the evidence upon which we confidently rely, is as follows.

Mrs. Lathan, a full cousin of Andrew Jackson, in a conversation with Benj. Massey, Esqr., stated, about 20 years ago, that she was about 7 years older than Gen'l Jackson, that she recollected very well when he, Jackson, was born, that she was present the night of his birth. That her Mother, Mrs. Lassley, who was sister to Mrs. Jackson, was sent for on that night, & took her (Mrs. Lathan) along with her to Mr. McAmies, where & when Andrew Jackson was born. Mrs. McAmie, Mrs. Crawford, Mrs. Lassley & Mrs. Jackson were sisters. That Jackson, the father of Andrew, & McAmie settled in N. C., Jackson on Twelve Mile Creek, & McAmie on Waxsaw, that Jackson dieing previous some months to Andrew's birth, Mrs. Jackson lived with her brother-in-law, Mc-Amie, & sister until after A. Jackson's birth; in a few weeks after which event, Mrs. Jackson moved to her other sister's, Mrs. Crawford's, the reputed place of Andrew's birth, in Lancaster Dist. S. C., where she and family remained until the revolution. Mrs. Lathan recollects the circumstance of Andrew's birth very well, she remembers walking with her Mother to McAmie's the

---

[57] Samuel Huey Walkup, of Union County, state senator, 1858-1860 and later colonel of the 48th N. C. regiment, C. S. A.

night of his birth, & taking the near road thro' the field, & many other little incidents. She was a woman of unimpeachable reputation.

This testimony I learned from Benj. Massey, Esqr., of Lancaster Dist., S. C. You can see his letter in the Charlotte Journal & Mecklenburg Jeffersonian, dated about the same of this letter. His testimony is incontrovertible, for he is one of the most honorable and intelligent citizens of Lancaster Dist., S. C., & has frequently represented that Dist. in the Senate & House of the S. C. Legislature, with distinguished credit to himself & his Dist.

If it was necessary, others could easily be found, who have heard from Mrs. Lathan similar testimony, & among them Thos. & Sam'l Faulkner, of S. C., her nephews; which last two state that their Grandmother, Mrs. Lassley was a midwife, & very probably officiated on the occasion above alluded to. Every person about here knows that the McAmie place was & is still in N. C., about one mile from Waxsaw Creek, & ¼ mile from the State line, on a plantation now owned by Mr. Jackson Cureton.

Mr. John Carns, a very respectable old gentleman, of Lancaster Dist. S. C., heard Mrs. Lassley state many years ago, that A. Jackson was born at George McAmies, in N. C. & afterwards moved to James Crawford's, now in S. C. (see his letter or statement in papers of same date.) Mr. Sam'l Givens, of N. C., an old revolutionary soldier of strict veracity, has often heard old Charley Findley say, that Jackson was born at McAmies in N. C. Gen'l Jackson's own opinion was founded, probably, merely upon his infant recollections, and rambles, & those youthful associations which make localities so dear in mature years, & which compose those "greenest spots on memories' waste" around which it delights to "linger" & which distance, of time & space only renders more enchanting, & opinions founded upon such circumstances should weigh nothing against the much more conclusive proof we think we have adduced. But we wish others to be satisfied, and lay it before you, if you think proper to notice it.

But suppose that in fact and in truth Jackson was born at James Crawford's, the reputed place of his birth; even then we think we can establish that he was born in N. C., for that part of N. C. was given to S. C. in running the State line, after the Act passed in 1803, for there are old land deeds farther South & West than that,—Grants dated 1752, & calling for land lying South and West of James Crawford's, in N. C., Pickens County. I conceive that this amounts to proof positive, as far as oral testimony & *records* can prove anything. Will Mr. Kendal & other biographers of Gen'l Jackson state whether they had as strong proof as the above for the assertion that Jackson was born in S. C., or whether they had any proof, except Gen'l Jackson's mere opinion? If you, honorable Sir, would ask the question, you would get an answer which would satisfy all of us, and confer a lasting obligation upon your humble servant.

Please, Sir, excuse the bungling manner in which I have so long trespassed upon your patience, & be assured of my high esteen & regard for yourself personally, & politically, & present, if you please, my respects and compliments to your private Secretary, Henry Graham.

Your Excellency's humble Serv't

*From Elisha Mitchell.* A.

[Chapel Hill.
August 28th. 1845.]

$400.00.

Rec'd August 28th. 1845, of His Excellency, William A. Graham, Governor of the State of North Carolina, four hundred dollars for services already rendered, and to be rendered, in carrying on a survey of certain roads from Raleigh west to the Georgia line, and from a point, or points, in these to Fayetteville, directed to be executed by the last legislature.

E. Mitchell.

To Gov. Graham.

Dear Sir:

I send you above a receipt for the money with which you were so good as to furnish me. Also I have put into the hands of Gov. Swain something I have written for the Fayetteville paper, an article in which, you may have noticed. This, will you please read, and either suppress, altogether, modify, or continue, as your own judgment, and that of Gov. Swain shall direct. I suppose that such squibs as this are neither absolutely fatal and deadly, nor to be altogether despised. I had not time to attend to the punctuation.

I say now what I should have said before, that any suggestions you may make, in regard to the best modes of conducting the survey—or persons to be employed in it—will receive due attention. I left a map in your office, exhibiting the geological formations of the State, which I shall need in instructing the class now in hand. Will you please ask Gov. Swain to bring it up if he can.

The contribution from your Father's pen to our revolutionary history I regard as amongst the most valuable that have been recently made, filling a blank for which I had supposed there were no materials remaining. The men who fought at Kings Mountain seemed to rise suddenly out of the earth, and as suddenly disappear, no one could tell how, whence, or whither.

*To David L. Swain.*         U. Swain Mss.

Raleigh,

Sept. 2nd, 1845.

I believe I neglected on the hasty mem. sent with Burke's Messages, to state that he received a vote of thanks from the Gen'l Assembly, which seems to have been a customary compliment to a retiring Executive in those times.

I am induced to write, however, by the discovery of new matter from him, which I regret cannot now be inserted in its proper place in his correspondence. In examining the writings of Caswell, I find in one package a series of letters from Burke, as State delegate to the Continental Congress, reporting to the Governor the progress of events, and transmitting reports of the debates of Congress taken by himself on all important subjects.

These papers begin in Feby. 1777 and are numerous during that year—less so, in the years following. They are more elaborate than any productions that I have seen from his pen, and evince a rightmindedness, high spirit, and patriotism, surpassed by no member of that body, and a political wisdom, and conversancy in the philosophy of Government which would be creditable to Edmund Burke or Sir James McIntosh. He seems to have taken an active part in the debates, which besides being conducted in secret, could not be divulged, even by the members of the body except upon subjects which had received final action.

His course is marked by a vigilant jealousy against the encroachments of Congress on the States, great energy in relation to the conduct of our Military operations, devotion to North Carolina, which not unfrequently breaks out into indignation at the supposed arrogance or injustice of other States (especially Virginia) and great mental intrepidity which did not dread collision with the master spirits of the times.

One of his letters gives a detailed account of the Battle of Brandywine, in which he was an amateur, having gone out from Phila. in the expectation of a brilliant victory. This, he says, would have been attained, but for the singular and stupid blunders of Gen'l Sullivan, and asserts that although our troops and officers under the grade of Major General were admirable, there was no officer of that high grade in the service, who was worthy of his place, except the Commander in Chief.

Speaking of an excitement in Penna. growing out of the Constitutional provision of a single Legislative body, he declares, that he has heard that Dr. Franklin carried that article by representing that two bodies engaged in the lawmaking power would operate like a waggon with two horses drawing at each end, in opposite directions. Upon which Burke adds, that the propriety of two bodies in Legislation, might be much more truly shewn by a simile of four horses attached to the front of a waggon assisting each other in pulling up hill, and in bad places, but when going down hill, the hindmost horses counteracting the dangerous effect of the situation of the ground and force of those in front.

I have found all the papers of Caswell, mentioned in his memorandum, handed to me by you, that relate to subjects of much moment, except his Messages to the Legislature; that is, the packages with corresponding Numbers are here, but they have been searched heretofore, and some of the letters, I think, are abstracted.

The letters of Burke, before mentioned, will be of course copied in Caswell's correspondence, but such is my estimate of them from a hasty perusal, that had they been discovered in time, I would have had them also inserted among the present labors of Mr. Scott.

I will box up the Caswell papers, and retain them untill I shall have more leisure for their arrangement than I can command for a month or two to come.

I will probably go to Hillsboro' about the middle of this week— say Thursday,—and will remain ten or twelve days.

I send by this mail to Professor Mitchell a check for Four Hundred dollars, for outfit of his Turnpike Mission.

*Request from Committee.*                                U.

University of North Carolina,
September 6th, 1845.

At our last Commencement, several of the Trustees, who were in attendance, having noticed the very great inconvenience which we were at, to entertain visitors, suggested that we build by subscription, a large party room for their better accommodation. The students having taken the matter in hand, and appointed us as a Committee to obtain such pecuniary aid as we may be able, and believing that you would willingly contribute in any way to promote the interest of the University, we have selected you as one, who, in our opinion, would aid us in this matter.

Any sum that your liberality may suggest, will be kindly received. Please let us hear from you soon, as we wish to accomplish the work by our next annual Commencement.

Yours with respect

W. K. Blake[58]        E. W. Hall[61]
W. A. Daniel[59]       W. H. Manly[62]
W. J. Duke[60]         D. T. Tayloe[63]
                       Committee.

*To Messrs. Gales & Seaton.*                            U.

Raleigh, N. C.,
October 4th, 1845.

To the Editors of the National Intelligencer:

Your paper of the 1st. of August contained a grossly defamatory article, in ridicule, of the character of the late General Joseph Graham, of this State.

[58] William Kennedy Blake (1824-1897), of Fayetteville, graduate of the university, later a lawyer, teacher in women's colleges in North Carolina and South Carolina.
[59] William Alexander Daniel (1827-1893), of Halifax, graduate of the university, farmer and teacher.
[60] William James Duke, of Mississippi, a graduate of the university.
[61] Eli West Hall (1827-1860), of New Hanover, a graduate of the university.
[62] William Henry Manly (1826-1848), of Raleigh, who died in less than a year after his graduation.
[63] Thomas David Tayloe (1826-1884), of Beaufort County, a graduate of the university, M. D. of the University of New York, a physician of widespread reputation and popularity, later surgeon in the 61st. N. C. regiment.

This was the more surprising and offensive, by reason of the fact that independently of his Military services in the Western part of the State, and elsewhere, being well known, to those having an intimate knowledge of the British invasion in that quarter, he was described in the prefatory remarks of the Editor of the Union, from the narrative in that paper, on which your article professed to be a criticism, as "the Father of the present Governor" of this State.

Being aware of no motive which could have prompted such a publication, and presuming that possibly this description had been overlooked, I was content simply to expose the injustice of the assault, not doubting that a sense of propriety on your part would at once have made proper reparation. This was done in a communication to the Union of the date of the 20th. or 21st. of August, which has been generally copied by the newspaper presses of North Carolina, with observations of their own, calculated to vindicate the truth of History. Your failure to recur to the subject, after it has been thus brought distinctly to your consideration, evinces a disposition to persevere in the injury, whatever may have been the motive of its origin.

And to avoid any inference of acquiescence in such a course, I have to request that my subscription to the National Intelligencer be discontinued. The amount in which I may be in arrears will be paid as soon as ascertained.

Your Obedient Servant.
Will. A. Graham

*From Edward W. Johnston.*          U.

Washington,

Oct. 11th, 1845.

My friends, the Editors of the National Intelligencer naturally made me, as the writer for their columns of the Notice of Aunt Suzie's Revolutionary Anecdotes, acquainted with the displeasure which they learned that you had conceived at an article certainly never imagined by any body connected with the Intelligencer, to relate to any person of whose fame you were bound to be jealous; and once again, the other day, at receiving your letter of the 4th, they communicated to me that fresh token of your continued anger. To their respect for you, and their habitual good feelings towards every body of any merit at all, the affair was painful, and the answer to be returned you, embarrassing. Perceiving this, I proposed at once that they would allow me, as the original cause of the strife, to explain to you the facts.

If you will recur to the original notice (of Aug't 1st.) you will find, in the preliminary remarks, indications of the whole history of the paper. It was enclosed to the E. E. by some anonymous person, with a request to republish it. As a thing of doubtful claim to admission, it was only glanced at, and referred to me, as things of a historical sort often are. My impression is very decided that it came without any prefatory remarks of the "Union." Besides, had such, mentioning your Father, accompanied it, it is well-nigh impossible that both Mr. Gales and I should have remained (as we did) without a suspicion who "Jo Graham" was. As originally appearing in the "Union," we had all overlooked it. The political articles of that sapient Journal, one must read, of course, however *multum gemens;* but for any thing historical or literary or scientific, we all look on its columns as the securest hiding place a-going. Consider, too, I pray you, how complete a travestie of your Father the act of the narrator or of her Secretary had made; and imagine if, through such a disguise, any body was to be expected to recognize Gen'l Graham.

Mr. Gales, Mr. Seaton, Mrs. Seaton, are all familiar with the Revolutionary families and histories of your State. To me, the son of an officer of Lee's Legion, those names and events are the minutest household memories of my boyhood. And yet, I assure you that not an idea of your Father was ever suggested to any of us, by the person made to cut so absurd a figure in Aunt Suzie's legend. I think you will find, on fairly re-examining my article, that all this is plainly betokened by its tenour.

In truth, I looked upon the whole story as probably meant merely to glorify Gen'l Jackson; and therefore paid very little attention to "Jo Graham," whose very existence, you should have perceived, I considered problematical; for I looked on Aunt Suzie's whole story as apochryphal.

Greatly, therefore, were we all surprized to find that you regarded this very trivial and innocent matter in a deeply offensive light, and attributed it to personal hostility on the part of men, as you know, signally exempt from influences of that sort, and never indulging in their Journal the few personal resentments which they have. I know that your public career here, under their eyes, had commanded their high esteem. They admired your unusual calmness of sense, your unvarying maintenance of the Senatorian temper & dignity, your unpretending but solid ability. Believe me that the hastiness & unjust rancour which I am sorry to say I think you have displayed in this affair, are the only things that ever diminished you in the opinion of the Editors of the Intelligencer.

I know full well that you think them the enemies of your family, because in the late contest between your brother and Mr. Clingman, they, who thought the independent course taken by Mr. C. on the 21st. Rule,[64] deserved an unusual public favour, for this reason alone, and out of no personal preference, desired his success. But surely, Governor Graham, you know that honest men can prefer one man to another, in public life, without being even unfriendly to that other.

You perceive, my dear Sir, that I am writing to vindicate them, not to apologize to you for them. I may the better do this because if any offence has been committed, it should be transferred from them to me. Yet I too, am innocent of having had any thing but a very high opinion of you, & the best feelings, when this imputed injury and affront was perpetrated.

You appear to think that you have a right to expect that your very intemperate and causeless letter against them in the "Union" should be re-published in the Intelligencer. Its terms and temper did not permit it. As it is not their habit to print personal abuse against other people, they ought surely to be allowed to include Gales & Seaton in that rule. Recollect that, in an article of the 29th. of August they made all the amends that could be desired to the shade of Gen'l Graham. They should be held in no manner responsible for the innocent—nay, natural, mistake in the Intelligencer. That, it seems to me, you should visit upon the foolish people who, in their tale, tricked off in harlequin attire a brave gentleman, nickname him "Jo," and are then astonished & indignant if people mistake a really gallant and distinguished man for a Jackpudding.

My dear Sir, let me hope that this needless feud between people who can so easily find worse folks to quarrel with, may be dropped. You have the devil to differ with, and the Locofocos; be content.

---

[64] The writer was in error as to the rule, which was the 25th. rule. Clingman made a speech on the subject, on January 6th., 1845, which attracted much attention. He, however, opposed the 21st. also.

I do not know that you will consider my explanations exactly the most soothing; but you may remember that, in the Iliad, when Jove and the Queen of the skies get to very high words, the uncouth Vulcan limps in between, laughs at both parties, and makes peace.

Very sincerely your friend and servant

*From John M. Morehead.*                    U.

Greensboro',

Oct. 15th, 1845.

I had a set of measures made in Phil'a & sent me as a sample upon trial, I found them not correct, nor of good quality. I pointed out the defects, & told the persons to try it again; they did so, & sent me a second set, which I disliked more than the first. So I paid them for the two sets, & dismissed them & afterwards employed Price of Danville to make the ½ bushel & Gall. & parts of Gall. measures; one for each County. I thought the two sets on hand might remain in the office, for some new County, as they are frequently making them, & these sets could be easily altered by a coppersmith or tinner so as to make them correct. They would not be very good sets, but it is difficult to get a few sets of weights or measures made.

I have seen Kirkman & he says that Price himself was to take the set for Wake down when he called to get his money, & he thinks he did so, & left them in the Executive Office. I recollect Price did send some boxes up from the Hotel when he came down for his money, but whether this was included, or the boxes were only the *return of the originals* by which he made the duplicates I do not recollect. If the box for Wake was included, it ought to have been handed over to the Standard Keeper of Wake, who is, I believe, Col. Reeder, of your city.

If, therefore, you have 3 sets of copper (not brass) capacity measures in your office, one of them is for Wake, and it may be known by the half Bushel being out of stronger copper and not so high as the other two, & the Gall. Pot is more like a cannister than a Gall. Pot. This set is already tested and correct & may be handed over to the Standard Keeper.

We have Badger, Dewey, & Lucas all here; it seems quite like Raleigh—also Kerr, Waddell, Davis, Jones, etc.

Court is in full blast, but not much doing.

I think there is but a poor chance for you to don your chapeau as Commander in Chief & guard our coasts against the hostile Mexicans. Poor fellows, President Polk cannot kick them into a war.

\*    \*    \*    \*    \*

*From James W. Osborne.*                    A.

Concord,

Oct. 22nd, 1845.

We have been waiting with some anxiety to see what suggestions will be made in the papers at Raleigh concerning the political canvass of the approaching year. Thus far there has been no intimation that a convention of the Whigs is desired within any short period, or that such a thing is expected to take place. So far as your position is concerned I have no doubt—the nomination—let a convention meet when it will wish at your disposal.[65] The only question will be personal, and must be decided by a reference to those considerations which are wholly within your bosom. That you will be more acceptable to the great majority of the people than any one else can not be doubted. And that your election to the office for a second term is highly probable.

Some resolutions have been adopted at a public meeting at Asheville,[66] under the lead of Clingman, which may seem to have a construction unfavourable to you. How far this feeling may

---

[65] Graham's hesitancy about accepting the gubernatorial nomination, 1844, gave rise, in 1845, to the question if he would accept one for a second term. The *Standard,* on August 20, 1845, as part of its persistent sniping at him, asked if he would consent to serve a second term, or decline to do so. Graham, of course, ignored the question, but the *Register,* on August 22, replied that they did not know, and had never spoken of the matter to the governor. It continued: "Indeed, no one with the sensibility of even a dray horse, would think of mentioning the subject in his presence. It is not for him to say at present whether he will or will not. When the party, who nominated him for office, shall tender him again the honor of being their standard-bearer, the first occasion will arise when he can, with propriety, announce his determination. His whole life gives the assurance that he will then act as he always has acted since his entrance upon public life—"without fear and without reproach." The present day commentator can only reflect that times, indeed, have changed—and by no means always for the better.

[66] A Whig meeting in Asheville, on October 7, 1845, passed a series of resolutions, the first of which was: "*Resolved,* That we entirely approve of the administration of His Excellency, William A. Graham." The *Standard,* on October, 22, remarking, after quoting it, "As cool as the summit of Pilot on a January day," went on to declare it anti-Graham. Thomas L. Clingman had just been defeated for congress by James Graham, and his prominence in the meeting excited suspicion among some of the Whigs. Another view is seen in a letter of John Gray Bynum to Graham, Nov. 4, 1845.

exist with him I do not know, or whether he feels it at all. I am informed that some of his friends do sustain a feeling of opposition, but I am satisfied that it does not embrace any large number, and that it will pass away before the canvass begins. In the present state of the Whig party our press should be reinforced with more than its ordinary share of vigour and ability. But 'tis a deplorable fact that at this time it seems to give way to the general depression, and yield to the adverse course that seems to have befallen affairs In this district I fear that the Whig party is defeated. It will be so for Congress at the next term. We can still rally a majority in the canvass for the office of Governor, but it will be reduced. Outlaws & Banners districts, both of which are considered as lost, give fifteen hundred of the majority we claim in the State. Something must be done or we are defeated. Dockery and Worth did nothing to elevate the character of politics, in their canvass for Congress and the number and enthusiasm of that district have been impaired by it. The prospect is not it must be admitted encouraging, but I still believe we can carry the Governor and probably the legislature at the next election. My object at present is to urge the expediency of holding the convention in January next. At that time many members of the bar from this region attend the Supreme Court, and by this means a full representation may be secured. This is in the highest degree important. The concurrence of the west must be secured to any successful nomination. The time which would best suit the convenience of that region will be the period referred to, and I think now would be a favourable opportunity to respond to the Asheville resolutions in regard to that branch of the subject. In 1842 the Whigs of our State nominated Mr. Clay. Our circumstances are now different from what they were at that time, and we have no individual upon whom the nomination can be cast with so much propriety; but shall a nomination be made, a rally under some name is desirable, at the special terms of Cabarrus & Iredell—do not give us Dick—or Settle. Neither of them will work.

*To Edward W. Johnston.*                                    A.

Raleigh,

Oct. 22nd, 1845.

I regret that my engagements have prevented an earlier reply to your letter which came to hand nearly a week since.

I hasten at once to correct a misapprehension into which I know not how you have fallen. You state that you "know full well" that I consider the Editors of the Intelligencer the enemies of my family because of their preference for a particular candidate, at the recent election in the Mountain district of this State. This is certainly a strong mode of averring as a fact, that which can exist only in imagination. I am aware of no part taken by them in that election, which can be the occasion of offence to the member elected or to any of his friends.

In the notice I have felt obliged to take of the lampoon in the Intelligencer on Genl. Graham, I have but obeyed the ordinary dictates of self respect & filial duty—And although the explanations of your letter shew an absence of any offensive design in that publication, how stands the matter now before the public view?

The 'Unions' introductory remarks had described the person alluded to in the sketches as my Father. This I, (and as I presume the generality of readers of the article) did not overlook though you and Mr. Gales appear to have done so. Whatever therefore was said of this person after such description would be naturally presumed to be with a knowledge of this connexion.

But independently of this, had history been examined, or information sought as carefully as the Intelligencer's criticism professed, there would have been no room for the doubts or sarcasms of the critics. Hundreds of readers of the paper familiar with the British invasion of Mecklenburg, would readily understand who it was, that was attempted to be held up to public ridicule although the editors were ostentatiously ignorant.

As to your remark that the caricature by the "sketches" was calculated to disguise real character, there is a very simple view of the matter which guards against that.

The stories of the old matron, however badly executed & encumbered, purport to concern persons with whom the reader has already some acquaintance. And while no injury can be done by the loquacity a female octogenarian indulging a very pardonable vanity in telling how she had acted the part of the good Samaritan towards one who attained some distinction as a soldier, the case is widely different when persons of the intelligence & character of the Editors of the Intelligencer, neglecting the most obvious means of information, appear before the public not only denying the truth of the narrative, after a professedly minute examination, but trifling with the pretensions even of the chief subject of the legend.

I did not, as you intimate, make any requirement that my letter to the 'Union' should be republished in the Intelligencer. I forbore, for a fortnight, to reply to its article in the expectation that there might be some correction. This not being done, I noticed it in such way as I thought it merited; whether the offspring of design or negligence. And sufficient time having elapsed to shew that no amends were intended, I wrote the letter which you have seen. It is therefore simply a case of injury from negligence and a refusal of reparation.

With an entire reciprocation of the kind feelings you are pleased to express, I see nothing to change the views I have heretofore taken in relation to this subject.

I am very Respectfully<br>Your Obedt. Servt.

*From William Henry Foote.*[67]    A.

Raleigh,<br>October 30th., 1845.

The enclosed, from President Swain of Chapel Hill, will explain the object of my visit to Raleigh, & calling upon you, with the addition of a single sentence—that I undertook the preparing a history at the request of the Synod.

I shall feel myself under great obligations upon receiving from you an attested copy of the Declaration from the "Davie Paper." I wish to use it in my volume which I wish to send to the press soon.

Judge Cameron thinks he can identify the hand writing of John McNitt Alexander.[68] The paper I left with President [Swain] I found at Robert Alexander's in Mecklenburg, among the papers of B. Alexander. I think there is no doubt of its authenticity.

---

[67] William Henry Foote (1794-1869), of Virginia (now West Virginia), a graduate of Yale, and of the Princeton Theological Seminary. He filled pastorates in several places in Virginia, was agent for the Presbyterian Board of Missions, was an intense Unionist, and later a Confederate chaplain. He was the author of *Sketches, Historical and Biographical, of The Presbyterian Church in Virginia,* and *Sketches of North Carolina.*

[68] John McKnitt Alexander (1733-1817), of Mecklenburg, a native of Pennsylvania, trained as a tailor, who moved to North Carolina and, very successful as a surveyor and business man, became quite wealthy. His attempt to reproduce from memory, many years later, resolutions adopted at a meeting in Mecklenburg, on May 20th., 1775, with the names of the signers, brought about the first publication of the Mecklenburg Declaration of Independence, and the beginning of discussion of its authenticity, which has continued ever since. He served in the third and fourth provincial congresses, and was, in 1777, Mecklenburg's first state senator.

I shall also feel under obligation on receiving one of those copies that are referred to by President Swain.

I should have been gratified in receiving your recommendations and criticisms upon the Chapter referring to your father, and any other Chapter you may have chosen to inspect.

Very Respectfully yours, Sir,

P. S. My Post Office is Romney, Hampshire C'ty, Virginia.

[*Enclosure*]

*From David L. Swain.*

Chapel Hill,
October 28th., 1845.

The bearer, the Rev'd W. H. Foote, of Va., has nearly ready for the press, a History of the Presbyterian Church in this State. I have read a great portion of his manuscript, with much interest, and have advised him, if he should find you sufficiently at leisure, to submit some of his Chapters to your examination, especially those in relation to your father, the Rev'd H. Hunter, and Dr. Hall.[69]

He obtained in Mecklenburg some days since, from the representatives of your brother-in-law, the late Mr. Alexander, the original instructions for the delegates of Mecklenburg County, which I consider important collateral testimony in support of the Mecklenburg Declaration of Independence. I have induced him to leave the original manuscript, evidently that of John McNitt Alexander, in my possession, and have promised that you will give him, instead of it, one of the three printed copies contained in Charlotte newspapers published, I think, in 1839, and preserved in the bundle of papers which you exhibited to me during my recent visit to Raleigh. One of the Chapters mentioned above relates mainly to the Mecklenburg Declaration. This, he intends to recast, and before he does so, is anxious to examine the "Davie paper," and the memoir of the Rev'd H. Hunter.

[69] The Rev. James Hall, D. D. (1744-1826), of Iredell, a native of Pennsylvania, who was brought to North Carolina in 1752. He was educated at Princeton, where he studied theology under John Witherspoon. He was a Revolutionary captain, and chaplain, and is said to have declined promotion to brigadier general. He became a famous minister, was a missionary in the West, going as far as Natchez, and writing an interesting account of his impressions of the country, but his chief reputation rests on his work as a teacher. His school, "Clio's Nursery," and, later, "Academy of the Sciences," trained many distinguished men. They were famous too, for the number of men they furnished the Presbyterian ministry.

I hope you will find leisure during the two days I have advised him to remain in Raleigh, for full conferences, in relation to the general subject, and on numerous points of his history.

Yours very sincerely

*From John Gray Bynum.*                               U.

Marion, McDowell Co., N. C.,

November 4th, 1845.

\* \* \* \* \*

If I may be pardoned for alluding to the subject, I wish you to understand that the meeting at Asheville & the resolutions there adopted, are by no means a true index of the feelings of the Whigs in this district

The conjectures of the Standard are true. The Editor doubtless obtained *authentic* information before the appearance of his editorial article. Clingman wrote the resolutions, & they were palmed off upon the meeting (not over twenty in number) after night, not more than two or three knowing that the object was to prepare the way for Mr. T. L. Clingman's being nominated for the office of Governor of N. C.! ! ! The Whig party with us is entirely united, save for some few boys, and will give you a hearty & zealous support. Our only anxiety is as to the time when the convention is to be held, so that we can attend.

If that is fixed at a time when the West can attend we shall have a large delegation present.

We are now holding the first Superior Court in McDowell & commence on the criminal docket with two murder cases.

*From James W. Downey.*[70]                           A.

Abrams Plains, [N. C.]

Nov'r 7th., 1845.

I feel very grateful for your kindness in forwarding me a letter of introduction to Mr. A. Whitney,[71] which, however, did not

---

[70] James Webb Downey, of Granville, a graduate of the university.

[71] Asa Whitney (1797-1872), of New York, a native of Connecticut, who became a buyer in Europe, and later in China for mercantile houses in New York. Eager for trade development, he began to advocate a railroad to the Pacific, scouted for suitable routes, conducted a great newspaper campaign, addressed the legislatures of most of the states, and unceasingly wrote articles on the subject. His wife was one of the well-known Moore family of the Cape Fear.

reach Milwaukie before I left. The individuals of our small party
of *six* found no difficulty in introducing themselves to each other,
& the Wildness of the Praries made us afterwards fast friends. I
found Mr. Whitney gentlemanly and scientific. We had a pleasant
and exciting excursion—leaveing Lake Michagan at Milwaukie.
We traveled due West, Crossing the Mississippi at Prairie du
Chien. Thence due West some 800 miles to the great Missouri,
& down the same in a log Canoe some 950 miles, before we
reached a Steam boat. From Lake Michagan to the Mississippi &
for a hundred miles beyond it the country is well timbered, but
thence West to the Missouri is almost entirely Prarie. We traveled over no poor lands, & found the soil strongly impregnated
with lime, well watered and admirably adapted to agriculture.

I send you a copy of A. Whitney's Memorial. The object of
our excursion was to see the practicability of his scheme. We
learned from the trappers & traders that the Country West of the
Missouri was favourable for the enterprise. Mr. Whitney is now
on his way to Memphis to attend a Convention for Western
internal improvement, he is trying to engage the influence of this
Country in advanceing his project, & seems to be succeeding.

This letter is partly an application for the same purpose from
him, through me, to you and to others who may concur with him
in the scheme, & feel disposed to lend their influence. Mr. Whitney is very anxious, if convenient, to procure your opinion & that
of others with whom you may converse on the subject. I shall be
pleased to give you any information as to the Country in my
possession, at any time when you may request it. If you express
any opinion on the subject, it will reach Mr. Whitney by being
directed to me. If convenient to yourself, a letter from you would
afford me much satisfaction.

P. S. My post office, if you *should* wish to be aware of it, is
Abram's Plains, Granville, N. C.

*From William H. Foote.*                                    A.

Romney, Hampshire Cy., Vir'a.,

Nov. 19th, 1845.

The last mail brought the printed document inclosed in your
favour of the 12th. That document is in many respects more
remarkable than the Declaration, for it tells what Government was

denied and defines religious liberty; & neither have been better defined in the same brief space.

I had for years heard that there was an Autobiography of Dr. Hunter, but the family could not tell its fate further than it had been put in the hands of Judge Murphy. I collected from his family many facts respecting him, from Dr. Morrison the history of his Captivity, the death of DeKalb, & many other smaller incidents.

When at the University this last month President Swain suggested the thought that perhaps the paper might be in your possession. If so, & you are willing to risque it by mail it will be a favour not only to me but to others if I can have the reading of it before my Manuscript goes to the press. If you feel under any disability or there is any difficulty I cannot press the matter however much I may wish the papers for a perusal.

I have determined to use the copy of the Declaration you may send as being the copy of the genuine. Judge Cameron puts Davie's Copy beyond all doubt.

Those inhabitants of Mecklenburg were a marvellous—truly wonderful set of men. The next generation will honor them as the present does not from want of knowledge.

At M. R. Alexanders I came across another paper of some interest; The Constitution and rules of the Agricultural Society formed in Mecklenburg in 1788. Mr. Caldwell took it to the printer & promised to send me a copy when printed. The paper has not yet reached me, though the printer promised that it should appear some two weeks ago. It was as unique as the other old papers of that set of men & had the names of the leading men of that day.

Very Respectfully, Sir, I am
Yours in the Service of the Lord & his truth.

*To William H. Foote.*                                           A.

Raleigh, N. C.,

November 22nd., 1845.

I send herewith a copy of the paper requested by you, with a kind of "facsimile." It is, you are aware, a mutilated paper. The manner of its being torn is explained by Dr. Samuel Henderson's certificate, attached thereto. The copy of the Mecklenburg Resolutions published by our Legislature in 1831 was obtained only in part from this document. There are two other papers among those collected by Dr. Joseph McKnitt A.,[72] relating to the same subject,—one in the handwriting of John McKnitt, and the other in an unknown handwriting, but found among his papers. The last corresponds with the Davie paper, as far as that is preserved, but is more full. There is, among the papers of Jo. McKnitt, which I lately perused in Mecklenburg, a letter from him to Gov. Stokes, dated April 5, 1831, referring the latter to these three papers, as materials from which to prepare the publication directed by the Legislature, and requesting that all the manuscripts should be returned to him when the pamphlet was finished, he having procured and sent them all, in the first instance. If you desire copies of these also, I will have them made out, and forwarded. I regret I had not the pleasure of a personal interview with you. I believe I am in as full possession of the Revolutionary accounts of the Mecklenburg declaration as any one now living, and, as it is to occupy some place in your work, I would be glad to see justice done to it.

*  *  *  *

*From James W. Osborne.*                                       U.

Charlotte

Dec. 9th. 1845.

It has been several weeks since your kind letter was received, and it has been owing to my incessant engagements at Courts that it has not received an earlier notice. The question whether you will accept the nomination at the Convention in January next, is one altogether at your own disposal. My impression is that your nomination will be without any opposition whatever, from any quarter, and will be the result of the conviction that it will do more than any other which can be presented to cause a successful rally of the Whigs. Bynum tells me that in the quarter where some hostility might have been expected, you will be as strong as formerly, and probably stronger. He is, however, the only person from the mountain region whom I have seen, and his

---

[72] Dr. Joseph McKnitt Alexander (1774-1841), physician, son of John McKnitt Alexander, a graduate of Princeton. His son, Dr. Moses Winslow Alexander, married Graham's sister, Violet.

opportunities of judging have been limited. Assuming, however, that your nomination would be universally acceptable, another question presents itself which is wholly personal to you; whether you ought to accept it, if tendered. I place out of the question all considerations arising from the labour and exposure of the Campaign, and the hazards of the result. But the effect it may have on your future prospects. If defeated, the Whig party goes down to be submerged under a long night of Loco domination. Should you succeed, the enjoyment of the office, however nominal the advantages may be to the incumbent—and indeed how great—soon the sacrifices made by him for the public is used as a bar to other and more valuable elevation. At the next Session of the legislature a Senator must be chosen for the term of six years next succeeding. That position is an exalted one, and your ostracism from it by the accidental supremacy of the opposition places your claim to it on high grounds. Your election to the office of Governor for two successive terms will, in the judgment of most persons, be a compensation for the disappointment thus incurred, and your occupancy of the office immediately after the popular election will place your claims for the vacancy in the Senate out of the question. Writing only as your personal friend—and truly solicitous for your welfare, it does strike me that you should weigh well these views of the subject before you consent to be a candidate. Your reluctance to enter the office of Governor is well understood; your declining it now when the occasion on which it was accepted has passed, cannot be the subject of complaint on the part of your friends or your party.

Fisher will be the candidate of the democracy, if the West can force him through. This determination is announced, not only by the spirit of their organ in his region—but the temper of private conversation, as manifested by the leading men of the party, bears the same aspects. Jealousies already exist of the aspirants in the Centre and East, and I do not doubt but by representations of his superior popularity in this region, and the result of the Canvass for Congress in this district, that his nomination will be secured. His popularity is greatly overated and his efficiency as a stump orator far from being formidable. The Counties in the West will be generally represented in the Convention in January. I was in hopes that I could myself be present, but it will not be in my power. The young lawyers from our region, of whom there are numbers, will go down. Could it be possible to induce Gov. Morehead to go down and act as its president. It would probably be attended with good effects.

*From James Graham.*                                    U.

H. R.,

Dec. 18th, 1845.

\* \* \* \* \*

We have no news of interest here beyond what you see in the Papers. The Oregon question appears to be the great question of the session; and it is a delicate and dangerous one. I think some Bill extending the Civil and criminal Jurisdiction and laws of our territories over that region; so as not to violate the existing treaty until 12 month notice be given of its termination, so far as joint occupancy is concerned.

I feel very sure the Sub Treasury will be passed before the end of the session. The majority of the party will go for it. The party is well organized and drilled.

There appears much indifference among the dominant party with regard to Polk's and Walker's opinions on the Tariff, except among the Calhoun wing of the party. They rejoice and triumph, but no others.

The Tariff will probably be postponed until a late period of the session.

The *Caucus* has in this House, appointed all the officers here, and elected their Printer too, although it was expressly proposed by another to do it for $35. or $40. thousand Dollars less. But the party determined to elect their organ, and thereby make the people pay for the party papers they needed.

Many of your old friends have enquired after you very kindly.

1846

*From James Graham.*                                    U.

Washington,

January 4th, 1846.

You perceive Texas is admitted as one of the States of this Union. All the Whig members South of the Potomac voted for

Texas, and the opposition to its admission proceeded mainly from the Abolitionists, who objected to it because [it] was a slave State.

Pinckny Henderson (son of Lawson) is elected Governor of Texas. We have not yet heard who the Senators and representatives will be. I presume they will be here about the first of Feb. to take their seats.

The Oregon Question is still the great question of the Session. No vote has yet been taken to indicate the sense of the House, or Senate on that subject. The discussion, I presume, will come off about a week or ten days hence, and continue until a decission is made of it. There is great anxiety here to hear how the President's message will be received in England. Mr. Adams, you see, goes strongly in favor of giving Notice to Great Britain to terminate our commercial convention in Oregon. He says the Treaty of 1818 gave only a permissive right to either nation to trade with the Indians in Oregon, but that Treaty gave no right to either party to permanently and exclusively occupy that Territory, so that before we can rightfully do any thing we must *give notice* that our former Treaty is at an end.

*Charles Fisher is here.* He came from the State of Mississippi, through Alabama, Georgia, Charleston, and Wilmington, to this place. He has not been in Salisbury since last summer. I think from all I can learn, he will be the Democratic Candidate for Governor. He professes to be greatly pleased with President Polk's Message. The Tariff is his Hobby before the people.

I think you should act with great prudence & circumspection in the management of the Rail Road. *Your political enemies will watch you very closely.* You should have as few Agents as possible, and let them be competent, diligent, and faithful. Can't you increase the speed, and avoid the long and too frequent stopings at the Depots ? and also lower the freight so as to induce Merchants & others to transport goods by that conveyance; and try also to make the Merchants at Petersburg more *punctual* and attentive in forwarding goods. All the freight cars at the different Depots should be fully ready before the train arrives. Perhaps you have not the power to reduce the Tolls, or price of freight. I would not exceed my powers or even exercise doubtful powers where you can get along without doing so. Some repairs I presume you must make, and that should be attended to in due time. Let a plain Report make all you do with the Road, make your conduct plain and satisfactory, so that Demagogues can't misrepresent you.

The Whig members of the Whig Convention at Raleigh ought to be fully apprized of the importance of nominating suitable candidates in each County for the next Legislature. They should be men who are *personally popular,* and who will exert themselves to the utmost to carry their respective Counties. Let the Whigs in every County be united, and make a good and popular nomination early in the Spring, after consulting the different parts of each County. Let the Whig watchword be in '46 what it was in '76 "united we stand, divided we fall." Let the Whigs make no false issues. Let them wait until this administration presents distinct issues. Let them approve what is right; and condemn *only* what is wrong. The Whigs have often injured themselves by a sort of *general faultfinding* disposition. That temper weakens us very much on great questions; we thereby *loose the confidence* of the people.

The Democratic party will try to get us to fighting false issues, but we should not join issue on such false and fatal questions. They will *try to press* Texas into the discussion in the hope that *inconsiderate* Whigs will oppose anything which they advocate. I hope our Whigs will not be caught by such traps. Milton Brown, a Whig, offered the Resolutions which passed Congress, for the admission of Texas; a number of Southern Whigs voted for them then, and now every Southern Whig voted for the admission of Texas, and several Democrats to the North *now* voted against the admission of Texas. The sub Treasury and the Tariff will be the main substantial issues. Every Whig is opposed to the sub Treasury, and the people have solemnly pronounced their verdict against it.

So far as I can learn, the Whigs here now, do not intend at this Session to take the ground that the Tariff of 1842 is the only true or proper Tariff. But they intend [to] stand on the ground that *the Labor of the Country ought and must be protected by Government as near equal as possible to all working classes in the Union.* Hence Mr. Stewart[1] of Pa. was advised and consented to withdraw his instructions to the Committee of Ways and Means requiring them to stick to the Act of 1842, so that now they are at liberty to report a better bill, if they can; and we will consent to any modification which makes it better, if it be demonstrated to us that the part so altered is for the better. In this way the *labouring on* is on the Locos. They must not only point out defects, but

---

[1] Andrew Stewart (1792-1872), of Pennsylvania, a lawyer, Federal district attorney, and Democratic member of congress, 1821-1829, 1831-1835, 1843-1849.

present and apply the remedy. In that way we admit the Act of 1842 is not perfect in all its parts and details, and then we call upon the majority now in Congress to give us *a perfect Bill free from all Defects.* I begin to think that the odds and ends of ultraism in Pa. and S. C. will not very soon agree in the policy, principles, or details in a Tariff Bill. It is easier to find fault than to mend. The *Western interest* has become very strong in Congress. It is the ruling star at this time. The True policy of the Whigs is to wait the developments of coming events; to abide their time. Let the administration present its measures, and its system of measures fully and in detail, before a general condemnation and opposition is made. A *premature* opposition only drives *the party* close up together, and serves to unite them at every step. The leaders and cliques of the party are now suspicious and jealous of each other. I am anticipating a loco-foco-volcano in the Democratic party before the end of this Session. I deeply regret that the Whig Editors at Raleigh and in N. C. are so inefficient and have so little popular tact. Their late opposition to me precludes me from writing any Editorials for them, which I used to do. Had you not better keep a private Journal of the events that are transpiring here? Note the Date and the Deed and state the objection to it in a plain simple manner.

I will write you often, and give you the news here.

Your affectionate brother.

*From David L. Swain.*                                                    A.

Chapel Hill,

Jan. 6th., 1846.

Gov. Graham will oblige me by having the printed copy of the Mecklenburg instructions compared with the original paper, which was left in his possession, and having Mr. Foote advised whether any material variation exists.

I do not suppose that the name of Ezekiel Polk[2] became connected with the Mecklenburg Declaration in the manner he suggests. I think it not improbable that he was a delegate to, or a member of the Committee that adopted the Resolutions, and that his name was stricken from the list in consequence of his subsequently taking a Protection from Lord Cornwallis.

---

[2] Ezekiel Polk, a native of Pennsylvania, lived in North Carolina for a time, and also in South Carolina, later removing, permanently, to Tennessee. He was President Polk's grandfather.

[*Enclosure*]

*From William H. Foote
to David L. Swain.*

Romney,
Hampshire C'y.
Virginia.

December 28th., 1845.

I some time since received from Governor Graham the printed paper purporting to be a copy of that Manuscript I left in your hands last fall on my return from Charlotte. Upon a careful perusal of the printed paper, it appears to me that there are some errors. At least, I can scarcely think the original reads like the copy I have.

I would therefore be greatly obliged by a corrected copy of the original papers, as I wish to be as correct as possible, in my volume. I lay some stress upon that paper. Perhaps my young friend, Philips can spare time enough from his law office to copy out the paper for me without encroaching upon your time, so much occupied in the affairs of the University.

While in Charlotte, I found another paper in the hands of a descendent of McNitt Alexander (the Secretary) which I left in Charlotte, and which has since been published in both the Charlotte papers. It is the Constitution and Rules of an Agricultural Society, established soon after the Revolution. To it are appended the names of a large number of gentlemen in Mecklenburg, among others is Ezekiel Polk. Can not that be the paper that the gentleman in Tennessee saw with the name of Ezekiel Polk on it, and which, after years had passed, he thought was the Declaration.

I have not yet written to the Book makers or Printers. Some long expected manuscripts, etc., which I had given out all hope of seeing, met me in Petersburg on my return to Virginia; these, and some letters I expect daily, delay me a while. The book will be all the better. I have no doubt that when the book shall see the light—if it ever does—that many manuscripts of importance will be brought out, of the existence of which we are ignorant at present. I shall not therefore delay any great length of time.

I have remodeled the Chapter on the Declaration, & can but think it improved by the change. I have left out all discussion of the authenticity of the Documents, & have merely given the facts of the publishing of the Declaration & the consequent paper on the 30th. of May, & have reserved the discussion for another paper or Chapter, & even thus make but a short matter of it. It would perhaps be better to let all defence or discussion about it alone—'till it be denied—an uncalled for defence is acknowledged weakness.

My attempts to set up a proper school in Romney have as yet been prospered. There is a prospect for a flourishing institution.

Very respectfully, Sir, yours in the Service of the Lord's work,


*From Jacob Siler.*                                       A.

Agency Office,
for the collection of
Cherokee County.,

Jan. 7th, 1846.

as you will be informed of the excitement occasioned in Cherokee by the proposition of the State to rent the lands released by the Insolvent purchasers. It may be proper for me to communicate an opinion not strictly demanded by my duty as agent. —Comparatively few of the citizens of Cherokee County seem to have examined the act of our last Legislature in which it appears that they are so much interested. And I have found that law, with your explanation, of the 8th. ultimo, enough to sattisfy almost every individual, whith whom I have conversed, that by virtue of releas deeds the property passes again into the possession of the State, and that as her agent, I ought to secure it to the best advantage. I think it due to these people therefore, to say that in my opinion a few days opportunity for inquiry and reflection will lead them to appreciate your motives correctly, and submit to what is right.

Mr. Finch had passed on his way to Raleigh before I was apprised that he was the barer of a memorial of a public meeting, held in Murphy a few days since. It is to be hoped that an alternative spoken of by him in this County was not designed by the people who met at Murphy as an appendage to these proceedings. I can not believe that any degree of excitement which may of prevailed there could have prodused a suggestion of resistance from any but a few reckless individuals.

I expect, pursuant to your instructions, to proceed in a short time, with out interruptions, to visit the improved lands belonging to the State in Macon and Cherokee Counties, for the present year, to which I shall attend as faithfully as I may be able.

*From Hezekiah G. Spruill.*            A., G.L.B.

Plymouth, N. C.,

January 8th., 1846.

Presuming on the readiness with which the Regiment was raised, under the requisition in May last, I made no effort to procure Volunteers under the last requisition.

I am informed by Mr. Halsey, that only two companies have offered themselves, and that fears are entertained in Raleigh that the Regiment will not be made up.

One great difficulty in procuring Volunteers, here, can be removed, probably, by answering a few questions. I know of no one else to apply to. Should this Brigade, composed of the Counties of Washington, Tyrrel, Beaufort & Hyde, or those counties with one or more of the adjoining counties, raise a company, would they be authorized to assemble in the Town of Washington, preparatory to organizing & marching to Wilmington?

Will each company adopt its own *Uniforms?* Or, must each company be regularly equipped for service when tendered, & marched to the rendezvous? Much difficulty would arise, (if indeed it would be possible) in procuring proper military dresses, both for officers and privates, where there are no military stores. Or, are the companies to rendezvous at Wilmington in citizen's dress, and then select a uniform? Or, are the clothes to be furnished by the Government on the arrival of the Regiment in Mexico? Will each Volunteer have to provide himself with a knapsack? Where will the arms, accoutrements, etc., Cartridge boxes, bayonet scabbards & belts, etc., be furnished? Will the officers have to provide themselves with side arms? Should a company be formed in this Brigade, could funds be placed under my control, or under the control of some one else, to pay the travelling expenses of the Volunteers to Washington? And, should they have to equip themselves, will funds be advanced? These inquiries are frequently made of me, and I am unable to answer them all; they are important, in order that the Volunteers may know what preparations to make.

If they have to carry sufficient clothes & baggage to serve them to Wilmington, & then adopt a different dress, it would be both expensive & troublesome.

You have doubtless heard from all the State, & know whether the Regiment will be made up without another effort. If not, and I can have sufficient time to visit the adjacent Counties, I will make an effort to form a Company.

Our State must not be behind in this matter. The Regiment must be formed.

Pardon me for troubling you.

I did not know how to avoid it.

### Resolutions, Whig State Convention.[3]

#### January 12th., 1846.

Resolved, that this Convention has full confidence in the integrity, ability, and devoted patriotism of WILLIAM A. GRAHAM, the present Governor of our State, and that, for the faithfulness and impartiality with which he has performed the duties of the high station which he holds, he is entitled to the gratitude, and should receive the support of the people of North Carolina, at the ensuing election; and that, entertaining as we do, admiration for the virtues he has exhibited, in the fulfilment of the duties of every public station with which he has been entrusted by the people of his native State, we do not hesitate to declare our belief, that his re-election will advance the best interests of "North Carolina."

Therefore, be it resolved unanimously, That the Honorable WILLIAM A. GRAHAM be, and he is hereby nominated as a candidate for Governor of North Carolina, for re-election; and that we recommend him to the support of that people he has for years so faithfully served.

Resolved, that the President of this Convention appoint a committee of five, to communicate the above resolution to his Ex-

---

[3] The Whig state convention met in Raleigh, January 12th., 1846, and nominated Graham by resolution, On the following day a resolution was adopted, asking him to canvass the state during the campaign. Later, the delegates were entertained by Graham.

cellency, Gov. GRAHAM, and earnestly urge his acceptance of the nomination therein made; and that they report to this Convention as soon as convenient, the Governor's reply.[4]

*From John D. Hawkins.*[5]          A.

Washington City,

Jan'y 15th., 1846.

In accordance with your views expressed to me in your letter of the 30th. ult. in relation to four Horse Coaches from Raleigh to Campden, (I presume you meant Columbia) I have had an interview with the Post Master Gen'l and handed him your letter. In your letter to him, you asked him for the Four Horse Coaches, to aid the facility of the Traveling community. To do that, he is forbidden by the act of Congress, and as that was your main object as thus expressed, he viewed the increased speed asked for as a minor consideration with you, upon which consideration *only,* he could comply with your request. He then turned to the profits to the Department from Raleigh to Fayetteville, etc., etc.,

---

[4] The *Hillsborough Recorder* of January 22nd., 1846, described what followed: "Accordingly, in a short time, the Governor entered the Hall, and never have we seen any man greeted by such marked demonstrations of popular attachment. It was some minutes before silence was sufficiently restored to enable the Governor to address the Convention. Sensibly affected by the enthusiastic reception given him, he proceeded to respond to the nomination which had been tendered, in a brief, but most eloquent and impressive speech. Without affectation, he promptly accepted the call, and declared his readiness again to represent the Whigs, as their standard-bearer, in the coming contest. And no one there, whatever his politics, who looked upon his fine, intellectual face, and heard his words of truth and soberness, could have failed to pay a silent tribute to the dignity and elevation of his character—those attributes which render him so deservedly an object of pride to his party and his friends—or have resisted the conviction that with such a candidate as William A. Graham, before such a people as North Carolina can boast of, defeat is impossible."

The *Fayetteville Observer,* of January 20th., 1846, thus commented: "Gov. Graham's response to the nomination was, like everything he says and does, sound, sensible, and dignified; full of affection for his native State, and of devotion to the Whig party. His character is a perfect emblem of that of North Carolina. His hands are clean, his heart pure, his head clear. Modest and retiring, he never thrusts himself forward, but has always obeyed the call of those who had a right to require his services at whatever sacrifice. More sound than brilliant, he moves on in the even tenor of his way, commanding the respect and confidence of all who are capable of appreciating his practical common sense, his unsullied character, his public and private virtues. May the good old North State ever have at the helm so true a representative of herself as WILLIAM A. GRAHAM."

[5] John David Hawkins  (1781-1858), of Warren and, later, Franklin, a graduate of the university, who studied law under Judge John Haywood, but became a planter on a large scale, and business man. He was a devoted supporter of internal improvements, and was active in promoting the Raleigh and Gaston Railroad Company. He represented Franklin in the state senate, 1834, 1836-1840,

which he said would not justify the increased expense of the four Horse Coaches, *taken in that single point of view*. But he said he had come to the conclusion that if the Raleigh and Gaston Rail Road Company and the Stage Contractors on to Columbia and to *Hamburg,* would agree to carry the *Big Mail* upon fair terms, he would send the Big Mail upon our Road immediately, "for it was out of the question to rely any longer upon the Wilmington Rout, which had failed 3 times out of 4." He then asked me for propositions for carrying the *Big Mail*. I told him I was not authorized to make any, and read to him that part of your letter to me upon that subject. But I told him I would address you immediately, and give him your answer, as to the Rail Road Company, and through you, I expected, we could procure the answer of the Stage Contractors, as far as Columbia.

Before I waited upon the Post Master Gen'l, knowing his great disposition to Husband the public money pertaining to his Department, and that no ordinary influence would reach him, if any could, to move him from his determinations—I drew up an application to him to gain your object, *only* for the avowed purpose of increase of speed to the mails, which I got 16 members of Congress to sign, and to which I believe the most of the Southern members of Congress would have signed, expressing *only* for an increase of speed in 4 Horse Coaches. Mr. Haywood and Gen'l McKay refused to sign it, but agreed to go with me to the Department, and to confer about it. I wrote to Mr. Dobbin,[6] and got him along, and we have just had that conference which resulted as I have intimated. Mr. Haywood, as well as Gen'l McKay, friends, I suppose, or nutrals, in relation to the Lower Road, declined taking any part to the prejudice of the Lower Road. And Mr. Haywood said he never liked to argue a cause after the Judge had decided it. And therefore, if Col. Johnson[7] had decided to remove

---

[6] James Cochran Dobbin (1814-1857), of Cumberland County, graduate of the university, lawyer, was a Democratic member of congress, 1845-1847. He was a member of the commons, 1848-1849, where he had a large part in securing the establishment of "Dix Hill," the state's first mental hospital, and the charter of the North Carolina Railroad. He was again in the commons, 1850-1853, in 1852 nominated Pierce for President, and became secretary of the navy, where he carried out the plans of Graham for the expedition to Japan, and made many improvements in the navy.

[7] William Johnston (1817-1896), a native of Lincoln (now Gaston) County, attended the university, studied law under Judge Pearson, but, after a short period of practice, gave it up, and went into business. He was an active promoter of various types of transportation. He was a member of the convention of 1861, and author of the ordinance removing the disability of Jews to hold office. He was defeated by Vance for governor in 1862. He declined appointment of commissary general of the Confederacy. After the war, he was a powerful figure in the work of restoration.

the *Big Mail*, he had nothing more to say. Then it was Johnson said it must be so, because the failures were 3 out of 4 trips. Mr. Haywood & Gen'l McKay showing some sensation, and McKay seemed suspicious that our application carried with it indisguised hostility to the lower Road, though very politely insinuating it.

I stated to the Post Master Gen'l that I disclaimed any such intention, that I had not, nor did I intend to ask him for the Big Mail, that all I asked was for a four Horse Coach in place of the two, with increase of speed, and that the Post Master Gen'l would do me the justice to recollect that that was my language in the summer upon that subject. But that, if he thought proper, unsolicited, to put the Big Mail upon our rout, we would certainly carry it, upon reasonable terms, but what they might be, I could only say I would write you to obtain them & when had, he should be replied to upon that subject. Mr. Haywood & Gen'l McKay than proposed to have the act of Congress altered, to allow the Post Master Gen'l, in the way of exception to increase the speed, Coaches, etc., upon our Road, to carry the mail there as it is, which they contended could be done immediately. Col. Johnson said that would open a door that would give the Department infinit trouble; as every road would claim a change under the precedent. That he was willing at once to put the Big Mail upon our rout if the Terms could be agreed upon. It was, however, finally settled down among us, that I would write you for terms, which I expected could be procured speedily, when Col. Johnson could get an answer. It was then required, that your propositions should be of a two fold aspect, (but this requirement was mainly by Haywood and McKay, for the Post Master Gen'l seemed bent, or decided, upon transfering the Big Mail) first, what would you carry the present mail for in four Horse Coaches, with speed increased to six miles per Hour? And 2ndly, as he would with the first, or under the first, proposition, claim the priviledge of sending on the Big Mail when he pleased, then upon what terms would you carry the Big Mail? I wish to be understood by the word *you*, not only you, but the Stage Contractors, that their proposition must also be made in connexion with those of the Rail Road Comp'y. Col. Johnson furthermore remarked that if a contract was made, it must be explicit, so as to avoid any future misconception. I suppose he spoke in reference to the misunderstanding with Capt'n Guion, I told him we should require that, also. I think there is no doubt of the settled determination of the Post Master Gen'l to send to our Rail Road the Big Mail, if the propositions to take it are reasonable, which will mainly depend upon the Stage Contractors. And it is to their interest, and they will find that interest to increase, to carry the mail upon fair terms. I verily believe a great deal more travel will be thrown upon the Road than one Coach can carry. You know the number of Coaches upon the Cumberland Road to Wheeling are enough for any emergency. Let it be so understood upon our Road, and you may rely [on it], a large Travel will go the line. This is a very important time to add prosperity to the Road, and I think its prospects are better now for the future than I have ever known them. Get the Big Mail, as you can do, if you offer fairly, and reasonably, increase the travel, as it will do, and I hope the State may put the Rail Road to a company for a sum equal to both her Loans.

In a conversation I had with Mr. Calhoun and Mr. Holmes,[8] of Charleston, together, they both expressed a great wish for No. Carolina to extend the Road to the So. Car. line. And Mr. Holmes told me he would with much pleasure aid about the 4 Horse Coaches, etc. This I had not supposed, for I reviewed him as inimical to any change which might in any manner affect Charleston. As he may be violently opposed to the removal of the Big Mail from the Lower Road, and in favour of that Road, they can raise a strong party. But if you offer reasonable terms for carrying the Big Mail, I fully believe you will get it. But to insure your object of a 4 Horse Coach, I deemed it most prudent to show disinterestedness about the coming of the Big Mail, showing a wish not to conflict about it. To be ready to take it, however, if they will send it. Haywood & McKay, under this state of things, will I think insure the 4 Horse Coach by moving for & procuring partial Legislation to allow of it.

I have endeavored to show you this case as it has presented itself to me, that you may the better Judge of it. And if you think proper to make an answer through me, I shall, I expect, remain here long enough to receive it, and will attend to it with much pleasure.

---

[8] Isaac Edward Holmes (1796-1867), of Charleston, a graduate of Yale, a lawyer, served in the lower house of the legislature, 1826-1833, was a Democratic member of congress, 1839-1851, when he moved to California. He later returned to South Carolina.

*To Cherokee County Committee.*                     A.

Executive Office,
Raleigh,
Jan'y 17th., 1846.

Gentlemen

I have considered with all due attention and respect, the memorial preferred by you, as a Committee, appointed by the citizens of Cherokee County, in relation to the proper disposition to be made of the lands surrendered to the State, according to the provisions of the Act of the General Assembly at the last Session, entitled "an Act more effectually to secure the debts due for Cherokee lands, and to facilitate the collection of the same."

Had the good citizens whom you represent, been fully acquainted with the interpretation given to the Act, or the instructions sent to the State's Agent by this Department, respecting those lands, I cannot believe that they would have entertained the apprehensions expressed in their memorial.

It is the obvious design of the Legislature to rescind the contract of sale between the State and the description of purchasers mentioned in the Act. The terms of this rescision are, on the one hand, a release of title & all claims for monies heretofore paid, as well as a surrender of possession by the purchaser; and, on the other, a delivery of, or cancellation of the bond for the purchase money, by the State. Upon the fulfilment of these conditions, on both sides, the purchaser is out of possession, and although he should continue to occupy, would not be able to maintain an action for trespass on the lands. The lands being thus, by force of the Act of Assembly, devolved on the Agent of the State, it becomes his duty, under that provision of the Act of 1840, which requires him to "guard & protect the general interest of the State in connection with these lands, whether sold, or unsold;" to make such disposition of them, untill the further direction of the General Assembly, as shall be just to the State, while it is liberal towards the citizens. Accordingly he has been instructed to lease the lands untill the 1st. of January 1847. Not however, (as seems to be the impression of the memorialists) by public auction to the highest bidder; but he is expressly directed to give a preference to those making surrenders of the land, and to treat them with liberality in the amount of rent demanded—it being understood that the premises shall be in as good a state of repair at the end of the year, as at present.

The Supreme Court, being now in session has afforded me an opportunity to take the opinion of the Attorney General on the proper construction of the Act of Assembly, and for your satisfaction it is herewith enclosed. Had I found the opinion of that officer in conflict with the instructions heretofore forwarded to the State's Agent, I would have been pleased to modify [them,] so as to make them conform to it. Not doubting that these will be carried out in the spirit in which they have been dictated, I indulge the hope that no great hardship can result from such a course; or at least that if there be any disappointment in the benefits expected from the Act of the Legislature, that it is not fairly attributable to a want of liberality in those charged with the execution of the law, since they act but in obedience to the requirements of duty.

You are requested however, to say to those you represent, that if there be any error in this view of the duties of the agent, the General Assembly will be in session before the expiration of the year, and can administer the proper correction.

I desire only to add, that having been a member of the Legislature at the time of the survey, and sale of the Cherokee lands, and aware that they were sold at high prices, from causes not necessary to be now stated, I have not been wanting in sympathy for the situation of the people of that section of country, and in every step of the execution [of] the law of the last session, have sought the interpretation most favorable to their relief, when consistent with the language employed.

I am, Gentlemen,<br>
With high respect,<br>
Your Obed't Serv't

To James W. Bryan.                    U. Bryan Mss.

Raleigh,

Jany. 24th, 1846.

I have neglected for some time past to write you, though often intending to do so.

Some time during the last summer on the recommendation of Mr. Attmore and yourself, I appointed a Mr. Hunter Notary Public at Ocracoke. Subsequently I received a letter from Mr. A. S. complaining of the appointment, as he was a Notary residing there, and representing that one officer could transact all the business, that Mr. Hunter from a connexion with the Custom House, had control of the Revenue Cutter, and could get on board of vessels coming in, so as to engross every thing pertaining to the office of a Notary, and that the appointment was equivalent to removing him (Mr. S.) from office. Latterly Mr. E. S. has been here, and mentioned the same matter to me. I told him, I desired to deal with him frankly, and supposed the recommendation had been made, of Mr. H. because the habits of his brother were perhaps intemperate, and unfitted him for business. He said it might be so, for he was really ignorant upon that point now— some time ago he had been intemperate. He mentioned however, that Mr. Hunter was a deputy Collector at the Port, a Federal officer, recognized by the acts of Congress, and that the appointment was probably on that account void, under the Constitution. I would be obliged to you, to let me know, confidentially of course, what are the habits of A. S., and that you would consult with Mr. Attmore in regard to the supposed ineligibiliy of Mr. Hunter to the office of Notary, and inform me of the result. I have not looked into the acts of Congress on the subject.

Since writing the foregoing, I have turned to my Letter Book, and find Mr. Attmore's letter of July 21st '45, in which he says in reply to inquiries of mine, made through Mr. J. H. Bryan, as to whether an appointment was needed there, "I have seen Capt. Hunter since, who informs me that the Custom House is kept there, and that there is no one commissioned there at present, that Major Stanly did reside there, but has recently removed from the Island." Is there any mistake in these facts? Did Mr. Stanly remove and return again?

You have, no doubt, heard of the doings of the two Conventions here recently. The conduct of some persons among our opponents has produced a bitterness of excitement which is not likely to subside soon.

You will perceive that I am again in the unenviable predicament of a Candidate. When one gets into a scrape of the kind it is difficult to get out. Our Friends hereabouts have been very urgent, but I apprehended there was hardly any attention to public affairs in the State generally. Our Convention, however, was very spirited and argues a fine state of feeling in the different sections of N. C. There are contradictory accounts as to Mr. Caldwell's accepting. I have no doubt myself that he will be forced in, however unwillingly.

The news of the dissolution of the British Ministry on the Corn law question, has produced quite a sensation here. Corn is rising in price, and above here, there must be some suffering.

\* \* \* \* \*

There have been many lawyers from a distance attending the Supreme Court the present term, remaining however but a few days, and attending the Conventions during the time. My advices from Washington are, that the Subtreasury Bill will pass. Some Bill extending our jurisdiction over Oregon, not conflicting with the Convention of 1818 may also pass.

Only the friends of Calhoun take much interest in the Antitariff movement, and it will probably be postponed, untill late in the Session,—final action doubtful. You see, however, that Mr. Hudson,[9] a prominent member from Mass. writes home that it will be repealed.

Mr. Senator H[aywoo]d came home yesterday, to attend the Supreme Court, as I hear. I have not seen him, or learned his news, of which, he doubtless has much.

I hope our friends will be attentive to bringing out suitable Candidates in the different Counties, and at any early day.

With the Sub-treasury folly before us, I think we can crush Loco focoism in N. C.

*From James Graham.*                    U.

H. R.,

Feb. 2nd, 1846.

Dear Brother

On this morning at six o'clock *a Duel* was fought near Bladensburg, between Jones (son in law of Tom Deverux) and Dr. Johnston,[10] in which the latter was killed at the first fire, being shot through the Head, and entirely through the head. A Mr.

---

[9] Charles Hudson (1795-1881), of Massachusetts, a Universalist minister, who served in the lower house of the legislature, 1828-1833, in the state senate, 1833-1839, was a member of the executive council, 1839-1841, and was a member of congress, 1841-1849. He edited the *Daily Atlas,* and served in several capacities in the Federal revenue service.

[10] Beyond a short news notice of the duel, and the names of the principals, Thomas F. Jones and Dr. Daniel Johnson, I have found nothing concerning it. Dr. Johnson, who was killed, was from Perquimans County, N. C.

White was the second of Jones; and Dr. Henderson,[11] of Salisbury, was the second of Johnston. Johnston did not discharge his pistol.

Yours truly

Jones is said to be in custody.

\* \* \* \* \*

*From James W. Bryan.*                                         U.

Newbern,

Feb'y 8th, 1846.

Your favour in relation to the appointment of a Notary Public at Portsmouth was succeeded by one from Mr. E. S. on the same subject, and I should have replied to your letter forthwith, but for pressing engagements, and necessary absence from home on my circuit. This matter has assumed an importance that I little thought of when I gave Capt. Hunter the letter to you. I must detail to you my connexion with the matter, for it does seem to me that it is making a mountain out of a molehill. I was in the Street here, and Capt. Hunter came up to me, and said he had been advised by Mr. Attmore to apply to me, to give him a letter to you, in aid of obtaining for himself the appointment of a Notary Public at Portsmouth, & as I understood him he said that there was no Notary there; that Mr. A. S. had removed to Hyde County. Knowing Capt. H. to be a worthy man, although he was opposed to me in politics, I had no hesitation in giving him the letter, and considered the appointment pretty much as a matter of course & an office of little or no profit or consequence, but I did not fancy, ever, that I was interfering with the rights of others, much less of being privy to making an illegal appointment. The last time Mr. A. S. was in Newbern he was exceedingly intemperate, . . . What are his habits now, I am unable to say. I have not been able to refer to the act of Congress which makes this appointment incompatible with that of Deputy Collector. I presume however that it is so, as Mr. E. S. reiterates it in his letter to me. I have however, advised Mr. Attmore, if it be so, to cure the vice of the appointment of Capt. Hunter, by inducing him to send his resignation to you; and in the meantime I will turn my attention to A.

---

[11] Pleasant Henderson.

We are very quiet here in the way of politics, and it will require something very extraordinary to excite the Whigs again in this Section of the State. I fear they will let the Legislature go by default. My health and habits, and my desire to retire as soon as I can from my profession, have withdrawn me entirely from any active participation in political matters, and I do not now appear in public in such matters, when I can avoid it.

\* \* \* \* \*

Our Market is most abundantly supplied with fine Shad and oysters; we often wish you were all with us to enjoy these fine "sea vegetables," as our sailors call them. Ann says that she sent a bundle to your good wife by Mr. Jno. M. Washington, and trusts that it has come safely to hand. We have been induced by certain rumors to believe that you intended to make us a visit this winter, we should be happy to see you, and I think it might have the desirable tendency of arousing the Whigs & infusing a new spirit into them.

We have no news in our town, as the progress of things with us is downward; but for the article of Turpentine, we should have squally times in the Eastern Section of the State.

\* \* \* \* \*

Mr. Hubbard[12] rec'd the Book from you, and is much obliged to you indeed; he is making progress in the work he has on hand.

*From James Graham.*                    U.

H. R.,

Feb. 20th, 1846.

You have seen the vote on the subject of *Notice* to Great Britain to terminate our Treaty with her in relation to Oregon. An effort was made to make it a party question, but it failed.

Twelve months ago Mr. Adams was the *first person who proposed* to give that *Notice*. It was then voted for by all the Whigs in the House, and some of the Democrats, but not a majority of them. A majority of the House then voted the Notice, and the Senate rejected it by two votes only. Now when the President

---

[12] The Rev. Fordyce M. Hubbard, who was then engaged in writing the biographical sketches of William R. Davie and Samuel Kirkland.

recommended us to give the notice why then a large majority of
the Democrats vote turn over and vote for it; and the Whigs
divide about equally on the subject of Notice.

Notice was right, in my judgment, because we could rightfully
do nothing efficiently until we untied ourselves from the joint
Treaty; we can *negotiate, legislate,* and *emigrate, better after
notice.*

The Virginia and So. Carolina locos were very severely handled
by their Western brethren during the long debate. Notice will
pass the Senate certainly, in some shape.

We have not yet got the proposed new Tariff bill before the
House. The Party have much trouble in agreeing on the details.

There is a good deal of manoevering here among our Whig
friends about get [ting] up a candidate for the next President.
Gen'l Scott's friends and Judge McLean's friends are sounding,
and some other persons. I have resolved to abstrain from all
pledges and expressions on that subject at this time. Mangum is,
I think, not improving in his habits. He is spoken of as a Candidate for Vice President; and is obviously pleased at such notice.

The Locos have many aspirants for the Presidency, and much
jealously among them. The Calhoun wing of the Party are much
dissatisfied and discomfited. I presume however, when the Tariff
comes up they will claim all the credit of the lead in free trade
doctrines.

\* \* \* \* \*

To James W. Bryan.             U. Bryan Mss.

Raleigh,

Feby. 23rd, 1846.

\* \* \* \* \*

Our news from Europe received today is of great moment. You
will no doubt have rec'd the same before this reaches you. The
reduction and prospective abolition of the Corn laws in England,
the immediate repeal of the duties on Indian Corn, Pork, and the
promise of abandoning protection in every aspect, by Sir Robert
Peel, and the order of the House of Lords to print Walker's
report on our revenue system for their use, are likely to cause
quite a sensation on both sides of the water, and what is to be the
result of it all, will be a matter of speculation for some time to
come.

The Locos have not yet agreed on a Candidate for Governor. Mr. Leak [13] has been nominated at a meeting in Anson, & Jas. Shepard by a meeting at the Co. Court of Wake last week. Either, I presume, would accept with but little provocation. There are said to have been 18 persons present at the meeting here—one of whom (McRae) opposed the nomination. They are much at fault, but will probably concentrate on some body before a great while.

Our Railroad earned a few hundred dollars beyond expenses in the month of Jany. (usually a dull season for business) and I hope will turn out better than the croackers predicted.

Judge Battle passed a day or two since on way to his Circuit. He says it is all a hoax that the College Students have joined the Temperence Society, as the newspapers have recently reported.

\* \* \* \* \*

I wish to visit the States lands in Hyde about the 1st. of May, and may possibly return through New Bern. It is however, somewhat uncertain. I would have gone down the river, as proposed to me last fall at Smithfield, had the Steam Boat come up so high this winter.

We have had a severe winter, and scarce a sign of Spring yet.

*From James Graham.*                            U.

H. R.,

March 13th, 1846.

We have but little of interest here, more than you have seen in the papers. Haywood's speech [14] has produced great excitement and ill feeling among the Democracy—He said many good things and some very foolish ones. It seems to be believed here he spoke by the authority of the President, and he obviously desired to encourage that belief. I do *not believe* he spoke by

---

[13] Presumably Walter F. Leake (1799-1879), of Richmond County, briefly a student at the university, member of the commons, 1831, state senator, 1832. He was a member of the convention of 1861.

[14] The allusion is evidently to an extended speech, begun in the senate on March 4th., 1846, on a proposed resolution to give notice to Great Britain of intention to annul the agreement for joint occupation of Oregon, in which he defended the course of President Polk.

authority. But the Allen and Henegan [15] clique of ultras who have made so much noise do not exceed 7 or 8 Senators. Our Whig friends *as usual* acted indiscreetly in *interposing* and preventing the war from going on among the Locos in the Senate. Evans got the floor and moved the adjournment, and made a strong speech against the American Title and in favor of the British Title. I think no Whig in the Senate was pleased with Evans for his *premature* interference.

President Polk is turning gray faster than any man I ever saw. He is very thin, and looks careworn. He must give dissatisfaction to some of his own friends. There is much suspicion and jealousy among the party. If the Whigs had any common sense, any prudence, they could soon gain a great victory.

There is a rich scene going on in the debate on the River and Harbor Bill among the Democracy, one wing saying they are pledged to them, and the others that they are not pledged to that system.

*From Robert B. Gilliam.*          U.

Oxford,

March 29th, 1846.

I had been writing to you and had nearly finished my letter, when I received yours of the 25th. inst. The object I had in view, was to suggest the danger of meddling with the Penitentiary question[16] in the approaching canvass. My own opinion, is that popular sentiment is very fast forming against the establishment of such an institution, and inasmuch as one wise acre, of the last Legislature, thought proper to present the question to the people for their consideration and action, it seems to me that the candidates for office have nothing to do with it, except to give their own votes. I know nothing of the state of feeling in other parts of the State, except from hearsay, but hereabouts,

[15] Edward Allen Hennegan (1807-1859), of Indiana, a native of Ohio, who was educated in Kentucky. After service in the lower house of the legislature, 1832-1833, he was a Democratic member of congress, 1833-1837, again a member of the legislature, 1841-1842, United States senator, 1843-1849, and minister to Prussia, 1849-1850.
[16] The question of a penitentiary had been discussed in the state since Governor Morehead's first administration. The legislature at its previous session submitted the question to the voters, and Governor Graham, acting under legislative instructions, had, on February 23rd., published the result of an inquiry made to every state maintaining a penitentiary. Notwithstanding favorable reports, the voters rejected it.

I think I understand something of it, and I entertain no doubt that it is decidedly averse to a penitentiary. Why it is so, I am unable to speak with certainty, but I incline to believe it is owing to the uncertain condition of our finances, growing out of our liabilities for the R & Gaston R Road. In some instances, I have heard references made to your publication, as evidence of the expensive character of such institutions; and occasionally to other causes of opposition. But from whatever cause it proceeds, I am satisfied that a determined opposition to the measure exists in the minds of the people, and that the better course for the Whig party will be to make no issue upon it, and to suffer none to be made.

I concur with you entirely as to the Democratic nomination for Governor. It is manifest to my mind that the party do not count upon success; if they did, Mr. Shepard would never have been nominated; and as they anticipate defeat, they doubtless consider him as well qualified to be beaten as any other man. But it is not our policy, as you well remark, to regard him in this light. He comes out as the candidate of the party, and is therefore to be regarded as formidable, and we should be as active in our exertions to secure his defeat, as if he were entitled to some consideration on his own account. Indeed, we have some reason to know, that a candidate is not to be despised because he is obscene.

I did not go to Henderson to hear Mr. Shepard, but I learn from a sure source that his exhibition was all but contemptible, that the company was ominously thin, and that not the slightest *"enthusiasm"* was excited. His vote in this county must fall greatly below the party strength, though this is a subject upon which we ought to be cautious in speaking, as it might enable the central leaders to know where there is likely to be defection, and upon whom to exercise the party drill. I have heard two of the prominent and leading democrats in this county, say they intended to support you, at all hazards, and that was when they expected to have a *regular* candidate of their own.

I am sorry I cannot give you as flattering an account of the prospects in regard to the county election. I believe we can carry the County, if the right men can be brought out, but I apprehend great difficulty in this respect. Our strongest men seem to have an invincible repugnance to coming out. We shall endeavour to form our ticket at or before May Court.

When you find it convenient to visit us, I will be glad, if you will give us ten or fifteen days notice, by a publication in the Raleigh papers, and we will give you a proper reception.

*From Theodore W. Brevard.*          U.

Tuskegee, Macon County, Ala.,

March 30th, 1846.

Dear William

I have applied to our Cousin the President for the appointment of Judge of the District Court of the United States in the Eastern or Southern Division of Florida. I understand that there must be three Judges for that State. Now I have been a long time a lawyer—admitted in S. Ca. before I came here. I practised but one year there with Ex. Gov. Hammond when I removed to this State to plant, and did not resume it—the law—untill within the last 5 years. I was appointed by the Gov. Fitzpatrick [17] Judge of the County Court which has here common law jurisdiction to the same extent of the Circuit except in a few cases and in all criminal proceedings.

At the following session of the Legislature I was elected to the same office for 6 years, which term has not expired. This much I thought I should say to you before asking the favour or your employing any means to assist me in my application to Polk. I think several of the members from this State as well as the Senators will probably use some influence in my favour. If you can be of service in this matter I shall be very much your debtor as I am very anxious to remove to Florida and have but a few hands to plant with and withall understand that there is nothing as yet to be made there by the practice of the law. I shall leave the course to be formed by you in the event you should decide to do any thing for me entirely to yourself. I have a wife and four Sons, the oldest 11 and the younger one 2. I regard them all as promising well but may not be a competent judge.

I have written several letters today and am a good deal wearied so that I must close and at some other time and upon some other occasion write you more fully.

---

[17] Benjamin Fitzpatrick (1802-1869), of Alabama, a native of Georgia, lawyer, planter in Autauga County, was appointed as a state rights Democrat to the United States senate, and served 1848-1849. Later, he was again appointed, and elected and served, 1853-1861. He was nominated for vice-president on the Douglas ticket in 1860, and declined. He was president of the Convention of 1861.

I ought to say to you that I am a Democrat. I hope you will pardon but how can you bear to hear, my cousin & schoolfellow, that both myself and wife are Baptists

I know if you had not been so long away from the Furnace that Farr and Low, colliers of our fathers, scarcely distinguishing B from a Bull's foot, wouldn't rise in judgment against me. I do hope though you are a Whig that North Carolina has no Democrat whom you cannot distance in the coming races.

So much for my consistency

*From James Graham.*                                         U.

H. R.,

April 7th. 1846.

I received your letter asking me to send you a copy of the Dorr Constitution. I immediately wrote to Simmons, [18] who is now in Rhoad Island, requesting him to send me a copy; and I will send it to you as soon as I get it.

You perceive the Sub Treasury has passed the house by a strict party vote. But 2 or 3 days were allowed for its discussion, and its friends consumed nearly all of that short time. Our Whig papers are almost silent on that subject, and indeed it was the great question in 1840, which was so generally condemned by all the Whigs and a considerable part of the Democrats. I made an effort to address the House against that Bill, but could not obtain the floor. I am astonished at the indifference of the papers concerning the Sub Treasury; when I am sure if the attention of the people were called to it, it could not fail to meet their condemnation. My old speech on that subject had a decided influence on the public mind, as it was plain in its reasoning and simple in its illustrations, so that any man of common sense could see the unequal and unjust opperation of that measure. In that speech I did not advocate, or apologize for *base Banks,* or their *suspension* of specie payments; but I showed that, the *then* administration and the Pet Banks were *Twin-sinners.* The then administration *advised* the Pet Banks to loan the public money largely, that it might acquire a *large popularity,* and the Pet Banks did so, that they might acquire *large* profits. *I condemned*

---

[18] James Fowler Simmons (1795-1864), of Rhode Island, manufacturer and farmer, member of the lower house of the legislature, 1828-1841, United States senator, 1841-1847, 1857-1862.

*both acts,* and then took the ground that I was for Gold and silver coin for currency, and circulation as far as it was practicable to introduce it, but as there was not enough of the precious metals to supply the demands of the Government and the people both; therefore I was for a mixed currency, that is, for Gold and silver, and good sound specie paying Banks. That the Government and the people ought to share and share alike, and that public men and Tax payers, ought to fare and fare alike.

The Whigs ought to keep *the true and only issue before the people.* They should not advocate or apologize for Bad Banks. They should not permit their adversaries to make up false issues. No man can, or ought to stand successfully before the people who will advocate the conduct of Bad corrupt Banks. I would not either permit any man in discussing the Sub Treasury *to draw me* into a discussion and defense of the United States Bank, particularly that corrupt Pennsylvania Bank; because sufficient for the day is the evil thereof, and sufficient for the Sub Treasury is the evil thereof. I expect C. Hinton or Manly or Badger have a copy of my old Sub Treasury speech.

I have written to Ohio to get a Democratic Paper containing a copy of the Democratic Resolutions passed on the 8th. of January last, declaring that they are in favor of the Sub Treasury for the *State governments* as well as the general governments. That is, for an exclusive metalic money out and out. So soon as I get that paper, I will send it to you.

I *approve* of President Polk's course in relation to Texas. He acted wisely and promptly in consummating the *expressed will* of Congress. But to Milton Brown, a Whig, will forever belong the merit of Texas annexation. For after 15 or 16 different sets of Resolutions on that subject had *all* failed, then a Whig stept forth, and presented Resolutions embodying *terms* and *conditions* totally different from any that had been offered; but *right* and *just* in themselves, and they passed; and they were the propositions presented to and accepted by Texas.

The Oregon question has caused more difference of opinion among the Democrats than among the Whigs.

Indeed the Democratic party differed on the final vote for the annexation of Texas; they differ entirely about Oregon; about Internal Improvements; about the Tariff, and indeed about every great question but the Sub Treasury, and even on that, they differ about the specie Clause; for both Clark and Dobbin, voted against the specie clause when incorporated into the Bill;

but afterwards voted for the Bill. Mr. Calhoun himself, in his speech on Oregon, admitted if we got into a war the Banking System would be forced again on the government, so that the Sub Treasury is a peace measure only; and yet Gen'l Washington told us in peace prepare for war, and money is the sinew of war, and without which no war can be prosecuted for any length of time.

I think our friends here are willing to prune and improve the Tariff of 1842. They are willing to see it made better, but not destroyed. And when we put the Locos on the defensive, and tell them to present a better substitute on which *they themselves can all agree,* and then we will consider it, we find they can't agree among themselves, and that is the reason even up to this day they have not presented their scheme or Bill. For a man to say he is for Free Trade, or a Judicious Tariff is too indefinite, that fixes no rate of duty, that establishes, nor proposes any policy. But when you call on such men to propose some specific rate of duty, and make them shew whether they are for cash duties, for specific or advalorum duties, or minimums, or horizontal, or discriminatory duties, then they begin to expose their ignorance, and they get into deep water far beyond their depth. The right plan to pursue is to keep those men *defending* their new schemes all the time, and let the people see they are opposing the opinions and policy of Washington, Jefferson, Madison, Monroe and Jackson, all of whom said we must protect American Industry; But no class at the expense of any other class.

I presume it will be necessary for you so soon as you know your only competitor, to visit some parts of the State and make some speeches. You should be well prepared to sustain the Acts of your own administration, and call upon your adversaries if they disappove of it to point out their objections, and then call on them to shew their hands and inform the people the policy and measures they would pursue if elected. Call upon them to go minutely into and explain what they propose to do, if elected, for the people. They will try to keep the discussion mainly on the Tariff, and try to evade the Sub Treasury. Do not permit that; keep the Sub Treasury, the exclusive hard money policy, distinctly before the people, and shew its grinding and oppressive tendency. On the Tariff, state your views distinctly. For a Revenue Tariff, with no more money to be collected than is necessary for an economical administration with such discrimination in imposing duties as will encourage and protect equally and justly all kinds of useful labor and industry in our own country. We are opposed to taxing one class for the benefit of another; or one section for the benefit of another. But we impose duties in such a manner as [to] sustain the Independance and prosperity of our own Republican country against foreign Countries. You should state that your notions on the Tariff are not new or original, but that you got them from Washington, & Jefferson, & Madison, & Monroe, and Jackson, While your opponents are running after new and untried theories which will operate to the injury of America and to the benefit of England. The Democrats, I mean the Southern wing, say they want to have the priviledge and pursue the policy which will enable them to *sell high* and *buy low*. And so I say; yes, that is just what I say. If we want to sell high, *the more markets* we have the better. The more bidders we have, the better chance to get a high price. *"Competition* is the life of Trade." To have an American market at home, as well as an English market abroad, *is better* than to have *one* market only. The more the better for the Planter; but the nighest market is generally the best, because the shorter the distance you haul your produce, the less tax comes out of your load, and the more money you will realise from your Crop.

So in buying. If there was but one Store in the world, and that was *in Old England;* goods would be very high in America, because they would be expensive to carry so far and nothing which the farmer makes here would buy them there. So they would get all our Gold and silver.

If there was but one Store in each County, that store would sell high, and we could not buy low; but just as you increase the number of stores in each place, just in the same manner you lower the price of goods, because again, *Competition* is the life of trade. It brings the farmer's produce up, and the merchant's goods down, & the *nigher home* the better.

I have rambled on so far & will now stop.

[P. S.]   In N. C. popular men should be brought out as Candidates in every County by the Whigs, especially in the doubtful Counties, such as Granville, Stokes, Surry, and others.

I would not expose myself by long travels in bad weather. I would treat every one with respect, but if any one candidate or other opponent *attacks you crudely,* I would *promptly pay him off in compound interest.*

You ought to have side Arms with you to be ready for any contingency, but of course you will seek no quarrel with any one, but be ready to act on the defensive.

I presume the Rail Road subject will be discussed this Summer, that is, which party has involved the State in its present liabilities. You had better look at the Journals.

The conduct of Fisher, Caldwell, Leak and Sheppard, [19] as well as Sanders [20] and Henry, are all proper subjects of enquiry about Internal Improvements, et al. Dockery [21] informed me that after the great Internal Improvement Convention in Raleigh where Sanders and Henry figured, there was a County Convention to Ratify their acts in Leak's County, and moved in that the Resolutions approving of all that had been done in Raleigh and was appointed and did go through the County to explain it all to the people, so as to get them to approve it ! ! !

But what is the advantage of having low priced goods when the farmer has nothing to buy with. If all the goods in old England were in America, if we, the farmers and laboring men, had nothing to buy with, it would not help us much. Before we farmers buy anything, there is another more important Question, and that is, can we first sell anything for money to buy those cheap goods? I could buy anything for sale, *if I had the money,* to buy is easy, but to pay is the Devil.

The locofoco policy gives us a good policy to buy cheap, but it provides no means to make payment. There's the Rub. There is the Error and defect of their System. They make the people poor; and then tell them goods are very low.

I wouldn't give much for a bottle of liquor if I couldn't get the Cork out of it. A man can't buy goods who can't pay for them. But give him the means of payment, and he will buy all he needs.

*From Augustus Moore.*    U.

Edenton,

April 9th, 1846.

Upon my return from Gates Court last week, I received yours of the 29th. of last month, since which time I have seen the letter of Mr. Leak.

---

[19] Probably James B. Shepard.
[20] Romulus M. Saunders.
[21] Alfred Dockery (1797-1875), of North Carolina, farmer, member of the commons, 1822, delegate to Convention of 1835, state senator, 1836-1841, Whig member of Congress, 1845-1847, 1851-1853, candidate for governor, 1854, 1866.

I trust this family quarrel may be of service to the Whig cause. If Mr. Leak has the independence that a man ought to have, he cannot retreat. The only result I fear, and that seems to be a very improbable, if not an impossible one, is, that they may endeavour to prove that Leak is a Whig, and thereby secure to him the support of a portion of the Whig party. The more absurd any position they assume may be, the more strenuously will they insist upon it.

We had a visit from Mr. Shepard and a speech from him today in the Court House. The company which he addressed was very small, and nearly all Whigs. He spoke of the distribution of the proceeds of the sales of the public lands, the tariff, and the rail roads of the State. Of the public lands and the tariff you can readily conjecture the character of his remarks; upon the subject of the rail roads, I did not clearly apprehend his statements. He alleged, however, that the State would lose some $500,000. for which you and the Whig party were alone responsible. That the last Legislature did wrong in prescribing the amount that should be bid for the road, that had you not been limited, the road could have been purchased for our dollars, and more than $300,000. saved to the State, as the bonds of the Stock holders, held by the State, would have been good for that amount.

The speech I thought, produced no impression—in fact he had no persons present who could be influenced. Nearly every one present was decided in his opinions. It was not to be expected that those of his own party who were present should change; and I am sure there was nothing said that could change the opinions of a single Whig present.

If you can find it convenient to visit this part of the State, I am sure it would be very gratifying to us all. If you did not gain converts, your visit would have the effect to excite energy, increase activity, and awaken the party to a sense of duty. I have thought it best to make no appointments for you, fearing that I might thereby interfere with arrangements already made. You can best judge how to direct your labors. Should you direct your attention to the Counties East of the Chowan River, Perquimans County should receive a portion of your attention. We have lost greatly in that County, and I fear we shall not be able to recover our loss. The County Court of that County sits in Hertford on the 2nd. Monday of May. The 3rd. Monday is Gates County Court; at which place there is always a very large collection of persons. By reference to the Almanacks and by consultation with

Mr. Iredell, you could make your appointments for this Section of the State.

I fear we shall have some difficulty in getting out an efficient set of candidates. I hear very little said upon the subject, from which I infer that the business does not engage the public mind. I hardly think I can be prevailed upon to offer. The injury which I sustained more than twelve months ago almost forbids it. Since I returned home in January last, I have improved very much, and I fear the fatigue of standing as much as I should be obliged to, would greatly retard my recovery.

Individually, it will give me unfeigned satisfaction to have you in this part of the State.

*From James Graham.*                                               U.

H. R.,

April 18th, 1846.

The Senate, as you have seen, has passed the Notice. And all the Whigs in that body voted for it but two, Evans and Thomas Clayton.[22] The form of the Senate Notice is that presented by Crittenden. The House Notice and the Senate Notice are substantially the same; but the different wings of parties are trying [to] make capital out of the difference.

The House this day has amended the Senate Notice so as to make the terms more imperative on the President.

I will continue to vote for Notice, in any form, because it is "the brush always in our path." It is *in the way* of negotiation, of legislation, and of emigration. *It will surely pass.*

A Bill this day passed the House to extend the (our) Jurisdiction and Laws over Oregon, fixing no boundaries. I voted against the Bill, but did so with much hesitation. I finally resolved to do so, because until the Notice was given, to terminate the joint occupation, we could not rightfully pass a good and efficient Bill to protect our citizens in Oregon; and then it appeared to me that a feable, ricketty and temporary Bill might rather embarrass than aid our citizens in that Territory.

---

[22] Thomas Clayton (1778-1854), of Delaware, a native of Maryland, who had a long career as a legislator and state officer before his service as a Federalist representative in congress, 1815-1817, and senator, 1824-1827. After a decade of service as a state judge, he was a Whig United States senator, again from 1837 to 1847.

I am anxious to extend our Laws whenever we can without violating Treaties.

[P.S.] The Locos can't [make] capital out of Oregon, because they differ much among themselves.

*To James W. Bryan.*  U. Bryan Mss.

Raleigh,

April 19th, 1846.

I will leave tomorrow on a tour of four or five weeks, to the Eastern section of the State;[23] and must beg of you the favor to hand the enclosed notice to the Editor of the New Bernian. I would gladly forego this expedition, and am very sure that I will never be engaged in a like canvass again.

From Beaufort I must come home, and could take Jones, Wayne, and Johnston in the way if deemed important. I could be at Wayne Court, but I attended a Court there two years ago, and Gov. Morehead had given them a like attention but all without effect—I may go to Johnston the 4th. week in May.

The Fayetteville paper received to day contains a letter from Mr. Leak addressed to Mr. Shepard proposing a reference to their Central Committee, provided the Committee shall assemble in Raleigh as soon as practicable, but if any member can't attend, he may signify his preference by letter. It is in rather a subdued tone, and does not comport with his former gasconade, but the Lincoln paper has warmly espoused his cause recently, and he has published appointments untill the last of May. I think they will probably make some compromise in the course of the next month. **The only impediment in the way of our entire success, is the**

---

[23] Graham campaigned actively. Among the counties in which he spoke were Granville, Northampton, Chowan, Pasquotank, Washington, Pitt, Craven, Beaufort, Greene, Orange, Cumberland and Buncombe. The *Register*, May 12th., 1846, published an article entitled "Chronicles for Granville County," in which the following appeared: "And, moreover, know ye not, that the Governor of the Province, even William, whose name is Graham, hath stolen the hearts of the people, and behold all men go after him.

For the Governor of the Province made an oration to the people, at the chief village of the lesser Province of Granville, and much people of both tribes were assembled.

"And although he sprang from the Whig tribe, which are hated, and treated by the other tribe as 'sheep-stealing dogs,' yet they could not gainsay or resist the power and wisdom with which he spake.

"And while he was yet speaking, . . . the countenances of the leaders of the Democratic tribe was as the giving up of the ghost."

difficulty of getting out suitable Candidates in the different Counties.

Affairs at Washington are likely to operate to our advantage. You see the 54s are completely routed on the Oregon question. I think they will not be able to disturb the Tariff, after four years of conflict and the Subtreasury will not help them in this State.

I regret to learn that there are new cases of Small Pox at Hillsboro', and I fear it may spread through the Country—

\* \* \* \* \*

A poor old woman from Wilkes, the Mother of a man under sentence of death, came and quartered herself upon us last night with a Petition for his pardon, having travelled alone on horseback, or on her blistered feet, 180 miles in four days. It is, however, a direful case of Guilt, I fear, and no relief can be given.

| | | |
|---|---|---|
| Plymouth | Friday | 8th May |
| Washington | Sat. | 9th |
| Greenville | Monday | 11th |
| Snow Hill | Tuesday | 12 |
| Newbern | Thursday | 14th |
| Beaufort | Sunday | 16th. |

*From James W. Bryan.*                                    U.

Newbern,

May 9th, 1846.

. . . I cannot learn that Mr. Shepard has made any impression of a favourable character among us, by his speech; in truth, from what I have heard, his efforts are disparaging to the reputation he had acquired. Sagacious and discriminating men all say, that they are sadly disappointed, and that he has heretofore been greatly overrated.

I have had every publication given to your intention of addressing the people here, on Thursday, and they are looking for you at Carteret, with much anxiety.

*From Alexander MacRae.*                                    U.

Wilmington,

May 17th., 1846.

Seeing that our country is involved in a war with Mexico, it would seem to be a proper inquiry to make, whether we run any risk from the war. May it not be a possible thing for the Mexicans to fit out Privateers to prey upon our Commerce? And if they should, it might very reasonably be asked, what is to hinder them from entering our ports and burning our Towns? If the rest of the Towns along the Coast are in the situation of Wilmington, a 10 gun vessel might destroy them. At the fort at the mouth of our River there are no men, in Wilmington we have not a piece of Ordinance fit for use, there is therefore no means of defence. It may be supposed that the Mexicans are too insignificant for us to fear them, I hope it may prove so. I fear others may, for the sake of Plunder, take commissions from them. I would suggest whether it would not be a dictate of wisdom to be prepared. It will cost less to put ourselves in a state of defence than to rebuild a Town. The news from the South this morning is very exciting, and creates an intense interest here.

If you think it advisable to call the attention of the Gen'l Government to the defence of our harbors, or feel disposed to take action by sending us some Artilery & Artilery Stores, we will trye and take care of them until we hear further from you.

And here permit me to tender my services to you, if you should have occasion for them. I do not do it in the spirit of Bom bast, but because I consider it to be the duty of every man holding a Commission in the Militia of the State, to hold himself in readiness in case of need, or else resign and let some one take his place who will do so.

I have two vacancies in my Staff, please send me two blank Commissions, that I may fill them.

Respectfully,

Your ob't Serv't.,

Alexander MacRae

Major General 6th. Division

of the Militia of North Carolina.

*From James G. Martin[24] to James Iredell.*    U.

Cambridge,
Maryland,
May 23rd., 1846.

I have understood to day that several Officers of the Army have received appointments in the Volunteer Regiments now being raised in this State, with the understanding between themselves and the proper authorities of the Government, that they shall receive their present Commissions when discharged as Volunteers. One Lieutenant not much older than I am, has been appointed Brigadier General.

It immediately occurred to me, that, on the same conditions, I would like to have an appointment of Colonel, Lieutenant Colonel, or Major, in one of the Regiments to be raised in my own State. In regard to my claims to, or fitness for, such an appointment, I can only say, I am a native of North Carolina, and, since Graduating at the Military Academy, have served with my Regiment (The First Artillery) nearly six years.

Of course I would prefer having Command of a Regiment to holding any subordinate situation, though as I have said above, I would take a Majority.

If you can at all advance my wishes by presenting my name to the Governor, you will much oblige me by adding this to the many favors you have already conferred on our family.

If letters from Mr. Wm. B. Shepard, or General Ehringhaus would be of any service, they could be obtained at the shortest notice.

Any communications will be received by me at Baltimore, Md. until Saturday next, after that time at Prince Frederick P. O., Calvert County, Md. I have been on duty on the Survey of the Coast for several months, and am at present employed on the Chesapeake Bay.

\* \* \* \* \*

P. S. If the recommendation of Bishop Ives would be of any service to me, I feel confident he would gladly give it.

---

[24] James Green Martin (1819-1878), of Pasquotank, graduate of West Point, brevet major in the Mexican War. He resigned in 1861, and was appointed adjutant general of North Carolina. He made a notable reputation there for his organization of troops, and through his suggestion that the state engage in blockade-running. As a result, the North Carolina troops were better clothed and otherwise supplied than any of Confederate troops. In 1862 he became a Confederate brigadier general. After the war he became a lawyer.

*From N. G. Harrell.* U.

Rossville,

Cherokee County,

May 23rd, 1846.

Some six weeks since, I removed from Haywood County to this County, and have been passing and repassing among the people of this County. I find they are generally displeased in consequence of they having to Rent the Lands they were compeled to surrender to the agent and commissioner of the State, or at Least sevral persons that I heard speaking about the matter seems to blaim you pretty much, they say whin they surrindered to the Agent and Commissioner they ware told by both that they should stay in possesion of the Lands, & all would be required of them would be to take good Care of the same. I did not expect to have any Rents to pay, I think from what I can discover in the Conversation of the people, they seem to blaim you for ordering those Lands surrendered. This is and has always been, a Whig County, but from the above mentioned Circomstance the most influential Whigs will not vote in the Governor's Election this summer without they should be some removal of the obsticle now in the minds of the people, it would be well as you are canvassing the State to fall into Cherokee County.

I have no interest [in] the Renting of the Land maters but I would like to see you appear before these people. We live in the back woods here we are strong to believe, but not hard to remove from Error. I have brought the Interest in a renter of this County and intend at the first opportunity afforded by the State to perchase Lands and settle in this County. If you should come to Cherokee I should like for you to call on me, I will be in sight of the public Road as you will go to Murphy five miles from Murphy.

*From James A. King.* U.

New Orleans,

May 26th., 1846.

* * * * *

I did not succeed in getting my Company for the Mexican War. The better opinion seems to be that we shall terminate this contest in a very short time, unless we should determine to penetrate into the heart of Mexico. We could now, of course, dictate such terms of peace as we ought to be content with, but there exists a most irrepressible propensity to invade Mexico.

\* \* \* \* \*

*From John Gray Bynum.*                     A., G. P.

Lincolnton,

May 28th., 1846.

I had the honor of addressing you a letter from Cleveland a week since, tendering my services to command such forces as might be raised in No. Ca. to serve in the War against Mexico. I yesterday received your proclamation, & I beg leave to renew my offer. I presume I am the only officer in the State who has had an opportunity of serving at all, tho' my own tour of service was quite short, & attended with no danger, but it afforded me the means of learning the routine of Camp and Garrison duty.

I am now reviewing my division, and anticipating a call upon the State for troops have been making efforts to raise volunteers, & have now one or two companies in process of being formed. If your Excellency however, will pardon me for a few suggestions I shall make, I think I can point out the proper & the only mode of raising our quota of volunteers. I think the Colonel ought to be appointed at once, & that he should be specially charged with raising the Companies. Unless it is made the special duty of some one person, it will not be attended to & the ten Companies will not be raised. I am sure that will be the case from what has occurred under my own observation, & I am sure, without meaning disrespect to other portions of the State, that much the largest portion of volunteers will be raised from the West. Very few will be found from the East except in the Cities and towns. In addition to that, the organization of a company is a matter of the greatest consequence. The Captains will not know how to constitute it properly. They know nothing of the importance of the non-Commissioned officers. The efficiency of a Company depends almost as much upon the capacity of the first, or orderly sergeant, as upon the Captain. His duties are more laborious, and almost as important, requiring intelligence & business habits. None of our officers have the slightest conception of the duties of that officer

& unless they are particularly instructed at least one half of those officers will be found incompetent, & the Colonel when called to service will have to send them back to the ranks, creating thereby jealousies & dessensions which will detract much from the effectiveness of the whole regiment. Those things I discovered in my short tour of service operated much against our troops in the expedition against the Cherokees. I would respectfully make another suggestion. There is no call for Surgeons. Each regiment is entitled to one Surgeon and 1 assistant Surgeon. Without these the troops ought not to be moved one days march. If they are in one month, one half will be upon the sick list some where on their march to the place from which they are to be transported to the scene of action. This I *know* to be true. A suggestion of this nature to the President would insure you the liberty of appointing those officers. I am sure it was only an oversight in the Secretary at War.

Should I be selected to command, I should prefer making it a rifle or light infantry Regiment. From the character of the forces already sent, I am sure a Reg't of that character is most needed.

I will have forwarded to your Excellency at Chapel Hill, testimonies upon which I have presumed to ask the command sought for.

*From Robert B. Gilliam.*                                    U.

Oxford,

May 28th, 1846.

Franklin Court sits on the 1st. Monday of June. Would it not be judicious to take a flying trip to Louisburg, to make an address to the people of that County? I presume you will scarcely set out on your Western expedition within two or three weeks, and if you can find time, I think you would do good by a visit to Franklin.

I should like to hear from you, in person, your views as to the state of things in the East. Accounts from other sources are of the most encouraging character, but I confide in your observation and judgment, more than in the opinions of the Editors. The truth is, I cannot doubt that you have given the fullest satisfaction wherever you have been. The impression made by you in this County, was of the most favorable kind, and one that will last. I believe it is of very great importance that you should address the people as often as possible. Good will follow, wherever you go, and I trust your official duties will enable you to get off by the middle of June, at the latest.

Unless there is a change in this County, and I do not anticipate one, you will go over the party vote here, from one to two hundred —and I should not be surprised if the difference was still greater.

Our friends here are preparing for the County election with a good deal of spirit. At present, the prospects look well. Dr. Russell,[25] I think, will certainly be elected, and unless this war question injures us, I see no reason to dispair of the Commons ticket. The Whigs, indeed, are almost as sanguine in relation to the Commons, as to the Senate. It is a sort of uphill business with me; but you may depend on it, I shall do my best.

I intended, until within a day or two, to meet you at Chapel Hill; but the weather is likely to be so hot, that I have determined to reserve all my resources for the sweltering heats of July.

*From John H. Wheeler to James Iredell.*    U.

Beattiesford, N. C.,

June 3rd., 1846.

My esteemed Sir,

I must be allowed to congratulate you and my State, at the spirit and enthusiasm of your meeting in Raleigh[26] on the 26th. ult'o, on the subject of our existing difficulties with Mexico. It reminded me of the early days of our acquaintance, when you led, during the War of '12 a gallant band of volunteers in defence of liberty and independence.

To no one can I enclose more properly the enclosed letter, and very sincerely request your earnest co operation with my friends, if consistent with your views of propriety, to have my wishes gratified.

Our Western Country is all alive. Last Friday at a general Muster we raised 40 Volunteers. I can enrol my name here, as I have expressed a willingness to do, but should prefer when the field Officers are appointed for the Regiment, to receive from

---

[25] James A. Russell of Granville County, member of the commons, 1840-1842, state senator, 1846.

[26] James Iredell presided over a public meeting where resolutions were adopted pledging the support of the state in the war with Mexico.

the Commander in Chief some suitable appointment to my age and character in the Reg't.

By the 9th. Sec. of our State Law, (Rev'd Statutes, page 398) each Regiment is entitled to one Col., one Lt. Col., and one Major, one Adjutant, one Quarter Master and one pay master; I am willing to receive from the Governor a commission for either of these appointments, except the first, which I would decline.

Let me hear from you by return mail, and believe me, as ever, very truly

Your sincere well wisher & old friend,

[*Enclosure*]

*From John H. Wheeler.*

Beattiesford, N. C.,

June 3rd., 1846.

As suggested by the proclamation of your Excellency of date the 22nd. ult'o, I beg leave to tender through my friend, Gov. Iredell, who will hand you this, my services as one of the Field Officers in the Regiment already raised, or to be raised, for the prosecution of the War between the United States and the Republic of Mexico.

Your fellow citizens of your native section of our State are roused, without distinction of party, by the condition of our common country, and at the recent outrages of the Mexican Government, a Government whose conduct for years has been a continued series of wrongs, in the commerce, rights, and interests of our Republic and our citizens; and we rejoice in an opportunity of visiting these outrages upon a nation whose whole history is marked by tyranny, and perfidy.

We hope to report within the course of 10 days the formation and enrollment of a company of volunteers from this county, ready to be mustered into the Service of the United States, with the names of the Company Officers.

I would suggest to your Excellency, with great respect, the propriety of appointing and announcing publicly, the field Officers of the Regiment, that they might aid in recruiting and rendezvousing the troops. In this opinion, I am coincided in by Maj. Gen'l J. G. Bynum, who reviewed our Regiment on Friday last.

Be so kind as to allow me to receive an immediate reply, or as early as may suit your convenience, and accept, Sir, assurances of the respect of

Your faithful servant,

P. S. By the 9th. Sec. of our Militia Statute (398) each Regiment is entitled to: One Col., one Lt. Col., one Major, one Adjutant, one Quarter Master, one Pay Master and others; as I have stated to Gov. Iredell, I would accept a Commission from you for either of these, except the first.


*From Edward Stanly.*          A., G. P.

Washington,

June 3rd., 1846.

I presume you will appoint some of the "field officers," if our proportion of Volunteers for the Mexican War is raised.

I write to solicit the appointment of my brother, James G. Stanly, Jr., to some one of these places. Generals and Colonels will probably be offered to experienced persons, but I suppose some Majors, Sergeant majors, (if there is such a rank) will also be necessary. If so, I hope you will confer the appointment of one of them on my brother. He is about 25 years old, of good health, & has had some experience as a Lieut. in a Volunteer Company. He has volunteered to go to Mexico, and I dislike to see him go as a common soldier.

Pardon me for trespassing on your valuable time.

There is very little War feeling among us. Politically, we go on smoothly.

SCHEME OF THE EXERCISES
AT THE
C O M M E N C E M E N T [27]
OF THE
UNIVERSITY OF NORTH CAROLINA
JUNE 4th, 1846.

FORENOON

1. Sacred Music.
2. Prayer.
3. Salutatory Oration, [in Latin,]
   FREDERICK A. SHEPERD, Wadesborough.
4. Oration. "Life and Character of Howard."
   RICHARD T. WEAVER, Northampton.
5. Oration. "English Tragedy."
   DAVID S. JOHNSTON, Caswell.
6. Oration. "True Glory."     JAMES S. AMIS, Granville.
7. Oration. "True National Greatness."
   SION H. ROGERS, Wake.
8. Oration. "The Shade of the Past."
   TURNER W. BATTLE, Edgecombe.

AFTERNOON

1. Oration. "The Reformation."   JAMES R. WARD, Chatham.
2. Oration. "Influence of Fiction."
   RICHARD N. FORBES, New Berne.
3. Oration. "Free Institutions Favorable to Literature."
   OWEN H. WHITFIELD, Mississippi.
4. Oration. "Highland Character."
   WILLIAM K. BLAKE, Fayetteville.
5. Annual Report.
6. Degrees Conferred.
7. Valedictory.     WILLIAM S. BRYAN, Raleigh.
8. Sacred Music.
9. Prayer.

---

[27] Brief biographical sketches of the graduates can be found in the *Alumni History of the University of North Carolina*.

ILLUSTRISSIMO GULIELMO A. GRAHAM, ARMIGERO:[28]
CAROLINAE SEPTENTRIONALIS REIPUBLICAE
G U B E R N A T O R I;
HONORANDO DAVIDI L. SWAIN, ARMIGERO, LL.D.
FACULTATIS PRAESIDI;
OMNIBUSQUE SENATUS ACADEMICI SOCIIS;
UNIVERSIS DENIQUE HUMANITATIS CULTORIBUS;
EXERCITATIONES HASCE JUVENES HODIE
PRIMI GRADUS IN ARTIBUS HONOREM PETENTES,

Jacobus—Saunders Amis,
Turner—Westray Battle,
Guliemus—Kennedy Blake,
Alexander—Franklin Brevard,
Guliemus—Shepard Bryan,
Guliemus—Franklin Carter,
Johannes—Napoleon Daniel,
Guliemus—Alexander Daniel,
Guliemus—Jacobus Duke,
Solomon—Jacobus Faison,
Jacobus—Sterling Ruffin,
Johannes—Vicar Sherard,
Jacobus—Riddle Ward,
Benjamin—Franklin Whitaker,
Hillory—Madison Wilder.

Guliemus—Alexander Faison,
Ricardus—Nathan Forbes,
Edwardus—Hubbel Hicks,
Robertus—C. T. S. Hilliard,
Johannes—Lyon Holmes,
David—Saunders Johnston,
Guliemus—Belvidere Meares,
Thomas—Mullen Newby,
Stephanus—Farmer Pool,
Sion—Hart Rogers,
Fredericus—Augustus Sheperd,
David—Thomas Tayloe,
Ricardus—Thomas Weaver,
Audoenus—Holmes Whitfield,
REVERENTER DEDICANT.

DIE JUNII QUARTO ANNO SALUTIS
MDCCCXLVI.

Anno Libertatis LXX.

*From Nicholas W. Woodfin.*                                    U.

Asheville,

June 11th, 1846.

On yesterday the Regiment in this County East of the river,
met for the purpose and raised a full Company of Volunteers for
Mexico, & elected their officers at once. They elected E. H. Hughes

---

[28] The following is an extract from a letter written in 1873 by Mrs. Cornelia
Phillips Spencer, according to Kemp P. Battle, for a "leading Raleigh journal."
See Kemp P. Battle, *History of the University of North Carolina*, II, p. 38.

their Captain. Heretofore, on the West side of the river one full Company and perhaps twenty more volunteered, and are to meet on next Saturday to elect their officers. I have assured them all, that if they would step forward that they would at least have an equal chance with others to be received, and further, that if they would make a full Company from each of the Regiments in the County, that I hoped it would give them some more favorable consideration. I assured them that if in the disposal of your Excellency that one or the other would be chosen. I now write at their request to ask for them the most favorable notice and, if not improper, to ask that our two Companies should be allowed to draw only as between themselves, so as to insure at least one. I do not know whether this be admissable, but if so, we would be much gratified.

We have two large and fine looking Companies indeed. And all seem so eager for the acceptance and orders for marching that I do hope both Companies will not be disappointed. It will be remembered that Henderson and Yancy both recently taken from Buncombe, have each made up a full Company and in the Burke part of Yancy they are making another. In my Senatorial District we shall then have five Companies, and I hazzard nothing in saying that they will compare favorably with any five in the State, and do as much service, and do it as willingly as any Companies in and out of the State.

Allow me to enquire whether they might not all be sent if tendered the Government tho' the ten Companies were completed? If so, we will be greatly obliged for the suggestion, and directions as to the mode.

The Whigs here are not disposed to stop now to enquire into the propriety of geting into the War. They will not be behind in prosecuting it. We are willing to wait for a proper occasion and settle that account at home.

When can you visit the Western Counties? Tho' without you must get a larger vote than you did against Col. Hoke we can not give it up. We all think that you must come, and more especially

"I have before me one of three Commencement programs to read, which brings back a gush of warm, sweet Spring air, crowds the silent campus with glowing, ardent youth, and lights the halls with the fresh beauty and grace that once adorned them, sends the music of the drums and trumpets floating through the tree tops, and crowns our riven old Poplar again with bud and bloom. *Illustrissimo Guliemo A. Graham, Armigero. Carolinae Septentrionalis Reipublicae Gubernatori.*

"Can we not see him? Certainly the noblest figure there, calm, self-poised, and firm, his dark eyes gleaming over the crowd, not one of whom but is proud that day of him as a representative North Carolinian."

go to Macon and Cherokee. In those Counties it is really important to go.

*From Charles N. B. Evans.*[29]    U.

Milton,

June 15th, 1846.

Understanding that Maj. W. A. Whitfield [30] contemplates going to Raleigh this week, I avail myself of the opportunity offered to address you a line soliciting his appointment as an officer of rank in the N. C. R. of Volunteers. He was the *first* in Caswell to enroll his name as a *private*. But at the urgent solicitation of his numerous friends in Caswell, he has consented to apply to your Excellency for a field office, and I presume this is one of his objects in going to Raleigh, though I do not know. Should he apply, your Excellency will greatly gratify the wishes of a large portion of the most respectable citizens in Caswell to honor him with an appointment. And you may rest assured that *he* will honor the office, however great and important it may be.

Maj. W. is *proficient* in knowledge of the science of Military tactics (which you know is very important, and which can be said of but few men in our State.) He has served in the Navy, and, I learn, has been engaged in action with Mexican forces. I think he would make a splendid officer—possessing as he does all the requisite traits. And there prevails among your friends here, a general desire to see him promoted.

I sent your Excellency, per Mr. Boyd, my a/c for advertising the Penitentiary. You however, deemed it too large, and *docked* it. Of this I will not complain, but, lest you might regard it as a disposition on my part to *gouge* the State, I beg leave to explain. I charge $1 for the first insertion of 12 lines (advertising matter). Owing to the *shortness* of my *columns,* and the *largeness* of my type, the article made almost double the number of lines (in *my* paper) that it made in the Raleigh papers, because their columns are *wider* and their type much *smaller*—hence the difference. Now there are type so small that the whole article could be put in

---

[29] Charles N. B. Evans, was editor of the *Milton Chronicle,* which was probably the most ably edited and influential weekly paper ever published in North Carolina. He was later, very briefly, editor of the *Hillsborough Recorder.*

[30] I have been unable to find any record of W. A. Whitfield's name in the North Carolina troops in the Mexican War.

36 lines in my paper, but then I had not these type. I trust, Sir, this brief explanation will satisfy you that I had no desire to *gouge,* (as it *may* seem to *you* I had) and that in making out my a/c I made it out strictly in accordance with my Advertising terms.

Allow me, in conclusion, to assure your Excellency that Jas. B. Shepard, Esq., will not get *all* the votes in this part of the State— (he lost several by speaking in this county, to my knowledge).

Trusting that I shall be pardoned for any *too great* familiarity in addressing you.

*From Burgess S. Gaither.*                                    U.

Asheville,

June 20th, 1846.

Gen'l Edney is very desirous of participating in this Mexican War, and request me to write to you upon that subject to see whether you can do any thing for him. Immediately upon the commencement of hostilities, he wrote to Messrs. Graham and Barringer to procure from the Secretary of War permission and authority to raise either a Regiment or Brigade of Volunteers from this region and march forthwith to the scene of action. This application has failed, and he then resolved to be a candidate for the Command of the Regiment required from this State, and expected the officers of the same to elect their own field officers, but he has learned through the News papers that you have appointed Gen'l Pasteur. His death has produced a vacancy, and you now will have to make another selection. Gen'l Edney has been making War speeches from Cherokee to this place and has succeeded in geting out a great number of Volunteers, a very large number of whom (probably all) wish him to command the Regiment. Edney has considerable Military talents and I have very little doubt is one of the best Militia Officers in the State, and would do himself and the State credit, in the Army. I presume if you have not filled the vacancy caused by the death of Gen'l Pasteur, that you probably will not do so until you get back to Raleigh and you will have the means of knowing public sentiment in the West on this subject, during your visit among us. We are very much pleased to learn that you are on your way West, and particularly so to see that you are to meet Sheperd at this place. I hope you will find it convenient to extend your visit as far West as Cherokee. The matters growing out of the Cherokee bond question require that you should go to Macon and Cherokee if possible, otherwise, it would be a matter of little moment. The party in the District at present need rousing up, and some excitement to bring them out, and I think we will give our usual majority. The selection of Candidates for the Legislature are good, and our success almost certain.

*To Michael Francis.*                          A.

Waynesville, Haywood Co.,

July 4th, 1846.

I must beg of you the favor to offer my apology to the citizens of Macon & Cherokee for my failure to extend my visit to those Counties. When I left home, I expected to be able to do so. But owing to the accidental circumstance that a letter written by me to a friend in Asheville, did not reach him in time to make appointments for me as early as I desired, I have not now time to go further West, and return as early as necessity will require. It would have afforded me great pleasure to have paid my respects in person to the good people of those Counties. And I especially desired to meet the citizens of Cherokee, that I might have explained more at length than could be done in reply to their memorial, in a written communication last winter, the considerations which required, in my opinion, the course then taken under the act of the General Assembly of the last session. I also wished to ascertain from actual observation, and conference with them what policy is best to be adopted in the future in relation to the Cherokee lands.

In the circumstances which surround me, I beg them to be assured that my failure to come among them does not arise from any feeling of indifference or neglect.

I am very Respectfully
Your Obedt. Servt.

*From Charles L. Hinton.*                    A.

Raleigh,

July 10th, 1846.

Yours of the 3rd. Inst was recd by last mail, which together
with the HighLand Messenger and several letters of the same
date has produced quite a sensation among us—Our prospects are
encouraging from every section. The Loco claim Halifax, but
Batt Moore who is here think there is but little doubt of our
success there. Rainer has no opposition. Erringhouse, Augustus
Moore says will be elected—these are the most doubtful cases.
In Johnston the Whigs have a strong ticket, Adams[31] in the Senate, McLeod[32] & Sanders[33] in the Commons.

We wish you could visit Johnston before the election, it is
thought you might do much good. If you do not return before
the election would it not be as well to be in Orange on that day.
John Norwood tells me he thinks there is much to be dreaded
there. Carr however thinks differently.

There is nothing of an official nature that requires your immediate attention here. You have recd I suppose a copy of the letter
of the Sec of War saying the troops from N. C. will not be called
out. Senator Haywood who is here on a visit says the same.


*From James Graham.*                    A.

H. R., July 29th, 1846.

The Tariff Bill this day passed both Houses of Congress and
only waits the Signature of the President to become the Law. It
is as you know on the *ad valorem* principle in opposition to
specific duties. It is opposed to protection to American labor and
discriminates against our Country and in favor of England and
Europe. Haywood has resigned. His *conscience* would not let him
vote for it, and he did not wish to incur the displeasure of voting
against it.

Senator Niles said in the Senate yesterday that he knew the
proposed Bill was not approved by one third of the Senators, but

---

[31] Jesse Adams, of Johnston County, who had been a member of the commons
in 1840 and 1844.
[32] Probably John McLeod, of Johnston, who was a member of the commons,
1832-1833.
[33] Ashby Sanders, who was elected.

still they were going to vote for it to please the party. He made a bold strong common sense speech. *Dallas*[34] gave the casting vote in the Senate. He is *cursed* and denounced by every Pennsylvanian and they say he will be burnt in effagy in a 1000 places in *Pa.* Bob Walker I think is the ruling spirit in the Cabinet. He is artful and managing. The Democrats from Pa and Jersey say they are betrayed by their own Party.

You will see the papers.

*The* party has passed the Bill by aid of the *party screws.* and some of the members are now quite sick of it.

*From John A. Gilmer.*                    A.

Greensboro',

August the 8th., 1846.

I have been to Randolph Court, returned by Jamestown on Thursday, and did not get home until late at night. Hence the delay in answering your letter of the 2nd. I am under many obligations for the evidence of your kind partialities, and have given the subject a full consideration. And, after looking on my wife and little children in connexion with the much and many matters of business which I have to do, and which none can do but myself, I have deemed it my duty to decline the honor of a Commission,[35] which under other circumstances, I would readily and gladly accept.

Any Election news which we conceive will not reach you by this mail otherwise, will be put on the way Bill.

Please accept assurances of my high regard and esteem,

*From Samuel F. Patterson.*                    U.

Palmyra,

*Private*                                        August 8th, 1846.

Your favour of the 1st. instant reached me by an indirect route on the 6th., and I embrace the earliest leisure moment afforded me after getting through the bustle of the election, to reply. Be-

---

[34] Vice President George Mifflin Dallas (1792-1864).

[35] No trace can be found of a copy of Graham's letter offering a commission to Gilmer. It is probable that such an offer was made in a personal letter of which no copy was kept.

ing the Adm'r on the estate of my late father-in-law, which is yet
in a very unsettled condition, and having important private engagements of my own on hand, requiring my almost constant
personal attention, I could not be absent from the State at this
time for any considerable period, without heavy pecuniary sacrifices. I am compelled, therefore, though with great reluctance, to
decline the acceptance of the appointment [36] so politely tendered
in your letter, and permit me to add, that for this distinguished
mark of your confidence and esteem, you will be pleased to accept
my most profound acknowledgements.

Could I be pardoned for suggesting the name of a gentleman
who in my opinion would do credit to the station, and to himself,
I would venture to bring to your notice that of Gen'l Wm. F.
Jones,[37] of Rutherford County. He was one of the aids to Gov.
Hayne of S. C. during the troublous times of nullification, and
afterwards a Major Gen'l for several years of the militia in Mississippi. He returned to Rutherford, (his native County) some
four or five years ago, and is now the Commandant of one of the
Regiments in that County. Although a connexion of mine by
marriage, I have no hesitation in stating that, in my judgment,
he is the first Military man in Western Carolina. Knowing as I
do his fondness for Military pursuits, I think it probable that he
may be among the numerous applicants to whom you allude,
altho' I have heard nothing from him on the subject.

I take the liberty to enclose herein, a statement of our election
returns, knowing that you will feel considerable anxiety on the
subject. By a comparison with the vote of 1844, you will perceive
that we have increased your number 108 votes, and diminished
that of the democratic candidate 36 votes. If other Counties have
done even half so well, your majority must be greatly increased
over that of 1844, and upon the prospect of so glorious a result,
permit me to offer you my hearty congratulations.

Having but a weekly mail here, and our mail day not occurring
until Thursday next, I shall send this by a special Messenger, to
Wilkesboro', that it may be forwarded at the earliest possible
period.

---

[36] In the Graham Papers, in the North Carolina Department of Archives and
History, and those in the Southern Historical Collection, no trace can be found
of any letter offering a commission to Patterson. Probably no copy was kept.

[37] William F. Jones, of Rutherford, and later of Polk, member of the commons,
1846.

[*Enclosure*]

Return of the election in Caldwell County 1846.

### For Governor

| | |
|---|---|
| Wm. A. Graham | 651 |
| J. B. Shepherd | 222 |

### For Senator

S. F. Patterson _____340  no opposition

### For Commoner

| | | |
|---|---|---|
| Elisha P. Miller[38] | 440 | ) |
| Thomas Isbell | 392 | Elected ( all Whigs |
| William Puett | 104 | ) |

### For Sheriff

| | |
|---|---|
| L. Ballew | 416 |
| E. S. Moore | 355 |
| James H. Collett | 172 |
| For Penitentiary | 185 |
| No Pen'y | 585 |

*To James W. Bryan.*          U. Bryan Mss.

Raleigh,

Aug. 9th, 1846.

* * * * * *

Locofocoism has never sustained a more overwhelming defeat than in our late election. I think my majority may exceed 10,000 votes. We have heard from the West as far as Salisbury, and today from the Edenton district. And in every County except Johnston there is a gain upon the Whig vote of 1844, and even there the Loco's gain is small. I have a majority in Cumberland of 21,

---

[38] Elisha P. Miller sat in the commons, 1846-1848, and in the senate, 1858. The other names listed do not appear.

where there was at the last election a contrary majority of near 500. There is also a gain of 300 votes in Randolph, 200 in Chatham, 200 in Person, &c &c.

We have lost two members of the Commons in Halifax, 1 in Orange, and one in Moore—in all 4—and have gained Senators in Granville, Franklin, and (as we hear) in Craven, and a Commoner in Person, in all 4 also. So that our majority of 22 on joint vote at the last session remains, unmoved: except that there is a majority in each house in consequence of the late changes.

Poindexter[39] is, no doubt, returned, as Senator from Stokes, having no opposition when I was there, a fortnight since. Which makes the majority in the Senate considerable. Waddell is Senator from Orange, Moody[40] from Northampton, and Sanders Whig Commoner from Johnston, each elected by 4 votes. The Whigs ran a ticket of real loafers in this County (Wake) but stood up to it, and came nearer electing it than they have done for years. Shepard's majority here was but 41 votes. Eringhaus[41] has beaten Granberry[42] handsomely, and the Whig Commoner[43] is elected in Perquimans, Paine[44] in Chowan, and that district seems to be reclaimed. There is even a chance for the Senator in Currituck & Camden.

My "honorable opponent" came to town yesterday evening from his long tour in the West, saying that when the mountains are heard from he expects yet to be elected. When passing through that Country he told several persons that, if there were changes there equal to what he had wrought in the East, he would be elected by 10,000 majority. His travelling a day in attempting to go from Ashe to Yancy and getting back at night to the house from which he started in the morning, caused much laughter among the mountaineers, and in all the West, I am sure he would have run better if he had never been seen there.

---

[39] John F. Poindexter.
[40] John M. Moody, who was the incumbent.
[41] John Christoph Blucher Ehringhaus, of Pasquotank, attended for a time the university, was a member of the commons, 1842-1844, and was state senator, 1846.
[42] Josiah T. Granberry, of Perquimans.
[43] Tristram L. Skinner, of Perquimans, member of the commons, 1844-1846.
[44] Robert Treat Paine (1812-1872), of Chowan, a graduate of Washington (now Trinity) College, Hartford, Connecticut, became a lawyer and business man in Edenton. He served in the commons, 1838-1840, 1844-1847, and was colonel of a North Carolina regiment in the Mexican War. Afterwards he was a member of the commission on Mexican claims. He was a member of congress, 1855-1857, and then moved to Texas.

My family is now well, though we have had some fever and ague among the children. We will go in a few days to Hillsboro' and stay some time.

[P.S.] Mr. Haywood has not yet returned. Mr. Busbee just from Washington says he will triumph over the Locos, and has convinced him that the new Tariff is highly objectionable.

*From James W. Bryan.*                                    U.

Newbern,

Aug. 9th, 1846.

Your majority in Craven is 100—in Carteret between 80 & 100—in Jones 49—in Pitt we learn about 200—in Beaufort Co. (official) 414—in Washington County 237—in Wayne the vote, we learn, stands Graham 317, Shepard 884.

Street [45] is elected over Chadwick,[46] Whig, to the Senate in this Co. by two votes; this election can easily be set aside in favour of Chadwick if it should become necessary. Street has received a number of illegal votes, and Chadwick is truly and honestly elected.

Washington[47] and Guion[48] are elected (Whigs) to the Commons, by large majorities. Howard [49] is elected in the Senatorial district of Jones and Carteret, and Foy,[50] Whig, from Jones, in the Commons. Piggott,[51] Whig, is elected from Carteret. Wm. Ferrand,[52] Loco, is elected to the Senate in Onslow, & Cox in the Commons. We have gained a member in Lenoir;[53] he has heretofore been an "independent", but will vote with the Whigs now. Speight [54] has beaten Taylor[55] (Whig) in the Senatorial district

[45] Nathan H. Street, of New Bern, state senator, 1846, 1860.

[46] Samuel Chadwick, of New Bern, member of the commons, 1854.

[47] William Henry Washington, of Craven, member of congress, 1841-1843, of the commons, 1846, and of the state senate, 1848-1852.

[48] Henry T. Guion, of Craven, member of the commons, 1846.

[49] James W. Howard, of Jones, member of the commons, 1831, 1834-1835, state senator, 1842, 1846.

[50] William Foy, of Jones, member of the commons, 1844-1846.

[51] Jennings Piggott, of Carteret, member of the commons, 1846-1850. In December, 1862, he was elected to the Federal congress in a so-called election, ordered by Edward Stanly as military governor, but was not seated.

[52] William Pugh Ferrand, of Onslow, briefly a student of the university, a physician, member of the commons, 1826.

[53] Jesse Jackson, of Lenoir, member of the commons, 1844-1846.

[54] Edwin G. Speight, of Greene, member of the state senate, 1842-1850.

[55] John W. Taylor, of Greene, member of the commons, 1840-1842.

of Greene and Lenoir, and Edwards[56] has beaten Horn, Whig, in Greene. This is all the election news we have.

We reached home safely and leave for Beaufort the last of this week. I have only time to write you this short note.

\* \* \* \* \*

*From Felix Axley.*[57]                                    A.

Murphy, N. C.,

August 11th., 1846.

On Thursday last, the Political battle come off, the Whigs come up most Gallantly to the Charge, & have andmistered to the *Lo Cos* of this County such a rebuke, that if they can ever organize again it will have to be like the *Phenix;* below is the state of Poll.

| | |
|---|---|
| Graham | 489 |
| Sheppard | 238 |
| Majority | 251 |

This is at Least one hundred over former Whig Majority. Brittain,[58] the democratic candidate rec'd only 136 votes. Hays[59] elected by a Powerfull Majority, notwithstand a few days a few days before the election an old broken down Whig who we taken from tract two years since for want of both wind and heels, permitted his name to be run for the purpose [of] dividing the Whigs ranks. Our Mountain Whigs are to good hunters to be cought by so shallow a devise, and it was go I have no doubt the old man is taking Wheeling distance in favor of Loco Focoism. If it is consistent I should like much to have your views on the subject of our land affair. We are preparing to have a convention in fall for the purpose of Memoraling the Legislature. We will ask that the releasors and other occupants have a preference at such price as they can pay *down,* this to my mind is the only practicable plan that can be adopted that will finally settle the

[56] James G. Edwards, of Greene, member of the commons, 1844-1848.
[57] Felix Axley was one of the pioneer settlers of Murphy, and "Father of the Bar."
[58] Benjamin Brittain was a member of the commons from Haywood, 1827-1828, and of the state senate from Macon, 1832-1835.
[59] George W. Hays, a prominent man in Cherokee County, was a member of the commons, 1842-1850, 1860. Hayesville, the county seat of Clay was named for him.

matter between the State and the people, this will put it in the power of those who have improved the country to get titles to their lands, and then they will become permanent citizens of the State. As I before remarked, I should very much like to have your views on this subject at as early a period as suits your convenience.

P. S. Our Company of Volunteers are very anxious to hear Whether they will have to march to Mexico or not.

*From Theodore W. Brevard.*                                    U.

Tuskeegee,

Macon County, [Ala.],

August 18th, 1846.

Dear William

I suppose I may venture to congratulate you upon your success in the recent Gubernatorial election. I should have written you before this, but concluded to defer doing so until I had decided whether I would remove to Florida, and until I could learn the result of the election for Governor, in North Carolina. I do assure you it affords me great pleasure to hear of your well doing. In early life we were a good deal together, nearly related, and at this distance of time to ascertain that early associations and attachments are still so vividly revived and the best feelings of our natures called into exercise, is truely a gratifying reflection.

I thank you, sincerely thank you, for the evidences of attachment manifested by your letter. I can never forget the part you have taken in endeavouring to further the object which lead to our present correspondence, and it affords me real pleasure to know the anxiety with which my brother looked forward to your success in the race which you have so lately won. The objection made by the President to my nomination was that of non-residence. I am unable to say whether a bill has passed Congress dividing the State into Judicial Districts. If not, I shall be a Citizen before it does. I think I shall remove at all events, and settle in or near Talahassee, with the view of practising my profession, and commencing a small farm or plantation, as circumstances may make most practicable.

To this course I am urged by the constitution of my wife, and some of my children, with whom I think a Southern climate will better agree.

The office I hold here is a very good one, worth, if all dues were collected regularly, from Eight hundred to a thousand dollars, with the priviledge of practising in the higher Courts, which however, is allowed with many restrictions. For instance, I could sue no note, or institute no suit where no Admr: Exr: or Guardian was interested whose licenses I have to approve, and as there are two County Courts, propper held between the two Circuit Courts for each year, in the former of which I preside, and as they have concurrent jurisdiction in all civil cases to any amount, and in all actions, with very few exceptions, you must at once perceive that a Judge of the County Court would necessarily do a very limited business in the higher Courts. In the Commissioners Court of Roads and Revenue he is the presiding officer, & four Commissioners, elected by the people acting with him holding together four regular Courts for each year and sitting from day to day until the business before them is disposed of, with the authority to call special Court.

As Judge of the Orphan's Court, one regular Term is held each month and a great deal of business is transacted in vacation. As Judge of the County Court he holds two terms, each year, extending to some six weeks each.

Thus you perceive if all the duties appertaining to the office are well attended to, it[is] no sinecure, and I may say to you that my attention has been such as perhaps the habits of my boyhood would not have authorized an acquaintance to believe, the result of a conviction of duty imposed by the office itself. But enough of myself, though from friends details of this character please me most. I wish very much that our wives could meet. To be honest, I am very proud of mine, & I think not without reason. My four boys too I hope may do well should they live, and I educate them properly. Caroline is anxious that one at least should become a Preacher. It may be that with this in view she has taught the two elder to play tolerably well upon the piano. I tell her that this accomplishment may suit the highest but not the lowest Church to which she gives her preference.

Isaac Hayne has returned to Charleston, South Carolina, and gone into a firm of some standing there. He must do well any where. He is industrious, and intellectual, generous and a credit. All who know him admire him. I don't think they could do less.

He left a large practise here, and carried with him good will of all of the associates. He has a wife and four children, not much property, and a life of labor before him, with a good constitution to sustain him. As soon as your leisure will allow you, I should be glad to [hear] fully from you. I did not tell you that when in Florida I saw Matthew Davidson. He has a house full of very large children, and one grown, beautiful daughter, with a profusion of glossy curling hair, the belle of Quincy. You recollect how Matthew's head in his youth was uncertain as a weather-gage. Whether his hair was a proper subject in his youth for ridicule or not, I assure you his daughter has no reason to complain of the inheritance.

We all join in love to you and yours.

Affectionately,

From James W. Osborne.                                    U.

Charlotte,

Aug. 30th, 1846.

\* \* \* \* \*

Mr. Haywood's address has done very little to mitigate the animosity of his friends. At a meeting of the democracy held in Mecklenburg a few days since, resolutions strongly denunciatory of his course were adopted. Wheeler—the force of whose oratory you have some reason to appreciate—delivered a violent harangue on the occasion, interlarded with the current phrases of "treason" —"traitor"—"vile dust"—"damnation"—"infamy", etc. The sentiments are warmly felt in our region, where it seems that Haywood had some popularity.

The Whigs, I hope, will not feel it their duty to take his case into their special keeping. The Register, if encouraged, would be gratified with such a work. I would rather estimate Mr. Haywood by the uniform tenor of his public life than by a single feat of morals, however stupendous. We of North Carolina do certainly know that whatever political corruption we may have among our people Mr. H. is the author—His conduct in the campaign of forty and to some extent in forty four was characterized by a degree of baseness which with us had been unequalled. For my part, I have no objections to his political dissolution as I believe the Country can prosper and flourish as well by substituting for him some intelligent Whig who will faithfully represent the wishes of his constituents.

From James Graham.                              U.

Rutherfordton,

Sept. 15th, 1846.

\*     \*     \*     \*     \*

Would it not be well in your Message to propose to destroy the County Courts, as *Jury Courts;* and let the Magistrates in each County hold *a Court of Probate* on the first Monday (one day only) in every month. And instead of Jury County Courts; Let the Superior Courts be holden *three times* in each year. That would require two or three more Superior Court Judges; but it would save a great deal of time and money to the people. In many counties they now hold *six Jury Courts in the year,* when I think *three,* (well held by good competent Judges), are quite sufficient to transact all the business. Three weeks time of every Farmer and taxpayer in the State spent every year in useful labor, instead of lounging about county Courts, would add much to the productive industry and substantial wealth of the country, as well as to the public morals of the people. The State of Tennessee has abolished the County Courts, *as Jury* Courts; and substituted three Jury Superior Courts. They are well pleased with the change. The profession and the people of that State regard the Jury county Court system as a nuisance, I believe the most respectable States in the Union have abandoned the Jury county Court system, because it produces double delay, double costs and *wastes time which is money.* It is a *nursary* for petty-foggers, dissipation and idleness.

The Clerk of the County Court, or Court of Probate, might also perform the duties of County Register, and the last officer be merged in the first. I think the large majority of the people desire the County Courts, as Jury Courts, to be abolished; and Superior Courts to be established in lieu of them. What a blessing it would be if all law suits could be tried and ended in the same year they were commenced; instead of being transmitted from father to son, and grandson, to be tried often when the original parties and witnesses are dead; or removed to some distant State. Delay and denial of justice are nearly the same thing to a poor man involved in law. The State should provide speedy and competent tribunals to try all cases at issue, and then the State should impose a *high State Tax* on any party that is not ready or asks a continuance.

A Mineralogical and Geological Survey of the State would be attended with great advantages and develope the resources of the State, and consequently *add to the value of Taxable property* in the State much more than to *defray the expenses* of the Survey. We are rich in mines and minerals, but poor in practical knowledge of the quality and character of our natural resources; we seek extensive information of other States & foreign Countries, and why should we be ignorant of our own State, where we believe our mineral region is excelled by none.

I think your Message should recommend the fostering hand of the legislature to all Gold Mines, Silver Mines, Copper Mines, Iron Mines. Marble, Limestone, lead and coal mines, and indeed to all useful industry which has a tendency to develope the resources, and enrich the State of North Carolina; whether engaged in Agriculture, manufactures, commerce, navigation or mining.

Our Road laws ought to be revised, new modeled, simplified, and new vigor infused into them.

The Legislature might employ an Engineer one year only, who with two commissioners, might lay out five or six leading State Roads that should be opened and kept up by the statute labor on each side of the line of Road so marked off. There would be no expense but the Engineer, and 2 or 3 dollars a day to Commissioners. A Road well laid out, is half made. It would be on the right ground and be permanent, and those who would use it most would make it, and dispense with their old road which ran near to it on worse ground, so that the number of Roads would not be increased. They would be worked at leisure times—say one Road from Raleigh to Salem, one from Raleigh to Asheville, (if the Turnpike does not succeed) one from Fayetteville towards Concord—one from Raleigh to Newbern, and so on wherever needed. One Engineer to lay off all; but have *new* Commissioners on each Road and each one of them to live, one at each point of the contemplated Road. There his interest would be the best way. That is the only practical plan to obtain good Roads for our Stages and Travel at present. The Legislature will not appropriate large sums to make Roads and still less *long* Roads. Then by and by, the Legislature might make small appropriations for some Bridges and bad parts of Road. At all events the Road would be well layed out & susceptible of future improvement, either by the overseer and his hands, or the State.

The Legislature ought to pass a law giving to volunteers when called into the public service, the right and privilege of Electing all their officers from a Colonel down.

And all Militia officers ought to be required once a year to camp out 3 or 4 days and be drilled thoroughly. That would be a school in which to learn Tacticks. I would also recommend Militia discipline and Tacticks as a part of Education in all our Acadamies where males are taught. The South Carolina Militia are said to be the best in the Union. They owe it mainly to Camp, and drill musters, where the officers of each county meet and drill in Camp, and learn every part of discipline.

The Legislature ought to provide for collecting the valuable statisticks of the State. I should like to know not only how much corn, wheat, cotton and so on we raise annually; but how much Gold, Silver, Copper, Iron, Lead, Marble, Plumbago, and where it is found. I should like the same information about our Flour Mills, Cotton Mills, and Iron Works, Paper Mills.

I have made the above *as suggestions only,* reflect on them, but if they do not fully and entirely coincide with your own views, of course they will be omitted. Let your Message be plain and simple, not too long, nor embracing too many subjects.

*From Benson J. Lossing.*[60]          A.

13 Chambers St.,

New York,

Nov. 16th., 1846.

I take the liberty of addressing to your excellency an enquiry respecting an asserted fact in the history of our country, which, if true, reflects great honor upon your State. I allude to a convention, said to have been held in Charlotte, Mecklenburg County, on the 20th. of May, 1775, at which a series of resolutions declaratory of Independence of all allegiance to the British Crown were

---

[60] Benson J. Lossing (1813-1891), of New York, started life as a wood engraver, and, later, made a reputation as a prolific author. His best-known work—as well as his best—is *Pictorial Field Book of the Revolution.* He wrote similar books for the War of 1812, and the Civil War. He also was an editor of documentary works.

adopted, and transmitted by Special Messenger to the Continental Congress, then in session at Philadelphia.

My object in making the enquiry is briefly this. I am preparing a work for the press, to be entitled "1776, or the War of Independence;" and, of course, I am desirous of obtaining every *new* fact that may be developed, in relation to that period. A publisher put into my hands a few days since some proof-sheets of a work entitled "Sketches of North Carolina" in which a full history of that convention is given, together with subsequent events growing out of its action, and which bears *prima facie* evidence of truth. The author states that the original document containing the resolutions then and there adopted, were preserved by Mr. John McKnitt Alexander, Secretary of the convention, until the year 1800, when they were destroyed, with his dwelling, by fire. But, he says, Mr. Alexander had previously given a copy of them to General Davie, "which copy is now in possession of the present Governor of North Carolina." I have no reason to doubt the veracity of the author referred to; but, as neither Pitkin,[61], Marshall,[62] or Sparks, as far as I can discover, has alluded to that convention, I am anxious to have corroborative evidence of the truth of the narrative, from a reliable source like the one to which I am now applying, before I shall feel warranted in incorporating it into the text of my history.

Will your Excellency therefore do me the favor to answer this at your earliest convenience, and inform me whether there *is* documentary evidence of the transactions in question, and if so, whether they are in your possession. If they are, and it shall be compatible with your engagements, or inclination, to send me a certified copy of the same, you will confer a great favor. If North Carolina (or any other State) can claim the imperishable honor of first raising the shout of Independence, that honor should be freely awarded by the historian. "Honor to whom honor is due."

I will state that I am preparing this work with much care; and my publisher intends to spare no pains or cost in making it a valuable one to the American public. It will contain upwards of forty portraits of the distinguished men of the period, twelve plans of battles, and between twenty and thirty miscellaneous

---

[61] Timothy Pitkin (1765-1847), of Connecticut, a graduate of Yale, twice member and speaker of the lower house of the legislature, member of congress, 1805-1819. He wrote profusely on various subjects and was the author of two well-known works: *A Statistical View of the Commerce of the United States of America* and *A Political and Civil History of the United States.*

[62] John Marshall, chief justice of the United States.

illustrations; not introduced as mere pictorial embellishments, but as illustrations of fact.

I have the honor to be,

> With sentiments of high regard,
> Your ob't Servant,

*From William L. Marcy.*[63]                    A., G. P.

War Department,

November 16th., 1846.

In my communication of the 19th. of May last, your Excellency was requested to organize one regiment of Volunteers under the Act of the 13th. of that month, to be held in readiness for public service.

The President now directs me to notify your Excellency that one Infantry regiment of Volunteers from your State is required for immediate service, and to be continued therein during the War with Mexico, unless sooner discharged. The regiment will consist of

| | | |
|---|---|---|
| Field and Staff | ( | 1 Colonel. |
| | ( | 1 Lieutenant Colonel |
| | ( | 1 Major |
| | ( | 1 Adjutant—a Lieutenant of |
| | ( | one of the Companies, but not |
| | ( | in addition. |
| | | |
| Non Commissioned Staff | ( | 1 Sergeant Major |
| | ( | 1 Quarter Master Sergeant |
| | ( | 2 Principal Musicians, and |
| | ( | 10 Companies, each of which to |
| | | consist of |

---

[63] William Learned Marcy (1786-1857), of New York, a graduate of Brown University, who became a lawyer and editor. He was successively adjutant general of New York, comptroller, judge of the supreme court. He was a Democratic United States senator, 1831-1833, governor, 1833-1839, secretary of war, 1845-1849, and secretary of state, 1853-1857.

( 1 Captain
( 1 First Lieutenant
( 2 Second Lieutenants
( 4 Sergeants
( 4 Corporals
( 2 Musicians, and
( 80 Privates.

Should the number of privates, on being mustered, not fall below sixty four effective men in a company, it will be received.

Wilmington is designated as the place of rendezvous for the several companies, as fast as they shall be organized, and where they may be further organized into a regiment, if not already done under a previous call. The regiment will be inspected and mustered into service by an officer or officers of the United States Army, who will, in every case, be instructed to receive no man who, is in years, apparently over forty five or under eighteen, or who is not of physical strength and vigor. To this end the inspector will be accompanied by a medical officer of the Army, and the volunteers will be submitted to his examination. It is respectfully suggested that public notice of these requirements will prevent much disappointment to the zealous and patriotic citizens of your State, who may be disposed to volunteer.

By the enclosed copy of an Act authorizing the President to call for Volunteers, it will be perceived that all the field and company officers, with volunteers taken into the service of the United States, are to be appointed and commissioned, or such as have been appointed and commissioned, in accordance with the laws of the State whence they are taken; and I would suggest the extreme importance to the public service that the officers for the above regiment be judiciously selected.

By the Act of Congress, above referred to, it will also be seen that the terms of service are for twelve months, or to the end of the war, unless sooner discharged, and it may be that the regiment which has been enrolled in your State, and is now in readiness to enter the service, may regard their offer as made with reference to the former period. Should this be so, your Excellency will cause them to be informed that the engagement required by this requisition is to the end of the war with Mexico, unless sooner discharged, and on this condition only, will their services be required. With this understanding the regiment will be accepted. If the modification suggested should not be acceptable to the regiment which has tendered its services, you are respectfully requested to proceed without delay to enrol and organize one in fulfilment of this requisition.

It may be proper to remark that the law provides for the clothing (in money) and subsistence of the non commissioned officers, musicians, and privates of Volunteers, who are received into the service of the United States.

In respect to clothing, the law requires that the volunteers shall furnish their own clothing, for which purpose it allows to each non commissioned officer, musician and private, three dollars and fifty cents per month, during the time he shall be in the service of the United States. In order that the volunteers, who shall be mustered into service under this requisition, may be enabled to provide themselves with good and sufficient clothing, the commutation allowance for six months, (twenty one dollars) will be advanced to each non commissioned officer, musician and private, after being mustered into service, but only with the express condition that the volunteer has already furnished himself with six months clothing—this fact to be certified to the paymaster by the Captain of the Company—or that the amount thus advanced shall be applied, under the supervision of his Captain, to the object contemplated by law. In this latter case, the advance commutation for clothing will be paid on the Captain's certificate that he is satisfied it will be so applied.

In respect to subsistence before arriving at the place of rendezvous, and for travelling home from the place of discharge, the allowance is fifty cents for every twenty miles distance.

The President requests that you will be as prompt as possible in the arrangement of this whole matter, in order that the Volunteers may be ready for immediate service. Officers of the Quarter Master and Subsistence Departments will be immediately ordered to the place of rendezvous, with funds to defray the necessary expenses which may be incurred.

> Very respectfully,
> Your Ob't Serv't
> Secretary of War.

*From William Henry Foote.*                    U.

Romney, [Va.],

Nov. 17th, 1846.

The volume I have been preparing respecting the past generations in Carolina, is now ready for public perusal. I have
reason to expect that a box of the copies will soon be in Raleigh.
The Title is—*Sketches of North Carolina.* I can but feel anxious
for its reception, while I hope it may be favourably received by
those under whose auspices I undertook the work.

Permit me to commend the volume to your attention; and if
it meet your approbation, to ask your public commendation, at
least so far as to draw the attention of the Gentlemen assembled
in Raleigh from different parts of the State.

Lacy[64] will give notice when the box arrives; and if the volume
in the perusal shall interest the reader as much as the collection
of the facts has interested the writer, the purchasers will not
complain of their bargain.

For the assistance rendered me in procuring the necessary
documents, please receive my thanks privately, as you have already
publicly.

Very Respectfully, Sir, I remain,

Yours in the cause of truth and uprightness


*From George Talcott.*[65]                    A., G.P.

Ordnance Office,

Washington,

Nov. 18th., 1846.

Orders have been sent to-day, from this Office, to Capt. J. A. J.
Bradford,[66] commanding Fayetteville Arsenal, to issue to the
commanding officer of the North Carolina Regiment of Infantry,
called into the U. S. Service by the letter to your Excellency from

---

[64] The Rev. Drury Lacy.

[65] George Talcott (d. 1862), of Connecticut and New York, who served in the
army, 1813-1851. The *Army Register* notes him as dismissed, but he was later
given brevet rank of brigadier general.

[66] Captain James Andrew John Bradford (d. 1863), of Tennessee, a graduate
of West Point, who was colonel of a North Carolina artillery regiment in the
Confederate army.

the War Department, dated Nov. 16, 1846, the following Arms, accoutrements & ammunition; viz—

880 Muskets, National Armory, with appendages complete.
42 Non Commissioned Officers' Swords.
22 Musician's Swords.
880 Sets of Infantry accoutrements complete.
40 N. C. Officers' Sword belts, with double frogs, for Sergeants of Companies.
24 N. C. Officers' Sword belts, with single frogs, for Principal Musicians, Musicians of Companies, and Non Commissioned Staff.
35200 Musket Cartridges.
1760 Musket flints.

All the foregoing articles have been directed to be sent to *Wilmington,* the place of rendezvous appointed for the Regiment, for distribution by it's Commanding Officer amongst the several Companies.

Not knowing the address of the Officer who may command the Regiment, I have to request that you will give him early information of the arrangement, which has been made, for supplying it with arms, accoutrements, and ammunition.

> Respectfully,
> Your Obed't Serv't
> Lt. Col. Ordn'ce

*From W. G. Freeman*[67] *to R. D. A. Wade.*[68]     U.

Adjutant General's Office,

Washington,

Copy.                                        November 19th., 1846.

Sir:

A requisition has been made on the Governor of North Carolina for one Regiment of Volunteers (infantry) to *serve during*

---

[67] William G. Freeman (d. 1866), a native of Virginia, graduate of West Point, who served against the Creeks in 1836, and the Seminoles, 1836-1838, and attained the rank of major by brevet. He was assistant adjutant general, 1841-1849, and chief of staff to General Scott, 1849, with the rank of lieutenant colonel. He resigned in 1856, and lived thereafter in Washington.

[68] Richard Dean Arden Wade (d. 1850), a native of New York, who served in the Florida Indian war, and the Mexican War.

*the war with Mexico,* unless sooner discharged. The Regiment will rendezvous at *Wilmington,* and you have been designated to inspect and muster it into the service of the United States. In the execution of this duty, I am directed by the General in Chief to give you the following instructions for your guidance.

The Regiment will consist of—

|  |  |
|---|---|
| | ( 1 Colonel |
| | ( |
| | ( 1 Lieutenant Colonel |
| | ( |
| Field and Staff | ( 1 Major |
| | ( |
| | ( 1 Adjutant, (a Lieutenant of one of |
| | (    the Companies, but not in addi- |
| | (    tion.) |
| | ( 1 Sergeant Major |
| | ( |
| | ( 1 Quartermaster Sergeant |
| | ( |
| Non Commissioned Staff | ( 2 Principal Musicians, and |
| | ( |
| | ( 10 Companies—each Company to |
| | ( |
| | (    consist of— |

                   1 Captain
                   1 First Lieutenant
                   2 Second Lieutenants
                   4 Sergeants
                   4 Corporals
                   2 Musicians, and
                  80 privates.

Should companies of less than 80 privates offer themselves to be mustered, they may be received, provided the number does not fall below *sixty-four.* You will be careful to accept no volunteer who is in years apparently over forty-five, or under eighteen, or who has not physical strength and vigor. Assistant Surgeon *McCormick* will attend at the muster as examining surgeon, and in any doubtful case, the volunteer must be submitted to his examination.

The field and company officers of the regiment taken into the service of the United States, will of course be appointed and commissioned, in accordance with the *State* laws.

Fifty blank rolls for mustering into service, and four blank regimental returns, were sent you yesterday. *Four* rolls are required for each company, and an equal number for the field and staff, (including the non Commissioned Staff,) —the same blanks being used for Companies and for the field and staff. One of these rolls must be transmitted to the Adjutant General, one given to the Captain, (and in the case of the field and staff rolls to the Colonel,) and two, delivered to the United States paymaster, who will be at the rendezvous to pay the volunteers their travelling allowance, and six months advance for clothing. In the last blank of the caption of the roll, and also in the mustering officers certificate, the words *"during the war with Mexico,"* will be inserted. Great accuracy must be taken to insure accuracy in the rolls, particularly in ascertaining the distances from the *"homes"* of the volunteers, to the *"place of general rendezvous."* The information in the three columns under the heading—"Joined for duty and enrolled," must be inserted by the *Captain,* or under his supervision. The first, will show the date when, and the second, the place at which, each volunteer joined the Company, and the third, the name of the officer who enrolled him. The mustering officer will himself be responsible for the correctness of the information embraced in the other columns. The regiment not being mounted, the first *eight* colums only, will be filled up, and the last three will be left vacant. On the back of the roll, the *"Date"* and *"Station"* refer to the *time* and *place* of the muster of the Company, which must be noted by the mustering officer.

Herewith I inclose you copies of the acts of Congress of May 13th., and June 18th., 1846, authorizing the President to accept the services of volunteers, and fixing their organization, pay, and allowances. These acts, and also the Rules and Articles of War, must be read to every Company.

You will perceive that the Act of June 18th., allows to each non commissioned officer, musician, and private of Volunteers, fifty cents in lieu of subsistence, for every twenty miles, by the most direct route, from their homes to the place of general rendezvous, and three dollars and fifty cents per month for clothing, during the time he shall be in the service of the United States. The Volunteer must, however, furnish his own clothing, and cannot receive it in kind. To enable the Volunteers called into service to provide themselves with good and sufficient clothing, the Secretary of War has authorized the commutation allowance for six months (twenty one dollars) to be paid in advance to each non commissioned officer, musician, and private, after being mustered into service, but only with the express condition that the volunteer has already furnished himself with six months clothing, which fact is to be certified to the paymaster by the Captain of the Company—or that the amount thus advanced shall be applied under the supervision of his Captain to the object contemplated by law. In this latter case, the advance commutation for clothing will be paid on the Captain's certificate that he is satisfied it will be so applied.

When you have completed the muster of all the Companies, you will make out a *consolidated return* of the regiment, as required by paragraph 463 of the regulations, and transmit it with one roll of each company to this office.

Measures will be taken to supply the Volunteers with the infantry tactics, and the General in Chief desires you to impress upon them that not an hour ought to be lost in acquiring a knowledge of the tactics and all camp duties; and, as far as time will permit, it is expected you will give the volunteers at the beginning of their service, all the advice and counsel upon every matter of duty and instruction in your power, so that the Volunteers may enter upon the service to the best advantage that circumstances may allow.

You will immediately address his Excellency, the Governor of North Carolina at *Raleigh,* signifying your readiness to enter upon the duty of mustering into service the regiment from that State, and requesting to be informed at what time your services may probably be required. You will notify this office of the time appointed, in order that directions may be given to the examining Surgeon to be in attendance in due season.

I have the honor to be, Sir,
Very Respectfully,
Your Obedient Servant,
W. G. Freeman,
Asst. Adjt. Gen'l.

To
Bat. Maj. R. D. A. Wade,
    3rd. Artillery,
        Mustering officer,
            Fort Moultrie,
                Charleston, S. C.

*From Gaston H. Wilder.*[69]     A., G. P.

Raleigh,

Nov. 19th., 1846.

I have this moment seen in the "Union" of the 16th. inst., that a call has been made on N. Carolina for one Regiment of Infantry of volunteers to serve during the Mexican War. I have never asked for an appointment in my life; but being a friend to this war, and anxious—deeply anxious—to see our Country come out of it victorious, I desire to place my name before you for any appointment you may think me capable of filling in this Regiment. Should you deem me worthy, and confer an appointment on me, it will be gratefully remembered, and its duties faithfully performed by

Your Ob't Serv't.

*From Charles Lee Jones to Kenneth Rayner.*     A.

Washington,

Nov. 19th., 1846.

I am exceedingly anxious to join the Army in Mexico, and perceiving that the Government has called upon the Governor of N. Carolina for a regiment, I have thought it quite possible that I might procure one of the field officers' appointments from your State, were it not for the difficulty of my not being a Citizen of the State.

If you think this difficulty not insurmountable, please inform me to that effect, and if you think it not so, I will immediately come to Raleigh to make my application to the Governor, backed by strong recommendations.

I have made application to the Gov. of Virginia, where this objection does not exist, as I am legally a citizen of that State, but I fear that I am too much tainted with Whiggery to meet with justice or favor from that State.

---

[69] Gaston Hillary Wilder (1814-1873), of Johnston and Wake, a graduate of the university, who served in the commons, 1842-1846, 1852, and in the state senate, 1854-1856. He was major and paymaster of the North Carolina troops in the Mexican War. He spent much time in Alabama, where he acquired considerable business and planting interests, but retained his connections in North Carolina. He was, for a time, president of the Raleigh and Gaston Railroad. During the Civil War President Davis made him receiver under the Sequestration Act.

*From Edward J. Hale to Weston R. Gales.*     A.

Fayetteville,

Nov. 20th., 1846.

I rejoice most sincerely at the honor our Whig friends in the Legislature have done themselves & the State, by nominating Judge Badger. I trust that the good work has by this time been consummated.

I write you in great haste to say, that since I see the N. C. Regiment is called out, a young friend of mine, Alex'r F. Mallett, who is said to have a peculiar aptitude for Surgery, is anxious to obtain the place of Assistant Surgeon in the Regiment.

Will you do me the favor to mention his name to Gov. Graham, & say, that he will follow up this application by proper testimonials?

*From J. Q. Perkins.*     A., G. P.

Elizabeth City,

November 20th., 1846.

A requisition having been made upon this State for a Regiment of Infantry, I would respectfully ask of you an appointment as Chief Surgeon, or Medical Officer. Any testimonials required will be submitted either from Citizens of this Section of Country, or from members now composing our Legislature. My health has been delicate, & I should be pleased to visit such Sections of the Country as the Army would necessarily pass through, believing that such a tour might be attended with relief to myself.[70]

I am, my dear Sir,
Very Respectfully Yrs

---

[70] This is an excellent example of numerous applications for office of this period, with an almost unbelievable indifference to the needs of an army in war.

*From Louis H. Marsteller.*                    A., G. P.

Head Quarters 3rd. Brigade,

6th. Division N. C. Militia,

Wilmington,

November 23rd., 1846.

In obedience to orders issued by me, to fill vacancies in the posts of Field Officers of the 30th. and 39th. Regiments of Militia attached to the Brigade under my command; I have the honor to inform you of the following results, and request that you will transmit to me Commissions for them, viz:

30th. Regiment

| | |
|---|---|
| Colonel Commandant | — Robert G. Rankin[71] |
| Lieutenant Colonel | — John McRae, Jr.[72] |
| Major | — David Williams[73] |

39th. Regiment

| | |
|---|---|
| Colonel Commandant | — Henry H. Watters[74] |
| Lieutenant Colonel | — Henry N. Howard |
| Major | — George W. Potter |

I have appointed John L. Meares[75] as an Assistant Surgeon to my Brigade, in place of James F. McRee, Jr.,[76] resigned; I should be glad to receive a Commission for him. William W. Harriss[77] the other Assistant Surgeon, had the misfortune to have his Commission burnt in the fire that destroyed his Mother's residence some time since, and is anxious to have another in place thereof, which you will please forward at same time.

I have also the honor to inform you, that they have organized in the County of Duplin, a very handsome Uniform Cavalry Company; that on the day of my review last week, they turned out thirty eight men in full dress (Arms excepted) that they have

---

[71] Robert G. Rankin, of Wilmington, was chairman of the safety committee, 1860-1861. A Confederate captain, he was killed at Bentonville in 1865.

[72] A prominent citizen of Wilmington, active in many public enterprises.

[73] David Williams, of New Hanover (now Pender), later a Confederate captain.

[74] Henry Hyrn Watters, one of several of the same name, members of a prominent New Hanover family.

[75] John L. Meares, a physician of Wilmington, and a member of a prominent Cape Fear family.

[76] James F. McRee, Jr., was a well-known and socially prominent Wilmington physician.

[77] William W. Harriss, of Wilmington, a graduate of the university, and an M.D. of the University of New York. Active in the militia, he was later a Confederate surgeon.

elected for their officers the following persons, for whom Commissions are also requested, viz:

| | | |
|---|---|---|
| Captain | — | Daniel B. Newton |
| 1st. Lieutenant | — | Luther Wright |
| 2nd. Lieutenant | — | Buckner Bowden |
| Cornett | — | William J. Kornegay |

I have also to ask of you as a particular favor, for this Cavalry Company, that if you can consistently, with a sense of duty to other portions of the State, furnish them with sixty stand of arms, viz: Swords and Pistols, you would do so; they are a fine set of young men, and bid fair to make an efficient and handsome company.

> Very respectfully,
> Y'r Obed't Serv't
> Brig. Gen'l—

*From Alfred Dockery.*                                    A., G. P.

Dockery's Store,

Nov. 23rd., 1846.

Your very kind favor, dated the 11th., postmarked the 13 instant, reached me last week's mail. (We have but one a week.) I hasten to answer by sending this to Rockingham that it may reach you a few days sooner than if mailed at this office. With much distrust of my ability to sustain the character of the Old North State in the event of active Service, I accept the offer of Col. Commandant of the regiment of Volunteers, called from this State to prosecute the Mexican War. I expect to stop a day or two next week on my way to Washington, in Raleigh, you may have my Commission ready.

I received the tender of the command as proof of the warmest friendship on your part, added to an over estimate of my claims to so high consideration.

*From Andrew Joyner.*                                    A., G.L.B.

Raleigh,

November 23rd., 1846.

I learn it will soon be necessary, if not already done, for you to appoint the Field Officers of the Volunteer Regiment required to be furnished by the State of North Carolina, by the President of the United States. With one exception only I have no information whatever as to the persons from among whom these appointments are to be made, and of course disclaim all right to interfere with the full exercise of your sound discretion in this regard under any circumstances; and the more especially so, as the volunteers are generally residents of the Western portion of the State. I trust however, I shall be pardoned for submitting to your consideration the name of John A. Fagg,[78] Esquire, of Buncombe, for the office of Leu't Colonel, who I learn from Western gentlemen is well qualified for the office.

*To James W. Bryan.*     U. Bryan Mss.

Raleigh,

Decr. 1st, 1846.

I received a week or ten days since, the Petition for the pardon of Daniel O'Raferty, and also the solicitations of the Judge and Solicitor of the Circuit recommending him to mercy.

In deference to the sympathy in his behalf which so generally pervades your Community, and the opinions of the Judge and prosecuting officer, as well as of the bar generally, in his favor, I am induced to relieve him from the extreme penalty of the Law. This, however, will be done with reluctance. The crime of which he has been convicted is one of great injury to society, and is becoming of very frequent occurrence. Within the last six months several instances of its successful perpetration have happened within the sphere of my acquaintance. It must be also recollected that from failure in duty by the authorities of the nonslaveholding States to surrender up fugitives who escape thither, our only reliance for protection against such injuries consists in the rigorous execution of our own law. I would feel less embarrassment in granting the prayer of this Petition could the prisoner be punished in some other mode, upon being relieved from the penalty of death. For his correction as well as for the sake of example, I must require that he suffer the only punishment, short of death, which can now be inflicted, by remaining in prison untill the next term of the Superior Court of Craven.

---

[78] John A. Fagg (1807-1888), of Asheville, who was a member of the commons, 1844-1846, 1852, lieutenant colonel of the First North Carolina regiment in the Mexican War, and postmaster of Asheville, 1873-1879.

The appeal to the Supreme Court which he has taken, will entitle him to a respite untill that time, and then only, in my view of his case, should he be delivered out of custody.

[P. S.] My family is quite well.

Several members of our Congressional delegation are here on their way to Washington. . . .

The elections of Treasurer and Comptroller and Atto. Gen-will take place tomorrow. No opposition for the two first. But, Moore and Stanly are likely run for the last, unless the matter can be adjusted by Caucus tonight.

There are many things of which I would be pleased to write you, but am in haste from backwardness in the business of the office, and must postpone at least for a few days.

*From Denison Olmsted.*                                                     U.

Yale College

Dec. 11th, 1846.

A few days since I had the pleasure to receive the Message of your Excellency to the Legislature of North Carolina, which I read with great interest and satisfaction. I believe it is a weakness common to all *old* teachers, to take a great deal of pride in all the good and great things any of their quondam pupils ever happen to do in the world, and to take a large share of the credit of them to themselves. Although it might be difficult to show how teaching you a little Chemistry should have been the means of producing so enlightened a message, yet I think the power evinced in it of first viewing the various interests of the State in their individual elements, then compounding them into one whole, and finally investigating their relations to the General government, was plainly derived from that part of your education which fell under my province, which taught first to analyse compounds into their elements, then to re-unite them into compounds, and finally to trace their relations to the great powers of Nature.

The part which urges upon the good people of the State the importance of a Geological Survey would of course interest me deeply. When I first went to North Carolina, in 1818, the impression among mineralogists and geologists was that the State had no useful minerals, except a little gold scattered among the sands of Cabarrus. I had thoughts of performing the journey in a

Jersey wagon, in order that I might collect specimens of the minerals on the road, but was told that "I might as well mineralize among the waves of the ocean." I had not been long at Chapel Hill before I was well convinced of the injustice done to the State in so under-rating her mineral treasures. Subsequent excursions in different parts of the State greatly strengthened my convictions, and I have never ceased to believe that there is no State in the Union whose Geology would better reward the labor and expense of an accurate and thorough geological survey. The little that I did in that way is hardly entitled to the name of "Survey," yet it was a *beginning*, and was referred to several years since by the President of the "Association of American Geologists" at their annual meeting at Philadelphia, in his official address, as the first attempt of this kind to investigate the geology of a State under the patronage of its Legislature. I rode hastily over the State, intending, by this general and rapid examination of the whole, to determine where the points of greatest interest lay, and afterwards to give these a more special and scientific examination.

It was also necessary and reasonable to hold up to the people of the State a full picture of the advantages, in an economical point of view, which might be expected from a geological survey of the State, and my Reports therefore made to the Agricultural Society of the State (under whose immediate direction I acted) were written more in reference to the people at large than to men of science, and in a freer and more popular style than would comport with good taste in Scientific & official reports.

The youngest of my sons, who was born in North Carolina, (Denison Olmstead, Jr) at a very early age indicated a passion for the studies of Chemistry and Mineralogy, and during the last year received a Commission from the State of Vermont as Analyst and assistant in the Geological survey of that State, now in progress. I am pained to add that, while prosecuting the analysis of the minerals collected in that survey, he was arrested, last March, by symptoms of pulmonary consumption, which rapidly ran its course and terminated in his death the 15th. of August. He had, at my suggestion, long cherished a wish of one day going to North Carolina, and under the direction of Professor Mitchell, or whoever might be the State Geologist, helping to complete a work so imperfectly commenced by his father. This was indeed with myself a fondly cherished idea; but it has pleased a wise Providence to call him to follow his two elder brothers (Francis and Howard) to another, and I trust, a nobler sphere.

I shall never forget the intense interest which your honored Father took in the proposed geological survey of the State. Few men whom I have even known had finer powers of observation than he, and no man, situated as he was, could have more justly appreciated the advantages of such an enterprise.

Accept, my Dear Sir; my best wishes for the success of your efforts for the good of your native State, and for your personal happiness, and believe me

Very Truly & Respectfully Yrs,


*From Daniel M. Barringer.*                                    U.

Ho. of Reps.,

Dec'r 18th, 1846.

In a conversation with the President of the U. S. this morning, he said that if you would suggest that it would be more convenient for the volunteers to rendezvous at Wilmington and at *Charlotte,* the order would be made by the Secretary of War accordingly. As it is probable that most of the Companies will be from the Western part of our State, I think a rendezvous at Charlotte would be more desirable, and if it were understood that such an order would be, or was made, it might have the effect of inducing some to volunteer that would otherwise refrain.

I trust the regiment will be raised. A failure would be the subject of much unjust reflection and calumny on our State.


*From S. A. Andrews.*[79]                              A., G. P.

Goldsboro',

Dec. 30th., 1846.

It may appear strange to your Excellency that an humble individual so little known to you as myself should address you on the subject I now do. But its great importance, and (however we may differ in politics) my perfect belief in your patriotic love for the honor and welfare of North Carolina emboldens me to make to you the request that if in your power you delay a few days the appointment of Colonel of Reg't. of U. S. Volunteers.

---

[79] S. A. Andrews was a Goldsboro physician.

My reasons are these. I am informed that an application was made by Capt. Richard S. Gatlin[80] to the Adj't Gen'l U. S. for leave to be a candidate for the office, & if appointed, to hold at the close of the war his proper rank in the army, & that this application was refused. I am in possession of evidence which induces me to believe that this decision may be reconsidered. The bare possibility of which I hope would be sufficient inducement to justify a few days delay.

I need say nothing to your Excellency on the importance of securing the services of such a man in so important a station. You will readily agree an old campaigner as Commandant, of his experience in all the necessaries for an inexperienced reg't, as ours must necessarily be, will be worth & 100 men. I feel a deep personal interest, having many friends and neighbors & a beloved son among the Volunteers from this County, & like every other citizen, an anxious hope that this Reg't will do honor to our Beloved old State.

1847

*Inaugural Address.*[1]

January 1, 1847.

With profound gratitude to the people of the State for the renewed expressions of their favorable opinion, I am here a second time, under public and sacred solemnities, to assume the office of their Chief Magistrate. The trust is undertaken with diffidence. Its weights, its cares and responsibilities have been felt, and are therefore appreciated. Conscious of my deficiencies, such humble attributes as I possess will be exerted to deserve the continued confidence of my fellow citizens, and in all that may depend on a just sense of obligation, rectitude of intention, devotion to the public welfare, and an ardent admiration and attachment for

---

[80] Richard Caswell Gatlin (1808-1896), a native of North Carolina, a graduate of West Point, and a veteran of the Indian war in Florida, 1839-1842. He declined the appointment of colonel of the North Carolina regiment in 1847, but was in active service and was made major by brevet for gallantry at Monterey. He served against the Seminoles, 1849-1850, was in the Utah expedition, 1858-1860. He resigned in 1861, and rose to the rank of brigadier general in both state and Confederate service. He was a highly efficient adjutant general of North Carolina for several years of the war. After the war he was a planter in Arkansas.

[1] From the *Hillsborough Recorder*, January 14th., 1847.

the free Constitution which I am called to administer, their partiality shall be justified; happy if in yielding up authority at the close of the prescribed period, the prosperity of the State shall have been, in however small a degree, advanced by my efforts, and her honor preserved inviolate.

To a casual reader of the Constitution it must be obvious that the powers and duties of the Executive, though important and arduous, are in a great degree subsidiary merely to those of the General Assembly. The jealous spirit of liberty which characterized our fathers, not only annulled all power in that department to veto or suspend the execution of the laws, but an essential provision of the Bill of Rights requires it to be "kept separate and distinct" from the function of legislation. To effect the public policy, therefore, for good or evil, the origination of measures, as well as their perfection, belongs to the Legislature.

To the Executive in this sphere of public agency, is permitted only the province of recommendation. I have too recently exercised this priviledge respecting the present condition of our affairs to detain you with repetitions now. It is deemed, however, not inappropriate to the present point of time, the termination of one administration and the commencement of another, to inquire of ourselves and of each other what is the actual posture of the great interests committed to our charge on this day? What is the condition of our finances and revenues? Has suitable provision been made to meet the public engagements, and preserve the faith of the State? Is our system of education equal to the wants of the community, and does it diffuse the blessings over the country, which ought to flow from it? Is our agriculture, the greatest source of our wealth, properly encouraged by public authority, and has it been supplied with that necessary desideratum, cheap and easy access to market? Are our highways such as a free people in this age are entitled to? Does our commerce prosper? Have our mineral resources been sufficiently explored, and do our mining and manufacturing interests flourish as they might? Is justice dispensed speedily and cheaply, so as to maintain right, suppress crime, and uphold the public morals? Is our militia system upon a footing of usefullness and efficiency, answering the designs of its establishment? In fine, have our population all the conveniences and advantages which they may justly expect from an enlightened and parental Government?

How do we compare in all of these respects with the other members of the Union?

These are questions of moment to us and our constituents, not propounded to imply defectiveness or inferiority where it may not exist, but to awaken attention to those domestic and important concerns (too little respected possibly in our conflicts for political ascendancy) which lie at the foundation of the prosperity and happiness of the people and the true glory of the State. Such an examination is due to the generous confidence reposed in us, and should it reveal defects, it is the office of the statesman to determine in what, with the resources at our command, we can meliorate the condition of things. It is not alone sufficient that we have a republican constitution equal in wisdom of provision, as we firmly believe, to any in the world, mild and equal laws and representative government, derived from the popular will.

These are our inheritance from the past generation, agencies in the hands of public men for the promotion of the public good, our own obligations to preserve, to amend, to improve to the utmost of our faculties and resources, are but increased by their possession and by the example of those who have transmitted them to us. In whatsoever measures for the public weal your inquiries may result, my hearty cooperation shall not be wanting.

Relying on the indulgence I have heretofore so liberally experienced in the service of the State, and humbly trusting in the protection and guidance of that Deity, whose superintending care is over nations as well as individuals, and who has so bountifully favored us in all past time—on his holy oracles as a witness of truth, I now take upon me the oaths of loyalty to the government and fidelity and impartiality in my official trust.

*From William B. Lloyd.*[2]     U.

Washington,

Jan. 2nd., 1847.

I am, with others, about forming a Company to be called the Washington & New Orleans Telegraph Company, for the purpose of constructing a line of telegraph from Petersburgh, Va. to New Orleans.

Mr. Badger has done me the favour of reading a short act of incorporation to Mr. Rayner, & some other friends of his, in your

---

[2] William B. Lloyd's attempt to establish a Washington-New Orleans telegraphic connection failed at the time, but a company of the same name was in successful operation by 1860.

Legislature, with view to procuring its passage before the adjournment of that body. I take the liberty of asking the favourable consideration of the subject by your Excellency.

The project is one intended to be of incalculable public benefit, as well as of advantage to individuals, and conflicts with no rights or interests of any kind whatever. It is possible that some aid may be rendered towards its construction by the Gen'l Gov't as a war measure, but the control and management will remain in our hands.

In any event, the passing an act incorporating the Co. by your Legislature, is of great importance to us.

> I have to honor to be,
> With great respect,
> Your ob't Serv't

*Message in Relation to the History of North Carolina.*[3]

January 8, 1847.

*To the Honorable, the General*

*Assembly of North Carolina:*

By a Resolution of the last Session of the Legislature, the Governor was authorized and empowered to collect such papers as might be necessary, to complete the series of Letter Books in the Executive Office, and have them copied and arranged; and to obtain, as far as practicable, either the original papers, or copies of the proceedings, of the several Town, County and District Committees, organized in the Province of North Carolina, in compliance with the recommendation of the Continental Congress of 1774; and the proceedings of the various Committees and Councils of Safety, subsequently convened under the authority of the Provincial Legislature. And an appropriation was made to defray the expense which might be thereby incurred.

Soon after their adjournment, a notice of this Resolution was published in all the Newspapers of the State, of which, a copy is transmitted herewith.

The period for which no Letter Books are preserved, extends from the organization of the present Government in 1776 to 1784,

---

[3] *Executive Documents, Printed for the General Assembly of North Carolina, at the Sessions of 1846-1847.* The message was actually transmitted, January 8th., 1847.

and comprises the administrations of Governors CASWELL, NASH, BURKE and MARTIN.

The correspondence of Governor BURKE, preserved by his only descendant until her removal from the State, and then left in the possession of a highly respectable citizen of the County of Orange, was readily obtained, and was found to be a most interesting contribution to our Revolutionary History. Finding that he was a distinguished member of our own Provincial Congress, a delegate from the State to the Continental Congress from 1776 continuously, until he was elected Governor in 1781, and that during a part of the year for which he had been chosen to the latter office, he was detained as a prisoner at James' Island, near Charleston, S. C. by the British Commander, having been captured in a descent of the Tories upon the Town of Hillsboro' and that his correspondence threw much light upon the history of public events, both State and Continental, during this whole period. I directed it to be transcribed entire, at an expense of $225. The two folio volumes in which the transcript is contained, are in this Office, and will well repay a perusal by any reader, and furnish abundant resources to the future historian. It is regretted, that a most interesting portion of the letters of Mr. BURKE, were not discovered in time to be copied in their chronological order in these volumes. It consists of his letters, while a delegate in the Continental Congress, to Mr. CASWELL, then Governor of the State, on the condition of public affairs from 1776 to 1780, and contains sketches at some length, of the debates of that body, which sat with closed doors. It seems that the proceedings were required to be kept secret until final action on any measure, but not afterwards. And that his memoranda were preserved, and furnished the basis of reports to the Governor, of the debates on all subjects of interest. These letters have been discovered among the papers of Governor CASWELL, and will be copied with them.

A memorandum of the latter gentleman, left with his family, and describing his papers "deposited in the office of Secretary of State, at the request of the Legislature", has led to the discovery in that office, of all these documents in a good state of preservation. My own leisure has not been sufficient to make the selection from these, and give directions to have them transcribed. And it is my intention, to place them in the hands of a gentleman, who has paid much attention to that period of our history, that they may be properly revised and copied.

Of the letters of Governor NASH, and the first year of the administration of Governor MARTIN, I have been able to procure but few. These however, which relate principally to the British invasions in 1780-'81, are of deep interest, and serve to increase our regret that the residue have not been preserved.

I have not been so fortunate as to collect any documents of the kind mentioned in the latter branch of the Resolution of the Legislature, i.e. the records of the Town, County and district meetings, except those pertaining to the memorable Declaration of Independence, in Mecklenburg in May 1775, from which the publication of the Legislature was made on that subject in 1831. After that pamphlet was compiled, the various original papers referred to in it, were returned by Governor STOKES to Dr. J. McKNITT ALEXANDER, of Mecklenburg, at the request of the latter, by whom they had been collected and furnished to the General Assembly. These were obtained from the family of the only son and Executor of Dr. ALEXANDER, (both father and son being now dead,) in the Autumn of 1845, and are now in this office.

I respectfully recommend to your consideration, whether it is not expedient to publish a new edition of this pamphlet, with notes containing the additional evidence of the authenticity of the declaration. And also the Journals of the various provincial Congresses and Committees of Safety, from 1774 to 1776 inclusive, together with the Journal of the Board of War alluded to in the advertisement appended hereto. I am satisfied from a casual reading of these latter papers, that no State of the original thirteen, can boast of a documentary History, more creditable to itself for spirit, statesmanship, or enlightened love of freedom, and a valorous defence of it, than is to be found in these unpublished manuscripts.

WILL. A. GRAHAM.

Executive Department,    )
    Jan. 8th, 1847.    )

*From James Graham.*                                      U.

Washington,

Jan. 10th., 1847.

By last night's mail I received yours of the 7th. inst.
I am distressed and mortified that the Legislature have been so
dilatory on the subject of Field officers for the Volunteers, and
the Bill to aid and facilitate raising the Regiment. I still hope
they will pass the law authorizing the Company officers to elect
their Field officers, or that the Legislature will themselves make
the appointments. It is, after so much delay, better for you and
the Whig party, that they should do it. At all events, every patriot
of the State should aid and encourage persons to volunteer, and
fill up the Regiment forthwith. A number of the ultra Whigs of
the North and West will vote against the supplies of men and
money. I regret that. For myself, I totally disapprove that course;
and if persisted in to any considerable extent, it will *ruin* the
Whig party. I learn from good Whigs in Pennsylvania, we have
now sustained much injury in that State by or from several Whig
speeches. I shall vote supplies liberally to prosecute the War. The
Question before the Session of Congress is not how we came into
the War; But *how we are to get out of it?* It requires *two* to make
a peace; and I do not know that Mexico is willing to make peace.
They are a faithless, perfidious people. If we were now to bring
our troops on this side of the Rio Grande, she might pursue and
prosecute the War on the East side of that River, if not by open
fight, by secret murdering and plundering expeditions. Those
who oppose the prosecution of the War *now,* will take the responsibility from the shoulders of the Administration and *shoulder* it themselves. We have ultra Whigs, ultra Democrats here,
and it does seem to me, in both of them, every vestige of Patriotism is lost in blind devotion and bigotry to Party. You see the
Locos have introduced the Slavery or Abolition Question, and I
believe they intend to press it. They have Also introduced the
Lieut. Gen'lship, and from the speeches of Ficklin[4] of Illinois, and
Thompson of Miss., I presume they are determined that Scott
and Taylor shall not gain Laurells enough to make either of them

---

[4] Orlando Bell Ficklin (1808-1884), of Illinois, a native of Kentucky, graduate of
Transylvania, lawyer, a soldier in the Black Hawk War, who served in the lower
house of the Illinois legislature, 1835, 1838, 1842, as a Democratic member of
congress, 1843-1849, 1851-1853, and was a delegate to the Charleston convention,
1860, and the Chicago convention, 1864.

President—or win victories that shall enure to the benefit of the Whig party. Such conduct is provoking, and may react and rouse the indignation of the people. But still the true policy of the patriot is to give all *proper* supplies to carry on the War. It will make no factious opposition to the Administration, when Whigs oppose everything, and propose nothing. The people will not then put confidence in them, when they rightfully oppose evil measures. The Administration is obliged to break down on the Sub Treasury and Free Trade, and nothing can save them but the wildness and madness of *ultra* Whigs about this War. When a House is on Fire, the first duty of every good Citizen is to exert himself to extinguish the Fire; and then enquire into the mode by which the Fire was Communicated. I anticipate a great pressure and probably a suspension by the Banks. *The want of Confidence* is thickening every day, & the Sub Treasury screw is running down and contracting the Specie Banks. It will soon be very *tight*.

There is still a good deal of intriguing about Candidates for the Presidency on both sides, but no man appears to be preeminent. The Locos are in deep trouble about how to raise more Revenue. *Low* Taxes and *expensive* Wars don't coinside, or lye side by side very well. To fill empty Treasuries out of the people's pockets is not a very popular vocation. They must raise the Tariff; but it will be a bitter Pill just after this very Congress reduced it. There is no escape for them, if our friends would wait patiently until these damnable measures develop their own folly and imbecility. But my fear is that our *ultras* will render the Whig party so odious by their general opposition to *all* War measures, that the people will not confide in them.

I think there is great want of confidence among the Locos, in each other, the different wings are distrustful of each other. Calhoun is holding back & waiting to take advantage of events that may arise. He is not considered cordial with the administration.

On tomorrow, the House will vote to raise *10* more Regiments of Regulars. I wish to present some names for officers but I scarcely know who to nominate.

I hope our Legislature will do something about the survey of the State—and the employment of an Engineer to lay off Roads.

\*    \*    \*    \*    \*

I presume the Legislature will not set more than another week. You will have to exercise as much patience as you can with them.

But so far as you can with propriety, urge them to act finally and at once as to the Volunteers.

I am at Coleman's Hotel this winter. Badger is on the Hill, with a Mess of Gov. Davis, Evans and others. Mangum is doing very well.

There are fewer strangers than usual here yet. Capt. Walker of the Texas Rangers is here on a visit to his Brother, who lives here. He looks much like Dick *Allison*.

I think we shall have a very exciting Session, and the news from the seat of War is daily looked for with intense interest.

*From George E. Badger.*                A., G. P.

Senate Chamber,

Jan. 14th, 1847.

I send you by this mail a report from Treasury department on light houses, accompanied by drawings, etc., thinking it ought to be in the State Library. If you concur, please have it presented to the Library.

We have just had a message from the Pres't recommending the appointment of a *Gen'l in Chief* during the war with Mexico. That is, to appoint Mr. Benton (as is understood) Lieut Gen'l to supersede Scott, Taylor, etc., & make him President of the U. S.

I don't like the looks of things here—and will endeavour to make myself understood in a few days.[5]

At present I write in haste and have not the time.

I beg you to have Gilliam's resolution[6] about pay't of the Volunteers passed in both houses, *with the preamble unaltered in a word.* It is I think of a good deal of importance that this should be done.

---

[5] See the letter from James Graham, January 17, 1847, for a brief notice of the fulfillment of the promise.

[6] The resolution appropriating $10,000 to pay the expenses of the volunteer troops to their places for assembling was introduced in the senate by Dr. John R. Gilliam, who was then serving his only term in the legislature. The preamble, which so delighted the Whigs, began: "Whereas, by the action of the Executive and the subsequent action of Congress, this Republic is involved in a foreign war. . . ." The resolution had already been passed and ratified when this letter was written.

*From James Graham.*                                            A.

Washington,

Jan'y 17th, 1847.

Dear Brother

I have rec'd your letter informing me of the Death of brother John. Death has thined the numbers of our family very much. I was not surprised to hear of his death from his general bad health last Summer and Autumn.

\*    \*    \*    \*    \*7

I will make one more effort to get Franklin Graham in at West Point.

I think you ought immediately to employ two men to go right-a-head and fill up the Regiment of Volunteers. Let each one have a *Carry-All with him* & take his new Volunteer right along with him to the Rendezvous. Let him go to each County and inquire for those who did volunteer and will go.

Badger made a good speech on the Lieut Gen'l & has well sustained his reputation.[8] Would it not be well to have Military Science taught at our University?

*From Alfred Dockery.*                                          U.

H. R.,

Jan'y 18th., 1847.

\*    \*    \*    \*    \*

I see in the last Register the legislature, after a 7 or 8 weeks march up the hill, suddenly marched down again, leaving the power to appoint field officers where it was, and I presume you have by this time performed that duty but for the threatened action of the Legislature and the advice of a hundred kind friends I should have without hesitation, taken the command, and as it

---

[7] The omitted portion of the letter relates to the distribution of John Graham's estate. His children were: Charles Connor (1819-1886); Joseph Montrose (1823-1871); Henry William (1825-1857); James Franklin (1829-1851); Alexander Hamilton (1835- ?); and Robert Clay (1843-1911). The daughters were: Mary Ann Graham Orr (1816-1855); Isabella Davidson (1817-1831); Malvina Sophia Graham Young (1821-1894); Martha Caroline Graham Rounsaville (1827-1853); Elizabeth Poythress Graham Sloan (1831- ?); and Julia Adelaide (1833-1876).

[8] Badger, on January 15th., 1847, made a powerful argument against the bill to appoint a lieutenant general, but did not mention Benton. At its conclusion, upon motion of Mangum, the bill was tabled.

has turned out, I regret I did not, but perhaps it was the prospect of some other Gentleman geting the command that changed the minds of the Legislature.

I had no doubt from the start that the opposition arose mainly from considerations personal to me and felt so confident the power would be removed from the executive—until I read the Register. I abandoned all idea of the command. I desire again to assure you I feel under obligations to you which I can neither repay nor forget.

*From Hugh Waddell.*                                            U.

Hillsboro',

Jan. 22nd., 1847.

I write to ask y'r interposition in behalf of my Nephew, James F. Waddell,[9] in regard to whom I dropped you a line a day or two since. It seems that he volunteered, (although I am not certain that his name is on the list) & was no doubt persuaded that if he did so, he would certainly be elected one of the Officers of the Company raised in Orange. In this expectation he was disappointed, and his Mother has written me a most touching letter lamenting his determination, but adding that, sorely as she was grieved at his leaving her, she could have borne it, if she could see her son go in a capacity worthy of his name, his education and his high character for moral deportment. But to see him a Private in *such* a Company to command which would have been but a small distinction, was more than her pride could bear.

In most of this perhaps the Mother speaks, but I can assure you that in point of character, in upright, moral bearing, intelligence, and spirit she speaks no more of her son than all others concur in, so far as I know, and I have no doubt of its truth. Had I been made acquainted with his purpose of volunteering while I was in Raleigh, I might have done something towards aiding him, but as it is, I really do not see what I can do, beyond an earnest appeal to you in his behalf.

As I learned before I left Raleigh that there were more Volunteers than were required, it has occurred to me, that in that event James might be considered as discharged, or at any event as

_____
[9] James Fleming Waddell (1828-1892), who attended the university, 1841-1843, was a lieutenant in the Mexican War, and a major in the Confederate army. He afterwards moved to Russell County, Alabama.

suspended from the necessity of going on to Wilmington 'till he could hear from Washington on the subject of his application for a Captaincy or 1st. Lieutenancy in the new Levy of U. S. Troops, to be raised under the act of Congress just passed.

I believe in the hasty note I addressed you a day or two since, I mentioned that it was the purpose of J's friends to apply to the Pres't or Secretary at War for an office for him, and my purpose is that he may not be hurried off with the N. C. Regiment until he can hear from Washington as stated above. But it is only justice to the lad to state that in the event of his disappointment in the expectation of receiving an appointment at Washington, that he intends to go on with the N. C. Regiment.

I need not add, my dear Sir, how deep is my anxiety on the subject of this young man's fate. You can imagine it all.

With a perfect confidence in y'r doing all which y'r sense of duty will permit, I subscribe myself, as ever

truly y'r friend and servant.

P.S. It is suggested that there is yet a Captaincy vacant in the N. C. Regiment, & perhaps James might, by proper recommendations be elected to this or to a 1st Lieutenancy, & this I would prefer if practicable. Of course this can only be done by the men, but perhaps some recommendation directed by you might have some effect.

I speak of course under the profoundest ignorance, and ask pardon for any errors.

*From John A. Gilmer.*                                    U.

Greensboro',

January 23rd., 1847.

In this County is encamped Capt. P. M. Henry,[10] with a full grown company of Volunteers, raised from the Counties of Guilford, Stokes, and Rockingham. They have elected all their officers, as you have been already informed. These Volunteers have been in Camp a week, and are exceedingly anxious for leave to march. Capt. Henry, who is a very intelligent gentleman, and a good Whig, is exceedingly anxious that he and his men may be received.

---

[10] Patrick M. Henry, captain of Company G., First North Carolina regiment in the Mexican War.

Capt. Henry has spent some time in the Army, and exerted himself to get up the Company. If you get the power, or there is any possible chance for it, do give him a commission.

No Captain, in my opinion will do that State more credit than Henry. He is a grandson of old Patrick Henry. Several of our citizens went to Salisbury and joined Long's[11] Company. One of them came home to day, and says that Long, on hearing that the full officers were appointed, disbanded his men, gave each $3., told them that they might go home, or join another Company. Got on his horse and left. If this be so, & I believe it is, from what the Volunteer says, & my knowledge of Long, then there is certainly an opening for Henry. It is important that the fate of this Company shall be determined at once. Please answer by return mail, and if by any means possible, accept this Company. I am exceedingly anxious that our Brigade shall furnish one Company, and particularly that Guilford shall have Volunteers in the service.

I regret that I was not at home at the proper time. Please write fully, so that Henry may know whether to hold on, or disband. Also, in case he gets a Commission, whether he shall march, etc.

*From Daniel M. Barringer.*                    A.

Ho. of Reprs.,

Jany. 26th, 1847.

*Private*

I am mortified to hear there is discontent among the volunteers at Charlotte, & that there is some probability of an effort to have them disbanded. If so, there will be an effort to embarrass you & cast odium on the Whig party. Let me know the facts, if in your power. I have heard that they object to the field officers & the preamble to the $10,000 act.[12]

If they refuse to be mustered into service, cannot we get a sufficient number of Companies from other Counties to make up the regiment? If so, there will be a reaction against this move-

---

[11] R. W. Long, who raised the company within a few days after the call. After organization, the company went to Charlotte to be mustered into service. The men were badly housed, and provided for, and, after three weeks, no move having been made to muster them into service, Long finally resigned, and the company disbanded.

[12] The state legislature, by resolution, on January 12th., 1847, appropriated $10,000 to equip and pay the expenses to Wilmington and Charlotte of the companies composing the regiment of volunteers required by the United States for the war with Mexico.

ment. And our party will go unhurt. Do let me know how the matter stands; I feel a deep concern in relation to it. Write me *in confidence,* if you choose. I have heard that Caldwell is going to tender his Company to the Pres't under the new 10 reg't bill which will pass.

*From John A. Gilmer.*                                    U.

Greensboro, N. C.,

January 27th., 1847.

We are under many obligations to your prompt kindness in sending the Commission to Capt. P. M. Henry & the other officers of our Volunteers. They were waiting with great anxiety for them, and Officers, men, and Citizens greatly delighted at the arrival of your messenger.

Company, all full and complete, will leave in the morning, and will arrive in Raleigh on Monday, agreeably to expectation, and leave by the cars on Tuesday morning. Please have all the orders given that you can conveniently, to get them on to Wilmington, with as little delay as possible. Our young men here are trying to raise another company to be ready to take the place of Caldwell or any other Capt. that may happen to shew the white feather. How far they will succeed I cannot say, but to day, I am informed, that 18 of our best young men listed their names.

The contributions to Capt. Henry have been some $560. If, after settling off his Bills in the morning, he shall conceive that he needs more money, I will advance it to him, & take his draft on you, and remit the same by mail.

*From James Graham.*                                    U.

Washington,

Jan'y 31st, 1847.

I have just seen the letter you wrote to Baringer, stating the conduct of the Volunteers at Charlotte. I heard a Rumor in this City some days since that Capt. Green Caldwell's Company would not muster into service under *Fagg;* and that they would present themselves to the President under the *Ten* Regiment Bill, so soon as it became a law. I think I understand all that manoevering at Charlotte. They have two objects in view. One is, to make political capital; and the other is, *"to strike for higher wages"* and to get *higher* appointments from the President, and more money out of the Treasury. Men sometimes volunteer on one day, and regret it on another, and then they conjure up objections, and try to make the most of their position. I shall expect to hear that Green Caldwell is an applicant for Colonel in one of the Ten Regiments to be raised.

I hope the Whigs will try to raise the remaining Companies of the N. C. Regiments as soon as possible. I do not think you ought to call a Court Martial on the refusing companies; but leave them to be tried by public opinion. But it is due to you to publish the names of the Democratic Members who recommended Fagg for the benefit of the Democratic party, who are now objecting to the appointment of a man whom they recommended for that very appointment. Surely if you appointed him on their recommendation, they and their party have no right to object to it.

Publish the list of names of those who recommended Fagg, with as few remarks as possible. Short and plain, so as to fix the public mind on the *insincerity* and *inconsistency* of the objections and objectors.

If rabid partizans have a right to object to the acts of the Governor, they have no right to object to the acts of the Governor when based on their own Recommendations, signed with their own hand and pen.

The Ten Regiment Bill will pass in a day or two, I believe. It has been under discussion about three weeks in the Senate, where the Democrats have a majority as well as in the House.

Now before Democrats deliver lectures and censure Whigs in N. C. for wasting time in our Legislature, they had better lecture and censure their own party in Congress for delay.

P.S. You ought to be very careful of the disposition of the $10,000. and have good vouchers for every dollar. Your political enemies will try to make political capital out of that too, after a while.

*From Shepard K. Nash.*[13]                              U.

Wilmington,

Feb. 3rd, 1847.

I was extremely sorry to learn from your letter received yesterday by Gen'l Haywood, of the continued indisposition of Capt.
Cameron.[14] I trust that he will soon be here to take charge of the
company, as I find that they are beginning to grumble at his
absence.

Our numbers are increasing slowly, being now fifty five, all
told. In consequence of the absence of Lieut. Fremont,[15] his
agent here did not think himself authorised to muster us into the
United States service, not being a full Company, and we are now
in Wilmington awaiting his return. Upon our arrival at this
place, we found no preparations made to accomodate the volunteers, and it was with great difficulty that I could get a room in
which to lodge them. I at last, after some difficulty, rented a large
room, and we are here upon our own expense, Lieut. Fremont's
agent saying that he could not issue rations to us. I suppose however, that the bounty granted by the Legislature will defray all
expenses. I do not think that much can be done in Randolph in
getting volunteers. In Granville I understand that more can be
done. We have now in our ranks some five or six from Granville,
who say that there are others there anxious to volunteer.

We have heard nothing as yet from the Bertie men, but I will
keep an officer at the Depot to look out for their arrival.

*From Robert B. Gilliam.*                              A.

Oxford,

Feb. 10th, 1847.

\*    \*    \*    \*    \*

I had before heard of the defection of the Rowan and Mecklenburg companies, and I was apprehensive that you would be

---

[13] Shepard Kollock Nash, of Hillsboro, a son of Judge Frederick Nash. He was a
student at the university, 1838-1839, and was a lieutenant of Company D., First
North Carolina regiment in the Mexican War.

[14] John Cameron, a son of John Adams Cameron, and a nephew of Judge
Duncan Cameron.

[15] Sewall L. Fremont (born Fish), a native of Vermont, was appointed from
New Hampshire to West Point, was a lieutenant in the Mexican War, and rose to

placed in some embarrassment in determining what measures to adopt in relation to them. Their backing out is a most inglorious one, and I am extremely gratified to find that it has given you but little trouble.

Before your letter reached me, some sixteen or seventeen of our people had volunteered & repaired to the rendezvous at Wilmington, amongst them Cal Mitchell, whose name I mentioned to you in Raleigh. I am sorry to say that this number has exhausted the material in this County who are willing to be made into *Soldiers* for the present war. If the Government were to call for a regiment of Colonels, Majors, and Captains, I think it likely we could furnish our quota without much trouble or delay. Of the small number which left this County, all but three are Whigs, and I think it very likely that if a count could be made of all belonging to the two parties, who have volunteered for the war, the whole army would be found to be made up pretty nearly in the same proportion. This is the kind of "aid" which the Whigs give to the enemy, to fight the Country out of a war, brought upon it by the blundering folly or the selfish ambition of the President.

The clamor made by certain democratic presses in relation to your appointment of Field officers does not surprise me. They would have complained of any appointments made by a Whig Governor, or a Whig Legislature. As to the appointment of Fagg, about which they raise the greatest noise, I still believe it to be a good one, and I have the strongest confidence, should the occasion offer, that he will sustain himself in such a manner, as to bring shame upon his defamers. But let it turn out as it may, your skirts are clear, and there is not a fair minded man in the Country who is not obliged to admit that you did right "with the lights before you" to make the appointment. The recent publication in the Register, giving the names of the indorsers of his claims, puts the matter, so far as you are concerned, at rest.

We are beginning to move in this district, with a view to the selection of a Candidate for Congress. In this County the public sentiment seems almost universally directed to Mr. Kerr, and I have some reason to believe that, if called on, he is willing to take the field. The district is fairly laid off as a democratic one, but there are several of their aspirants that, in my opinion, Kerr can beat.

---

captain. He resigned in 1854, and was an engineer in North Carolina when the Civil War began. He was commissioned by the state a colonel of artillery, and engineers, and later was in the Confederate service. After the war he was superintendent of the Wilmington and Weldon Railroad.

*From James Graham.*                    U.

Washington,

Feb. 28th, 1847.

I have received two letters from you since I answered you. I have been somewhat unwell with Influenza, which brought back my old acquaintance, the *soar Throat* which annoyed me very much about a week. I am now quite well, but a little weak.

I recommended James F. Waddell some two weeks since to the President for 1st. Lieut. but have no answer yet.

Constantine Davidson has been here about two weeks, pressing the claims of the Charlotte Company on the President. I am informed the President has sent all the names of the Charlotte officers to the Senate, but there is no confirmation yet.

Constantine has been somewhat shy of me. I called to see him, and treated him civilly, but told him frankly as he had joined in the Resolutions passed at Charlotte denouncing the Whig legislature and Whig Governor, I could do nothing to aid him here in procuring appointments, but said to him I would exercise no influence against him. I said I thought he did wrong to unite in that *insubordination* at Charlotte, but as he was quite a young man, I would do nothing to injure him.

Junius Alexander[16] is *not now* attached to the Charlotte Company.

I think I will stay here about one week before I set out for home. I will stay perhaps two days in Raleigh on my return. I have some business in the Departments which I must transact before I leave. We sit early and late now, and have no time to spare from business. I will do what I can to keep up the four Horse Post Coach Line from Raleigh West, but still I fear under the left handed economy of Cave Johnstone[17] it will be reduced to a Hack West of Salisbury.

---

[16] Presumably Junius Montrose Alexander (1826-1855), then a student at the university.

[17] Cave Johnson (1793-1866), of Tennessee, lawyer, judge, Democratic member of congress, 1829-1837, 1839-1845, postmaster general, 1845-1849, president of the State Bank. He was a Unionist in the Civil War.

*To John A. Fagg.*[18]                              **A.**

Executive Office,

Raleigh,

Mar. 20th, 1847.

I am gratified to learn from your letter of the 15th. inst. the success which has attended your efforts to raise a company of volunteers. As soon as the company is complete you will direct the Captain to make return to the Adjutant General at this place, including officers.

I wrote you to Morganton by the last mail, inclosing Five Hundred dollars to pay expenses of the company, & informing that Capt. Martin Burke,[19] a recruiting officer at Salisbury, was appointed to muster in this company at Charlotte, & that I had requested him to advise you at Morganton by mail whether he would consent to muster them at Salisbury. On all those points I have only to repeat the instructions contained therein. After the company is mustered in, it will be subject to the orders of Capt. Burke. He is allowed, I presume, only to receive a full company, and hence the importance, as I stated in my last, of not leaving the mountains until you have the minimum number of 64 privates besides the officers. There is no detachment remaining at Wilmington. Col. Paine sailed in the Florida with the last about the 4th inst. A few men, two or three, in this county wish to join the Buncombe Company, and will be sent to meet you at Fayetteville.

I concur with you in opinion that by Fayetteville is a preferable route for the Company, to that by this place, the more especially if they must needs be mustered in at Charlotte. On that, however, Capt. Burke will determine. As the U. S. will bear all expense after the muster into service, it will be the best arrangement so far as regards monied matters that you simply indorse the draft I sent you, & remit it to Mr. Woodfin with $100 of the monies you have, to indemnify him; and let the troops receive the balance at Wilmington. All funds have been withdrawn from the Paymaster at Charlotte. This, however, I only suggest, as I do not know how long you may be detained at Morganton to fill up the company.

---

[18] From a copy in the Graham papers.
[19] Martin Burke (d. 1882), of Maryland, who rose to the rank of colonel and after retirement was promoted brigadier general.

Be so kind as to write me as soon as the company is complete, and to present the especial thanks of the Commander in Chief to the officers & men of this company for the promptness and gallantry with which they have turned out in this emergency. Lieut. Fremont writes me that if you bring down another such company as those we have in service, it will form a Regiment of which the State will have much reason to be proud, and from which she may expect a good account in the field.

*Invitation from Literary Society.*    U.

Hamden Sidney,

March 22nd, 1847.

It cannot be denied that all true happiness is the result of virtue and intelligence, for the promotion of which the Philanthropic Society was instituted, and being desirous of obtaining your cooperation in the attainment of this object, and also giving a proof of its esteem for you, it has taken the liberty of conferring on you the title of Honorary Member of this body. We hope therefore that you will so far honor us as to accept the appointment, and happy at all times participation of your friendship, and experience, we would be glad if at your convenience, you will attend to be initiated and receive the priviledges to which you will be entitled when you have done so. We flatter ourselves, therefore, that you will consider yourself a member and feel an interest in the Philanthropic Society.

By order of Society
S. Frederick Venable[20]
Extra Clerk.

*To Daniel Webster.*[21]    A.

Raleigh,

March 27th, 1847.

Learning that it is your design to pass through the Southern

---

[20] Samuel Frederick Venable was a graduate of Hampden-Sidney, in the class of 1848. He became a civil engineer, was a Confederate captain, and, later a public school superintendent, and principal of a classical school. He died in Asheville in 1902.
[21] From a copy in the Graham papers.

States, as far as New Orleans, the present Spring, I flatter myself with the hope, that it will suit your convenience to spend a few days *en route* in Raleigh. And in advance of your setting off, I write to request that will have the kindness to present the respectful compliments of Mrs. Graham and myself to Mrs. Webster, and to say that we will esteem it a great favor if she and yourself will make your home with us at the Government House while you may remain here. Be assured that we will be much gratified to have your company, and be pleased to advise me at your early convenience, when we may probably expect you.

> With the highest consideration
> and respect I am very faithfully
> Your Obed't Serv't.

*To David L. Swain.*              U. Swain Mss.

Raleigh,

March 27th, 1847.

The Executive Committee, having understood, that it is the intention of the President of the United States[22] to visit the University, at the next Commencement, have adopted the suggestion of one of the Professors, as to a suitable and respectful reception of him, by the authorities and students of the Institution, and propose as follows, viz—that Professor Green,[23] attended by a Committee of the Senior Class, appointed by the two Literary Societies in equal numbers, not exceeding twelve in all, shall proceed to Gaston in season to receive the President, either at that place, or at the line of the State, and accompany him thence by Raleigh to Chapel Hill. This Committee will be expected to provide conveyances for the President, and suite, and for themselves, between the two latter places. The expense of which will be defrayed by the Board of Trustees.

They will also make arrangements for his reception on arriving at the University, with such ceremonials as the Faculty shall prescribe, and will, if rooms be provided for him in the College buildings, have a general superintendance of his quarters and accommodations.

The Executive Committee will not undertake to prescribe, but

---

[22] James K. Polk was an alumnus of the university, of the class of 1818.
[23] William Mercer Green.

they all unanimously recommend, that a Ball, as a part of the entertainments of the occasion, be omitted; and that an illumination, on the evening of Commencement be substituted. This will be readily admitted to be the more appropriate, when it is remembered that a portion only (and that a small one) of the large concourse who are expected there, could participate in a Ball, in any building of the College or village.

We have thought proper to communicate these general suggestions, expecting the faculty to fill up the programme & make such additions as may be expedient.

I am very Respectfully
Your Obed't Serv't.

*From Daniel Webster.*                          U.

Washington,

March 30th, 1847.

I had the honor of receiving your very friendly letter, last evening. Mrs. Webster & myself have contemplated a visit to the South, leaving this City the first of April. I am afraid that circumstances may detain us a few days longer, but we hope to get away by the 5th.

The journey before us is a long one, and as the season is advancing, our stay at the several Cities thro which we pass, must necessarily be short.

We have contemplated the pleasure of a day at Raleigh, & accept, most readily, the proffered hospitality of your House.

I will take care that you are informed, in advance, of the day of our arrival, agreeably to your wishes.

Mrs. Webster joins me, in grateful acknowledgements; & we both desire our kindest regards to Mrs. Graham.

Very truly & cordially,
Yours.

*From David L. Swain.*                                        A.

## Chapel Hill,
### April 7th., 1847.

Your letter of the 27th. ult., in relation to the anticipated visit
of the President of the United States to the University, was received by the mail of the following day, and submitted to the
consideration of the Faculty on the morning of the 29th. A Committee, consisting of Professors Green and Deems, and Tutor
Phillips, was appointed, to arrange a programme of proceedings
proper to be observed upon the occasion, and to report upon the
subject generally.

At the first regular meeting of the Faculty thereafter, Friday
the 2nd. inst., the Chairman stated in reply to enquiries in relation to the matter, that with a view to obtain some necessary information, he had addressed a note to the Hon. W. H. Haywood,
and would avail of the earliest opportunity, after receiving a
reply, to comply with the instructions of the Faculty.

The contractors for the additions to, and improvements on, the
East and West Buildings, have given me notice, that they regard
themselves as having completed the work in the manner required
by the laws of their contract, and that they desire an examination
at the earliest practicable period. I hope it will prove convenient
for you to make me a visit in the course of a few days, in order
that we may confer upon this, and other subjects connected with
the University. It will afford me great pleasure to lay before you
on this occasion an authentic copy of the 20 Resolutions adopted
by the Mecklenburg Committee on the 31 May, 1775. They fully
sustain the assertion in Gov. Martin's letter, on file in the State
Paper Office, London, dated Fort Johnston, June 30th, 1775, in
which he speaks of sending a newspaper containing the "Resolves
of the Committee of Mecklenburg—which surpass all the horrid
and treasonable publications, that the inflammatory spirits of this
continent have yet produced." I have just finished a note to Prof.
Sparks requesting a copy of this letter in extenso, and suppose
that the entire series of Resolutions (but six of which, and some
of these not the most important, have been published by Mr.
Force) and the letter of Gov. Martin will form interesting additions to the materials of which the Legislature have requested you
to prepare a volume for publication.

*From E. L. Winslow.*                          U.

Fayetteville

April 9th. 1847.

Many of our citizens are Very desirous that Mr. Webster Should pass a day With us. They recollect With lively gratitude the part he took in Boston in 1831, When We Were laid low by Fire.

If you Would Send him to Mrs. Barclay's, We Will have a carriage there for him, and from this We Will See he departs Comfortably to Wilmington, if that be his route.

Should he conclude to come, Will you drop a line & let us know the number of his family with him.

*From David L. Swain.*                          A.

Chapel Hill,

April 20., 1847.

The cause of delay in arranging a programme of the order of proceedings to be observed in the reception of the President of the U. S. having been removed by the receipt of a note yesterday from the gentleman referred to in my last communication; Prof. Green, the Chairman of the Committee of Arrangements, has been requested to proceed to Raleigh immediately for the purpose of conferring with you, and the Executive Committee, upon the subject.

On the 8th. inst., I addressed you a note advising you that the contractors for the additions to, and improvements on, the East and West Buildings, had notified me that they regarded themselves as having completed their work according to the specifications, and were anxious to have it passed upon in the manner pointed out by the contract. In addition to their anxiety on the subject, since the use of these edifices, the dormitories at least, will be important to us at Commencement, an early determination with respect to them, is very desirable.

Prof. Green has been requested to confer with you in relation to other improvements, which cannot be executed in time unless undertaken immediately, viz—the enlargement of Gerard Hall, in the manner he will explain to you; putting one or more coats of paint on the outside of the four houses occupied by members of the Faculty; and rewashing the old portions of the East and West Buildings, repainting the window sills, and lintels.

I regret that it has not been convenient for you to visit us, and decide upon these matters after personal inspection. In addition to other engagements, I am much occupied at present in attending the examination of the Senior Class. The three last days in this month are assigned for the Senior speaking, (as it is termed here) and the Report of the examination will be read on the 1 of May.

*From David L. Swain.*                    A.

Chapel Hill,

April 23rd., 1847.

Your favour of the 20th. was received yesterday.

I would very cheerfully acquiesce in the arrangement you propose in relation to the new Halls, and undertake a settlement with the contractors, if I did not fear it would result in disappointment. I apprehend, from intimations that have reached me indirectly, that they and I understand the contract differently in some respects, and that they hope for liberal extra-allowances, in cases where I think a naked performance of the contract can only be found in a judgment of charity. Fortunately and wisely, the terms of the contract enable us to over-rule pretences of this character. They "are to deliver up the said buildings in the most perfect order and condition, fit for use and occupation, which is to be judged of by the President of the Board of Trustees, and the President of the University, or such agent as they may appoint.

Notwithstanding the notice given to me, and communicated to you on the 7th. that the work was ready for inspection, I doubt very much whether you will consider it entirely complete, should you visit us as suggested about the 1 of May, so that the contractors will not even then have any just cause of complaint of not having received prompt attention at our hands.

*From Daniel Webster.*                                    A.

Washington,

April 24th, 1847.

Saturday, P.M.

Circumstances have detained me here a great while, but I think I can now name the day of my departure, with some certainty.

I expect to leave this City on Wednesday the 28th. instant, & hope to be in Raleigh the next day. I suppose this can be accomplished, in the regular course of conveyance, & it is not my purpose to make any stay on the way.

Yrs. very truly

*From J. C. Washington.*                                  U.

Kinston

April 30th. 1847.

Below you will find the acct of your negroes here. I will annex a statement shewing the balance due you to be $255.38, for which amount I enclose you J. M. Roberts' check.

Hire for 1838 due 2nd. Jan'y 1839.

| | | |
|---|---|---:|
| Caesar | Jesse A. Gregory | 75.50 |
| Rose and child Ann | Ditto | 20.50 |
| Barbary | Warren Kilpatrick | 45.00 |
| Juno | Harrison Pollock | 11.25 |
| Richmond | Ditto    do | 10.00 |
| Ben | Ditto    do | 5.50 |
| Jim | Jesse A. Gregory | 22.00 |
| Willis | Warren Kilpatrick | 50.00 |
| Sally | Ditto    do    45.00 | |
| Sally was taken from Kilpatrick | | |
| 12th. May for which I deducted    30.00 | | 15.00 |

254.50

Hire for 1839 due 8th. Jany 1839.

| | | | |
|---|---|---:|---:|
| Barbary | John B. Hardison | 53.00 | |
| Juno | Harrison Pollock | 3.00 | |
| Ben | Ditto    do | 5.50 | |
| Jim | John Williams | 50.00 | 111.50 |

*From John McRae.*[24]                          U.

Fayetteville,

May 3rd, 1847.

I have the honor to communicate to you the enclosed, by the desire of the Gentlemen of the Bar, with the request that you will cause it to be handed to Mr. Webster.

You will readily understand the reason of the delay of this invitation, now cordially tendered. Having long been in contemplation, it was deferred until the arrival of Mr. Webster in the State should be certainly known. His arrival having having now been made known, this earliest opportunity has been taken of forwarding it.

Permit me, Sir, as the organ of this communication, to express my personal gratification in the discharge of this duty.

On a recent passage from the North, I had the pleasure of meeting with Mr. Webster; and being aware that preperations were being made for his reception at Fayetteville; and supposing that their result had been communicated to him, I took the liberty of urging upon him the acceptance of the invitation which I imagined had been tendered. Having, as I now find, anticipated at that time, the expression of the public sentiment, it affords me the greatest pleasure to act as its organ, and to assure Mr. Webster, in behalf of the citizens of the place, of a hospitable entertainment here, and a provision for his comfortable transportation to Wilmington.

A Carriage will be in waiting for Mr. Webster, at Mrs. Barclay's, on Wednesday night, (or at such a time as he may designate) which will conduct him to Fayetteville, if he shall consent to gratify us by his presence.

*To James W. Bryan.*        U. Bryan Mss.

Raleigh,

May 4th, 1847.

\* \* \* \* \*

Mr. and Mrs. Webster have been with us from Saturday untill this morning, when they took their departure for Goldsboro and

---

[24] John McRae, of Fayetteville, was an important local business man and was postmaster for many years.

direct to Charleston. He was tendered a public dinner but declined.

A large number of the good people here, as well as a few strangers who came on purpose, called on them, and they professed to be much pleased with their sojourn. By previous invitation, they took quarters in our house, and we found them exceedingly agreeable.

On yesterday while at dinner, with a good many gentlemen, whom I had invited, the Military of the City came down, fired a salute in front of the House, and sent in a message, saying that they desired to be introduced to him. On which we repaired to the door, and Col. Manly[25] made him a speech to which he responded in presence of great crowd of all sorts and colors. This was his only approach to a speech, except a little talk to the Military School boys, who had visited him in the morning.

A leading Loco foco, who heard him, I understand, insists that he is far from being equal to John Manly.

Invitations came to him today, from the people of Fayetteville, and the Bar of that Riding to spend a few days there, but after he had left Town. From this new opportunity of observing him, and much familiar conversation, I am more than ever impressed with the power of his mind, and the depth and variety of his knowledge. Though he never can acquire ease and gracefulness of manner so as to pass currently in a crowd.

I carried him to see our old friend Mrs. White, who remembered some of Mrs. Webster's relatives, the Carvells (her maternal ancestors) at New Bern in early times. Gales accompanied him to Goldsboro today, his niece Miss Seaton travelling with Mrs. W. Southward. You may expect a full account of them in the next Register.

On the whole, the City has been in quite a buz—though a quiet one. The good citizens have had their curiosity agreeably gratified, and I hope their visiters have experienced a like satisfaction, as they professed was the case.

The next great event, I presume, will be the arrival of the President. The faculty at Chapel Hill are quite agog in relation to him. Will you not come up to Commencement? I perceive you are on the Committee of visitation.

---

[25] John Haywood Manly, of Raleigh, a son of Governor Charles Manly, who, after a brief attendance at the university, became a lawyer, and settled in Texas, where he became mayor of Galveston, a legislator, and judge. He was a Confederate colonel in the Civil War.

The publication of the acts of the last Legislature, exhibits most stupendous errors in the enrollment of Laws. Such as directing a new County (Polk) to be erected by a Co. Court to be held the 6th. Monday after the 6th Monday of June. An omission of entire sections of the new Supreme Court Law, requiring a term to be held here on the 3rd. Monday of May, So that it will meet again, 2nd. Monday of June, although everybody well knows, the Assembly enacted differently, etc.

The papers will inform you of the meeting to present a sword to your nephew,[26] on account of Buena Vista.

*From James Graham.*        U.

Rutherfordton,

May 10th, 1847.

I received your letter last week, when I was confined to bed by severe illness. I am now on my feet but feable. . . . I am getting well. I have not declared myself a Candidate since my return. I had intended and *determined* to be a candidate again, *if* Clingman were my only opponent; but on my return I learned that Gen'l Bynum of this place was a candidate, and several other persons (Whigs and Democrats) were in keeping for the Congressional race. I then told my friends I would suspend my determination a few weeks to see if there would be any other candidate beside Clingman, if he were a candidate, (he was not then out.) Gen'l Bynum came to me and told me he was a candidate, but out of no unkind feelings to me, saying he had always been my friend, personal and political, and he was so now, and that he had no objection to my public general policy. He simply desired to be elected, and he thought I had been in long enough. I found several others fishing and sounding to ascertain their strength, among others McKesson[27] and Sam Fleming.[28]

I waited four weeks 'till Burke Court, expecting Bynum to *faint by the wayside;* but he did not, he held on cool and sober, assuring his friends that a total reformation in his future life had commenced. At Burke Court, I learned with absolute certainty, if I were a candidate in addition to Bynum and Clingman,

---

[26] Presumably Francis Theodore Bryan (1823-1919), a graduate of the university and of West Point, who was a staff officer in the Mexican War. He lived to be the oldest living alumnus of each institution.

[27] William F. McKesson, of Burke, who served in the commons, 1846, 1954.

[28] Samuel Fleming of Burke.

so as to have three Whigs in the field, then a Democratic candidate *was certain* to enter the contest. There are about 10,000 votes in this District; of which 3,500 are Democratic. With three Whig candidates the success of a Democrat would be very good, with their drill and discipline.

Under these circumstances, and in feeble health, I would not run. All I desired was a single race with Clingman. I feel sure I could have beaten him 1,000 votes, if we were left alone.

I also felt great confidence that I could have beaten him and Bynum both; though to *give two* in the game in *three up* is large odds. But the Idea of having any agency in a contest which was to result in the election of Sam Fleming I could not endure. Especially when I was tired of Congress, and would have declined before this year, but for the purpose of another race with my last competitor. Bynum's wife's relations, McDowells, are very numerous and scattered over the District. He and they are very active. Still, a large number of our best citizens say between the two candidates they will not vote; others say they will only vote for the one, to keep the other out. There is a great desire for a new candidate, and I think it probable some one or more will yet be out.

Rutherford and Polk Counties are still much excited, and in great confusion, about the division of the County. The Whigs in Rutherford are bitter in their denuciations of the last Legislature. Already two more new Counties are in contemplation to be formed out of old Rutherford, and Plans are being devised to effect that object. These local questions you know, absorb and supersede all others, I have stood aloof from them and shall. Still old Francis[29] tried at Raleigh to *lie me into it,* for the benefit of the Transmountain clique. That clique are unscrupulous, and fann any falsehood to gain power and to injure those who will not be subservient to their designs. In spite of all their efforts and falsehoods, I am stronger, much stronger, over the mountain than two years ago. There is much jealousy getting up among them, who is the *greatest* man among all the great men over there. They are a contemptable faction of selfish politicians. They go for themselves, and not the Whig party. I have heard of one or two acts of your administration that some of that clique have been endeavouring to make capital of, but they were unavailing, *intended to catch Democratic votes.*

---

[29] Michael Francis.

I will next week go to my Plantations, and remain some weeks. I desire now to devote myself to my own private business, which is much neglected and in great confusion.

*From William W. Morrison.*[30]                    **A.**

Cottage Home,

June 3rd, 1847.

Dear Uncle

I received your kind letter of the 14th. of last month a few days since. & agreable to your request will answer it immediately.

I have thought a good deal about the appointment of private secretary & as I am not engaged in any important business, have concluded to accept it. I do not know very much about the office but presume it is not a very difficult one to fill. I do not write as fair a hand as is desirable, & am somewhat doubtful about the other qualifications; but hope with care and attention to be able to fill it. I will be in Raleigh by the last of June or 1st. of July. I would rather go down before that time & learn something about the office before I would commence transacting the business of it; but cannot conveniently leave home before that time.

\*    \*    \*    \*    \*

I am very much indebted to you, for the kind offer you have made, & the unsolicited interest you have manifested in my welfare.

*From James Iredell Waddell.*[31]                    **U.**

Naval School,

Annapolis,

June 15th, 1847.

M't Excellent Sir

Your kind letter of the 12th. instant—enclosing a *draft* of one hundred and fifty dollars, has reached me; I am at a loss for language to express my gratitude. My situation was a *very fearful*

---

[30] William Wilberforce Morrison (1826-1865), Graham's nephew.
[31] James Iredell Waddell (1824-1886), a native of Chatham, who became a midshipman in 1841. He served in the Mexican War, and fought at Palo Alto. He

one, and as I posessed no quarter to which I might appeal, I deemed my future prospects as utterly destroyed, without a kind hand extended the necessaries for my soul's delivery; *You Sir!* *have saved me, I thank you.* I may never have it in my power to reciprocate this friendly offering, but, Sir, I can place such a *price* upon your goodness and friendship for my *name,* as will linger in my heart's core 'till it slumbers in the Earth. I shall use every effort to refund this amount, as soon as possible, which I trust will be in six months.

With my esteem and friendship for yourself and family.

> I am, kind Sir,
> Your Ob't Serv't


*From David Reinhardt.*                                           A.

Greenville, S. C.,

June 18th., 1847.

Soon after I wrote you, I left this place to travel for the Benefit of my health, through Polk, which is a very pretty Country and fine Lands, Rutherford, where I had some old unsettled Business, into Lincoln, where I remained 2 weeks. There I found the people much excited at the prospect of the Rail Road from Columbia to Charlotte. The prospect is very good, and the Success is, I think, Certain, the probability is the Road will be extended to Danville so as to monopolise that trade to Charleston.

Before I left Lincoln in '42, I had the R. Road in contemplation, from Fayetteville to the Narrows, which was surveyed, & which would soon have pushed its way to the Mountains, but North Carolina did not see her interest, at the time. This would have taken the trade along the N. C. line to Wilmington, the project of the new Road to Charlotte, is calculated to Sap the State of N. C. and make her more tributary to So. Ca. I have sent you a publication of the Intended Road to this place, the Charlotte Road, encompassing a greater extent of Country, will receive the greatest support from Charleston and Columbia, and this will have to struggle for the want of means.

---

was then sent to Annapolis for special training, and rose to the rank of lieutenant. He resigned in 1861, and joined the Confederate navy. He commanded the "Shenandoah" on its famous cruise. He lived for a time in England, after the war, and was then in the service of the Pacific Mail Company. He spent his last years in Annapolis.

All this shows the necessity of North Carolina exerting her power to have a port of her own. A Rail Road from Beaufort to Newbern, 36 or 40 miles, would be one step, and one from Newbern to the Wilmington Road would be an important Connexion, this would cause our native State to begin to feel her Importance, and Roads would be extended into the Interior. The length of this Road from Beaufort to the intersection of the Wilmington R. would not exceed 100 miles, when in this State they are trying to make the Road 110 miles to this place, and at least the same distance to Charlotte, in all, 220 miles. Surely No. Ca. can find means to make 90 or 100 miles to so good a port as Beaufort, a more healthy location than Charleston, with, I understand, a better harbour.

The effort making in this State will be a good time to stimulate N. C. into action, and the opportunity should not be neglected. Georgia is reaping a rich reward in the construction of her Roads. The Corn of the Interior as high as Cass, has swelled the Exports of that State the last Winter, and will continue to Enrich the State. I have been told 60 Cents pr. Bushel was readily obtained in Cass, where heretofore, from 12½ to 20 Cents per Bushel was formerly the price, & Sales dull at that. Such has been the effect of the Road to the Interior, in Georgia.

If I am not very much mistaken in the Report from the Patent Office, in 1844 the quantity of Cotton made in North Carolina excelled that of this State. I recollect calling the attention of a gentleman to the publication, I have not access to the Document. (Perhaps it was taken from the Census of 1840, but I suppose you can refer to the Report, and see if that be the case,) Corn & Wheat, the amount was much greater, and it would in many other products, perhaps all but Rice; in Mechanical productions I suppose No. C. would much excel, all would clearly indicate the necessity of having a port of the Importance Beaufort would be to the State, and the necessity of Developing her Immense Resources. By the small expenditure in making a Rail Road of 90 or 100 miles, the manufacturing interest of the Counties in the middle of the State, clearly proves its advantages, and with this Road made, water power would become in demand on many of the streams lower down, affording plenty and valuable water power, (now running waste.) N. C. is finely adapted to manufacturing, with an admirable climate and many advantages over any of the Eastern States, but she suffers herself to be persuaded her Coast is Iron Bound, and with perfect composure Suffers the adjoining

States to Draw lines around, and through her teritory, to Suck the heart's Blood of her great Vitality, Carrying out the plan, Divide and Conquer.

The R. Roads already made in N. C. Show the practicability, but those that have been made, are calculated only to pass the traveller through; (Wilmington only, receives a benefit, and but a small one.) Such are my imperfect ideas on this subject. Without the aid of Documents or Statistics, with only a desire to See my native State take the position She is capable of commanding among her Sister States.

I had hopes I could induce Capitalists in Charleston to take an interest in Beaufort, but I fear the grand object of extending a Rail Road to Charlotte, and to the Dan River, will monopolize all the available Capital.

My misfortunes and disasters in moving to Arkansas in 1835, a great part of my means was lost on the Mississippi, and the only too disastrous second attempt, to Florida, Exausted my means, so I have to Struggle for an Existence. My house and lott in Lincolnton will again become valuable, and my lands in Florida will come into value on account of their favourable location, and Very Rich Soil, and adaptation to the Culture of Sugar, but these means are yet only in prospect. If I knew any place or Business where I could make a living at Newbern, or Beaufort, I would very much [like] & would give my poor efforts Cheerfully, to aid this Valuable devellopment to the State.

I had Contemplated in going on a Collecting Tour to the South West, even to Texas, if I can raise the means to travel, and contemplated perhaps in trying a Commission Business, in New Orleans, but I am yet undetermined. I find the want of Funds produces a want of [illegible] even in those who should remember gone by days.

The Essays of William Gregg,[32] of this State, on domestic manufactures, is applicable to North Carolina, is of more real Value than all the political fervors which have for years been produced. He is acting under it, and a company has been formed in Charleston, with a capital of $300,000. They will soon be in operation, at Graniteville, near Aiken. He came into possession

---

[32] William Gregg (1800-1867), of South Carolina, a native of Virginia (now West Virginia), watchmaker, cotton manufacturer—first in Georgia, and then in Columbia and Edgefield. He lived in Charleston, 1838-1846. He founded the famous Graniteville Manufacturing Company, and became the leading cotton manufacturer in the South. He was progressive in his handling of labor, and wrote quite extensively on economic subjects.

of Vacluse Factory, at the same place, which he has made so profitable as to induce this large Investment at Graniteville.

I had written to J. W. Bryan at the request of James Graham, & Yesterday received a drawing of the Port of Beaufort. I should have very much liked to be with you at the sales in Hyde County, but your letter came after I had left this place. You will observe I have given you my views at some length. I hope they may give an Impulse to Benefit our Native State.

*To Robert Nash Ogden.*          A.

June 21st., 1847.

It is stated in the Southern Quarterly Review, published at Charleston, So. Ca., on the authority of Judge Bullard [33] of La., that the late Judge F. X. Martin of your State, had continued his History of North Carolina to the year 1815. Having been authorized by a resolution of the Legislature to collect documents pertaining to our History, I addressed a line to Judge Martin in the year 1845, requesting information in regard to any papers of this description, in his possession, and especially such as related to the Revolution. The reply, written by Paul A. Martin, was quite respectful, but very brief and unsatisfactory, stating in substance, that the History written by the Judge terminated before the commencement of the Revolution, and no such documents as I desired were in his possession.

An impression prevails extensively among the acquaintances of Judge M., in this State, that he carried with him to the South a large mass of material for the History, and that a considerable portion consists of public documents.

My purpose in troubling you with this communication is to beg your intervention with his personal representative, or the custodian of his effects, to endeavor to procure for the use of the State, whatever papers he may have left pertaining to the History of North Carolina. His publication, bearing this title, closes in 1774, or '75, and it may be that a third volume has been prepared, but not, as yet, published, extending to 1815, according to the declaration attributed to Judge Ballard. If this be so, his

[33] Henry Adams Bullard (1788-1851), a native of Massachusetts, and a graduate of Harvard, a lawyer, who, after service on the staff of Toledo, the Mexican revolutionary general, settled in Louisiana. He was a member of congress, 1831-1834, 1850-1851, secretary of state, professor in the Louisiana Law School, and a justice of the state supreme court, 1834-1846. He was the first president of the Louisiana Historical Society.

Legatees will, of course, expect the profits of the work to be derived from publication. But the collection of papers which served as materials for it, can be of little pecuniary value, and not much interest, I presume, to those concerned in his estate. We, on the contrary, take great interest in their contents, and are exceedingly anxious to obtain them.

I will therefore be greatly obliged by the intervention of your kind offices in the manner indicated above, and be enabled at least, to satisfy public curiosity in respect to the collection of Historical documents made by Judge Martin.

*From Robert Hall Morrison.*                A.

Cottage Home,

July 2nd, 1847.

My Dear Friend,

I had intended to write to you when William Started, but owing to various reasons delayed doing so.

Although I interposed no objection to his accepting the appointment, which in your kindness you have given him, I have felt some reluctance to his going. This has arisen chiefly from a dread of the temptations which such a place as Raleigh, must present to young men.

His habits, I have reason to believe, are thus far correct & moral; and I would deplore it as the heaviest of calamities, if they should become impaired in their purity.

I apprehend but little danger, except from the too common propensity of young men to be persuaded into compliances, at first apparently harmless, but leading in their results to the formation of dangerous habits.

It is to me, however, a great source of satisfaction, that he will be so fully under your supervision, and to know that your influence over him, will be for good, as far as he may yield to it. I have great confidence that he will pay the utmost regard to your counsels as it regards business & deportment.

May I therefore ask that you will feel no hesitation in giving him all the advice which he so much needs, and pointing out to him the dangers against which he should guard.

I have every reason to believe, that suggestions from you will be Kindly received, and have great influence over him, not only in the circumstances in which he is now placed, but through life.

All such interest in his welfare will be duly appreciated, as the highest manifestations of friendship to us.

*   *   *   *   *

The Season has been cold and wet. My crop looked very finely, until within a few days; successive floods having marred its appearance very much. The Oat Crop wh. was very promising, has been very much destroyed by heavy rains.

We have nothing of Special excitement in the community, except the projected Rail Road from Charleston to Charlotte.

This awakens much interest and the prospect is now fair, that the enterprize will succeed.

It will afford us much pleasure to hear from you when convenient.

*   *   *   *   *

May every blessing crown your lives & descend upon your Children.

Very affectionately Yours,

*From Robert Nash Ogden.*                               A.

New Orleans,

July 8th., 1847.

Your favor of the 21st. of June has been unanswered for a week, during which time I have been waiting to receive, from Mr. Paul B. Martin, the remaining papers & books, relating to North Carolina, of which he had, under the instruction of his brother, given me already the greater portion. Judge Martin repeatedly assured me during his life, that if he should leave his work unfinished & unpublished, he would bequeath to me his materials & manuscripts. His brother, who by his will is his sole heir, has given them to me since his death. I have, since receiving your letters, examined them carefully, & can find none which could appear to belong to the State. On my return from my last visit to North Carolina, I mentioned to Judge Martin that either you or Gov. Swain had intimated to me that he had probably some papers or documents belonging to the State. He, however, assured me that such was not the case, & that all he had was his own property. Will you be so good as to designate such as may be missing, or as you may imagine to have been in his possession? If there are any in my hands to which the State can have the remotest claim, I would desire to deliver them up immediately to any person authorized to receive them. I am very anxious to see the unfinished history completed, & did intend, if my leisure would permit, to attempt it. I shall write to my Uncle, Judge Nash, more fully on the subject.

*From Sophia G. Witherspoon.*    A.

Brookland,

July 28th, 1847.

My Dear Brother

It is a long time since I have heard from you, & still longer since I have written. My son Thomas Franklin not being engaged in business this Summer has concluded to visit you; his health heretofore has not been good; at this time is in better health than he has been for years past, but thought it advisable not to spend the Summer here. My youngest son William Alfred has gone on to Virginia & I have enjoined it on him also to call on you on his return to Alabama. I am exceedingly gratified that after so long a time some of my children can visit you, & become acquainted with some of my relations.

I hope Thomas will go up to Lincoln & see all my kindred. My Daughter Eliza with her six children has been spending two Months with me, she leaves in a few days & takes with her my youngest daughter Louisa for a twelve months to go to school. My oldest son John has returned from Mexico after a twelve months tour, my son Joseph Graham has settled in Arkansas on Big Black, or rather at the junction of the Black & White River— he is a Lawyer. Robert Sidney lives with us and attends to our plantation, is very industrious and a good manager. Thomas is next. Mary Sophia has gone North as far as Boston she travels with Mr. Campbell and family of Mobile. I have given you the names & ocapations of my family—& greater part of the time widely scatered.

Thomas & Alfred are both engaged in winter in the Cotton business in Mobile so that the Doctor and myself and Sidney are all that lives at home in the winter.

Louisa has been at school boarding out, and Mary stays a great deal with Eliza. I am in hopes that as long as I live we will hear oftener from each other. I confess it was altogather my fault my great avertion to writing and when I do write my children claim letters from me. I am sensible that it is not so great a task as I imagin before I begin. I hope my Dear Brother that you have not entirely given out coming to see us—nothing would give me greater pleasure than a visit from your family. As I never expect to visit Carolina again, unless you could come, I suppose we will never meet again in this world but if we can meet in a better where all will be happier it will be far better.

We occasionally receive letters from Mr. Morrison and Mary—no material change since Brother John's death that I have heard of; that was a solom warning to us all the survivors of that once large family, and I often ask myself which of us will be the *next;* but if we are only prepared for that change it does not matter.

＊  ＊  ＊  ＊  ＊

My Husband's health is generally good but is subject to violent attacks of fever in the fall and every one leave him more helpless and stiff, does not go much from home accept every winter to Mobile & spend a month or six weeks with Eliza, confines himself to the house for the most part is now in his 74th year. I can perceive his mind failing him altho on most subjects he has as good judgment as ever.

Eliza has 5 sons and one daughter; her oldest son she calls John Witherspoon, the next Thomas, the next Henry, her daughter she calls Mary, the next son Joseph Graham, the youngest George; the most healthy children I have ever seen for the number. She lives 1 mile out of the City is comfortably setled does not come up but once in two years and brings the children.

*Invitation from a Committee.*[34]          A., G. P.

Charleston,

August 2nd., 1847.

SIR:—We trust that we shall not be considered as taking an unwarrantable liberty in addressing to yourself, and some others, in whose discretion we rely, the following communication. We make an appeal to you, irrespective of Party Politics, as one having a common interest with ourselves, upon a matter, as we conceive, of momentous concern to every Southern man.

---

[34] Printed circular.

You cannot but have observed the rapid progress of the Anti-Slavery spirit, for some time past, and the alarming influence it has exercised on the politics of the country, as exhibited at Washington, and throughout the non-slaveholding States of the Union.

The inundation of Congress with petitions for the abolition of slavery in the District of Columbia, though the act of petitioning for such a purpose assumes an inferiority in the Slaveholding States, and the language of the petitions is replete with vituperation and insult, has been persevered in until it has almost ceased to arrest attention. The application in the United States, of the principle of the English case of Somerset, decided by Lord Mansfield, by which it is declared that the relation of master and slave ceases as soon as the parties pass the jurisdiction of the local laws which authorize slavery—a principle which isolates and degrades the slaveholder, has been more than half acquiesced in. We have seen State after State legislating, with a view to avoid the act of Congress in regard to fugitive slaves, and prevent its interference with the above principle, until we are so familiarized with such legislation that the public are scarce aware that the Pennsylvania Legislature has recently nullified this act of Congress, and affixed a heavy punishment to the attempt to enforce it within the limits of the State.

The missions of Hoar[35] and his compeer to South-Carolina and Louisiana, by which Massachusetts undertook, on the very soil of these States, by agents resident in Charleston and New-Orleans, to obstruct the execution of the local laws in regard to the introduction of free colored persons, though met promptly by the States respectively, to whom particularly the insult was offered, excited in the South but a passing interest, and is now almost forgotten.

Apathy on our part, has been followed by increased and still increasing activity on the part of the enemies of our institutions.

The introduction at the close of the session of Congress before the last, of the *Wilmot Proviso,* and its passage then in the House of Representatives, by a vote of 85 to 80; the provision, at the last Session, against Slavery, in the bill, organizing a Government for Oregon; and the repudiation of the principles of the Missouri

---

[35] Samuel Hoar (1778-1856), of Massachusetts, a graduate of Harvard, served in the convention of 1820, in both houses of the legislature, and as a Whig in congress, 1835-1837. He became a distinguished lawyer. He was sent to Charleston in 1844 to test the constitutionality of the acts requiring the imprisonment of free Negroes entering the state, and was virtually expelled from the city.

Compromise, evinced by the rejection of Mr. BURT's[36] amendment; the renewal of the Wilmot proposition by Mr. PRESTON
KING,[37] the vote on this; and the adoption finally of the Proviso,
as shaped by Mr. HANNIBAL HAMLIN [38] of Maine, in the
House of Representatives, by a large majority, are facts, which
leave no shadow of doubt as to the utter disregard of Southern
rights in that body. The defeat of the obnoxious measure in the
Senate, gives us no security in the future. Senators, in their
places, openly proclaimed their approval of the principle it
contained, and placed their opposition, distinctly, on the ground
that, though right in itself, the "time and occasion" rendered its
adoption inexpedient. The Legislatures of eleven States have, with
singular unanimity, urged a renewal of these efforts. Delaware,
Pennsylvania, New-Jersey, New-York, Rhode Island, Vermont,
New-Hampshire, Massachusetts, Ohio, Michigan, and more recently Maine, have all, through their Legislatures, spoken still
more explicitly than by their Representatives in Congress.

The tone of the Press, Whig and Democratic, Agrarian and
Religious, in every non-slaveholding State, manifests a fore-
gone conclusion, that the Abolitionists are to be conceded to,
at least so far as to forbid the extension of slavery in the United
States, beyond its present boundaries.

While clouds thus gather, what preparation do we make for
the impending storm? Are our people even aware of its approach?

How have the Abolitionists, so inconsiderable in numbers, and
themselves without official station, effected so much? The answer
is obvious. They have *adhered to principle*. They have made it
paramount to party organization, and temporary policy, and they
have thus held the *balance* of *power* between the two great parties. They have on this account been courted alternately, and together, by Whig and Democrat, until it has come about that no
politician on either side, is considered as "available" who cannot
enlist in his behalf the necessary vote; and they are actually at this
moment controlling the destinies of this great Confederacy? Shall
we not profit by their example?

[36] Armistead Burt (1802-1883), of South Carolina, lawyer, farmer, a Democratic
member of congress, 1843-1853.
[37] Preston King (1806-1865), of New York, a graduate of Union College, editor,
legislator, Democratic member of congress, 1843-1847, 1849-1853, Republican senator,
1857-1863.
[38] Hannibal Hamlin (1809-1891), of Maine, served in the assembly, 1836-1840,
1847, and was twice speaker. He was a Democratic member of congress, 1843-1847,
and United States senator, 1848-1857. He became a Republican, and was governor,
1857-1861, and vice president, 1861-1865. He was again senator, 1869-1881, and
minister to Spain, 1881-1882.

The Abolitionists have throughout the non-slaveholding States pressed zealously, ably, and efficiently, enforcing their views, and presenting *their* paramount principle—and they have lately established an organ in the City of Washington.

We have, in the South, papers of both parties worthy of all confidence, but these are but little read elsewhere, and there is no one of them of very general circulation, even in the Southern States; and we have not one paper in a non-slaveholding State, and none in the City of Washington, which, in this emergency, has proved a fast and fearless friend; not one which habitually reflects *the public sentiment of the* SOUTH on this question. The Intelligencer blinks the question; the Union rebukes equally the spirit of Abolition, and the spirit which resists its aggressions; and with ALL, except the Abolitionists themselves, *party success*, with its triumph and its spoils, is the absorbing, if not the sole consideration.

The object of this communication is to obtain your aid, and active co-operation, in establishing, at WASHINGTON, a paper which shall represent Southern views on the subject of SLAVERY —Southern views of Southern rights and interests, growing out of, and connected with this institution.

We want a paper whose polar star shall be the sentiment, "that danger to our Institutions can only be averted by jealously watching our rights under the Constitution; by insisting upon the proportionate influence intended to be secured to us by the compromises of that compact; and above all, by maintaining at all times, and at all hazards, our equality full and complete with whatever other communities we hold connection." We wish a paper which we can *trust*, firm and fearless, which cannot be bribed, cajoled, flattered, or frightened, into furling, for an instant, the Banner of SOUTHERN EQUALITY.

To effect this, we must render the press free from party influences, and unite in its support others besides politicians. We would therefore desire to engage in the undertaking men in every way *independent*; and whose means and positions are such as free them from all temptations of profit or place.

If you concur in our views, please confer with us, as soon as practicable; and inform us what amount in money you are willing, yourself, to contribute to effect this object, and how much you think can be raised in your immediate neighborhood.

Enclosed you will find a subscription list with a heading, setting forth the principles on which it is proposed to establish the paper. If you approve of it, please obtain such signatures as you can, and return the list by mail to this place, by the 15th. September next.

Address your communications to ISAAC W. HAYNE, Esqr. No. 3 State-street, who has consented, until the proposed association is fully organized, to act as Secretary and Treasurer.

Respectfully, your obedient servants,[39]

DANIEL E. HUGER, NATHANIEL HEYWARD, WADE HAMPTON, R. F. W. ALLSTON, JACOB BOND I'ON, JNO. P. RICHARDSON, JOSHUA J. WARD, J. HARLESTON READ, WILLIAM POPE, JOHN S. ASHE, H. W. PERONNEAU, HENRY BAILEY, DANIEL HEYWARD, W. W. HARLLEE, W. F. DESAUSSURE, HENRY GOURDIN, JAMES GADSDEN, CHARLES T. LOWNDES, JOHN RUTLEDGE, ROBT. W. BARNWELL, JOHN S. PRESTON, ANDREW TURNBULL, WM. BULL PRINGLE, JNO. L. MANNING, M. C. MORDECAI, WILLIAM F. DAVIE, WHITMARSH B. SEABROOK, GEO. W. DARGAN, W. H. TRAPIER, JOHN R. MATHEWS, P. W. FRASER, ALEX, ROBERTSON, N. R. MIDDLETON, JAMES H. ADAMS, WM. A. CARSON, GEO. A. TRENHOLM, JAMES ROSE.

## U.

*List of Negroes.*

4th. Sept. 1847.

| | |
|---|---|
| Dick | Cynthia |
| Joe | Evelina |
| Isaac | Sarah Ann |
| Jim | Mary Jane |
| Willis | Edmund |
| Alfred | Moses |
| Richard | Sam |
| Ben | Amey |
| Frank | Haywood |
| Ephraim | Kitty |
| Abram | Lettis |
| Dave | Henry |
| Mike | Lizette |

---

[39] The names signed are, in the main, those of well-known men in South Carolina, and any attempt to furnish notes for them would mean the inclusion of a "Who's Who in South Carolina."

| | |
|---|---|
| Betty | George |
| Ann | Roxana |
| Maria | Elick |
| Fanny | Shepard |
| Eliza | Hannah    ) |
| Lucy—born Sept. 1847. | Lewis      ) |
| Rose | Fred        ) |
| Barbara | Sally R. |
| Juno | Harriet |
| Mima | Leah |
| Lizzy | Sally B. |
| Martha | Mary |
| Sally Ann—infant of Maria | Ann |
| Susan | |

*To James Graham.*                            U.

Hillsboro',

Oct. 10th, 1847.

I had expected before this to have seen you, on your way North, but as the Season is so far advanced, I presume you have declined going at present.

*    *    *    *    *

A letter to Alfred Witherspoon from his Father came to my care, since he & Thos. left here, with a request, that I would open it if he had left. I learn from it, that the Pres't on the application of Judge Goldthwaite, had commissioned John Witherspoon[40] a Lieut. in the Army, and that he has gone to join the Army of Gen'l Scott. The Dr. says he will make about 130 bales of Cotton this season, and has not been much affected by the worm or other disaster this year. His Crop last year was 78 bales.

Judge Cameron returned to Raleigh last week from a three months absence at the North. . . . He was at the Aqu'ct Fair at Saratoga, where he was introduced to Mr. Van Buren, also saw Mr. Clay at Cape May; regrets to think that the latter is anxious to run again for the Presidency.

---

[40] Sons of Graham's sister, Mrs. John Witherspoon: John James (1818-1847) a lieutenant in the Mexican War; Thomas Franklin (1825-1909) a captain in the Civil War, who lived at various times in Alabama, California, Kentucky and Tennessee; William Alfred (1830-1861) of Mobile.

Pres't Polk has been very ill with bilious fever. McKay, who had been North, came on with Judge C. from Washington, and said he was barely able to speak in a whisper, when he left, but the crisis of the disease was supposed to be past. He is certainly in a bad situation, for an invalid. Our anxieties are at the highest pitch, for the Army in Mexico, and I don't see how a levy of at least 30 or 40 thousand more men is to be avoided, if the prosecution of the war is to go on actively.

\* \* \* \* \*

My wife's family have been greatly afflicted by the death of Dr. Washington, and I myself feel his loss, as that of one of the best and most valued friends I have ever known. His family will retire from the City to Schenectady, where Mrs. W's father resides, as well for comfort and economy, as the better education of his children.

You have heard, no doubt, of the birth of my sixth son,[41] now about two months old, a fine hearty fellow, and all doing well. We have named him, George Washington.

My three eldest are going to School, and are sufficiently advanced in learning for their ages.

Very affectionately Yours

*From Calvin H. Wiley.* U.

Oxford,

December 13th, 1847.

When I returned from the North I was in excellent health after three months of constant exercise. I came home and immediately became a fixture in my office, writing from early morn till late at night, and am now paying the penalty of this change of habit. My old friend, the Dyspepsia, has returned upon me, and my health seems rapidly declining. *Exercise and recreation are absolutely essential to my bodily and mental welfare,* and it is my wish to write a series of North-Carolina historical Novels, and also to publish some other sketches of the men and events of our State.

---

[41] George Washington Graham (1847-1923) who was later a graduate of the university, and of the University of New York Medical School. He lived and died in Charlotte.

I have determined to get upon a horse and travel over it, or at least over part of it. I have a great desire to see it's Coast and it's swamps, and to familiarize myself with the legends and traditions of those parts, but the important question occurs, how am I to bear the expense? I am now engaged in another and more elaborate Fiction, and many of its scenes will lie on the Cape-Fear, in the Swamps, and among the mountains of N. C., and this, as well as a regard for my health, renders it important that I should travel. Is there no kind of public employment which could pay the expenses of an economical traveller? The truth is, I could endeavor to pick up, without travelling, what information I now need, but for the precarious situation of my health, which will drive me to the back of a horse whether I am able to bear the expense or not.

I do not know myself of any public employment in which I might be engaged, but I have never kept the run of offices, State or Federal, and hope that you may be able to find something for me to do.

Please let me hear from you at your earliest convenience.

*From Edward J. Hale.*                                    U.

Fayetteville,

Dec. 14th, 1847.

I ought sooner to have acknowledged my obligation to you for your favor received a week ago, which enabled me to take a proper and much more effective notice of its subject matter than I could have done without its aid. And allow me to repeat a request which I made of you some years ago, that when anything can be furnished me, to the advantage of the Whig party or my friends, I will always be glad to receive it and make it available. I know that there are many cases in which I either have not access to the requisite facts, or want time to use them, or which, indeed, escape my attention altogether, when I might [be] of good service by the assistance of a suggestion or a fact from the Capitol.

I am careful to keep the authorship of such things to myself. I copied your article,[42] so that it went to the compositor in my own hand.

---

[42] Undoubtedly Graham wrote many editorials, and other communications, which were published without mention of his name. I have found many, which seem indisputably to be from his pen, but of course, have not included them in these papers.

1848

*From William Johnston.* A.

Charlotte,

Jany. 7th, 1848.

\* \* \* \* \*

I have just returned from a trip to Memphis, Tenn. I went via Atlanta, Gunter's Landing, Decatur, Tuscumbia, and Holly Springs. I found the Atlanta and Chattanoga railroad a work of much greater magnitude than I had supposed  The iron is laid to within about 30 miles of the latter place. It passes over the most hilly and mountainous country that I have ever seen penetrated by railway, the Cumberland road not excepted. For three fourths of the way to Kingston the cars are either on a fill or in a cut  The cost of bridges and culverts must have been very great. That portion of the country however is for its unevenness of surface comparatively free from the granate—a partially decayed slate being the princepal formation encountered in excavating.

All along this rout I found the cotton crop very abundant, and from observation and inquiry elsewhere, am induced to believe that the present will considerably exceed the average production of the country. There was however a general disposition among producers not to sell at present prices. This has, in the cotton markets, increased the rates of exchange and tightened money matters generally.

Memphis now contains a population of 10 or 12,000 inhabitants and appears to be increasing as rapidly as ever. Two fine boats ply regularly between that place and N. Orleans. The flat bottom boat trade is perhaps equal to that of N. Orleans  Its being a cotton market however has given the impulse.

I remained at and in the vicinity of Memphis more than a fortnight and visited the farm belonging to the heirs of Genl Jos. Graham. It is well managed by Mr. St. Clair. He expects to make 100 bales of cotton by the present crop of 450 lbs, each. . . .

Upon my return via N. Orleans I met with Genl Taylor at Natchez & travelled with him down the river to Baton Rouge. There not being many gentlemen on board the boat, I had several opportunities of conversing with him. I mentioned Col Paine in the service as of No Carolina. He then spoke freely of the mutiny in his regiment; said that he sustained Gen. Wool [1] in all his proceeding consequent upon it; expressed his disapprobation of the President's course in resisting Pender [2] and said that he "considered Col. Paine as one of the best officers sent to Mexico." The General is plain, frank, & familiar in his manners and [torn] and apparently very amiable in his disposition.

\*    \*    \*    \*    \*

To James W. Bryan.            U. Bryan Mss.

Raleigh,

Jany. 11th, 1848.

\*    \*    \*    \*    \*

Mr. Wm. Washington wrote me recently, that the leading Whigs in your section would present your name to the Convention, to be assembled, for the nomination of a Candidate for Governor, and he thought you might be induced to consent to accept it. Though so situated as to have no public voice in the selection, I deem it due to our relations to inform you of the present condition of the Candidacy in the State so far as known to me. Since Mr. Rayner's declination, (and I believe before) there is no settled public opinion in favor of any Candidate. It seems to be generally understood that some one in the lower section of the State is to be selected, and the delegates from that region will have the choice very much in their power, if they can agree. In the circle here, Col. Joyner has been, perhaps, the most conspicuously presented in conversation. But the newspapers, you see, present new names every day. The Convention will, no doubt,

---

[1] John Ellis Wool (1784-1869), a native of New York, who entered the army during the War of 1812, and who distinguished himself in the Mexican War by his training of troops, and by a march which has been compared to Xenophen's, but which was far longer. He served until 1863 in the Civil War, and is credited with saving the navy yard at Norfolk for the Union cause.

[2] Josiah S. Pender, of Edgecombe, who, after a year at the university, was appointed to West Point. He did not complete the course but was probably the most highly qualified officer in the North Carolina regiment, in which he was a lieutenant. For some reason he was out of favor with Colonel Robert Treat Paine who commanded the regiment. A mutiny of the troops occurred, caused by Paine's rigid discipline, which was often accompanied by personal violence on his part. Pender was sick and not concerned in it, but he and Lieutenant George E. B. Singletary later joined other officers of the regiment in suggesting Paine's resignation. The latter reported the matter to General Wool, who ordered them and two privates dishonorably discharged from the service. When the facts of the case reached the President, he reinstated both officers. A court of inquiry later sustained Paine, but another exonerated Pender and Singletary.

require a canvass by their nominee, whoever he may be. If you obtain your own consent to accept, if the tender is made, your friends should move with energy, in your own and the neighboring Counties, and attend the Convention in respectable numbers. At present it is most likely that the Convention will meet on the 22nd of Feby.; a later period would be preferred to allow affairs to settle down at Washington, in relation to a National Convention, and the Whig Candidate for the Presidency, but it is feared that after the Court Circuits commence, and the crop season of Spring opens, there cannot be a full Convention assembled. The democrats have but little hope of success in their election of Govr. and are evidently waiting to see what the Whigs will do, before assembling a Convention of their own. I have no doubt they would willingly dispense with a Canvass, in the hope that they might thereby carry the Legislature, while the Whigs, being in the majority, will insist on it, for a like reason. Waddell, Guion, Aug. Moore, Stanly, & Gilliam are here at the Supreme Court, but I have not been enough among them to hear what are the views of their respective sections—if they have any—in regard to the Candidate, except as the newspapers indicate them.

On the whole my conclusion is, that the selection of a Candidate will depend rather on the composition of the Convention than on any decisive demonstration of public sentiment beforehand.

Presuming that these desultory hints might possibly be of service to you, I have communicated them, in the confidence, however, which the propriety of my own position dictates.

*From John W. Norwood.*                                           A.

Hillsborough,

Feb'y 26th., 1848.

At the hazzard of being considered "out of order" (for I am ignorant of what is customary on such occasions,) I have concluded to write to you in behalf of our friend Pearson for the appointment of Judge of the Supreme Court.

Possessing a legal mind of a high order, with sufficient consciousness of his own powers to render him entirely independent upon the bench, with great ambition, and confirmed habits of study, he would not fail, I think, in such a station, to become an eminent Judge. His appointment, too, would probably give strength and stability to the Court in the West, where it most needs aid of that kind. For I have always considered the opposition to the Court, which is manifested in the Western part of the State, as far more formidable in its character than the dissatisfaction which is occasionally exhibited elsewhere.

And I know you join me in thinking it of immense importance to the State that the Supreme Court should be preserved. Allow that to be broken down, and where will the mischief end? If the appointment is to be from the West, I have little doubt that he will have most voices in his favor, if from the Superior Court Bench, then he is one of the oldest of that Class of Judge, and just at the suitable age to render important and probably long continued service.

These things of course you have thought of before, and may have passed them by, but still, judging from myself, it must be of some interest to you to know what your friends think in relation to so important an appointment.

*From Joseph Allison.*                                      A.

Mount Sterling,

March 5th., 1848.

I have thought it would not be amiss to communicate you the feelings and wishes of the people of this section of the country, as far as learnt, respecting the appointing of Judge to fill the vacacy on the Supreme Court Bench occasioned by the death of Judge Daniel.

As a friend, the information is offered for what it may [be] worth to enable you the better to form your judgment in the Selection of the individual to fill the place. And not for the purpose of interfering with your judgment, but because I have heard that representations prejudicial to the character of our mutual friend, Judge R. M. Pearson have been presented to your consideration against his claims to the appointment, and if so, I have the right to advise on the matter, as my opportunities of knowing are better than yours, since I have been intimately associated with him from our academic days, up to the present. And if these representations have biased you against him it should be removed, for his moral character is as good as any man whose pretensions may be presented, come from where he may, though

I have heard of only one charge specific, & that is, that he drank too much. Now I have never seen him drunk, though he, like all of us in the social intercourse may become lively, but never more than to be good, social company. And it is an evidence of a mans worth, that his personal enemies are reduced to the necessity of holding us to account at the festive Board. And as an evidence of his moral worth, (and if any one knows his habits it is the members of the Bar) all the Bar, and I have been told they are unanimously in favor of his appointment. So here you have recommendation loud, as to his moral character & qualifications for the Station, but as to qualifications that is before you, and we offer nothing, and you want nothing from us, for your opportunities of appreciating that is better than mine, and it is not my object to assist or forestall your choice on the merits, but to disabuse your mind and if that is done & merit is not with us, we must use the public aright; but if our friend has all the qualifications requisite to fill the place, I would be highly gratified to find that your choice had fallen on our mutual friend & school mate. All your friends in the West are the friends of Pearson, & are particularly in favour of his appointment as a man the best qualified & who would be independent of that Raleigh Clique, to which the people are getting strongly opposed, for using power because they have it, and are particularly opposed to Pearson for daring to think for himself.

Again permit me to make a suggestion. I have understood that the people in the East are dissatisfied that all the judges have removed from that section, then in case a judge is taken from the Circuit bench, you might find in Bat Moore a friend and a man well qualified to fill the place, & give to the people in that section particularly, satisfaction, as he has landed interests so great that he would probably not leave, as Judges Battle and Baily have done; in such appointments it strikes me the public could not be served better, while at the same time we are noticing our friends, & I think they are entitled to notice when they possess the qualification and merits that others may present.

As to the appointment of Judge Caldwell, none wish it except it may be his blood relations & not many of them. He is not considered to be qualified, & if he was, he is too much the dupe of Prejudice, of interminable malice, and so syncophantic that he would be always bowing to the Raleigh Dictators, and he is not the man that may be a credit to the place, but to be honored by the place. And the public want a man that may become the station, & not to give it to one for the sake of giving him credit. Pearson is his senior in office, & superior in every respect, except that of a *Mock dignity*. He, Caldwell, has been sounding and begging for recommendations for the place, he puts [illegible] he has got too old and feeble to ride the circuits, just [illegible] the man is capable of to think that merit is out of question, and all goes by favour, but I hear he has met with little or no encouragement. Pearson is the appointment that would give general satisfaction to the West, as being the best qualified in every respect for the People even murmur that Manly is from Raleigh, but will go for him for Governor, though, as he is a clever fellow & good Whig, but they would rather the nomination had been some [one] out of the influence of Raleigh.

*From Patrick M. Henry.*                                    A.

Sattillo,

Mexico,

March 6th., 1848.

Some few days since I took the liberty of addressing your Excellency quite a long communication, setting forth an application on my part for the Majority in our Regiment, which will be in a few days, vacated by the resignation of either Colonel *Paine,* or Major *Stokes.*[3]

In connection therewith, I beg leave to address you once more, in as much as some circumstances have recently come to my knowledge that would seem to make it highly necessary for me to do so. A number of *Subaltern Officers* of our Regiment who are now in Camp at Arispe's Mills, and who have heretofore been most active in opposing and reviling Col. Paine, hearing that *I* would be probably recommended to your Excellency for the office alluded to, by all the *respectable* portion of the Regiment, have, as I understand, written to your Excellency a *remonstrance* against my appointment, and a downright *proscription* of myself, who have never done any thing to incur their displeasure, except by giving, when occasion offered, my unqualified disappro-

---

[3] Montfort Sidney Stokes (1810-1862), of Wilkes, son of Governor and Senator Montfort Stokes, entered the navy as a midshipman in 1829, and resigned as a lieutenant in 1839. He was a member of the council of state, 1851, colonel of the First North Carolina regiment in the Civil War, and was mortally wounded at Mechanicsville.

bation of their generally unofficerlike and insubordinate conduct, since being in this service. Now, Sir, I beg of you to disregard such a communication until you can hear from those (and especially Col. Paine) in regard to my own character as an officer, and qualifications for the appointment.

The *"Court of Inquiry"* appointed to investigate the conduct of Col. Paine and Lieuts. Pender & Singeltary, has closed its sessions here, and will proceed forthwith to Monterey in order to take the evidence of General *Wool* & others. Col. Paine will also go, and I am certain he will not return to the Regiment, but will proceed to his home in N. Carolina. Thus, Sir, will the service have been deprived of one of it's most valuable and indefatigable officers by the bitter persecutions of a set of men, who, having no military qualifications themselves, cannot know how to appreciate those qualifications in others. I tremble for the future safety of our Regiment, on account of it's invaluable Commander being thus lost to it.

I think, Sir, there is but a poor prospect for peace, as the rumor has just reached us that the Mexican Congress has failed to reassemble in *Queretaro*. But, Sir, on the other hand, the opinion prevails here that the whole Country will, finally, have to be occupied by our troops, etc.

I presume, Sir, we shall in a short time "see what we shall see." Please present me to all my Raleigh friends—especially to *General Haywood,* etc.

*To James Graham.*       U.

Raleigh,

April 5th, 1848.

* * * * *

Wake Superior Court is in Session this week, Judge Caldwell presiding. Stanly informed me yesterday that he would resign the office of Attorney General at the close of this Circuit. The reason assigned is that he does not desire to live in Raleigh, and thinks he should not hold the office, unless he did so. Quite a difference has arisen between him and Badger on the one side, and Rayner on the other, owing to the opposition of the latter to S's nomination for Governor, and the circumstances connected therewith, too tedious to be here detailed. Badger was here last week, having come on to argue a criminal case in Johnston. He speaks despondingly of the success of the Whigs in the Presidential election, and manifests great asperity towards Clay. He is, on the whole, however, evidently pleased with public life. Manly seems disposed to take the field, and make a thorough canvass. His nomination is not acceptable in many quarters, and he may be hard run with serious opposition. He is by no means well informed in politics.

Four of my boys are going to school, and making pretty good progress. Susan has been thinking of visiting Lincoln this Spring, but has nearly given out the idea, owing to the inconvenience of leaving home. We were at Hillsboro' last week, and are arranging our home affairs for the period of our return.

I have only sold a part of my last crop of Flour, holding up for a better price, but I fear the French Revolution will derange all the markets abroad, and that grain will feel the depressing effect, as cotton surely must. I will not be surprized that it leads to a general war throughout Europe, and that we become involved in it before 12 months. Though the Revolutionists thus far have shewn great moderation.

Paul Cameron leaves here today, to carry two families of Mr. Bennehan's negroes, whom he liberated, to Baltimore, to ship for Liberia.

The Council of State will meet me on the 20th. of May to confer on the appointment of Judge of the Supreme Court, etc. I have not fully determined on the appointment as yet.[4] The little patronage attached to my office is like "a little learning," "a dangerous thing." At least not a pleasant one, when the selections necessarily imply discriminations on the pretensions of my friends. The public interest, however, must be my sole guide in the matter.

I will be glad to hear from you soon.

Affectionately Yours

---

[4] Graham and the council of state appointed William H. Battle to fill the vacancy on the supreme court, but the following legislature rejected the appointment and named Richmond M. Pearson.

*From Jonathan Worth.*                                    A.

Asheboro',

April 8th., 1848.

Presuming that it is desirable to you and your counsel, previous to filling the vacancy on the Supreme Court bench, to collect what you can as to the wishes of the bar, I take the liberty of saying to you that the subject was a good deal spoken of here during our Sup'r Court last week, and nearly all the gentlemen attending this bar have a decided preference for Judge Pearson. I am of opinion that his appointment would give almost universal satisfaction to the bar, and the public, within the range of my acquaintance.

*From James G. M. Ramsey.*[5]        A., G. P.

Mecklenburg,

near Knoxville,

April 8th., 1848.

I take the liberty of informing you that I shall visit Raleigh about the 10th. proximo, with the purpose of procuring from the archives of North Carolina such information as they furnish in relation to the early history of Tennessee.

A predecessor of yours, (Gov. Swain) once assured me that I might examine for that purpose the Executive and Legislative records of that period. I hope I am not making an improper request when I respectfully ask permission from yourself to do so.

A portion of our history is shrouded in such obscurity as to require an examination into the records of our Parent State. And if not incompatible with your views of propriety, & State usages, I persuade myself you will allow me to make it.

---

[5] James Gettys McGready Ramsey (1797-1884), of Tennessee, a graduate of Washington College, Tennessee, who studied medicine with Dr. Joseph C. Strong, and at the University of Pennsylvania, began practice in Knoxville. He quickly became active in business and internal improvements, was an active promoter of railway communication with the Atlantic seaboard, became president of the Knoxville branch bank of the Louisville, Charleston, and Cincinnati Railroad, and was agent for the State of Tennessee in selling its bonds for the East Tennessee and Georgia Railroad. He was an ardent pro-slavery man, a secessionist, and an active supporter of the Confederacy. Towards the close of the war, he came to North Carolina for refuge, but returned home in 1872. Deeply interested in history, he wrote *Annals of Tennessee.*

P.S. I notice in Foote's N. C. that the original Declaration of the Charlotte Convention, or a copy in the hand-writing of my Grandfather, J. M. Alexander, is in the Executive office at Raleigh. I need not ad that I will ask also the priviledge of seeing it.

[*Enclosure*]

CIRCULAR

of

THE E. T. HISTORICAL AND ANTIQUARIAN SOCIETY.

---

The Executive Committee of the "East Tennessee Historical and Antiquarian Society" again invites attention to the object and design of the Association. It is desirous of procuring and perpetuating all that relates to the early History and Antiquities of Tennessee. For this purpose it requests again from its members and all others disposed to contribute to its collections.

1st. Authentic accounts of the Aboriginal inhabitants that have resided within our boundaries—their wars—whether among themselves, or with the adventurers and emigrants that first visited the country. The Aboriginal names of the water courses, mountains, districts, and their English signification—the traditions, relics, laws, customs, religion, etc. The names and exact locations of their towns, war paths, battle grounds, territorial boundaries of the different tribes, with an account of their head men and warriors.

II. The first approaches of civilization to the present State of Tennessee, embracing the adventures and exploits of the hunter, trader, traveller, Spanish, French, or Anglo-American, their routes, discoveries, journals, privations, captivities. The time and place of the first permanent settlements in the country, the names of the first emigrants, the roads and manner of their travel, the difficulties encountered, their reception by the natives, first causes of hostility, the names and exact location of the several stations, forts, and garrisons built upon the different frontiers, the battle grounds, the several campaigns, the routes pursued, the treaty grounds, the names of those who held them, the treaties themselves.

III. The incipient efforts of the first emigrants to form their civil and political institutions, local histories of towns, counties, churches, schools of learning, and private associations, the part taken by the infant settlements in the Revolutionary war, the history of the ancient commonwealth of Franklin, embracing the civil and military transactions of its government, during that period of our political orphanage, sketches of the lives of all eminent personages, who have lived in the State, or who are identified with its history, and the private papers and letters of the leaders of the day, and files of early newspapers and journals that may illustrate it.

The Committee acknowledge with great satisfaction the contribution to the Library and Museum of the Society, from some of its honorary members and similar associations abroad, of rare and valuable books, pamphlets, manuscripts, relics, curiosoties, etc., they invite to its collection like additions from the liberal and curious.

As a further means of promoting the objects of the Association, they beg leave to suggest the formation of County Lyceums, auxiliary to it.

The task of rescuing from oblivion the early history of Tennessee is not without its difficulties. Much of it is already forgotten, or but indistinctly remembered, or handed down by vague and uncertain tradition. No archives of State, no portfolios of Ministers will assist our investigations. The narratives of our oldest citizens who have *"ab urbe condita,"* resided in the country, must be procured, the papers of their deceased contemporaries which may have survived the ravages of time or accident, must be examined. The emergency admits of no delay. Whatever can be done in this laudible undertaking, must be done soon. The slow, but certain, operation of time is yearly removing from the theatre on which they have so long and so nobly acted, many who could have given valuable additions to our knowledge of the *past.* In a few years more, the last of these venerable relics of another age will have retired from the scenes of earth, and their lamp of life, already feeble and flickering, be extinguished forever, by the dampness of the grave. Let us hasten to redeem the time that is lost. From every citizen we expect a whisper of encouragement. From the intelligent and enlightened we allow ourselves to hope essential and efficient assistance. Upon our members we depend for prompt and active co-operation. We appeal to the gratitude of every son of Tennessee; we appeal to his State preferences and to his ancestral pride.

By order of the Executive Committee.

J. G. M. RAMSEY,
Cor. Sec. E. T. H. & A. S.

*From Augustine H. Shepperd.*                          A.

Washington,

May 10th, 1848.

A friend of Massachusetts has expressed a wish to learn the condition of the ruins of the Statue of Washington that lately adorned our Capitol. He would also like to learn some particulars of the time of its execution cost, etc., time of destruction. I am unable to answer these inquiries & take the liberty of asking of you the favor of furnishing the information to me.

You know the time of the Democratic National Convention is near, and as it approaches curiosity is more and more excited amongst us to conjecture the result.

All along I have thought Cass had the best prospects of success, but within a few days there has been much talk about Woodbury & many are saying that if the "two thirds" rule should be adopted his chance is the better one The southern Wing of the Democracy is known to prefer him & although diminution in point of numbers the opinion obtains that it will have great influence in determining the nomination.

The Democrats may & probably will have their troubles in Convention & *we* are not without apprehension that in this particular at least the Whig Convention will not be more fortunate than the Democratic. I think the contest will be between Taylor & Scott; no one here at least very few think for a moment of Mr. Clay's success. Many that were apparently for him have in my confident opinion *never* looked to nor desired his nomination. What temper and disposition will the delegates from our State bring with them? Doubtless many of the good old pannel will come into [illegible] thinking of nobody but Clay, but when they exchange a few thoughts with their neighbors from New York, Massachusetts, etc., etc., they will wake up to the conviction that *Clay is not the man.* Who then; will they look to Taylor or Scott, or will they cast about for McLean? I am more and more convinced of an early impression that the North and slave holding States generally are strongly disinclined to support Taylor, on account of his geographical position. The feeling of the free States is any thing but friendly to the South.

Pardon these mere thoughts of the day, & believe me to be Your friend truly.

[P.S.] Have you read the two last letters between Scott & Marcy? [6] all agree that the Secretary's reply is a very able one.

### From David L. Swain. A.

Chapel Hill,

May 13th., 1848.

After various efforts during a period of more than 10 years, I succeeded on Tuesday last in obtaining a box of papers constituting a portion, if not the whole, of Judge Murphy's collections. I have examined them cursorily, and if there are none in reserve, the collection is by no means so extensive, nor is it altogether so valuable as I had hoped to find it. I am anxious to ascertain by an examination of your descriptive list, which I have never seen since the time it was published, whether there is no other box, at Mr. Kirkland's, or elsewhere.

The largest and most valuable portion of the collection, are public property, and ought, I suppose, to be deposited in your office. You no doubt remember how unwilling I was to undertake the arrangement of Governor Burke's manuscripts untill it could be ascertained that there were no remaining ones among the Murphy papers. I had no expectation, however, that I should find, as I do, a larger number of valuable papers, drawn from his files, than from any other single source.

Judge Murphy turns out, too, to have been the last depository of the long lost papers of Gov. Nash, and these, I suppose, from a letter copied in Burke's Letter Book, now before me, and written immediately after his entrance into office, (28th. June, 1781) these he must have received from Miss Burke, at the same time he obtained her father's manuscripts.

The following is an extract from the letter from Gov. B. to Gov. N., "I request you, Sir, to transmit to me by the bearer, all the public accounts, returns and other papers which are incident and belonging to the office—to furnish me with an account of the warrants issued by your authority, and the persons who are accountable for the expenditure of public monies, or supplies

---

[6] The allusion is to the attempt of the Polk administration to discredit General Scott, which was thwarted by overwhelming adverse public opinion.

under your orders, of such orders as you have issued and not yet completed, and of such stores as have been procured by your orders." etc., etc.

The Nash papers are put up in separate bundles, with labels in Judge Murphy's hand writing, the first label as follows, "Governor Nash's papers for January, February, March, April, 1780." There are seven other bundles with similar labels, for May, June, July, Aug. Sep. Oct. & Nov. 1780, but none for any subsequent month. The files from Dec. 1780 to June 1781, both inclusive, may, it is hoped, be yet discovered in Hillsboro'.

Next to the executive papers, the largest contribution to the collection came from Gen'l Sumner. There is a considerable bundle obtained from Gov. Johnston,[7] & Judge Iredell.[8] A few uninteresting papers from Gov. Franklin.[9] Collections of letters written by, or obtained from, W. Hooper,[10] A. M. Hooper,[11] &

---

[7] Samuel Johnston (1733-1816), of "Hayes," Chowan County, a native of Scotland, was brought as an infant to North Carolina. Educated in New England, he became a lawyer, served as clerk of the court, 1767-1773, and quickly, by force of intellect and character, became a leader in the province, who ever commended the respect, but not the love, of the people. He served either as borough or county member in the assembly, 1760-1775, was a member of the first four provincial congresses, of the state senate, 1779, was a member of congress, 1780-1782, and was president of the conventions of 1788 and 1789. He was intensely conservative in his political thinking. He was governor, 1787-1789, and was the state's first United States senator, serving from 1790-1793.

[8] James Iredell (1751-1799), of Chowan, a native of Sussex, England, came as a youth to Edenton, where he studied law under Samuel Johnston, and married his sister. Of great ability, he soon acquired reputation. He was a member of the commission, appointed in 1776, to revise the laws, was made a judge in 1777, was attorney general, 1779-1782, and was appointed to make a new revision of the laws in 1787. He was a Federalist delegate to the convention of 1788, and with William R. Davie had its debates published. In 1790 Washington made him a justice of the supreme court, where he served until his death.

[9] Jesse Franklin (1760-1823), of Surry and Wilkes, a native of Virginia, and a revolutionary soldier at seventeen. Sent by his father to select a place of settlement, he chose Surry County, and there became captain and adjutant of the regiment of his uncle Benjamin Cleveland. He distinguished himself at King's Mountain, and, later, at Guilford Court House. He was captured by Tories and hanged, but his bridle broke, and he escaped. After the war he moved to Wilkes, and was a member of the commons, 1784-1787, 1789-1791. Returning to Surry, he sat in the commons, 1793-1794, 1797-1798, and in the state senate, 1805-1806. He was a member of congress, 1795-1797, and United States senator, 1799-1805, 1806-1813, presiding at the impeachment trials of Pickering and Chase, and voting for conviction.

[10] William Hooper (1742-1790), a native of Massachusetts, graduate of Harvard, who studied law under James Otis and settled in Wilmington, where he rose rapidly, becoming deputy attorney general, and an officer in Tryon's expedition against the Regulators. He was borough member of the assembly from 1773 to the end of the colonial government. He was a member of the committee of correspondence, of all five provincial congresses, of the continental congress, 1774-1777, and a signer of the Declaration of Independence, and of the commons, 1777-1782. He moved to Hillsboro, and was in the commons, 1784.

[11] Archibald Maclaine Hooper, of New Hanover, grandson of Archibald Maclaine, a scholarly man with a gifted pen, who for a time edited the *Cape Fear Recorder*. His father, George Hooper, a Loyalist, was a near relative of William Hooper.

Harnett,[12] & A. McLaine,[13] are interesting. There is also a letter from your father, a letter & other papers from Gen'l Lenoir,[14] a few ante-revolutionary & very interesting manuscripts by Waightstill Avery.[15]

The printed Journal of the Provincial Congress of Aug. '75, The sermon delivered by Micklejohn[16] before Gov. Tryon's army at Hillsboro', a little tract by Maurice Moore[17] denying the right of the mother country to tax the colonies, and the official account

[12] Cornelius Harnett (1723 ?-1781), of Wilmington, probably a native of Chowan, an eminent figure in revolutionary North Carolina. He was a member of the assembly, 1754-1775, chairman of the Cape Fear Sons of Liberty, and led the resistance to the Stamp Act, which nullified it in North Carolina. He served in the last four provincial congresses, and was vice president of the fifth. He was the author of the resolution instructing the delegates to concur with the delegates of other provinces in declaring independence, which was the first official utterance on the subject. He was a member of the provincial council, and the council of state, and member of the continental congress, 1777-1780.

[13] Archibald Maclaine, of Brunswick and New Hanover, was a native of Scotland, who, after serving as an apprentice in Dublin, came to Wilmington, and became an eminent lawyer. He was one of the leaders in nullifying the Stamp Act, was an active member of the Wilmington committee of safety, signed a call for the first provincial congress, and was a delegate to the fourth. He was a member of the commons, 1782-1786, and of the senate, 1777-1803. He was fearless, outspoken, and had a fiery, uncontrollable temper. He was notable as a letter writer.

[14] William Lenoir (1751-1839), a native of Virginia, came to Edgecombe County as a child. Moving to Surry (now Wilkes) County, he entered revolutionary service with enthusiasm. He was in General Rutherford's expedition against the Cherokees, waged partisan war against the Tories, and was wounded at King's Mountain. He was for many years major general of militia, was a justice of the peace for sixty-two years, was clerk of the court, surveyor, land speculator, and chairman of the county court. He served in the commons, 1781-1784, and in the senate, 1784-1794. He was a delegate to the conventions of 1788 and 1789, and was president of the original board of trustees of the university.

[15] Waightstill Avery (1741-1821), successively of Mecklenburg, Jones, and Burke, a native of Connecticut, a graduate of Princeton, who came to North Carolina in 1769. He is listed among the signers of the Mecklenburg Declaration of Independence, but this cannot be made to accord with his taking the oath of allegiance to the Crown shortly thereafter. He was a member of the second and fifth provincial congresses, and was a particularly important figure in the latter. He represented Burke in the commons, 1782-1785, 1793, and in the senate in 1796. He was probably the most learned lawyer in North Carolina of his day.

[16] George Micklejohn, an Anglican clergyman, who came from Scotland to Hillsboro in 1767, who loved liquor and money, and hated women. When Thomas Person was jailed, the parson rode all night to destroy papers that would prove him a Regulator, and was back in Hillsboro the next morning. He was selected to open the first provincial congress with prayer, but, like most of his cloth, he was a Loyalist. He fled to "Goshen," Person's plantation, when the revolution began, and spent the rest of his life there.

[17] Maurice Moore, of Brunswick and New Hanover, distinguished lawyer, colonial judge, member of the assembly, 1754-1760, 1762-1774, and of the fifth provincial congress. He was highly talented, versatile and witty, and had a wide reputation as an orator.

of the trial of Gen'l Howe[18] before a Court Martial at Philad'a, are the only pamphlets of any value. There are about a dozen newspapers containing revolutionary incidents, and the letters of Florian[19] in Bundles.

There is a letter in relation to the Mecklenburg Declaration from Gov. Israel Pickens,[20] but I find no paper reflecting new light on the subject. There is also an account of the expedition against the Cherokees, written by Lewis Williams, at the request of his father, presenting the reminiscences of the latter.

These imperfect notes, when compared with your particular account, will probably enable you to determine whether the entire collection is here.

Yours very sincerely,

*From James Madison Leach.*[21]    **U.**

Salisbury,

May 17th., 1848.

At the hazard of being thought importunate, I again drop you a line in regard to the forwarding blank commissions. The election has come off in Rowan and I have lost 5 or 6 votes for the want of commission although I am 21 votes ahead in this

---

[18] Robert Howe (1732-1786), of Brunswick, educated in England, became a wealthy rice planter. He was placed in command of Fort Johnston, in 1766, and was a liberal member of the assembly, 1760-1775, and in the last session was chairman of the committee to reply to the governor's message, and prepared it. In 1773 he had joined with Joseph Quincy and Cornelius Harnett in planning resistance to the policy of the mother country. He was a member of the second and third provincial congresses, and wrote the reply to Governor Martin's proclamation. He organized a regiment, and commanded the troops that captured Norfolk, and was promoted to brigadier general. He was excluded, with Harnett, from Sir Henry Clinton's amnesty proclamation. Placed in command of the southern department, he served in South Carolina. Refusing to recognize the authority of Governor Houston, of Georgia, he was courtmartialled and acquitted. He was in command later at West Point, and was a member of the court that tried Major André. He rose to the rank of major general. He was elected to the commons in 1786, but died before taking his seat.

[19] "Florian" was a character created by Archibald D. Murphey to serve as a sort of lay figure whom he alleged himself to quote in numerous writings of his own, usually signed "Philo-Florian."

[20] Israel Pickens (1780-1827), of North Carolina and Alabama, a graduate of Jefferson College, Pennsylvania, a lawyer, who represented Burke County in the state senate, 1808-1809, and was a Democratic member of congress, 1809-1817. He moved to Alabama, and was governor, 1821-1825, and United States senator, 1826.

[21] James Madison Leach (1815-1891), of Lexington, a native of Randolph County. He was twice a cadet at West Point, but never completed the course. He became a lawyer, served in the commons, 1848-1856, and in congress, 1859-1861. He was a Confederate lieutenant colonel, and a member of the Confederate congress, 1864-1865. After the war, he was a member of the state senate, 1865-1866, 1879, and a conservative member of congress, 1873-1875.

County. Davidson and Davie are yet to vote. In Davie, the Col. Commandant is a bitter Democrat, and is therefore doing his best against me, was even over here today electioneering might and main against me today. He informed me on enquiry that there have been 19 or 20 new officers elected recently, who have not been commissioned, and that he only had some 10 commissions. Well, I am perfectly certain he will commission *Clemmons* men, & pass over those who would vote for me if commissioned, and my election may depend on getting a dozen blank commissions as they are making desperate efforts to beat me in these Counties, thinking and fearing my success will have a tendency to strengthen the Whig party. I do hope therefore, that commissions will be forwarded to me, directed to Lexington, *immediately* on the receipt of this, and if there should be no blanks in your office, I hope you will be so good as to have several *writen out.*

The election comes off in Davie on Tuesday next. I presume you have received the lines I wrote you from Lexington on Saturday last, and be assured I would not trouble you again, except from what I conceive to be the urgency of the case.

*From James Graham.*                                    U.

Rutherfordton,

May 19th, 1848.

\* \* \* \* \*

This is Superior Court week here, Judge Battle presiding. The Candidates are beginning to come out for the Legislature, and this County is again to be agitated and convulsed with *new* County questions. I will leave here to day for my Earhart Place, as I am to have Father's old Dwelling House *painted* next week.

\* \* \* \* \*

I would go to Raleigh and stay awhile with you now, but as I expect to do so in a month or six weeks, I must devote my time to business and prepare for a long absence.

Gen'l Bynum has removed to Columbia, S. C. he is here this week, *sober.* Col. Mills has returned from Florida in health and spirits greatly improved. Wm. McKesson of Burke is to marry the Daughter of Charles McDowell next week.

Rich discoveries of *Gold* and *Limestone* are being made about the Little Mountain near Vesuvius Furnace.

The *low* price of Farming and planting produce will turn a large number of laborers into the Mines. If you could come up the Country and bring your family or a portion of it, come to my Earhart Place and stay all the time. From that point you can make such trips of business or pleasure as may be agreeable; or avoid society if you want rest and retirement. I have no White family at my Earhart Place. I have a single man for an Overseer, and the whole house is at the disposal of your family for any length of time. If you should find it necessary to return quickly to Raleigh, you might leave your family and let them go down with me when I go North, or remain at my place all Summer if convenient.

*From James W. Bryan.*                        U.

Newbern,

June 1st., 1848.

\*    \*    \*    \*    \*

Politics are beginning to excite our people somewhat, and there is quite a stir being made in Craven on the subject. Our friends only await the action of the National Convention to burst forth in favour of the Whig Candidate. The Whigs have not formed a ticket in Craven yet, and the Democrats have not selected a candidate for the Senate in the place of Street, who declines the nomination for that appointment. Messrs. Washington & Guion have consented to become Candidates for the Whigs, but they are put to their trumps to select the third man. In the Senatorial district of Carteret and Jones the Whigs are unable as yet to agree upon a Candidate. Howard's [22] death has confused matters and things there very much, and I fear that they will delay the matter so long as to produce some difficulty in the Whig representative of that district. Our people seem to like Manly much, but he creates but little enthusiasm among them. I trust they will give a better account of themselves in August. The extreme pressure and want of money, seems to affect their energies very much.

---

[22] James W. Howard.

*To James Graham.*                                    U.

Raleigh,

June 9th., 1848.

I was glad to receive your letter from Rutherfordton, and would be pleased to go to Mecklenburg, in this month, as you propose, but shall not be able to do so—I have had this Spring, an attack of pneumonia, which confined me to my room, more than three weeks, and has left me much debilitated, and sensitive to cold on the least exposure. I cannot therefore, bear travelling at night in the Stage, and have not the time to make the journey in my own conveyance. I wish to go to Hillsboro' next week, to look after my wheat harvest, which is quite promising, and about the middle of July to go by Richmond, etc., to the White Sulphur Springs in Va. Susan's health is by no means good, and she will accompany me, if possible. I must, therefore, defer my visit to Sister Violet untill the fall. . . .

We hear by Telegraph from Philadelphia, that Gov. Morehead of this State is President of the Whig Convention. Two dispatches were received, saying Taylor would be the nominee. The last, however, from G. W. Haywood (a Taylor man) says there would be no balloting untill this morning, and the nominee was very doubtful. If any further intelligence is received before the departure of the mail, I will append it. Judge Mangum was here a few weeks since, and thought Gen'l Scott would be nominated; in which event he hoped to go on the ticket as Vice President. The N. C. delegation to the Convention, however, do not seem inclined to his support.

We are glad to hear that you are coming this way to the North, and hope you make arrangements to spend some time with us. Judge Cameron and his daughters have gone to Philadelphia, to remain as long as there is any hope of benefit to the invalid, from the physicians there. Paul C's family are spending the summer here. The Judge resigns the Presidency of the Bank the 1st. of Jan'y next. He apprehends great pressure on the Banks & indebted class of the Community, and has ceased to make loans here. His theory is that so long as we have a low Tariff, causing specie to be exported from this Country to pay balances against us, the Banks will be in straightened circumstances, and can only be prosperous from accidental causes, such as the famine in Europe last year, causing a heavy demand for exports of grain from our side of the water.

Manly & Reid addressed the people here last Monday. The friends of each seem to be well satisfied with their candidate and Reid will make a better rally than I expected, though he must, of course, be beaten. Many of the democrats disapprove his proposition to amend the Constitution, but I believe they will still vote for him. I would not be surprized if Wm. Haywood came out here, an independent candidate in opposition to that doctrine. He is conscious of his mistake in resigning his seat in the Senate, and this will be a good opportunity to come out as the defender of the Constitution, with which he claims a near connexion, in consequence of his efforts on the Convention question.

You have probably heard of the death of Rob't Martin, of Rockingham. He has left his negroes (of whom he has a large number in Miss.) to his daughter, Mrs. Douglass[23] & her children, if she has any, if not, to be all liberated, at her death. Judge Douglas has now gone to Miss. to look after the estate.

By Telegraph at 1 o'clock this morning—Two ballots in Convention yesterday—

|       | Taylor | Clay | Scott |
|-------|--------|------|-------|
| 1st.  | 111    | 97   | 43    |
| 2nd.  | 118    | 86   | 49    |

Still later

Taylor is nominated on the 4th. ballot;—particulars not given as yet.

Very affectionately yours

*From Robert B. Gilliam.*     U.

Oxford,

July 8th., 1848.

I desire to ask your views, confidentially, in relation to the course to be taken in the approaching Canvass.

When I saw you in Raleigh, I supposed that the Democratic Candidates in this County would eagerly seize upon the issue which Mr. Reid had furnished for them, on the subject of equal suffrage, and, as I informed you, my own mind was fully made up to meet the question, and to discuss it upon its merits before

---

[23] Mrs. Stephen A. Douglas.

the people. Since my return home, I have been informed, that, under the advice of some of their leading friends, they have determined not to make it one of the issues of the Campaign, unless it is brought up by our side.

Whilst I am fully determined to sustain the conservative grounds upon which our Constitution is founded, yet I confess to you that I have felt a good deal apprehensive lest a sufficient number of the Whig non-freeholders might be captivated by this new priviledge, offered to them, to decide the election. Our opponents seem to be quite as apprehensive, that they may lose a portion of their freehold strength. Now I have very little expectation that the issue can be kept out of the Contest, whatever may be the wishes or determination of the Candidates. Nor have I any reliable assurance that such is the purpose of our opponents. But, in the event that they should indicate a disposition to give the subject the go-by, I desire to have your counsel as to the safe and proper course to be adopted by us in such a contingency. I am in that state of uncertainty about it, that I am unwilling to rely upon my own judgment.

So far as the County election is concerned, I should have no hesitation in permitting the subject to pass without discussion or notice. We have other issues which are likely to be more profitable, and in which there is less risk; and the only circumstance which induces any indecision in my judgment, is the influence that may be exerted on the Governor's election—the doubt being whether Reid would sustain more injury by the apparent abandonment of the issue by his friends, than the benefit to be derived from the silent operation of the humbug.

It may seem strange that I should go from home to seek counsel in regard to the mode of conducting our County election; but you have not now to learn the estimate I place upon your judgment, as well as your candour.

You will probably receive this letter tomorrow, and you will be able to reply to it by Monday, or Tuesday at furthest. If practicable, I should be glad to hear from you by Monday, as the campaign opens on the day following. Whether you write on Monday or Tuesday, direct your letter to me at Henderson.

The Whigs here are quite sanguine, I believe sincerely so. The democrats appear to be in good spirits, and for aught I know, they may be equally sincere. I have been a good deal bedeviled, about my defence of the Slave recently tried in Person, and I fear it will be impossible to remove all the dissatisfaction on that subject. Some of my friends think that the silly clamor has expended all it's force, and that I shall make quite as much as I shall lose by it.

To James W. Bryan.                    U. Bryan Mss.

Raleigh,

July 13th, 1848.

I take the liberty to inclose you [a letter to] the New Bernian, which I have supposed might be of some service in the Canvass for the Legislature in the Eastern section of the State.

Please look over it, and if you concur, hand it to Mr. Mayhew. Of course in my present position I would not like to be known as an essayist, especially in a sectional appeal. It may be, also, that it conflicts with the ground taken by the Candidates in your County. If so, suppress it, or make any alteration you think proper. Strange to talk such demigogueism [illegible] Convention in the East than in the West as far as I can hear.

And the Whig Candidates are said to have given way in Johnston, on this question. Manly reports very favorably of himself in the West, but thinks the Legislature in some doubt owing to the folly of the Whigs in running several candidates in some of the large Counties there.

We are all well, and send love to your family. We hope to get off to the Springs next week, taking our own carriage, and the rout by Hillsboro'. The telegraph is out of out order & Susan is fearful of being delayed in getting the articles ordered from N. Y.

[Enclosure]

Senatorial Suffrage.

To the Editor

I am surprized to find in this section of the State, and in the Eastern Counties generally, that the proposition of Mr. Reid, the democratic Candidate for Governor, to alter the Constitution has excited so little examination. It is said by the democratic press in your town, to be a popular doctrine in that quarter, and that Mr. Reid will gain votes by its agitation. While I am unwilling to believe this, I am yet apprehensive that the people of Eastern

North Carolina are not sufficiently aware of its mischievous tendency.

The proposition is, that the Constitution shall be so changed, that any man who now votes for a member of the House of Commons shall vote for a Senator also. And the argument to sustain it, is, that every White man should have equal priviledges without regard to his property.

I shall not here undertake to defend the present system of Representation, under which we have lived nearly three quarters of a century, nor to account for the new born zeal of Mr. Reid in favor of the rights of poor men, whom in 1840 he voted to sell (if convicted of vagrancy & unable to pay costs) see Senate Journal 1840-1 page 283. But I design to shew by incontrovertible facts and figures, what will be the effect of his proposition if carried out in practice, on this region of Country, and the whole Eastern part of the State. The advocates of this amendment, or change of the Constitution, say, they ask no other change of the fundamental law, except that all persons who now vote in the Commons shall also vote in the Senate. But, if the reason for this change be, the one assigned, that all White men should have equal priviledges without regard to property, it necessarily involves another. And that is, that the Senators shall be apportioned among the people according to numbers, and not according to the taxes paid by them, as is now the case.

To make this plain: the County of Onslow with a white population of 4,735, now elects one of 50 Senators, because she pays one fiftieth part of the taxes of the State. While Wilkes & Burke (also including Caldwell and McDowell) with a white population of 23,295 elect only one Senator, for the same reason their amount of taxation entitles them to no more. But if property should not be considered in the qualification of voters it surely follows, that it is entitled to no weight in laying off communities of voters, or districts. And if the amendment of Mr. Reid is to prevail, it must of course be accompanied with a change of the basis of representation in the Senate from taxation, to White population. In which event, Wilkes and Burke would have 4½ times the weight of Onslow.

Now let us see what would be the result of the change, on this quarter of the State. The number of Senators is Fifty. The total White population of the State is 484,870 persons.

1/50 th. of this, is 9,695

Consequently, every County containing a White population of 9,695 White persons, would be a Senatorial district, and every County falling below that number, would be united with some one, or more, other Counties, to make a district.

The County of Beaufort has a White popn. of 7050

Craven    ”   ”   ”   ”   ” 6624

Pitt      ”   ”   ”   ”   ” 6128

Wayne    ”   ”   ”   ”   ” 6754

Beaufort combined with Hyde would still form a Senatorial district, but Craven, Pitt and Wayne (each now a district of itself) would each fall, about one third short, of the number required, and would have to be joined to neighboring Counties in composing a district.

Take any other Counties in this end of the State, now forming Senatorial districts of themselves, and see what would be their fate. Look to the largest of them.

Edgecomb has a White popn. of 7915

Johnston has a White popn. of 6996

New Hanover has a White popn. of 6371

All considerably below the required ratio of 9695. Even Granville, classed as an Eastern County, fails to come up to the ratio by 3 or 400, Her White population being 9,309. Thus the effect of this wonderful step in the progress of modern democracy would be to disfranchise every County East of Raleigh, which now forms a separate Senatorial district, and amalgamate it with others, and to take away some half dozen Senators from the people composing them, and transfer them to the Counties of the West, with their more numerous White population.

Craven, now a separate district, would then be not quite equal to a district after taking on Lenoir.

Washington, Tyrrel and Martin, now forming two districts, would then not be equal to one.

But, the basis of representation in the Senate is taxation, in the lower House it is Federal population, every five negroes being counted as three White persons. The same abstract equality which requires that all free White men shall vote for Senators, also demands that only free White persons shall be represented in the Commons. The same Convention, or Legislature, therefore, which gives us Mr. Reid's amendment in the Senate, will likewise, if true to his principles, establish White population as the basis of representation in the other branch. There being 120 members of the House of Commons, and the White Population of the

State, as before mentioned, 484,870, it follows that 4040 will be the ratio of White population for a member of the Commons.

Every County, therefore, having a White population of twice that number, will be entitled to two members, of three times that, to three members, etc.

Thus Craven, Johnston, Wayne &c now represented as large Counties of the East, would probably each be deprived of one of their present members of the House of Commons, besides losing three separate Senatorial representation. I have heard heretofore of a scheme for relieving the people, which would have ended in bringing them in debt without the means of payment, and this project of extending our priviledges (as far as the Eastern people are concerned) would ultimate in taking away the weight we now have in our Legislative Councils. At present, it is represented as a contest between the freeholder and nonfreeholder, among ourselves. Resolve it into its true elements, and it becomes a contest between the free White men of the mountains, and his fellow citizens of the lowlands. By a fair compromise with our Western friends, after a controversy of thirty years, our fundamental law on these subjects was settled. That controversy can never be renewed without injury to us. The smallest of our freeholders derives political weight from the taxes paid by his wealthier neighbor, and the poorest citizen among us derives like weight from the number of slaves owned in his County. The owner has the property, the political power which it confers belongs to the Community. I ask whether any man in this County desires to see her deprived of the power she now has as a separate Senatorial district, or to see her reduced to a single member in the House of Commons. I make the same inquiry for Johnston, Halifax, Northampton, and all the Eastern Counties.

I desire that the people shall question the Candidates on these subjects, and remember that "it is the first step that costs," that the proposition of Mr. Reid, attempts to break up the Compromises of the Constitution, and to deprive our section of the State, of the guarantees which that instrument affords us.

It may be sport to him to trifle with the great interests of society in a Canvass for votes, where he has no hope of success, but the people in this region, who hope for long years of prosperity and happiness under the wise institutions of our fathers should mark well the public men among ourselves who shall give any countenance to his mischievous suggestion.

A Citizen.

*From George E. Badger.*                                    U.

Senate Chambers,

July 13th., 1848.

The President yesterday communicated to us the proceedings of the Court of Enquiry, held in Mexico upon the mutiny of the Reg't, which was ordered to be printed. The record being very voluminous, there is no prospect of getting it from the printer for several weeks. I had a copy made of the finding of facts, & the opinion of the Court thereon, by one of our Clerks, & certified as a true copy, which I furnished to Outlaw to be sent forthwith to Edenton for use and publication. It furnishes a complete vindication of Colo. Paine, asserting that the dissatisfaction in the Reg't, & in those of Va., proceeded from the faithful and energetic discharge of his duty by Col. P., that a mutiny existed, & that in starting his men on the 15 day, he acted strictly in the line of his duty, that Gen'l Wools discharging and rejecting, etc., was an act dictated by the best motives demanded by the state of the case, & proved to have been right by the effect produced upon the troops. This is the substance. The result of the other Court of Enquiry upon Paine for putting a man out of Saltillo has also arrived, & is, I learn, a full acquittal. I am only waiting for the title to move a call for these proceedings also. These things are melancholy, as affording evidence of the spirit which prevails with the Adm'n, but they may have a good effect ultimately.

We hear here bad news from N. C., intimating that by division among ourselves we may lose the legislature. I hope there is no such danger, but shall be glad to have your opinion, & to know if anything can be done here. I am at your command if you can suggest a plan of aiding us.

We begin to fear that Morehead's letter to Gen'l Taylor has been suppressed through the Post Office. I have written to M. to send copies by every mail until assured one has reached him, & to send one to Balie Peyton at N. O., with a request to him to have it sent to the Gen'l by express. I wish you would also write to Morehead.

*From Robert B. Gilliam.*                                    U.

Granville County,

17th. July, 1848.

I send my nephew, R. B. Gilliam, to Raleigh, to procure, *if possible,* the Journals of the U. States Senate from the time of Gen'l Cass' election to the Senate, to the close of the last Session of Congress. It is very important to me to have them, and I would incur any expense or trouble to get them. My object is to point out from the Journals themselves, all the votes of Cass on Internal Improvements. I have seen it stated that he has uniformly supported that system in Congress, and reference has been made in the Register (Mr. Miller's speech) to the Journals, which I suppose must be in Raleigh. I hope you or Mr. Miller will procure them for me, and I will return them *safely,* as soon as the contest is over. I should be glad, if you have time, to point out for me all his votes on the subject of Internal Improvement. I shall write, also, to Mr. Miller, to request him to unite with you in procuring the Journals.

I pray you to pardon me for troubling you. The matter is of much importance in this Campaign. The Democrats are very sensitive in regard to the charge made, and will endeavour to get some evidence from Washington to contradict it; I wish to have the Journals in readiness for them.

Writing in much haste, I fear you will scarcely decipher what I write.

*From John M. Morehead.*                                    U.

Greensboro,

July 17th, 1848.

Your favor of 12th. was recd day before yesterday. I inclose to you open a letter to Balie Peyton, which with its contents you will please to read, & then seal & forward it forthwith by Charleston. This will show you what I have done, & you may cause your papers to take notice of my action in endeavouring to get a communication to Genl Taylor.

I have forwarded to the Intelligencer for Publication Mr. Fillmore's reply. I delayed its publication hoping to have Genl Taylor's to go with it.

*From James W. Bryan.*                                    U.

Newbern,

July 18th., 1848.

You will find your communication in the Newbernian. I think your fears as to the ruinous progress of Mr. Reid's demagoguical doctrine of free Suffrage in the East are rather groundless; they are a *brutum fulmen* in this quarter.

The Whigs were never in better spirits, and their success never more certain, the entire ticket will be carried with ease in Craven. Our accounts, too, elsewhere, are very cheering, & I think our friends were never more active, in any previous Canvass. You will find your communication in all the papers, as Mayhew has put the "printer's mark" upon it, in his exchanges.

I hope you will bring to the attention of the Legislature this winter our system of Equity practice, and the constitution of those Courts in general. A more villainous system in practice for the purposes of justice, the wit of man never devised. We ought to have a separate and distinct Court of Chancery, our Circuit Judges know nothing about it, & our Clerks, nine tenths of them can neither write a legible hand, or state an account.

The devotion of Saturday afternoon, too, to the Equity docket, completes the farce of the system. I know not how it is in your section of the State, but with us, the system is a reproach to the public justice of the Country. Why can we not have a separate Chancery Court in each district, with an Injunction Master for each district? It would not only be a credit to the Court, but of vast public utility. Many of our Courts or Counties furnish so little business that nobody seems to want the office of Clerk, and in all such instances the office is filled by incompetent persons; our people could have no objection to a District Chancery Court, as the witnesses are not required to attend and a Jury is never needed. Do think of this matter, and let us have a Chancery Court that will reflect credit on the State, make good Chancery lawyers, and promote the public justice of the Country.

Our people are greatly oppressed for the want of money, several of our merchants have failed, and others are thought to be in a bad way. There seems to be quite a gloom spread over the Country, the pine trees are dying up, the valuable oak trees have all died, and our people see nothing in the perspective to cheer or relieve them.

\*    \*    \*    \*    \*

*From George Cavallor Graham.*                    U.

Memphis,

July 27th, 1848.

My Dear Uncle

Your very kind and affectionate letter came to hand a few days since. In which I was very much pleased to hear from you and your family. As it has been several months since I have had the pleasure of doing so.

I departed from Lincoln County, N. Carolina, about 25th. of January and arrived at Memphis the 4th. of February. I was accompanied by Uncle James as far as Collumbia, S. C. I had quite a pleasant travel through the northern part of Georgia and Alabama, principally on Steam cars. I am at present residing at my Father's old place near Memphis. It was my design when I first returned to the State to have engaged in the mercantile business in Memphis. But as I could not succeed in getting in such a house as I should have liked to have done, I have declined getting in at all. My present intention is to remain on the plantation until the latter part of August, then I think of going up to Georgetown Colledge Kentucky to remain some twelve or eighteen months. My Brothers and Sisters are staying at Uncle Kimbrough's near Germantown. Albert and Joseph and Mary, my youngest sister, are going to school in the neighbourhood. Lydia Ann has just returned from Jackson. She has been going to school there for the last fifteen months. They are all in very fine health, and are very anxious to go to N. Carolina. We have very promising Crops of Corn and Cotton at the plantation, we are cultivating 200 Acres of Cotton and 125 Acres of Corn this year. Working twenty six hands. We have a man overseeing by the name of St. Clair, he was formerly from Pitsboro, N. C. he is a very good Manager. There was 106 Bales of Cotton made on the plantation last year, it was sold in Memphis at Six and Seven cents a pound.

One of our Memphis Banks broke about eight months since, the Farmers and Merchants, and I am fearful that our Estate will sustain a loss of about eight thousand dollars, Six thousand which was invested in Bank stock, and two thousand deposited for safe keeping. These Bills are selling now for about fifteen cents in the Dollar. There is no hope of it being restored again. All of the other Banks are rather suspicious; Memphis is in quite a flourishing condition. I think it is nearly twice as large as it was when I departed from this Country in 1844. The Navy Yard is progressing rapidly. There are some two hundred hands engaged on it. The walls are built principally of sandstone, which they obtain from Ohio and Kentucky, and transport it down on Steam boats. It will no doubt add greatly to the improvement of the old part of the town. There are two Medical Colleges recently located in Memphis. A Mineral and Botanic College both in a flourishing condition.

There are three thousand volunteers in Memphis, just returned from Mexico, and several distinguished officers, they are the most wretched looking set of men I have ever witnessed. I suppose at least one third of them were diseased. Generals Quitman[24] and Butler[25] left this City a few days since.

Mr. Rounsaville of Lexington, N. C. spent several days with me last week. He is on his way to Arkansas on a visit to his Mother. General Taylor seems to carry the day in this part of the State. There are two Teligraphs runing to Memphis one from St. Louis and the other to Nashville.

\* \* \* \* \*

*From   William   W.   Morrison.*                          U.

Raleigh

July 7th. 1848.

[August 7] [26]

\* \* \* \* \*

The election returns are very discouraging to the Whigs. We have heard from about twenty Counties, and Reid has gained

---

[24] John Anthony Quitman (1798-1858), a native of New York, studied law in Ohio, and settled at Natchez, Mississippi. He served in the lower house of the legislature and in the convention of 1832. He became an intense defender of state rights, and, as a "Nullifier" served in the state senate in 1835. He took a company to aid Texas against Mexico, but did no fighting. Returning, he became a brigadier general of militia, and was active in politics, opposing the repudiation of the Union Bank bonds. He entered the Mexican War as a brigadier, and, serving with distinction, was promoted to major general. He advocated annexation of Mexico. He was elected governor in 1850, and opposed the compromise of that year, advocating secession. He wanted the annexation of Cuba and was offered the command of the revolutionists. Indicted by a federal grand jury in New Orleans, he resigned as governor. He served in congress, 1855-1858.

[25] William Orlando Butler (1791-1880), of Kentucky, a graduate of Transylvania, and a law student, rose from private to captain, and brevet major in the War of 1812. He became a lawyer, was a member of the legislature, 1817-1818, and a Democratic member of congress, 1839-1843. He was a major general in the Mexican War, and received swords from congress and Kentucky for gallantry at Monterey. He was Democratic candidate for Vice President in 1848. He was an ardent Unionist in 1861, and was a delegate to the peace conference.

[26] July was evidently written from force of habit, since the election came at a later date.

near 1200 votes, over the vote given for Hoke in 1844. If Reid gains as much in the Counties to be heard from as he has done in those already heard from, he will certainly be elected. The Whigs generally believe Mr. Manly will be elected by a very small majority, probably less than a thousand votes.

We have lost ten members of the Legislature, & gained only four.

We have gained 2 in Halifax, 1 in Granville, 1 in Davidson, and lost 2 in Northampton, 2 in Surry, 2 in Orange, 1 in Davie, 1 in Franklin, 1 in Johnston & 1 in Person. In Orange Waddell was elected by the casting vote of the Sheriff. Mebane elected, and the other Whigs defeated. Col. Paine is elected over both his opponents by 29 votes. Ellis[27] re-elected in Rowan. Orange gave Reid a majority of 12 votes & Guilford only gave Manly 1200 majority. Murchison[28] elected over Cameron[29] in Cumberland by 100 votes. R. Barringer[30] and Scott [31] are elected in Cabarrus & Manly's vote increased.

Rogers (Whig) elected Sheriff in this County. I will write again as soon as the other returns are made.

\* \* \* \* \*

*From Charles L. Hinton.*                                  U.

Raleigh,

August 8th, 1848.

In 43 Counties heard from Manly has fallen behind Graham 2497 votes.

---

[27] John Willis Ellis (1820-1861), of Rowan, a graduate of the university, who studied law under Judge Pearson, was a member of the commons, 1844-1848, a judge of the superior court, 1848-1858; governor, 1859-1861. He was a convinced secessionist, but returned the forts in North Carolina which were captured by hotheads. After the call for troops, he acted as if secession was accomplished. He died during the first year of a second term.

[28] Alexander Murchison, of Cumberland, state senator, 1848, 1852.

[29] Thomas N. Cameron, state senator, 1844-1846, 1850.

[30] Rufus Barringer (1821-1895), of Cabarrus County, a graduate of the university, who was a member of the state senate, 1848-1850. In the Civil War he was a dashing and able cavalry officer, who rose from captain to brigadier general, he took part in seventy-six engagements, was twice wounded, and had two horses shot under him. Captured in the last days of the war, he stayed in Fort Delaware until July. After the war, he returned to the practice of law, became a Republican, and was a delegate to the convention of 1875. He married one of the daughters of the Rev. Robert Hall Morrison.

[31] Joseph W. Scott of Cabarrus.

Reid behind Hoke 877.

Nett gain for Democrats 1,666.

They have a gain of 6 on joint ballott.

We have not heard from Randolph or the Counties West, nor Craven or below Beaufort.

In Guilford we fell off about 500, in Chatham our majority was only 154. In Pitt Reid gained 238.

I have very little doubt of carrying the Gov. and Legislature, the first by less than 1000, the last by two or three votes.

We have the Senator in Davidson, they have a gain in Davie, Craven as it was, but we have not heard whether Washington or one of the Commons is defeated. We claim Stalling's[32] district, & Rutherford, they in Francis,[33] and the Ash[34] which I suppose is somewhat doubtful—They think they have a fair chance for Buncombe one. Jones and Carteret, Commoner in Macon and Curituck, & Camden Senator, but we have strong reasons to believe Bernard[35] is elected.

Deep interest is felt on both sides. I suppose you will have heard that Waddell is elected by the casting vote of the Sheriff. We saved Mebane in the Commons. We have the entire ticket in Halifax, carried three of the four in Granville. We took N Hampton & Johnson.

Our town very healthy. Stone[36] about as you left him.

Our young people generally going to Shocco.[37]

*Invitation from the Dialectic Society.*          U.

Chapel Hill

Dialectic Hall

Aug. 11th, 1848.

At a late meeting of the Dialectic Society, we were appointed a committee to inform you, that you were unanimously elected to deliver an address before the two Literary Societies at the ensuing Commencement, and to ask your acceptance.

---

[32] Whitmel Stallings, of Gates, was state senator, 1842-1846. His district also included Chowan.

[33] Haywood and Macon composed this district. William H. Thomas was elected.

[34] "Ash" may refer to New Hanover, where William S. Ashe was re-elected, to Ashe County, where George Bower was elected, representing Wilkes also, or to Asheville, where Nicholas W. Woodfin was re-elected.

[35] John Barnard, of Currituck, state senator, 1846-1850.

[36] David W. Stone.

[37] Shocco Springs, in Warren County, was then a popular summer resort.

In discharging this duty, permit us to add our personal solicitations to the earnest wish of the body we represent, that you may find it convenient to comply with this request.

> With sentiments of respect,
> Your Obedient Servants
> H. McDusenbery[38]
> E. J. Mallett [39]
> George V. Young[40]

*From William W. Morrison.*                    U.

Raleigh,

August 14th, 1848.

I have postponed writing to you much longer than I intended, hoping to be able to give you the final result of the State elections.

We have received returns from all the Counties in the State except Currituck, & Mr. Manly's majority is about 1200. Currituck will probably reduce it to 800. We are still doubtful about the Legislature; it is a tie in the House & the Whigs have a majority in the Senate, if Waddell retains his seat, if not, it will also be a tie in the Senate. It is rumored here that a mistake was made at one of the precincts in Orange, in adding up the votes & that Berry[41] received five votes more than Waddell. I presume the seat will be contested.

\*    \*    \*    \*    \*

The Volunteers have all returned to N. C. & many of them have passed through Raleigh on their way home. Major Stokes and several other Officers passed through last Friday.

A letter was received from Colonel Paine last week, stating that he would retain the Colors of the Regiment & deliver them to

---

[38] Henry McRorie Dusenbery (1829-1862), of Davidson County, then a senior at the university.

[39] Edward Jones Mallett (1827-1865), of Fayetteville, then a senior at the university, who became a planter. He was a Confederate lieutenant and was killed at Bentonville.

[40] George Valerino Young, of Mississippi, then a senior at the university. He was a Confederate major in the Civil War.

[41] John Berry (1798-1880), a builder and contractor and farmer of Orange, who represented the county in the state senate, 1848-1852, 1864, and 1866; in the commons in 1862; and in the conventions of 1861 and 1865. He was comparatively uneducated, but was possesed of "hard sense" and considerable ability.

you, or to the Legislature, as you may prefer. He intended coming to Raleigh, but heard you were absent.

A letter was received to-day from a Committee of the Dialectic Society at Chapel Hill, requesting you to deliver the next annual address before the two Literary Societies. I enclose a letter from the citizens of Mecklenburg Va.

No other letters of importance.

Mr. Stone was burried on last Thursday.

*From William W. Morrison.* U.

Raleigh,

Aug. 22nd, 1848.

\* \* \* \* \*

There was a letter received today from the Sheriff of Duplin stating that James K. Hill,[42] the Senator elect from that County, died on the 18th. inst. I presume you will be at home in time to order an election to fill the vacancy.

Nothing of importance has taken place since I last wrote to you. We have received all the election returns, and Mr. Manly's majority will be about one thousand. The Whigs will have a majority in the Legislature of two on joint ballot.

The Rough and Ready Club meets every week of late and we have very enthusiastic meetings. Both parties are doing all they can to get up a great excitement.

No very important business in the office.

*From John R. Witherspoon.* U.

Brookland, near Greensboro', Ala.,

October 4th., 1848.

My Dear Friend,

Owing to the circumstance of my being pretty much engaged for the last eight or ten days, at the solicitation of the Synod of South Carolina, in preparing a History of the Churches of my native District, Williamsburgh, with a view to its publication, I have delayed longer than I could have wished to forward the en-

---

[42] James Kenan Hill, of Duplin, was a member of the commons, 1834-1835, and of the state senate, 1838-1840, 1844-1846.

closed letter.[43] I may also add that I have been much interrupted with a more than usual routine of company.

\* \* \* \* \*

Eliza, with a view of avoiding the usual prevalence of yellow Fever in Mobile, has been spending the summer on a small Farm [page torn] between this [place and] Greensboro', a fine, healthy situation, with [page torn] improvements, excellent water, and in a very agreeable society, one mile from Greensboro'.

Our son, Jos. Graham, has been residing for the last three years in Arkansas. He writes me that he enjoys good health, and that his Practice at the Bar is steadily improving, though the Country, like Mississippi and Alabama, in many respects, miserably poor, especially as to money, being entirely under *Democratic Rule.*

In regard to the present condition of this State, I can say but little in its favour, on the contrary, I consider its present condition, in comparison with what it ought to be, miserable indeed, especially as regards its Politicks, its fiscal operations, and these owing to the extreme ignorance of the great mass of the people, and the want of moral honesty among the better informed, nor can it be thought strange that, with such a population, this State may reject the honest, firm, patriotic, and virtuous Taylor, and yet give its vote for that miserable *War-hawk* or 54°-40', late of the Senate of the U. S.[44]

But I cannot think that any of the common herd will be found so debased as to vote for that miserable and contemptible Paltroon, the little Magician, now associated with the insignificant, self-styled Barnburners. I entertain no doubt, however, but that the honest and virtuous Taylor will receive an overwhelming majority, unless God, in his Righteous Displeasure, should, on account of the great depravity of many of our chief Rulers, scourge this Land and Nation with his just indignation. My humble and feeble Prayer is, that He may visit us in Mercy.

The crops of cotton, at least in this Section of Country, and as far as I have been informed, have been more or less injured with too much Rain during the past Summer, or with the Caterpillar. Still I think there will be a tolerably fair crop made.

The Corn Crop, I am induced to believe, will be abundant, and this [is] a very favourable season for gathering both, but the prospects of sales very discouraging. The Season, as far as [I]

---

[43] The letter was an application for an appointment. The omitted paragraph also relates to that.

[44] Lewis Cass, the Democratic nominee.

have learned, has been one exceedingly favourable to health, perhaps no one more so within the last ten years. We have had no case of Fever as yet in our family, either white or coloured, that has required medical aid. One of our near, and an old Neighbor, Mr. Thomas Webb, brother of the Doctor in Hillsboro', died on the 23rd., ult., no other recently.

Having [page torn] proper place above, to express my honest opinion of Jas. K. Polk would [page torn] him to be one of the vainest or most ostentatious [torn] our Country, hence his great *imbecility*, and the *cause* of the consumate fooleness of all the prominent measures of his administration, being scarcely *adequate* to manage the civil affairs of a single State, he has the vanity, or foolery, to think that he was competent for thirty, and the half of Mexico and Oregon besides. As well might my son, who manages for me, undertake to manage ten or twenty of the largest plantations in this, or any other, County in the State, nor can I think any better of that Warhawk who *stupidly* and *pertinaciously* held out for his 54, 40 in the Senate, as if to destroy the Southern States, I hold *both* in equal *abhorrence*.

A report having, through some channel reached us, that you will visit us soon after the 1st. Jan'y next, I need not attempt to express the sincere gratification we will all feel to see you, and every other member of your much esteemed family, to whom we cordially unite in our best regards, and shall be pleased to hear frequently from you.

*From James W. Osborne.*                                      U.

Wadesboro',

October 11th., 1848.

Yours reached me just on the eve of my setting out for this place, to address the Whigs of Anson, and I tho't it advisable to postpone my reply until after I had performed that duty. From the indications in my District, I am impressed with the conviction that we will sustain the vote given in 1844. The chances are that it will be increased. I hear of many democrats who will vote for Gen'l Taylor, and no Whigs who will vote for Cass. From the manifestations at the large meeting which took place on yesterday, I incline to the belief that the full Whig vote will be given. You can assure the central Committee that this district will do its duty. It in August last, under the melancholy defection of the Whigs of the State, increased the vote for Governor over that of '44, and I anticipate a similar result in the presidential election.

I observed some remarks on the state of this district in the Register, which I thought were inappropriate—calculated to place me unfavourably before my brother Whigs in the State, and based on information manifestly erroneous. Favours from that quarter I do not expect; unwarranted censure, however, I might hope to escape. This District is probably more reliable than any other in the State. Such at least, has been its uniform character, and I do not doubt such will be the case in November.

As to the Rail-Road project to which you refer. I can only say that all my preposessions are in favour of the Raleigh scheme. I think I once urged the subject in your presence, and Gov. Swain's, at the University in June, twelve months since. It has my warmest wishes as a North Carolinian, but I fear it is wholly impracticable. In the first place, there is no hope of obtaining the necessary means for its construction, unless the State will take 2/5 ths., or 3/5ths. of the stock. Is this, in the present state of feeling in North Carolina to be expected. I am convinced that all efforts to connect the State with the work will be failures, and I am equally convinced that there is no hope of success but in that principle. Besides this, shall the road take the direction of Salisbury, Greensboro', Raleigh. If this should be the case, it will pass within 40 miles of the Danville Road, and nothing can prevent the connection between the two roads. The source of proffit to it from travel will, in this way, be in a great measure cut off, and this will greatly increase the difficulties of obtaining subscriptions for stock. From Richmond to Charlotte by the way of Danville is not less than thirty miles more than by Raleigh. This consideration must be decisive as to the course which travel will be likely to take. I have not now time enough to present the considerations which I think conclusively show the Road to Raleigh to be impracticable. The question then resolves itself into this; whether it is better that the West should be without a Rail Road at all than to run to Danville. In that alternative, I do not think there can be any hesitation among fair-minded men. All that is asked is that the Legislature would give us a Charter to construct the Road to Danville. We can build it, we believe, by the capital which we can command at home, and that which we can obtain abroad. A refusal to grant a Charter will be unheard of in an enlightened age, and will utterly destroy the Whig party—indeed the organization of parties as it now exists—and divide us in sectional factions, which will embarrass our legislature, destroy our harmony for years to come. I repeat, Sir, that in labouring to construct the Charlotte Road, I was most anxious to effect the connection with Raleigh, which I hoped would be its necessary consequence. I deeply regret, however, to come to the conclusion that this work is wholly impracticable, and that for the West, there is no scheme left but the Danville Road. I am satisfied that this is the Western view of the subject, and that no other plan is likely to be acceptable to them.

*From John Stafford.*[45]                                        U.

Snow Camp, N. C.,

October 19th., 1848.

I have rec'd your communication of the 11th. Inst., and must express my gratification at its mild and manly terms, compared with the insult and abuse received from others on the subjects referred to. I can say to you with truth that your information so far as the Election of Mr. Waddell and State Officers is concerned is without any serious foundation. The Society of Friends, to which you allude, will vote for Mr. Waddell as heretofore, except such as attend their yearly Meeting in the County of Guilford on that day, which may deprive Mr. Waddell of some five or six from this neighbourhood. As for myself, I am not at all connected with that Society, and therefore shall not attend the Meeting. I expect not only to vote for Mr. Waddell but do all I can honestly do to secure his Election. I think it important for various reasons, but one prominent reason is his order of talents. I can not however say quite as much for the prospects of Gen Taylor just in this section. It is not the Society of Friends only that will not vote for him, but many others. I do not mean that they will vote for Cass, or Vanburen, but they will not vote atall. The Society of Friends are all Whigs because they voted against General Jackson (I presume it is so with your Excellency and myself) and not because they voted for Jackson and then turned against Mr. Vanburen and Mr. Polk. I could name many who will not vote for Gen. Taylor, but such as are his admirers need not fear, he

---

[45] "Squire" John Stafford, of Orange (later Alamance) County, noted for his sound sense and sober judgment.

will get a great number of Democrats, and it will all turn out right in the end. I think it not best that men should be elected by too large majorities, for to that cause I attribute the self willed and self irresponsible course of Gen. Jackson. Had he been Elected by a small majority, he would have taken less "Responsibility upon himselfe." Ex Governor Morehead, Mr. Waddell, and Senators Mangum & Badger were as anxious for Gen. Jackson's Election in 1828 as they were for Gen. Taylor's now. I shall be now like I was then, I will hold off untill they wish to get out of their difficulties, and should I live I shall be as willing to help them as ever. They may possibly live out their day of Military Glory and be willing to fall in with me again, not for the sake of my company, but for the sake of my path.

Both History and observation teaches me that it is not good policy for Republics to place Military men at the head of affairs. I pass by what History teaches, and ask what else has brought Mexico to her present condition. Any comment on the subject by me would be useless to you, if it could even be included in the space of a letter. I must however, examine for a moment the subject of Washington and Taylor being Military men of the same character, as stated in your letter. You know I never study law further than to know how to keep out of it, and will therefore excuse me if I err in that science, then you will understand me as believing that Washington's war was strictly defensive and therefore justifiable by the Law of Nations. On the other hand, if I as a Magistrate of Orange, order an inferior officer or private individual to bring him who misbehaves, before me, he is bound by Law to do it, but if I tell the officer or individual to take a stick and knock the third person down, I then become a "whitened wall," and the officer or individual is under no obligation to obey what I say to him as a Magistrate. And as I understand it, when the citizens of a republic are aggrieved so that they are willing to jeopard their lives and property in a war, and they, through the mouth of Congress, their proper representative, say we will incur the danger and expense rather than suffer the injury, the Executive has the right to say to inferior officers go and execute, and they are bound to obey. Now it seems to me that if my position is reasonable there is no need of argument to show that General Taylor's war was not ordered by legal authority, but by the Mandate of him who was set to Judge according to Law, and ordered him to smite, contrary to the Law, therefore the war was unconstitutional and aggressive. But it is said that if Gen

Taylor had not went into it, he would have been called a coward, therefore it would not do for him to resign, and what if he had been called a coward; if doing right is cowardice, who ought not to be a coward? Does your Excellency or any body else expect that if President Polk had ordered Gen. Taylor to go and capitulate London instead of Monterey, that he would not have waited for Congress to have spoken, even at the risk of having been called a coward. Did not Mr. Duane, Secretary of the Treasury under Gen. Jackson's administration, and Senator Mangum, resign before they would obey unconstitutional Mandates without asking whether they would be called cowards. The limits of a letter forbid my saying any thing respecting Gen Taylor's talents, but you know that honesty first, then ability was Republican creed. In reference to the subject of slavery mentioned by you, there is an entire mistake in your information. Slavery as existing under the constitution and laws is part and parcel of what we are bound to obey, its existence in the State renders it necessary that laws should be passed to regulate it. Therefore the withholding votes of any kind from State affairs is not the case. But with respect to the propriety of extending Slavery over the Territories under the jurisdiction of the general Government, which are now free, there is certainly a great difference of opinion amongst the honest citizens of North Carolina. I am always inclined to speak my opinions frankly and without impugning the motives of others and therefore I must say that I cannot reconcile it with justice to take that Territory from a Sister Republic under duress, and all the time be promising the citizens of these Territories that if they would submit and come under the Laws of the United States that they should have its protection, and be entitled to the right of Habious Corpus, and trial by Jury, and as soon as we get the power establish against their will and wish Laws which they have abolished which will deprive many of them of the Elective Franchise, and compel them to carry the evidences of their freedom in their pockets. The colour of the skin by the Laws of African Slavery being primafacia evidence that the person is a slave, and will therefore throw the Burthen of proof on him. No sensible man can doubt that if slavery is extended over New Mexico that the citizens there will be much harrassed by pursuit after runaways if not themselves subjected to slavery. I must adopt the Language of John Kerr, Esq., Elector on the Taylor Electoral Ticket in this District when I say that "no Christian community can wish to see the evils of slavery enlarged." I but adopt the language of the sage of Ashland when I say "no good man can wish to see Slavery extended over the Mexican territories." I but adopt the language of the sage of Monticello when I say "no slavery or involuntary servitude (except for the punishment of crimes) ought hereafter to exist in any Territory under the jurisdiction of the General Government," and in view of this subject "I tremble for my Country when I reflect that God is just, and that his justice will not sleep forever." If Slavery be an evil (and so it is admitted by many) I can see no advantage in its extension. If it is right and profitable I think those who enjoy it, ought not to complain at its monopoly, consequently I would say, leave it where it is, but never extend it where it does not exist. It is no advantage for a man of my age to labour in Error, and I am glad to receive admonition from Your Excellency, or any other person in any thing like good taste. , but the late attempts to put to shame every thing that was not favourable to give Taylor even at the expense of truth, and by Mob violence and threats in this neighborhood, and the casting aside of Mr. Clay in the Philadelphia Convention, because he was not in favour of extending Slavery over Mexico, has caused me to adopt the motto of No mob violence, or unconstitutional Law, No Division of the Union, No extension of Slavery. But Free Soil, Free Labour, a Free Press, and Free Men. This I conceive to be in perfect harmony with the Spirit of the American people, should I be wrong, it will only be necessary to convince me of my error and I will leave it immediately, for I have no idea of "fighting it out, right or wrong." Common observation, Natural and Moral Philosophy have long ago taught me, that error can never be cured by pursuing the course of error, any more than falsehood can be made truth by adding yet another falsehood. I would be extremely happy to know your opinions respecting Slavery as it exists in this Country, whether it is right between man and man, and whether you believe it can always exist in its present form without danger both to Master and Slave.

With sentiments of the highest regard, I remain,

Yours in much hurry.

To *James W. Bryan.*    U. Bryan Mss.

Raleigh,

Nov. 9th, 10 P.M, [1848]

The following Telegraphic dispatches have been recd here in reference to the election—

| | | | |
|---|---|---|---|
| Vermont | Maj[ority] Taylor | | 5,000 |
| Massachusetts | " | " | 13,000 |
| Connecticut | " | " | 3,000 |
| New York | " | " | 30,000 & |
| | 30 Whigs to Congress— | | |
| Pennsylvania | " | " | 10,000 |
| Maryland | " | " | 3,000 |
| Louisiana | " | " | 2,000 |
| Tennessee | " | " | 8,000 |
| Kentucky | " | " | 15,000 |
| Ohio | Maj[ority] Cass | | 10,000 |
| New Hampshire | " small maj. | | |
| Michigan | " do but I Whig to Congress | | |
| S. C. | " do | | |

Returns from Virginia induce the belief that Taylor has carried that. Nothing yet from Georgia. In N. C. 15 Counties heard from shew a gain on Manly's vote of 1800, & the State is safe for 5,000 maj. Waddell is beaten 7 votes but will contest the election. Taylor's victory will equal Harrison's.

*From Hugh Waddell.*    U.

Hillsboro',

Nov'r 19th., 1848.

Your favour of the 17th. inst. reached me on yesterday. What *can* I say in return for the fraternal spirit which is breathed in every line of it? *Thanks* for individual acts of courtesy or kindness are common, and according to the forms of this cold and ceremonious world are usually deemed a sufficient return. But a *chain* of acts, the kindest, most generous, & most disinterested, continued through 20 years, & through every reverse of Fortune, without one link wanting, even from temporary alienation or unkindness, binds me to you with a power which I could not break if I would. I will not pray God to place us in such relative situations as might enable me to shew my sense of your friendship, for this were to invoke evil on your head, for the selfish purpose of exhibiting how joyously, and with what alacrity I would fly to your relief. But if I may innocently implore his aid, I do so, to enable me to manifest, not to you, but to the world, how deeply, how indelibly, your affection has engraved itself on my heart. Perhaps His inscrutable Providence may yet put it in my power to aid in binding other and still fresher laurels on your brow, for you may remember a very inconsiderable animal in the Fable once rendered a very important service to the King of the Forest when in the toils of the net.

As to the proper course to be pursued in the odious contest with Berry. I am wholly at fault, but supposing that notice should be given him, I ordered it and gave to the Sheriff a written notice to be served two days after the result of the election was announced, but it so happened that that Officer did not see him on the day I furnished him with the paper, but went on the day after to his house, and found he had left home for Goldsboro'. He then went the day following, & left the notice at his house, & on his return home served another Copy personally on him.

You say (I observe) that if the result of the election, if legal votes only were counted, would have been favourable to me, I owe it no less to my friends than myself, to persevere in the contest. In answer I will only remark, that after the strictest scrutiny into the Books by the Sheriff, aided by some of the most intelligent Whigs of the County, 26 men have voted for B. who had *no* Land, & 8 or 10 who had made Deeds of Trust, did the like, & the Sheriff assures me that after searching his Books *carefully* he cannot find three votes for me which can be successfully assailed by the Democratic party.

You know the Sheriff, and I have implored of him not to mislead me, that I would not contest the election unless he was certain of my success, & after this appeal he still insists upon the truth of the above statement. In addition to this, I may state, that the return from C. F. Faucett's precinct was not properly authenticated, & that I objected to the Sheriff's receiving it.

The case was this: 2 of the 3 Inspectors certified that Berry had rec'd 67 votes, and I 27. Bennett Hasell refused to join them, but wrote under their certificate one of his own, in which he stated that he concurred as to 60 votes, but protested as to 7, whose names he gave, & his reasons for refusing to accept or receive them. 3 were without Land, & 4 had made Deeds of Trust. I objected to the Sheriff's receiving the entire return, it not being "signed by the Inspectors" as the Law requires, but also, that if accepted at all, it could only be for *60* votes, as that return was signed by the *Inspectors*—the 60, if that were accepted as the return, would make a *tie*—the Sheriff, however, accepted the return. I deem him wrong, but was glad for my *own sake* that he received the return. He said he thought it would be taken before the Legislature by one or the other, & he preferred to put it out of the power of the Democrats to charge him with party motives. I have sent a *very short* Memorial to Gilmer to present to the Senate, & asked him to shew it to yourself & Badger, & if wrong, that you would have one drawn right, & present it for me. I thought it might give offence to the overzealous Democrats of the Senate if I gave a full statement of the frauds practiced by the party, although I *had drawn* a full and pungent Memorial, setting forth all these things, & upon a "sober second thought" concluded to take the matter by the *smooth handle*.

I suppose the Committee to which the case will be referred will direct a Commission to certain Justices here to take Depositions, & have requested Gilmer to have certain persons appointed, & if at difficulty, to obtain the aid of Giles Mebane. The Chairman ought to direct the Commissioners here what notice Dep'ns might be taken upon, & I have requested Gilmer to see to it. I know the Democrats will throw every obstacle in the way of a speedy determination. But if the Whigs cannot elect a Senator without doubt, I should be extremely pleased that they would postpone the election 'till my case is determined, and I would thank you to suggest this to our friends. As to the Supreme Court Judge, I am also anxious, but of the propriety of postponing any thing, our judicious friends are the best judges.

I might say that, in addition to the facts above set forth, that there were 4 persons who insisted that they were entitled to vote, at Wilkinson's, & at J. R. Holt's, & were refused by the Inspectors, although they were unquestionably entitled, and offered their Deeds, and also to swear to their qualifications to vote.

There were 2 Precincts where the Democrats knew by *previous concert,* the *Trustors* would be permitted to vote. C. F. F's, & Hurdle's (Nichol's) & they all flocked there. Such votes were *rejected* elsewhere. Where the Democratic Inspectors presided, the false and *fraudulent* votes *were received.* So much are our friends excited, that even John Newlin told some Democrats that if he had belonged to the party *before,* after seeing the frauds of this election he would leave the party forever. They have said that they knew that the men *presented* would vote again, for they knew they would be permitted, and the *fines for voting could be easily raised* by friends, and they would carry the election *in spite of the Whigs.*

*From James Graham.* U.

Earhart Place,

Nov. 22nd, 1848.

On my return from Raleigh I learned that nothing was doing for Gen'l Taylor in the mountain district. So, I went directly to Rutherford to attend Gen'l Logan's Musters, and make speeches for Taylor. At the second Muster, where I made a speech; or rather the day after, I was taken very ill with Bilious Feaver. . . . Gen'l Taylor got a capital vote in Rutherford, and in the State and Union. I am *delighted* with the result. Now the *impracticable* Whigs will again try to Rule, or Ruin, our Party. If they Rule they Ruin it, and if they can't rule, they still try to ruin it. No man ever had greater cause now than Gen'l Taylor to say "God save me from my friends."

I shudder for the anticipated conduct and character of the Legislature. Both branches are equally divided unless unforseen accident decides otherwise. Will you direct the *"Semi-Weekly Register to me at Vesuvius Furnace,* during the session of the Legislature; from the first of the session. If you have time, write me about the 1st. of Dec'r to this place. I wish to go to Columbia so soon as I can gain a little more strangth, to sell, or give away some Cotton.

*Extract from Message.*[46]

Nov. 27, 1848.

\* \* \* \* \*

In surveying our territory, with an eye to the present interest and wants of the people, I am more than ever impressed with our destitution of facilities for cheap and speedy transportation. In this regard, however unpleasant may be the admission, I am

---

[46] *Journal of the House of Commons,* 1848-1849, 375-379.

forced to the conviction that we labor under greater disadvantages than any State in the Union: And that we can never be equal competitors with their citizens in our Agriculture, the predominant pursuit among us, until these disadvantages are in a great degree overcome. The man who is obliged to transport in waggons over no better roads than ours, a distance varying from sixty to two hundred and fifty miles, at the speed of twenty-five miles per day, can no more contend for profits with him who has the advantage of Railroads, or good navigation, than can the Spinning Wheel with the Cotton Mill. Had we ever been in a more favorable situation in this respect, and had the impediments which now beset us been imposed by human power, no sacrifice would be esteemed too great to effect our deliverance and restore our prosperity. It is therefore a theme for the profoundest consideration of those enjoying the confidence of a constituency thus situated, and intending to requite it by a faithful devotion to their interests, what can be done, or ought to be undertaken, to remove these grievances and place their industry and labor on an equal footing with those of their fellow citizens in other States? It must be admitted, that from Geographical causes, the question was originally one rather difficult of solution. And our former enterprizes in Internal Improvement, having failed from causes not necessary to be now commented on, the State has of late years taken no action in constructing works of this kind, and many good citizens appear to have concluded that further efforts were in vain, as our doom to privation in this particular was fixed fate. Meanwhile, other States have pushed forward their improvements (some of them with a rash and extravagant hand, it is true, but in the main with the most beneficial results,) overcoming obstacles far greater than any which impede us, and obtaining for themselves still greater advantages over us in the competitions of the market. We are therefore impelled not only by all the more obvious considerations which appealed to us in former times, but by a reasonable self defence, to abandon further hesitation and adopt at once a system of improvement, commensurate with the wants and interests of the State. Too much should not be undertaken at once, but what may be attempted, should be thoroughly completed. As the commencement of such a system, and a basis, on which other works may be engrafted, to any desirable extent, as our means may from time to time permit, a Railroad from Raleigh to Charlotte by way of Salisbury, appears to me of the first moment. This scheme has not been much considered heretofore, and derives much of its importance from a kindred work, now in progress from Charlotte to Columbia, South Carolina. Already from Raleigh Northward, continuous lines of Railroad and Steamboat transportation stretch through the towns of Virginia, and the great cities of the North, to Portland in Maine, and Buffalow on Lake Erie. Similar works also exist, or are in progress, with a certainty of completion in the course of a year or two, extending from Charlotte Southward through Columbia, to Charleston: and again from the former of these through Augusta, and the interior of Georgia, and Tennessee to Nashville, as well as to the Mississippi, at Memphis, and to New Orleans, by way of Montgomery and Mobile. Through a part of North Carolina alone, a link is wanting, to complete the grand chain of communication, from one extremity of our Country to the other, and to furnish to the whole nation those facilities of intercourse which the inhabitants North and South of us, enjoy in their several sections. The connexion proposed therefore, being, as it were, a bridge over a space now impassible by steam cars, having at either end the great highways of the North and South, with their numerous branches for a thousand miles in both directions, promises a reasonable remuneration for the outlay of its construction, from "through" transportation: and in a military and other points of view, would be of great national advantage. Had nature supplied us with navigable rivers like the Mississippi, flowing from Raleigh and Charlotte, respectively, to New York and New Orleans, or even to Charleston, all would at once perceive the benefit of the junction of the two, through the interior of the State, as clearly as did the genius of Clinton, that arising from the union of the Hudson with the great Lakes. The parallel may not be yet perfect in the present state of Railroad conveyances, but is destined to be at no distant day.

But the foregoing are merely incidental inducements to undertake this work. It is commended to us as a great North Carolina improvement, appealing to our interest and State pride, by arguments which it were almost criminal to overlook. 1st. It would open to the market of the world an extensive region of the State, reaching from the Capitol almost to the Blue Ridge, of great fertility, and capacity for indefinite improvement, by reason of its Agricultural, Mineral and Manufacturing resources; containing in the Counties within twenty-five miles of the most direct route, more than 230,000 souls; and within fifty miles, more than one half of our whole population, who are far removed from places of trade, and dependent entirely on the common waggon and common road for all their transportation. The occasion will not permit me to dwell on its numberless benefits in this regard, which will readily occur to any one who looks on the Map of the State with the eye of a statesman and patriot. 2nd. It would add incalculably, to the business and value of one at least, (and ultimately of both), of our present Railroads, in which the State has so deep an interest, and make them productive Stocks. 3rd. It would unite the middle and eastern with the western section of the State, in a domestic trade, and exchange of productions too cumbersome for the present mode of conveyance, besides facilitating travel for health, and social intercourse. 4th. By running over the most practicable route from Raleigh to Salisbury, and thence turning southwestward to Charlotte, it would bisect the State for more than a hundred miles, bringing the most remote on either side within fifty miles of the Railroad, and would be in a favorable location for being extended still farther west, from the former place, and to connect advantageously by means of Turnpike roads with all the Northwestern part of our territory.

Whilst it would confer these benefits on the interior Country, now depressed and partially excluded from all profitable commerce, the objection has not been overlooked that it does not point immediately to the seaboard of our own State, and to an increase of the prosperity of our market towns. Let them, however, not despair. Its advantages will be afforded to them in due season. After the completion of the main track, a branch to Fayetteville, or other point on the navigable water of the Cape Fear River, will be of easy accomplishment. Its extension from Raleigh to Goldsboro' would be invited by the connexion thus to be formed, between Wilmington and the upper Country, and eventually it might realize that scheme of a central Railroad, consecrated by the patriotic labors of Caldwell, in an extension from Goldsboro' to Beaufort. Whether, therefore, we regard it as a single work, or as the groundwork of an extensive plan, the Road from Raleigh to Charlotte appears to be the important improvement which should first engage our attention, and our energies. And I accordingly recommend it to the patronage of the Legislature, to the amount of one half, or at least two fifths of the capital, necessary or its construction. The distance is about one hundred and sixty miles by the mail route, and the cost of the Road and equipments over such route as may be selected would probably not exceed $1,600,000. As an inducement to aid this scheme, it presents an opportunity for disposing of the Raleigh and Gaston Road, as has been intimated in the preceding remarks, on that topic. A Company might be organized to embrace the entire line from Gaston to Charlotte, and the Road now owned by the State transferred to them at a fair valuation, in payment of her subscription for stock. Of the particulars of such an arrangement, if favored by the Legislature, no delineation is here required. I have already treated of this subject with more minuteness [than] may be appropriate, in an address of this kind, because it has as yet attracted but little of the public attention, and from a deep impression of its utility in alleviating the condition of our industry, and reviving the waning fortunes of our countrymen—while it gives an assured hope of profit on the capital invested.

\* \* \* \* \*

*From William H. Battle.*                                   U.

Chapel Hill,

Nov. 28th, 1848.

From the enclosed note you will discover that our friend, Waddell, thinks that I ought to go to Raleigh. Our friend Gov. Swain is inclined to be of a contrary opinion, but he advises me to send you the note, and to ask you to advise what, under the circumstances, I ought to do. I have great reluctance to appear in the character of an electioneerer for so important an office as that of Judge of the Supreme Court, but I am willing to yield my objections to the opinions of those in whose judgment and sense of propriety I have entire confidence.

An answer at your earliest convenience will add another to the many obligations conferred upon me.

*[Enclosure]*

*From Samuel F. Phillips*

*to William H. Battle.*

Rich'd Ashe came to R. Saturday Aft. and came away Sunday Morning. He said that he heard nothing about the Judge-ship— except: that it was very doubtful who would be elected. Judge

Strange's friends were pressing his claims. He saw Judge Pearson & *asked him to take a drink which the Judge declined.* Lillington took Pearson off & very evidently had a private chat with him.

Mr. Waddell—who has *not* been to Raleigh—says that he knows of nothing but that Judge Pearson is moving Heaven & Earth for himself. Judge P. sends Mr. Waddell word that he hopes he, (W.) will beat Berry—& that he is even willing that Judge Battle should gain his vote (W's).

Mr. Waddell says that he thinks you ought to go to Raleigh. He knows that (abstractly speaking) it is improper to electioneer for that office, but as Judge Pearson is there exerting himself, he thinks that upon the whole he would go. This is the substance of a private chat he gave me in the St.

With much Respect

*From William E. Anderson.*          U.

Wilmington,

Dec. 1st, 1848.

*   *   *   *   *

And now, my dear Sir, will you permit me to appeal to the remembrance of our boyhood days for a personal favor; one which will cost you nothing but the exercise of that influence which your position commands, & which your more unfortunate friend has never acquired. My brother[47] obtained from Mr. Polk the unsolicited appointment of Navy Agent at Pensacola, an office which had been vacant *many months* before he received it, & of course no one was displaced for his benefit. It constitutes the chief means of supporting his large family, but as he has been a friend of the present administration, he apprehends that he may possibly become the victim of political proscription in favor of some friend of the party about to go into power. He can obtain the testimony of a large majority of his fellow citizens of the Whig party in Pensacola of the perfectly satisfactory manner in which he has discharged the duties of his office, & of the high & honorable character of his conduct throughout the Presidential campaign; though decided in his preference, yet on all occasions

---

[47] Walker Anderson (1801-1857), a graduate, and briefly, a professor of the university. Strangely enough, in the light of this letter, he was three years later chief justice of Florida.

expressing a high appreciation of General Taylor's character, & in fact, taking no more active part in the matter than every high minded man in our country has a right to do, by giving expression to his preferences whenever it was incumbent upon him to do so. Yet I, his brother, a good Whig, and a warm supporter of General Taylor, feel some apprehension that the contamination of proscription for political opinions will not be wholly inactive in our party. I have determined to use my humble influence with those of my own party, whose position is more commanding, in his behalf. To Judge Nash and yourself, first, have I applied, I beseech you refuse me not. I merely wish one or two letters expressive of your personal knowledge of my brother to persons I will presently designate, and your influence with our present Senators. Mr. King[48] of Georgia, and Mr. Badger are both looked to as probably filling the office of Secretary of the Navy under the coming administration. This is the department which has the entire control of the appointment, and a word from you would be powerfully effective on the subject. One or two letters to influential Whig members of Congress, say Mr. Clayton[49] and Mr. Winthrop, or any other whom your better information would suggest, would greatly favor my wishes, and above all, should it be the pleasure of our legislature to displace Mr. Badger from his present high position and make you his successor, as I have heard it thought probable, you can do every thing, my dear sir, to promote the ardent wishes of an old personal friend, and a zealous friend of our mutual political opinions.

Permit me, then, to enlist your friendship in my brother's behalf. He has seen much of misfortune, but his integrity and his highminded honor have never abondoned him, and I trust that those whom fortune has more kindly favored will not feel reluctant to use their influence for one whom in other days they admired and respected.

---

[48] Thomas Butler King (1800-1864), of Georgia, a native of Massachusetts, lawyer, and planter on St. Simon's Island. He was state senator, 1832, 1834-1837, 1850, a Whig member of congress, 1839-1843, 1845-1850, collector of the Port of San Francisco, 1850-1852, and was active in the building of the Southern Pacific Railroad. He was commissioner of Georgia and the Confederacy, 1861-1863, to encourage trade with Europe.

[49] John Middleton Clayton (1796-1856), of Delaware, a graduate of Yale, who studied law at Litchfield. He served in the lower house of the legislature, 1824, was secretary of state of Delaware, 1826-1828, National Republican United States senator, 1829-1836, chief justice of Delaware, Whig senator, 1845-1849, secretary of state, 1849-1850, and negotiated the Clayton-Bulwer Treaty, and was again senator, 1853-1856.

To James W. Bryan.          U. Bryan Mss.

Raleigh,

Decr. 5th, 1848.

\* \* \* \* \*

B. F. Moore has been elected Atto. Genl by one vote over MacRae.[50] Gaither reelected in mountain riding. W. N. H. Smith [51] of Hertford in Edenton, three or four trials for a Judge of Supreme Court, but no election—Strange getting most of the Democrats about 77, Pearson 57, Battle 39. Result very doubtful. Pearson still here, and he and his friends sanguine. Strange attended the Federal Court and went home. The democrats can elect whom they please; among the Whigs. Pearson, I learn, calculates on a majority of them, but I think it doubtful how they may go eventually.

There has been one trial also for a Judge of the Superior Court. Bragg, W. A. Wright,[52] A. Mitchell [53] voted for, against Moore but no election. I hear today that your Senator[54] may be in the field, before the matter ends. Two refractory Whigs from Buncombe & Henderson still hold out, I learn, against Badger. But I am told that one of them will resign in a few days. By the last accounts there is a prospect of electing a Whig from Yancy—and Waddell thinks he will establish his claim to a seat. There is a favorable disposition to adopt my recommendation and abolish County Courts, and I believe it can only fail, for want of agreement about details. There is also some favor shewn to my project of a Railroad Westward.[55] It being a part of the central scheme

[50] Duncan Kirkland McRae, 1819-1888), of Fayetteville, a distinguished lawyer, educated at William and Mary, and the University of Virginia, was Federal district attorney, Whig candidate for governor, consul to Paris, where he was secretary of the Ostend Conference. For a time he was a Confederate colonel. Later, he edited the *Daily Confederate* in Raleigh. After the war, he lived in Memphis and Chicago.

[51] William Nathan Harrell Smith (1812-1889), of Hertford County, graduate of Yale, a lawyer, who served in the commons, 1840, 1858, 1865-1866, and in the state senate, 1848. He was a Whig member of congress, 1859-1861, and narrowly missed being elected speaker. He served in the Confederate congress, 1862-1865, and was chief justice of North Carolina, 1878-1889.

[52] William Augustus Wright (1807-1878), of Wilmington, distinguished lawyer, director W. & W. R. R., bank president.

[53] Anderson Mitchell (1800-1876), of Wilkes County, a graduate of the university, state senator, 1840, 1852-1854, member of congress, 1842-1844. He was a judge of the superior court, 1865-1875.

[54] William H. Washington.

[55] Graham, in reply to a senate resolution, sent a special message to the legislature at this session, urging the construction of a railroad from Gaston to Charlotte. The final bill for the North Carolina Railroad directed the construction of the road from Goldsboro to Charlotte.

and holding out hopes towards Beaufort, if the members in your quarter would espouse it, it can be carried. Wm. Sheperd informs me, that he will go for it, and I hear from Salisbury that in that region, they will abandon the Danville project, if the State goes heartily into this. Genl. MacRae of Wilmington Road is here, and favors it, if the link from here to Goldsboro' be made a part of the original plan. I told him if his section of Country would come up to aid the scheme, that could be done.

The Electors are generally here, and meet tomorrow. The question is mooted, whether members of Assembly vacate their seats, by acting in that capacity.

*    *    *    *    *

*From Hugh Waddell.*                                            **U.**

[Hillsboro'],

Dec'r 10th, 1848.

I know you feel such interest in the result of the contest in which I am now engaged, that you will pardon me for sending only a *half sheet,* as excuse for a letter, as it is all I have time to write by this mail. We have proved some 12 of B's voters to be *without* land, some 12 who had made Deeds of Trust, 4 who being fully entitled to vote, offered to vote for *me* & were rejected by Demo: Inspectors.

On Monday, I feel confident we shall shew 6 or 8 more of the *Lackland* men among Berry's friends.

So far we hear of no attempts by B's party here to shew spurious votes among the Whigs, except that the G. Jury at Nov'r Court presented 2 & one of them (Mann Patterson's son) was so clearly entitled to vote that Mangum told me he refused to send a Bill. But if we had any fears before, the conduct of Mr. R. today would have removed them. He gave me notice for Wednesday next, which I accepted instanter, & in a few minutes after he went to Norwood to take it back & say they could not begin before Monday week!! & insisted they could not have their witnesses here by Wednesday, but N. treated this admirably, by replying that they should not have the excuse of absence of their witnesses to offer, for he would himself engage to have every witness here by Wednesday, 10 o'clock! Furnish me the names, Sir, said N. The

Shff & 3 Deputies are now in Town & they shall all be in the saddle in 10 minutes!

After much fluttering, Mr. R. agreed if the Shff would deputize some *Democrats* he would try to have his s'pos executed. N. gave him notice that he should regard B. bound by the notice already accepted by me, & should treat his failure as a virtual *abandonment* of the contest.

They probably have had but one hope from the first, & that was to prop their spurious voters by proof of their qualifications rather than to attack any of mine. But I am told they can do neither.

I asked the Shff this morning whether they could help themselves or hurt us & he is certain they cannot.

They cannot produce 5 on the Whig side, he says very confidently. I think now I will not go down before the end of next week, as I can do nothing till the proof is there.

*From Robert Hall Morrison.*    U.

Cottage Home,

Decr. 18th, 1848.

\* \* \* \* \*

Receive my thanks for your kindness in sending your Message. After a careful perusal I have no hesitation in regarding it, as one of the most dignified and able State Papers I have seen for many a day.

I congratulate you on the very high estimation in which your administration is held by the public.

We are all well at home. Majr. Hill [56] and Isabella went by

---

[56] Daniel Harvey Hill (1821-1889), a native of South Carolina, graduate of West Point, was a lieutenant in the Mexican War, and came out a brevet major. He resigned in 1849 to become a professor at Washington College, where he remained for five years. He was, briefly, a professor at Davidson, and then became superintendent of the North Carolina Military Institute. As colonel of a North Carolina regiment, he was in command at Bethel in 1861. He rose successively from brigadier in 1861 to lieutenant in 1864. He was removed from command of the Western Army because of his protest against Bragg, and had a bitter quarrel with President Davis for refusing him a court of inquiry. After the war he was an editor for some years, president of the University of Arkansas, 1877-1884, and then of the Georgia Military and Agricultural College. He was one of the three distinguished Confederate soldiers who married daughters of Graham's sister, Mrs. Robert Hall Morrison.

Salem and left Mary Anna and Eugenia there. We have not heard from them since they left Danville.

Your Bro. James is still in delicate health.

May every blessing crown your life and rest on your family.

1849

*From Patrick M. Henry.*                                      U.

Leaksville, N. C.

Jan'y 5th, 1849.

I take the liberty of addressing you a few words concerning a matter of deep interest to my future welfare and in regard to which I beg of you a little aid.

You may well remember, that, a short time previous to the close of the War with Mexico, a Bill for the raising of ten New Regiments for the further prosecution of that War, was brought up for the action of Congress, and that it failed to pass. I was recommended by a considerable number of Officers of high rank for the position of a *Field Officer* in one of them; but the failure of the Bill to pass, and the uncertain chances of any Civilian of whatever claims and merits to get in our Regular Army since it's reduction to the old Peace Establishment, have caused me to abandon all attempts to obtain an Appointment of a military character. But, my friends have induced me to apply for a Civil Appointment under the coming Administration, since they know that both in a Civil and Military consideration I can bring many strong points to bear well on the future President.

I have the satisfaction to know that some very influential friends are now exerting themselves in my behalf at Washington, and I hope, Governor, that I am not asking too much at your hands, when I request you to confer with *Col. Paine* and *Mr. Gilmer* (who, I am certain, are my friends) on the subject-matter of this communication, and who have been recently addressed by me on the subject. Any suggestion you may jointly make for my guidance will be most thankfully received, and acceded to.

I am particularly anxious to get also the co-operation of Governor *Morehead*, Messrs. *Badger* & *Mangum*, which co-operation and your aid, Sir, will ensure me a good opportunity to be heard and favourably received in my application.

I am desirous to obtain a *Minor Bureau,* or a *Clerkship,* in one of the Departments at Washington, which may afford me an opportunity to obtain hereafter such a position in our Army as I may seek.

I would be glad to have some suggestion from you, Sir, on the subject, and, if convenient, please address me at Leaksville, N. C.

### *From Hillsborough Committee.*[1]    U.

Hillsborough,

January 12th., 1849.

Your friends and neighbors, anxious to evince their great satisfaction at your return once more to renew the social relations of which your absence in the service of the State has for some time deprived them, have appointed the undersigned a Committee to tender to you a public dinner, at such time as may suit your convenience.

They perform the duty assigned them with great pleasure, and would only add, for themselves individually, the hope that you will not decline at their hands, this public but simple and heartfelt testimonial of their esteem for private worth, and public fidelity.

Very respectfully, your friends,

Stephen Moore, Jno. W. Norwood, Pride Jones, W. A. Norwood, H. K. Nash, P. B. Ruffin.

Committee.

### *To Hillsboro' Committee.*[2]

Hillsborough

January 13th. 1849.

Gentlemen

I acknowledge with great pleasure your favor of yesterday, expressing the gratification of my friends and neighbors on the occasion of my return among them, after an absence of four

---

[1] From the *Hillsborough Recorder,* January 17th., 1849.
[2] From the *Hillsborough Recorder,* January 17th., 1849.

years, and tendering me, a public dinner, as an evidence of their esteem, and a renewal of the social relations which have so long, and happily, existed between us.

I cordially assure you, and those in whose behalf you offer this hospitable civility, that the reunion cannot be more agreeable to them, than it is to myself; and although no demonstration could add to my sense of the kindness and attachment of a Community to whom I am indebted for so many, and repeated favors, I do not feel at liberty to disappoint their wishes, by declining the invitation. The time may be at your convenience, rather than my own, on any day after the ensuing week, which will be occupied by necessary attention to my private affairs.

*From Giles Mebane.*                                    A.

Raleigh, [Jan. 18, 1849.,]

Thursday morning.

I introduced your scheme [3] for a Rail Road in the Commons and immediately after the bill offered by Mr. Ashe[4] was introduced with an amendment of Col. Joyner; these last measures have gone through the Commons & await the action of the Senate. It is believed here they will go through. Joyner's amendment will re-establish the Raleigh & Gaston Road. The State takes two millions on the Central road, it runs by Raleigh and Salisbury to Charlotte. An appropriation of forty thousand dollars for the Neuse, & twenty five thousand for *tar* River were added on to the bill to give it more *momentum*. Now if the million of individual stock can be subscribed, all will be well. My colleagues voted against the measure, but Jones has since pronounced a *eulogy* upon it, and opposed Dobbin's plank road because it might injure

---

[3] A bill, drawn by Graham and introduced into the commons by Mebane, provided for the charter of a railroad from Raleigh to Charlotte and conveying to it the state's interest in the Raleigh & Gaston Railroad. It failed in the senate, and heavy pressure was exerted upon the legislature to charter a road from Charlotte to Danville—the "Danville Connection" as it was called—but the East was violently opposed, and Ashe prepared and introduced into the senate a compromise measure, which Mebane introduced in the commons where it was passed. Defeated in the senate, it was reconsidered and passed by the deciding vote of Speaker Calvin Graves, who, as it happened, was fully aware that he was thereby terminating his political career.

[4] William Shepperd Ashe (1814-1862), of New Hanover, lawyer and planter, a state senator, later a member of congress, 1849-1853, again state senator, 1858, and a delegate to the convention of 1861. He was an eager advocate of internal improvements, and was for some years president of the Wilmington & Weldon Railroad.

the great Central scheme. Dobbin's measure has failed in the Commons.

The Senate referred the constitutional questions between Waddell and Berry to the Supreme Court. The opinion [5] was written by Judge Ruffin, and is in favour of Mr. Waddell, he is now believed to be entitled to the seat.

We shall adjourn Monday week, if not earlier.

*Speech at Hillsboro' Reception* [6]

January 23, 1849.

Mr. President & Gentlemen

I tender you my heartfelt thanks, for the kindly greeting which has hailed my arrival at home; for this occasion of conviviality, on which, so many of my friends and neighbors, without regard to differences of political opinion, have left their usual pursuits and business, to extend to me, the hand of welcome; and for the cordial and friendly spirit, in which, the sentiment just announced, has been received, by the company. Such demonstrations of regard, from a community, with which I have been connected in the intercourse of business, in the conduct of public affairs, and in the offices of good neighborhood, since my first entrance on the stage of manhood; which, indeed, fostered my youthful aspirations, and has uniformly cheered me, with encouragement and confidence, give rise to emotions, which language cannot express, and command the best return, of my gratitude and affection.

Called to administer the government of the state in times of high political excitement, I cannot hope the performance of that duty has met the approbation of all; and therefore I accept the compliment you convey, as a tribute to the purity of my intentions rather than my abilities, and to the neighbor and fellow

---

[5] A reference by the legislature to the supreme court was most unusual, and, ordinarily, would have been refused, but as Judge Ruffin said, in opening his opinion, the question, while not official, involved purposes of a judicial character, and the court decided to consider them and give their opinion. The reply is printed in 40 N. C., 422.

[6] From the *Hillsborough Recorder*, January 24th., 1849. Graham was introduced with the following toast: "It is not to the successful partizan, the able and distinguished statesman, or the patriotic Executive Officer, that we are here assembled, to tender our warm and sincere congratulations: but to welcome back a tried neighbor and friend, to his own home, and to our homes and firesides, with our hearts in our hands."

citizen, rather than to the chief Magistrate. I should however, be untrue to myself, not to avow that it has the approbation of my own conscience, on the most dispassionate review, and I cheerfully submit it to the arbitrament, of that matured and chastened public opinion, which in the end, is apt to settle all things aright. But the scene before me is an evidence, that the widest difference of opinion on public affairs, is not inconsistent with personal respect, and that the social intercourse of our community, is not Poisoned with the rancour of political faction, I trust, it will be always thus. Howsoever diverse may be our views of national politics, the ties of a common interest, and daily familiarity, our mutual dependence and connection in society, render the good wishes and opinion of political opponents at home often as important to our happiness as most of friends at a distance. While the proprieties of this festival forbid any allusion to the topics which divide parties, and are too apt to excite unpleasant feeling, they, I trust, allow, and it may be expected from the position I have occupied, that I shall submit a few brief observations on the domestic concerns of the state. It is remarked by a philosophic historian that "that public virtue, which the ancients denominated patriotism, is derived from strong sense of our own interest, in the preservation and prosperity of the free Governments, of which we are members". If this were true, as applied to the republics of antiquity, it is eminently true of our own country and times. Governments to secure and preserve the affections of the people, must not only guarantee and protect them, in the enjoyment of political and social rights, but afford them the means of rearing and educating families, and making reasonable gains from their labor; and we are taught by observation that unless these facilities are afforded him, the American patriot, has no escape in breaking off all local attachments, in leaving the graves of his ancestors, and the home of childhood, and removing to a country more favored in these respects. In the language of a statesman of the last age, "to make us love our country, it must be lovely," it must be such as we would desire it to be. And, what nature has not provided, must as far as practicable, be supplied by our own efforts. The state must therefore in an age of civilization and progress, not content itself with the exercise of its ordinary functions of dispensing justice, and suppressing crimes, but must look to the interest of universities of education and improvement. It has been my fortune to put in operation at the seat of Government, a school for the Deaf & Dumb, recommended by my predecessor. Seconding the efforts, of that christian philanthropist, Miss Dix of Massachusetts, I have recommended, and have rejoiced to see the Legislature enact a law for the erection of a Lunatic's Hospital. As the advantages of education in a university are to the country, and in colleges and schools of the higher order, the state and our immediate neighborhood is highly favored, but I regret to repeat here what I have urged, I fear in vain elsewhere, that our system of common schools is yet exceedingly defective, and I fear at the next decennial census of the Union, it will not have elevated us above the grade we occupied at the last, of being among the lowest in the scale of education in the whole union. And I am clearly of opinion that it will never be what it ought to be untill a general superintendant shall be appointed, to supervise and administer it throughout the state. But even facilities of education will not retain and control our population here without prosperity and success in their pursuits of industry. In our present situation, therefore, the important inquiry is now, can we better our condition and promote our prosperity. Doubtless much may be done by an improved Agriculture, the primary and important pursuit among us, and by a more general introduction of Manufactures and the Mechanic arts. But in an age when the world around us, has made and is making such wonderful strides in cheapening and quickening transportation, when states are embarked in the glorious rivalry of increasing the wealth and civilization of their people, we must be left behind in the race, unless we employ the means which they employ. In my opinion, therefore, we can do nothing half so beneficial to the farmer of the interior of North Carolina, as to make a Railroad which shall give him free access to the markets of the seaboard. And if he who, by improving agriculture, "makes two ears of corn or two blades of grass to grow, where but one grew before," is to be reckoned among the great benefactors of his country, he who shall enable us to carry a thousand pounds at the same price, and in less time, than we carried one hundred before, is hardly less entitled to our gratitude & esteem. Entertaining these views I have freely recommended bold measures on these subjects by arguments, and considerations which I have not time to dwell on here. As the Chinese who has never employed the horse as a beast of burden but uses the power only of the human animal, excepting the aid of a most inferior species of ox, is far behind the European or American, who makes one of this most useful of animals, perform the service of a dozen men, so we who employ the old modes of transportation over roads, not much better now than when they were lumbered over by the baggage wagons of Cornwallis on his way to the memorable fields of Guilford Court house, cannot compete with the Iron horse, whose food is fire, and whose breath is steam, which carries at a load from 50 to 100 Tons at the rate of 10 miles the hour against 2 Tons with a good waggon & team at the rate of 20 to 25 miles per day. All must own as experience has abundantly proved elsewhere, that if in 24 or even 48 hours a planter of this, or the counties west of us, could go with his produce to Wilmington, New Bern, Norfolk, or Petersburg, buy his supplies & return in a like time with even 50 cents on the Hundred weight in each direction, that produce would be worth here within 50 cents on the Hundred weight of what they are worth there, and on the contrary the heavy groceries would be cheapened by the diminished cost of their freight here. Our productions are chiefly the food of man, the heaviest articles in proportion to value that are consumed, corn, wheat, live stock, &c. Our competitors are in New York, and the Northwest, we meet in the seaports. He who gets them cheapest can realize the most profit. Example before completion of New York Canal and now. But not only produce but live stock, whole droves of cattle, hogs, &c., sent from Michigan to Boston arriving with regularity of mail.[7]

*From Hugh Waddell.* U.

Raleigh,

Jan. 26th, 1849.

I have been intending to write you for several days past, but delayed doing so with the hope that I might give you the pleasing intelligence of the passage of the Central Rail Road Bill, & have now that pleasure. It passed the Senate last evening by the casting vote of Mr. Speaker Graves!! & such was the surprize and delight of the friends of the measure, as well members as others, that all hands raised a shout of joyous acclamation, which was heard by me in my room. I fear it may be reconsidered to day, as the opponents of the Bill have been making desperate efforts all night,

---

[7] At the conclusion of his speech Graham offered a toast:
"Our true policy at the present juncture—The improvement of the mind, the improvement of the soil, and, above all, improvement in the means of transporting the fruits of the soil to the best markets."

I hear, & there are two or three who dodged, but may be in their places perhaps, & yet defeat it. It is said that its fate will depend upon the success of the Bill for the improvement of the Cape Fear & Deep Rivers, which is in the Senate, & may be killed on its 3d. reading, especially as it involves the appropriation of $15,000, to Lumber river & which if rejected will so offend two Senators that the great measure will fail.

I have no time now to go into particulars of the other matters of general interest, still before the Legislature, as the mail is about being closed, but will conclude by informing you that I deem it certain I shall *not* obtain my seat. The vote is to be taken this evening at 3 o'clock, and Lewis Thompson[8] having gone home, and Albright and Halsey[9] both confined to their beds, will leave me in a minority, for these wretched creatures have made it a *party* question. Excluding Bargainors in Trust, Trustees, & cestui que agreeably to the unanimous opinions of the Judges of the Supreme Court, Gilmer demonstrated two days since that I was elected by 12 or more votes, & yet the Democrats pretend to believe that Berry is elected by 5 votes.

No one doubts, as I understand, that if Halsey and Albright were in their seats I should be given the seat. My friends think of giving it the "go bye" if they find I must be defeated on account of the absence of those Senators—

Hawkins *refuses to vote,* & I shall therefore be defeated by the casting vote of the *Speaker.*

Complaints are idle, indeed contemptible, & I shall not indulge in them, & have not uttered a word of impatience since my arrival, but my position has been more painful than I can describe. I have not visited the Senate Chamber (or called on any of the members) except once when I went there in company with some strangers & remained but a few minutes. The heavy expense I shall incur is a source of real distress to me, but it is inevitable. It has been suggested that the expenses of the contest & the per diem of the contestant ought to be paid by the State, but I doubt if Democrats will listen to it.

---

[8] Lewis Thompson (1808-1867), of Bertie, a graduate of the university, an extensive planter in North Carolina and in Rapides Parish, Louisiana. He was a member of the commons, 1831-1832, 1840, and of the state senate, 1844, 1848.

[9] Joseph Halsey, representing Washington and Tyrrell.

*From Charles L. Hinton.* U.

Raleigh,

Jan'y 26th, 1849.

All of the Internal Improvement schemes have passed. The Central Road Bill by the casting vote of the Speaker in the Senate, the Wilmington bill by a considerable majority in the House, the plank road, Deep River, and all have gone through the third readings. Last night there was great rejoicings, the crowd seemed to think the State was redeemed.

Really I could not enter into it with any spirit. I endeavoured to look to consequences, in doing so, I could see the benefit that *might* result to Wilmington, and the Deep River, but to no other section. One half of the Gaston road is given to the old Stock holders and bondsmen if they will put it in thorough repair, the bondsmen to be released from their obligations to the State.

I doubt very much whether they can do it. That portion of the road from this place to Goldsborough will prevent the Stock being taken in the Central Road. It is a dead weight, which can't nor won't be carried. Yours was the only practicable scheme, it would have succeeded, this can not.

The Legislature have authorized the Pub. Treas. to borrow money to pay off the old Rail road debts, they will do nothing more, and the road must stop very soon.

Halsey and Albright of the Senate are confined to their rooms, fifteen of the members have left, and many more will leave to day and tomorrow.

The Legislature may adjourn Monday night, they can't get through sooner.

*From Patrick M. Henry.* A., G. P.

Leaksville, N. C.,

January 27th, 1849.

Some few days ago I took the liberty to address You a few lines on a subject of all-absorbing interest to myself, and presuming that you may not have received it on account of your removal to Hillsboro', I take the liberty to say a few more words in regard to the same.

274 N. C. DEPARTMENT OF ARCHIVES AND HISTORY

You may remember that during the last Session of Congress a Bill was offered to raise and organize *ten additional Regiments* for the prosecution of the War, and that it failed to become a law. I desire to state to You, that I had the honor to be recommended to the President for the *command of one of those Regiments* by all the principal officers (General, Field and Staff) on our line of Operations; but, as anxious as I may have been to enter permanently the *Military Service* of the Country, the failure of Congress to authorize those Regiments, and the reduction of our Regular Army, since the confirmation of peace, to the Standard of the old *peace-establishment,* have rendered my prospect for doing so quite remote and uncertain. Having abandoned, for the present, the attempt to get an Appointment in the Military Service, I have entered upon the experiment to obtain a *Civil* appointment of a senior grade under the coming Administration, —a *Clerkship* in one of the Departments at Washington, where I can watch for a favourable opportunity to attain to the *Military* promotion so much desired, should one occur in a reasonable length of time. The marked discipline of my Company of *N. C. Volunteers* in Service in Mexico, brought me particularly to the notice of Generals *Taylor* & *Wool,* Colonels *Hamtramck,*[10] *Paine, Butler, Temple*[11] and *Tibbalt,*[12] and of all other Superior Officers under whose command I served. Indeed in a communication to you from Mexico, I took the liberty of sending you a *portion* of the evidence which I was able to produce in order to establish what I now say; to which I *now* invite your attention. I mention these things, Sir, because I think they may present me in a favourable manner before General *Taylor* or his *Secretary* when I apply for the office alluded to; and I feel proud in being enabled to say to you, that I will be fortunate enough to get the aid and influence of a portion of our Delegation in Congress and of some distinguished friends in *Civil life.*

I am very solicitous to obtain from yourself, Gov. Morehead and Judge Badger some little aid in the forwarding of my object.

---

[10] John Francis Hamtramck (1798-1858), of Virginia, a native of Indiana, a sergeant in the War of 1812, who, for distinguished service, was appointed to West Point. After graduation he remained in the army until 1822, when he resigned. He was a planter near Shepperdstown, Virginia, 1838-1846, and a captain of militia. He was colonel of the First Virginia regiment in the Mexican War, and was governor of Saltillo, 1848.

[11] Robert Emmet Temple (1809-1854), of Vermont, a graduate of West Point, who served in the Seminole War, and resigned in 1839, and practiced law in Albany, New York, was adjutant general, 1846-1847, and colonel of infantry, 1847-1848, returning afterwards to his practice.

[12] John Williston Tibbatts, of Kentucky, colonel of infantry, 1847-1848.

I have no right I will acknowledge, Sir, to *ask* any thing of you of such a character, yet, Sir, I hope that you can grant it without any violation of rules prescribed for yourself in matters of the kind. I have received flattering letters from the two gentlemen alluded to, and hope that it will be compatible with your feelings to co-operate with them in giving me a letter recommending to the *Head* or *Chief* of the Department to whom I may apply. The aid and influence of Yourselves in Connection with the action in my favour, of a goodly number of our Members of Congress and of the State Legislature, will, I am Certain, place me in a favourable position before the Secretary, and cause me to count upon almost certain success. In regard to my qualifications to fill such an office, permit me to say, Sir, that a long experience as a *Classical Teacher,* and the advantages resulting to me every way by several tours of service in *Florida* & *Mexico,* have rendered my education a *systematic one,* so well adapted to the duties and functions of the Office alluded to.

I refer you to my friend Col: Paine for an exposition of whatever claims I may have to the small boon now sought for, as I am certain that he would be glad to communicate with You on the subject.

I beg of you, Sir, to pardon the liberty I thus assume; but in consideration of the *past,* I hope to find a favourable response on your part. If you should be disposed to address me in reply, your communication will find me at *"Leaksville, N. C."*

## Editorial Tribute[13]

## GOVERNOR GRAHAM

### January 31, 1849.

The distinguished statesman who for the last four years has filled the Executive Chair, has closed the duties of his station, and is about to retire to private life. A sense of justice constrains us to say, that so far as we have heard an opinion expressed, the sentiment is nearly universal, that the duties of Governor have never been discharged with more ability, fidelity, and zeal for the honor and interests of the State, than by the late incumbent. The friends of William A. Graham, on his accession to office, were ardent in their anticipations of an able and satisfactory administration. A review the most scrutinizing, of the manner in

---

[13] From *Hillsborough Recorder,* January 31st., 1849. Quoted from the *Newbernian.*

which he has discharged the duties of his office, would demonstrate, we are satisfied, that Gov. Graham is one among the very few statesmen of the present day, who has not, in one iota, disappointed even the predictions of his warmest political friends. The reason is obvious, Mr. Graham belongs to a class of statesmen, (too rare in these days,) who have built their reputation upon a solid basis. The ground work of real statesmanship is laid in sound moral, as well as political principles. No man can be a true statesman who does not carry into office a consciousness of inflexible integrity, a generous, self-sacrificing spirit, and an enlarged view of duty, that looks beyond mere personal, temporary, or public advantage. If we have read the character of Gov. Graham aright, as presented to the eye in his actions, he possesses all these high qualifications, in an eminent degree. Hence, we have seen in the conduct of his administration, no littleness, no temporising, wavering line of policy, no truckling to party dictation, on corrupt influence, no unjust favoritism. Party spirit has in vain assailed his acts. Brought to the scrutiny of truth and reason, his political actions have stood forth as conspicuous for the purity of motive that prompted them, as for the wisdom that foresaw their operation. With others, we have believed that some of the measures of the Internal Improvement of the State, which he has recommended, overlooked the existing state of things among us, and were unfortunately too far in advance of the spirit and enterprize of our citizens to be of practical utility. But, on the whole, have not the measures which he has adopted in order to meet the consequences of a previous injudicious expenditure of public money, been the very best, that under the circumstances could have been adopted?

Governor Graham will carry with him into private life the proud consciousness of having served the State faithfully, and of having deserved and won, the approbation of those who called him to fill the Executive Chair of his native State.

*From James W. Osborne.*                                         U.

Charlotte,

Feb. 17th, 1849.

Since your relief from gubernatorial duties, and your return once more to the great interests of private life, I hope the advantages and pleasures of the change will not entirely withdraw your attention from the great interests of our good old State. It is certain that a crisis at present exists in her affairs which must exert a most material influence on her destiny. The Rail Road scheme which has been proposed, is certainly the best which her condition admitted, and more completely meets the demands of her business than any other which can be devised. Its accomplishment will however I fear be attended with the greatest difficulty, & the intrinsic difficulties which lie in its way have been greatly augmented by the awkwardness and illiberality of the charter. If the copy of the charter published in the Register is correct the second and seventeenth sections are contradictory, and however they may be construed when taken together—and the object of the work is considered—will create great difficulty in the minds of many persons. By the one section the work is directed to be constructed to Charlotte; by the latter to stop at Salisbury. Another omission in the charter of great importance to the success of the work is a provision that the company should have corporate existence when [a] sum short of a million of dollars is subscribed.

Organization on the subscription of a small amount of stock is necessary to secure the remainder by creating offices whose incumbents are specially employed in the business of procuring subscriptions. But the material difficulty is the provision which gives the entire government of the road to the State. She appoints two thirds of the directors, and it is impossible but personal prejudices and political attachments should control each administration. But the directors chosen may not be, and probably will not be stockholders, and can have no interest in the work, beyond the discharge of their official duty. Had the charter provided that one half the directors chosen on the part of the State should have been stockholders, this difficulty would have been obviated. Capitalists will refuse to embark in the work to any great extent, and foreign capital will be wholly withheld. The provision that five hundred thousand dollars shall be paid in is placed so unintelligibly in connection with the provision to the same clause that I feel great difficulty in understanding it. The legislature with great patriotism and a most unexpectedly liberal spirit seems to have been sadly deficient in business talent. With all these which I have refered to only with the hope that wiser men may suggest some move in which they may be obviated. I am most anxious for the success of the great enterprise which will work the political, moral, intellectual, and commercial redemption of the State. It is, [and] has been with me a cherished idea for several years, and while I lay claim to no share of sagacity, beyond the most ordinary of my race, I foresaw that the construction of the Charlotte road to Columbia would drive our reluctant Legislature sooner or later to some great effort for North Carolina. You will observe that a convention is to be called at Salisbury in June. It was the earliest period at which the occurrence of the Courts would permit the participation of the bar in the deliberations of such a body. It will, if fully attended, and rightly conducted, exercise a most important influence on the success of the work. Let me suggest to you and our friends in the centre to respond to it warmly and promptly. Really when I look at the condition of the State, and the prospect held out to her by this greatest of State enterprizes, it does seem to me that her sons should do little else than labour until it is accomplished. I have no fears if we do not become dispirited. There is so much of fact and argument connected with the enterprize (and the difficulties to which I have referred are so much within the reach of time and wise legislation) that I have no doubt but that the sober, reflecting, intelligent, Presbyterian people will build the work. I rely on their intelligence, their virtue, for everything noble in the future welfare of the State, as all that is glorious in her past history, has been accomplished by them. Let me state to you a fact, that in the obtaining of subscriptions of stock for our Charlotte road, there was not a Presbyterian minister in this Community who did not subscribe, and who did not urge his people to do so. I have written you a long letter on this most important subject. Commit me in the glorious struggle for the good old State for any duty which I can perform, and which the absolute necessities of my situation will permit.

I will deform this letter by a single word as to the Mint. I need not say to you how many painful personal considerations make that office desirable to me at present. To ambition it has no attractions. A seat in Congress, which this district would give me with enthusiasm would be certainly more agreeable to my tastes, and be more condusive to that desire. But it is impossible that I should accept it. I must labour or be irrevocably ruined. The office at the Mint is worth $2000 per annum, and comes in aid of my profession, which it will be my duty and my pride to pursue with industry, and I hope success. A letter from yourself to Mangum would probably secure his influence in my behalf. I have written but have had no reply.

*From George Washington.* U.

St. Augustine,

Feb'y 19th., 1849.

I presume of course, that you have heard before this of my removal from New York, and of my present location in Florida. Having succeeded so badly Merchandizing, I have again taken up the Law, and passed my examination last Fall, when I was admitted to all the various Courts of the State; and so far I think my prospects flattering. As a natural, or I should rather say, unavoidable concomitant with Law, in this country, I have also taken up the subject of politics, I was one of a few who originated a Rough and Ready Club in this City, which I think has rendered some "aid and comfort" to the good Whig cause. And it has so happened, that we have had three elections this past Fall, which afforded a plenty of warm and steady work. In the second election, the Presidential, we reduced the majority of the democrats here, (which had already been reduced a good deal from the previous year) to one half; and at the next election, (that for Corporation officers of the City) we succeeded in electing Gen'l Hernandez,[14] Mayor, which in this City, that has always been considered the Gibraltar of Democracy in this State, was a great achievement. He is the first Whig Mayor the City has had, I believe, since the cession of the Territory. As, from some cause or other, I was led to take a prominent part in all their trials, the good people of this vicinity have expressed a wish to send on representation to Washington, with the view of getting me an appointment to some office. The office of Surveyor General was first spoken of, and I have determined to accede to it; but some circumstances have occurred within the last few weeks, which have induced me to change my views of the office, and the determination now is to apply for the Live Oak Agency, of East Florida. This suits my situation much better than the other. Instead

---

[14] Joseph Marion Hernandez (1796-1857), a native of Florida, and a Spanish subject, who was naturalized when Florida was acquired; delegate to congress, 1822-1823, member and speaker of the territorial legislature, brigadier-general in Indian War, 1835-1838, and capturer of Osceola.

of conflicting, its duties will rather accord with my legal pursuits at this time, and in addition it gives me facilities for forming extensive and valuable acquaintances in the various sections of the State. Now, as it is delicate to undertake a hazzardous business, it is particularly unpleasant to meet defeat when once it is undertaken; and I have therefore taken the liberty of asking your assistance in the matter; which, from your acquaintances in Washington, I am disposed to believe will be very valuable to me, and which, if not inconsistent with your views and feelings, will be conferring a great obligation upon me. A letter from you to Judge Mangum and to Mr. Badger requesting them, if not inconvenient, to take some interest in my behalf, provided (as I suppose they will not recollect me, tho' I believe I have had the pleasure of being acquainted with both of them) the representations that go on from here are satisfactory, will, I think, be of much advantage. Also, if you are sufficiently acquainted with Mr. Thomas Butler King, of Geo'a to feel justified in writing him on such a subject, a few lines to him, of the same purport, will be of still more advantage.

The office I am seeking for, is an appointment made by the Secretary of the Navy, and the impression seems universal that he will be called to fill that Department; at any rate, he is Chairman of the Naval Committee of the House, and from a neighbouring State, and I think a word from him on such a matter will carry much weight. I have mentioned these gentlemen as those of influence with whom you were perhaps on terms of sufficient familiarity to induce you to write to them on such a subject, but if there are others to whom you think a line would be of service, may I beg that favour. If you conclude to write Mr. King, may I beg that you will write him soon, as the present incumbent's term of office will expire shortly, and in addition, if Mr. King is appointed Secretary of the Navy, I should not like to be forestalled, especially in that quarter.—

. . . We have had a most delightful winter here—up to this time we have had no frost at all.

*From Patrick M. Henry.*                    A., G. P.

Leaksville, N. C.

Febry. 24th, 1849.

I was truly gratified to receive a reply to my two communications to you in regard to my application, and beg leave to return heartfelt thanks for the lively interest manifested by you in my behalf.

I entertain opinions similar to your own in regard to letters of Credit generally presented by those who seek *place* at Washington, Yet, Sir, permit me to say to you, that although *you* may not be *personally* known to Genl Taylor, yet I am certain that your *name* is well known to *him,* and I desire your aid more than that of any other distinguished Civilian in the State in presenting my claims before him, as little as I may have the right to ask it &c

Since my last communication to you I have had the satisfaction to receive the most flattering letters from the following distinguished gentlemen directed immediately to Genl Taylor. Viz—

| | |
|---|---|
| Col. R. T. Paine | Hon. Kenneth Rayner |
| Col. Andrew Joyner | Hon. J. C. Dobbin |
| Hon. Edward Stanly | Hon. D. S. Reid |
| Hon. W. H. Washington | Hon. W. B. Sheppard, |

and also very flattering ones from 20 other Members of the Legislature. From *Hon. A. H. Shepperd* I hear very good accounts in Washington, and from him and Messrs. *Venable* and *Boyden,* I expect considerable aid.

If, Sir, *after all,* you deem it inconsistent with the line of action prescribed for yourself in matters of the kind to give me a letter to *General Taylor's Secretary,* I would thank you much indeed for such letters to Messrs. *Mangum* & *Badger* as will fairly introduce me to them and such as you may deem to be most expedient, or may choose to give me under the circumstances. As I expect to proceed to Washington quite soon after the Inauguration, I would be glad to receive them so soon as may suit your convenience.

## RESOLUTIONS

### ORANGE COUNTY RAIL ROAD MEETING[15]

March 15th., 1849.

*Resolved,* That this meeting is gratified in commending the liberal spirit in regard to Internal Improvement which characterized the last General Assembly, and that they look to a completion of a Central Rail Road through the State as a work of

---

[15] From *Hillsborough Recorder,* March 21st., 1849. The resolutions were written by Graham, who offered them.

the utmost importance to her character and honor as a sovereign, and to the prosperity and best interests of her people.

*Resolved,* That in the opinion of this meeting, the most eligible route for the construction of such a road, from Raleigh westward, whether regard be had to the greater number of persons to be accommodated, the quantity and value of productions to be transported, or its practicableness and cheapness in being graded, will be found through the counties of Orange and Guilford; and its success is therefore a subject of peculiar interest to the citizens of these counties.

*Resolved,* That if, (as we have no doubt will be the case) the route shall be selected which is above indicated, the members of this meeting will use their best exertions to raise a sufficient subscription to grade the road, so far as it may pass through the territory of this county.

*Resolved further,* That ten delegates be appointed by the Chairman of this meeting, to attend a Convention on the subject of this Rail Road, proposed to be held in the town of Salisbury in the month of June next.

The resolutions having been read, the Governor addressed the meeting at some length upon the subjects embraced in them. He spoke of the necessity of works of improvement in North Carolina, to enable our citizens to compete, with any hope of success, with the citizens of other states; and of the importance of this work as a link in the great chain of communication between the Lakes on the North, and the Gulf of Mexico on the South. He expressed it as his opinion that the best location for the road would be through the counties of Orange and Guilford, thence by way of Lexington and Salisbury to Charlotte. He said it was too late in the day to discuss the benefits of such improvements; we had but to look at Georgia and other States, to see the life and energy and prosperity that they impart to the citizens, by facilitating and cheapening transportation. And how is the road to be built? He did not know whether it would invite capital from abroad or not, his opinion was that we need not rely much upon capitalists in other states, nor upon the few at home. It must be done by the bone and sinew of the country, by those who will take a small amount of stock, and pay for it by the sweat of their brow. It must be engaged in as a work to improve the condition of the State, and to enhance the value of the land, and not as a scheme of speculation on the money invested, though the stock may, and probably will, yield something. When the books were opened for subscription, he hoped all who could afford to contribute anything, whether little or much, would come forward and take stock, not enough to injure them, if the stock should not be profitable, but as much as they would be willing to pay for the advantages which such an improvement would afford them.

We have attempted only to give a slight sketch of a few of the subjects upon which the Governor dwelt, and are very sensible that, even in this, we have not been able to do him justice.

*From James W. Osborne.*                          A.

Charlotte,

March 20th, 1849.

I received your kind letter when at Washington and am greatly obliged to you for the interest expressed in my behalf in your letter to Judge Mangum. If I receive the appointment which is of greatest importance to me I shall be much indebted to you. Mangum did not take much interest in the matter. He however wrote a letter to the Secretary of the Treasury, enclosing yours to him and endorsing its statements. He urged as a reason why he should not participate in the matter—his old friendship for Alexander—and the neutrality which he was desirous to preserve between myself and Gaither—who to my surprize through Clingman became an applicant. The only difficulty will be the probability that no vacancy will be created. Mr. Badger does nothing. Indeed his deportment towards North Carolinians in the City was so supercilious—and any efforts to serve them rendered so ungraciously—as to make it my duty to abstain from any application to him. I think indeed if it were not that considerations of a public nature might render it unwise, that it would be only just that his conduct should be exposed in the newspapers. The arrangement of the Cabinet was to him in the highest degree offensive as it must be admitted that some of the appointments were not to be accounted for on any ordinary principles. The only fear in Genl Taylor is that his inexperience in his new Theatre may subject him to imposition by flatterers and cliques. It is clear that the "original Taylor men" are endeavouring to usurp his confidence and divide out the spoils among themselves. It is this circumstance which places the appointment of our friend Mr. Waddel as Minister abroad in a hazardous position. It must however be admitted that the vehemence with which the name of Mr. Stanly is pressed by Mr Badger is another difficulty, which from what I have learned Mr. W. did not have reason to expect. At present the chances of Mr Barringer are decidedly in the ascendant. He has enlisted in his behalf a number of influential friends in other States, whose exertions in his behalf are very active. In the mean time the two Senators do not agree on any one name.

The delegation in the lower house are equally divided, and the result is to place him decidedly in the vantage ground. It is altogether uncertain however whether the foreign minister of the highest grade will be given to the State at all. Events have shewn that in the disposal of important offices the State is not likely to secure much consideration. When all the circumstances are considered it is not a matter of much surprize. The temper of one Senator—and the habits of the other—are equally hostile to such a result. I hope we will have a good administration, tho it does not promise as favorably as I could have desired. The tolerance given to democratic men and democratic opinions do not indicate any decisive reformation or any lasting good.

In the meantime we in North Carolina have enough before us in the great work which has been authorized by the late legislature. Notwithstanding the defects in the Charter and the objections which may be urged against the work on other accounts we can never obtain one so favourable for the interests of the State. Indeed, my impression is, that a work which does not connect the West with Wilmington can never be supported by either section, and it is our duty to get this stock subscribed by all the appliances which we can make use of. I am convinced we can arouse the community, and if arrangements can be made to give labour for stock that we may obtain the amount necessary.

The Convention at Salisbury will take place in June. It is desirable that we should have a full assemblage from all parts of the State, and I hope that the Counties on the road—Guilford, Orange, Wake—will come up to the Convention that we may at least discuss the matter, and take steps necessary for its advancement.

*From Edward J. Hale.* U.

Fayetteville,

April 23rd., 1849.

I am very much obliged to you for your favor, which put me in possession of facts which it would have given me some trouble to hunt up, even if I could have proved them at all, having lost many of my public documents and papers by fire in 1845. Mr. Shepard makes his assertions with so confident an air, that it makes one cautious about contradicting him, except with the proof at hand.

It has given me great pleasure to set the matter right, and I trust that it is done in a *manner* unobjectionable to you. I thought I might, with propriety, enter into the details, even though you deemed it unnecessary, since I was able to refer to your previous denial on the same subject.[16]

Allow me to assure you, that it will give me great pleasure to hear from you on any subject in which you may feel an interest, & that I know that your views of public men & measures will be valuable, whether communicated for the Editorial columns of the Observer, or otherwise. I regret that I am so seldom favored in that way, by those who might benefit the public—& the Observer.

*From William Mercer Green.* A.

Chapel Hill,

May 11th., 1849.

Our friend, Walker Anderson, who received the appointment of Navy Agent (at Pensacola) from Mr. Polk, is threatened with "removal" on account of his politics. To a man with so large a family as he has, this would be a serious blow. His Whig, no less than his Democratic friends, are anxious to prevent it; and would seek the aid of every one who is likely to have influence with "The Powers that be." Among all those of my acquaintance favourably known at Washington, I doubt whether any could render Mr. Anderson more efficient service than Gov. Morehead, Mr. Badger, and yourself. To Mr. Badger I have already written;

---

[16] *Fayetteville Observer,* April 24, 1849.

by the next mail I shall write to Gov. M; and my object in obtruding this communication upon you is to beg your kind assistance so far as you feel at liberty to give it.

Inasmuch as the Office is one not sought for by any of our own citizens, as no one was turned out when Mr. A. was turned in, as he is admitted on all hands to be "honest" and "capable," and as he has faithfully discharged his duty thus far, I flatter myself that you will find no difficulty in giving him the weight of your recommendation. As to the manner or measure in which it is given, you alone must decide.

It has occurred to me that a paper briefly setting forth the capability and honesty of Mr. Anderson, his well known character as a Scholar and a Gentleman, the claims of his large and lovely family, and the fact that his reappointment would be gratifying to a large circle of Whig friends, as well as others, would hardly fail to gain the attention of the Sec. of the Navy. Gov. Swain says that he will cheerfully sign a petition of that kind, and I hope that Gov. Morehead will do the same. If such a paper were drawn I would take pains to have it circulated among Mr. A's friends of all parties in Hillsborough and elsewhere.

I hope, my dear Sir, that I am not imposing either an unpleasant or improper task upon you. If so, do not hesitate to tell me, and I will fully excuse you. In this Academic cloister a man ought not to be expected to know all the etiquette and forms and influences that belong to such an occasion. I may be asking an unreasonable or unwonted favor at your hands, while thinking only of serving an old and dear friend.

Permit me to add, that whatever is done should be done *quickly,* inasmuch as the appointment is expected to be made in a few weeks.

*From Charles L. Hinton.*                                         A.

Raleigh,

May 24th, 1849.

Yesterday I wrote you, saying, it was the particular desire of the friends of the Central road in this place that you should go to Salisberry. Since then I have had a further conversation with Gov Swain who takes a deep interest in it, and says that he will not go unless you do, if you both decline, Messrs. Boylan & Mordecai I think will do so & probably no delegate from this section.

Now, my Dear Sir, I do believe the fate of the road depends on you, by going, the Charter may be secured trusting to such modifications as may be necessary to be made by the next Legislature.

### From William Ward.                    U.

Norfolk,

May 26th, 1849.

I had hoped that my engagements would have permitted my visiting your section of the State, and attending the Convention of the friends of the Central Rail Road, which will convene at Salisbury on the 14th. proximo; the difficulty of getting there, and the time it would occupy, makes it impossible for me to be present, as I had anticipated.

It is probable that the citizens of Norfolk & Portsmouth will have a meeting within a few days, and pass resolutions upon the advantages which will accrue to your State, and to them, by the opening of Rail Road communication between you, and that they will also appoint delegates to attend your Convention to express personally the interest which is felt here, in the construction of the N. C. Central R. Road, and their desire to co-operate to the extent of their ability, by pushing forward the Seaboard & R. Road to meet you, at your terminus.

Hammond Whiting, Esq., the Treasurer of the Seaboard & Roanoke R. Road Co., will attend as a delegate, to whom I shall take the liberty of giving a letter, for the purpose of introducing him to your acquaintance.

He is a gentleman of high standing, a graduate of Harvard University, and has a high estimate as to the advantages which will attend the opening of the improvements contemplated by the friends of Internal improvement in your State.

### From Robert T. Paine.                    A.

Washington City,

June 1st, 1849.

I was told by the Secretary of State that the Mission to Spain would be given to you, and I hope for the honour of our State that you will accept the appointment.

This result (I suppose I may say so different from the expectations of all) was brought about by no recommendations in your behalf; but it is solely the consequence of the estimation in which you are held by the Executive in which the Secretary of State entirely concurs.

Knowing that you took an interest in Mr. Waddell's appointment, in which I most heartily united, I have, though often pressed by the Secretary of State, refused to answer enquiries which I could have answered in relation to your appointment, without in the least laying aside any interest in Mr. Waddell's appointment.

I do not think our friend has at any time stood a chance to get such a situation as we & his friends generally desired for him, and I would have written to him to this effect, but for fear of being misunderstood.[17] I say that I hope you will not decline the appointment if it is tendered to you, yet I do not write for the purpose nor with the wish of receiving an *answer* that you will accept. As I have done or said nothing in the matter, I do not wish to know even your views about it. I may be permitted however to express the very great gratification I shall feel at your appointment to such a post & I feel confident that the appointment of no other gentleman will meet with so hearty a concurrence amongst the people of the State at large. As this will be a spontaneous offering to your merits as well as to the opinions and wishes of the public, I do not think you can be at liberty to decline.

Remember that when I received at your hands the important yet responsible and dangerous office of a Military Command, in a Service beyond the limits of the Country, I sacrificed every domestic duty, every selfish feeling, to the public service, you cannot do more in accepting the post of honor & service that will be tendered to you; I would not wish you to do less.

---

[17] Willie P. Mangum wrote Graham, on May 25, 1849, that, after the most strenuous efforts of his life, he was beaten. "Waddell cannot be appointed abroad." He went on to add that only one North Carolinian could be appointed—Graham himself, stating that he was to be appointed minister to Spain or Russia, "at your choice."

*From Robert T. Paine.* A.

**Washington City,**

June 6th, 1849.

I have learned with unfeigned regret that you had written to Judge Mangum intimating that you could not accept the Mission to Spain if tendered to you. I write now to beseech you to reconsider the matter because it is of the utmost importance that you should not decline the Mission. I saw the President last night, & he spoke very freely & frankly about the matter, & when I expressed my fears lest you might not accept the appointment, he spoke of the probability of such a course as a matter which he would much regret. I repeat now what I wrote in my former letter, that the determination of the President to appoint you to this Mission, is not the result of the recommendation of *any* friend in your behalf; but it has been formed totally independent of such a thing & solely from the high regard he entertains of your character &c.

I am no hand at bestowing compliments & I am sure such would have on you only their proper effect. I shall therefore only say it is of very great importance that you should accept the appointment. If your predilections for Mr. Waddell have any influence in determining you to decline, I assure you honestly & sincerely that he stands no chance, under such circumstances, to get the appointment. I say to you that if you decline the appointment it will be conferred on some other than Mr. Waddell. I have done all that I could do in his behalf; but our old Chief has his own opinion about these matters & I think his opinions are most right and proper. He will listen to no argument or appeal in these appointments, based on sectional views or considerations in the State; but he looks to the views & interests of the Country at large.

Mr. Waddell is not known to the Country.

I continue to hope most earnestly that you will not shrink from the discharge of this public duty. I desire you will say to Mr. Waddell, that I do not think it proper his friends should press him farther for a Mission. The President has frankly expressed his opinion in the matter & has as frankly given his reasons therefor & those reasons I must admit, are good & with me sufficient. I regret as much as any one the failure of our efforts to succeed in our friend's behalf.

## ADDRESS [18]
### DELIVERED BEFORE THE
### TWO LITERARY SOCIETIES
### OF THE
### UNIVERSITY OF NORTH CAROLINA,

### JUNE 6, 1849,

### BY HON. WILLIAM A. GRAHAM.

### PUBLISHED BY ORDER OF THE DIALECTIC SOCIETY.

DIALECTIC HALL, *July* 29, 1849.

SIR:

The undersigned have been appointed a Committee, to tender to you the grateful acknowledgements of the Dialectic Society, for the very instructive and appropriate Address which you delivered before the two Literary Societies, in Gerard Hall, on the day preceding our Annual Commencement, and to request a copy for publication.

Permit us, sir, personally to express our wishes that you will comply with the request of the body which we represent.

With very high respect,
WASHINGTON C. KERR,[19]
HENRY HARDIE,[20]
SAMUEL E. WHITFIELD.[21]

Hon. William A. Graham

---

[18] Reprinted from the pamplet published by the two societies.

[19] Washington Caruthers Kerr (1827-1885), geologist and educator, a native of Guilford County, later a graduate of the university, a professor at Davidson College, and, from 1864 to 1882, state geologist and professor in the university. He was an author and a member of the American Philosophical Society.

[20] Henry Hardie (1823-1868), of Raleigh, who after graduation was a Presbyterian minister.

[21] Samuel Erwin Whitfield (d. 1869), of Aberdeen, Mississippi, who belonged to one of the far-flung lines of the prominent North Carolina family.

HILLSBOROUGH, *August* 13*th*, 1849.

GENTLEMEN:

I have had the honor to receive your favor, expressing the acknowledgements of the Dialectic Society for the Address delivered by me, under their appointment, at the late Commencement of the University, and requesting a copy for publication.

Actuated by the sense of duty which prompted the undertaking of this task, I do not hesitate to comply with the request you have so politely communicated, though satisfied that the Society has estimated the Address above its merits.

I am, Gentlemen, with high respect,
Your obedient servant,
WILL A. GRAHAM

Messrs. WASHINGTON C. KERR, )
HENRY HARDIE, ) Committee.
SAMUEL E. WHITFIELD, )

ADDRESS.

GENTLEMEN OF THE DIALECTIC AND PHILANTHROPIC SOCIETIES:

I come to acquit myself of an obligation I could not disregard, and to attest my sense of the distinction you have been pleased to confer, however much I regret that the cause of letters, and this occasion of ever recurring interest, have not a more fit representative. Though poor must be my contribution to the annual festival of the friends of learning, so redolent of pleasant, but mournful remembrances of the past, and joyful hopes of the future, so cheering to our country and our University, in view of the intellectual harvests which have been here gathered, and of those which are in promise, I could not decline the grateful office of welcoming forth those, who, having finished with approbation their course here, now go forward to the duties and trials of manhood, and of speaking a word of encouragement and counsel to the ingenuous youth, who continue in these peaceful shades, pursuing the same liberal studies.

It would, doubtless, be a most agreeable communication, could one, who after a long separation, returns to bear a part in the ceremonies of this day, and finds in these classic halls, a new generation, emulous in every ennobling quality, announce any discovery or improvement, in an age so abounding in wonderful changes, by which the student could be relieved of the toil and labor now deemed indispensable for his discipline, and by which, youth could be at once invested with the wisdom and learning, thus far attainable only by long years of industrious application. Insomuch as might depend on the suffrages of Collegiates, such an improvement would certainly entitle its author to a place in the most delightful region of those Elysian fields, which VIRGIL has consecrated to Heroes and Sages and the inventors of other useful arts. But however sincere would be the pleasure enjoyed, as well as imparted, by the bearer of such tidings, I am charged, my young friends, with no such mission. It was the consolation of the scholar, under the afflictions of neglect, persecution and poverty, in the monarchies of the old world, that "there was no royal road to learning." Whatever other advantages we have gained under our freer institutions, we have found it equally true, that there is no popular road. The acquisitions of liberal scholarship are neither elective or hereditary, but the results only of the patient toils of genius. Neither place, nor power, nor wealth, can bestow them—no canons of succession transmit them. They are the purchase only of the ingenuous mind. Yielding, therefore, to that necessity which is our common lot, let us not lament nor despond; but rather rejoice, that they are prizes held out for the free competition of all, and endeavor to alleviate our labors, and illumine our path, in their pursuit, by a cursory review of the objects of a liberal education. The subject has no claim to novelty, but it may not be unprofitable, occasionally to examine the grounds of our opinion and practice, though they challenge general approbation.

The objects of a Liberal Education! Why the endowment of Colleges, and establishment of Professorships, and the tedious and laborious course of studies required for graduation?

When Omar, the Mahometan Caliph of Egypt, was entreated not to consign to the flames the magnificent Library at Alexandria, the repository of the productions of the human mind for forty-six centuries of the world's history, he replied: "If there be that, contained in these books, which accords with the Koran, the latter is all sufficient without them; but if there be any thing repugnant to that sacred book, we can have no need of them. Order them, therefore, all to be destroyed." The historian informs us, that they were accordingly made to supply fuel for the luxurious baths of that Capitol, for more than six months, until the whole were consumed. Perhaps, in impatience and despondency of mastering the ponderous volumes prescribed to him, the modern student may sometimes indulge a momentary regret, that a summary, alike compendious with the Koran, had not been digested of the discipline and knowledge required for his instruction, and that all other books, if not doomed to the fate of the Alexandrian Library, had been at least postponed from his tasks, until, with a more matured mind, and greater conversancy with the world, he could perceive the advantage, utility or pleasure he was to derive from learning their contents. If we, like the fanatical and destructive Caliph, aspired to nothing more than a life of conquest, rapine and violence here, and sensual indulgence hereafter, we might readily content ourselves with like views of the extent and utility of study and information.—But formed for a nobler destiny, we are impressed with the necessity of cultivating our powers for its fulfilment, as reasonable and immortal creatures.

The design of all education being to prepare the young for the duties and employments of life, the system has no doubt varied with the phases and progress of society in different ages. When the strongest arm, the most dextrous spear, lance or scimetar, or even the successful combinations of embattled hosts, were the tests of human excellence, and HERCULES or ACHILLES, SAMPSON or RICHARD COEUR DE LION, were the impersonations of all that commanded the admiration of men, there was but little need of a refined taste, a critical knowledge of Languages, of Mathematics, or of Physical or Moral Science. Even in times and countries where learning was esteemed and cultivated, the zeal and energies of its votaries were too often wasted in futile speculations and vagaries, and the aspiring youth, fired with a noble ardor for intellectual distinction, was doomed to wear out his life in the intricacies of a vain philosophy, or a false theology, which has been dissipated, as the mists of the morning, before the light of the Christian and reformed religion, or in the labyrinths of metaphysical disputation, serving no other end than to whet the mental appetite, without furnishing it any appropriate food. And since the establishment of Universities, which were unknown to the Ancients, and have arisen consequently to the revival of letters, after the dark ages of history, much that once engaged their attention, and procured for their sophisters high Academic honors, has been found unequal to the scrutiny of common sense, and of that new philosophy of which Lord

BACON was the founder, and has been exploded as obsolete pedantry.

Having our lot cast in a period favored beyond all others, because blessed with the light of their experience, and the researches and inventions of our own, our scheme of instruction is, of course, designed to fit us to act well our parts, in the maturity of knowledge, and the higher civilization which it is our privilege to enjoy. With Governments of vast and complicated affairs, appealing to justice, truth and reason, instead of force, in every step of their administration; with systems of Law, attempting to define every individual right, and the appropriate remedy for its infraction;—a Medical Art, which puts in requisition a knowledge of the minutest functions of our bodily organs, and calls on all the kingdoms of nature for its remedies;—a Theology, which, though simple and easily intelligible in its essential features, runs back in its details and history, through all the learned languages of the world, to the very origin of our race;—with a Literature, preserving for our use the wisdom and learning of past ages;— when Commerce brings us into acquaintance and friendly competition with all the nations of the earth, and every Art is becoming illustrated, adorned and dignified by the discoveries of Science; a system of Education, corresponding in its provisions with this stage in the progress of mankind, is obviously necessary. And modern nations, sensible of this necessity, instead of leaving such provision to be made by the voluntary and unaided efforts of the friends of learning, as was the case even in the most polished ages of Greece and Rome, have established Universities in their fundamental systems of Government. Not to supersede inferior Schools, but as a part of the same system; to supply the wants of the noble aspirants, whose thirst for knowledge has not been quenched at these humbler fountains of learning. Not that it is expected that every youth can participate in their teachings, however desirable it may be among a free people that all should, but because the State will be remunerated for their endowment, if those who do, shall become worthy representatives of their age and country, in useful and elegant erudition and good morals.

If, in the estimation of CICERO, himself "a sublime specimen of the perfection to which the best parts, with the best culture, can exalt human nature," the education of an Orator, the finished scholar of his day, should comprehend "a knowledge of every thing in nature or art, worthy to be known," this standard ought, at least, to be kept in view, in an age near two thousand years subsequent, and enriched by the prodigious advancement in knowledge of things human and divine, which has been made in the mean time. Tried by this standard, the systems of our Universities are rather deficient than redundant. For, although it were extravagance to suppose, that he expected an education to be completed in the period allotted for graduation with us, yet the foundations here laid, in all their length and breadth, are barely sufficient for the superstructure which he recommends, and of which he afforded so brilliant an example. But if such a model of a thorough education is to be reached, or approached even, in the course of a studious life, it can only be after the mind has been strengthened and furnished for the work, with all due preparation. The course of Collegiate instruction, therefore, while it expands the thoughts, stores the memory with useful truths, and forms and corrects the taste, is carefully arranged by a series of gradations, to discipline the understanding to the habit and the love of study, so that it may acquire the power to labor with perseverence, if not with pleasure, on whatsoever subject its faculties may be employed. And although in its pursuit, we may often stand in need of the consoling advice of Sir EDWARD COKE, to his pupil in the Common Law, that "albeit the student shall not at any one day, do what he can, reach to the full meaning of all that is here laid down, let him no way discourage himself, but proceed, for on some other day, in some other place, his doubts will probably be removed," we must constantly bear in mind, at least in the earlier stages of our progress, that these exertions have not been made by the fancies of pedantic schoolmen, but have been devised with care and deliberation by the concurrent opinions of the scholars and statesmen of our own age, as well as those who have gone before us; and that they being judges, he who hopes to excel in any intellectual employment, will be helped forward to the goal of his ambition by complete proficiency in this course of preparation.

The time would soon fail us, to pass in review the branches of study it embraces, and to vindicate the claim of each, to the place it occupies in the system. But avoiding such tedious recital, and without presuming to invade the province of the learned and zealous Instructors, whose enlightened labors are enjoyed by this Institution, I may be permitted to say, that so much as is here taught in any department, is useful, nay, important to be learned, by every one who aspires to liberal scholarship, without reference to the idea he may have formed of the peculiar adaptations of his genius, or the course in life he may contemplate. Those who consider this a mere Procrustean process, and contend for fostering only the natural inclinations of the mind, must be reminded, that, as the first rudiments of learning are to be overcome by all, these are but rudiments to him who would attain to the higher departments of knowledge, and the generous culture of his faculties. Independently of the difficulty of pronouncing too early, and without sufficient trial, on the peculiar powers we have derived from nature, true genius will not be impeded in her celestial flight, nor shine less brightly in her destined orbit, for having disciplined her strength in the circuit of science, and adorned her plumage with the graces of general literature. That many of these studies have no immediate connexion with the actual business of mankind, makes them no exception. It has been strikingly remarked by a writer of our own day, (in vindication of the study of the ancient classics) that a course of education for the young, "should form a distinct mental character, from which the professional character of after years may derive liberality and warmth, to correct its natural selfishness and exclusiveness." If some of them be found dry, uninteresting, severe and difficult, it must be recollected that they are exercises which may qualify us to grapple with the more abstruse branches of knowledge, or for the exigencies which await us in life; as the Roman soldier of those armies which conquered the world, was always trained in arms of double the weight, required in real action, and these trainings were so unremitted in all seasons and under all circumstances, that the very name of army became identical with that of *exercise*. It is the duty of instruction to endeavor to awaken interest and curiosity in their pursuit, so as to render them as attractive as possible to the noviciate mind, and I doubt not that office is well performed now, as heretofore, within these walls. It has been the reproach, however, of collegiate learning, that it is acquired too much as a task and by rote, and that graduates even want the familiar and dextrous use of it, which shows it to have been thoroughly incorporated with their stores of knowledge. And it seems to be reserved for the philosophic Germans, with whom the *art of teaching* (not the quantum of acquirement in the teacher) is among the highest objects of ambition to discover and apply the true corrective for this defect. But with all the adventitious aids of Professors and Universities, the acquirements of the Student must depend, at least mainly, upon himself, and unless he shall master these studies, and make the knowledge, spirit and taste of the authors of his text-books his own, his labor will be in a great measure in vain. I by no means design to inculcate, that the attention to these studies should be so exclusive that no other knowledge should be sought during the collegiate term; on the contrary, in the intervals of leisure enjoyed by the diligent Student, much may be added to his treasures of various information, without encroachment on his hours of recreation and amusement. But I have been thus emphatic in the expression of my conviction, that they should be the primary object of pursuit, because I doubt whether there be any error more injurious in its effects to the literature of our country, than the too frequent one of the early choice of profession or pursuit in life, by young men of genius, and there consequent neglect of all liberal studies, unless their direct connexion with this one pursuit is obvious and manifest. Where this mistake has been committed, a liberal education, if attempted by, or forced upon, the impatient aspirant, is not sought with the alacrity which his natural parts and spirit would inspire. He devotes no more attention to those branches of which the utility to him is not clearly perceived, than is necessary to obtain a degree, and narrows the energies of his capacious mind to a single end. To him Professorships, and all the appliances of instruction, beyond his chosen field, are of no value; and his favorite studies could be carried on with almost equal advantages elsewhere as here. The effects of such a course are too visibly before us everywhere, to require mention. It makes us artisans in our several callings, not scholars—useful men, of intellectual acumen and professional intelligence, but without the varied learning and polite accomplishments we might have acquired by a proper improvement of our opportunities. It perverts the intention of our system of instruction, and gives it a wrong direction. It has been objected to the Grecian system, of which the Roman was but an imperfect copy, that it bestowed too much attention on mere elegance and accomplishment, while the pursuit of useful knowledge was neglected. Ours, intended in its theory to embrace both of these objects, tends in its actual prosecution to the merely mechanical and utilitarian.

Most persons excuse themselves for the curtailment of their course of preparatory study, and taking this nearer way to fame and fortune, by their supposed want of time for greater attainments. And considering the briefness of our active life, and the necessary interruptions to which the most vigorous plans of application are subject, it is important that none of it be wasted.

But by acting on the sentiment of the Italian philosopher, mentioned in one of the essays of the Rambler, that "time was his estate," which yielded nothing without culture, but made rich returns to diligence and labor, much more may be accomplished in the space allotted to us, than is generally imagined. Others apprehend that such a course of mental exercise and discipline, is calculated to

"Freeze the genial currents of the soul,"

and doom them to austerity and servitude—forgetting that a life of diligence and industry, is not by any means a life of drudgery. Labors, it is true, are demanded; but they are the labors of Hercules, triumphing over obstacles—not the ineffectual exertions of Sysiphus. And although they were multiplied twelve-fold, they would be well imposed, did they but subdue sloth, that wicked foe to all generous effort and enterprize, and give us active, intrepid, and well furnished minds. But as every advance in knowledge opens a new scene of delight, the toils so appalling to indolence and despondency vanish away in our progress, *et labor ipse est voluptas.*

But the eager desire to leap into the arena of affairs, and participate in the stirring events of the learned professions, or of politics, is in our young and adventurous country, one great obstacle to the liberal culture of the mind. In such a country, life itself is a school in which practical affairs are practically taught with but a limited course of previous education, and with its keen competitions and excitements daily before us, it is difficult to command the patience and perseverance necessary to profound and extensive erudition. And unless the habit of study and taste for generous learning has been established in early life, it will be in vain to look for them afterwards. It is in the department of public speaking that the candidate for distinction usually makes his *debut* before the world. It has been said of the British empire, that since the restoration of the second CHARLES and the practical changes wrought in the Constitution by the Revolution which preceded it, eloquence has usurped the place of wisdom; and the Government has been under the control of Parliamentary debaters, many of whom have been profoundly ignorant of the departments of the public service, which, on account of this species of talent alone, they have been called to administer, and that "a Premier who can make a successful speech, need trouble himself little about an unsuccessful expedition." Making every abatement for the overdrawing of this picture, it must be admitted that in that counry, and in his, public affairs are in a great measure controlled by oral discussion. Hence the natural wish among us to excel in this qualification; and although but few, comparatively, have attained to the higher grades of eloquence, no nation probably ever presented so great an array of ready public speakers. But by far the greater part seem content with this one acquirement, and push their intellectual exercises no further. We abound much more in speakers than writers—satisfied with the temporary success and renown obtained with the freest indulgence of the Oratorical license, the larger number have little claim to the taste, discipline and accuracy of thought required for correct and elegant composition. Both speaking and writing, however, are but arts, designed to portray the productions of the mind. Unless it has been inspired with a true taste, enlarged and exercised by study, and stored with generous knowledge, no rhetoric can supply its deficiencies, nor give excellence to its effusions. And although the public and professional affairs, to which allusion has been made, may be conducted without liberal learning, yet he who aspires to high eminence or permanent fame in these pursuits, will be greatly advanced by its aid. BURKE had many rivals among his contemporaries, who successfully contested with him the palm of eloquence on the floor of Parliament, but from the inexhaustible resources of his philosophic and cultivated mind, and his brilliant attractions as a writer, he has left them far behind in the race for posthumous distinction, and has embalmed even the ephemeral party controversies of his day in a diction which will preserve them to future ages. Other examples of the advantages derived to statesmen and men of affairs from liberal learning, will readily occur to the reader of the history of all enlightened nations. And he who neglects it in our country, under the impression that it will be needless to him in these pursuits on which he is so anxious to enter, usually discovers his mistake at too late a period of life for its correction.

By spending the collegiate term in the generous culture of all the faculties, and the acquirement of a liberal store of knowledge, the horizon of the emulous Student becomes enlarged, the field for selection of a path in life is extended; perchance that once contemplated is not found best suited to his capacities and tastes, and he enters upon the journey in whatever direction, *animis opibus que paratus,* for noble exertion and continued improvement. He regards his collegiate exercises as but a preparation for self-education, and impressed with the true dignity of science, he continues his devotions at her shrine, no matter where necessity or choice may demand his chief attention. Only such a course of education deserves to be styled "liberal"; by such only is the intellectual character of our country to be elevated, and our *alma mater* to be "honored in her children."

No system of education, however, would be complete, which aimed merely at intellectual culture and attainments, and neglected the morals, the heart and the affections. Fortunately for us, the culture of these is attended with no difficult and painful study, but is taught in the pages of revealed truth. Commencing in infancy around the knees of the mother, our duties are learned in the precepts of the decalogue; and the heavenly charities of imperfect obligation inculcated in the maxims and parables of the New Testament. All the ethics of the schools, and pure systems of morality among men, but confirm and illustrate these sublime doctrines. And the virtues which are their fruits give to the human character all its loveliness and real dignity. While, therefore, generous studies are assiduously pursued, an enlightened moral sense, and an inflexible determination to conform your conduct to its dictates, should be habitually cultivated. In this connexion, perhaps it is not below the dignity of the occasion, to commend to your attention the culture of the "lesser morals," or a proper standard of manners and conversation, for the same reason assigned by ARISTOTLE, for the study of music by the young Greeks, "that so the mind may be taught how honorably to pursue business, and how creditably to enjoy leisure; for such enjoyment is, after all, the end of business and the boundary of active life."

The time will not permit us to enlarge on the boundless fields of knowledge which lie open to the man of liberal culture, or the fame, satisfaction or advantage to be derived from reaping the harvests they afford. Suffer me, my young friends, to conclude these undigested remarks, with the expression of my sincere hope, that each one of you may realize the fond desires of his parents, by attaining the highest excellence in all generous learning and good morals, and that our University may long continue the nursery of genius, the pride and ornament of the State.

GENTLEMEN OF THE GRADUATING CLASS:

Though it is near a quarter of a century since I was honored with the degree you are about to receive, and quitted these scenes for the active pursuits of life, I well remember the emotions of that day, and can readily participate in your hopes and apprehensions, your joys and sorrows. Thus far, you have lived under the kind direction of your parents and of the authorities of this institution. You are now to be segregated from the College community of which you have formed an important part, and to assume the control of your own conduct, as members of civil society. Each one of you is an object of affectionate regard to his family and friends, who have looked forward to this period of his life with deep interest, and from the certificate of liberal scholarship and good morals, now conferred, becomes at once an object of mark and distinction in his sphere of acquaintance.

Bearing the testimonial of superior opportunities of improvement enjoyed, you will be expected to possess corresponding acquirements and qualifications. Favored beyond most of your contemporaries in the enjoyment of these opportunities, they will be regarded as a talent committed to your charge, of which you must render an account in your subsequent life. At such a point in your existence, I would that I could furnish any precepts to be chronicled in your memories, that might direct you with safety, honor and usefulness in the scenes through which you are to pass. In the ever varying circumstances which attend us, the principles of moral and religious truth, in which you have been so often instructed in this place, afford the only reliable chart for your guidance. These, I may not presume, "can come mended from my tongue." There are a few suggestions, however, on other topics, which may not be wholly useless. In our stirring, active, energetic nation, with every thing tending to the practical affairs of life, we have not as yet, and are not likely soon to have, a body of Professors of literature and science merely. And if we wait the coming of JOHNSONS, GOLDSMITHS, HUMES, or MACAULEYS, exclusive devotees of learning, to establish a literary character for our country, we shall probably enact the fable of the rustic described by HORACE, who sat by the river's side, and expected it to ebb away. Without pensions or patronage from Government, with the engrossing demands of public affairs of the professions and of business, calling for new employe's in their departments, liberal learning among us, for a long time to come, at least, is to be cultivated not by a separate order of writers, but by those who snatch time from other avocations for its pursuit; and its chief dependence for preservation at all must be upon the *alumni* of our Universities. I conjure you therefore, for "the studies' sake," to which you are indebted for your present distinction, not to permit your tastes in letters to become extinct, but to add to your present acquirements on every fitting opportunity. This will be an easy task, if undertaken with a moderate degree of attention now, but will become more and more difficult the longer it may be deferred. I fear it argues, however, a gross negligence of generous studies, or that our courage is unequal to our capacities, that there is not a more general diffusion of polite learning among the men of education in our country. Instead of apologizing for the want of it, by necessary attention to the demands upon our time by public trusts, our professions or business, we ought to remember that some of the most eminent votaries of elegant and profound learning were persons, who, at the very time when pursuing these studies, bore their full share in similar employments, and equally laborious. Not to recur again to CICERO, (whose excellent biography by MIDDLETON cannot be too often read by men of affairs, to overcome sloth and revive their courage for mental labor) it may be sufficient to particularize BACON, BURKE and BROUGHAM, in English history, LAMARTINE, GUIZOT, THIERS and ARAGO, at the present day, in France, and omitting many others in our country, MURPHEY, TAYLOR and GASTON, in our own State. These were persons not slothful in business, but who adorned business as well as leisure, with the charms of polite erudition. Whatever, therefore, be your plans of life, whether to embark in the Professions, in Agriculture, Commerce or other business, or whether you entertain an honorable desire for distinction in public employment, a true taste, love of learning and a desire for further advancement in knowledge, should be habitually cherished.

But if these be neglected or deemed impracticable, and the fair flowers which have been here nourished should bear no such fruit, remember, that there can be no excuse for a failure to illustrate your lives by enlarged views of integrity, justice, truth, honor and benevolence, in your several spheres of action. Not by an abstract and outward admiration of these virtues, but an inflexible adherence to their impulses, under every variety and change of circumstances. And your education will have proved defective in its most essential object, if with the precepts of religion and of reason, and the examples of history, it has not imparted to you the force of will to maintain  right and resist wrong, come what may.

As citizens of a Republic who have been by your studies made acquainted with the Constitution and Government of your country, and who have also been

"By ancient learning, to the enlightened love
Of ancient freedom warmed,"
you feel a natural admiration of her noble Institutions, and a just pride in her fame. It will now devolve on you to bear your parts in giving direction to her Government, and in upholding these Institutions. The study of her history, the trials, perils, and sufferings through which she has passed, and of the characters of the sages and patriots who founded her Governments, and under the Providence of God, conducted her affairs to the most favorable results, will engage your attention, not only as subjects of liberal knowledge, but of personal interest and duty. In these you will learn what sacrifices were required to achieve our National Independence, and what anxious days and sleepless nights it cost the Father of his Country, and his associates, to establish our National Union. You will thus be inspired with true loyalty and attachment to that country, and prepared to hold fast to that Union 'as the sheet anchor of our peace at home, and safety abroad." For sixty years it has secured to us justice and domestic tranquility, and conferred on us a renown and prosperity unexampled in the history of nations. If cherished and defended in the spirit of sincere patriotism, wisdom and forbearance which characterized its framers, it will preserve the blessings of liberty to our remotest posterity. Such of you as may be called to administer its public trusts, should bear always in mind, that they are designed to confer only "the power to do good", the "true and legitimate end of all aspiring." But whether in public or private station, from your course of education you will exercise an agency in the formation of public sentiment, and will be in some measure accountable for results. May you so appreciate this responsibility, as to keep always in view the precepts of justice, wisdom and patriotism, and to derive additional lustre to your own characters, from the brightness of that career which, under the blessing of heaven, we trust awaits our country.

*From James Graham.*    U.

Memphis, Tenn.,

June 7th, 1849.

I reached this place yesterday, on Horse back from N. C. I came to Chatanooga, on the Tennessee River, to take a Steamer and descend that River to a place called Savanah. But on my arrival at Chatanooga I learned the Cholera was on the Boats in the Ten. River, so I came all the way by land.

\*    \*    \*    \*    \*

This place is dull and dreary from the *Cholera* being here and on the River.

The weather is distressingly hot. I will act prudently and avoid exposure. I find I can do nothing here at this Season. I am obliged to return the same way I came, and will be off in a week or ten days.

*From Richard Lee Fearn.*    U.

Mobile,

June 13th., 1849.

I have just seen in the Washington news papers that you are, or likely to be, appointed Minister to the Court of Spain. Fitness and probability confirm my belief in the rumor. Under the impression, therefore, that it may be true, I presume upon old College acquaintance, to offer a suggestion for your consideration.

I have a son, now at Yale College, who has, from the peculiar circumstance of our mixed population, acquired a full and familiar acquaintance with the French and Spanish languages; reading, writing and speaking them with accuracy and ease, very unusual in one so young, or indeed of any age.

He also reads and writes the German, but has had little opportunity of conversing except with his teacher.

In other departments, Latin, Greek, Mathematics, &c. he has sustained himself very creditably and honorably at Yale, he is seventeen years old, with much more general knowledge than is usual at that age.

With your knowledge of the modern languages, which is probably confined to the reading and writing, without the Coloquial and free use of them, you might find it exceedingly agreeable & important to have one near your person, under your immediate influence and confidence, possessed of the qualities above stated.

I could not trust my only child with any one whom I might know less, or less confidently, than I do you.

If this suggestion appears worthy of attention, a personal interview might be had with my son in New York, or Washington City.

Will you do me the favor to write in answer, at your earliest convenience.

*  *  *  *  *

*From Robert T. Paine.*                                    U.

Washington City,

June 14th, 1849.

I have the pleasure to acknowledge the receipt of your answer of the 9th. inst; and although you have given the best of reasons for declining a high public office, I cannot refrain from expressing my deep regret that you should be forced by any circumstances to decline public service.

The President, to whom I have made known your acknowledgements and your decision, regretted very much that the Country would not have the benefit of your services abroad. He is desirous of elevating the character of the Diplomatic Corps of the Country, and in seeking for persons to fill these offices, I know that in his selections he is animated by the strongest desire to promote the honor and interest of the Country at large. The President is fully satisfied of the sincerity and strength of your reasons for not wishing to go abroad; yet I would be very glad if, when you have leisure, you will come on and see him. I feel sure that he is every way worthy the confidence of the Whig party and of the Country, and I am equally as sure that his Administration will go very far to root out the heretofore corrupt practices of the Government. It is so rare a thing to see one decline a high public station, that I know your conduct will create surprise and admiration, whilst it will not diminish the President's confidence in you, nor his estimation of your character.

Is there no way by which you can prevail on our Senator to return home? This a thing very greatly desired, and if you can accomplish it, I beseech you do so, for his sake and for North Carolina's.

Wishing you prosperity and happiness, I am

With great respect
Truly your Obed't Serv't

*From Cadwallader Jones.*                                U.

[Hillsboro,]

July 19th, 1849.

As Mr. Norwood is absent, & neither Mr. Johnson nor myself are speakers, & indeed as I shall set out for the Springs early next week, I must beg that you will address the people at Chapel Hill on the 26th.[22] and here on the 31st. on the subject of the R. Road. I have written to Gov. Swain to the same effect, but have had no answer from him, and have invited several distinguished speakers from neighboring Counties, from none of whom I have heard except Mr. Mordecai, who possibly may come, tho' it is doubtful. He seems to think, as possibly others may do, that Orange is so well provided with able men as not to require aid from abroad. I am somewhat of his opinion, & shall be quite satisfied if you and Gov. Swain will take the business in hand. This I trust *you* will do, especially as the paternity of the measure is laid at your door.

In behalf of Committee.

---

[22] Graham spoke in Chapel Hill on the 26th, and the following comment in a university student's diary is interesting: "The former (Governor Graham) made a very instructive and entertaining speech pressing the importance of the subject upon the minds of the people. He endeavored to bring the public mind to act upon it, made use of many illustrations affording proof of the opinion he entertained, and endeavored to persuade the people to embrace the opportunity of creating the work proposed. . . . Gov. Graham [is] a man of considerable influence amongst the public, a man in whose judgment the people put explicit confidence, with a view to the advancement of the public good, and that the people may be correctly informed with regard to this matter and their minds aroused to a proper sense of their duty." Nearly two months later he wrote: "Gov. Swain mentioned the name of Gov. Graham of this state as an instance of a great man who has balanced his education according to the maxims of Lord Bacon. His writings and speeches show that he has not neglected Rhetoric, or has he failed to employ his time in useful reading." Diary of Thomas Giles Garrett, July 26, and Sept. 20, 1849. The diary is in the Southern Historical Collection.

*From George Washington.*                    A.

St. Augustine,

July 30th, 1849.

Your letter of the 12 inst. was received by me while in the Country some miles South of this place, and I hasten to answer it at my first opportunity

To begin, I should appologize for my neglect of your former kind letters, but that it admits of no excuse, and I must therefore beg you to pardon it. The fact is that I was somewhat deceived and a good deal disappointed. The first office urged upon me to make application for was that of Surveyor General, but on my return from a short absence in the Country, I found that a man of much influence here had already taken his departure for Washington and thought by some with the same view. It was thought advisable that I should yield and turn my attention to the Live Oak Agency. I did so and wrote to you, but afterwards I found that Mr. Tracy, President of the last House of Rep. of the State, was making a move for the same office at Washington, and had obtained the promise of Mr. Cabbel's[23] influence. On the whole therefore, I though it best, with the concurrence of my friends to drop that matter also and remain quiet for the present.

Give Sister my most hearty congratulation on the birth of a seventh son,[24] which is a happy omen.

The engrossing topic here just now is the probability of another Indian War. The Indians have attacked and broken up the Settlements at Indian River, numbering some dozen families in all, and killed in the attack a Mr. Barker, who married a Miss Bullock, I believe, of North Carolina,—at any rate she is the Sister of the wife of Mr. Russell, whom Sister Susan knows very well—and also wounded Mr. Russell himself in the left arm, which has been amputated since he came up to St. Augustine.

---

[23] Edward Carrington Cabell (1816-1896), of Florida, a native of Virginia, who attended Washington College (now Washingtgon & Lee University) and was a graduate of the University of Virginia. He settled in Florida, was a delegate to the constitutional convention, 1838, became a lawyer, and in 1845 was elected to congress and served until 1846, when he was unseated. He was again elected, and served, 1847-1853. He moved to St. Louis, and was a Confederate colonel in the Civil War.

[24] Augustus Washington Graham (1849-1936), who was the seventh son of a seventh son. After graduation from the university he became a lawyer. He was secretary of the Virginia—Maryland boundary commission, a judge of the superior court, and member of the state house of representatives, 1901-1911, (speaker, 1909-1911), 1913-1915.

The settlers all were much alarmed—more so I fear than the occasion justified, as they could only count four Indians—and escaped in much confusion and suffered many hardships on their way up here, a distance of over 200 miles, but none were injured except those I have mentioned. I am pretty well acquainted with Mr. and Mrs. Russell. Mrs. R. begged to be remembered kindly to Sister. Mr. R. is doing pretty well since the amputation of his arm.

About four of five days after the attack on Indian River, another attack was made on a settlement on Pease Creek, on the West side of the Territory and some distance South of Tampa Bay. One person was killed and several wounded. This attack was also made by four Indians.

There is great diversity of opinion as to the Character of these attacks Some look upon them as preliminary to a general War; others think them only the effects of private revenge—I can't say which is true, but I think the latter opinion more likely correct.

*   *   *   *   *

List of Taxables.                    U.

July 1849.

White Poll—Self _____ 1
Black Polls

| ( Dick | Rose, hired to Emma Taylor _____ 1 |
| ( Joe | Martha, hired to Sam'l Stubbins _____ 1 |
| ( Isaac | Mary, hired to Wilkerson _____ 1 |
| ( Richard | Willis, hired to Wm. F. Strayhorn _____ 1 |
| ( Frank | Barbara, hired to Dan'l Phillips _____ 1 |
| ( Ephraim | Ann, hired to John Laws _____ 1 |

—

| ( Maria | | 6 |
| ( Fanny | Rose, over age _____ 1 |

—
5

( Betty
( Harriet
( Ann
( Leah
( Sally (of Betty)
( Jim
( Bob

( Eliza
( Juno
( Cynthia
( Abram
( Dave
( Mike
( Sally
( Lizzy
( Hannah
( Mima
( Alfred
( Evelina

27 in possession—Deduct Dick and Mima over age 25.

### From James Graham.                                    U.

Charlotte, N. C.,

August 1st, 1849.

Dear Brother

I am here for one day at an Extra Court, having returned from Ten. about ten days since. I came home in good health and remained in Ten. a shorter time than I anticipated in consequence of the Cholera in the West.

\*    \*    \*    \*    \*

I heard the candidates for Gov. in Ten. address the people and feel sure the present able Gov.[25] of that State will be re-elected. The contest for Congress and the State Legislature will be close and warmly contested.

Clingman has no opposition. I was strongly and generally solicited to run against him, and believe, I could have beaten him with much ease, but my business and inclinations did not allow me time and opportunity to go to Congress; and still less, to canvass the District. My former *ultra* Whig opponents were most anxious for me to be a candidate. They now see their folly in supporting Clingman heretofore, and whose crazy course is about to sacrifise

---

[25] Neill S. Brown (1810-1886), governor of Tennessee, 1847-1849, a lawyer, soldier of the Seminole War, a Whig at this time. He was minister to Russia, 1850-1853, and in the latter year was speaker of the lower house of the Tennessee legislature. He became a Democrat, but was a Unionist in 1861. Graham's prediction was not verified, as he was defeated for re-election by William Trousdale.

the Whig party in the District, and perhaps in the State. For Bob Love,[26] the last Democratic Member from Haywood county has *boasted,* "that Clingman's course before the last Legislature was worth *1000* votes to the Democrats in the next election in this State for Gov." The leading Democrats in the upper district are open in their advocasy of Clingman at this time. The *West* side of the Mountain is rapidly giving way, in support of the Whig cause. Gen'l Bynum has lately removed back to Rutherford from Columbia. Gov. Manly is much censured in Rutherford, Lincoln and Cleveland for the appointment of the Commissioners whom he has designated to lay off the Turnpike, the Road. The people say that, by that appointment, the Gov. *has himself located* the Road through Statesville & Morganton.

In this, (the Charlotte District) I think Deberry will be elected, but some Whigs hereabouts, are going to vote for Caldwell.

The Rail Road from here to Columbia is progressing rapidly in construction. Public opinion is not yet formed on the subject [of] the Rail Road from here to Raleigh & Goldsboro'. West of Salisbury the people do not seem to feel much interest in that Road. Still, I think there will be more animation felt on the subject when the matter is more discussed and understood. In Ten. I was pleased [to] see and hear that Democrats and Whigs *united* Cordially in the support of their Rail Roads now being constructed.

The candidates declared themselves warmly in favor of all their internal improvements and said expressly, there was no difference of opinion between them on that subject.

I will remain about the Earhart Place about two weeks, when, if I do not learn of your intention to come up the country in this month, or next, I will probably go over for a short time to the Buncombe Springs.

Your affectionate brother

*To James W. Bryan.*     U. Bryan Mss.

Hillsborough,

Aug. 26th, 1849.

\* \* \* \* \*

We are all as well as usual, except, some of our servants. My children have recovered from measles, which they have had, with

[26] Robert G. A. Love, of Haywood County, member of the commons, 1848-1854.

great severity. Mrs. Washington says her health is better than it has been for several years. We were for a week or two under great apprehension that Dr. Knox had fallen a victim to Cholera. Maj. Gatlin[27] wrote Gov. Swain that such was the rumor in St. Louis, from Rock Island, whither the Dr. and family had gone. A letter from Mrs. K. at the latter place, however, has removed our anxieties. He had had the disease before leaving home, but recovered.

Our crops of wheat are equal to the average, though injured by too much rain. And the Corn exceedingly promising.

We are making efforts to get the stock taken in the Railroad, but is hard work in this County. Guilford and Davidson will perhaps raise each a subscription of $100,000. but I fear no others will do as well. The Virginians from Richmond to Danville are busy in discouraging the work, saying that if it can be postponed untill another Session of the Legislature, the Charter can be repealed, and then the Danville and Charlotte road will certainly succeed.

I have lately subscribed for "the Republic," and find it an effective party paper, and think it worthy of the patronage of our friends. With the discord now prevailing from various causes among the Whigs, we are in great danger of losing our ascendancy in the State.

* * * * *

*From David L. Swain.*

Chapel Hill,

Sept. 10th., 1849.

I met with Dr. W. R. Holt,[28] at the C. H. in Alamance on Tuesday last, and received from him a paper of which the enclosed is a copy.

This paper will serve to indicate the basis on which the Company is being organized to make the road, through the County of Davidson. Dr. H. informs me that our friend Thomas[29] was exceedingly anxious to unite with him and take the whole $100,000.

I have no doubt that upon similar terms, men of energy and *capital* (owners of land, slaves and provisions) such men as your

---

[27] Richard C. Gatlin.

[28] William R. Holt, of Davidson County, state senator, 1838.

[29] Probably John W. Thomas, of Davidson County, member of the commons, 1831, state senator, 1842, 1848, 1854-1856.

neighbour Josiah Turner[30] & my neighbour C. W. Johnston,[31] might, by taking stock to the amount of $10,000 and contracts to the amount of $20,000. pay for their stock without inconvenience, and without the expenditure of a dollar in money, beyond the 5-per-cent necessary to secure the subscriptions.

I intimated to J. Hargrave,[32] Esqr. the other day a willingness to join him in a $10,000 subscription. He is thinking about it.

The day of the meeting at Providence was gloomy and unpleasant. Mr. Gorrell and I delivered addresses. The rain was falling in torrents at the time I arose, and this caused dispersion of the persons assembled, and allowed me no opportunity to judge of public sentiment. Col. Carrigan[33] authorized me to state, at presiding, that he would increase his subscription from one—to $3,000.

*From John B. White.*[34]                                    U.

Wake Forest College,

Forestville,

September 13th, 1849.

At a meeting of the Trustees of this Institution, held in June last, you were unanimously elected a member of their Board.

The Communication of this has been delay[ed] as I supposed it would be made by the new Secretary appointed at the same Meeting.

Allow me to express the hope that you will accept of the appointment, and if convenient, that you will attend the Annual meetings of the Board.

With sentiments of esteem,

---

[30] Josiah Turner (1782-1874), native of Caswell County, a prominent citizen and long sheriff of Orange County.

[31] Charles W. Johnston, a substantial citizen of Orange County, and a friend of Graham and Swain.

[32] John L. Hargrave, of Davidson County, state senator, 1836.

[33] William Adams Carrigan, of Orange (now Alamance) County.

[34] John B. White, agent and later trustee of Wake Forest College.

*From James F. Waddell.*                    U.

Hillsboro',

Nov. 11th, 1849.

My dear Sir!

No sooner have your kind exertions in my behalf been crowned with success, than I find myself again compel'd to seek assistance at your hands. My appointment as Consul for the Port of Matamoras, I need not tell you, has found me with no funds at my command. I have no relatives to whom I can apply in this emergency, and I have thought that, under the circumstances, I might procure funds through the influence of your name. I mean, of course, funds to defray the expenses of my journey. The office which I have received is worth, as I learn from the very best authority, at least $3600. It will be necessary for me to procure $150. or $200. With sufficient security I have thought that this would not be very difficult, for if my situation be so lucrative, I could return it in a very short time. My deep sense of the obligations already conferred upon me by your disinterested kindness leaves me not the slightest apology for this second application. But I feel, my dear Sir, that you know my situation, and will appreciate my motives.

In conclusion, permit me to express the hope, that some opportunity may yet be afforded me of expressing to you my gratitude, and I feel that I can in no better way do so at present, than by striving to excel in the performance of the duties of that Situation your influence has been so instrumental in procuring for me.

1850

*From Edward J. Hale.*                    U.

Fayetteville,

Feb. 8th, 1850.

Let me assure you, that so far from deeming any apology necessary for writing to me as you did on the course of the Observer, I owe you my hearty thanks therefor, and only wish that you would often favor me in the same way. Almost at the same time that your letter came to hand, I received long and earnest letters from Judge Pearson and Mr. Badger, taking the same views, and urging the same course. Could I feel otherwise than grateful for such an evidence of regard from three such sources, and flattered at the importance thus given to the Observer? I shall show my appreciation of it, and my respect for your sound judgments, by making the best kind of a *back out* in my power.

I am fearful of the effect upon the Whig party of a position of hostility, or even of neutrality, upon this Convention question. But that consideration may not be weighed against disunion, or anything calculated to promote it. It is the course of true patriotism, therefore, to go for the Union at the hazard of party supremacy. The Whigs have often sacrificed the last upon much slighter grounds.

I would have replied to your letter sooner, but for the press of business, and company, consequent on Seaton Gales's[1] wedding. I write now in haste, only to assure you [how] glad I have been, and will always be, to hear from you.

P. S. Feb. 9th. I have submitted to a couple of friends here the article I have prepared on the subject, and they advise against its publication, for the present at least. They think the proper course for me is silence. I differ; but will hold the subject under consideration.

### *Invitation*

New York,

March 1st, 1850.

You are cordially and earnestly invited to attend a Ball, given by the citizens of New York, on Tuesday Evening, March 19th, at Niblo's, in honor of Henry Clay, whose patriotic and self-sacrificing course, through a long and well spent life, attaching him personally to the devotion of millions of the people, now irradiates with brightest promise the difficult and thorny path, over which he fearlessly tracks his way, unawed by faction, undismayed by threats, looking calmly and steadily aloft, bravely, unfalteringly battling for "the Union," his whole Country, and nothing but his Country.

Our people are desirous of mingling socially, and of interchanging those sentiments which commend their National views, to all sections of this broad and exceedingly prosperous country.

---

[1] Seaton Gales (1828-1878), son of Weston R. Gales, graduate of the university, editor of the Raleigh *Register*, 1848-1858, Confederate major and brigade adjutant, associate editor of the Raleigh *Sentinel*, 1866-1869.

The favor of an answer at your earliest convenience, is requested.

We are, very respectfully,

Your Obed't Serv'ts,

(Caleb S. Woodhull,

(

(Frederick A. Tallmadge,[2]

(

Committee of Invitation.          (Thomas Carnley,

(

(Theodore E. Tomlinson,[3]

(

(Charles Riddle,

*From Joseph Montrose Graham.*[4]          U.

"Little Bay," Ouchiata County,

Arkansas.

March 20th, 1850.

Nearly five months has elapsed since my arrival in this State. The time, however, has passed away so rapidly that I can't realize that it has been more than one. We had quite a pleasant and successful trip out, and arrived in good time, as the roads became very bad immediately after our arrival.

The winter here has been unusually wet and the water courses have been all extremely high. We pitched our tents and remained in them for some four or five weeks (after getting here) having no houses on my place, and but seventeen acres of Cleared land. We had a pretty rough time of it. But I believe my own health and that of the negroes were never better than since we left Carolina. We have been constantly—but slowly—moving along, and I have been my own overseer, and have paid particular attention

---

[2] Frederick Augustus Tallmadge (1792-1869), a prominent lawyer of New York, a native of Connecticut, graduate of Yale and the Litchfield Law School, a captain in the War of 1812, recorder of New York City, superintendent of police, and Whig member of congress, 1847-1849.

[3] Theodore Tomlinson was a New York lawyer, who had been a member of the legislature in 1838.

[4] Joseph Montrose Graham (1823-1871), son of John D. Graham. He married Mrs. William A. Graham's youngest sister, Mary Ann Gartha Washington (1824-1888).

that the negroes should not be exposed more than we could possibly avoid untill they got acclimated to this Country.

They have, however, done a great deal of work, having erected four good & comfortable negro houses, a Smoke house & Black Smith Shop, & have our dwelling under way.

We have also cleared about one hundred and Thirty acres of land, and in the course of Two weeks will have it ready to plant.

I hope, if nothing unforseen prevents, to make this year about thirty Bales of Cotton, and some Corn to spare. So many persons are daily migrating to this Country that Corn readily sells at 50 cents per Bushel, and in the summer at $1.00. I am much better pleased with this Country than I anticipated and particularly with my land and location. I am only a mile & ½ from Little Bay on the Ouchiata, where Boats stop almost daily as they ascend and descend the River, which brings me within four days of New Orleans.

This is one of the finest Stock Countries that I have ever seen. Persons here never think of feeding their Hogs with Corn and they are killed from the woods as fat and large as the Kentucky Hogs that are driven to Carolina. I have bought about a hundred head; & a little salt, and the Bear, and Panther, serves to make them gentle, and causes them to come up every night. Rice Potatoes and vegetables of every kind grow here luxuriantly. As we are near navigation every thing of that kind that we have spare, we can find ready sale for on the Steam Boats.

Henry[5] arrived here about two months since, and remained with me for some time. He has purchased a house & lot in the town of Camden (at the head of navigation on the Ouchiata, a business place & containing about 2500 inhabitants) and opened a Drug Store, and will practise in copartnership with Dr. N. S. Graves, of Caswell, No. Ca. who has quite an extensive practise in Camden, & whom I suppose you are well acquainted with.

Mr. Rounsaville[6] & Martha landed at Little Bay about Two weeks since. They remained with me a day on their way to Princeton, where Mr. Rounsaville's Mother lives. Mr. R. has obtained License to practise Law, & will settle in Camden. Frank[7] came out with Mr. R's negroes, spent about Twelve days here, & in Dallas, the adjoining County. He left the other day for Carolina

[5] Dr. Henry Wilson Graham (1825-1857), a younger brother of the writer.

[6] Peter King Rounsaville (1834-1867), who married Martha Caroline Graham (1827-1853). They lived in Camden, Arkansas.

[7] Presumably James Franklin Graham (1829-1851), another younger brother of the writer. He was drowned in San Francisco Bay.

via Memphis, where he will stop a short time to see George and Uncle Jo's family. His intention is, I think, to go in with Mr. McCollum (formerly of Richmond, N. C.) into the Mercantile business at Little Bay, also to furnish wood for Steam Boats, & as a receiving and forwarding Business there.

Negroes hire here quite high, men from $150.00 to $200.00 and women from $100.00 to $120.00. I have hired out two women at Ten dollars per month each. And I believe any interest on money that a man would ask, and get land as security. I have entered in my own name some Five hundred acres of land for Persons, and they give me their notes bearing 20 per cent, & I their bond for title when the money is paid.

Say to Mother that I have some Three hundred dollars subscribed to build a Baptist Church in our neighborhood. That we hope to have the Church completed in about six months, and that we would be pleased if she would send us a minister. We have not a Church now where they have regular service within 20 miles of us. And it is a rare thing to hear a sermon.

\* \* \* \* \*

P. S. Will you please see if you can sell those Kettles I left in Hillsboro' at any price. Let me hear from you at your earliest leisure. Say to Aunt S. & Mother that I should be pleased also to hear from them.

Direct to "Camden", Ark.

*To James Graham.*                                              U.

Hillsboro',

March 24th, 1850.

\* \* \* \* \*

My family is in good health, except that William has had a violent inflammatory attack, similar to that he had last year when you were here, but he is now convalescent. The rest of us have had violent colds in this month, which in this Climate is productive of disease of that kind, as September is of bilious fever in the low Country. Having gone to Greenville Court on horseback, I returned somewhat unwell, and was confined to bed for a day, but became able to attend to my business in Court, the remainder of the week. The business of the profession is greatly depressed in Orange, and as I look for employment only in the more important part of it, the Court here, with the exception of a few causes, is hardly worth attending. The truth is, that the whole business of the County is on so contracted a scale that there is nothing to produce litigation. Granville on the contrary is to me, a very profitable Court, and I am doubting whether I will not attend the County Court there, instead of the Superior Court in counties of less business.

You have probably learned through the newspapers that the stock of the N. C. Railroad has been all subscribed. It yet a matter of some doubt whether the 1st. instalment of five per cent will be paid in immediately as required. I will go, the last of this week, to Greensboro', to meet the Commissioners of the road, where, if the whole instalment has been paid, a General meeting of the stockholders will be called at Salisbury, to elect Directors and organize the Company. The County of Orange has taken about $114,000 of the stock, which we think will insure the location of the road by this place. I am a subscriber to the amount of $4,000. and with Chas. Johnston[8] in a like sum, make one of the 100 Companies of $8,000 each, who expect to work out the subscription. Paul Cameron has taken $18,000. and his Father $4,000. more. Unless we succeed in this enterprize, I have come to the conclusion that I must remove my negroes from this section of the Country.

Judge Cameron has much revived in health and spirits. Dr. Webb continues to decline, and, I fear, cannot survive much longer. . . . Dr. Knox[9] has concluded to take his negroes and go to California in April, expecting to be absent from his family for two years—the negroes agreeing to serving him during that time, in digging Gold, or any other business he may direct, and then to receive their freedom. I don't know how it may result, but if any one can make such an adventure successful, he can.

It seems now to be understood among the Whigs that Manly must be their candidate for Governor again. Dobbin, or Reid, will probably be run against him. It is difficult to excite much interest in the contest. Webster's speech[10] will, I hope, do much to allay excitement on the subject of slavery. The democrats in this quarter have been endeavouring to get up meetings to send delegates to Nashville, but it has thus far proved a failure. Calhoun, as usual, is weakening the true interest of the South, by the

---

[8] Charles Johnston was a well-to-do farmer of Orange County and an excellent citizen.

[9] Dr. Reuben Knox (d. 1851), who married Mrs. Graham's sister, the widow of Richard Grist.

[10] The allusion is, of course, to Webster's famous Seventh of March speech.

extravagance of his views. We hear nothing from Mangum, who you know, has not been at home for more than twelve months. Stanly, in a letter to Waddell, fears that he will go with the extremists against the admission of California, while he and Badger are in danger of injuring us, by not being zealous enough, for the right of slavery, or at least by appearing too tolerant of the Abolition feeling at the North. I believe I mentioned in a former letter to you that Mangum last fall refused to see Maj. Hinton & Paul Cameron at Washington (who were passing through, and sent for him to Gadsby's) because Hinton and Judge C. had written him to come home, in the vacation of Congress. The matter has never been explained, or reconciled. Maj. Hinton was here, and staid at my house during the Railroad Convention.

\* \* \* \* \*

### From Edward Stanly. A.

Ho'. Reps.,

April 2nd, 1850.

*Private.*

An effort is being made by Clingman to have his man Edney[11] appointed Consul at Glasgow, in case one here recommended should be rejected.

Will you tell me *confidentially*, from what you know of Edney's character, whether such an appointment would be agreeable to the Whigs in the Western part of the State? Is he qualified for such an appointment? It seems to me that to give such a place to Edney, the particular friend of Clingman, would be to encourage a spirit of disunion and make our friends sick at heart.

If you think it would not be prudent or proper to write me on the subject, say so; I know whatever you do, will be from pure motives.

### From James Graham. U.

Earhart Place,

April 21st, 1850.

\* \* \* \* \*

I have been closely confined to business during the past Winter. I have made two trips with cotton to Columbia, (one the middle of Dec', another the first of March). The Roads and weather were

---

[11] Bayles M. Edney.

as bad as they could be. I got $9.50 for my first two loads: and $11.51 for the last two. Beside I sold, during the last trip, Eight fat-beef-cattle. I have got an overseer from Guilford, John Gillaspie, at my South-Point-Place. He does very well so far. I have no overseer at this Place; because I can get no one worth having, although I have had numerous applications. I have had more work done at both plantations since New Year than ever was done before in the same space of time by being generally present directing and encouraging the hands. I have still some cotton on hand. The Roads and weather have rendered it almost impossible to wagon since last fall: and busy season of planting has now commenced, so that I must try and sell the residue of my Crop to the Factories.

I have been but little of late among the people; except at Lincoln Supr. Ct. last week. The approaching election for Gov. has been but little talked of in my presence: and that little is mostly *un*favorable to the nomination of Manly. The citizens of Lincoln, Cleveland, and Rutherford are all dissatisfied with his appointment of Commissioners to locate the western Turnpike Road. They now expect the public Stage to be withdrawn from them, and placed on the Morganton Road. Beside Manly was so nearly defeated before, that the Whigs generally now appear to have no confidence in his ability to succeed again.

If Dobbin should be the Democratic Candidate for Gov. (and present indications point strongly to him) he will be hard to beat. As the vote goes at the next election for Gov; so, in all probability will the majority of the Legislature go. And if the Democrats have the power, they will District the State to suit their own Party purposes; and fetter and embarrass our U. S. Senators with all sorts of odious instructions. The Whig party of our State suffers greatly for the want of an efficient Press in the State, particularly at Raleigh; to which point the Village Papers look for leading articles, stating clearly and concisely and in a popular manner, the issues, reasons and arguments which divide the two parties. Some too, who aspire to be Whig leaders, are personally unpopular, are a dead weight to carry in the political race.

*    *    *    *    *

Congress is constantly discussing the Slavery Question. It is a great Question to the South. I think and hope sincerely now, and indeed the recent indications from Washington justify the belief that the Wilmot Proviso will not be passed by the present Congress. Webster's speech did more to avert the Proviso, or to stop it's folly and madness than any other speech; and yet, I do not give him as much credit as some do, for even he has heretofore disputed with Davy Wilmot[12] his right to be the first inventor of that Proviso. Webster claiming it himself. The difference is this. Webster being a man of sense, sees clearly that the *discovery of Gold* (and consequently an immense White population immediately flocking to California) has decided the question in favor of the North and against the South, and therefore it is unnecessary to insist upon that being done, which is already done without the aid or exercise of any political power. But Wilmot, a silly man, still claims the Proviso as his thunder; and he desires to hear it roar, though it should dissolve the Union. It is glory enough for him to Nullify the Abolitionists though he should nullify the Union. Webster, however, went further than any Northern man dare go, and I feel greatly obliged to him for his views, and sentiments in relation to fugitive slaves, and the future disposition of Texas Territory as slave states.

The Charlotte and Columbia Rail Road is progressing well. The contractors are all at work. If the Central Rail Road in N. C. be begun soon, as I presume it will, Western N. C. will begin to look up and improve. A good Engineer to give the Road the right location at first is all important, after a thorough examination of the ground and country over which it is to pass. Our Relation Dr. John McLean was lately married to Miss Bigger just below where he lives, 7 or 8 miles. Uncle Wm. Lee Davidson also Married the widow of Hiram Huston. They have gone to Alabama.

I am informed John Hoke[13] of Lincolnton, son of old John, is to be the Candidate for the Senate in place of Maj. Connor. He is a lawyer by profession, without practise. He is a right good negative fellow.

The war has commenced again between Col. Wheeler[14] and Alfred Burton. Wheeler has committed three of Burton's negroes under the charge of Burglary. . . . There is a new Bridge *now contracted to be built* over the Catawba River (near the Horse-

---

[12] David Wilmot (1814-1868), of Pennsylvania, lawyer, Democratic member of congress, 1845-1851, Republican United States senator, 1861-1863, judge of the Federal court of claims, the author of the famous proviso that slavery should never exist in any of the territory acquired from Mexico, which precipitated the great quarrel over slavery which ended in the Civil War.

[13] John Franklin Hoke (1821-1888), of Lincoln County, a graduate of the university, state senator, 1850-1856, member of the commons, 1860-1861, 1865-1866, captain in the Mexican War, Confederate colonel, and adjutant general of the state.

[14] John Hill Wheeler.

Ford) where the River divides Caldwell and Catawba Counties. The Bridge is intended to facilitate the Trade and Travel from Ten. and Kentucky, by Lenoir, Newton, and another Bridge about the Mountain Island, to Charlotte. This Road is to become the formidable rival of the Buncombe Turnpike. I think it will pass through this neighborhood.

I think I will go to the Virginia Springs next Summer, but I am not fixed in my mind. I wish to go to Memphis in the Fall. . . .

*From John Newlin.*[15]                                            U.

Lindley's Store,

Alamance, N. C.,

May 1st., 1850.

Respected Friend

Thine from Raleigh on the 6th., of Last month had a long passage, and did not reach me in time to go to Hillsborough in the week of the 15th. It appears to me that by 'Freeing' the negroes before leaving the State will Place me in an unpleasant Situation. I will be required to give Bond, and Security to remove them out of the State. When they are free and I can have No legal Control over them, besides they are all now hired out, untill I call for them, which I did not wish to do until a few days before Starting them out of the State free them, and they are under no restraint, and would be verry likely to look out for homes for themselves. If they are sent to a free State I would prefer to Free them after I got them there (the Society of Friends have removed a large number of Slaves to the Free States but did not Free them until after they got them there) If I send them to Africa, which I think is most likely, I cannot see any necessity to Free them here, because when they arrive there, they are free of course because Slavery does not exist there, but I expect there are two circumstances that may occur that makes it advisable to Free them without delay, one the uncertainty of life, the other in case of an adverse Claim. If there is no safe way of managing without Freeing them, it must be done, but if we can manage safely without Freeing them here, I prefer to do so.

I suppose if they are Freed that all their names and ages will be required. Please to let me hear from thee as soon as convenient,

---

[15] A member of a numerous Quaker family of Alamance and Guilford counties.

and give me the necessary instructions in regard to the Case.
I am so Circumstanced that I cant conveniently go to Hillsborough besides the uncertainty of finding thee at Home.

I am Respectfully.

From John M. Morehead.          U.

Chapel Hill,

Wednesday, May 15th.,

1850.

Having received no official returns from Cabarrus, although
Gen'l Means[16] informs me that $12,300. has been paid in, having
ascertained that there was a deficiency of $18,500. any how, and
being informed by Gen'l Means that neither he, nor Mr. Wilson
could attend at Lexington this week, I did not call a meeting of
the Commissioners, as proposed.

You will perceive by the Greensboro Patriot that I have ordered
the books to be opened again until 1st. June, that the Gen'l Commissioners meet at Chapel Hill on 5th. June, and that all subscriptions and Books be returned to them at this place at that
time. I think we can then get a majority of the Commissioners,
and the balance of the Stock taken if there is still a deficiency.

Architect Davis[17] is here, and goes with me this morning to
Raleigh. I informed him of your desire to see him, and of your
*whereabouts* for the next week and week after, he will probably
visit you about the time he expects to find you at home.

From David L. Swain.[18]          U.

Chapel Hill,

May 15th., 1850.

Gov. Morehead, at the moment of starting, handed me the foregoing note, with a request that I would add a postcript. Mr. Davis
has been at our house since Friday, until this morning. I would

---

[16] W. C. Means of Cabarrus County.

[17] Alexander Jackson Davis (1803-1892), who began as an illustrator and drafts-
man and became an eminent architect, noted for his daring experiments and his
meticulous care. He designed the library building at the university which is now
the Playmakers' Theatre.

[18] Written on the same sheet with Governor Morehead's letter, preceding.

have sent him up to Hillsboro' on Monday, if I had supposed you to be at home. He says that he has pressing calls to Richmond and other points, and does not think he can return with Gov. M., as the latter desires him to do, but that he will leave Raleigh on Monday. A note by Sunday's mail addressed Alexander J. Davis, Esq. Architect, Raleigh, would find him.

A description of your grounds, and a pencil sketch of your house, exhibiting doors, windows, stair case, dimensions of rooms, etc., might enable him to make important suggestions, though I would greatly prefer having him on the ground. He will probably find it necessary to come to Raleigh again during the year. He expresses great anxiety to visit the mountainous region of N. C.

\*    \*    \*    \*    \*

*From  Samuel  Field  Phillips.*[19]                                    U.

Chapel Hill,

June 20th., 1850.

Gov. Swain recommends me to apply for the place of Secretary in the North Carolina Rail Road Company. By his advice, and with the assurance that your influence will be of great assistance to any one that you may think proper to aid in this respect, I write to inquire if you think that I can hold the office of Secretary, with benefit to the Company?

And, if so, whether you will be so kind as to give me the weight of your influence?

I should certainly entertain serious doubts as to my qualifications for the position, had not Gov. Swain given me his unsolicited advice to make the application.

Will you be pleased, Sir, to act the part of a friend in advising me whether I can properly become a candidate for this place?

With very great Respect,

Your obedient Servant,

---

[19] Samuel Field Phillips (1824-1903), of Chapel Hill, son of Professor James Phillips, and a native of New York, a graduate of the university, a lawyer of distinction, member and speaker of the commons, state auditor, delegate to the convention of 1865, and solicitor general of the United States.

## THE NEWSPAPERS OF NORTH CAROLINA [20]
### 1850.

1. Aurora, Wilmington, by Henry I. Toole.
2. Albemarle Bulletin, Edenton, T. C. Manning.
3. Asheville Messenger, Asheville, J. M. Edney.
4. Buncombe Dollar News, Atkin and Sherwood.
5. Biblical Recorder, Raleigh, Thos. Meredith.
6. Common School Advocate, Guilford, N. Mendenhall.
7. Carolina Watchman, Salisbury, Bruner and James.
8. Christian Sun, Pittsborough, Com. Christ. Church.
9. Charlotte Journal, Charlotte, T. J. Holton.
10. Communicator, Fayetteville, William Potter.
11. Deaf Mute, Raleigh, W. D. Cooke.
12. Fayetteville Observer, Fayetteville, E. J. Hale.
13. Goldsborough Patriot, Goldsborough, W. Robinson.
14. Goldsborough Telegraph, Goldsborough, W. F. S. Alston.
15. Granville Whig, Oxford, George Wortham.
16. Greensborough Patriot, Greensborough, Swaim & Sherwood.
17. Halifax Republican, Halifax, C. N. Webb.
18. Hillsborough Democrat, John N. Bunting.
19. Hillsborough Recorder, Dennis Heartt.
20. Hornet's Nest, Charlotte, J. L. Badger.
21. Lincoln Courier, Lincolnton, Thomas J. Eccles.
22. Lincoln Republican, Lincolnton, J. D. Newson.
23. Milton Chronicle, Milton, C. N. B. Evans.
24. Mountain Banner, Rutherfordton, Thos. A. Hayden.
25. North Carolina Standard, Raleigh, W. W. Holden.
26. North Carolinian, Fayetteville, Wm. H. Bayne.
27. North Carolina Herald, Asheborough, R. H. Brown.
28. North Carolina Farmer, Raleigh, Thomas J. Lemay.
29. Newbernian, Newbern, William H. Mayhew.
30. Newbern Republican, Newbern, Wm. B. Gulick.
31. North State Whig, Washington, H. Dimmock.
32. Old North State, Elizabeth City, S. D. Poole.
33. Primitive Baptist, Raleigh, Burwell Temple.
34. Plymouth Times, Plymouth, Wm. Eborn.
35. Raleigh Register, Raleigh, Seaton Gales.
36. Raleigh Star, Raleigh, T. J. Lemay & Son.
37. Raleigh Times, Raleigh, C. C. Raboteau.

---

[20] From *Hillsborough Recorder*, July 3, 1850.

38. Religious Intelligencer, Wilmington, J. McDaniel.
39. Spirit of the Age, Raleigh, Alex. M. Gorman.
40. Southern Advocate, Raleigh, Burwell Temple.
41. Tarborough Free Press, Tarboro', Geo. Howard, Jr.
42. Wilmington Chronicle, Wilmington, A. A. Brown.
43. Wilmington Journal, Wilmington, Fulton & Price.
44. Wilmington Commercial, Wilmington, T. Loring.
45. Wadesborough Argus, Wadesborough, Samuel Fulton.
46. Weldon Herald, Weldon, Jas. F. Simmons.

*From Augustine H. Shepperd.*               A.

House of Rep.,

July 11th, 1850.

Will you regard what I write as strictly confidential—*never to transpire?* The death of Gen'l Taylor may lead to an entire change of the Cabinet—such at least is the hope of many who wish to see it so organized as to favor the adjustment of the Slavery question. No one yet knows, nor indeed has the President determined what he will do. Mr. Clay is *known to be invited to see him*—amongst others. Your friends have informally mentioned your name among those who should be considered of as worthy of a place in his Cabinet—just say to me (never to be repeated unless it becomes necessary) whether you would accept a place in the Cabinet, so that I might upon a certain contingency be at liberty to speak.

Rest assured that you are safe in my hands.

Very truly and confidentially
Yours.

Write me immediately.

*From Charles L. Hinton.*               U.

Raleigh,

July 14th, 1850.

The report by Tellegraph yesterday morning, stating that your name is confidently spoken of as a member of Filmore's Cabinet was confirmed yesterday evening by a very intelligent gentleman direct from Washington.

I hope and trust it may be so, and that you may find it consistent with your feelings and interest to accept.

If Mr. Filmore is judicious in selecting his Cabinet, he may do much for himself, his party, and the Country.

By the mail that carries this I have no doubt you will receive letters from Washington on this subject.

I returned yesterday from Henderson. Young Amis[21] it is said is making a most favourable impression, it is believed that the Whig Ticket with the exception of one will prevail in the county.

Spier Whitaker[22] is in opposition to Col. Joiner[23] for the Senate in Halifax.

I very much fear the reports of Manly's coming out for the White basis will seriously affect his election in the east.

*From Augustine H. Shepperd.*    A.

**Washington,**

**July 16th, 1850.**

There is a union of action here in yr favor. Have just seen the president. He fears that the sudden withdrawal of the Cabinet will force upon him immediate appointments. He is not only disposed but (unless compelled to change his mind) determined to tender an appointment to our State. I telegraph you through Hon John H. Bryan asking that you may be in your friends hands. I have just advised the President of our concurrence. I could not directly ask whether you accept as there is not at this moment absolute certainty.

I wrote you a week since. I have roused from a sick bed to act in this matter.

Yours truly

I have telegraphed at the request of the President himself

[21] James Sanders Amis (1825-1903), of Granville County, a graduate of the university, who was a member of the commons, 1850-1854, 1862-1864.

[22] Spier Whitaker (1798-1869), of Halifax County, who attended the university, became a lawyer, was a member of the commons, 1828-1840, and was attorney general, 1842-1846.

[23] Joyner.

[Enclosure]

*From Augustine H. Shepperd to John H. Bryan.*[24]    U.

Washington,
July 16th, 1850.
1 O'clock, A.M.

Will Hon. Wm. A. Graham place himself in the hands of his friends as to a Cabinet appointment?

*From William S. Bryan.*    U.

Raleigh,
July 17th, 1850.

The enclosed telegraphic dispatch for my Father reached here yesterday. As he was not at home I opened it. Being unable to answer Mr. Shepperd's question myself, I send the dispatch to you. If you should wish to make any communication to Mr. Shepperd by the telegraph, I will take charge of the matter for you with great pleasure.

*From Charles L. Hinton.*    A.

Raleigh,
July 17th., 1850.

I enclose the within, just rec'd. I have answered I take the responsibility of say he will. I have said if necessary I will send an express to you this evening. I am waiting an answer.

My Dear Gov don't decline. I think know your situation, and consider your private interests, as well as the public good you may render.

Yours in great haste,

[Enclosures]

*From A. H. Shepperd to Charles Hinton.*[25]

Washington City,
July 17, 1850,
3 o'clock.

Know if Graham will permit his friends to use his name for Cabinet appointment? Answer soon.

---

[24] Telegram.
[25] Telegram.

*From A. H. Shepperd to Charles Hinton.*[25]

Washington City,

July 17, 1850.

Let Graham be reached tonight. Answer soon.


*From Charles L. Hinton.*      A.

Raleigh,

July 18th, 1850.

I suppose you recd by mail the first telegraphic dispatch I recd. & inclosed to you yesterday. I now inclose the second and should have sent it by express last night but could get no one to bear it, and learning that you were probably at Greensboro, I replied to Sheperd that you were probably attending Guilford Court and several days would elapse before we could hear from you. It is believed here that the War Department will be tendered you. I suppose you have recd letters on the subject.

Any communications you wish to make by Tellegraph shall be attended to.

You know your interest too well for any opinions of mine to have any weight on this subject. I can only say it is the *general wish here that you accept.* I think your position requires it of you.


*To James Graham.*      U.

Greensborough,

July 19th., 1850.

Stopping here, on my return from the Salisbury Convention, to attend a special Sup'r Court, I have rec'd a confidential letter from Mr. A. H. Shepperd, saying that Mr. Clay had been called into consultation by the new President, as to the formation of a Cabinet, that my name had been canvassed as a probable appointee to one of the Departments, and asking permission to my friends there to present my claims for his consideration. This letter is dated the 11th. inst., and no reply being rec'd, owing to my absence from home, on yesterday I rec'd a Telegraphic dispatch, from Mr. Shep'd to Maj. Hinton, dated the day before,

---

[25] Telegram.

requesting him to make the same inquiry and reply to him immediately. Maj. Hinton writes that gentlemen from Washington, who had arrived at Raleigh, state that my appointment is generally spoken of there.

I am taken altogether by surprize, in receiving these communications, and have felt much embarrassment, as to a reply, especially as it was required before I could see and consult my family. Conceiving, however, that the appointment, if designed to be made, was intended as a compliment to the State, rather than to myself, I have concluded that I was not at liberty to refuse for her an honor, to which, from a thousand considerations, she is eminently entitled.

I have, therefore, very briefly replied, by the mail of last night, saying, in substance, that if President Fillmore should think proper to require my services as a member of his Cabinet, the consideration above stated would prevent me from declining, however diffident I sincerely am, of my fitness for the station, and conscious of a sacrifice of personal interests, and domestic comfort.

I will write you again, after my return home, (whither I go today) if anything further has transpired on the subject, and would be glad to see you, provided the appointment be made, before undertaking its duties. I am afraid I may be required to leave home within a very short time, though I think it desirable that the present incumbents should remain in their places untill the end of the Session of Congress. I have thought proper to communicate this to you, though you will perceive it is all uncertain as yet.

\*    \*    \*    \*    \*

*From Charles L. Hinton.*                                      A.

Raleigh,

July 20th, 1850.

I enclose Shepperd's telegraphic dispatch dated 3 o'clock yesterday which is probably later than any you could receive by mail. I regret they did not assign you the War Department as we were led to believe was intended.

You will receive a letter from Shepherd which was enclosed to the Post Master here by Friday's mail but too late for the

Western Stage, that I suppose will give more detailed and satisfactory account than anything we have here.

We learn that Mr. Fillmore requested the Cabinet Officers to remain for one month on the discharge of their official duties which they all declined, so I suppose the heads of the Bureaus are vacant.

This will necessarily require your speedy departure for Washington.

I should like to know by return mail what day you will probably be here, and should be glad if you would stop at my house while in Raleigh.

We hear nothing of the Gov election from the east.

[Enclosure]

*From A. H. Shepperd to C. L. Hinton.*

Ho. Rep,

July 20th, 1850.

I am assured in words that leave little or no doubt that Graham will be today sent to the Senate for the Navy or War Department Can he not be reached? I have been unfortunate in the extreme in not being able to hear directly from him. No time nor expense must be spared Upon your ans'r. I saw the President again & repeating the assurance that you gave: he has concluded to consider it an acceptance.

If the wires are restored I will telegraph you.

[Enclosure]

*From A. H. Shepperd to C. L. Hinton.*[26]          A.

Washington,

July 20th, 1850.

3 O'clock.

D. Webster, State.

T. Corwin, Treasury.

J. A. Pearce,[27] Interior.

---

[26] Telegram.

[27] James Alfred Pearce (1805-1862), of Maryland, a native of Virginia, graduate of Princeton, legislator, Whig member of congress, 1835-1839, 1841-1843, United States senator, 1843-1862. He declined the appointment mentioned.

E. Bates,[28] Missouri, War.
Wm. A. Graham, Navy.
John J. Crittenden, Attorney Gen'l.
N. K. Hall,[29] New York, Post Master Gen'l.
Just sent in to the Senate.

*From Augustine H. Shepperd.*    A.

House of Reps.,

July 22nd, 1850.

Your early arrival here is very much desired. Should any thing detain you let me known by telegraph. I congratulate you most sincerely upon the universal approval of your appointment. Some things I wish to say to you when I have the honor & pleasure of seeing you here.

I have written to Raleigh also, thinking you might be found there.

*From Augustine H. Shepperd.*    A.

House of Reps.,

July 22, 1850.

I was not a little gratified to learn through our friend Major Hinton your willingness to accept a place in the Cabinet, some other than that assigned might have been more desirable, yet I hope you will find no special objection to it, indeed there are some considerations that would I hope make it decidedly acceptable.

I take great pride and pleasure in assuring you of the universal satisfaction with which your appointment has been received. My Colleagues have united with me—*some of them,* however, *looking to your locality in our State took early steps to honor my own modest District.* Well enough—*I write in strick confidence.*

[28] Edward Bates (1793-1869), of Missouri, a native of Virginia. He was a soldier in the War of 1812, was a member of the constitutional convention of 1820, and a member of congress, 1827-1829. He declined this appointment. He was attorney general in Lincoln's cabinet.

[29] Nathan Kelsey Hall (1810-1874), of New York, who had been a law student with Fillmore, and had been a state legislator, judge, a Whig member of congress, 1847-1849. He was a Federal district judge, 1852-1874. He and Graham became attached friends.

Hope you will be here as soon as possible. Your nomination was determined on before the last telegraphic dispatch giving assurance of your willingness to accept. I having taken the liberty of expressing the opinion that you would yield to the wishes of your friends.

Let me know when you will be here. Should be gratified by a frank and confidential interview immediately on y'r arrival.

Your sincere and confidential friend


*From Millard Fillmore.*                                    A.

July 22nd, 1850.

I have the honor to inform you that you were on Saturday, "by and with the advice of the Senate," appointed Secretary of the Navy. Time did not enable me to obtain your consent before this was done, but I trust that you will accept the office, and enter upon the discharge of its duties at your earliest convenience. I am sure that the appointment will be highly acceptable to the country as I can assure you your acceptance will be gratifying to me.

I have the honor to be
Your Obedt Servt.


*From James W. Osborne.*                                    U.

Charlotte,

July 22nd., 1850.

The intelligence has just reached us that you have been called to the Cabinet of President Fillmore to fill the office of Secretary of War. In common with your many friends, indeed with the feeling of North Carolina, allow me to offer you my warmest congratulations on this distinguished honor. I have, however, felt some fears lest you might feel it a disposition to decline the appointment, from considerations by which you were governed in regard to the Mission to Spain. Tho' I feel that there are other duties more important than the claims of official station, and that the path of public usefulness does not always lie in the way of political distinction. I do believe that you cannot decline the appointment tendered you by the President without mortification to your friends, and disappointment to the State. A connection of long standing with the Whigs of the State, in which you have truly spent much time in their service, and they have rewarded you with their fullest confidence, makes it incumbent on you to represent them on this occasion. The omission of Gen'l Taylor to call a North Carolinian to the Cabinet, his unfortunate course with regard to the Territories, had weakened his administration in the State, and something is necessary to inspire the Whig party with zeal, and attach their confidence to the new President. I am convinced that your appointment will have that effect. The considerations which led to that conclusion are so obvious that I will not press them further.

But there is a wider and more comprehensive view of this subject which cannot but influence the Patriot Statesman. It cannot be doubted but that difficulties lie in the way of the National Administration, and peril to some extent the National existence. Should moderation, modern conservatism, and an enlarged nationalism (if I may use the phrase) characterize the Administration, it will achieve a glorious destiny. To harmonize sectional discord, to rebuke and if possible stifle, and extinguish, the fanatical spirit which is found every where, to do justice to all interests, and reestablish the energy of the Constitution will be a glorious work. I believe that President Fillmore, with the Cabinet advisors whom he has chosen, can do so. He has the proper character, and is in the proper location to do so. A Northern man, conceding to the prejudices of his Southern brethren, will have much more influence in the work of conciliation than a Southern statesman contending only for principles in the justice of which he has confidence. His influence both at home and abroad, in all sections of the country, will be greater and more beneficial.

I think the Country calls you to advance this glorious work, and that patriotism, with her preeminent authority demands of you the sacrifice. Surely there is but one ambition that can actuate a noble mind. The ambition of usefulness. For this high station, with all its cares, is desirable and in this crisis of the Country, that laudable desire has a brilliant prospect of gratification in the position to which you have been called.

A bright career is open to those statesmen who adjust on equable terms the present controversy, and I may with justice, and certainly without flattery, say, that to no one is the prospect fairer than to yourself.

It is true that there is a crisis in the condition of good old North Carolina in which you could be eminently useful. But, with effort on the part of her sons at home, I think you can be spared. I hope, with trembling, that the Central Road is safe; at least I believe she can be made so, and your former services in her behalf will discharge you from further duty.

All your relatives here, and I have conversed with several of them, are anxious that you should accept the appointment, and regard it as indispensable that you should do so.

\* \* \* \* \*

*From Charles L. Hinton.*                                    U.

Raleigh,

July 24th, 1850.

I send by Judge Nash a Telegraphic dispatch dated 1 Oct. yesterday saying the nominations are confirmed.

Up to that time Shepherd had not rec'd your letters. I telegraphed him saying you would accept and wrote him on Saturday enclosing yours from Greensboro also the one sent by Hill was mailed on the same day. I also wrote and telegraphed him on Monday after the receipt of yours by the mail of Sunday. You see he is anxious for you to go immediately on.

I go to my plantation in the morning and shall not return untill friday evening.

In my absence I shall request Roulhac[30] to attend to communications directed to me. I fear I may miss you on your way to Washington as I suppose you will go as early as possible.

We hear that the publications in the Standard will probably materially affect Manly's election in the East. Gales rec'd a letter from him last night denying that he has expressed or entertains such sentiments as are attributed to him in the Standard.

An extra from the Register Office will be issued this morning on the subject. I have no doubt it will produce a reaction in the East.

[P. S.] Let me know when you expect to leave for Washington & I will telegraph Shepperd.

---

[30] Joseph B. G. Roulhac, now a resident of Raleigh and a devoted Whig.

[Enclosure]

*From A. H. Shepperd.*[31]

The following Communication was Despatched
from Washington at 1:45 o'clock, P.M.
Dated July 23rd. 1850.
For Chas. L. Hinton, Esqr.

Cabinet confirmed. No letter from Graham yet.
He should come immediately. Let me know when.

*To James Graham.*                    U.

Hillsboro',

July 24th., 1850.

Dear Brother,

By the last mail I received a note from Maj. Hinton, enclosing
a Telegraphic despatch from our friend, A. H. Shepperd, saying
that President Fillmore nominated to the Senate, on Saturday
last, the following Cabinet officers—viz:

Dan'l Webster Sec. State.
Thomas Corwin Sec. Treas'ry.
Edw'd Bates, Missouri, War.
W. A. Graham Sec. Navy.
Jas. A. Pearce, Maryland, Sec. Interior.
J. J. Crittenden, Atto. Gen'l.
N. K. Hall, New York, P.M. Gen'l.

I received by the same mail, a letter from Mr. Shepperd, the
third or fourth that he had written, the others failed to reach me
in time for immediate answers, owing to my absence from home.
In it he says that his Telegraphic despatches were sent at the
instance of the President himself, who had determined from the
first to offer an appointment to N. C., and that there was a "union
of action in favor of my nomination."

Maj. Hinton learns that the retiring Secretaries have been
invited to remain untill the end of the session of Congress, but
have declined. Such being the case, I shall probably be required
to repair very soon to Washington. I have received no official intelligence as yet, but expect a notification by the mail tonight;
but as it will be too late for me to write you afterwards, I drop

---

[31] Telegram.

this line to keep you advised of my information thus far. I would be very glad if you could visit us before I may go. I cannot take my family with me at present, and am taken so much by surprize in the whole matter that I shall be obliged, in going, to leave my affairs somewhat deranged. I dislike exceedingly to quit my profession a second time so soon, as I have recently added considerably to my Library, and have business on hand from which I have expected handsome remuneration. And it breaks in upon my plans of life, and the education of my family in such way as to render new devices necessary. The State, however, has complained so much of neglect in the past, of the Federal Government, and as it is the second instance in which a high distinction has been tendered to her, in my person, I have conceived that there was no choice left me. Having "put my hand to the plough" I cannot "look back," and must needs accommodate myself to the new situation as best I may.

The Whig candidates in this County are sanguine of success. It will require, however, much effort in the State to carry the election of Governor. Reid, however, is not as strong as he was before, and I am not without hope of the election of Manly.

\* \* \* \* \*

Your affectionate Brother

*To Millard Fillmore.* A.

Hillsborough, N. C.,

July 25th, 1850.

I avail myself of the earliest opportunity to acknowledge your favor of the 22nd. inst. announcing my appointment "by and with the advice of the Senate" as Secretary, of the Navy, of the United States, and requesting my acceptance thereof.

Permit me, in reply, to express my profound obligations for the proof of your confidence, and favorable opinion, and the assurance that while I accept it with a sincere diffidence, in my fitness for the office, nothing shall be wanting in the discharge of its duties, which can be supplied by assiduity and diligence and zeal for the public service.

I trust shall be pardoned for the delay of a few days in reaching the seat of Government, in consideration of the suddenness of the call from my private and professional affairs. I design to set out for Washington City on Monday the 29th. inst. and shall hope for the pleasure of waiting upon you on the 31st or at farthest on the 1st. of August.

I cannot close this communication, Mr. President, without the tender of my cordial congratulations, on your accession to the first office of the Republic, however deeply regretting the melancholy event which has occasioned it, and my ardent wishes that your administration may redound to your own fame, to the peace, prosperity and glory of our Country, and the perpetuity of the American Union.

I have the honor to be
With the highest respect

Your obedt Servt.

*From Hugh Waddell.*                                        U.

Hillsboro,

July 28th, 1850.

My dear Friend

I had intended to see you again before yr. departure, but have been disappointed, and now write to make my adieus & to assure you that few incidents could have occurred, in the few remaining years of my life, in which my feelings could have been more deeply interested than in that of yr. recent appointment. Feelings too of mingled pleasure and pain; of pleasure & pride at yr. elevation to a Post reflecting honour on yr. native State & of treble honour on yourself who have never sacraficed either your principles or yr personal independence to obtain any of the many distinctions which have been showered upon you—& of pain to myself at the loss of yr. society for so many of the years yet left me.

I may safely say you take with you the respect, confidence & affection of as many friends as have ever accompanied a Public Officer with their benedictions on his departure from among them.

May God bless you & crown yr. official labours with success. Write me as often as yr. engagements will permit & believe, that wherever I am you will there have a sincere, constant, & ardent friend.

*From W. F. S. Alston.*[32]                    U.

Goldsboro',

July 30th., 1850.

My object in this communication is to get an office. I am Editor
and Proprietor of [the] Whig paper in this place. You know the
strong opposition with which I am surrounded, to wit: *Nash,
Edgecombe, Duplin, Lenoir,* etc. I have a very fine circulation in
the Eastern Counties, but my subscribers are scattered over such
a large territory that it does not pay to collect, etc.

I am no printer by trade, & have to hire my work done. It
took all my capital to buy my stock, & my subscribers "go on
tick," while I have to pay cash for all I buy. I can sell out to a
*Whig*—a man of talent and a good printer—but can get nothing
in return until he makes it. I shall stop the publication of my
paper. I have a family to support, and I can't work for nothing.
I can get recommendations from *all* the prominent *Whigs* of the
State. I have received lately several flattering letters in relation to
the ability and tack with which I Edited my paper.

North Carolina has never had any of the publick officers. Why
should she not? I want an office worth $500. or more, not less. I
am anxious about it. I do not expect to hold it but two years, &
then I will return to N. C. & have capital sufficient to keep up
a *Whig press.* I am a young man, and a determined politician for
life.

If you will let me know where I can get a situation, I will
come forthwith to Washington City. I expect to come the first
of Sept: anyhow. I must have an office, I have spent what little
I had for the party.

I was raised in Wake Co: my father was raised near "Stagsville"
in the North West corner of Wake Co. Hon. Willie P. Mangum's
wife was my father's cousin.

Ask W. P. Mangum concerning *Geo: L. Alston, of Wake Co:*
near *Rogers' Store.*

My Mother was a *Warren*—Sister to Nath'l Warren, Dec'd, of
Wake Co: who was a candidate for the Legislature in Wake Co:
vs J. B. Shepherd & *Sam'l Whitaker.*

I have said probably too much.

---

[32] Editor of the *Goldsborough Telegraph.*

*From Thomas Corwin.*                                    U.

Treasury Department,
Washington,
Aug. 2nd, 1850.

This will introduce you to Dr. F. Lieber,[33] of the S. Carolina College.

I have the pleasure to assure from a very long acquaintance with Dr. Lieber that he is a gentleman in every proper sense of the word.

Truly your friend

*From Daniel Webster.*                                    U.

Aug. 3rd, 1850.

This note of introduction I give to Dr. F. Lieber, Professor in the College at Columbia, with whose high reputation for learning and ability you are probably acquainted.

Yrs truly

*From William B. Rose.*                                    U.

Washington,
Pennsylvania.
August 3rd,
1850.

I avail myself of this early occasion to congratulate you upon your recent appointment as a Cabinet Minister; a position well calculated to call forth those eminent talents which have been so frequently exhibited in the councils of your State and Country, and to express the fond hope that your great abilities may be fully proportioned to your disinterested patriotism.

Being a native of Windsor, Bertie County, N. C., I feel the

---

[33] Francis Lieber (1800-1872), of South Carolina, political scientist, author, a native of Germany, a Ph.D. of Jena, who served in the Greek war of liberation, was the tutor of Niebuhr's son, was imprisoned in 1824 for his political activity, and, released, came to America in 1827. He founded and edited the *Encyclopedia Americana*, was professor in South Carolina College, 1835-1857, and in Columbia College, 1857-1872. He was a profuse and able writer, and his "Instructions for Armies in the Field," written for the war department in the Civil War, was a pioneer work.

deepest possible interest in the proper appreciation of her distinguished sons, and assure you that I shall never cease to respect—nay, to honor her.

You will do me the justice to be assured that the above sentiments most sincerely declared, are not intended as a propitiatory offering, or as constituting a claim on your respectful consideration of my eligibility for Office, tho' I should be exceedingly happy to serve you in some subordinate situation connected with the Department over which you have been called to preside, and can produce as strong testimonials as any other poor man in our Country. I have no doubt but that the Hon. R. R. Reed,[34] the present worthy Representative of this District in the Congress of the United States, and your former compatriot T. M. T. McKennan,[35] will sustain my application by a tender of the most decided testimony as to my humble qualifications and character.

Scarcely inducted into office, you cannot have fully ascertained your wants, I shall therefore, not presume to press the matter, but patiently await your relief from the confusion attendant on your succession.

I would respectfully remark, in conclusion, that I am a widower, and have four little children to support and educate, and am only receiving for incessant clerical service, four dollars a week. So that if it were prudent to urge my claim, there would be some ground from necessitous circumstances. Perhaps you may need a messenger. I would most cheerfully compound for that humble part, tho' qualified for some more important situation.

> I have the honor to be,
> Very respectfully,
> Dear Sir,
> Your Friend & Serv't

I can refer to, Hons. R. R. Reed, Ed. Stanly, D. Outlaw, R. L. Rose,[36] T. M. T. McKennan & Rev'd B. T. Blake of Raleigh, and tho' last, not least, Hon. Kenneth Rayner.

[34] Robert Rantoul Reed (1807-1864), of Pennsylvania, a graduate of Washington (now Washington and Jefferson) College, M.D., University of Pennsylvania, Whig member of congress, 1849-1851, state legislator, 1863-1864.

[35] Thompson McKean Thompson McKennan (1794-1852), of Pennsylvania, a graduate of Washington College, lawyer, Whig member of congress, 1831-1839, 1842-1843, president of the Baltimore and Ohio Railroad. He accepted the appointment to the cabinet a few days after this letter was written, but resigned almost immediately.

[36] Robert Lawson Rose (1804-1877), of New York, a farmer and manufacturer, who served as a "Clay Democrat," 1847-1851.

*From William Robinson.*                                    U.

Washington,

August 4th., 1850.

I hope you will take my claims into consideration, for your predecessor would not, he continued to keep in his office the locofocos, to the entire exclusion of the friends of the administration, "who fought the good fight," he refused to turn any of them out, altho' he knew that many of his party were suffering for want of means to support themselves. Now, Sir, I believe there is no man who can say any thing with a semblance of truth, against my character, while I can produce you every evidence of my entire fitness for your consideration, and qualification for the place. I now beg at your hands. I ask for the Messenger's place, which is now held by a rank loco foco. He and his *son* were of the *Club,* they both were in hopes of Gen'l Taylor's defeat. You can learn this in every quarter.

I would not trouble you, Sir, or do anything calculated to injure that man, but I know he & his family are well to do in the world—even the negro, who is the assistant Messenger, is far better of, in a pecuniary way, than many hundreds of us poor Whigs. Still they are kept in office to our exclusion. I most respectfully ask the honorable head of the Navy Department if this is proper?

I have a large family to support, and I have taken the liberty to address these few lines to you, that my application may be laid before you in time, and that the letters I may present to the Department may follow in due order.

In the hope that I may give satisfaction to the Hon'ble Secretary, I subscribe myself his dutiful,

and ob't Serv't,


*From Maurice Q. Waddell.*                                 U.

Pittsboro, N. C.,

August 4th., 1850.

\* \* \* \* \*

The elections in N. C. are just over, and Chatham, I am sorry to inform you, has behaved very badly. Hackney,[37] Whig, is

---

[37] Daniel Hackney, who served this one term.

elected for the Commons. Cotten, Democrat, next, and Brasier,[38] quasi Whig, being an independent candidate, the 3rd. man. Bynum[39] and Clegg, regularly nominated by the Whigs are both beaten. Haughton is elected over a deranged man, . . . by nearly 3 hundred votes, but ought to have beaten him 7 hundred.

Democratic Sheriff is also elected over Harman, Whig, Manly's majority over Reid about 250. You will no doubt receive authentic information from all sources very soon, but I fear the Whig State of N. C. is fast becoming Democratic, and I hesitate not to ascribe it to the neglect of her by the Government, when giving out the loaves and fishes a year ago. Had you occupied (as you were entitled to) the position you now do, it would have appeased our Whig friends, and they would have rallied this Summer, as they ever have done.

*From Friederick Schmidt.* U.

Washington,

August 5th., 1850.

Permit me to address a few lines to you on a subject the importance of which is the only apology I can plead in thus trespassing on your time.

The German population wields in this Country, a very great political influence, and this influence having been thrown hitherto entirely in favor of the democratic party, has caused its almost uninterrupted success during the last twenty years. The popular party of Germany is called the democratic party, and, hence, the German immigrant ranges himself at his arrival here under the banners of that party, which bears an appellation so familiar to him from former associations, a circumstance the democratic party knew well to profit by, and turn to its own account. Hence, they represent the Whig party as being opposed to popular Government, and *aristocratic* in its tendencies and principles.

In order to keep the German population under its sway, the democratic party established German papers throughout the length and breadth of the United States, and has so well succeeded to enthrall and fetter them, that a German, who acknowledges himself to be a Whig, loses caste, and is shunned and avoided as a traitor and enemy to popular rights.

[38] G. M. Brazier, who also served only the one term.
[39] Turner Bynum, who served in the commons, 1852-1854, 1856-1858, 1860-1862.

The German democratic press is well organized and ably conducted. Great numbers of well educated persons, who conducted the publication of political papers in Germany have arrived here as fugitives, and were received with open arms. They are the active leaders in the Socialist movement, and in their hands is the German democratic press. But this press is equally well organized. It is a formidable array. There are 4 daily German democratic papers in New York, 1 in Buffalo; Philadelphia 3; Baltimore 2; Pittsburgh 2; Cincinnati 3; Columbus 1; Cleveland 1; Wheeling 1; Louisville 1; St. Louis 3; Charleston 1; New Orleans 1; Detroit 1; Milwaukie 1; Dubuque 1. These daily papers issue Weekly editions for the country. Besides, there are in the country towns in most of the Middle and Western States, Weekly papers of minor importance; in Pennsylvania more than 60; and in Ohio an equal number; the same is the case in the States of Indiana, Illinois, Missouri, Iowa, and Wisconsin. To cap the climax, the democratic party established under the administration of Mr. Polk the "National Democrat," published here in Washington, and edited by Francis Grund, which was especially established to furnish leading articles for the other papers, yet so discreetly was this done, that the National Demokrat was actually forbidden to get a large subscription list, so as not to come into competition with the local papers, and excite their jealousy. It was, however, amply rewarded by becoming the choice paper of the President, and thus receiving all the Government advertisements. The National Demokrat was discontinued in Spring 1849, but is now about to be resuscitated. These are well established facts, proving that the German democratic press is well organized, ably conducted, and efficient.

What force has the Whig party in the field to remove prejudices, to counteract the influence of this well organized press, and to disseminate, diffuse, and establish Whig principles and measures among this vast and continually increasing German population? We have 1 daily in Cincinnati, which is very ably conducted, and well supported; but for more than five years it was mainly kept in existence by aid from english Whigs. We have another daily in the City of New York, established four months ago by the Whig Young Men's Society, with a slender list of subscribers, needing and receiving its main support from said Society. A third daily is published in New Orleans, established February last, but already discontinued for want of support. We have 1 weekly in Buffalo, 1 in Allentown, Pa., 1 in Lancaster, Pa., 1 in Pittsburgh,

Pa., and this is the entire Whig force against 25 dailies, and upwards of 200 weeklies!!!

The Volksblatt in Cincinnati has a larger list of subscribers than the *entire German Whig press,* and the New Yorker Staatszeitung has even a still greater circulation.

In the face of such facts, it seems to be no miracle that the German population is entirely ranged under the democratic flag, and the more so, as the consuls in Germany are known to have used their influence with emigrants even before they left their own country.

When the Whig administration came into office, I was urged to establish a German National paper at the seat of Government. It was expected that the administration would cordially assist it with its entire influence, such a paper being thought desirable and even necessary for the success of the Whig party. I opened a correspondence with German Whigs in all parts of the United States, who promised to co-operate with me. I engaged a number of travelling agents, who were to canvass the middle and Western States at the appearance of the first number, and I moved to Washington before the meeting of Congress in order to commence my operations. I soon learned, however, that the "Union" and the "Intelligencer" had the Government advertisements *by law,* and the "Republic" *by the choice* of the President, and that I was precluded from getting any Government patronage. The members made some efforts to produce some change in this arrangement, but without success. I was then encouraged to procrastinate and to issue my paper semi-monthly, because some change in the Cabinet being expected, which might exercise a favorable influence. Such a change has now happened, and I would now most respectfully address you as member of the new Cabinet, and invite you to investigate the merits of the following proposition: Is it more advantageous to the Whig party to have two English organs at the seat of Government, or to adopt the policy of the administration of Mr. Polk, by giving the Government patronage to the German Whig paper? If the former is decided upon, then I have to desist, and can only say "Ut desint vires, tamen laudanda est voluntas"! If the latter, then I shall publish a Semi Weekly during the Session of Congress and a Weekly in the recess, and at such a low price, as to insure a large circulation.

In the hope to receive soon an answer, I remain, with sentiments of the highest regard.

*From J. W. Clay.*[40]                                    U.

South Bend Post Office,
Arkansas City,
Arkansas.
"Desha Place,"
**August 6th.,**
1850.

This will renew to your notice an old collegiate friend,[40] whom circumstances and vocations have separated for 28 years. Yet oft have I heard from you, publicly and personally, through our mutual friends and mates, "Lucius" and "Bishop" Leonidas Polk.

I, too, as yourself, have worked in the great *Whig cause,* tho' in different fields, and if all had pursued and properly appreciated its principles, a protective growth to this confederacy would now be echoed over this fairest fabric of earth's habitable globe, but progressive and insipid Jackson-Democracy won otherwise, and wisdom, always redundant, has now placed a Whig constituency at the helm, if they are as we have preached, they will win, if otherwise—the millenium is not at hand. I now wish to add to the association of our youth the acquaintance of manhood, and that we should know our "whereabouts," **and you may ask why this long** silence—answer it yourself, my friend—and I will abide its decision, **and in all refer you to John Bell of Tennessee, Gentry**[41] **and others, and now I am a planter in Arkansas to Col. Rob't A. John- son**[42] **of Arkansas and of the home.**

Another object, and one I feel much interest in, is for a naval friend, whose interest now demands locality and station—one whose service for the last 18 years has been chivalrous, arduous, and ever prompt to his duties, and is ever ready to the call of Country, but our Country is oft prolix in giving "naval" merit than Just reward, and as he now has the duties and cares of an old Mother and sister he asks the *naval station at Philadelphia.* The gentleman I introduce as applicant is "Paul Shirley[43]—Passed Midshipman of the Navy."

---

[40] No trace of him can be found in the records of the University of North Carolina.

[41] Meredith Poindexter Gentry (1809-1866), of Tennessee, a native of North Carolina, lawyer and planter, legislator, Whig member of congress, 1839-1843, 1845-1853. He was a member of the Confederate congress, 1862-1864.

[42] Probably Robert Ward Johnson (1814-1877), of Arkansas, a native of Kentucky, a lawyer, member of congress, 1847-1853, United States senator, 1853-1861, member of the Confederate provisional congress, and later senator.

[43] Paul Shirley (d. 1873), entered the navy in 1839. He rose to the rank of captain.

As I said to Mr. Clay, I will partly repeat to you. It is the first application for a friend I ever made, and I am sure its the last, and I expect to be heard, for no man has spent more in behalf of the Whig cause, yet always eschewed office for myself, & I am vain enough to think my application then—*but once*—will be countenanced, and of course acquiesced in, as my applicant is in all respects the chivalrous officer and gentleman. If your views correspond with mine, after consultation with Messers. John Bell, & H. Clay, I shall be fully compensated for a life of political exertions *in the Whig cause.*

We here groan much at the heavy dispensation our country has to mourn, in the death of our good and great chief, "Taylor," but, it is so, and our comfort is sustained by the President's retention of such men as "Webster, Graham, and J. J. Crittenden," and we do hope that, after so many "breakers ahead," a calm may come in which we Southern planters may have a peaceful respite evermore.

I hope this hasty scrawl may induce you to reciprocate, and *every now* refresh the days of "Auld Origin."

*From William Smith.*                                U.

Warrenton Springs, Va.,

August 6th., 1850.

I hope you will excuse the liberty that I take in writing to you I do it by the advise of my friend Judge Mangum I riten to him to beage you to give me the place as your private messenger I heard from him to night and he ses that I must write to you and refur you to him for my Character. I was the body Servant of the late Judge Gaston of N C & now lives in Washington if you Sir will be so kind as to give me the place I will be inatennance in your family in the time of your Dinners and parties free of all Charge to you and try and do every thing satisfaction to your wishes I will refer you to Mr E. Stanly he sed he would trye and see what he could do for me I remain your umble Servant.

the body Servant of the Late Judge Gaston

*From Millard Fillmore.*                               U.

August 7th.,

1850.

Please to accept my thanks for the books which you sent me this morning, in reference to the Navy.

I intended to ask only for such as you could spare conveniently, because you might have several copies.

I perceive, however, that you have sent me one which I think must be an *"heir loom,"* being the rules and regulations printed in 1818.

I presume this is essential to your office, and therefore return it.

Truly yours,


*From Rufus Haywood.*[44]                               U.

Tuscaloosa,

August 7th, 1850.

Alabama in common with the rest of the States of the Union, felt a sincere and profound regret at the Death of our venerable President Taylor. Apart from the natural regret we (the Whigs) felt his loss most sensibly, and we had our apprehensions that Mr. Fillmore might not carry out our principle as fully as he would have done.

Since the selection of Mr. Fillmore's Cabinet all appear to be content, and it gives me pleasure as an old North Carolinian to say that I am proud that she is represented in the Cabinet, and feel doubly gratified that the selection has fallen on you.

This Letter will be handed you by my friend Mr. Robert Jemison[45] and as he will be in Washington probably some time, I take the same pleasure in giving him this introduction to you that I did letters to Messrs. Badger, Mangum, and Stanly.

I would be glad that you would make his acquaintance. He represents this County in the Legislature, is a leading member

---

[44] Rufus Haywood (d. 1883), a native of Raleigh, was briefly a student at the university. He became a physician and settled in Tuscaloosa.

[45] Robert Jemison, Jr., (1802-1871), of Alabama, a native of Georgia, he was a graduate of the University of Georgia, became a lawyer, and moved to Alabama. A planter and successful business man, he served frequently in the legislature, and though an opponent of secession he was a delegate to the secession convention, and later a Confederate senator.

of the Whig party and will confer with you freely on such subjects as may interest you about our Southern country.

There is one subject that I hope will claim the serious attention of the present administration. That is, the placing of Whigs in office. In this State they have been in the minority Ever since it was received into the Union, and Even when it was a territory. We have fought against every disadvantage and maintained a respectable position. But we can't get the majority. The opinion I think is Universal amongst the Whigs that If they can have and Manage the offices through this Administration that we shall have the State. In this Country office gives influence, and every office holder commands many votes.

We have as good, as Able, as true and Honest Men in the Whig party as in the opposition, and as such no one here would stop for a Moment to consider If this was a Democratic Administration where the Patronage would go.

I will here take occasion to remark that for myself I am no applicant or candidate for any office. I know of none that I either desire, or would accept. But I feel an interest in some of my Whig friends who I feel confident well deserve the offices they apply for. I wish to bring to your notice two of my friends—(Viz) Mr. Thomas J. Burke[46] of this place who is an applicant for Receiver at the Land office in this place. Instead of Ed. F. Comyges[47] who is desired to be removed for his violent opposition to the party, and also by the grossly improper Language used by him on the arrival of the news of the Death of the Late President.

My Other Friend, Mr. E. M. Burton is an applicant for Register at the Land Office at this Place, In place of Monroe Donoho whose appointment was improperly obtained and been always a source of Dissatisfaction to our Citizens. I will not detail the particulars of his appointment, but refer you to my friend the bearer of this Letter, who will no doubt confer with you freely on the subject.

I would ask you the favour to interest yourself in their behalf.

\* \* \* \* \*

[46] Thomas Jefferson Burke (1813-1857), a native of Ireland, a lieutenant in the Seminole War, lawyer, editor, and banker.
[47] Edward Freeman Comegys (1797-1875), a merchant and banker.

*From Robert B. Gilliam.*                    U.

Oxford,

August 8th., 1850.

\* \* \* \* \*

If you will pardon the liberty, I will venture to mention the case of Mr. J. W. Syme, Editor of the Petersburg Intelligencer. I understand that, until towards the close of Mr. Preston's[48] administration, Mr. Syme enjoyed a portion of the printing patronage of the Navy Department. He took a decided stand for the Compromise Bill, and he got no more printing for the Department.

I will mention further, that Mr. Syme is one of the few Editors out of North Carolina, who has thought any thing in this State worthy of particular consideration. He has always spoken and written of us in a proper spirit.

Though out of place, at the close of a letter, I must, nevertheless, express the high gratification which I felt at the announcement of your nomination to the Navy Department. And that, by the way, is a common feeling with both parties in this section of the State.

The storm is clearing up, and we find ourselves terribly damaged. As the election returns come in, things grow worse and worse. We have stood our ground better in Granville than in other doubtful Counties, which is some consolation, though a poor one.

*From Frederick Nash.*                    U.

Morganton,

August 8th., [1850.]

I write to you at the request of my nephew, Robert Ogden, of New Orleans. When Gen'l Taylor came into office, he was an applicant for that of District Attorney of the United States, for that District. Before his application reached the President, the office was disposed of, to a Mr. Hunton. His nomination has

---

[48] William Ballard Preston (1805-1862), of Virginia, a graduate of William and Mary College, and, in law, of the University of Virginia. He served frequently in the state legislature, was a Whig member of congress, 1847-1849, and secretary of the navy, 1849-1850. Later he was a member of the secession convention and of the Confederate congress.

never been before the Senate, & is still to be acted upon. Robert laid before the proper department recommendations from the highest sources, & they are now on file in the State department, & to which he begs to draw your attention. They are letters from Judge Eustis,[49] Judge Buchanan,[50] & Judge McCaleb.[51] There is another paper, which he denominates a remonstrance against the appointment of any man to such an office, who does not speak and understand the French & Spanish languages. With both of these languages he is familiar, having resided in New Orleans since early manhood. What course the President will feel himself constrained to pursue, as to present incumbent, I, of course, can form no judgment; whether or not he will nominate him to the Senate. If he does, of course Robert must await their action.

I know very well, Sir, that this is an appointment over which you have no immediate control, but I also know that the good opinion and kindly feelings of Gov. Graham will be felt, whenever and wherever known. I hope you will not consider me as acting officiously in this matter. Robert has always been to me a son, I raised him, and necessarily feel a deep interest in all that concerns him.

The papers will have informed you of result of the recent elections. I deeply feel for Gov. Manly. He has been abused, vilified, slandered, in the most outrageous manner. There were three prominent causes of his signal defeat: his location, his Church & internal improvement. The latter, from what I can learn, was the most efficacious instrument—as is proved by the result of the legislative elections.

The crops of corn in this portion of the State, are very promising, & while poor old Orange is literally consumed with burning heat, showers fall here almost every day—abundantly.

If there was a railroad from this to Raleigh—but a large majority even of those in this region is opposed to it,—and in a government like ours nothing can be done to which the popular

[49] George Eustis (1796-1858), a native of Massachusetts, graduate of Harvard, secretary at The Hague. Moving to Louisiana, he became a distinguished lawyer who served in the legislature and as attorney general. He was associate justice and chief justice of the state supreme court. He was a delegate to the convention of 1845, and was largely instrumental in the establishment of the University of Louisiana which became Tulane University.

[50] A. M. Buchanan of New Orleans.

[51] Theodore Howard McCaleb (1810-1864), a native of South Carolina, educated at Exeter Academy and at Yale, became a lawyer and settled in New Orleans. He was Federal district judge, 1841-1861, and professor in the University of Louisiana, 1847-1864.

will is opposed. I hope the company will surrender their charter to the Legislature at its next session, & let us sleep on, as we have heretofore done.

We have just received the news of the defeat of the compromise Bill. I begin to dispair of the Republic.

Pardon me for taking up so much of your time.

[P. S.] Oh that I were a young man, how I should like to grapple with this fiend disunion.

*From Joseph F. Battley.*    U.

Norfolk, Va.,

August 9th, 1850.

After my best respects, and congratulations, upon your accession to the Navy Department, am I mistaken when I state, that you once resided in Abingdon, Washington County, Virginia, in the year 1824 and 25, if not longer, my reason for making this inquiry is this, I was raised in that section of Virginia, being the son of John Battley who carried on the Cabinet Makers business in that place, and I, being a Boy, then only Ten Years of Age, recollect well Mr. William A. Graham, who I think studied and finished a thorough course of Law, under Judge Benjamin Estill,[52] now of the General Court of Virginia, he also had a brother by the name of Archibald, and always being glad to hear of Citizens of my native place rising to fame and pre-eminence, I hope Sir, is a sufficient apology for troubling you with this letter, of one thing I am sure off, that you are one of North Caroilna's brightest Whigs, and distinguished Statesmen.

Mr. Graham moved from Abingdon to North Carolina, in the neighbourhood of Raleigh, I think 1825. Your appointment as Secretary of the Navy, has given General Satisfaction, in this section of Virginia, I am well assured, as also the Whole Union, particularly the Whig party. hoping you will gratify my desire at your earliest convenience, and trusting in God that your Superior Mind will be extended to aid in the preservation of our Glorious Union, from Anarchy and disunionism, I remain, with sincere regard,

---

[52] Benjamin Estill (1780-1853) was educated at Washington College (now Washington and Lee University), became a lawyer and served in the legislature, in congress, 1825-1827, and as a judge.

*From James Graham.*                              U.

Earhart Place,

Aug. 10th, 1850.

I received lately from you three letters, the last of which informed me you were appointed Secretary of the Navy, and expected to go to Washington immediately. I would have been pleased to have gone to Hillsboro' to see you before your departure, but from the fact which you mentioned in your second letter, that you expected to be ordered off promptly; so I anticipated you would be gone before I could reach your residence.

Your family, I presume, will remain in Hillsboro' until November. Washington is unpleasant and unhealthy until the first or second frost. In the mean time, you look out an agreeable residence for next winter. A new house, you know, is regarded as the most healthful. It may be you can't get a house to the end of the year, as the present leases may not be out, if so, you could board your family at a good private boarding house a short time. If the Cholera gets to Washington soon, and I think it will, I would take my sleeping quarters over in George Town (friend Carter could tell you where). Avoid the hot sun, and the night air, and unhealthy vegetable food, and I should apprehend no danger. Your office will be confining, and you must take *regular exercise,* if in no other way, by slinging dumbells, or weights. A small bottle of Saratoga water in the morning, during the hot season, would aid you in keeping your bowels open. Too much ice is used in the Cities in water. The stomach is often chilled and cramped by the *excessive* use of ice. I believe Harrison and Taylor were both killed by indulging in the irregular habits and constant exposure and being oppressed by crowds, and worried, doged, day and night. Polk did not die in office; but he was killed by having filled the Presidential chair.

President Fillmore and his Cabinet have to administer the government under great difficulties and trials. Your office being new to you I think you should adopt Bonepart's plan, on new and difficult questions. He expressed no opinion hastily but called together officers and those who were supposed to be well informed and experienced on any subject on which he wanted light and had it discussed publickly; or took their opinions privately, and *then* He gave his opinion, having had a full view and accurate knowledge of the whole subject. That is similar to a trial in Court, where the Judge hears the witnesses and parties through council before he gives his judgment. Be careful about promising appointments to any body, or committing yourself before the time of action. Pledges are often tried to be obtained before you have had time to hear all about the matter. Beware of that.

The Slavery question is the only embarrassing question before the President and his Cabinet. The President in nominating his first Cabinet officers showed much liberality in taking *four* from Slave States, and Three from non-Slave holding States. However, I must say Maryland and Kentucky do not feel strongly and act with much zeal on that Question. They have but few Slaves, and they are leaving quite fast. Firmness and moderation are the requisites to settle that question.

The vote of N. C. is sufficiently full to learn that Reed has beaten Manly about 3000. I think the Whigs have also lost the Legislature. Burke has elected Avery,[53] and Buncombe has elected a Democrat. I deeply regret all this, but I am not surprised. The Whigs have *im*practicables among them. The western District has been giving way for 2 or 3 years past. Clingman is now a great favourite with the Democrats of that District. Gen'l Bynum is elected in Rutherford, who took open ground against Manly. It was most unfortunate to nominate Manly. He committed several blunders, all of which were turned with effect against him and the Whig party.

You ought, as soon as you can, [to] employ a good overseer to take charge of your negroes this coming fall and next year. You will have to give from 2 to 300 for such a man, and you ought to have him under the controul and direction of some business practical man near your plantation. Perhaps your partner in the Rail Road Contract would superintend your overseer. You had better do something like that, or hire out your negroes next year. If you have surplus stock too, you should order them to be sold as soon as convenient, so of surplus produce, in your absence your negroes will not make you much on the farm; so you had better place things in a condition to loose as little as may be.

---

[53] William Waightstill Avery (1816-1864), of Burke County, a graduate of the university, studied law under William Gaston, and became prominent in his profession and in politics. A state rights Democrat, he served in the commons, 1842-1844, 1850-1854, and in the senate, where he was speaker, 1856-1858. He was a delegate to the Democratic conventions of 1856 and 1860, and was a member of the Confederate provisional congress. He was killed by Union bushwhackers in 1864.

\* \* \* \* \*

My soar throat is better since I had Dr. John McLean to give it divers burnings with Caustic, as suggested by Dr. Knox. My general health is improved, and I have been devoting my time to my farm here, and my plantation on the River, where I have a promising prospect of a good Cotton Crop. I desire early the coming fall to engage me two overseers so as to give me more command of my time the following year than I now have.

The society is so indifferent in this section, that I do not feel satisfied to make a permanent settlement here; and yet I am well pleased with my lands at both places, and have made considerable improvements since you were here. But I find negroes will do little or nothing unless superintended and directed every day.

Brumby, Professor of Chemistry in Columbia College, and his family (9 children) are staying with Ep Brevard this summer. The country all through this section is healthy.

I expect in the next Legislature of N. C. the Democrats will undo much that has been done in 10 or 12 years. There is no telling what they will not do.

When you have leisure I should be glad to hear from you.

Give my Respects to Mangum, Badger, Shephard, Deberry, and Jo Caldwell and accept for your self the well wishes of your affectionate brother.

*From Richard C. Gatlin.*                    U.

Jefferson Barracks,

August 13th, 1850.

I take the liberty of drawing your attention to an application, made some time last winter, for the appointment of Midshipman for G. M. Plympton,[54] and to ask for it your favorable Consideration. He is the son of Col: Plympton,[55] of the 7th. Infantry, a Soldier of near forty years service, is sixteen years of age, healthy and intelligent, and is extremely anxious to enter the Navy. His aged Father would be much pleased to see his son gratified in this particular. As the Father is in the Army, the son might be appointed *at large*. He may be addressed at this place.

I had not intended to have addressed you at this time, on my own affairs, but as I leave tomorrow with my Regiment for Fort

[54] G. M. Plympton served briefly in the navy as assistant engineer, resigning in 1854.

[55] Joseph Plympton (d. 1860), of Massachusetts, who was promoted for gallantry at Cerro Gordo.

Leavenworth, for service on a distant Frontier, probably New Mexico, I take the liberty of doing so, fearing that a letter I addressed to Gov'r Swain not long since, may not have reached him. You were so kind last summer as to join with Gov'r. Swain in recommending me for the appointment of Pay Master in the Army. For some reason, unknown to me, the Hon'l Mr. Badger, to whom the recommendation was sent, failed, or declined, to lay it before President Taylor, at least, such is my impression. I am still anxious to obtain the appointment, and must ask your good offices in my behalf. As appointments have heretofore been made in the Pay Dept. almost immediately after a vacancy, it seems to me that the only way to secure an appointment is to get the President's promise before one occurs. By giving this matter your consideration, you will confer a great obligation upon me.

*    *    *    *    *

*To Susan Washington Graham.*                          A.

Washington City,

Aug. 13th, 1850.

My dearest:

I have this evening taken possession of the house formerly occupied by Mr. Preston, and have taken Thos. Witherspoon[56] with me to keep bachelor's Hall. I believe I have written you that he was here. I have hired a cook, formerly Mrs. Madison's at $8. per month, and a man servant, belonging to Mr. Lee,[57] a son-in-law of Mr. Custis[58] at $12. I have also agreed to take a coachman at $15, but he will wait untill my carriage is here. I find the house not so well furnished, as I had expected, although there are a good many things in it. But it is unfit to be tenanted without some articles immediately purchased. For example, there are no knives, forks, spoons, table ware, bed furniture &c. there are beds and pillows, but no sheets, blankets, pillow cases, &c. What other deficiencies I do not know. I have ordered two pairs of sheets and a bed spread, today I have gotten one of them. I hope in a day or two to be tolerably comfortable. Mr. Preston has left articles

---

[56] Thomas Franklin Witherspoon (1825-1909), Graham's nephew, who lived at various times in Alabama, California, Kentucky, and Tennessee.

[57] Robert E. Lee, then a captain of engineers with headquarters in Baltimore.

[58] George Washington Parke Custis of Arlington House.

in the house, of which he furnished me the Bills, and which cost him upwards of $1,000—consisting of a large French mirror, $89. over parlor fire place—two chandeliers in parlor and dining room $96. carpet for parlor $153—cut glass and china $222. etc., etc.— all of which he proposed to me to take at my own price. I told him they depended so much on taste and opinion, to which I make no pretension, that I would not purchase untill you could see them, or I could hear from you—that if he chose to let them remain, untill I could consult you, I would make him an offer for such as suited me. And they remain, for the present, on those terms, but the Glass, etc. locked up. The Glass and China I think very nice, and has only been used since last Winter. The mirror and Chandeliers, I think, suit the house very well, I can't say I like the carpet—though I have seen it imperfectly.

The House is near the North East corner of Presidents Square, and on the next street North of the Avenue. It fronts North, has three rooms, capable of being thrown into one, on the first above basement, besides a stair case, a passage. A Piazza the full length of the South side opening into a garden of about a quarter of an acre with some fruit trees—Above are two large chambers with fire places, two small ones, one with, and the other without,— then two garret rooms, besides closets, etc., there are two hand-some Mahogany presses, in the small room, which I use as an office, besides Center table, desk, Girandoles etc. In the parlor, a sofa, chairs, but not enough, nothing on the floors, and carpets, but that for parlor changed to dining room, but I have not room to be more minute.

If you can make the arrangement I would prefer that you come on here, about the 1st of next month, so as to determine what you will take of Preston's, and what else to buy, and let us re-turn for the children in Oct. If however you cannot come then, write me what to do, in regard to the furniture, whether to take any, and what. The rent of the house is too high, but considering everything, I conceived it best to take it, and, though solitary now, I am glad to get away from the Hotel, and not a little disgusted with the extortion of the landlord, who for a small parlor and bed room, made out my bill at $6. per day, for the time I have been there.

I am invited to dine tomorrow with Mr. Webster—Mrs. W. has gone to New England—and the day following with Genl. Scott at Boulangers. The Genl. is thus far Secr. of War, has been with me at the Hotel, and given me many scenes of the Mexican War, and earlier Military history.

There is no telling when Congress will adjourn, the Senate is making progress, has passed the Texas boundary Bill, and the Bill to admit California, and will go on, to pass all the other measures in detail, which were embraced in Mr. Clay's general Bill. In the house there is a fractious feeling of discontent, opposing today what it advocated yesterday, and afraid to let the Country be tranquilized, lest the agitators shall sink into insignificance. My time is much occupied. I have not yet been to the Capitol, but will go up in a day or two. I have called, by Card, on the Senators, and received visits from some foreign Ministers, and members of the house, and citizens. Mr. Mangum's daughters spent a few days here last week. I called to see them, but they had returned to the Country. . . .

It is late, 11 o'clock at night.

Give my love to my sons, and to Mother and Sister E. I intended to give some instructions about home affairs, but must defer it till another time.

Within three weeks my attention has been wholly withdrawn from suits at Law, and my domestic pursuits, and has been wholly engrossed with War Steamers, mail steamers, Squadrons in the East Indies, & on the Coast of Africa, with the wonderful changes produced by the addition of our Pacific possessions, on the commerce of the world, and anxieties about future events, which have been the subject of Cabinet Councils.

Mr. Conrad,[59] of La. will be nominated tomorrow as Secr. of War, and Thos. McKennan, of Penna. Secy of Interior, and thus the Cabinet will be complete.

Tell the boys I am going before long to the Naval School at Annapolis, where Wm Kirkland[60] is. I can go over in the morning and return in the afternoon. I have lately appointed a full set of Professors there.

Take care of your health, and write me at once, whether you can come on. It seems a great while since I left you.

Kiss my sons & believe me

Ever Yours most affectionately.

---

[59] Charles Magill Conrad (1804-1878), a native of Virginia, a lawyer, who moved to Louisiana. A Jackson Democrat, he became a Whig on the issue of the bank. He was United States senator, 1842-1843, a delegate to the constitutional convention of 1844, member of congress, 1849-1850, and was secretary of war, 1850-1853. He was a member of the Confederate congress, 1861-1865.

[60] William A. Kirkland (1836-1898), of Hillsboro, entered the navy in 1850 and served until his death, rising to the rank of rear admiral.

*From Daniel Jenifer.*[61]

Port Tobacco, Md.,

Aug. 18th, 1850.

Seeing that President Fillmore's Cabinet is now complete, allow me to congratulate you and the Country upon his selection of it's members.

I rejoice to see returning to the Councils of the Country, men who have the confidence of the whole Whig party, and whose association together bids fair to put to rest the disquietude which has prevailed not only in the North, but in the South.

President Fillmore has been happy in the selection of his Confidential friends, and I am satisfied that they are endorsed by the whole Whig party, except those of the ultras, consisting of the Northern *abolitionists* and the Southern *fanaticks.* They cannot, will not, be satisfied.

Altho' not having the pleasure of so intimate an acquaintance with you as I have had with your brother, with whom I served in Congress several years, yet my knowledge of you is sufficient to estimate the judgment of President Fillmore in selecting you as one of his Confidential friends and advisers.

I hereby send my hearty concurrence in his selection, and the belief that we may approve entirely of the Cabinet.

*From Oscar T. Keeler.*[62]                                U.

Columbus,

Mississippi,

August 20th, 1850.

*Private.*

Can you at earliest convenience inform me if in your power, if the descendants, or persons having the correspondance and papers of Wm. Hooper, Jos. Hewes, Jno. Penn, Wm. R. Davie, Willie Jones, Alexander Martin, R'd D. Speight, or Hugh Williamson are residing in N. Carolina, and if so how a letter addressed would reach them.

Excuse the liberty I have taken.

---

[61] Daniel Jenifer (1791-1855), of Maryland, lawyer, state legislator, Whig member of congress, 1831-1833, 1835-1841, minister to Austria, 1841-1845.

[62] Oscar Keeler was an assiduous autograph collector.

*From P. K. Rounsaville.*                                   U.

Princeton, Arks.,

August 20th., 1850.

In compliance with my promise I take this occasion to give you some account of ourselves, our adopted State, and such matters of general interest as may occur to me. We have been passing this year with my Mother, near this place, visiting and enjoying ourselves, though I have had a crop of corn and cotton raised with a part of my force, equal to any in the Country. The others I have hired at $10. per month for men, and $7. for women. We will move to Camden, 35 miles South on the Washita river the 15th. of next month. I purchased one of the most desirable lots of 8 acres, with ordinary improvements in a half mile of the Court House in the place, and at half its value. The situation is commanding, and it can be made a beautiful place. The water is cold, and good—freestone. I am just out of the corporation—exempting me from its onerous taxes. The City contains one thousand inhabitants, has Steamboat navigation from De. to Jul—ships 12,000 bales of Cotton & is rapidly improving. A plank-road to Fulton or some eligible point of Red river is now under consideration, which will much enhance the importance of the place. Its citizens are well educated, intelligent, and enterprizing. We have recently visited the place together, and Martha is much pleased with its Society. I have some commissions, merchants and planters in the place, and county, who have influence, and they have received us with great kindness and hospitality. We anticipate a happy life there, and I hope to get into a good practice in a year or two.

Dr. Graham has settled there, and is associated with Dr. Graves in practice, and a drug-store. His prospects are very flattering, and he is making himself very acceptable to all. He goes North, and thence to Carolina, in Dec.

Joseph lives 18 miles down the river, is well, has a fine crop, and has one of the most desirable farms in Arks. He is in 1½ miles of Little Bay landing. He will move to Camden in two or three years, I think. We left his house the last of June, but heard he was well when in Camden a few days since.

At present we are in 7 miles of Chapel Ridge, a settlement of Granville & Caswell people equal to any in the South. I have had several occasions at their festival days of extemporising when called upon, and we have met with much kindness and hospitality amongst the Smiths, Eatons, Summervilles & so on. They recognized Martha immediately by your face, and many of them are related to your brother Joseph's wife. They have flourishing schools. George Eaton was elected Representative by 50 votes in this County on the 5th.—a reduced maj. one half.

The Southern part of this state is settling rapidly with a most desirable population. The soil is generally kindly and productive and it is healthy, and the water good. It is also cheap, and hence its settlement. But in the northern parts of the State, on the rivers and in the valleys, the lands are described as very fertile, but unhealthy, and are settling with foreigners, and an inferior class of people.

There is little to encourage a liberal and enlightened Statesman in Arks. at present. The Government and all its offices are, and have been, in the hands of men who have recommended themselves more for zeal and party drill in democracy than integrity and efficiency in their public conduct. Hence the State has been involved in an enormous debt of 4 mils. The internal improvement fund of 500,000 acres of land, frittered away amongst the Counties and the State has enacted in her Constitution that there shall be no banks. There is then shavings at the rate of 25 per cent—10 per cent per contract is legal, and if usury is practised, the excess of interest only, is forfeited. The Seminary fund is gone. The taxes are very high, and democracy is still in the ascendant. But those of us who are settling here, live in better hopes and in a pecuniary respect we have much to encourage us, as compared with Carolina.

The Cotton crop will be a fair one, in South Arkansas, but in the South a worse failure than last year. It commands 11 and 12 cents at Camden, at present.

We are highly gratified to hear of your elevation at the helm of Government, and hope that your usual good success will attend you.

*To Susan Washington Graham.*                    A.

Washington City,

Aug. 20th, 1850.

I have neglected writing you several days longer than I intended. Thomas Witherspoon has left me, and gone to the Virginia

Springs in Fauquier. I am therefore all alone. From 9 A.M. to 4½ P.M. I spend at the Department, then come home and dine, and spend the evening alone when no friend comes in, or go to visit some one else. I believe I wrote you that I dined last week with Mr. Webster, (Mrs. W. having gone to New England) and afterwards with Genl Scott. The Genl has been exceedingly kind & civil, since my arrival, and today paid me the unusual honor, when he and his Officers now in the City, assembled to pay their respects to the new Head of the War Department, of marching them in a body, in full feather, to the Navy Department, to render a like tribute, to the other "fighting Secretary", as he expressed it. They were a noble looking set of men, and constitute the very flower of the conquerors of Mexico.

I am to dine with the President, in the White House, on Thursday of this week. He still spends the nights in Georgetown.

I have been endeavouring to think somewhat about home affairs, in view of your leaving. And think you should get some friend, Dr. Long or Mr. Kirkland, to sell my Buggy and Harness, and the Horses, Clay, & Crockett, & the grown steers at both plantations except the bull and four oxen. I wish also to sell the crop of wheat, but that may be deferred later. Your letters say nothing of the crops of corn, but if the drought has continued in N. C. as it has been here, I fear they are to be very short. If the Bacon I ordered from Petersburg has not been received, after using the wethers at the Estes place, and the old ewes at the Ray, you should kill some of the steers already mentioned.

After threshing out the wheat, I wish Hill and Alfred to put up the Stable at the Estes place, and after doing the work, laid off for them at home, I want the shed put up to the stable at the Ray place, for which the timbers were gotten last year.

Give directions to have all the fodder & tops saved, and the meadows cut about 1st. of Oct. . . .

Ask Mr. Kirkland to ascertain on what terms I can obtain the services of Garrett, or of Campbell, or some other suitable person to overlook and manage my affairs, generally, in my absence. I have thought if I could not get a suitable person in Orange to write to some friend in Caswell, to engage an overseer for me.

I regret that you are so desponding in regard to your health. Had I supposed it would be seriously endangered by a return to this climate, I would not have accepted, the distinction which the President thought proper to tender to the State in my person. If you feel sufficiently well, I think you had better come on, with Mr. Webb, or some other friend, by the earliest day, that may be convenient. Bring Hannah or some other servant with you. If you find after staying a month or six weeks here, that your health does not improve, we can make arrangements for your spending the winter in the South. It will be well to bring with you a few articles of furniture. I have but half a dozen knives and forks, ½ a doz. Brittania or German silver Tea spoons, and two Table spoons, finding no article of the kind in the House. Also two pairs of sheets & two bed spreads. You might bring a Doz. Tea Spoons, and such other things as you find convenient. I have not been to see Mrs. Page who owns the house, intending when you come and have seen her furniture that if you prefer it, we will take the house without the furniture. It needs a thorough cleansing and painting. Write me when you will be here, and I will meet you at the Boat. It is hardly safe, I think, to drive Jim a days journey in the carriage. Before leaving home you should see that Mother and Sister Eliza have a sufficient supply of every thing, untill you return. I think we will get back between the 1st and middle of Oct. to stay not more than eight or ten days. If Dr. Strudwick wants a carriage, perhaps he would buy ours, at a reasonable price. Otherwise, if varnished up, I think it will suit us here & I will send it to Baltimore for that purpose. You should give directions to have it aired, and the wheels kept off the ground while you are absent.

Hill can remain in my employment till the plantation buildings are finished, and the crop of wheat is sown, unless I get an overseer before the wheat is sown. I shall not want him longer.

I have not yet been to the Capitol, and have made but few visits. Mr. and Mrs. J. H. Bryan & Betty B. & Miss Pettigrew are here on return from Canada. Mr. Rayner also called to see me today, going to New England.

Shew the boys the letter in the National Intelligencer, which has been recd. at the Navy Department, and I ordered it to be published, from Lieut. DeHaven,[63] commanding the vessels sent in search of Sir John Franklin, and let them search out the "Whale fish" islands on the Map. There is said to be a fine school in my neighborhood, here, taught by Mr. Abbott.

As I wish to get this letter in the Post Office tonight, I have not time to write more. I would that I could look in upon you

[63] Edward Jesse DeHaven (1816-1865), of Pennsylvania, was an experienced explorer. He saw active service in the war with Mexico, and had been attached to the naval observatory. On this expedition he was in the ice for nine months, and discovered Grinnell Land.

tonight. My love to my dear boys, and to Mother & Sister Eliza, also to Miss Julia Miner for her kindness in remembering me.

The Senate has passed Bills on all the distracting questions of the time, and thrown the responsibility on the House, where there is much disorder & bad feeling, but I think a majority there will eventually do their duty. Write me on receipt of this and let me know when you are coming to relieve my solitude.

*From Silas E. Burrows.*                                   U.

New York,

August 21st., 1850.

I have the honor to enclose Gov'r Graham the within correspondence,[64] which I have been induced by my friends to allow published, previous to leaving America, that all may know the author of the Arctic Expedition, which I hope is destined to add lustre to the character of our Country, and gratify the present Secretary of the Navy.

With high considerations, I remain,
Your most ob't serv't

*From Winfield Scott.*

August 21st., 1850.

My dear Mr. Secretary:

An old brother soldier, who served with me in the War of 1812, will send in to you this note. Major Saunders, (his name) wishes a midshipman's Warrant for a son. He has strong recommendations from the Governor of Pennsylvania, etc., etc., and I beg to add mine.

Please read his papers.

Very truly yrs.

----
[64] The enclosures are not to be found in the collections of Graham papers.

*From Daniel Webster.*    U.

Department of State.
Washington,
August 22nd., 1850.
Thursday morning,
9 o'clock.

It is thought advisable that the Heads of Departments should hold a conversation together, to day; and it is proposed that they assemble at this Department, at 2 o'clock, P.M.

Very respectfully, Yours

*From Charles L. Hinton.*    A.

Raleigh,
Augst 22nd, 1850.

I thank you sincerely for your kind favour of the 18th which reached me yesterday. The more so as it was unexpected from the great press of business which I know occupies your time.

Yesterday I sent you the Standard containing the card[65] of Thomas Ruffin, jr., & the certificates of others about Gov Manly's Wentworth speech. Manly will reply in tomorrow's Register, but I very much fear it will be difficult to extricate himself before the public. He says he has no doubt he was so understood by those Gentlemen, but such opinions he never intended to advance—but his defence you will see.

I feel very much for him personally, chagrined at his defeat appearing before the public on a point of Veracity, & having to retire on a limited income, gives much for deep concern. If the charges of his notions about the distribution of the school fund & White basis had been generally credited, he could not have gotten two thousand votes east of Raleigh.

---

[65] Governor Manly had charged with falsehood Ruffin and others who had signed a certificate concerning the governor's statement in his speech on the basis of representation in the state. The card which had just been published included letters from Whigs as well as Democrats testifying to the truth of Ruffin's statement.

After his speech at Wentworth, Rawley Galloway[66] and other Whigs refused to vote, so with many it is said that Collins[67] in Washington took the stump against him.

It is believed there will be a general change of State Officers. Several are spoken of for my station, Green W Caldwell, I think, is the most prominent—really I feel very little concern about it, for on a pecuniary point I don't know that I am anything gainer by remaining here. Majr Clarke[68] will oppose Collins.

I learned last night that Gov. Morehead has had a fall from his horse which made it necessary to call in several physicians, but is now improving and believed nothing serious.

Swain, P Cameron, & Jno Norwood are with us, the accounts of crops in Orange are distressing, indeed in all the section of Country from Haw River to the Yadkin. It has been cloudy for the last 24 hours & we hope for good seasons.

*    *    *    *    *

*From B. R. McKennie & Company.*

True Whig Office.

Nashville, Tennessee,

August 24th., 1850.

(Private)

We trust you will excuse us for trespassing upon your time one moment, in reference to a subject, to us of something more than mere pecuniary import, one that addresses itself to our pride and our sensibilities as members of the great American Whig party.

For the character and position of the Nashville True Whig, we respectfully refer you to the enclosed copy of a statement *voluntarily* tendered to us by the Whig members of the last Legislature of this State, (with only two exceptions, and they from sickness or absence). Nevertheless, by some strange influence, (we know not what) the True Whig has been excluded entirely (with the exception of a single small item) by the late administration, from

---

[66] Rawley Galloway (1811-1872), of Rockingham County, a planter, a graduate of the university, who was a member of the commons in 1860.

[67] Josiah Collins was the Whig candidate for the commons in Washington County.

[68] William John Clarke ( -1886), of Wake County, a native of Perquimans, who also lived in Craven, a graduate of the university, captain and major in the Mexican War. He served as comptroller, 1851-1855, was a colonel in the Civil War, and was state senator, 1870-1871. He was also a colonel in Holden's "detailed militia," of evil memory. He was a judge of the superior court, 1871-1874.

the patronage of the Federal Government at Washington. We are well assured this is not in accordance with the popular feeling of the Whig party in Tennessee, or with common justice and propriety.

We ask simply an equitable division. As that patronage has been bestowed almost exclusively upon another establishment for more than a year, we respectfully request that it shall be bestowed in like manner upon the "True Whig" for the next twelve months, and then equally divided between the two Whig presses at Nashville. Even this would leave a balance against us, as the post office advertising, the most desirable, and occurring but once in four years, has already been bestowed entirely on the other establishments.

With earnest solicitude for the speedy adjustment of the sectional difficulties which unhappily threaten to disturb the peace and harmony of the country, we subscribe ourselves,

Most Respectfully.

[Enclosure]

Nashville, Tennessee.

Feb. 4th., 1850.

The undersigned members of the Tennessee Legislature, have been earnestly impressed with the superior energy, ability, and efficiency of the Nashville True Whig, over any other Whig newspaper in the City, and perceiving that large Government patronage has been bestowed on other Nashville papers, to the exclusion of the True Whig, feel called on by justice and sound policy to make this suggestion.

| | |
|---|---|
| R. W. H. Bostwick | F. K. Zollicoffer |
| P. G. Stiver Perkins | A. Tipton |
| Jno. F. Henry | W. Sunnell |
| E. Thompson | Gayle H. Kyle |
| G. D. Crosthwait | H. S. Kimble |
| J. B. Palmer | M. R. Hill |
| S. M. Campbell | S. M. Fite |
| J. A. Rogers | J. W. Gillespie |
| G. D. Searcy | Y. M. Brashear |
| Alex. Jackson | J. Hamilton |
| W. R. Kenner | M. Thornburg |

W. Heiskell

H. Barham

H. V. Murphy

Jo. Parsons

M. J. Clay

C. W. Nance

Geo. Maney

E. S. Smith

Jno. W. Burton

S. W. Seriter

M. Carriger

G. A. Harrell

Robt. C. McRee

Y. Snodgrass

W. Woodward

W. Galbraith

R. D. Allison

Y. Foster

B. S. Allen

Jno. Phillips

W. Duggan

M. Benham

J. C. Tipton

A. G. Shrewsbury

Ed. Cooper

N. B. Stokes

A copy of the above has been forwarded to each member of the Cabinet. (A true copy.)

B. R. McKennie & Company.

*To James Graham.*                                               U.

Washington City,

Aug. 25th, 1850.

Dear Brother

Your kind letter of the 11th. inst. has been received. After my arrival here, I remained two weeks at Willard Hotel. My predecessor, Mr. Preston, being about to vacate a house, with which I was better pleased than any I had examined, I agreed to take his lease for nine months, with the priviledge of continuing for another year, if I think proper. It is a house, built by Mr. Rush, on H. Street, West of President's Square, and was occupied by him when Sec'y of the Treasury, and by Mr. Poinsett, when he was in the War Department. It is partially furnished, and I have taken by the month two servants that he had hired, and am now keeping house. Preston had other furniture of his own, which he wishes me to take on some terms, but matters of that nature depend so much on taste and opinion, to which I have no pretensions, that I told him they might remain till my wife came on; and if she were pleased with them, I would make him an offer, otherwise, he could dispose of them, and they are thus left. I have written her of my arrangements, and advised her to come on with some friend going North about the 1st. Sept. and remain with me a month or two, and that she could ascertain what furniture, etc., we want, and I would return with her, about the middle of Oct. and bring on the children, Mrs. Washington & Mrs. Knox remaining with them meanwhile. And I expect her perhaps the present week. A heavy rain last night reveals to me that my house leaks badly, and the servants say it has done so for a considerable time. Preston has left town; I will call on the landlady tomorrow, and must have it remedied. In good repair it will suit me very well, has good stables, carriage house, wood house, and a considerable plot of ground in a flower and fruit garden, and is situated conveniently to the President's house and the department.

You will have seen by the papers that the Cabinet has been completed. But McKennon seemed depressed, from the time of his arrival, and complaining of bad health, left the city yesterday, intending to send back his resignation as soon as he gets home. The President and Mr. Webster, entertaining a favorable opinion of my capacities for work, insisted on my taking the Interior, which ranks next to the Treasury, but I demurred, and the matter is adjourned for further consultation. I told Webster yesterday that the transfer was not to be thought of—that all the time I was in Congress I was buried under the Chairmanship of the Committee of Claims, and that the Interior department was next to it. The President desires to fill it with a Southern man, though I proposed Evans, of Maine, and Webster said last night that he thought we could get a proper man, from Georgia. We have canvassed over the South Western States several times before, after the declination of Bates and Pearce, & I regretted that being the only member of the Cabinet from the Potomac to the Rio Grande, I knew so little of the practical talent in that section. Since Conrad has come in, I find he is as much at a loss as I was, or, rather, he knows few men whom he thinks have the proper qualifications. A selection will be made in a few days.

I think light is dawning on Congress, after an Arctic winter of chaos & dissension, and that in ten days more, tranquillity will prevail every where except among Abolitionists and disunionists. The Senate on Friday passed the Fugitive Slave Bill, the last of the measures embraced in the general Bill of Mr. Clay, and now the responsibility is upon the house. The administration, though quietly, has thrown its whole weight into the settlement of the difficulties, and at a meeting of the Cabinet officers, at Webster's last night, to compare information, the result was that the Texas boundary Bill, the Bills for the establishment of Territorial Governments in New Mexico and Utah, without the Wilmot proviso, the Bill to admit California, and the Fugitive Slave Bill, will all pass without amendment, and by handsome majorities. The Clingman faction in the house, who threatened to call for Yeas and Nays, has dwindled far below one fifth. Corwin has joined us in this movement, and Webster feels as much or more interest in it, than a Southern man. He has had a great triumph in the election of Mr. Elliott,[69] of Boston, who is known as the author of the letter to him, signed by so many persons and approving his speech of the 7th. of March. And the recent arrival of Elliott, with his great weight of character, wealth and influence in New England, has had a happy effect on that delegation. Gen'l Scott told me that Winthrop advised him to see Jno. Davis, and persuade him to go for Compromise, that he mentioned it to Webster, who replied, "Mr. Winthrop is a good man—he means well, but wants moral courage, but d—n John Davis—We'll whip him in" — "don't trouble yourself about seeing him." I have been much with Gen'l Scott, sitting together at table at our Hotel, and he being Sec. of War untill Conrad's appointment, And have been much pleased with the soundness of his views on public affairs, his patriotic feelings, and personal kindness. I have dined with him at Boulanger's, also with Mr. Webster, the President, the Messrs. King,—two sons of Rufus King[70]—members of the House Reps., one from New York,[71] the other, New Jersey,[72] who are at Mrs. Gadsby's near me, corner of President's Square. I have been to the Capitol but once, except to attend preaching, on Sunday at another time.

The Senate has not more than ten members with whom I served, and there are but few in the House. It seems to be understood that

---

[69] Samuel Atkins Eliot (1798-1862), of Massachusetts, a graduate of Harvard, academic and divinity, who had already served in both houses of the legislature. He was in congress for only one term.

[70] Rufus King (1755-1827), of Massachusetts and New York, one of the most distinguished American statesmen. A native of Massachusetts, a graduate of Harvard, he became a lawyer, was a state legislator, member of congress, 1784-1787, delegate to the Federal convention, 1787. He moved to New York in 1788, was minister to Great Britain, 1796-1803, and Federalist candidate for vice president, 1804 and 1808, and for President, 1816. He was United States senator, 1789-1796, 1813-1825, a delegate to the constitutional convention of 1821, and again minister to Great Britain, 1825-1826.

[71] John Alsop King (1788-1867), educated at Harvard and in Paris, lawyer, soldier in the War of 1812, state legislator, secretary of legation in London, Whig member of congress, 1849-1851. He was a delegate to the peace conference in 1861.

[72] James Gore King (1791-1853), educated in England and France, Harvard and Litchfield, soldier in the War of 1812, he then engaged in business. He was president of the Erie Railroad, and of the New York chamber of commerce. He served only this one term in congress.

Benton will not be returned to the Senate, and I hear that he declares himself a Candidate for the House in the St. Louis district.

The late administration had lost favor with Whigs far beyond what I had supposed when I came here, and had they continued, Conrad assures me, that there would have been a break with them, equal to that with Tyler. Clayton[73] seems to have lost character for candor in a most extraordinary degree, and he was the only man among them, who was reputed to have talents, or capacity for affairs. Bayard, with whom I was always intimate, came the other day to see me (happening here), and he charges that Clayton & Seward had formed a complete alliance for a third party, to consist [of] Taylor men, and abolitionists, and there is no doubt of the fact that Seward had completely supplanted Mr. Fillmore with that administration, so much so that he procured the appointment of a Post Master for Buffalow, against the remonstrances of the Vice President, and the nomination of a Collector for the same Port whom Mr. Fillmore promptly withdrew from the Senate, on his accession to the Presidency.

Mr. Fillmore has admirable qualifications for a Chief Magistrate. Although I knew him favorably as a working member of the House when I was in Congress, I was very far from estimating at their true standard his ability, firmness, conversancy with affairs, and just appreciation of the high and enlarged duties of a Chief Magistrate. He is disposed to deal justly with all parts of the country, and with liberality, even, towards the South, as the weaker section. But his moderation will impose no check on his firmness, if action shall become necessary. I now feel a confident hope that Congress will adjourn in the course of the next month, having tranquilized the country in all quarters, except where there is a determination to be satisfied with nothing.

Waddy Thompson, who is here, says that all the members from his State are disunionists, *per se*. He begs me to say to you, that smoking a pipe will be a certain cure for your throat, and I think he may be right. It is at least worth trying. While others say that chewing or eating the horse radish will have the same effect. Many of your old friends have enquired for you, with much kindness, Corwin, Crittenden, McKennon, Jenifer, etc. Frank Graham wrote me from New York, saying he was disappointed in

---

[73] John Middleton Clayton (1796-1856), of Delaware, a graduate of Yale and Litchfield, state legislator and secretary of state, United States senator, 1829-1836, 1845-1849, 1853-1856, state chief justice, United States secretary of state, 1849-1850. He negotiated the Clayton-Bulwer Treaty.

getting a passage to California, and asking a pursership in the Navy, or Lieutenancy in the Marine Corps. I wrote him that there were no vacancies, and would not be for some time. He then came on here, asking to bear dispatches to California. But having regular mails to that country the Government sends no messengers of that kind. I asked him to take quarters with me, and stay a few days, but he said he would proceed on home. I think, however, that he is still at one of the Hotels of the City. An appointment of Naval Storekeeper has lately become vacant in California, worth $1500. a year, and requiring nothing but attention, care, and moderate capacity for business, and I had thought of giving it to him. But he has so unsteady a character, that I have not deemed it just to the Government to appoint him, and therefore have not mentioned it to him. Thos. Witherspoon was here a week since, and staid with me several days. He went to the Fauquier Springs, Va. and was doubtful about returning. He wanted a pursership or clerkship here. There being no purser to appoint, and Alabama having her full number, I advised him if he could make $1,000. a year in Mobile (which he said he could do) not to think of coming here, in a subordinate office. There are numberless applications for office, especially from N. C. and the impression prevails at home that there are no clerks here, from the State, whereas there is a very considerable number. Some changes will be required beyond what were made under the last administration, for the Whigs were greatly disheartened then, but there will be no indiscriminate proscription. In my own department I have constantly replied that there are no vacancies, and have not yet determined on any, but expect to make a few. I have labored seven or eight hours a day there, thus far, and coming in while Congress is in session, and the routine of affairs new to me, I shall have no time to spare untill the adjournment in March, except what time I shall snatch, to bring on my children.

The affairs of the department, and the service, require in my opinion, and I find that is the general one, thorough revision, and my regret is that I shall not have time, before the next meeting of Congress, to digest the subject properly. Our Pacific possessions give a new aspect to Naval affairs, and the transportation of the mail from Oregon to Panama, and from Chagus via Havanna, etc., to New York, and between New [York] and Liverpool, etc., in steamers built by individuals under the patronage of the Government, on such plan, as to be convertible to War Steamers, and to be taken at value by the Government when ever desired, and the comparative value of steam and sail vessels for War purposes, are all subjects of great magnitude, which now occupy and divide public opinion among Naval men—as well as the state of discipline in the service, and the proper instructions to our squadrons in the different seas of the world.

Isaac Hayne called to see me last week, in company with Judge Butler,[74] and Commodore Shubric,[75] who is the Uncle of his wife. I subsequently called at the Commodore's, and saw Mrs. Hayne, but Isaac was out. I presume he is deeply committed to the extreme opinions of his State. Gen'l Houston called at the department yesterday, and says he is going to notice on the floor of the Senate a violent attack upon him, in a letter published in the Southern Press by Wallace[76] of S. C. about the Nashville Convention and disunion.

\* \* \* \* \*

I will direct this letter to the Furnace. I much regret our election in N. C. though it is, in many respects, the result of accident. Clingman, I understand, exults over it, and cooperates altogether with the extreme democrats here. The Whigs of his district have either to cast him off, or he will them.

Write me frequently,
                    Your affectionate Brother.

*From Elisha Mitchell.*                                              U.

Chapel Hill,

Aug. 27th, 1850.

It is incident to the office you hold to place it in your power perhaps to benefit North Carolina in some small things without overstepping the bounds of what is just and right.

---

[74] Andrew Pickens Butler.

[75] William Branford Shubrick (1790-1874), naval officer, born in South Carolina, was educated in Charleston and Massachusetts. He entered the navy in 1806 and served with distinction. Sent to California during the Mexican War, he commanded the troops there. He also commanded the expedition to Paraguay, 1858-1859. He remained in the navy in the Civil War, but was too old for active service. He became rear admiral, retired in 1862.

[76] Daniel Wallace (1801-1859), lawyer and farmer, state legislator, Whig member of congress, 1848-1853. On September 9, 1850, Houston made the promised speech, which, however, was chiefly a defence of himself from a charge of malfeasance. Senator Butler, in behalf of Wallace, replied to him.

I suppose there are sometimes placed at your disposal, seeds and other things, which the national vessels bring in from abroad. When the Dead Sea expedition returned, there was, I understand, a multitude of such things that would have been interesting; no one of which so far as I know, made its way to North Carolina.

But what I have more particularly in view does not belong to your department, but to the Minister of the Interior, or Secretary of the Home Department, or whatever his style and title may be, and perhaps you may be able to attain the ends desired through him as readily as if the whole were under your own control.

The Buffaloe grass of the country east of the Rocky mountains must, from the size the animal attains, be both luxuriant and nutritive through growing in a dry and poor country. It might prove exceedingly valuable in North Carolina on our old fields. It produces no seed, and can therefore be propagated only in the way mentioned by Colnar—author of the Reports on European agriculture, in his letters on European Life and Manners, Vol. I, Page 132, where he speaks of the "invention of what is termed *inoculating* land, a process by which setting or planting small pieces of grass at some little distance from each other over a piece of land, the whole is soon converted into a close sward."

Cannot a sod of living Buffaloe grass be gotten into these parts, and is the thing not worth attending to. If you do not give me satisfaction, I will positively write to Mrs. Graham about it.

To encourage the Hon. Secretary of the Home Department to diligence in this business, you may tell him that though my wife is past child bearing and I shall therefore never have a son to be named after him, if he will get me the grass—the first big bull I shall fatten upon it I will testify my respect by calling by his name.

*From John S. Gallaher.*[77]    U.

(Confidential.)

Washington,

Aug. 27th, 1850.

I suppose I need not attach any importance to the confident outgivings of a correspondent of the Baltimore Clipper "that the probabilities in favor of Mr. Botts' being called into the Presi-

---

[77] John S. Gallaher, a newspaper publisher for twenty-eight years prior to 1849, when he entered government service. He was at this time third auditor in the interior department.

dent's Councils, *amount almost* to a certainty"; yet my interest in the success of the Administration, and your kindness, embolden me to drop an opinion.

I was friendly to the election of Mr. Botts as the Whig candidate for Congress; but a place in the Cabinet is a different affair. Mr. B. is an able man—but headstrong and self-willed. In short, of the "Rule or Ruin" stamp.

I know you will pardon these suggestions, even though there may have been no necessity for them.

*To Daniel Webster.*[78]                                    U.

Navy Department,

August 28th., 1850.

If you have half an hour to spare, I will be glad [to] see you, on a subject of some public importance, and, if it be agreeable, will call on you, at your department, at 1 or 2 o'clock today. The matter, however, is not urgent, and I would not have you postpone any thing else, on this account.

Very truly Yours,

*From Daniel Webster.*                                    U.

Department of State.

August 28th.,

½ past 12 o'clock.
[1850.]

My Chief Clerk is sick in bed, and I am sick out of bed, and therefore cannot well see you to day, but will call at your Department when I come from my house tomorrow morning.

Yours, truly always,

*From William W. Kirkland.*[79]                                    U.

Hillsboro',

Aug. 29th, 1850.

I hope that You will excuse the liberty that I now take upon myself in addressing You. I have always been anxious to obtain

---

[78] Copy.

[79] William W. Kirkland, son of John U. Kirkland of Hillsboro, received an appointment to West Point from which he was later dismissed. Jefferson Davis, in 1855, gave him a commission in the army, but as his class had not completed

a warrant for West Point, but as Yet have never been able to accomplish my wishes, and it is, Sir, to solicit Your influence that I now write. I believe that I am too late for the present Session, but should any vacancy occur in our district, I would hail the opportunity to fill it with the greatest pleasure.

\* \* \* \* \*

Hoping that You will grant my humble request. May I beg that You will honor this note with as speedy an acknowledgement as Your convenience will allow.

\* \* \* \* \*

*From David L. Swain.*                                                    U.

Chapel Hill,

Aug. 30th, 1850.

I do not know that I can make any better disposition of the enclosed letters[80] than to send them to you.

That from Maj: Gatlin requires no explanation; David W. Siler, the writer of the other,[81] is the son of Jacob Siler of whom you have some personal knowledge, and is a member elect to the House of Commons from the County of Macon. You will probably regard him as uncouth in manners, since he has had little opportunity for intercourse with good society. I know him well, and though he is my nephew, I feel myself at liberty to say to you, that I have rarely known so fine a man.

From a previous letter, I happen to know that he does not regard himself as a favorite with his immediate representative, Mr. Clingman, and suppose that to be the reason why he desires letters to our Senators. I will send his letters to Messrs. Badger and Clingman, and direct him to call upon you. The object of his visit to Washington he can explain. I merely know that it has some connexion with the Cherokee Indians resident in that region, whom he does not suppose to have been fairly dealt by.

the course at West Point, he was not allowed to accept. He then entered the marine corps as a lieutenant and served in China three years with some distinction, and in 1859 was eager to get a transfer to the army. In the Civil War he was colonel of the 21st North Carolina regiment, was a highly successful officer, and was promoted brigadier general in 1864.

[80] Siler's letter has not been found.

[81] David W. Siler (b. 1822), of Macon County, a tanner, member of the commons, 1850-1852, 1856-1858, 1860-1861.

204 matriculates are on our records, 31 more than at any previous period in our history. We are of course busy enough.

* * * * *

Judge Cameron is in Phila., Paul was there, Mr. Boylan had gone to the Springs. J. H. Bryan returned that day. The Governor, all things considered, sustains himself with a good degree of equanimity.

[Enclosure]

*From R. C. Gatlin to David L. Swain.*

Jefferson Barracks,

July 31st., 1850.

Gov'r Graham's appointment to be Sect'y of the Navy, encourages me in again asking your good offices in favour of my wish to enter the Pay Department of the Army. I can only hope to obtain the Appointment of Pay Master upon the promise of the President, that I shall fill the first vacancy, for I am too distant from Washington to give notice to my friends of a vacancy, before it will be filled, as was the case last January. You will therefore very much oblige me by writing to Gov'r Graham, making such suggestions as you may think proper.

Being a *Man of Family,* I am more anxious than ever to leave the line of the Army. It will never do, to be forced to drag my Wife and Child on distant Service, as I shall have to do, if I retain my present Office.

* * * * *

*From Daniel Webster.*                                    U.

Department of State.

August 30th., 1850.

It was not in my power to call upon you yesterday, pursuant to my promise in my note of the day before. This morning, however, I shall be here until 2 o'clock, and will see you with pleasure at any time before then.

I am, with entire regard,

Your obedient servant,

*From William Seawell.*    U.

Selma, Alabama.,

August 31st, 1850.

I am one of the Editors of a Whig Journal called the "Selma Reporter," published at this place. Selma is located on the Alabama river, within 24 hours run by Steam Boat from Mobile, is the Southern Terminus of the "Ala. & Ten. River Rail road" now in a course of construction, and intended to convene at the waters of Mobile Bay with the Tennessee River, & will be the point at which this road will be intersected by the "Southern Rail Road," which is to start at Vicksburg on the Mississippi River, and to traverse the States of Mississippi, Ala. & Georgia.

Thus you see that Selma is already a place of some importance, and upon the completion of these roads will become one of very much greater. The "Reporter" has already an extensive circulation in the State, and has the reputation of being one of the soundest & most conservative Whig Journals in Alabama.

Of course I have not been so presumptuous as to undertake the conduct of a public paper merely for the public good. My abilities are too humble for any such patriotic conceptions of duty. In plain English, I edit a paper to make money—which, by the bye, my shortened circumstances render it very necessary I should endeavor to make.

Therefore, my dear Sir, if you have any Executive crumbs to dispense in the way of advertisements from your Department, or any thing of the way which might help to nourish a poor Editor, allow me to say, that they would be most thankfully received by the "Selma Reporter."

The citizens of North Carolina are no less gratified at your being in the Cabinet, than are your numerous friends & acquaintances in Alabama.

I wish your services may redound to the happiness of our common Country, & to the advancement of your own reputation.

*Opinion*[82] *on the*    A.
*President's power with respect to New Mexico.*
*August, 1850*

The Executive, being that department of Government whose functions never cease, or undergo suspension, while the Govern-

---

[82] Copy in Graham's writing.

ment itself endures, is expected, not merely to execute written Laws, but to watch over the public interests, and to take care of the public property, by all the means which have been committed to its hands, by the Constitution, or the Laws made in pursuance thereof.

"The Executive power" of the Government of the United States is *in his verbis* vested in the President. The argument is certainly not without plausibility that such Executive powers as are necessarily correlative to the Legislative and Judicial authorities of the same Government pass to him, from the nature of the subject matter, by this single grant. And that while Congress possesses the power to declare War, it is an Executive duty to carry on such War, to wield the arms of the Country in battle, to preserve the trophies of victory, to secure and afford subsistence to prisoners of War, and to hold and keep possession of territories, or other property conquered from an enemy, or purchased from him, in consideration of peace, or of a pecuniary equivalent. And that if territories or other property pass from a foreign Government to ours, the absence of any statute regulating the subject (and none such can be pretended) they fall under the control and direction of the President of the United States, as a matter of course.

But the President, under our system, is not merely the general depository of the Executive power. He is, by express terms, constituted the Commander in Chief of the Army and Navy of the United States, and of all the Militia forces called to their aid for any service. He likewise is expressly authorized to appoint all agents of the Government to hold intercourse with foreign nations, and to make treaties with them, subject only to the concurrence of a majority of two thirds of the Senate. By virtue of these express powers, he not only plans campaigns in War, but provides, under general appropriations of money, all the necessary armaments and supplies, but when peace is concluded, he receives back property captured from us by our adversary, or an indemnity in money, as in the case of the Military posts in Oregon, and the negro slaves carried away from the Southern States, in the last War with Great Britain.

And when property or money, in lieu thereof, is thus delivered up to him, it is his duty to hold it, untill it shall be placed in other hands by a law of Congress. To this extent, there seems no room for doubt as to the powers of the President. But the question now presented in the case of New Mexico, is whether the President has power to maintain the municipal Government, which he found in operation when that territory was acquired, against a change of system demanded by a majority of the inhabitants. If that country be regarded as a conquest of our arms, it came into his possession as Military Commander in Chief of the Nation. If by treaty of cession, it came to him as the Chief negotiator of the Country. In either aspect, it came to him as President of the United States. And it is his duty to hold it, not only against foreign invasion, but to protect it against internal disturbance. For the execution of these duties he employs the Military force of the United States, which is under his absolute control, limited only by his sense of obligation to official duty, and his liability to impeachment, for any abuse of his powers. Thus Louisiana and Florida, respectively, were taken into Military occupation by marching troops into their borders, after their acquisition, and thus New Mexico continued to be occupied, after the conclusion of peace, by the troops who had invaded it in War. The rights of the inhabitants of the territory during this continuance of Presidential occupation or custody, are *civil* rights merely—rights *under* the law. They have no political rights, or rights *over* the law. In other words, according to the code and usage of modern civilized nations, they have a right to the continuance of that municipal system for the protection of life, liberty and property, which was found in existence when their flag was changed, and their allegiance transferred, but they have no right to abolish or alter that, except by the permission of the President. Admit to them any political rights, and where will be the limit? If they can form a State Government without the permission of the President, they can also form a monarchical Government—or at least, being without the restraints of the Federal Constitution, their isolated state may levy & keep any number troops, and render insecure, or onerous & expensive, the very conquest itself. Even the inhabitants of our organized territories enjoy very limited priviledges, and cannot change their municipal systems, except with the approbation of Congress. And it would be a strange anomaly if a people of a conquered or purchased territory in the Military possession of the Executive, before Congress has passed any law for their Government, have a right, without the permission of the President, to throw off his control, by establishing for themselves a new Government.

But the question remains, what system of Law is to be maintained in that country, the old code or the Kenney Code? The people were entitled at the peace, had they demanded it, to the re-establishment of the old Code. But no such demand was made.

There seems to have been a general acquiescence in the Code of Gen'l Kenney before the treaty of peace, and that, I presume, is to be considered as the system which was in force when our title to the Country was perfected by purchase.

The treaty guarantees to the inhabitants of New Mexico no political rights, therefore is to be tested by the law of nations, and the Constitution of the United States. But for the delay of Congress to provide for them a Government, in due season, the question to be solved would hardly have admitted a doubt. Can this delay, in one department of the Government, take away the powers, or diminish the responsibilities of another? Is the President to abandon the exercise of the authorities now possessed by him, because in his opinion Congress could, by legislation, give a better Government to a Territory? I conclude therefore, that it is the duty of the President, untill Congress shall otherwise direct, to continue the same supervisory authority, or Government, over this Territory, since the treaty of peace, that was established during the War; and that whilst under the law of nations, and the treaty of Guadeloupe Hidalgo, they are entitled to the preservation of their municipal system. They have no right to change it, except with his approbation. And that the contrary opinion arises from confounding the people of this subjugated or purchased territory, with an independent sovereign people, from whom, under our system, all political power emanates.

The administration of President Polk, though its ideas of this subject are not very clearly defined, seems to accord with the foregoing views, in the letter of Mr. Buchanan to Mr. Voorhees, on the          day of          after the treaty of peace. Gen'l Taylor, while he did not disaffirm them, seems to have yielded his permission to have encouraged the formation of State Governments in those territories, a preparatory step to direct admission into the Union. But in his Message of June last, he asserted the power of the Executive to maintain the *status in quo* of New Mexico, untill the intervention of Congress.

1. The power being established, it seems highly expedient not to permit a State Government to supersede the Military or Presidential Government, untill Congress shall provide for it. In the first place, there is no great evil now endured by the people there, which would be remedied by an independent State Government, not bound by the Constitution of the Union.

2. Such a Government, in the event of Congress continuing

to postpone any legislation for this territory, might become mischievous, and dangerous to the peace of the Union.

3. It would be highly offensive to the State of Texas, after giving her distinct warning not to attempt to establish any Government over this territory, (which she earnestly claims) to permit a State Government to be established there, which is no doubt intended, in some degree, as a fortification against her title.

4. There is no ground, or pretence, that there is a sufficient population there to entitle such State to a member, or even delegate, of the House of Representatives, much less, to two Senators.

*From Daniel C. Goddard.*[83]     U.

Department of the Interior,

Sept. 2nd, 1850.

I have recived your note of this date by the hand of Mr. Lafayette G. Brown, whom it was my misfortune to be obliged to discharge from the Pension Office on Saturday last.

I had no acquaintance with Mr. Brown, nor I believe with any other of the gentlemen who were included in the same list. The duty of making any removals was a very painful one, and one which I would gladly have avoided. But, since the responsibility was imposed upon me, I could not shrink from it. I have no doubt of Mr. Brown's efficiency and fidelity as a Clerk. It is not improbable that I made a mistake in removing him. But I understand he is a Democrat, and I could not very consistently retain him and dismiss a Whig.

If I had the power I would gladly restore him to the place he occupied, But I find myself obliged studiously to abstain from making any appointments—

Being a mere *locum tenens* myself, I do not feel authorized to deprive the Secretary who is to come in, of any portion of the patronage which belongs to his Department, and which he only, has a right to dispose of.

Under these circumstances, I think you will agree with me that it is impossible for me to reappoint Mr. Brown.

---

[83] Daniel C. Goddard was chief clerk and twice secretary *ad interim* of the interior department.

*From Daniel Webster.*                                       U.

September 2nd, 1850.

I send this for your private perusal, only; not supposing it a
case in which any thing is to be done. I believe Capt. Stockton[84]
feels very much chagrined.

[Enclosure]

*From C. A. Stetson to Daniel Webster.*            U.

Astor House,

August 22nd, 1850.

Is there anything wrong in regard to Capt. Stockton's resigna-
tions? He has been a splendid officer—Absent years—conquered
California—was entitled to a Navy Yard or a Furlough—was ordered to a Station, Valpariso—where he could not hear from home
as often as his great interests demanded, as a matter of annoyance
by the late Sec'ty.

He asked for a furlough—It was *refused.* He had a *Rule* of
action never to *disobey an order.* Therefore resigned on receipt
of refusal, to *avoid the order.* The Secretary answered at once,—
*accepted!!!* The most popular officer insulted by a fifth rate Virginia Lawyer! Thirty years Service and all his experience thrown
away as Easy and with as much want of grace as the Sons of the
Old Dominion exhibit in their yearnings after the Crib Drops
in Washington.

Can the Secretary accept? Must not the President Direct? Is it
*not* possible that the President knew nothing about it? That it
is illegal, and of course unjust and wrong.

I just suggest. I think Mr. Stockton is very much annoyed,—
would not have resigned but for the injustice in the action of
Mr. Preston. I have no authority to say one word, but I remember where your feelings are, and that amid the thousand things
you have to look after, this might escape until too late.

———
[84] Robert Field Stockton (1795-1866), of New Jersey. Educated at Princeton, he
entered the navy in 1811, saw service in the War of 1812 and in Algiers. He was
off duty, 1828-1838, and was active in politics, and declined appointment as secretary
of the navy. He was in the war with Mexico, taking possession of California. He
resigned in 1850, and was a Democratic United States senator, 1851-1853. He was
then a railroad president. He was a delegate to the peace conference in 1861.

I hope when you investigate it—*If you think it best*—that you will find he can be ordered to duty or to *await orders* upon the informality of the acceptance of his resignation.

> *From Daniel Webster.*                                    U.

> Washington,

> Septr. 3rd, 1850.

*Private.*

The object of this note is to introduce to you Mr. Samuel Kettell[85] and Mr. Chandler R. Ransom, both of Boston, Mr. Kettell is Editor of the Boston Courier, a Whig Paper of established reputation, and which espouses the cause of the present Administration with much decision and ability.

Mr. Ransom is one of the Editors of the Boston "Bee," a Whig penny paper of very large circulation, and which evinces zeal and talent, in sustaining the Administration. These papers deserve the countenance and patronage of all who desire to promote the Whig cause. I ought to add that the Boston Daily Advertiser is decided in its approbation and support of the measures of the Administration. This is one of the oldest and best conducted Whig Papers in the State.

> I am, with regard,
> Your obedient servant,

> *From James Buchanan.*                                    U.

> Wheatlands, near Lancaster,

> September 5th., 1850.

I know you will pardon me for the sake of our agreeable intercourse in the Senate, in addressing you a few lines in favor of Dr. Foltz,[86] an old and much valued friend.

He has been long a surgeon in the Navy, has seen much sea service on distant stations, and has always acquitted himself to

---

[85] Samuel Kettell (1800-1855), of Massachusetts, journalist, teacher, and traveller. He was a vigorous writer and was much admired by the Whigs. He was editor of the first anthology of native American verse.

[86] Dr. Jonathan M. Foltz (d. 1877), entered the navy in 1831, and became surgeon in 1838. In 1871 he became medical director and chief of the bureau of medicine and surgery. He retired in 1872.

the satisfaction of the Department and the officers and men with whom he served. In truth I consider him one of the very best surgeons and physicians in the Country, and the people of Lancaster where he was born and educated hold him in general esteem.

I understand he is desirous of being ordered as Surgeon on board the New Steamer Susquehanna, at Philadelphia; and I should esteem it a particular favor if you could grant his request, without injury to the just claims of others.

Should he enjoy the honor of your personal acquaintance, you will find him to be an agreeable and intelligent gentleman, possessing a mass of information on Naval and many other subjects.

> Yours very respectfully,

*From Joseph Graham Witherspoon.*[87]        U.

> Jacksonport, [Ark.],
>
> September 8th.,
>
> 1850.

I suppose that it will be rather a surprise to you to receive a communication from me at this late date, & that perhaps I had forgotten that I had such a relation as yourself, but the newspapers of the Country once in awhile reminds us of our duties, & also of distinguished individuals. I am in hopes that you will allow me the privilege of congratulating you upon the occasion of your acceptance of the office you now hold, & also of stating to you that it even meets with the approbation of your warmest political opponents.

I suppose that you have not been aware of my having located myself for the last five years in this State, pursuing the practice of the Law. But such is the case, nevertheless, & a rare time I have had of it. Manners, customs, inhabitants, in fact almost everything, entirely different from that to which I have been accustomed. The conventional Rules of Society have been heard of, but not known or practiced in this region.

My success has been very good in my profession, also once in awhile I am troubled *with a very great desire* after office, (I mean

---

[87] Joseph Graham Witherspoon (1820-1852), Graham's nephew.

direct from the people.) I once had the honor of being elected *Justice of the Peace,* and got by it the name of Squire, and at this time have the honor of being a Lycirgus in embryo, or in other words, a member of the Legislature. If at any time this winter I should take it into my head to make a speech or two, and be fool enough to have it published, I will certainly send you a copy, which you can read upon Sunday, being too much occupied, as I suppose, the balance of the week, attending the duties of office.

Arkansas at this time is increasing very rapidly in its population, having very nearly doubled its population within the last two years. It's soil cannot be excelled in any State. It's mineral resources boundless, & inexhaustible. It's streams are second to none, i. e. of Northern Arkansas, but we meet with a very serious inconvenience in regard to our postal arrangements through this section of Country, on account of the mails.

Accompanying this, you will find a petition to the Post Master General, in which I feel very much interested in having the routes extended to this place. It is the head of Navigation, & will eventually pay the Department well if it does not do so now. I would have enclosed it to Sebastion,[88] or Johnson, our Senator & Rep., but supposed that they had left Washington before the petition would reach there. I am well aware that it is usual to send such things to the department itself, direct, but such things, & *particularly* from this section, have received so little attention from that quarter that we have almost dispaired of ever being benefitted by it.

Those are the reasons why I have troubled you at this time. My acquaintance at Washington is quite limited, & more particularly so with persons of influence. I am in hopes therefore, that you will make all due allowance for my making the request, that you will present it to the Department, and ask that it be complied with. (Jacksonport is certainly a place of the greatest importance in Northern Arkansas, except Batesville, & in a business way now its superior.

\* \* \* \* \*

---

[88] William King Sebastian (1812-1865), of Arkansas, a native of Tennessee, lawyer, cotton planter, state supreme court justice, Democratic United States senator, 1848-1861. He moved to Memphis after the Civil War.

*From James Reid.*                                    U.

Yancyville,

Caswell County, N. C.,

Sept. 11th., 1850.

Under a sense of the Highest respect for you, permit me to approach the—as my political friend, in whose Judgment and opinions I have the fulest confidence. You will please indulge me in expressing my views, findings and wishes. I do this in confidence, from a conviction of the moral influence that Controlls the arder of your Spirit in the support of your country's rights, and sacredly garding her Charts and priviledges, secured to us as the price of the Blood of our forefathers. Hold up the hands of your President. We have confidence in President Fillmore, and may that being who has Long presided over the Consel of Princeses, and the Convulson of Nationa suspend the blow that would sever the Union, and with moral influences Nerve the arm of the President in guiding the Shipp of State. May the Cabinet be a unit in this support, and Triumphatly pass the Gulf of Disunion, again to enjoy the smiles of the Goddess of Liberty. in view of the passing scenes of the day. We, Sir, cannot shut our eyes against the fact that a Distracting Excitement is getting abroad in the South. I hold it as a principle that the good, the wise, the patriotic men of all parties are caled on to stand up, and arrest the course of events, that would lead to the formation of Leagues, for the overthrow of this Government, for myself, my maker, my Country, the union of the States, upon this platform I stand, or fall. The issue may some day be force upon us. I believe in the perpetuity of the Union rest all our blessings, Civil, Social, and religious. Destroy the Union of the States, and we are at once Launched on an ocean whose shores are shrouded in darkness, whose depths are unknown, whose sand bars and Rocks are unmarked, where the violent storms of passion will ever rage without Cessation. I cannot make an experimental voyage on so stormy an ocean with such a crazey Crew. I desire not to Lift the veil of the future, and expose to my own startled vision this Republic thrown into fragments. I affirm by the Blood of our forefathers, their sufferings, and by the spirit of the Illustrious Dead, to Defend and preserve the Constitution, as the fraternal compact which binds these States together. Let us resist that fanaticism to the Last, that would stop the wheels of Government telling us there is no danger. We, Sir, are not deceived. The spirit of Discord, in its wanderings, would Lead us to abandon A nerican freedom, and take a Leap into that Abyss whose Depths of Horror no eye can fathom, no Human Intellect can measure.

May heaven save my Country.

From perishing by Dissolution, Discord, or Civil War, bear with me, Sir, a Native of N. C., having Travel in ten States in the Last Twenty years, I field like I want to be on the wing, and to pour Oil on the Trouble Waters. Let me hear from the.

Dear Sir,

I now submits to your Calm Judgment, the following items.

In the Post Office Department they have agents. Let me go as an agent, please say to President Fillmore, and Mr. Hall of the Post Office Department, if they will employ me as an agent for this Southern Country I will do good work, and all your Interests shall be taken care of where ever I go. Any evidence wanting of Character, or Ability for the purposed work can be had. I have consulted no Human being Living. I submit this whole matter into your hands as a friend, to whose interests I still stand firm as in '44 & '46.

If you should Disapprove of my course, being unwilling to see me conected with the Department in any way, please send this back, and there the whole matter shall end. In the Navy Department I know your position, and I Doubt not but what the Department will be manage well.

From John Cameron.     U.

Hillsborough, No. Ca.

September 13th., 1850.

I dislike exceedingly to trespass upon your time, by forcing on your attention any matters of my own; but really, I am so circumstanced, as to be compelled to request the aid of my friends influence, (I can ask them for nothing else) in procuring such employment as will enable me respectably to support & educate my children.

I pretend to no particular claims, either upon my party, or upon the country. I have endeavoured to serve both, and if I have failed in my efforts, you at least will do me the justice of saying that the fault was not in me. That my *will* was good from first to last, however I may have erred in judgment. It was at your request that I offered my services to the government, & having done so, I never looked back, or relaxed my efforts, even when stricken down, a cripple, until thrust without question, or reason, from the position to which it was thought that my exertions had entitled me.

Why my after efforts were so unsuccessful, is plain enough. It was not intended that I should succeed. I was a Whig, and the President knew it.

Thirty days to raise an hundred men! The idea was preposterous, and I then, more than 300 miles from home, and no preparations made. I never should have accepted the terms, but that I thought a covert slur was aimed at my State in the *manner* of the proposition, and I determined not to be out bragged by the political gambler.

I some time ago, had the promise of preferment to a civil office, and I have lived on that promise until I have nearly starved to death. I am too poor now to pretend to be very choice, so that *any* opportunity is offered me of making a respectable livelihood; but were I at liberty to follow the bent of my inclinations, I would seek to be attached to the Dragoon Service in the West & Southwest, where there was a chance of being actively employed. My old Commission, received from you, is now in the War Office, where it was left in charge of Judge Mason,[89] who promised me to use his influence to further my views as regarded the Army then in Mexico. Could a similar position in the Dragoon Service be obtained, I should be highly gratified, if not, however, *any* aid which your position may enable you to render will be highly acceptable, & gratefully received.

Priestly Mangum has been very ill, but is much better, the congestion at one time was so great, as seriously to threaten apoplexy. The town is generally healthy. The Engineer part has crossed Eno, and are now making their way to Haw River; conjecture is still alive as to whether or no the road will pass through Hillsboro'. My own opinion is, that they will settle finally upon this route, though it is obliged to be a very expensive one.

Mr. Mangum and Mr. Badger will certainly not refuse to aid any exertion which you may make in my behalf, I am a poor beggar, and though I have not written to either very lately, they

---

[89] John Y. Mason.

are both acquainted with my necessities, and desire for employment.

With sincere respect and regard.

From *James Graham*    U.

*to Willie P. Mangum*
*and*
*George E. Badger.*[90]

Lincoln, N. C.,

Sept. 14th., 1850.

The people of Western N. C. are more neglected and worse treated by the General Government than any other part of the United States, in regard to mail-facilities. In Gen'l Jackson's administration, we had four horse post Coaches runing, and carrying the mail with quick speed in one half of the Western Counties of this State. Under Polk's and Cave Johnston's misrule, we were deprived of every single four horse post Coach, and cut down to a few *two horse shabby Hacks* travelling about *three miles* an hour. That is the sort of conveyance from Salisbury, by Lincolnton, to Ashville; and about one third of the time the Shabby Horses & Hacks break down, and fail, and loose the trip, to the great annoyance and vexation of the passengers and newspaper readers. This ought not to be so. Well now we have got rid of Polk, and Cave Johnston no longer sits astradle of the P. O. Department. I, in common with every reading man want a change for the better in the mode and speed of our Mail transportation. We want the Mail again transported in four horse post Coaches, at the rate of 7 or 8 miles per hour. So that we can get the News while it is new. An old newspaper is like an old Almanac. Its out of date, and of no value. The present line pays very little; because very few persons will take papers carried in such an uncertain, shabby, *Snail* line. But if the Department would put us on a par with other States by increasing the speed of conveyance, and give us a good four horse post Coach through the central Mail line of the State, then a large number of persons would take papers, and the post offices on the line would pay well to the Government. But Cave Johnston killed the Goose that laid the golden Eggs.

[90] Copy.

Now, Gentlemen, I ask the favor of both of you, or either of you, to go to the Post Master General, and insist upon our being restored to our ancient priviledges. All the people of all the States have had their Mail facilities improved and advanced, and increased in speed, but N. C., and we are treading backwards. We are worse off now than we were 12 years ago, in mail matters. We of N. C. get nothing from the Gen'l Government but Mail facilities, and surely we ought to demand and have our equal rights in that Department. If the Government can afford to send Mail-Steamers to the Pacific, and across the Atlantic to Europe, surely she can afford to put *one line* of four horse post Coaches on the great Central Mail Rout *through* the patriotic and union-loving State of North Carolina, & I think the mail ought to go faster than a man can walk. (or at the rate of 3 miles an hour.)

I think it is a reproach and degredation to the State to be thus treated. And I trust our Senators and Representatives will no longer submit in silence to it. Let us have a stageline from Raleigh to Ashville, travelling at the rate of 8 miles an hour; or any way 6 miles an hour. Then the small, lateral lines can diverge from *the main-Central trunk,* and supply the smaller Post offices.

Besides, a good Line of Stages through the Central route of the State would blaze the way for the contemplated Central Rail Road, from Raleigh, towards the Western part of the State.

I have an abiding conviction that the present Post Master Gen'l —whom I have the pleasure of knowing personally—will be disposed to do us justice, in making the mail line all we ask, and so much need. But he, a New Yorker, cannot understand the subject, and the changes and improvements proposed unless he have the explanations, and comments of a North Carolinian to develope the general advantages.

Your attention to this subject at your earliest convenience will greatly diffuse useful knowledge among our people, if your effort shall be crowned with success, and confer a peculiar favour on your friend.

*From  Richard Hines.*                                    U.

Raleigh,

Sept. 16th, 1850.

\*     \*     \*     \*     \*

Gov: Morehead was here a few days since. Majr. Guion[91] and himself had made a reconnaissance of most of the Country West of this through which the Central Rail Road must run. They were both much pleased with the prospects and the Majr. says he has no doubt the Road can be built with the $3,000,000. They represent the West as being very much alive to the subject and every thing promising well.

I and the Whigs generally have been delighted at the passage of the compromize bills and the approval of the President. The Administration is gaining golden opinions *from the people* of all parties in this State. I was particularly pleased at the passage of the bills even now as I am satisfied that many of the Loco foco leaders even in this State are rapidly becoming tainted with the disunion fever, and am inclined to believe that if the question had not been settled at this Session they would have exerted themselves to make it a party question before the next election. As it is, I believe if it is properly managed our members of Congress who voted against the Texas boundary bill can be killed off. Which I trust in God may be the case, and that their fate may be a warning to all future Traitors.

The Gov: bears his defeat badly. Neither his health or spirits has been good since he reached home. He has however much improved in the last week.

Our friend the Majr.[92] is—and is getting on much after the old sort. Always in his office, and when a Sheriff comes sending after Collins and hunting him up even at his plantation to avoid complaint. He has strong hopes of being able to retain his office as he has assurances from four Loco's that he thinks can be relied upon that will vote for him come what may. For myself I place little reliance on Loco foco promises.

From all I hear from the leaky vessels about the City I think the Gov: elect and the Legislature intend to make a clean sweep.

[91] Walter Gwynn, then chief engineer of the road.
[92] Charles L. Hinton.

And you may rely upon it the Whig cause has been much injured in the State by the retention of Loco's in office. But it would probably be best to let things be as they are until after the Session of the Legislature.

\*    \*    \*    \*    \*

*From William A. Wright.*[93]                                    U.

Wilmington,

September 18th., 1850.

You may recollect that Dr. Joseph Togno,[94] then of Phila-delphia, in June 1849 was at Chapel Hill during the Commence-ment of that year, when and where he stated that he had visited our State with the view of introducing among our citizens the culture of the grape, upon practical and scientific principles. The Doctor from the desired peculiarity of climate favorable to the growth and maturity of the grape, and from other considerations, was induced to establish his vineyard in our vicinity, and al-though but a year has passed since he commenced his operations, (in the woods) yet during the past month he has exhibited in our town grapes well matured, which were grown from vines re-ceived by him from Bordeaux but six months prior to gathering the fruit, and he has fifty foreign varieties, all imported by him-self, in addition to many different domestic, or native kinds, in fine condition. His general operations and his results are truly aston-ishing, and his example, his skill and science as a vine dresser, induce us here to regard him as a benefactor to our State. He is a gentleman of refinement, of extended literary and scientific acquirement, of indomitable industry, and energy, and well de-serves any aid which can be given him in his most praiseworthy undertaking. His great leading purpose is to introduce in the United States, all the valuable and most desirable varieties of the grape cultivated in foreign countries, and with this end in view he, during the past year, has made many importations, but owing to the want of proper care or skill in packing the cuttings, many of them were worthless when received. Mr. Clayton, with whom I think the Doctor is personally acquainted, while acting as Sec-

---

[93] William A. Wright (1807-1878), of Wilmington, graduate of the university, lawyer and banker, one of the founders of the Wilmington and Raleigh (later Weldon) Railroad.

[94] Joseph Togno was a French grape grower and wine maker who leased a part of the Love Grove plantation on Smith's Creek near Wilmington.

retary of State, addressed a circular to such of our Consuls residing at points where choice varieties of the grape are cultivated,
requesting them to aid the Doctor in selecting and forwarding
such varieties as he might designate, or as were considered the
most desirable at their respective places of residence—all expenses
incident to procuring the vines, packing them, etc., being defrayed
by Dr. Togno. The circular of Mr. Clayton was in the nature of
a letter of introduction, &, as his object was one in which the
whole country was to some extent interested, requesting them to
further his views as far as their convenience might permit.

As many of the kinds much desired by Dr. Togno, and ordered
by him last year, were destroyed in their transit to him, and as
there are many other varieties which he wishes to procure, he is
solicitous again to avail himself of the agency of our different
Consuls, and to enable him to do so, he asks the cooperation of
the Secretary of State.

We are much concerned as to the success of Dr. Togno's undertaking, and if you can aid him in the premises, I am satisfied a
benefit will result to our Country and more especially to our
State.

*From James H. Dickson.*[95]

Wilmington, N. C.,

Sept. 18th., 1850.

It gives me especial pleasure to introduce to your acquaintance
Dr. Joseph Togno, a gentleman of highly cultivated mind, and of
rare attainments, in literature, art and science, who has been
residing here for a year or more, engaged in the culture of the
grape.

He has selected this portion of the State, as best adapted in
climate and Soil for the experiment in which he has engaged, and
we are very solicitous that it should be successful, believing, as
we do, that it will be of great advantage, not to this section alone,
but to the whole Country.

Thus far his efforts have been quite successful, and his prospects
highly encouraging, but less so than they probably would have
been, from a failure in receiving at a proper season and in good
condition, cuttings of foreign vines, which were forwarded by our

---

[95] James Henderson Dickson (1807-1862), of Wilmington, graduate of the university, M.D., Columbia, a well-known and beloved physician.

consuls, resident in the vine growing countries of Europe.

He desires now to bring the subject to the attention of the Secretary of State (in a manner which he will himself explain) and the object of this letter is to solicit your good offices in his behalf.

I have not hesitated to assure him that you will take particular pleasure in aiding him, in the praiseworthy attempt to introduce a new branch of agricultural industry into our State, and that you will regard it as worthy to receive such aid as he requires on the part of our consular agents.

*A Recommendation.*　　　　　　　　　　　　　　　U.

Wilmington,

Sept. 18th., 1850.

For more than a year past, Doctor Joseph Togno has been actively engaged in the cultivation of the vine in the immediate vicinity of this place. Having understood that he is desirous of securing the agency of some of our consuls for the more efficient prosecution of his plans, which we deem very feasible, and believing him to be altogether worthy of the aid which he desires, it is with much pleasure that we now earnestly solicit for him such assistance as the Government may be able to afford through any of its foreign functionaries.

He is a gentleman of most excellent character, of very varied intelligence, and ardently devoted to the business to which we have adverted. Already he has achieved much, under most unfavourable circumstances, and we feel assured from the results which have followed his past operations that his future efforts will eventuate in complete success, if he is at all sustained as he deserves to be.

The nature of the application which he designs making, will doubtless be very distinctly developed in another communication, which he will send you, and though we are not very familiar with it, still we know enough, to feel no hesitation in cordially commending it to your most favourable consideration.

With the assurance that any thing done by you in furtherance of his very laudable enterprize, will be duly appreciated by us, and with the hope that you will pardon this trespass on your attention, we are,

Most respectfully,
Y'r Ob't Serv'ts

Josh'a G. Wright, Tho's H. Wright, N. R. Savage, Dan'l B. Baker, James S. Green, John McRae, Alex MacRae, H. W. W., E. B. Dudley, P. K. Dickinson, O. G. Parsley, T. Loving, James F. McRee, Mauger London

*From Whig Representatives*

*to Millard Fillmore.*                                        *U.*

Washington City,

September 20th., 1850.

Sir;

The undersigned, Whig members of the 31st. Congress, most respectfully invite your attention to the necessity of making such changes in the offices connected with the Navy Department as will place the several Bureaus under the charge and direction of persons connected with the Whig party.

Whilst we have a Whig President, and a Whig Cabinet, we believe it to be the desire of the People we represent, that the General Government should be administered, as far as practicable, by Whigs. And we therefore, most respectfully submit this paper to you, as an indication of the wishes and feelings of members of Congress, friendly to the present Administration.

Very Respectfully,

Your Obed't Serv'ts

M. Hampton, Geo. Ashmore, Edw. Stanly, David Outlaw, Jos. Casey, Sam'l Calven, R. R. Reed, J. W. Hone, Chester Butler, John L. Taylor, of Ohio, Walter Underhill, N. Y., Jno. R. Thurman, L. Burrows, N. Y., H. P. Alexander, N. Y., Wm. A. Sackett, N. Y., Wm. Nelson, N. Y., P. H. Silvester, D. A. Bokee, T. S. Haywood, H. Putnam, George Briggs, John W. Houston, Wm. A. Newell, of N. Y., John A. King, John Crowell, of Ohio, James G. King, of New Jersey.

[Endorsement]

Ref'd letter Sec'y of the Navy Oct. 5. M. F.

*From Francis Lieber.*                                U.

Columbia, S. C.,

September 20th., 1850.

I was unavoidably prevented from replying to the letter we had the honour of receiving from you, for some days. I now hasten to express to you my, and my son's[96] very sincere gratitude for the great kindness you have shown us in giving my son another appointment in the Naval School. I shall accompany my son to Annapolis, where I trust that his bashfulness will not be in his way. By constant occupation with him for a considerable period, I have gained the conviction that he is fully prepared to enter, and the only difficulty he labours under, is a want of self-confidence. I hope he will succeed, and do honour to his Country, which through your kind mediation, is willing to undertake his education.

My son begs me to present his respects to you, to which you will permit me to join my sincerest regards.

*From William L. Long.*                               U.

Halifax,

September 20th., 1850.

In October last, you presented my name to the favourable consideration of the late President of the United States. For that act of kindness, I thank you. You are now in a position to serve me, any influence you may exert in my behalf will be gratefully acknowledged, and duly appreciated.

The Hon. John M. Clayton promised me the appointment to Belgium, a country distinguished for its enterprising population, its agriculture and manufactures. Mr. Clayton is a warm-hearted and intellectual man, wanting, however, in moral firmness, and

---

[96] Hamilton Lieber (1835-1876), after his appointment to Annapolis, was dropped in 1851. He went to Ohio and became a farmer. He was an officer in the Union army during the Civil War. The general register of the navy does not list him, unless he was the Alfred H. Lieber, whose record duplicates his.

when Secretary of State, destroyed his usefulness and in a measure, the popularity of Gen. Taylor, by being entirely too profuse in his promises to applicants for place.

I prefer Belgium to any Court in Europe. If there be a disposition on the part of the administration, at this time, to do any thing for No. Carolina, I refer you to testimonials in my favor deposited in the archives of the State Department. Enclosed is a recommendation from our friend, Waddell, which you can dispose off, as you think best.

*To Millard Fillmore.*    U.

Norfolk, Virginia,

September 20th., 1850.

To his Excellency

The President of the United States.

The undersigned, speaking the sentiments of at least 7/8 of the Whig Community of this City & vicinity, respectfully beg leave to call your attention to the case of the Navy Agent at this place; and to request that you will, immediately after the adjournment of Congress, remove the present incumbent, and appoint Doct'r Francis Mallory[97] to the place. Mr. R. A. Worrell who visits Washington in our behalf, will fully and fairly represent to you the state of public opinion here, and make known the sentiments of the Whigs respecting this matter, and we respectfully ask that the wishes of the Whig Party may be carried out, by an Administration which it has been our pleasure, as well as our pride, to support.

We have the Honour to be, Very Respectfully,

Your ob't Serv'ts and fellow citizens,

A. B. McClean, Henry Moore, P. W. Hinton, Jno. C. Calvert Taylor, Simon Stone, S. Hartshorn, Rich'd B. Wright, Thos. G. Broughton, John Dickson.

---

[97] Dr. Francis Mallory (1807-1860), of Virginia, Whig member of congress, 1837-1839, 1840-1843, lawyer, physician, planter, state legislator, and railroad president. He served as a midshipman, 1822-1828. Graham appointed him navy agent at Norfolk, and found him tremendously helpful because of his knowledge and wide acquaintance.

*From Joseph Togno.*                              U.

Wilmington, N. C.,

September 22nd., 1850.

My name, though now most likely forgotten by you, was at least once sounded within your hearing. It was on a memorable occasion when you, Sir, addressed the Faculty and pupils of the University of N. C., and when I had the honor to follow you on that day, and then and there introduced to the consideration of your auditors, the utility and importance of the culture of the grape vine in their State.

I have examined many districts of your,—and now my State also; but none presented so many advantages for my ulterior views of diffusing information on this point, as the vicinity of this place.

The Hon. J. M. Clayton, with whom I had the honor of a personal interview in May, 1849, on this subject, did everything in his power to forward this "valuable undertaking." In consequence of it, he ordered a circular to be forwarded to all the American Consuls located in countries where the grape vine is cultivated advantageously, to cause to be sent to me packages of rooted grape vines, and cuttings of the best varieties. My wish in obtaining these vines from original sources, being to start a Model Vinyard, with a genuine stock, Cepage, entirely new so far as foreign vines are concerned.

From among the Consuls thus addressed and particularly requested to take into favorable consideration this undertaking, the Consuls of Bordeaux, Malaga, Oporto, Palermo, and Madeira only, forwarded rooted vines and cuttings; but unfortunately, (with the exception of the package from Bordeaux) they were badly packed, and rotted by watering them, and sent so late in the season that, by the time they reached our shores they were nearly all dryed up.

My design now, is to obtain from the American Consuls another supply of rooted vines and cuttings. I have borne the expense of the first importation, and as things were managed abroad, I was a great loser. My pecuniary means, Sir, for accomplishing this undertaking, being very limited, I would respectfully solicit your aid to obtain for this American Model Vinyard, that the articles wished for be forwarded to me free of all expense.

My undertaking, Sir, is to benefit ultimately the people of the U. S., and especially those of N. C., therefore the Federal Government may, with perfect propriety, assist and promote such a praiseworthy experiment. The success of it is now no longer a doubtful problem. I refer you, Sir, to the testimony of my fellow-citizens here, who have been eye witnesses of my daily efforts to naturalize the European grape vines to our climate, and especially by grafting them on our native vines with the most extraordinary success.

Will you, my dear Sir, be so kind as to interest yourself so far in my behalf, as to induce the Secretary of State, the Hon. Daniel Webster, to request the American Consuls to obtain and have put up and forwarded to me, rooted vines and cuttings to be put up in a careful manner, as the accompanying directions will instruct, and then forward them to me early in January, to the care of my friend, Wm. D. Lewis, Esqr., Collector of the Port of Philadelphia.

I remain,<br>Very respectfully,

N. B. Directions for packing cuttings or rooted vines. They ought to be well wrapped, in plenty of moss, and then in hay, and afterwards in long straw, and tightly tied together. They ought to be kept in a cool, but not damp, place, and they should be sent to this country before January. It is of the utmost importance that the above directions be strictly attend to.

*From Charles L. Hinton.*　　　　　　　　　　　　　U.

Raleigh,

September 23rd., 1850.

I must say to you, as I once said to Badger, when occupying the station you now fill, that he must bear with the letters[98] I write at the solicitations of others, and let them pass for what they are worth, for really, I have not the firmness to refuse so small a favor, tho' I know that they have no influence. The letter I wrote a few days since for P. H. Haywood,[99] and the one I now enclose

---

[98] The letters have not been found.
[99] Philemon Hawkins Haywood, who entered the navy in 1841, and was dismissed in 1849.

for Battle, contain nothing more than my feelings, but at the same time I feel as tho' I were intruding on your patience unnecessary. It can't well be helped.

You have seen in the papers the sudden & unexpected death of our friend, P. H. Mangum. Paul Cameron this evening told me that a few days before he was taken, he saw him, and had never seen him in finer health. He was taken with a congestive chill, which prostrated both mind and body, and he died in a few days.

I am now busily engaged in settling with the Sheriffs—the Revenue will be increased about one third over the last year. Wake will pay about $1,800. on interest, Edgecombe near $1,400. I suppose we shall probably have you with us the next week.

*From Robert B. Gilliam.*                                U.

Oxford, N. C.,

Sept. 24th, 1850.

\* \* \* \* \*

I am most sincerely gratified that the commencement of Mr. Fillmore's administration has been signalized by the success of all the great peace measures, which were so ardently desired by all the true friends of the Country. Thus far Mr. Fillmore has given the highest satisfaction to the Whig party, and in some quarters even the adversary seems to be disarmed. It is a singular fact, that his administration is more popular in this section than ever Gen'l Taylor's was, from the day on which his Cabinet was announced. He entered upon his office at a period of great peril, and universal alarm. His first step, the appointment of his Cabinet, inspired confidence. And in two short months, we have Peace, which fanaticism, either at the North or South, however it may lament, cannot disturb.

Your acceptance of a seat in the Cabinet has given universal satisfaction in this State, and contributes in no small degree to the favor with which Mr. Fillmore's administration is regarded. During a visit to the State of Virginia in the month of August, I was gratified to find the same feeling prevailing there.

*To James W. Bryan.*                    U. Bryan Mss.

Washington City,

Sept. 25th, 1850.

When I wrote you the other day, in relation to the office of district Judge, in California, I had just had a conversation with the President, in which he inquired, if I had any one to propose for the offices in that State, or the territories of New Mexico or Utah. I replied in the negative, saying that our people were so out of the current of Federal affairs, that they rarely heard when a place was to be filled, and when they did, they supposed there was but little chance for them.

Afterwards, when writing you, it occurred to me, that possibly you might be willing to go to California, and therefore proposed it. After receiving your reply, I mentioned it to Mr. Webster, who answered, that he had learned from your brother, that he desired the Judgeship in N. C. and that it would not be expedient to appoint both. In further prosecution of the conversation, I found he had talked with the President after my interview with him, and they had committed themselves to others. I did not inquire to whom—but he seemed much impressed with the notion of appointing persons familiar with practice under the revenue laws, and admiralty jurisprudence. He mentioned, however, that he thought those now in contemplation, might decline. No publicity has been given to the matter. I mentioned it only on the occasions already stated, and as I am urging George Washington for a Consulship with some hope of success, I do not deem it advisable to insist on too much personal accomodation. If the first appointees decline, I will revive it again. But the appointment is not now so probable as to delay your stay in New York longer than you intended.

\* \* \* \* \*

All is hurry here, in winding up the business of the Session. I hope the Country is quieted, but I think there is a mischievous spirit at work in S. C. and Ga. which may yet occasion trouble.

The Turk[100] is the Lion of the day here, as Jenny Lind [101] is Lioness in New York.

---

[100] Amin Bey, the Turkish diplomatic representative in the United States. He became an outstanding social figure, and was widely lionized.
[101] The famous concert singer.

I hope to see you, on your return home. Mr. A. C. Blount has declined going to San Francisco, and I have made another appointment.

\* \* \* \* \*

### From *William D. Porter.*[102]          U.

Washington,

September 26th., 1850.

Sir:

I herewith enclose you a few Seeds from the Mediterranean, which please accept.

The Turkish Tobaco is much better than North Carolina, and brings a better price in the European Market. I send you a Sample of Tobaco, and a pipe to try it.

Very respectfully,
Your ob't Serv't.

### From *John MacPherson Berrien.*          U.

Senate Chamber, U. S.

(Unofficial)                    Sept. 26th., 1850.

Fearing that the pressure of public business may have occasioned you to overlook the cases of the young midshipmen *Kell* [103] and *Hopkins,*[104] whose warrants you were good enough to say you would allow me the priviledge of forwarding, I trouble you with this note to recall them to your recollection.

Will you do me the favor also to say, whether the President has received the resolution in the case of Lieut. Anderson, and whether he has taken any, and what, action upon it?

---

[102] William David Porter (1809-1864), of Massachusetts, a lieutenant in the navy and brother of Admiral David D. Porter, and a foster brother of Admiral David Farragut. During the Civil War he served on the Mississippi and Ohio rivers, and attained the rank of commodore.

[103] John McIntosh Kell (1823-1900), of Georgia, a graduate of Annapolis, who served with Perry in Japan, and in the Civil War was executive officer of the "Sumter" and the "Alabama" under Raphael Semmes.

[104] Probably Alfred Hopkins of Georgia, who entered the navy in 1851. He remained in the service during the Civil War and attained the rank of captain.

*From David L. Yulee.*[105]     U.

Washington,

September 26th.,

1850.

Monday night.

I enclose you a copy of the Navy appropriation bill as it came from the House. Will be happy to receive any suggestions of amendment, which you may think will be useful to the public service.

The bill will be taken up tomorrow.

*From Robert Hall Morrison.*     U.

Cottage Home,

Oct. 1st, 1850.

\*   \*   \*   \*   \*

With your many friends I shared most sincerely in the great gratification which your appointment diffused throughout the Country. In accepting the appointment you are no doubt called to make many sacrifices; but there perhaps never was a time in which the counsels of wise and patriotic men were more needed to arrest the progress of discord and turbulent passion, than the present.

The conciliatory measures adopted since the formation of the new Cabinet, promise much for the peace and prosperity of the Country.

If the efforts to diffuse anarchy and fanatacism are not arrested I trust they are so far crushed and rendered odious as not to involve seriously the tranquility and safety of the government.

\*   \*   \*   \*   \*

Isabella[106] has a Son about 2 months old. She is recovering her health pretty well, and the child is healthy.

---

[105] David Levy Yulee (1810-1886), of Florida, born Levy, a native of St. Thomas, lawyer, Democratic territorial delegate in congress, 1841-1845, delegate to constitutional convention, 1845, United States senator, 1845-1851, 1855-1861, planter and railroad president.

[106] Isabella Sophia Morrison (Mrs. Daniel Harvey) Hill (1825-1904). The child, Robert Hall Morrison Hill, died in 1857.

Your brother James was here today, and is in tolerably good health. He complains none; but his throat is evidently disseased, and I fear he suffers more than he is willing to admit.

\*  \*  \*  \*  \*

The Season has been remarkably healthy throughout this section of the Country.

The Crops with us are not very promising. In some districts of Country the drought was very severe. A violent Storm in the month of Aug't, with a flood of unusual severity destroyed much of the best Corn. There was a great failure in Wheat generally. In some of our Western Counties Corn is now selling for $1. per bushel, and flour at $10. per barrel.

\*  \*  \*  \*  \*

May the richest blessing of a Merciful Providence ever Crown your path and rest upon your family.

*To James W. Bryan.*          U. Bryan Mss.

Washington City,

Oct. 1st, 1850.

\*  \*  \*  \*  \*

... The California Judgeships turn out to be not very desirable, after the reducing of the salary, by the House Reps. But the appointments would have been the same, at the higher compensation. The business has been greatly hurried, in the last few days of the Session, and the departments having patronage, of which mine is not one, have bestowed it, without much consultation.

I notice your remarks in regard to the share of our State in these things, and almost regret that I did not take the Department of the Interior, when repeatedly urged upon me, with a view to greater equality. Though I greatly prefer the duties of that in which I am.

I will, however, keep my eye upon the current of events, and may possibly make some change in its course. The President himself, I believe, has the most just and liberal feelings towards us.

Congress adjourned yesterday, but the recess brings but little leisure. In addition to the deferred and current business the annual reports of the Heads of departments must be completed within 50 days.

*From Oscar T. Keeler.*      **U.**

**Columbus,**

**Mississippi.**

October 3rd., 1850.

In accordance with your suggestions, I wrote to Dr. Murphy, and he informs me the papers collected by Judge Murphy were carefully packed in a box, and left at Hillsborough, N. C., to be left with Mr. Paul C. Cameron, but that he never received them, and he understands they are in care of Mr. John U. Kirkland, of the same place. Dr. Murphy has consented to my having the papers for my use, & then to return them to him, and suggests you might be able to aid me in having them forwarded. Will you visit Hillsborough soon? and if so, can you aid me so far as to have the box forwarded to me. Or, as all I wish are such letters as may be in the box written by any Governors, Senators, or Revolutionary Characters, could you not at the time of your visit, select all the letters, do them in suitable sized packages, and send them to me by mail, under your frank? If they are sent by box, they could be addressed as follows: Oscar T. Keeler, Columbus, Mi., Care of J. S. Marsh & Co., Mobile, Ala., and forwarded in that way.

Forgive me if I am asking too much or presuming too far on the kindness you have already shown me.

Please let me hear from you at earliest convenience.

Your obliged Serv't,

Annexed is a list of letters I most need.

Samuel Ashe, Nathaniel Alexander, Bedford Brown, Timothy Bloodworthy, William Blount, Hutchings G. Burton, John Branch, Thomas Burke, Richard Caswell, Arthur Dobbs, Wm. R. Davie, Richard Everard, Jesse Franklin, Gabriel Holmes, Wm. Hawkins, Rob't Howe, James Hogan, Wm. Hooper, Jos. Hewes, James Iredell, Sam'l Johnston, Gabriel Johnston, Wm. Jones, Francis Locke, Alexander Martin, Alfred Moore, William Miller, Joseph Martin, Nathaniel Macon, Abner Nash, Francis Nash, John Owen, John Penn, Matthew Rowan, Benj'n Smith, Montfort Stokes, Jethro Sumner, David Stone, R'd D. Spaight, James Turner, Wm. Tryon, Benj'n Williams, Hugh Williamson.

*From George S. Bryan.*[107]        U.

National Hotel,

Washington,

Oct. 6th., 1850.

Upon my return last evening from your recent residence, with Mr. Petigru, I found a letter from Charleston, making a request of me, which had been previously made by the Sisters of the Gentleman interested. The Gentleman has himself made the same request of you already, enforced by a letter from the Collector of our Port, Mr. Grayson.[108] It is a petition for leave of absence, from Lieut. Edgar O. Marden, of the Revenue Service.

Mr. Marden is the only male of his family, is to be married in Philadelphia, and is very anxious in company with his wife, to spend a week with his family in Charleston. I do not know a more deserving family, or a better brother or more faithful officer, and the occasion is such that I am sure it need only to be stated, to secure the boon so much desired by himself and his friends. He wishes the "leave" to date from the time of the departure of his vessel for Key West, until the 20th. of Dec'r. December is the only month which his sisters can command to receive his Bride and himself. They have a large Boarding School, and their time is wholly occupied with it, except in vacation.

Mr. Petigru and myself regretted exceedingly not being able to see you. We were not able to leave the Hotel 'til quite late, and it was so late when we got to your recent residence, and Mr. Petigru so unwell, that we thought it better not to attempt to see you. He felt particularly desirous of seeing you, and making your acquaintance. You are so much nearer home, that he, as well as myself, felt the sense of kin, as to yourself, which we could not have in reference to the other gentlemen of the Cabinet. Mr. Petigru is afflicted with the complaint which distressed him so much last summer. He is anxious to get home, and leaves here this morning. I go with him.

I had counted upon the pleasure of seeing very much more of you than I have done, supposing Mr. Petigru would remain some

---

[107] George S. Bryan (1809-1905), of South Carolina, was a Charleston lawyer, a Unionist Whig, who became Federal district judge in 1866, and served to 1886. During military occupation he came into conflict with the army officers, but successfully upheld the authority of the court.

[108] William John Grayson (1788-1863), of South Carolina, a graduate of Charleston College and South Carolina College, planter, lawyer, state legislator, Whig member of congress, 1833-1837, author.

time in the City. I congratulate myself in having made your acquaintance, and I shall ever remember, with gratitude, the kind consideration which, in the midst of business of larger importance, won your attention to a matter, only important as involving the feelings of a gentleman. We are both the more grateful— that matter of feeling—as it was, you acted with the caution and deliberation due to a proper and just administration. The obligation is enhanced and elevated by being the award of strict, impartial justice.

I had hoped to have shaken hands with you, and told you good bye in person.

*From Matthew F. Maury.*[109]          U.

National Observatory,

Washington.

October 7th.,
1850.

Sir:

In complying with the request which you did me the honor to make, that I would submit to you, in writing, my views concerning the Navy, & the reforms requisite to place it in a more efficient state, I am painfully impressed with the difficulties in the way.

The importance of the subject is great, and when I consider the magnitude of the undertaking, I am appalled by my own deficiencies. Yet, since my views are thought worth having, I do not feel at liberty to withhold them, be they never so contracted.

---

[109] From Hydrographic Letter Book, 1850-1851, p. 145, Naval Records, National Archives.

Matthew Fontaine Maury (1806-1873), a native of Virginia, naval officer, oceanographer, author, was carried to Tennessee as a child. He entered the navy in 1825, and from 1836 to this time had been intensely critical of the organization and operation of the service. His scientific work won wide attention, and recognition and honors of every sort poured in from all over the world as the tremendous benefits of his research became apparent. He became superintendent of charts and instruments and head of the naval observatory. He was the chief figure at the international congresses of 1853 and of 1855. There was great jealousy of him in the navy, and a board "to promote efficiency" recommended an indefinite leave for him as a way of getting rid of him, but in 1858 the President restored him to active service with the rank of commodore. During the Civil War he was special agent of the Confederate government in Europe. He lived after the war for a time in Mexico and England, and was then professor at the Virginia Military Institute.

Graham showed great wisdom in selecting him as an adviser, and based his important recommendations for improvement in the service upon this document and many interviews.

One of the difficulties that meet me at the threshold of the subject, is found in the circumstance that no official declaration has been made by the Government as to that system of Naval policy which is best adapted to our Country & its institutions, and which it is the intention or the duty of the government to preserve. So that, before setting out, I find myself at sea.

At the conclusion of the war of 1812, it was determined that the true policy of the Country henceforward, required the maintenance of a Navy; but as to the size of that Navy, or its rate of growth, the law was silent. A sum of money was annually set apart for its "gradual increase," but this money was applied to the building of ships. But ships without proper & well trained Officers to command them, are like forts without garrisons.

The number of Officers in the various grades was left to the appointing power; and the number of Midshipmen, to Executive discretion; consequently, the ratio between the ships and the Officers was a fluctuating one, and the proportion between the two, or between one grade and another, lost its bearings. Midshipmen were appointed *ad libitum*, and promoted without regard to the list of Captains; and Captains were made without regard to the number of ships; and in these promotions, after the grade of Midshipman was passed, no rule of merit was established. Discretion as to fitness was but seldom exercised; and all, good and bad, efficient and inefficient, were advanced alike, and promoted by the miller's rule of "each one according to his turn."

Under this system, the Navy began to grow sickly, for the seeds of disease were in it's system. Nevertheless, it continued to look vigorous, because it yet had the powers of growth; and these gave it energy.

But in 1842-3, Congress took those sustaining powers away, and fixed the number and ratio of Officers in the Navy as they existed, out of all proportion, on the first day of January, 1841. Since that time, it has been ordained that the Navy shall stand still; but nothing in this age, and, above all, in this Country, can stand still. Improvement and decay are alternatives. Nothing in the physical world is permitted to be in a state of rest and preservation too. When progress ceases, ruin follows. The moral world is governed by the same iron rule. Upward and onward, or downward and backward, are the conditions which it imposes upon all individuals, societies, and institutions.

It is impossible for this nation to preserve the *statu quo*; and, therefore, equally impossible is it, for its "right arm," or any other member of the body politic to stand still and not wither.

Since the passage of this law, promotion has ceased, except to fill up dead men's places. Incentives to professional exertion, there are none. No officer, however great his qualifications, can be advanced over his senior, however worthless. The result has been to set at work in the Navy, principles calculated to demoralize any set of men in the world, and to afflict every grade of Officers with senility. Our passed Midshipmen are too old for passed Midshipmen; our Lieuts., too old for Lieuts.; Commanders too old for Commanders; and our Captains, who, although they have done yeoman's service for the State, and have reached their three score and ten, are allowed no respite, and are often seen, after years of long and faithful services, to die with their harness still on.

The senior Passed Midshipmen in the Navy are now older men than Decatur, Perry, McDonough, and our other Captains were when they fought their battles & won their victories. The Senior Lieutenants have passed the prime of life; and the youngest Commander is some years on the down-hill side. They are kept waiting for dead men's shoes; and when, at last, they find them vacant, they are put in them, and it is called promotion. But it is promotion which brings with it no gladness, gratifies no feelings of pride, because it comes without any of those circumstances which must endear it to high minded men. It comes to the Officer first who has been drawing pay longest, and no talents, however eminent, no merit, however conspicuous, no services, however great, on the part of any officer, will hasten it to him a single day the sooner.

Such is the present system in the Navy, and such the present condition of it's *personnel*; and therefore, as it may be supposed, dissatisfaction among officers pervade the Service.

By this diagnosis, we may, I think, recognise one of the diseases, at least, with which the Navy is afflicted; but before we begin to prescribe remedies and treat the patient, let us examine the case a little further, and look into other parts of the system.

Let us begin with the Navy Department. I have been in the Navy 25 years, and, within that time, have seen no less than thirteen different persons filling the office of Secretary of the Navy. This gives, on the average, a new Secretary every two years, or a little less.

The person called to this Office may be a merchant, or farmer, or planter, or he may be a man of letters, a lawyer, doctor, or of any other of the various professions of life. But whatever be his calling, he is presumed—under the present system—to know at

THE PAPERS OF WILLIAM A. GRAHAM

once the official character, standing, & qualifications of more than a thousand Officers, not one of whom he has perhaps ever seen before. He is expected also to be familiar with all the details of a service, as to the technicalities of which, even, he is ignorant.

Besides this, he is annually charged with the disbursement of eight or nine millions of dollars, and is continually called upon to examine into, & decide the most intricate cases of martial, maritime, & national law, into the validity of contracts, the justice of claims, and to grant daily, personal interviews of greater or less duration. All of these consume time, and leave the Secretary no leisure to devise reforms for the service, or to propose well matured lines of Naval policy for the Country. He has no time for reflection.

The current business of the Navy Department is more than enough to engross the attention & constantly to occupy the mind of any one man, however eminent his talents, and great his powers of endurance may be.

The duties of the Secretary are susceptible of division, and a proper division of them would be highly beneficial to the public service.

Usage has proved the necessity of having, in every fleet, an Officer appointed especially to assist the Commander in its management. The fighting Captain relieves him of all the every day details of the fleet, and leaves him, thereby, time and opportunity of attending the more effectually to its efficiency, of maturing his plans of operations, etc.

The Secretary of the Navy is charged with the management or conduct of many fleets, and much more does he require an Officer of experience who is familiar with all the details of the service, & thoroughly acquainted with its *personnel*, to assist him as to those details of which his previous occupations & mode of life have necessarily kept him in ignorance.

The Navy is too large, and the business of the Navy Department, notwithstanding the subdivisions into Bureaus, is too heavy for the Secretary, without the aid of an Officer corresponding to the Adjutant General of the Army.

The establishment of such an Official for the Navy has been often urged. The importance of it, and necessity for it, are obvious to every one who reflects at all upon the subject.

You, no doubt, have already experienced the embarrassments and inconvenience arising from the want of such an Officer, therefore, it would be useless to say more upon the subject.

The Navy is without any code of laws at all suited to its condition, or the times.

The Naval code, crude at best, is of 50 years standing. Within that time, almost every State in the Union, if not all, have found it necessary to revise their code of laws, or to alter and amend their Constitution. They have been compelled to this, that they might keep pace with the spirit of the age. Within that time, there has been revolution after revolution, in almost all matters pertaining to Naval affairs.

First, there are the improvements which have taken place in Naval architecture. Ships are no longer the things they used to be. By the war of 1812, the United States effected a revolution in ship building; Great Britain learned then from this Country a lesson which induced her literally to sink her Navy, as it existed at that time, and to build up upon its ruins a new one. She razeed her line of battle ships to make frigates fit to cope with ours; her frigates were unequal to our first class Sloops, and her Sloops were too light for anything. The result was, she let them all go into decay, took pattern after our models, and rebuilt her Navy.

Next came steam, to strengthen the hands of maritime nations, and make them more terrible in war, by providing for their Navies a flying artillery at sea.

Add to these the improvements in navigation, in the condition of the sailor, the morale of the service, and in almost all the usages of the sea, and we may readily imagine that a code of laws which might have been very well adapted to the condition of the Navy half a century ago, is no longer suited to its government now. Grades of officers, ratings of men, classes of ships, implements of warfare, with modes of procedure, duties & responsibilities which were unknown then, are common now.

Some of the provisions of the laws now in force in the Navy are savage, cruel & barbarous, and are well calculated, not only to offend the spirit of the age, but to disgrace the statute book of any people. Take, as an example, the clause which relates to the escape of prisoners from the Master-at-arms, one of the petty officers of the ship, & therefore one of very limited authority. In case of a prisoner who is condemned to death, or to suffer any other punishment, or who is even charged with any crime—escaping from the Master-at-arms, he is liable to "suffer in such prisoners stead."

Attempts have been made from time to time to revise this effete & savage code. But the revision has always been sought to be accomplished by a board of Officers.

The history of the Navy will show, that the action of boards has seldom met expectations; moreover, the best codes of law, as well as the best commentaries have been the work rather of individuals than of boards, or commissioners.

Taking the lights of experience for my guide, I would recommend that the task of revising the code be first committed to some competent Officer of the Navy, and that the result of his labors be then referred to a Board, with instructions to point out faults and imperfections, and after the Secretary of the Navy shall have passed upon the whole, to refer it to Congress for adoption or rejection.

The Bureaus have never been properly organized. But, in my opinion, no legislation is required with regard to them. The authority of the Secretary is, it appears to me, sufficient to place them upon the proper footing &, to invest them with the proper degree of responsibility and efficiency.

But, before proceeding further, let us consider what is the true policy of the Country, with regard to its Navy. For, if that can be ascertained, we shall then have a foundation upon which to build.

According to my understanding of the spirit of our institutions, and my interpretation of public sentiment with regard to this subject, all war establishments are regarded as necessary evils; and we are compelled in self defence to maintain a Navy. The Navy has its mission in peace as well as in war, though the chief object of its existence is to serve the purposes of warfare. Therefore, the Naval establishment which is best adapted to the institutions of a Country like this, and which is most to be desired, is one—if it be possible to found such an one—with powers of expansion sufficient to meet all the emergencies of war, while in peace it is not more than sufficient to meet all the requirements of the Nation.

These requirements are in the display of a force which, while it shall not be so insignificant as to invite insult and aggression, shall nevertheless, not be larger than is necessary to maintain the police of the seas, to perform all the services required of it, to command the respect of other Nations, & to remind them that we are always ready and sufficiently prepared to repel aggression, to assert our rights & to maintain them.

Such a Navy would be truly economical, and in unison with our institutions; and such a Navy it is practicable to establish.

One of the first steps to be taken towards such an establishment, is to consolidate and enlarge the nucleus for it, by requiring the Navy to perform all those duties which it may legitimately and advantageously and economically perform in times of peace.

Some years ago, I think it was in 1841, Congress passed a law requiring the Executive to cause a *Hydrographical* survey to be made of the Northern Lakes. For some reason not known to me, this service was assigned to the Topographical Bureau of the Army. And what have we seen? Not the first chart yet, notwithstanding the Army has been building or buying vessels for this survey, while the Navy had them already there, manned, Officered, & equipped, and ready, without the expense of another dollar, to perform the service which is appropriate to it, & which legitimately apertains to it. It is believed that many thousands of dollars have been expended upon this work, from first to last, all, or nearly all, of which might have been saved to the Country had it been assigned to the Navy; for the Navy, or that portion of it on the Lakes, with all the means and facilities already provided and at hand, has been an idle spectator of it, and of course has been bringing itself into disrepute by appearing idle.

So with the Coast Survey. That builds, buys and repairs vessels under another appropriation, ships men, and employs Officers—besides Naval—when without the necessity of any such appropriation, the Navy has already on hand and unemployed, all the materiel & personnel requisite for the performance of the whole work.

Thus other laborers have been admitted into Naval fields to reap and bear off almost the only honors and distinction left within the professional grasp of Navy men in times of peace.

While strangers are thus brought in to perform those duties which the Navy ought to perform, the Navy to that extent is standing idle, and thereby incurring reproach and popular disfavor.

But even supposing that there would be, by transferring this service to the Navy, no saving of expense to the Government, the transfer would nevertheless be beneficial and wise; for it is required, according to the plan, of investing in peace, the Navy with powers of expansion to meet the emergencies of war, to employ its officers in preference to others in all things pertaining to their profession. The policy clearly is to make the nucleus from which this expansion is to take place, as large as can be usefully employed in peace. There would then be so much more occupation for the Navy, and while the Government would have the same amount of work done, it would, without additional cost, be sustaining its Navy exactly in the same proportion.

There is no want of talent or fitness among the Officers of the Navy, to take charge of those works. They are of the few kinds of work appropriate to the Navy, which have tangible results in peace, results that are obvious to the multitude, and useful to the public, and which, therefore, are the more calculated to keep the Navy in favor with the masses.

"The better to provide for the common defence," was foremost among the objects for which the federal government was created.

Such have been the improvements, the discoveries, the inventions, and the changes, since this government was formed, that plans of providing for the National defence which were then thought necessary, are now useless. We have means and facilities of defence & offence, with implements of war that were unknown to our fathers.

With railroads, the magnetic telegraph, & other works of improvement, individual enterprize has provided for National defences on the land, far more effectually than the government has been able to do.

With the railroads, which are now under construction, completed & projected, leading from this City far back into the heart of the Mississippi valley, to the far West, the extreme East, the remote South, & the distant North, what enemy would ever think of landing an army on the Chesapeake Bay, and of marching, as he did in the war of 1812, upon this City? Why, before he could reach the Capitol, we could assemble here to meet him, an army of mountaineers from your own State, while another army might be brought from as far as the Green mountains, in the opposite direction, to intercept and cut off his retreat to his ships.

The mere fact that we possess such powers of concentration, along the entire Atlantic sea-board, [illegible] secure against invasion.

An enemy may come with his ships, and with them attack our sea-port towns; but as for his invading the Country, or putting any considerable distance between him and his ships, or thinking of permanently investing any point on the mainland, is out of the question.

These works, therefore, have made necessary an entire and radical change in the plan hitherto pursued, of providing for coast defences. Instead of building a line of fortifications along the Coast from Maine to Georgia, we have now only to provide the forts and batteries necessary to defend our seaports against the great guns of big ships.

Equally important have been the improvements of the age in their bearings upon the true Naval policy of the Country. They have made necessary reforms and changes in this arm of the National defence, which, it appears to me, have not been sufficiently studied.

At the close of the last war, when the Country was flushed with pride for the Navy, a sum was annually set aside for the gradual increase of this branch of the public service; nurseries for seamen were encouraged by the government; and large bodies of the public land were reserved to supply the Navy with timber for ship-building. Under this policy, the keels of many fine ships were laid, which, to this day, remain rotting on the stocks, or going to decay at their anchors.

This policy, and a wise policy it was at the time, continued for many years, until it was found to be no longer necessary. When it was first adopted, the population of the Country was comparatively sparse, ship builders and mechanics were scarce, and therefore it was wise, in making ready by the time war should come, gradually to build ships in times of peace, when mechanics could be had at leisure.

But the commercial Marine of the Country increased rapidly and with it ship-builders and all the host of artisans concerned in Naval Architecture multiplyed exceedingly.

It was then discovered that our ships were beginning to rot on the stocks and as there were mechanics enough to put ships together in a hurry, and in any numbers, it was decided to stop building but to go on collecting timber, fitting it, and putting it under sheds so as to be ready for putting up on the first appearance of a war cloud.

But in the mean time the country went on increasing and improving, and other changes in our Naval policy have now become necessary.

I propose therefore to consider what those changes are, and in order properly to set them forth let us contrast the present with the former condition of the Country as it regards its Naval resources.

We may now consider ourselves the first Commercial nation in the world. For if our tonnages do not already exceed that of Great Britain it will before the end of another year.

When the policy of "Gradual Increase" was first adopted, the largest merchant ships in the Country did not measure over 500 or 600 tons, and there were but a few private building yards among our merchants. Now our sea shores and river banks are lined with them, and the largest vessels afloat anywhere upon the ocean are launched from them. We have sailing ships building for the Merchant service at 2000 tons, and steamers of twice, or nearly twice, that measurement. These private yards are well stocked with building materials, which would be on their hands at the breaking out of a war, and which on such an occasion, would admirably answer the purpose of the Government, towards building frigates and sloops-of-war.

The railroads and canals have converted every forest in the land into timber sheds for the Navy, ships of green timber would last through any war that we shall probably ever have. Such ships, so lasting, would be as good to us as the best,—for good or bad we should have no use, except for a remnant of them, at the end of the war, and should the fortunes of war throw any of them into the hands of the enemy, he would be neither enriched nor materially strengthened by his prizes.

Therefore these natural timber sheds, these private shipwrights employed in them, afford us a resource & a reliance in war the importance of which cannot ever be estimated. How unwise is it then to continue on in our uncertain course of naval policy, without regard to any such resource, & to go on building ships and collecting materials as though we had no such reliance.

Some years ago, when I was more at leisure than I have been since, I took the trouble of going into the official statistics of the Navy with regard to the cost of building and the expenses of keeping in repair live-oak built ships.

The sloops of war were the most numerous class, they have been kept more continually in active service than the Frigates, and therefore the sloops of war offered me in my enquiries a better guide than did the frigates.

I was startled to learn by this examination that to keep a live-oak built sloop of war in repairs for the first nine years of her existence costs on the average as much as it took to build her, and that it took nearly twice as much to build her of live oak as it would take to build her of white oak.

It is the planking and fitting up and not the live oak which requires repairs, the planking & fitting are the same in each. White oak timbers and knees are strong enough for ships of war; they can be had for about 30¢ the cubic foot, against $1.50 for live oak. Live oak is like iron, and is hard to work, and one shipwright will do on white oak knees, the work of several on live oak.

In repairing a live oak ship, the planking has to be ripped off, and the bolts that secured it have to be hacked out of the live oak, which is more difficult and expensive than putting them in, so that it is cheaper to buy the knees and timbers for a new white oak ship, than it is to rip off the planking & hack out the bolts & get a live oak ship ready for repairing.

After going into the merchant service for statistics concerning the durability of white oak ships, I was brought to the conclusion that one should, by adopting the plan of building our first class sloops of war of white oak, of running them till they began to decay so as to require repairs, and then, instead of repairing them, sell them, and build new ones, not only effect an important saving, but that the country would be the gainer also in other respects.

A white oak built merchant ship, of sloop of war size, will run from ten to twelve years before she requires any repairs from decay. She might then be sold for $20,000., which, deducted from $68,000., her estimated prime cost, leaves $48,000. for building and keeping in repair a white oak sloop of war for 9 years, against $223,000. for building & keeping in repair a live oak ship of the same class for a like period.

Subsequent experience & observation have confirmed me in these views, and convinced me that the best course to be pursued with regard to the live oak lands of the government is to dispose of them, and depend mainly on white oak for frames for our men-of-war, and especially for those to be built in time of war.

For further information upon the subject, see southern Literary Messenger, Vol. VII, Page 365 *et passim.*

The extension of our borders to the Pacific Ocean makes this change in the plan of ship building in times of peace, also essentially necessary at least for that part of the Navy to be stationed on that sea, and true policy requires that no inconsiderable portion of it should be sent there at an early day—and once on that side, that there it should remain.

So long as California remains essentially a mining country, so long will she continue to look from home, abroad over the sea for food and raiment & all articles of prime necessity, until a railroad be built across the country, these things must be brought to her by sea. Therefore, unless we have ships and guns there sufficient to drive the enemy away and keep her ports open, California will remain at the mercy of any 4th or 5th. rate Naval power that shall choose to send there & blockade her ports.

Until we have a railway to the Pacific in operation, succor from the rear is impossible, and long before succor could arrive from around Cape Horn, an enemy with an insignificant force before the ports of California might levy contributions upon our citizens there ad libitum, and starve her into any terms, however humiliating.

It is not generally known to the public & therefore it is here the more worthy of remark, that the distance in time by sea from our Atlantic to our Pacific ports, is greater than the distance between any other seaports on the face of the globe.

The distance from New York to China, to India, to New Holland, is nothing like the distance to California. In point of time, California is the most remote place on the face of the earth, to which ships can go by sea, and therefore it is out of the question to suppose that in war we should be able to succor California by sea from this side.

Labor in California is too high to think of building ships there. The ships must be built on this side for the present, at any rate, and sent there.

Besides these considerations, there are physical circumstances in favor of a white oak Navy, for the Pacific, and these circumstances are found in the smoothness of that ocean & in the entire exemption of much the larger portion of it from storms.

The trade wind belt of the Pacific is 3000 miles in breadth from north to south, & it extends from east to west entirely across. This region is never ruffled by storms, and any ship that will float is sea worthy there. Much of the coasting-trade of Peru is done on rafts with a pole stuck up between the logs for a sail—so smooth is the sea there.

In 1821 two white oak vessels of war were built for the Navy, they were duplicates of each other & alike. One was sent to the Pacific, the other retained for service in the Atlantic.

In a few years the repairs put upon the one in the Atlantic had doubled & trebled her original cost, whereas that in the Pacific continued 16 years in active service without any repairs whatever from decay, and was at the end of that time, sold for a considerable sum, and was a few years ago, & is I believe yet actively engaged as a merchant vessel in that sea.

We ship men in the Navy for three years—the voyage to California and back will occupy a year; therefore if we follow the plan hitherto pursued of sending vessels from the Atlantic to the Pacific ports and then of bringing them back vessel & all to pay off at the expiration of their term of service, it will be perceived that in order to get two years of actual service from ship and crew in the Pacific, we must actually pay for three, for the year occupied in going and coming is time lost.

It would be found a costly operation to bring a ship that requires repairs, home from the Pacific, the longest voyage in the world, and through the most stormy seas that are known. Why it would cost quite as much to bring her safely home as the ship was worth. A ship that is sea worthy for the passage around Cape Horn & the approaches to our Atlantic coast in winter, is good for several years of active service in the Pacific. Therefore, according to my judgment, the true policy is to keep the ships in the Pacific, to run them as long as they are seaworthy, & when they require repairs from decay, sell them there, build new ones here, & send them out.

The same causes which made the old law for the "gradual increase of the Navy," along the Atlantic coast, so wise thirty years ago, now call for a like increase along the Pacific coast.

We should gradually build on this side & send there more ships than were wanted for actual service, that they may be laid up there in ordinary, ready for any emergency.

Instead of bringing home via Cape Horn the crews of our ships in commission there when their times have expired, the country will find it most conducive to encourage the opening of railways or canals across the Isthmus, so that the crews, when their times are up may be brought home that way, leaving their ships behind.

Having lodged there, besides the force always in commission, a sufficient number of vessels with armaments to be held in reserve, the whaling business & the Merchant service would supply us with men sufficient to man & fight this reserved force in war. And to be completely prepared for any emergency it only remains to devise a plan for keeping in California and Oregon a sufficient number of officers to command in war the vessels which have been placed there in ordinary during peace.

This may be readily accomplished by transferring the Coast survey of the Pacific, and making it actually what it really is, a nautical work. This would call for quite a number of officers there, whose occupation as surveyors a war would suspend, and therefore leave them available for the ships in ordinary. This service together with a liberal course in encouraging Officers to seek occupation & residence in Oregon & California, & along their Coasts, would provide a corps of Officers at hand for as many ships as it may be judged expedient to hold in ordinary along our Pacific coasts for emergencies that may arise.

What this number ought to be, and to what extent we should go in providing our Pacific coasts with the means of defence, are subjects which require the most careful consideration, for they are subjects which admit of great diversity of opinion.

Present facts, and the lights which our own experience as a nation cast upon the subject, when consulted, will be found, I think, to be the safest guides that we can adopt.

When the States of the Union were all on the waters of the Atlantic, we had a sea front of only 2000 miles. But now, our Ocean front is more than double that. Then, the shortest way from State to State, was within our own borders, and by inland channels of communication; now, it is through foreign countries, and by a double sea voyage.

Then, our Navy could carry succor & bring relief from State to State in a few days, now, a voyage of circumnavigation can be performed in less time than it would take us to send a squadron around to drive away a blockading force from the coasts of California & Oregon—so widely has the Country extended its sea front, & maritime borders.

In 1841, when the existing limits were assigned to the Navy, a blockade of the entire sea coast of the United States would have been considered but as another kind of embargo. But now, the blockade of the ports of California would be both embargo & starvation.

Then, we were only the second or third commercial nation, and a fourth rate Naval power, now, we are the first in Commerce; and shall we be among the weakest for the means of defence?

The Navy must be enlarged, or we shall fail properly to provide for the common defence of the Pacific coasts; for I take it that the country is as ready to provide for the defences of one portion as another; and that it is willing to provide as liberally for the Pacific as the Atlantic.

As I before remarked, true policy does not require us to build ships on the Atlantic, any faster than they are required for present service there; for the private yards there, the abundant material, labor and facilities of all kinds there, will enable us, upon short notice, as to a state of hostilities, to equip a Navy as large as we shall choose to provide Officers, guns, and munitions of war for.

Not so on the Pacific—there are in California no ship yards, public or private, no timber sheds stored with timber, no railroads to fetch it from the forests; & no mechanics, except at exorbitant rates, to build them.

The centres of our Naval operations in the Pacific must, of necessity, be from the Harbor of San Francisco, & the mouth of the Columbia river. There, we should gradually collect ships & munitions of war, in peace, lay them up in ordinary, as a reserve, for the purpose of war.

If these views be correct, then it becomes necessary to consider whether a part of the ships which are now laid up in ordinary, in our Atlantic ports, ought not to be placed as early as practicable in ordinary in our Pacific ports, for, unless the Country means now without cause to abandon the policy which it has steadily pursued with regard to its Navy for almost fifty years, a considerable increase of the Navy is called for, on account of our acquisitions, & the settlement of our people on the Pacific coast.

The Pacific ocean is not the seat of any considerable Naval power, and the speedy accumulation there, in active service, and in ordinary, of ships enough in due proportion as to class—including steamers—to enable the Government to equip a fleet of 50 or 60 sail, would place us in the ascendant there, and give us the undisputed command of that grand Ocean.

There are something like 10,000 American seamen employed in the whaling business there. These are of the class of those Marblehead and Cape Cod men, who fought so gallantly, & gained such renown in the last war. These, together with the merchant sailors, who would be thrown out of their regular occupation in the event of war, would be ready to man these ships.

Therefore, the collection of such a number of ships, with stores of coals, guns, and all the imperishable munitions of war in sufficient quantities, would have the effect, in that Ocean, which our railroads have upon the land, viz:—by showing our means & resources, of preventing an enemy from giving us an opportunity for displaying that power.

With the exception of the vessels proposed to be laid up in ordinary on the Pacific Coast, and with the exception of the vessels which we now have on the stocks or laying in ordinary along the Atlantic Coast, we require no others in peace, except such as are requisite for the service, and state of preparation required of the Navy in such times.

As the Country expands & increases, its commerce becomes more valuable, its relations more complicated, and of course, its demands upon the Navy for active service greater and greater.

As a consequence, the Navy must keep pace with the wants of the Country, and when the means of doing this have been provided, and when the necessary number of guns and other imperishable materials shall have been placed in store to meet any probable emergency, we will have provided for all the "gradual increase" that is required, as to the *materiel*.

The merchant is a powerful auxiliary of the National marine. By a proper system of policy on the part of the Government as to its Navy, the merchant service may be made to support in times of peace, and to hold ready for the Government in case of war, all the elements, the materiel, the bone & muscle of the most powerful Navy in the world, and this the merchant service may be made to do, with advantage to itself, and without cost to the Government.

The commercial marine has in active service now, and in continual training, a hundred thousand able-bodied seamen. Its ship yards, mechanics, & the commercial resources of the Country, furnish all the materials for building any number of ships. So that by tomorrow, the Government might, were it necessary, cause the keels of a hundred frigates, sloops, brigs, & Schooners to be laid, besides steamers, in large numbers. These 100,000 merchant seamen are to the Navy what a corps of 100,000 regulars among the militiamen would be to the Army in times of war. A militiaman in the Army corresponds to a landsman in the Navy. They both require training to fit them for efficient service.

But the able-bodied seaman is like the well disciplined regular. They are both veterans, and he that has been trained in the merchant service, is as good a seaman as he who has served in a man-of-war. What tremendous powers of Naval expansion, therefore, does not our Commercial marine, constituted as it is, afford to this Country? Ought not the Navy to be so organized as to avail itself of these powers?

Such are the elements of the Naval strength of this Country. But where are the officers to command and direct and give them efficiency? The Merchant service does not afford them, the Navy has them, not in sufficient numbers; nor is it the policy of the Government to maintain in peace, Officers sufficient to command in war, the entire personnel of the Commercial marine. Whence, then, are the Officers to come, & how may they be obtained? My plan is to let the Government train them, and then let the Merchant service maintain them.

We may build ships in a day, & enlist crews by the hour, but not so with the officers to command them. They cannot be made without previous education, training, & discipline; and for this time is required. There is no hot bed from which competent sea-officers may be gathered at will for the Navy.

The great feature in the true Naval policy of this Country is still "gradual increase," and gradual increase it must be, as long as the Country, its powers, its resources, its grandeur, its wealth & its greatness continue to increase. But we have seen that gradual increase as to materiel is no longer required from the Government. The Merchants & ship builders of the land are, on their own account, increasing the materials for many such Navies as we shall ever require. The true system of gradual increase now applies more to the *personnel*. And this system is to be established simply by the expense to the public of supporting a properly organized Naval school.

The whole plan of reforming the Navy consists in providing the means for training Officers to command our ships, and squadrons while they are in the prime of life, and vigor of manhood, & of having in times of peace, a Navy no larger than the exigencies of the public service require it to be in peace, but invested with powers of expansion capable of meeting the most sudden emergencies of war. The entire plan for such a Navy rests upon, has root in, and grows out of, a properly regulated Naval school.

That I may be clear upon this, the most important feature in the plan of recasting the Navy, permit me to invite your attention to the present condition of it, (*personnel*,) while I endeavor to point out in the best way I can, what the causes are which have brought it to this condition. Then, seeing what these causes are, it will be the more easy to provide against them in the new plan.

As has been already remarked, all the active grades of the service are filled by Officers too old for their places. I have also said that the present system of promotion is demoralizing. Indeed, it offers a premium to sloth and idleness. That Officer is sure of the highest Naval honors the Country can give, who lives longest. He who shirks duty, and lives quietly on shore, has a better chance of a long life than he who is diligent in service, and is continually exposed to its hardships, privations & casualties.

The Navy of the United States is, I suppose, the only military establishment in the world in which no distinction is made between the efficient and inefficient; in which devotion to duty, zeal for service, and fidelity to Country, do not serve to advance an Officer. With or without them, he is advanced alike, no sooner with them, no later without them. And as far as promotion is concerned, it is as though he had them not.

If, in organizing the service as it now exists, the object had been to break down the spirit of the Officers, a plan more effectual for that end could not have been devised.

We want a system of promotion which, without favoritism or partiality, shall recognize zeal, and devotion to duty, and in practice give them preference over unfitness and indifference. We want a system which shall give us for our Commanders, not men of 50 & upwards; but dashing young fellows of not more than 30 or 35; and for Captains, we want men who are not great-grandfathers, but men who are in the prime of life.

Suppose, therefore, that the Naval school were properly organized;—for though the present organization is an improvement upon the old plan, yet it is such as no board of trustees of any college in the Country would submit to for an instant.

By the present arrangement, the Midshipman must stay there two years; then go to sea for two or three years; and then, when he is a bearded & traveled man, come back & be school boy again for another term.

The disciplined habits of study are difficult to acquire, and easy to lose; and that fact is, alone, a sufficient reason why the theoretical education of an officer should be completed before he is permitted to leave school.

What would the course of West Point be, in comparison to what it is, or what in comparison would be the value of that Institution, if the Cadets, at the end of the second year, were permitted to join their regiments, and, after roaming about the Country for two or three years, then to come back and complete the rest of their term at school.

What sort of an education would they get? Yet this is the plan for Annapolis, and as preposterous as it would be for the Army, it is proposed to tolerate it for the Navy.

I hope you will alter it, and make the term there four years, with a cruize of 3 months each year, in the school ship.

This being done, my plan for "gradual increase" is this: Let there be admitted annually into the School, two Midshipmen for each ship in the Navy. After each annual batch shall have been there four years and graduated, send them to sea for two or three years; bring them home; examine & promote as many of the highest on the list, & who are not over a given age, say 22, as are required to fill up the vacancies in the grade of Masters.

It will be six or seven years, (say six) from the commencement of this plan, before the first Master can be made under it, 9 years before the first Lieutenant, & 17 years before the first Commander.

We shall have, therefore, about 14 years in which we may gradually effect those changes that are necessary in the present *personnel* and grades of the service, in order to prepare and adapt them to the proposed new order of things.

It is easy to show that the grade of Pass'd Midshipman adds nothing, either to the discipline or the efficiency of the service. They are only Midshipmen waiting to be Lieutenants; and the grade was established under these circumstances. Formerly, when the powers of appointment were unlimited, midshipmen were admitted faster than nominations were made for promotions. Consequently, they accumulated, & then they began to be clamorous at being kept out of promotion so long; and as a concession to the justness of their claims, the grade of Pass'd Midshipmen was established; but their duties remain the same as those of Midshipmen.

Therefore, within the first six years of the school, and as soon as with justice & fairness to the Officers it can be done, the grade of Passed Midshipmen should be abolished, and the grade of Master established in its stead, to consist of two for each line-of-battle ship, & one for each vessel of every other class in the Navy, to which an officer of such a grade is allowed.

As vacancies ocurred in the list of Lieutenants, the Masters who were not over twenty-five years of age, and who had seen the most service, should be promoted. Those who were over twenty-five should be dropped.

It would be from 8 to 9 years from the commencement of this system before the names of any in the grade of Master could be dropped from the Register, under this rule.

In like manner, Lieuts. not over, say 23, should be promoted as vacancies occurred in the list of Commanders, not according to the date of commission, but according to quantum of service.

There is no good reason why A., who has been in the Navy 20 years, and on duty but 10, should be promoted before B., who has been in only 18 years, but has been on duty 15. On the contrary, every principle of justice, propriety, and public good, requires that fidelity should be rewarded, & that the honor should rest upon B.

The names of those Lieuts. who had passed the age of promotion should also be dropped from the Register.

In the meantime, the way to reorganization should be cleaned out & paved, by placing on a retired list all the incompetent or inefficient Officers of the various grades, except those who by long & faithful services, are entitled to the gratitude of their Country. Every consideration of public propriety seems to require that after a sea Captain, who has served his Country long, faithfully & well, and who has attained a certain age, should be released from further liability to service *at sea*. After he has passed the age of (say 60) his experience will be more valuable to his Country on shore, than his services can be at sea.

I announce this simply as a general rule, which has its exceptions—and take the age of 60 because that is the age at which judges in some of the States are ruled from the bench, and because there are but few men who follow the sea, that remain active in body, & vigorous after 60.

Therefore let it be enacted that no Captain shall be eligible for sea service after he is 60 years old and upwards. Let there be at all times, say 50 Captains, who are eligible for sea service, and let those who are over 60 be employed on shore as they now are, at our Dock Yards, in our Bureaus, and on other shore stations.

Those who had seen 30 years of service & upwards, might, at their own request, be allowed to retire on full pay, as a reward to their long and faithful services.

In like manner, reduce the list of Commanders eligible for *sea* service to (say 50); and that of Lieuts to (say 300); and for the first 6 years from the commencement of this plan, make Commanders of (say 55 years) & upwards, and Lieuts. of (say 50) & upwards, ineligible, either for *sea* service or promotion; and let those who are disqualified for the sea by reason of their age, be placed in honorable retirement, or be assigned to duty on shore, as they now are, according to the merits of the Officer, & the discretion of the Executive; and so gradually reduce the disqualifying age for promotion & sea service in these two grades, until, at the end of 14 years, from & after which it shall not be lawful to promote a Lieut. after he shall have attained the age of 33, as before provided, and his name shall be dropped from the list. So also for Commanders, the law should make them ineligible for *sea* service, or promotion after they had attained the age say of (38 or 40.)

Those of them who had seen 20 years of service & upwards, or who had distinguished themselves in any manner, it would be proper—though disqualified for sea service—to retain in the Navy, for duty at the Dock Yards, and other Shore stations, or to retire them on the leave pay of their grade.

Exempting all officers from the operation of such laws, who had failed to fulfill the requirements prescribed, by reason of injuries sustained in the actual performance of duty, or by wounds received in battle, we should, by this means, ingraft upon the Navy, a self-sustaining principle, and endow the junior grades with perpetual youth.

In England & France young men are lifted over the heads of their seniors and advanced to high places in the Navy through favoritism. And as hateful as this system is, its advantages to the *State* are most obvious. But for this feature in their Naval system, or some other by which the Crown could call men while in the prime of life to high stations in the Navy, the Navies of both these powers, as to personnel, would in all the grades, have become effete, & inefficient, long ago.

The plan here proposed will accomplish perpetual rejuvenation in all the grades, without any favoritism whatever. It will have an unerring index of merit, for it gives preference to him in the line of promotion who has served the Country the longest & the most faithfully. A better rule of merit it would be difficult to establish.

Let us now consider the practical operations of this plan.

At the end of the first six or seven years from the commencement of it, the Midshipmen who have been dropped from the want of vacancies in the grade of Master, will be candidates for the Marine Corps, the Revenue service, the Mail steamer service, & the Merchant service. Their education and previous training will have qualified them in an eminent degree for these various duties & places; but especially in the merchant service will they be sought.

The number of Navy officers now in the merchant service, and the number of applications on file in the Department from Officers seeking permission to engage in its callings, justify this conclusion. Therefore, it may be supposed that when a Midshipman shall be dropped for the want of room; and when Masters and Lieuts. are dropped because one is 25, the other 33 and upwards, and for no other reason than that they are beyond the required age for promotion,—it cannot, I repeat, be doubted, that men of such an education, as under the proposed reorganization of the school they would have, that men of such talents, acquirements, & abilities as the School would turn out,—that such men would not be most eagerly sought by our keen sighted merchants, as Masters and officers of their ships.

Having been brought up to the sea, it is natural to suppose that these rejected Officers would continue to follow the sea. Having been educated in the Navy, & imbued with correct notions of Naval discipline, they would carry with them, into the Merchant service, these habits and feelings.

The retired West Pointers, at the call of their Country in the Mexican war, started up like Roderick Dhu's men, and stood forth from their places of retirement to answer the summons, like brave men and true. All and more than those graduates were in that war, would these Navy men be in the next to our ships at sea.

Those graduates had, for the most part, been leading quiet, retired, and unmilitary lives, and therefore had become more or less rusty as soldiers. But these Officers would be leading the life of the sailor all the time, and would be acquiring as much experience as seamen in the Merchant, as they could in the Naval, service.

Those graduates had to do with Militia & raw recruits. But in war, these ex-Navy Officers with the 100,000 able-bodied seamen in the Merchant service, would stand as a corps of veterans in reserve, and enable their Country to put forth upon the sea any amount of force, and to display upon the Ocean any degree of power.

In war these same Officers would be recommissioned in the Navy, and these seamen of the Merchant service enlisted for the Navy, as required.

Thus the Navy would be invested with powers of expansion ad libitum in war; and by means of the school at Annapolis, the merchant service may be made, with advantage to itself & without further cost to the public, to maintain in peace a corps of reserve, consisting of ships, men and officers, with all the materiel except guns and munitions, for the largest Navy the world ever saw.

The nucleus, consisting of the permanent Naval establishment, or, if you please, the Naval peace establishment of the Country, around which such forces & powers are to be gathered in war, should therefore be compact and sound to the core—all its parts should be in the proportions due. Therefore in limiting the number of Officers eligible from the various grades, for sea service, authority should be given, as the number of ships in the Navy is increased or diminished, to increase or diminish the number of Officers in the various grades, according to the complement allowed by regulations to such increased or diminished number of ships.

Thus the Navy would be complete in all its proportions, with the power to expand & contract with the number of the ships, with the power to keep pace with the growth of the Country; or to contract without destroying its proportions, to suit any change of policy.

There is not the same physical necessity for having one set of ships for the Pacific, and another for the Atlantic, but the necessity for having them is almost as paramount as it was in the last war, for having a Lake fleet, and an Ocean fleet.

The necessity of proceeding to build a considerable number of ships to be sent to the Pacific, & be kept in ordinary, is obvious, and the propriety of the measure is clear.

The collecting of such material there, in such kind and quantities will make it necessary to have an officer, high in rank, and with enlarged powers, to be charged with its safe keeping, and to be responsible for its proper disposition, management and control. For obvious reasons, this duty could not be properly discharged either by the Commander of the Pacific squadron, or of the Navy Station at San Francisco. It could be properly discharged only by an Officer superior to both of these, and to whose orders not only they, but all the Navy Officers out there, whether on shore, or afloat, on duty furlough, or leave, should be liable.

In case of war, when communication would probably be interrupted, if not broken up across the Isthmus, months might elapse before the Government could communicate with that shore, and in consequence the most serious difficulties might again, as in the Mexican war, arise out there, by reason of not having there an Officer of enlarged and proper powers.

Therefore, as I said, it should be an Officer of higher rank & greater authority than any now known to the Navy, who shall be required to reside there. It would seem, therefore, that the creation of the grade of Admiral in the Navy cannot longer be delayed without laying the train for many drawbacks, inconveniencies and perplexities to the public service. For such an Officer will be required to have the control & management of the Navy. His powers over it should be that of a sort of Lieutenant Secretary, with authority to approve or disapprove in his own name, the sentences of Courts Martial on that distant station.

As to the true interests of the service with regard to steamers, sound policy seems to require both prudence & caution in proceedings for the future.

Improvements are rife, and ingenuity is active in devising new means and modes of propelling vessels at sea. If we proceed to build up a large steam Navy, after we shall have become fairly committed to this policy, we may find it invented into disuse by some new and important discovery. The true policy, therefore, seems to require that we should go into steam so far as may be necessary to keep pace with the improvements of the age, taking care always to occupy that position with regard to it as will enable the Country at all times to avail itself without inconvenience or loss, of the latest improvements and discoveries with regard to this or any other means of National defence.

As to how far and to what extent steam is to supplant canvass in maritime warfare, remains undetermined. So also is the value to the Navy of those mail steamers which the Government has encouraged individuals to build. But whether those vessels will answer the purpose of armed vessels of war or not, the encouragement has been most wise and beneficial to the commerce, & upon the Maritime greatness of the Country.

To American citizens belongs the honor of having built the first steam vessel that ever crossed the Atlantic. As far back as 1817 a steamer went from Savannah to England.

After that feat was accomplished, nothing more was done in the matter for twenty years. Then Great Britain took it up, and remained without a rival for ten years. American ship-owners were attentive lookers-on, but they were afraid to enter the field single handed against such a powerful rival as the British Government.

Under these circumstances, the Government contracted for the establishment, under Naval control, of a line of mail steamers to Bremen and Havre; and then, as a measure of Naval policy, the Liverpool, Chagres & California lines were established. The success of these lines demonstrated to our merchants & ship owners the advantages of Ocean steamers, and gave an impulse to this branch of business that has, in the course of a year or two, almost literally darkened certain parts of the Ocean with clouds of smoke from sea steamers.

Before this policy is abandoned, it is worthy of consideration whether the Government will not afford the encouragement necessary to establish a line to Brazil, touching at Para at the mouth of the Amazon; and another from California to China.

But, before the Government is committed to this system of Merchant Steamers as a permanent part of the Naval policy of the Country, it is desirable to know something further as to the actual economy of the system as regards the fitness of the vessels for carrying armaments, and the probable cost of putting them in a condition to receive those armaments.

I would suggest therefore, for your consideration, the propriety of having proper officers to examine the vessels of this class which have been running for some time, and to report to the Department as to their fitness for men of war, together with estimates as to the time and expense required to convert them into such, as well as to the length of time for which, when so converted, they would probably last.

Respectfully,

*From Matthew F. Maury.*[110]

Observatory,

Oct. 8th., 1850.

*Private*

I have put the suggestions which I have to make concerning the instructions to Lieut. Herndon,[111] in the form which I thought would be most convenient.

In case it should appear to you that the programme of instructions is not full enough, I enclose a copy of a letter from me to

---

[110] The enclosed letter affords additional evidence of the valuable aid rendered Graham by Maury. It is also indicative of Graham's readiness to use the navy for constructive purposes.

[111] William Lewis Herndon (1813-1857), of Virginia, Maury's brother-in-law, who had entered the navy in 1829, was now a lieutenant. He attained the rank of commander in 1855. He went down with his ship off Hatteras, while on leave commanding a Pacific Mail steamer. His report, "Exploration of the Valley of the Amazon," was a valuable contribution of geographical and economic knowledge.

Lieut. H. written some time since, in which the subjects worthy of his attention are treated of in detail.

By last advices he had not received this letter. I propose to send him this copy when you have done with it. Should you wish to make use of any parts of it, I need not say it is perfectly at your service.

[Enclosure]*

National Observatory,

Washington,

April 20th, 1850.

Dear Lewis

I wrote you some time ago and addressed the letter to San Francisco.

I have written you several letters, but the one of which I speak contained the copy of a long letter to the Secretary of the Navy upon the Valley of the Amazon.

He sent for me to day to speak of the matter, and has come in to my views fully as to the importance of the subject and the desirability of having some one to come down the Amazon with eyes and ears open.

He spoke of giving you permission to come home at once that way with a Pass'd Mid'n for a companion. This is Saturday, I am to see him again Monday, when he is finally to decide upon the matter.

Without speculating what his decision will be, or advising you on any course of action upon a hypothetical case, I shall talk over the subject with you to night so you may understand what I have done, what I am at, and where you are.

In the first place, Nannie is afraid for you to descend the Amazon, lest the Alligators will eat you, and Mib is rather timid about your crossing that way on account of vague apprehensions that cannot be defined, of danger and mishap in so long and lonely a journey.

In the next place I have often paused in my work of building up beautiful Castles for you to figure in, in setting forth your merits and in speaking of your qualifications for such an enter-

---

* Copy of a letter (April 20th., 1850) from Maury to Herndon, but which had not been received by Lieut. H. Oct. 8th., 1850.

prise. I have, I say, paused often in my zeal to bring you out to ask myself the question as to whether you would really like such service and whether you would not feel the Spanish saying in your heart, "Save me from my friends".

Since you sailed, Lewis, the turn which has been given to events in this Country has forced me to cast about and to take a comprehensive view of all those things and circumstances which are calculated to shape, control, or bear upon our destinies as a people. I have seen a cluster of things in and around the Gulf of Mexico in which are wrapped the germs of powerful influences upon the future well-being of Uncle Sam, and in that cluster the Valley of the Amazon looms up with great importance.

There too are the investigations as to the Trends and Currents, they have also called my attention to that river and its basin. Vessels travelling under Canvass from the Mouth of the Amazon to Europe, to Rio, to Africa, or around either of the Capes, must stand North, and pass not far from the West Indies. This fact you observe, makes that river basin nearer to us than to Brazil (if we call Rio Brazil) and puts practically the mouth of that river almost as much within the Florida pass and under our control, as is the Mouth of the Mississippi.

Reflecting upon this subject, and looking some distance into the future, I have seen the African slave population of America clustered in and around the borders of the Mediterranean Sea. I have seen this Sea, by Ship Canal and Isthmus highways placed midway between Europe and Asia. It is between two Continents, it receives the drainage of the two greatest river basins in the world, it is the natural for the produce of two hemispheres and I have therefore seen in it the Cornu Copia of the world, and this "Universal Yankee Nation" occupying upon its shores the very summit level of Commerce.

The question then comes up, Who shall people the great Valley of this Mighty Amazon? Shall it be peopled with an imbecile and an indolent people, or by a go ahead race that has energy and enterprise equal to subdue the forest and to develope and bring forth the vast resources that lie hidden there? The latter by all means.

And the object of your mission there, is to prepare the way for that chain of routes which is to bring this result about.

I care not what may be the motive which prompts the Gov't to send you there. Your going is to be the first link in that chain which is to end in the establishment of the Amazonian Republic, for when the Gov't has done what I have been urging it to do, and what it intends to try to do, viz, secure by treaty the right to navigate that river, it can no more prevent American citizens from the free, as well as from the slave States, from going there with their goods and chattels to settle and to revolutionize and republicanize and Anglo Saxonize that valley, than it can prevent the Magazine from exploding after the firebrand has been thrown into it.

That Valley is to be the safety valve for our Southern States, when they become over populated with slaves, the African slave trade will be stopped, and they will send these slaves to the Amazon. Just as the Mississippi Valley has been the escape valve for the slaves of the Northern, now free, States, so will the Amazon be to that of the Mississippi.

Thus you have one view of the subject, here is another.

Cotton is making England almost as dependent on us as though she were a colony in leading strings. She sees and feels that we have it in our power to create a revolution there whenever we choose to withold the annual supply of Cotton. The industrial pursuits of so many of her people are based upon this Staple that she cannot do without it, and it is of growing importance. How many people, think you, are in Great Britain that are entirely dependant upon the labor and occupations connected with this Staple, and whom the withdrawal of it would reduce to starvation?

A great and proud Nation, as she is, will not rest quietly under this state of things, and it is now thought in the best informed circles here, that she is casting about with eager eye for some cotton growing country, of which she may possess herself on this continent.

Some go so far as to say that if she can lay hold of such a country, she will even proceed to establish Slavery upon it. Such is the change of feeling wrought in that country by finding their dependence on our slave labor.

Now judging from the indications of the Wind Charts I am pretty clear that the only remaining Cotton growing country on this continent is to be found on the Southern tributaries of the Amazon, and in the regions thereabouts.

If we be the first to secure the right to Navigate the Amazon, your report will give our Merchants the information necessary to guide them in shaping their ventures and enterprises up that river. American influences will gain the ascendancy there, and the

Valley in a few years will become to be regarded for all commercial purposes as a sort of an American Colony.

The sort of Climate essential to the proper development of the Cotton plant is not a Climate that is divided into rainy and dry seasons, but it is a climate in which it may rain or be clear any day in the year, and that climate is South of the Amazon. Enquire about it.

The sort of labor necessary to the extensive cultivation of the Cotton plant is compulsory labor. If a country resting with its prosperity on the cultivation of this staple were to attempt its cultivation by free labor, the landlord would be at the mercy of the tenant or hireling, for at a particular stage of the crop, if the laborers were to strike or hold off for a few days, the whole crop would be destroyed. In India starvation follows a strike, therefore the labor there may be said to be compulsory, but in the two great American Valleys it will be many generations yet to come before population will be so crowded that loss of place and starvation will be correlative terms to the laboring man.

The energy, the science, and the civilization of the world have always been in the Northern Hemisphere. Do you suppose this is the result of chance? by no means.

The land as a general remark is all in the Northern hemisphere. Look at the condition of temperate Asia, temperate Africa, temperate Europe, and temperate America, and compare it with the condition of tropical Africa, America, and Australia. The feeble races that have peopled these portions have never been possessed of the Science, the skill or the energy to subdue the vegetation there. Look at the Northern continents with their fine relief and bold contrasts, the indentations of their Coast line, their finely articulated profiles, their inland seas, deep bays and gulfs favoring and inviting Commerce and the interchange of communication and compare them with the stiff outlines of the Southern Continents. Where in the South is your curtain of Peninsulas to relieve and diversify climates. Where your deep bays and extensive gulfs to multiply length of water line? No where.

My friend Guyot, of Neufchatel, in speaking of the duties of the North and the destinies of the Southern hemisphere, makes some remarks in a charming course of lectures called "Earth and Man", with which I have been so struck that I quote them for you, pp. 306-8:

"The three Continents of the South, outcasts in appearance, can they have been destined to an eternal isolation, doomed never to participate in the higher life of humanity, the sketch of which we have traced? and shall those gifts which Nature bestows on them with lavish hand, remain unused? No, Gentlemen, such a doom cannot be in the plans of God. But the races inhabiting them are captives in the bonds of all powerful Nature, they will never break down the fences that sunder them from us. It is for us, the favored races, to go to them. Tropical nature cannot be conquered and subdued save by civilized man, armed with all the might of discipline, intelligence, and of skillful industry, It is then from the Northern continents that those of the South await their deliverance, it is by the help of the civilized men of the temperate Continents that it shall be vouchsafed to the man of the Tropical lands to enter into the movement of universal progress and improvement, wherein mankind should share.

"The privileged races have duties to perform proportioned to the gifts they possess. To impart to other Nations the advantages which constitute their own glory, is the only way of legitimating the possession of them. We owe to the inferior races the blessings and comforts of civilization. We owe them the intellectual development of which they are capable, above all, we owe them the Gospel, which is our glory, and will be their salvation, and if we neglect to help them partake in all these blessings God will some time call us to a strict account.

"In this way alone will the inferior races be able to come forth from the state of torpor, and debasement into which they are plunged, and live the active life of the higher races. Then shall commence or rather shall rise to its just proportions, the elaboration of the material wealth of the Tropical regions, for the benefit of the whole world. The Nations of the lower races associated like brothers with the civilized man of the ancient Christian Societies, and directed by his intelligent activity will be the chief instruments. The whole world, so turned to use by man, will fulfill its destiny.

"The three North Continents, however, seem made to be the leaders, the three Southern the aids. The people of the temperate continents will always be the men of intelligence, of activity, the brain of humanity, if I may venture to say so; the people of the Tropical Continents will always be the hands, the workmen, the sons of toil.

"History seems to be advancing towards the realization of these hopes, towards the solution of the great contrast. Each Northern continent has its Southern continent near by, which seems more especially commended to its guardianship and placed under its influence. Africa is already European at both Extremities, North America leans on South America, which is indebted to the example of the North for its own emancipation, and its own institutions. Asia is gradually receiving into her bosom the Christian Nations of Europe, who are transforming her character, and beginning thence to settle the destinies of Australia. Lastly, the Christian Missions are organizing upon a larger and larger scale in the two leading Maratime countries of the globe, England and America, to whom the dominion of the sea seems granted for this end, and by engrafting upon all the Nations the vital principles of civilized societies, without which no real community can exist between them, are preparing and hastening the true brotherhood, the Spiritual brotherhood, of the whole human race".

You will thus see, Lewis, what a great work I have been chalking out for you. You are to be a pioneer, the humble workman if you please, in helping to get out from the quarry, and to lay the corner stone upon which such a magnificent, grand, and dazzling a superstructure is to be raised. I know your modesty and your merit, as great as is the latter, I know moreover, that in your composition the feeling of the former is so much in excess that your first impulse will be to decline the Mission with an unfeigned emotion of the heart that you are not equal to it.

I know too the dangers, the risks, and hardships of the voyage. But they will not be regarded by you, it will be the fear to touch so great a work, lest by failing you should do it harm.

But I have been called on to name the most competent officer in the Squadron for the undertaking, and I have named you without hesitation. I do not mean to persuade you to undertake the journey—I take it for granted that though you never would have sought the Mission, yet as it is offered on account of the estimation and the high appreciation of your abilities and talents I feel assured that you will not decline it without good and sufficient reasons.

In case you decide to go, and enter upon the journey with spirit, I take the liberty of offering a few suggestions as to some of the subjects which no doubt will occupy your particular attention. I know, Lewis, you will pardon me the liberty and appreciate the motives which prompt me. I am induced to offer these suggestions because I have been thinking so much more of the subject than you have, and because my notions will perhaps assist you in making your plans, modes and subjects of observation.

I shall speak of instruments and books after I have the interview with the Secretary.

*In the first place, the object of your journey should not be talked of.*

You should inform yourself as minutely concerning all the details of every branch of industry that you meet with in the way, as though you yourself intended to embark your fortune in it.

The mines of Peru and of Bolivia also, if you go through Bolivia, the average annual yield of gold and of silver, the profits, the companies, the machinery, the expense of transporting bullion to the sea coast, and the probable expense of sending it down the Amazon by Steamboat when we get there.

The feeling of the Peruvians and Bolivians tending the free navigation of the Amazon. Would they like to see an American line of Steamers plying between Para and the falls of Ucayale and St. Anthony on the Madera. and then above the system of falls to have more boats on the Mamosé and Guapuré rivers.

What facilities will the Gov't offer to American settlers and what inducements can citizens hold out to such an enterprise; What have they to send down the river, how long, and at what expense does it require to complete a voyage? What is the population?

Where do you find the Cinchona tree? What are the laws, if any, touching it? How is the bark collected? What are the forests worth? What is the bark worth when collected How much can one hand collect in a day? What is the season of the year for it? How much is gathered annually? How is it sent to market, and at what cost to the sea board Gutta Percha? Is it or can it be produced in the Valley of the Amazon? Where, and all about it, as tho' you intended to work at it for the rest of your life?

Tobacco—Is any grown? How much? Where sold? What its quality, and the season for planting, or do you cut and cure all the year 'round? How long does the same stock produce? You know with us the plant is killed by the first frost, and being not so killed, will produce suckers which in their turn will mature and produce good tobacco. What can it be produced for by the pound or is it produced at all, and why not?

You know that good rice lands must be where they can be overflowed at pleasure. The tide, they say, runs 700 miles up the Amazon. What then, is the capacity of the Valley for rice, how many crops in the year? What is the rice harvest period, and what the average yield per acre, and per hand? Is its cultivation considered unhealthy?

Note the implements of agriculture, the hours of work, the health of the Valley, and its diseases, the price of labor. I have a notion, gathered from the Wind Charts, that you will find no cases of consumption there. Inquire about it.

Cotton. How often is it planted? When is the best picking time? How much will one man pick a day? How much will one acre and one man produce on the average? Bring home samples of it, and some seed.

What are able bodied slaves sold at there? Is there any importation from Africa? to what extent and how do the untried slaves just from Africa compare in price with those who have been raised and trained in the country?

Sugar. How many crops in the year? What is the process for making? What proportion of the lands suited to sugar, what to Cotton, Rice, Hemp (will Hemp and Flax grow there) Tobacco, Indigo, Coffee, Cocoa, India Rubber, Gutta Percha, Ornamental and dye Woods, Cloves, Urucré, Sarsparilla, Drugs, balsams, Hides, Cattle and Indian Corn. Nuts, Fruits, and "Castanhoes de Maranham?"

As I said before, learn the value of each article, the extent of its production, the capacity of the region to increase it, the money that is to be made out of it, the cost and means of getting it to market, and every thing concerning, even to the minutest detail, as though you yourself were going to embark on that very business.

Do Crops ever fail, how often, what Crops, and from what causes?

When does the rainy, when does the dry season commence? What is the fluctuation one year with another, in the time of commencement? How much rain falls in the wet season? How much in the dry? Are not the dews heavy? Note the rains, the thunder and lightening as you come along. Does it ever hail in the Valley after you leave the vicinity of the Andes'. Note the size of the drops of the rain. The rain on the Andes I take to be rather fine rain, and the flakes of snow fine flakes, and, according to the Wind Charts, the drops of rain ought to be larger and larger 'til you get to the mouth of the river.

Get letters of introduction from the Bishop of Lima to the Missionaries and priests by the way. Cultivate them, they will give you information relative to soil, climate, quantity of rain, force of wind, botany, population, wealth, feelings of the people as to Steam Navigation on the Amazon, their dispositions towards the Americans, their feelings in regard to Slavery, and the slave trade, and information touching all other matters and Measures of policy which it may not be unexpedient to broach, and do not take any one man's opinion as sufficient upon any one of these subjects. Ask the same question of different people over and over again.

Of course you will not unnecessarily in such a country of ignorance and prejudice let the real object of your visit, and the authority under which you act, be known, nor would I speak of it at all to shipmates or others, it might embarrass you and cannot facilitate you in getting along with officials.

Find out all about the mines of Peru, and their yield. Get good letters to the leading men in all the river towns, and letters from the Gov't in Lima to Intendentes. You can ask the *Spanish* gentlemen, I think, freely, but of course upon your own hook, as to what they think of giving us such rights as they themselves have, to the Navigation of the Amazon, and the degree of encouragement they have their towns and Intendencies would be disposed to give to an American Steamboat Company.

Bring your questions home to them, when you can prudently do so, and get them to say that in case your country gets the right to navigate and that you or your agents appear there in the course of three years with one or more Steamboats, will they, if you stop at their place, furnish it with a given quantity of fuel gratis, or at a nominal price, or what amount of stock they will pledge to take in the Company. Take down names, pledges, and promises.

Notice the prices of every thing in Plazu and Tiena, by the way. Be particular to get statistics as to the quality, quantity, and kind of goods, English, French and American that are consumed in the different provinces. Get their retail prices with samples, and bring samples home, and learn as to the Channels thro' which they come.

Is there any coal fit for Steamboats, and how accessible is it? What are the rights of the State in regard to coal, iron, and other

mines? Salt—where does it come from? (Choco?) Extensive beds
of it are there, you know. Would it not be cheaper for them on
this side of the mountains to have salt sent them from the U. S.?
New York is but 25 days from the Amazon, and Charleston not
more than 15, under Canvass, and Canvass is almost as certain
as steam to and from the mouth of the Amazon because of the
regularity and certainty of the Trade Winds that are "Soldier's
Winds," they carry us there and fetch us back with equal celerity
and certainty.

Then as to the Tributaries that you will pass. Get the navigable
length of each one, and its tributaries, its extreme rise and fall,
and the periods of high and low water in each. Make a Map of
the Valley. The Intendentes and Missionaries will enable you to
do this with the help of the common map.

Get a fishing line or two from on board ship, about 50 fath's
long, have a lead to it of not over one pound weight, and run a
line of soundings with it from the base of the Andes to the
mouth of the Amazon, and map the river as you come along. You
will have a compass and a pocket chronometer. You can tell the
distance made daily, write it down on your chart, then sketch
in every day the mouths of the rivers passed, the bends of the
river, and the soundings, and the temperature of air and water
at 9 A.M. and at 3 P.M. Take the temperature also in the mouth
of each tributary, and if you keep watch, take temperature at
9 P.M. and at 3 A.M.

In this way you can do much to perfect the geography of that
region.

Note the color of the water of each tributary, whether it be
clear, milky, or muddy, and note all the way down the differences
between high and low water marks, what tributaries North &
South, and which are liable to the greatest floods and most rapid
rises and falls and which of them bring down most drift wood.

In short, Lewis, note down and take note of every thing that
you see, hear, feel or think while on the way down. Preserve specimens of all plants, bring home pieces of all rocks, and remark
on geographical formation. Hunt the rivers for fresh water shells,
and the trees for land shells. Bring along the seeds of fruits, and
plants, and when you embark at Para don't forget flowers and
my little green house, if by that time you be not worn out.

As you come down on this side of the Andes look at Steppes,
and consider them for sheep-husbandry—also the culture of the
grape and the manufacture of wine. Near the base of the Andes

the everlasting Wind Charts intimate the possibility of a wine country.

Be particular to ascertain how high up the tide ebbs and flows, the rate of the current above and below the tide water. Your lead line will serve you for a log.

Bores—high tidal waves 15 feet high are said to roll into the mouth of the Amazon on full and change days. Sometimes three rollers come in, sometimes four, it sounds fabulous to me, look to it. The rise and fall of the tide at the mouth of the Madera, will give you the descent of the stream, see if there be marshes back from the banks as in the Lower Mississippi.

Note too, if the Amazon cut away its banks as does the Mississippi.

As high up as the tide goes the rice country ought to reach, and that ought to be the greatest rice region in the world.

Pardon me, Lewis, for having been so tedious, but I am so anxious that nothing should escape you; whenever you can get information by the way, tarry there until you have satisfied yourself.

The rainy season in the main trunk of the Amazon, *according to the charts,* commences not until October or November, so you will have the dry season all the way, and as you come down, you will find the Northern tributaries most flooded. Would it not be well to make a trip of a few days, up each tributary, particularly those from the South?

You observe then that an important object of your Mission will be to collect political, Commercial, and statistical information relative to that immense region of country which has hereafter to play such an important part in the affairs of mankind and the world. Be full and minute and particular therefore, Lewis, in your inquiries and information as to the resources of that Valley, its soil, its climate, its productions and its capacities for productions. The labor to subdue the forests, the time required to open a plantation, the degree and amount of tillage to crops, the localities of marl beds and the facilities of manuring, the sites for Mills and water power on main trunk and tributaries, for as a general rule wherever there be falls on a river, there be water power.

Acquaint yourself also with the present obstructions to trade, political and natural, with tariffs and regulations. With the land policy. How much is owned by individuals and how much by the State? What is Gov't price of lands, the regulations under which they are disposed of to foreigners? The extent and fertility of the Valley of each tributary? The relative proportions of arable, barren lands and swamps, and lands subject to overflow in the valleys of the various rivers?

Pay attention also to the implements of husbandry, farming utensils, and the like.

May 2nd.

I have written the above and foregoing at odds and ends of time, a little now and then, interrupted by an attack of fever and ague, the business of the office, etc., so I am afraid you will find it a jumble out of which you will be able to make but little. I have had an interview with the Sec'y today, the matter was considered in Cabinet, and negotiation is to be tried. It certainly will be a brilliant achievement for any administration to secure the right to our people of trading and trafficking up and down the 40 or 50,000 miles of navigable tributaries to that river.

The Sec'y of State is to address a letter to the Sec'y of the Navy asking that an officer be directed to come down that river. I am to go in the morning to learn the result, but I consider the matter now as settled.

While I think of it let me say, inquire for letters at the Consul at Panama as you go along, for I may have something of importance to send you by that time.

Now for scientific matters. I wish I had a portable set of magnetic instruments to send you. By the way, I see Airy, the astronomer royal, has come round to my opinion expressed you know five years ago, to Sabine. You recollect the letter that those magnetic observations have been *"run into the ground."* That it is useless to follow British associations further.

I shall, if permitted, send you a pocket Chronometer, a Sextant, an Art Horizon, a few thermometers, a pocket compass and one of my steel Barometers for Elevations and Meteorlogical Observations. The Bar'r has gone to the makers on account of a leak. I shall not have time to describe it to you if I wait for it, so if you receive it you will be able to use it from this description.

Suspend it, unscrew the steel rod in the glass cistern, and screw it up to the shoulder in the arm which projects over the top of the Cistern.

To observe. Bring by means of the tangent screw the point of the steel rod and its image into contact and then read entering temperature. N. B. Always before proceeding to make an observation incline the Bar'r a little and then let it go free, so that the observation may always be made after the Mercury has been rising in the Cistern.

To adjust the Bar'r for transportation. Incline the Bar'r gently until all the Mercury except enough just not to uncover the hole in the tube, has escaped from the glass Cistern, then unscrew the steel rod from the arm, and screw it down *firmly* with the—don't force it into the place in which you will find it. It is now ready to be used as a walking cane.

It may be well before mounting always to assure yourself that no air has got into it. To do this, turn the Bar'r on taking it out for mounting, upper end down, and then right it slowly and in such a manner that if there be a globule of air it will be found on suspending the instrument to have crossed over from the steel part and to be resting in the short neck under the steel rod, or index. Now when you uncover the rod the air will rise and escape, if air there be.

Endeavor to take dew points every day, at least at 3 A.M. and 3 P.M. If you cannot conveniently provide yourself with the requisite refrigerating mixtures, give us *Wet bulb* all the way and all the time.

Endeavor to get copies of meteorological journals in any and every part of the valley, also the record of rain gauges.

Observe for Latitude at night by North, and South, Stars, e. g. suppose yourself on the Equator, that Star A is in 60° S and Star B in 60° N, and that A crosses the Meridian 10$^m$ before B. now the Alt. of A. will be 30°, and that of B will be 30°, and the result would show you to be midway between them.

I have selected in pairs all the Stars of 1st. and 2nd. magnitude that you will be able to observe on the Art Horizon, they are in the annexed table. When engaged in the observations and when you have got the first star of the pair, do not unscrew the telescope or remove the index but lay your instrument after you have read it, aside, having set it for the next Star. The advantage of doing this is, you do not disturb Collimation and the advantages of the method are you eliminate index errors—errors of eccentricity, division, refraction, etc.

As for Longitude and the other observations, you are *au fait.*

Provide yourself with a few gallons of alcohol, a number of vials of various sizes and a couple of reams of stout paper for botanizing, and a hammer for geologizing.

You will know how to preserve your plants, labelling each sheet with a full discription of the locality and of the specimens on it, and when you get a pile large enough, tie it between boards.

Every thing that you kill with a young in its belly open, and put the young away in your vial of alcohol. Your companion the mean while taking drawings of the old one. Break open eggs of birds, turtle and reptiles for their young in like manner. In the Embryological field you will perhaps gain more scientific reputation than in any other field of science down [which] you will fetch a swath.

The Specimens of Rock which you want to bring are:

Bring those which are generally the characteristic rocks of the locality. Bring sand from the river sides, and at the Mouths. Earth from the banks, and occasionally mud from the bottom, and label everything with care and minuteness. In selecting a companion have an Eye among other things to his skill with the pencil.

And before you decide to take a servant with you, think whether you would not prefer to take the allowance for him to ship in Lima. Some person accustomed to make collections in Natural History and bring him down with you. You certainly will not want a servant before you get to Lima. Get your Surgeon to put you up a medicine chest. I have estimated that $5,000. would cover the expenses. Companion and servant, *exclusive of pay* from California to Para, allowing you to purchase from it Chemicals, Arsenic, Alcohol, etc., and shall ask that a letter of credit be given you for at least that amount. This estimate allows you a boat's crew of six Indians for four months at $1.25 ea per day. Estimates in such cases are only guesses, and I have guessed double. Let me hear from you when you get to Panama, and again when you leave Lima, and tell me how you get on. In keeping your journal, don't fail to jot down at once, and just as things present themselves. You can fill up the picture afterwards. *You know* first impressions soon wear away or become stale familiars, always therefore seize first impressions and down with them while they are first impressions.

Get specimens of all ornamental and dye woods from the top of the Andes down. Bring home "Chunks" of them. I believe gold mines equal to those of California have recently been discovered on the head waters, perhaps of the Ucayale. Find out about them. Of course I have not pretended to remind you of one tenth part of the subjects which will occupy your attention. I have been merely trying to help you to open the way. You will see many flowers and many side paths that you will have to look after.

Upon an Expedition of this sort you must necessarily rely in a great measure upon parole information, therefore pump every traveller, trader and gentleman you meet with on the Amazon until he is dry.

A pleasant and profitable trip to you, Lewis. God bless you.

M. F . M.

Lieut. Wm. L. Herndon,

Pacific Squadron.

P. S. Here you have the list of North & South Stars:

| A Phinices | $0^m.19^m$ | $-43^0.7^1$ | and | A Persei | 3.13 | $+49.20$ |
|---|---|---|---|---|---|---|
| B Andromeda | 1.1 | $+34.50$ | " | T Caris Maj | 7.18 | $-29.1$ |
| A Aungue | 5.6 | $+65.50$ | " | Z Argus | 7.50 | $-39.25$ |
| O Argus | 8.5 | $-46.54$ | " | O Ursae Maj | 11.46 | $+54.32$ |
| A Ursae Maj | 10.54 | $+62.34$ | " | O Crucis | 12.23 | $-56.16$ |
| O Dracones | 17.53 | $+51.30$ | " | A Leonis | 21.59 | $-47.41$ |
| A Lyra | 18.32 | $+38.38$ | " | A Piscis Aus | 22.49 | $-30.25$ |

The rainy season at the Mouth of the Amazon will not fairly set in before the middle of December. Should I not be able to send you a Steel Barometer you will find an Aneroid, be sure that you do not disturb the index of the latter after you commence to observe with it, but bring it home for comparison.

*From Millard Fillmore.* U.

Washington

October 9th. 1850.

I hereby appoint the Hon. William A. Graham, Acting Secretary of War, during the temporary absence of the Hon. C. M. Conrad, Secretary of War, from the seat of government.

*From Francis Lieber.* U.

Columbia, S. C.,

October 10th, 1850.

You will have seen from the list of the passed candidates for the Naval School that my son, in behalf of whom you have shown so much kindness, has been passed by the examining board. I endeavoured to obtain a copy of the Laws and Regulations concerning the Naval School, but found that no copy could be easily spared at the School. As I wish to read them, in order to give, if necessary, some additional advice to my son, and to direct his particular attention to one or the other points, I make free to ask you whether there are any spare copies at the Department of which I might have one.

I hope I do not trespass if I give you the impression which the School has made upon me during the two and a half days which I have spent at Annapolis, being engaged in Education myself, and taking a deep personal interest in the Institution since my own son has become a member. This impression is altogether a most favourable one. Freshness and vitality seem to pervade the whole. A kinder and more appropriate person for the command of the whole than Capt. Stribling[112] it would be difficult to find. He seems to be a most excellent man and officer, and all that I have seen of the professors struck me as very favourable. The whole tone of the establishment seems to unite military strictness and order with gentlemanly amenity and brisk activity. We had a letter from my son in which he speaks with joy of the "kindness and politeness" he met with.

Of course so young an institution is capable of much development. We have only to look at Westpoint. Perhaps it has struck you already that the appointment of a national board of visitors, as the annual one at Westpoint, might be of an excellent effect. I am well aware that there would be many members of such a board, who would be little acquainted with the subjects on which they would be expected to report. But the great advantage, it seems to me, would be to make the School justly popular, and to obtain appropriations with a much better grace than the call for them could be made by any other party. When, some years ago, I was a member of the board of visitors at Westpoint, I saw that at least one half of us were little qualified to inquire into so important an institution; but I saw too, that a number of Western gentlemen, who had come to Westpoint strongly prejudiced against it, left it deeply impressed with its usefulness and resolved to diffuse this view among the people.

---

[112] Cornelius Kinchiloe Stribling (1796-1880), a native of South Carolina, who entered the navy in 1812, and was superintendent of the naval academy with the rank of commander. He retired as captain in 1861, but went back to active duty as a commodore in 1862, and was made rear admiral in 1866.

I take it for granted that Annapolis will stand in need of considerable appropriations for years to come. An observatory may be taken as an instance. Westpoint has one. Surely Annapolis ought to possess one on much stronger grounds; for what is true of all of us in a metaphorical sense—that only he who is familiar with the heavens can safely navigate the dangerous seas below— is literally true of the mariner. Now, if an observatory were strongly recommended by a board of visitors it seems to me that more ears would favourably listen than if the request came from the institution itself. I may be mistaken, but it strikes me so. Such a board would also raise the School more on a level with Westpoint, in the eyes of many people, than it is now considered.

I have seen from the Regulations, etc., that the midshipmen of the School are intended to pass the vacations on board a practice ship. This seems to me a very excellent idea. If a steam ship were taken, the boys might be taken to Europe—to Brest, Stockholm, London, where similar schools are, or where they might inspect navy-yards. They would be received everywhere with perfect international hospitality, and thus our lads would learn at once the real sailor's service on board, and, on shore, part of that international or representative character, with which every naval officer is, in a degree, invested when abroad. I can even imagine, without any exaggeration, that these trips would add their mite to that mutual good will and international kinliness upon which the peace of the world and the progress of mankind so much depend. Why, fifty or sixty sprightly American youths well trained and soundly taught, would be as fine and noble a representation of our country as could be found or imagined.

I have to ask you a thousand pardons for having detained you so long. My pen was carried on by a subject which, I own, deeply interests me. I consider our navy one of our noblest branches, and one too which will have to be much enlarged in the course of time; for the American eagle has to stretch its wide pinions over the Atlantic and Pacific at once.

With the highest regards

Your very obedient servant

*From James Graham.*                                    U.

Earhart Place,

Oct. 13th, 1850.

I rec'a your letter after you reached Washington, and was pleased to learn that you had declined the offer of Sec. of the Interior, for I presume it is a laborious appointment. I would prefer the place you have to any in the Cabinet, and think its importance must grow as the sphere of the Navy is now legitimately in the Pacific, as well as the Atlantic Ocean. But still I would caution you on the subject of increasing the expenditures in that Department too rapidly, otherwise it may cause a reaction and operate injuriously to the Navy, The increase should be gradual, with the growth of the commerce of our Country. Some plan or system should be devised, if possible, by which the officers and Sailors of the Navy should be *more actively* employed in time of peace. I know the Government ships are not well adapted to carry produce, but still I think it would be better so to employ a portion of them than to keep them 10 or 15 years idle, living in Dogaries and Brothels, and when war comes they are unfitted for action and useful service. Very few of the Revolutionary Officers who were appointed by Madison in the war of 1812 acquired any distinction either in the Army or Navy. Young and *active* men are the men for war, not the aged, indolent and dissipated. The respectability and popularity of the Navy must depend on its activity, and efficiency. I have always been the friend of the Navy, I am so now. I have served on the Committee of Naval affairs, and became satisfied that a necessary and popular arm of our defence would become unpopular, if permitted to do nothing but to live out of the Treasury. By enquiring how the British, French, Russions, employ their officers and sailors in time of peace, and also consulting distinguished, experienced and practical Merchants on this subject, I think you may receive some suggestions that would aid you in forming correct conclusions. I do not propose anything. I only suggest what is desirable, if it be practicable.

I am well pleased with the appointment of Stuart[113] as Sec' of the Interior. He is one of the ablest men I know in Va.

---

[113] Alexander Hugh Holmes Stuart (1807-1891), of Virginia, educated at William and Mary College, and the University of Virginia, lawyer, state legislator, Whig member of congress, 1841-1843, secretary of the interior, 1850-1853. He and Graham became devoted friends. In 1870 he was one of the "committee of nine" which cleared the way for the readmission of Virginia to representation.

The Whigs of this section are well pleased with the Cabinet, and the President. I have remained closely at business during the present year. I have the best Crop of Cotton I ever had on the River, and my Corn was very fine until the flood came & destroyed the greater portion of it. My Corn here is somewhat injured, but not to the same extent. The destruction on the Catawba River and South Fork is very general. That, added to the failure of the Wheat crop *by Rust,* creates a belief Corn will be scarce and high next year. My own Wheat was very good at both places.

* * * * *

If your Negroes are to be employed next year on the Rail Road, they should, as soon as they gather your Crop put your fences in good order in bad weather, and do winter ploughing for the next Crop, which I presume will be mainly worked by women and children. It would be well to order a good portion of your Hogs and Cattle to be fatted and killed early in the fall, and thereby save your grain. I expect to go to Raleigh about the middle of Dec'm, and if so, I will stop and look after your business near Hillsboro' a few days. I will be pleased to aid you so far as I can, if you will advise me of what you want done. In your absence you may count on making very little on your Farm, but you should try to save what you can, and prevent waste. If you have any bad Negroes, now is a good time to sell them. Likely Negro men are selling here from $800. to 860. To sell a bad one occasionally improves the rest, and saves much vexation to the owner. In your absence would be good time to put one or two of your young negro boys to learn Trades with good, honest mechanicks.

In your official station you are in duty bound to be civil and polite to all who have business with you; but, in your private family sphere you are not bound to ask any one to your house because he happens to be a member of Congress, or holds any other station. I wish President Filmore and his Cabinet would not always appoint hungry applicants and constant seekers to office; but look abroad and inquire for men of high character and high capacity, for appointments, and let office seek them, instead of the annoying applicant seeking the office. There may be a few exceptions, but as a general rule, I have observed men who are insolvent and bankrupt in property are apt to be so in character and confidence; and yet they constitute the largest number of office seekers. Having no corn in their individual Crib, they seek to live out of the public Crib. When Gen'l Washington wanted more forces in the field be beged *that men might be appointed to office who had some character to loose*. In your own Department, I think you should look out for meritorious men in our own State, and some in every part of it. You have a large acquaintance yourself; but by applying to such men as Outlaw, Deberry and Sheppard, you could select competent men and faithful officers in N. C. We ought to have our full share in the Naval Academy, and some in the West as well as the East. While in the N. D. you may have it in your power to do something for Wilmington, Beaufort, and Nags Head. I desire whatever advantages we have may be carefully examined, surveyed, and improved, if practicable. I have great doubts of the practicability of improving Nags Head, however desirable it may be. I have a strong and an abiding conviction that Beaufort has more natural advantages for a Sea-Port town than any place in our State; and would have been improved, as such, long since, but for the conflicting interests of Wilmington and Newbern. And also owing to the erroneous opinion of the olden time, that a Sea-Port town must be at the mouth of some navigable River. That was true before the invention of Rail Roads. But in these days of progress and improvement, water is not the only element on which travel, trade and commerce may be transported. Could not a survey or a resurvey be made by the most able of the U. S. Engineers, both of Wilmington and Beaufort? and their opinion of the most practical mode of improving each of them, and the amount needful for that purpose. I shall be pleased to hear from you whenever your leisure and convenience will permit.

*From Richard Hines.*                                        U.

Raleigh,

Oct. 14th, 1850.

\* \* \* \* \*

At the adjournment of Congress I flattered myself the Compromise measures which they passed would as soon as the excitement wore off, satisfy the whole Country. I have therefore been greatly pained and disappointed at seeing such exertions made North and South to keep up the agitation; and when I see a call for a meeting to agitate for the purpose of procuring the repeal of the Fugitive Slave law headed by such men as Josiah Quincy[114] of Boston I am compelled to believe there is breakers ahead. For if that law is repealed the South as one man would be in favor of a dissolution of the Union. From present indications I consider it certain there will be a Union of the Barn Burners and the Abolition Whigs in New York. Can they be counteracted by a Union of the old Hunkers and Union Whigs? If not, the State is gone! Here four fifths of all parties are perfectly satisfied with the present state of things, but it is impossible to say what effect constant agitation may produce.

I have been sorry to hear (not from him) that the Gov: intends in his Message to the Legislature to take ground in favour of distributing the School fund upon the White basis. which I consider worse than bad Policy, as it will be surely met by the bitter denunciations of every Whig in the Legislature from the Eastern part of the State, and will make his present unpleasant situation a still more painful one.

*  *  *  *  *

*From Millard Fillmore.*                                    U.

Washington,

Oct. 15th, 1850.

I hereby appoint William A. Graham acting Secretary of the Interior, ad interim, during the absence of Alexander H. H. Stuart from the city of Washington.

*From Robert B. Gilliam and James T. Littlejohn.*          U.

Oxford, N. C.,

Oct. 15th, 1850.

We take the liberty of addressing you in behalf of Mr. Daniel

---

[114] Josiah Quincy (1772-1864), of Massachusetts, a graduate of Harvard, lawyer, and actively partisan politician, state legislator, Federalist member of congress, 1805-1813, during the latter part of which period he engaged in disloyal activities with the English in the hope of defeating the national administration, delegate to the constitutional convention of 1820, mayor of Boston, president of Harvard, 1829-1845. An Abolitionist, he had an intense dislike of the South.

R. Goodloe,[115] now of Washington City, but formerly of North Carolina. We understand that Mr. Goodloe is now employed in the Treasury Department, but without any fixed grade or salary—and that he desires to continue his connexion with that Department.

We have known Mr. Goodloe intimately for many years, and we are therefore prepared to speak of him with confidence. He is a gentleman of highly respectable attainments, with a very decided talent for composition, especially in relation to statistical matters. His integrity is beyond all question, as he has passed through the ordeal of adversity, without leaving a stain upon his character. Though of not very prepossessing exterior, he is a man of many excellent qualities, and will undertake no duties for which he is not qualified. Should Mr. Goodloe have occasion to refer to you, you may say these things of him, without the slightest misgiving.

We flatter ourselves that you will not feel less interest in his case, from hearing that he is the personal friend of both of us.

*From James Fenimore Cooper.*[116]          U.

Otsego Hall,

Cooperstown,

Oct 16th, 1850.

I beg leave to express my thanks for the appointment of my nephew,[117] who, I trust, will be found qualified to enter the service.

This nomination has been particularly gratifying to me, as it gives my blood and name a fresh hold on the Navy, which lost

---

[115] Daniel Reaves Goodloe (1814-1892), of North Carolina, abolitionist, editor, and author, briefly a soldier in the Creek War, became a printer's apprentice. He became a lawyer, but printer's ink still drew him, and Mangum secured a place for him on the *Whig Standard* in Washington. He served on several newspapers, and was assistant editor of the *National Era*, an anti-slavery paper. He became editor, and the paper became an Abolitionist organ. Lincoln appointed him commissioner to pay for slaves emancipated in the District of Columbia. During 1865 and 1866, he was marshal for North Carolina, but broke with Johnson and became a full fledged Radical. Finding himself unable to accept the policies of Holden and the carpetbaggers, he broke from them in active opposition. He was a profuse writer on many subjects.

[116] James Fenimore Cooper (1789-1851), famous novelist who had served in the navy.

[117] Probably Edward B. Cooper, who was appointed to the navy in 1851 and dismissed during that year.

most of this connection with the service by the recent death of Commodore Cooper.[118]

The manner of this nomination has been so obliging and kind that I appreciate it quite as much as the appointment itself, and I sincerely hope the young gentleman may do us all credit.

Very respectfully
Your ob. Serv't

*To Susan Washington Graham.* A.

Washington City,

Thursday night,

Oct. 17th, 1850.

I have just received your letter of last Tuesday, it being the first intelligence I have had of you since your departure. On Monday night of this week Col. Britten, having bro't his daughter to school in Washington, delivered to me your trunk, which he had found on board the steam boat, having heard on a recent visit to Oxford that you had lost one. And the next morning he was kind enough to take it to Petersburg, and have it put on the Gaston car, I having marked it with your address, so that I hope it has reached you today.

I went yesterday to the Navy yard, accompanied by Com. Warrington.[119] had a turnout of the Marine guard, and the officers of the station went through all the works shops, laboratory, etc., and partook of a lunch at Com. Ballards.[120] Mrs. B. had with her the other ladies of the station, and is a very ladylike and agreeable person. I returned about 3 o'clock and kept up my labours at the Department untill 5, the hour to which I now labour, having both the War and Interior Departments on my hands.

I met Mr. Badger on the Avenue yesterday evening, and went to their house for Tea. Mrs. B. had heard of another Auction, and promised to ascertain the price of a set of extension tables, which she says is to be sold.

[118] Captain Benjamin Cooper, who entered the navy in 1809.
[119] Presumably Lewis Warrington (1782-1851), a distinguished officer, born in Virginia, educated at William and Mary, who entered the navy in 1800. He served against the Barbary pirates, and in the War of 1812, and was a captain in 1814.
[120] Henry E. Ballard (d. 1855), entered the navy in 1804, and became a captain in 1825.

Mr. Crittenden set off today for Kentucky. Judge Hall, Mr. Corwin and myself are all that are left of the Cabinet. The President showed me this morning a letter from Mr. Webster to Marshfield. He is still complaining of the score of health; but was expecting Amin Bey at his house the next day, and says it is somewhat embarrassing to entertain him; but that he will carefully conceal all swine's flesh, and give him beef, poultry, fish, and a plentiful supply of Coffee.

I am not surprized at the failure of the horse Jim, and don't think it safe to travel with him any distance. I regret to hear of the dearth of our Corn crop, and fear I shall be obliged to abandon farming in Orange.

\* \* \* \* \*

I have had no letter from Mr. Bryan since you left, I presume he is still in Phila. I recd yesterday a letter from Raleigh, saying that Miss Cora Manly was about to be married to Genl. Singleterry[121] against the wishes of her family. I am sorry to hear of the departure of Mr. Mangum's family, and fear we shall not find so agreeable a neighbor on our return. I find Anderson very attentive and faithful, and have a couple of wood sawyers, laying up a winter's supply of wood.

*From David Outlaw.*                                                    U.

Windsor,

Oct. 18th, 1850.

Allow me to introduce to your acquaintance, and favorable consideration, Dr. Edward Warren[122] of Edenton. Dr. Warren belongs to one of our most respectable Whig families, and is a gentleman of education, of fine manners, and of the highest integrity.

---

[121] George E. B. Singletary, whom she later married.

[122] Edward Warren (1828-1893), of North Carolina, physician, a native of Tyrrell County, was educated at the University of Virginia and Jefferson Medical College, and also studied in Paris. He edited the *Medical Journal of North Carolina,* and in 1860 became a professor in the University of Maryland. The following year he became a surgeon in the Confederate navy, and later transferred to the army, and served as chief medical inspector of the Army of Northern Virginia, and later was surgeon general of North Carolina. During this period he published "Surgery for Field Hospitals." He directed the revival of the Washington Medical School, and in 1873 entered the Egyptian army as chief surgeon to the general staff, and shortly after was made Bey, and chief surgeon to the war department. He retired in 1875, and practiced in Paris. Appointments, decorations, and other honors were showered upon him.

He desires to visit Paris in the farther prosecution of his medical studies, and wishes to obtain some situation (such as bearer of dispatches to that Court, or some one in the neighborhood) which would defray his expenses. In addition to his other qualifications for the situation, he understands and speaks the French language.

Any assistance which you may have it in your power to render him, will be properly appreciated by Dr. Warren.

*From William L. Long.*                    U.

Halifax,

Oct. 19th, 1850.

Your favor of the 12th. Inst. reached me a few days ago. I have been suffering with Chills and fevers ever since, although convalescent at this time. For your readiness to exert your influence in my behalf, please accept my sincere and grateful acknowledgements. To be tendered a chargé ship to any of our foreign Courts would be truly gratifying for many reasons,—but let that pass.

You well remember the noble stand of Mr. Clay, on the annexation of Texas; he raised the veil, and looked into the womb of futurity with a prophet's vision. If Mr. Polk and his friends had been governed by the policy indicated by Mr. Clay, in his letter published on the annexation of Texas in April 1844, we should have escaped the War with Mexico, the California discussion, and instead of agitation and heartburnings among the people upon the subject of Slavery, harmony and good will would prevail throughout the land. "The Country has passed through a severe trial"; and like you, I fear our troubles are not yet ended; though I sincerely hope that the passage of the Compromise measures at the last session of Congress will restore peace to the nation, and that fraternal feeling that ought to exist among our people.

The Union is consecrated to every true American heart by the best blood of the Revolution, by deeds the most heroic and daring; and if there be a man within the chartered limits of the United States who wishes a dissolution of the Union under our glorious Constitution, I would say to him

"If thou dos't Consent
To this most Crewel act, do but despair;
And if thou want'st a cord, the smallest thread
That spider ever twisted from her womb,
Will serve to strangle thee".

I earnestly hope that the administration of President Fillmore will be popular throughout the Union, and meet with the warm approbation of every patriot.

I regretted to learn through you that Mr. Webster had been indisposed. For his great effort in the Senate of the United States last Spring, in which he seemed "to gather the wisdom and patriotism of Centuries" may the earnest wishes of his soul be gratified; and the evening of his life be as tranquil and happy, as its meridian was brilliant with the noble creations of his intellect.

Enclosed is a letter[123] from our friend Senator Mangum, which I cheerfully confide to your care, to be used at your discretion.

### From F. Knox.[124]

Saint Louis,

October 19th., 1850.

A painful rumor, which has been in circulation here for three or four days past, has, this morning, made its appearance in the "Republican." It is to the effect that my Uncle, Dr. R. Knox, "was drowned in the Humbolt River."

I do not write to his wife, because I hope she *may* not see the report; and I write to you that you may be able to satisfy her, so far as the present state of the case will allow, if it should reach her.

All I can say is, that we think there is no evidence whatever, either direct or circumstantial, to sustain the report. It is like some forty others that have been in circulation, since he started, all of which we know to be false. It was not credited in San Francisco, and could be traced to no authentic source. So we are informed by a gentleman directly from there, who left there on the 1st. Sept.—the latest of any body, or any news which has arrived.

We shall doubtless have letters by the first mail from there, and as soon as we hear *any* thing, I will let you know it, or write to his wife at once.

I feel that the matter stands *in fact,* just about as if we had heard nothing; tho' we cannot avoid some anxiety, 'till we get positive intelligence, of course.

---

[123] Not found.
[124] A nephew of Dr. Reuben Knox.

You will please adopt the course your own judgment will dictate, as to any communication to Cousin Eliza. I have great confidence in her fortitude, but it is a pity it should be put to an unnecessary test.

From James W. Osborne.                                U.

Charlotte,
October 19th., 1850.

Your favour of the 8th. was received to day. I did not regard the application as a serious one, or likely to be successful. I am satisfied that my present position is really better for my interests than any office which the president could bestow—unless it were the Consulship to Cuba, or the D't attorney plan. I ought to be content, and hope by hard labour, and some patience, to extricate myself from my difficulties in a few years. It is a grievous thraldom, and blocks up the path of life—at least of ambition, with impenetrable barriers.

I deeply deplored the events in New York. But they did not surprize me. I am convinced that the South is content with the adjustment, I mean the popular mind at large. There [are,] of course, individuals, not a few, who would be gratified to use the occasion for the worst purposes. South Carolina is fully prepared to wreak her long cherished vengeance on the Union, and the national government. She will, I believe, stand alone in her treasonable efforts. Georgia will hold a Convention, but I anticipate good, not evil, from its assemblage. The unionists will largely predominate, and the action of the Convention will rally the conservative South—on a platform, the most liberal and salutary. It is important that the moderate and reasonable men of the South should go into this controversy—and I look to Georgia as leading the way in the right direction. It is true that the excitements which in some quarters at the North is created on account of the fugitive Slave Bill, may produce some alarms, and give to the disunionists some advantage. But I hope that this excitement will be found to be weak and transient, and that we may be permitted to enjoy the advantages of that beneficent measure. I believe Mr. Fillmore is personally popular, and I have heard many moderate and reasonable members of the democracy express the fullest confidence in his liberality and justice. It is difficult to say, however, what direction things may take, in the present state of confusion. I am inclined to fear the rashness and precipitancy of South Carolina. Memminger and Middleton,[125] with Rhett and Pickens, are open advocates for secession. And this too, without the cooperation of her sisters of the South. I know not whether to regard these proceedings as real, designed to draw after them the factionists in other States, and thus prevent the dispersion of the disunionists thro'-out the South. When Georgia speakes, affairs will assume a decisive character, and I trust that we will have peace. Our beloved North Carolina will, as ever, do her duty to the Confederacy. I am convinced that 99/100 of our population have but one sentiment, devotion to the Union and the Constitution. I to day saw Dr. Morrison and his family, on my return from Lincoln Court. They were well, and as you may probably be soon advised, your nephew, William Morrison, sets off to Washington next week.

I deeply regret that professional cares & pecuniary responsibilities scarcely allow me an opportunity to serve the administration at home. I think all things will come right, in '52. By the way, the movement is actively on foot to repeal the redistricting law of 1846. The attempts will be made, and in the house of commons will carry. There is some hope that it will be defeated in the Senate, as Thomas of Haywood, and Hargrave[126] of Davidson represent Whig constituencies—before whom the question was not made in the canvass, and whose known wishes they may not venture to thwart on a matter of so much importance.

*From Robert T. Paine.*                                      U.

Edenton, N. C.,

October 20th., 1850.

This will introduce to you Dr. Edward Warren, a citizen of this Town, & a recent graduate of the Medical College of Virginia.

Desirous of prosecuting his studies, he purposes visiting Paris, to obtain a thorough acquaintance with the practice of Medicine, & he is anxious, if possible, to obtain the appointment of bearer of despatches, if he can by such means secure his passage free, across the Atlantic.

I will vouch for his fidelity, & if you can, in any way, promote his wishes, you will confer an obligation on me.

---

[125] John Izard Middleton.
[126] Samuel Hargrave was state senator, 1846-1848, 1850-1854.

*From Kenneth Rayner.*                                    U.

Raleigh, No. Ca.,

October 21st., 1850.

You will please pardon me for troubling you in regard to a
matter of public concern to the people of my County, (Hertford,)
and to a considerable extent, the county of Bertie also. I allude
to our mail arrangements, as connected with the contract to carry
mail by steam-boat from South Quay, in Virginia, to Plymouth,
touching at the offices of Edenton & Winton.

Thompson, of Norfolk, the owner of the Boat, is under contract to deliver the mail at Winton, Edenton, & Plymouth. At
Edenton & Plymouth the mail is delivered *at the offices* by the
authorities of the Boat. At Winton heretofore, it has been thrown
off to a boy on the Wharf as the Boat went down, and put on the
Boat again in the morning as she went up. It seems from the enclosed letter of our friend, Mr. Anderson of Winton, who knows
all about it, that some misunderstanding having arisen in regard
to Mr. Bynums being unwilling longer to see the mail carried to
and fro, between the Wharf and the office, for $50. a year, (since
the new boat makes the trip in much less time, and consequently
keeps his boy on the Wharf for an hour or two before day) and
application having been made to the Gen'l Post Office department
to compel Thompson to deliver the mail at the office. That some
influence has been brought to bear on Hobbie by Thompson,
and hence it has been ordered, *or is to be,* that the boat shall no
longer be required to deliver the mail at Winton at all, but that
we must rely on the delay and uncertainty of an overland mail
from South Quay to Winton.

Now, if there be any such purpose in contemplation as to dis-
continue the mail to Winton, by the steam-boat, it is all wrong,
improper and unjust. We have had this mail for 12 or 14 years.
It is a great convenience, not only to the Winton Post Office,
but also to Murfreesboro', and the town offices in Hertford &
Bertie. It will disarrange all our conveniences for conveyance by
mail, and our direct communication with Norfolk, our people
feel greatly concerned about it.

The boat has time and to spare, in making the trip; and the
detention at Winton—even if some one on board had to carry the
mail up to the office, would be but a few minutes. Or, if Thompson will pay a *reasonable sum* for carrying the mail from the boat

to the office, there need be no detention to the boat at all.

I have no doubt it is, as Mr. Anderson suggests, this is the result of some *back-stairs* influence, exercised over Hobbie by Thompson. Thompson was no doubt offended by the application to the Post Office Department, to compel him to deliver the mail at the office, and now wishes to gratify his spite, by taking from us at Winton, a mail, altogether.

A word from you may be of service. We know not whom else to apply to. It is useless to apply to the Post Office department direct—for the communication would go in the hands of Hobbie, and that would be the last of it.

I am aware, my dear Sir, that it must be disagreeable to you to be thus annoyed, in regard to a matter appertaining to another Department, but the truth is, we need the influence and interposition of some one at Washington; and you must therefore pardon your old friends for applying to you in time of need.

To deprive us of this mail at Winton, by the Boat, would be an outrage, under the circumstances—and if it is done, it will be sacrificing the interests, and disregarding the wishes, of a large Community, from a disposition to gratify the revenge and pander to the avarice of one man.

If you can say or do anything to prevent this thing being done, you will confer a favor upon a large number.

*From Hugh Waddell.*                                              U.

Greensboro',

October 24th., 1850.

Your much esteemed favour of the 15th. inst., proposing, if agreeable to me, to present my name to the President for the Consulate at Havana, reached Hillsboro' on Monday last, & was forwarded to this place by express messenger.

I regret that this proposition has found me from home, & immersed in business, as it precludes the possibility of such consultation with my far "better half" as the importance of it demands; but as an early reply is required, & all the friends around me concur in the propriety of accepting such a post, if tendered me, I have concluded to write you by the first mail, & authorize you to use my name as proposed.

The position of Consul at that point must be one, just now, of difficulty and frequent embarrassment, & I doubt if the most experienced & accomplished Diplomat can succeed in satisfying the Spanish Government of the perfect *neutrality* of the U. States in regard to Cuba. Indeed, we can scarcely blame that unfortunate People, for want of *faith* on this subject, after recent events. It may well be doubted whether all the fame, & all the Territory acquired by the U. S. in her recent contest with Mexico, will be regarded in aftertimes, sufficient to remove from the National escutcheon the blots that contest has placed there. I fear that the impartial Historian should we continue such a course long, will place Americana with the 'Punica fides.'

Tendering to you my sincere thanks for the uniform kindness & esteen with which you have honoured me, & confiding my name most implicitly to y'r friendship & prudence.

[Enclosure.]

*From Hugh Waddell.*

Greensboro',

October 24th., 1850.

My dear Friend

Your most welcome letter of the 15th. inst. arrived in Hillsboro' on Monday morning, 4 days since, & was sent me by express, & I now reply to it by the *very first mail*, yet, as Mr. A. H. Shepperd asks me to do so, for fear of delays, I have written (by the mail which takes this) to Gov'r Manly, or Major Hinton, requesting one of them to Telegraph you immediately, & therefore I hope by day after tomorrow, you will be duly informed "that I shall be happy to receive the place y'r kindness has suggested."

I know nothing of the *proprieties* of these communications, but I shall write you on this half sheet what a warm heart, bounding with grateful pulses, may dictate, & on another sheet a more respectful and formal letter of thanks, which if *proper* may be shewn to the Pres't, though I suppose this would be more becoming upon being apprized of the appointment itself, *if at all.* You know what is proper, & will act as you deem best in regard to this, however.

And now permit me, my long tried and faithful friend, to say, that I have *no* language in which to utter the deep and soul-absorbing gratitude, which y'r constant and affectionate interest in me have inspired. Knowing as you do how important at this time such a post is to me, I regard it as the most fortunate event of my life that such a friend has had it in his power to procure it for me. It is but a moment since, that our friend Mr. Shepperd was stating to me how much and how deeply you were interested in my advancement, & to which, as you are well aware, I could only respond that I needed no assurances of y'r perfect friendship, and I had only to regret that I should never have it in my power to show you how sincerely and ardently I reciprocated it.

Accept all that I have to offer, the tribute of a heart overflowing with emotions of gratitude at the prospect of freedom from cares and anxieties which have preyed on that heart like a cancer, & would, ere long, have destroyed it.

Should y'r application be successful, as I suppose it will be, from all I hear of y'r position in the Cabinet, I suppose I shall of course be required to visit Washington, & will then talk over with you many matters which I cannot commit to paper. Some few friends are yet so sore on the subject of my treatment by the late Cabinet, as to doubt whether the present post is in *rank* suited to the claims pressed in my behalf for a Foreign Mission. But to this I have replied, that the post is quite equal, if not superior, to any *claims* I have, and I agree with you that, in my situation, the Consulate might be preferable on the score of pecuniary profit.

I rejoice to say, y'r fame is widening everywhere, every day, as I learn from strangers, & even Gen. Saunders, who is here, told me today that you were considered by Democrats as well as Whigs, the best and safest counsellor the Pres't had except Webster. May it's shadow never lessen, as the Spaniards say.

*From C. K. Stribling.*                                                    U.

U. S. Naval Academy,

Annapolis,

*Private*                                                    Oct. 26th, 1850.

I consider it alike due to you and others, that I should say, that my official letter to you of the 24th. instant, was written under the belief, that Political influence had caused you to order me to appoint Mr. Swann Steward to the Academy. I now have good reason to believe that no such influence was used to induce you to give me the order. But I am still under the impression that the course this affair has taken, is calculated to have an injurious effect upon this institution, in its interior discipline, and inducing persons employed here to look beyond the Superintendent, in all matters in which they are interested.

From John Strother Pendleton.[127]                    U.

Redwood,

[Virginia.]

October 27th., 1850.

Your favor of the 24th. inst. reached me by the mail of this morning, and I hasten to acknowledge it. I beg you to be assured that I never for a moment supposed that you were disposed either to disoblige me or to trifle with me. I fear'd that you had yourself been imposed on, as heads of Departments are liable to be, and, as I have had occasion to know, are very often, in respect to all sorts of appointments.

Since I had decided the question of propriety for myself, I regret that my friend, Gen'l Jones, interfered. I shall nevertheless not complain of him even—though I confess that his delicacy, rather than his judgment, commends itself to my approbation. I believe I could have performed the duties with proper impartiality, & I am sure I should have escaped any criticism, of the sort apprehended.

My object in writing so promptly, is to say to you, my dear Sir, that I have no complaint whatever against *you*, but, on the contrary, am very much obliged to you, for your disposition to serve me—as also to my friends Crittenden and Stuart, from whose ancient & intimate acquaintance, I had far more right to expect a favor, than from you.

And, secondly, to excuse myself to you for what has doubtless seem'd, in your eyes, an unbecoming solicitude on such a subject. This, Sir, is the *Fifth* occasion, since the 4th. of March, 1849, that it has been my fortune to experience a disappointment like the present, but on each of the other occasions, under far more provoking circumstances.

The first case was this: John M. Clayton at the close, or near it, of the last session of the last Congress, proposed to me to take

[127] John Strother Pendleton (1802-1868), of Virginia, lawyer, state legislator, diplomat. He was chargé in Chile, 1841-1844, Whig member of congress, 1845-1849, chargé to the Argentine Confederation, 1851-1854.

a mission of the first class. He did so without any request, recommendation, or intimation on my part, direct or indirect, or, that I ever heard of, from any friend of mine. I accepted his offer, and had such conversation with him, as to make, I thought, any future misunderstanding on the subject an impossibility. In a week afterwards, or less, he found reason to desire the accommodation of Mr. Wm. C. Rives, and forthwith adopted means of swindling me out of his own offer, so infamously dishonorable and base, that I shall ever reproach myself for consenting to the instance of his Cabinet associates, to refrain from making a public exposition of his conduct, through the press.

The second was a consequence of the first. Having declined a re-election to Congress, I was prevailed on, against my own judgment, to offer—on the heels of the election—and then, underating the strength of my opponent, who very unexpectedly united the entire vote of the Democratic party, though professing to be a Whig, I was, to the surprise of every body, beaten, losing four times as many votes by the matter of the mission as would have saved my election.

The Third instance, you will be most surprised at. Gen'l Taylor, and three of his Cabinet, viz: Messrs. Preston, Johnston, & Crawford,[128] annoy'd at the fate that had been brought upon me, agreed I should be then, in June 1849, appointed to one of the vacant Missions—provided Mr. Wm. C. Rives, who had been informaly notified that he should have the French Mission, would consent to post-pone his trip to France from the fall of '49 to the spring of '50. That gentleman having been twice saved in his re-election to the U. States Senate by my individual vote, & that of one other man, known to be influenced by me, against the united vote of our entire party, (Mr. Stuart will remember well the incident in one case, for he was present, when Chapman Johnson,[129] but for Broddus & myself, would have been elected). Having acknowledged to me a thousand times his obligation to me for those and a long series of other services through the whole course of the last thirteen years, it was supposed would cheerfully forego the gratifications of a Parisian residence for *six months*, to

---

[128] George Washington Crawford (1798-1872), of Georgia, a graduate of Princeton, lawyer, state legislator and attorney general, Whig member of congress, 1843, governor, 1843-1847, secretary of war, 1849-1850. He was later president of the secession convention.

[129] Chapman Johnson (1779-1849), of Virginia, graduate of William and Mary, able lawyer, state legislator, captain in the War of 1812, delegate to the convention of 1829. He had wide reputation in the state as an orator.

do me a great service, he was applied to, and declined, positively, to surrender a moment of his time.

The fourth case was one about which I don't know that I have any right to complain—except that it was a disappointment in respect to a matter I had not sought, or thought of.

In May, 1850, I was attending an Episcopal Convention in Alexandria. A messenger (a Clerk now in your Department) came to me with a letter from Mr. Preston, requiring me to appear immediately at Washington, by request of the President. I went— was informed that the President desired me to go immediately on an important and confidential mission *with full Diplomatic* dignity and powers. I must leave in forty-eight hours—the Cabinet would meet the next day, and agree upon my instructions, etc. It did meet, & determined to send no body.

Now, Sir, you will agree I had a bad run of luck—and will excuse me for getting a little nervous on such subjects.

A busy actor from my earliest manhood on the theatre of politics, and now in a fair way to be driven forever from that field, I would fain retire with the consciousness of preserving my own dignity, and the consolation of leaving behind me a respectable reputation.

I have therefore written you this—not because I suppose it can interest or amuse you, but for the reason that I would carefully avoid the forfeiture of *any* portion of your respect.


*From James Graham.*                              U.


Earhart Place,

October 28th., 1850.

Dear Brother

I have rec'd yours of the 20th. inst. I wrote the within before, and omitted to send it to you because of my leaving here suddenly for my South Point Place.

I wish we had the Assistant P. M. Gen'l from N. C., and from the Western part of it. We need mail advantages which we will never get while we have no prominent officer in the P. O. Dep't. Northern men no nothing of our localities.

Mr. Lord,[130] of Salisbury, would suit that appointment, if he

---

[130] John Bright Lord (d. 1851), a native of Wilmington, member of the commons, 1842-1846.

will take it. He is a man of wealth, and might like to be at Washington for a while.

Some man from Salisbury or Concord, or Charlotte, would be [in] a good location to render useful information to the Department. Baldy Caldwell, son of the Judge, (that is Arch'b'ld H. Caldwell [131]) after the legislature adjourns, I think would take it.

Is there no man in Davidson or Guilford that would do? Single men would be most apt to take appointments, as they loose little by moving.

*From "Boston."*　　　　　　　　　　　　　　　　　　U.

Boston,

October 29th., 1850.

Sir is there not a going [to be any] more removal in that Navy Yard in Charleston? Time that their should be, why i understood that it was a going to be entirely cleansed of those rabid Loco Focos who have been in office Long Enough, men who control all the Election after office, depriving honest Mechanics From Voting they want to for fear of Not Getting any Employment From them, if no More, Do for God Sake and the Whig Party Sake, Change them of to Some other Yard and put the other officers in their place.

Excuse this From an old Whig
Boston.

*To George C. Read.*[132]

Navy Department,

October 29th., 1850.

Sir:

Circumstances have occurred to prevent an earlier reply to your letter of the 18th. inst, which was duly received and submitted to the consideration of the President.

---

[131] Archibald Henderson Caldwell (1822-1861), graduate of the university, lawyer, member of the commons, 1850-1852, 1854-1856.

[132] From *Hillsboro Recorder*, October 6, 1852. George Campbell Read (1787-1862), at this time in command of the Philadelphia navy yard, a native of Ireland, who entered the navy in 1804, and was promoted captain in 1825. He served on the "Constitution" and the "United States" during the War of 1812. He retired as rear admiral in 1862.

In that letter you state that the judge of the district court of the United States had requested the assistance of the marines under your command to secure certain fugitive slaves, who have been claimed by their owners: and that calls upon the commandant of the Philadelphia navy yard to aid with the marines in the execution of the laws, by the civil authority, are often made, and you inquire as to your duty in rendering obedience to them.

That part of the inquiry which pertains to calls for military aid by officers acting under State authority it is not deemed necessary specially to answer, there being no present occasion to require it.

In reply to the other question presented by you, I am instructed by the President to say, that he deprecates any necessity for calling on the military forces of the United States to aid the civil officers in the execution of their proper functions: and he trusts that the patriotism of the good people of Pennsylvania will enable the marshal and other civil officers to command sufficient assistance from among those in civil life to serve any process in his hands, and to render it effectual.

But the President, feeling the full force of his constitutional obligation "to take care that the laws be faithfully executed," directs that, if the marshal, or any of his known deputies, charged with the service of process by competent authority of the United States, shall be unable to raise the necessary force for that purpose, or to prevent a rescue, or to make a recapture in case of rescue, by virtue of his authority to summon citizens to his aid, and shall call for the assistance of the marines, you will, in such event, promptly order them to accompany and assist him in the performance of his duty, having previously instructed the officer in command of the marines that during this service he will receive the orders of the marshal or his deputy, and act only in strict obedience to them.

Such will be your duty in applications from the marshal and his known deputies. But in the case of like applications from special deputies appointed by Commissioners of the United States to execute process under the act of the last session of Congress, entitled "An act to amend and supplementary to the act entitled 'an act respecting fugitives from justice and persons escaping from the service of their masters,' approved February 12, 1763," they will be required in each instance to produce to you a certificate of the justice or judge of the United States in their district, saying that the execution of the process in question has been actually resisted, or that combinations to resist it have been form-ed, too powerful to be overcome by the authority of such deputy, to call for the posse comitatus, in which event you will render to him the like assistance as if called on by a marshal or his deputy, observing the cautions above indicated.

Very respectfully, your obedient servant,<br>WILL A. GRAHAM

*From Haywood W. Guion.*                                    U.

Lincolnton,<br>October 29th., 1850.

A prompt answer to your very complimentary letter has been delayed by my absence from home, and I am unwilling to do more than barely acknowledge the receipt of yours at present, accompanying the same, however, with a few additional remarks.

At Charlotte Court, next Monday week, I shall have the oppor-tunity of conferring with your brother, and Messrs. Boyden & Osborne, and will then give you the result of our conference.

I do not believe that either Gen'l Patterson, or Col. Jos. J. Erwin[133] will accept the places proposed. The first has recently embarked largely in Milling operations, & is now engaged in erecting a Cotton factory, on the Yadkin, near his residence. Would he accept, I do not think that the place could be filled by a more suitable person. This is only *my* opinion, however.

The last, Col. Erwin, is now more deeply immersed in business than usual, in settling his late father's large estate. In his place, however, Mr. E. Jones Erwin,[134] of Morganton, with whom you are acquainted, might be a suitable person for the place. Mr. Erwin is brother to Mr. Adolphus Erwin,[135] one of Gov. Manly's Council, brother in law to Col. B. S. Gaither, & also brother in law to Col. Isaac Avery,[136] the father of Waightstill Avery. His

---

[133] Joseph J. Erwin (1811-1879), of Burke County, a graduate of Washington College (now Washington and Lee University), who was a gold miner, planter, clerk of the superior court, member of the commons, 1846-1848, 1864-1865.

[134] Edward Jones Erwin (1806-1871), of "Bellevue," Burke County, a graduate of Franklin College (now the University of Georgia), planter and banker, member of the commons, 1835-1840.

[135] Adolphus Lorenzo Erwin (1789-1855), of "Pleasant Gardens," McDowell County, lawyer and planter.

[136] Isaac Thomas Avery (1785-1864), of Burke County, a son of Waightstill Avery, lawyer, member of the commons, 1810-1811, planter, banker, member of the council of state.

appointment might be influential in a political point of view.

Mr. Benj. Sumner[137] contemplates removing to Georgia, and is now absent on a visit to that State in search of a suitable Cotton plantation. Were he at home, I would sound him upon the subject.

Suitable for minor Clerkships, I will mention the names of several young men. In Iredell, Rufus R. Templeton, now doing business in this place. He was trained by Rufus Reid at Mt. Mourne, and is well and favorably known in the lower part of Iredell. J. F. Alexander, of Statesville, is popular, a capital Clerk, and now Clerk of the County Court. Col. Thomas Allison,[138] one of the leading Whigs of the County, has a son named Richard,[139] just come to the Bar. I know nothing of his business qualifications, but have understood that he has been somewhat wild and frolicksome.

In McDowell, Young Alney Burgin, son of Gen'l Burgin,[140] of Old Fort, is a very worthy young man, and a good Clerk.

Mr. Adolphus Erwin has a son who is a fine Clerk, named Bulow.

I mention these names, thinking they may be useful to the party. An appointment, or even two or more to subordinate offices, might awaken a little enthusiasm with our friends in this part of the State.

As you have thought proper to use my name in Connexion with the office of Assist. P. M. Gen'l, & propound the inquiry whether I would be willing to take it, provided it is determined to vacate it, I deem it my duty to return you a positive answer. If you, knowing me as you do, especially in a physical point of view, think the post would be a beneficial one, to me politically, and not too arduous in its requirements for my corporeal powers —and moreover that I would fill the post in *every* way—I would not hesitate to accept it, and, if tendered to me through your influence, you may rest assured that you shall feel no reproach for having suggested my name, provided I am competent to discharge the duties.

---

[137] Benjamin Sumner (1801-1866), of Lincoln, a native of Gates County, teacher in Person, Granville, Lincoln, and Rowan counties, member of the commons, 1831-1833.

[138] Thomas Allison, who was state senator, 1842-1844.

[139] Richard Monroe Allison (1821-1884), who attended the university and Davidson College, and was later a Confederate lieutenant.

[140] Alney Burgin, Sr., was a member of the commons, 1830-1834, and state senator, 1842-1844.

In any event, whether tendered or not, I must return you my profound acknowledgements for having so kindly thought of one, whose aspirations have never looked to offices of this kind.

*From Hugh Waddell.*                                      U.

[November, 1850.]

Y'r favour of the 30th. Oct'r reached me by this morning's mail, & I desire even *before* I shall have the pleasure of seeing you, to say that the publicity given to the contents of y'r first letter was not only without my knowledge, or consent, but against my express wish. Deeming the proposition one of great moment, I asked the advice of one or two friends only, at Greensboro', & desired that it might *not* be mentioned. To my deep mortification I found the next day that it had got wind, & I then said to those who spoke with me that I thought it improper the subject should be mentioned until I should hear from you, & to all who spoke of it as something certain, I replied that it was not so, & I desired them to say for me that it was deeply regretted that it had got out. It is true that the friends whom I consulted judged from the language you used that the appointment could not be postponed as I was asked to answer immediately, & therefore it was that Mr. Shepperd insisted I should telegraph you as well as write; this, it seems, was a mistake of ours, yet I think if you were now to see y'r first letter you would admit that its language would bear out our conclusion that the appointment was to be made forthwith, or at least very soon. I am deeply mortified at this unfortunate mistake, but I was more than mortified, I was much displeased at finding, two or three days after my arrival at home, that without any authority from any one, & on rumour only, & against my express declarations to every one after my arrival, that Mr. Heartt had published "the appointment as already made, & that I was about to leave as soon as I could arrange my affairs." I remonstrated with him, and was so fortunate as to stop those papers which were to go to Washington, Raleigh, Wilmington, etc., in which Mr. H. promised the article should not appear. Mr. H. admitted that he was without excuse, as he might have known of me so easily. Take it throughout, I have never known a more annoying & mortifying affair than this publicity has been to me. I have required of Mr. H. to correct the error in his next issue, & especially to say it was without my knowledge, & contrary to my wishes, as afterwards discovered.

I sincerely hope it may not in any way cause the implication of y'r name unpleasantly, for this would be to me, more painful than any other circumstance connected with the unpleasant affair.

## From Edmund Coskery Bittinger.[141]

Sing Sing,

New York.

November 1st.,

1850.

(Confidential)
Hon: & Esteemed friend,

I feel truly grateful for your kindness & preference, & you may rest assured that it will be appreciated & cherished with heart felt emotion. I have been at Princeton, where I have a brother in Princeton Theological Seminary, & the Professors seemed highly pleased that I had received the appointment at your hands; for they remarked that the Episcopal Church had as many, if not more, than all the other denominations. There are now three Chaplains connected with our branch of the Church, & should vacancies occur during your Secretaryship, it is hoped that you will select Presbyterians to fill them, provided their appointment would promote the interests of the public service, & would meet with your entire approbation.

I would simply say a word in regard to a younger brother of mine, who is now settled in the Presbyterian Church at Tamaqua, Penns., & who could furnish you with the very highest testimonials from the most distinguished men in our Church. He was educated at Princeton, has been pastor of the Church four years, and is a very acceptable preacher in the estimation of the people of Washington, where he has often preached—his name is B. F. Bittinger.

I have been repeatedly asked whether the present rector of the Episcopal Church in Hagerstown, Md. (Mr. Jackson) [142] is still the Chaplain of the U. S. Navy?

---

[141] Edmund Coskery Bittinger (1819-1889), of Pennsylvania, a graduate of Columbian College, navy chaplain, 1850-1889, who had been connected with the Orange Presbytery in North Carolina and served as pastor in Washington, North Carolina.

[142] William G. Jackson, who was a navy chaplain, 1842-1850, had resigned in July.

The object of the present communication is simply to say that, should it meet with your approbation, that I would prefer being on duty than visiting orders, for I have never been accustomed to be unemployed since I have been a Minister of the Gospel; if I may be allowed to express a wish, I would prefer the Mediterranean Cruise to all others, or should my services be wanted at any of the land stations, I am always at your service at a moment's notice. I am willing to go, or stay where I may be instrumental in promoting the Glory of God, & the good of Man.

With sentiments of the highest esteem & regard,

I have the honor to subscribe myself,
Your friend forever,

*From Francis P. Mallory.*            U.

Norfolk,

November 5th., 1850.

*(Private)*

During the interview I had with you in Washington in September last, you were pleased to consult me in reference to an officer qualified to take charge of the Gosport Navy Yard on the 1st. Jan'y next, when the term of the present Commander will expire.

Circumstances beyond my controul have hitherto prevented a compliance with the promise I then made, and I hope the little information I am about to communicate will be in time to aid you, to some extent, at least, in making your selection.

The names of Commod's Morris, Shubrick and Perry[143] were mentioned in our conversation, and I have drawn from Officers of the Navy, in whose judgment all confidence may be placed, their opinions of these gentlemen in reference to the duties devolving on a Commander of a Naval Station. In speaking of the retirement of Comm. Sloat,[144] it was but natural to ask of them who was likely to succeed him, who was best qualified for this particular Station, etc., etc.

---

[143] Matthew Calbraith Perry (1794-1858), a native of Rhode Island, who entered upon a brilliant navy career in 1809. He served in the War of 1812 and the Mexican War, and is given credit for much of the development of the navy after 1830. An imperialist in spirit, he proposed the expedition to Japan which he later commanded, and as such he signed the resulting treaty.

[144] John Drake Sloat (1781-1867), of New York, who served in the navy, 1800-1801, 1812-1855, and attained the rank of commodore. Most of his service prior to 1844 had been routine, but, placed in command of the Pacific squadron, he landed troops in California in 1846, and declared it annexed.

The sum of the information thus obtained amounted to about this: All the gentlemen above mentioned bore a very high character. Morris was regarded as possessing thorough knowledge of the *details* of duty appertaining to a Bureau or Dock Yard, tho' some doubts were expressed of his adaptation to the Community with which he would be brought to deal. Shubrick is an accomplished officer, with pleasing address and popular manners, but rather easy, and too amiable for the *vicinage*—in which last mentioned particulars Perry was wanting, while in activity and energy he was superior both.

Owing to the peculiar characteristics of the population, amounting to some 900 or 1000 workmen, connected with what is termed its Civil Department, it is difficult for any Commander to perform the duties of the Gosport Yard in a satisfactory manner. Many of the workmen have lived in the large commercial Cities of the Union, and have brought with them notions of *social* democracy that conflict not a little with that discipline and subordination essential to the faithful discharge of duty. Aided by the demagogues who greatly infest that region, the workmen have been in the habit of appealing from the Commander to the authorities in Washington, who have too often interfered in matters which should have been left entirely to the discretion of the Commanding Officer. Portsmouth is almost entirely sustained by the Navy Yard, and more than one half of its population is directly connected with that establishment. The chief vocation of the Press in that place seems to be to pass sentence on all in authority who look to the interests of government, rather than the wishes of the Workmen. I represented this district 5 years in Congress, and the concerns of this yard employed 2/3rds of my time at home, or at the seat of Government, and was a source of such annoyance, that I was glad to retire from the position. But I will not enlarge on this topic, as I believe the real state of things there is not unknown to you.

To relieve the Department from the annoyance growing out of the petty disputes of the rival factions in & about the Navy yard, and which some of you predecessors were in the habit of trying to reconcile, requires an *active*, vigilant, prudent, and firm man, of good address and very cool temperament. An officer in the decline of life cannot sufficiently often inspect in person the numerous workshops in that extensive establishment, and must rely on the reports of others, instead of his own observation. One of *harsh* manners, however just and capable, would greatly injure the popularity of the Adm'r in that Section, without any corresponding benefit to the Naval Service.

From all that I can learn, Capt. Silas H. Stringham[145] of New York is perhaps better qualified for this position than any officer of his grade in the service. He formerly commanded at Brooklyn, where his administration was very much commended. He is gentleman of fortune, and has property in Brooklyn, where he resides, and would not, in all probability, be pleased with the order. He is a Whig, I am told, but no partizan. To me he is a stranger, it never being my fortune, when an officer of the Navy, to be associated with him.

Warrington Long commanded at Gosport, and managed well, he was rigid and yet kind, just, mild and firm. He is still much esteemed by the men, and if acceptable to him, no better choice could be made. I was under his command for a year, and speak from personal knowledge. Next to him and Stringham, I would name Morris and Shubrick, both of whom I know well.

Perry would answer admirably were it not for a somewhat imperious bearing that makes him unacceptable to the multitude. I never knew him, but when I was in the service he was considered *harsh,* and too rigid. In all other respects he is a fine officer, and in matters strictly military, he is equal to any of his grade.

I have just taken charge of the office which you were pleased to confer on me, and regret that I am compelled to send you such imperfect information. It will afford me great pleasure to assist you in any matter where, from your position, recourse must be had to the suggestions of others.

My predecessor received me very graciously, and, by my request, he continues to use the office and clerks in closing his returns. My appointment meets with little or no opposition in this quarter, and the extracts from the Whig and Democratic papers published here, which I take the liberty of enclosing, will show that, so far at least, your kindness and confidence have not been misplaced.

---

[145] Silas Horton Stringham (1797-1876), of New York, who entered the navy in 1809. He saw active service in the War of 1812, in Algiers, and in the Mexican War. In 1861 he commanded the blockading fleet, planned the attack on the forts at Hatteras, and carried it to a successful conclusion. He was criticized, and asked for retirement.

*From William K. Ruffin.*                                U.

Haw River,

November 7th, 1850.

\*   \*   \*   \*   \*

Permit me, my Dear Sir, to offer you my sincere congratulations upon the elevated honors to which you have attained, and to express my warmest wishes that, as the honors have been the reward of private and public virtue and useful service to the Country, they may lead to greater future ones. I am very sure that there is not an honest man in N. Carolina, who has not the most perfect confidence in the just administration of your Department of the Government, & whose hostility to the Administration will not in a great degree be disarmed by your connection with it.

I write amid the bustle of Huntsmen and Dogs, & can hardly express my own thoughts, or rather, collect any to express.

*From James W. Simonton.*[146]                        U.

New York,

Nov. 7th., 1850.

Designing to embark for California in the next Steamer, for the purpose of carrying out the design of the enclosed prospectus, I take the liberty of addressing you in relation to a subject intimately connected with the success of the enterprize.

You will readily perceive that a paper at the Capital of California will be deprived of that great element of success—Commercial advertising patronage. And yet the importance of having a sterling Whig Press at that point can hardly be overestimated. Having undertaken to occupy this interesting field, may I not rely upon your Department for such support, in the way of advertising, as you can, consistently, afford.

Soliciting the favor of an early reply

I am &c.,

Yours very truly

---

[146] James W. Simonton (1823-1882), of Washington, D. C., and California, a native of New York, journalist, one of the founders of the New York *Times.*

I most cheerfully add my testimony to the importance of the undertaking in which Mr. Simonton is engaged, and hope he may receive the patronage of the Departments at Washington.

T. Butler King

[Enclosure]

## The California Intelligencer

It is proposed to establish the *Intelligencer* at San José, the seat of Government of California, the first number to be issued on or about the 1st. December next. Its columns will be devoted to the dissemination and support of the principles and policy of the great Whig Party, casting aside all merely sectional considerations, and advocating such measures only as are worthy the approbation of the statesman of enlarged, liberal and national views, and deemed best calculated to build up, strengthen, and perpetuate the Democratic Institutions under which we live. To this end the conductors of the *Intelligencer* will avoid the control of all cliques, will pledge their position and influence to no individual interests; but, on the contrary, will assert the right to speak of men and measures as they may be presented, subject to no gauge but an enlightened consideration of the public good.

The *Intelligencer* will also pay appropriate attention to the interests of Labor, as developed in the wants of Agriculture and Manufactures, and to the cause of Literature, Science and General Intelligence—embracing under the latter head, especially, political news from every part of California, reliable reports of the proceedings and debates of the State Legislature, expositions of the laws passed by that body, and their bearing upon the existing state of affairs, accurate accounts from the Mining districts, &c., &c.

Argument upon the necessity for and advantage of such a publication at the point named, would be a work of supererogation. In looking over the new State—the youthful Queen of the Pacific—and considering her vast extent of territory; her yet untold mineral wealth; her commanding position, central between the Old World and the old settlements of the New, a position in which she may participate largely in the commercial advantages of both hemispheres, and command, almost at pleasure, the natural avenue to the riches of the East; and, above all, in view of the character of her population, already numbering hundreds of thousands of the most enterprizing, energetic, industrious, and persevering of our countrymen, whose numbers are receiving additions of thousands per week—all sovereigns, each possessing the right to participate in the grand scheme of Government;—in considering *all* these weighty matters, the discerning Statesman cannot fail to be impressed with a strong conviction that the day is not distant when the STATES of the Pacific will wield a giant power in the affairs of the Republic. How desirable, then, that Whig principles shall have, in such a field, and among such a people, an earnest, a consistent, and constant presentation.

Deeply impressed with the importance of this subject, and yielding to the earnest appeals of leading and intelligent Whigs of California, the undersigned has made arrangements to enter the field, and proposes to devot his time and best energies to the advancement of the good cause, relying with confidence upon the sustaining co-operation of those who believe principle worthy something more than mere words.

As a single evidence of the importance of prompt action, it may be stated that there is but one Whig Press in the entire State, while our opponents have six Presses; and at least three additional, of the same character, are proposed to be established during the present season.

The *Intelligencer* will commence publication as a tri-weekly, to be merged into a daily paper as soon as its arrangements shall have been fully completed. Terms, $10. per annum.

JAMES W. SIMONTON.

WASHINGTON, D. C., June 10th, 1850.

Believing the enterprize above set forth to be pre-eminently worthy of encouragement and support, and having full confidence in the integrity and capability of the gentleman who proposes to engage in it, we cheerfully recommend him and his undertaking to the favorable and liberal consideration of the Whig Party, and the Public in general.

H. CLAY, *Senator U. S.*

THOS. CORWIN, *do.*

DANIEL WEBSTER, *Senator U. S.*

WILLIE P. MANGUM, *do.*

TRUMAN SMITH, *Senator U. S.*

GEO. E. BADGER, *do.*

JAMES COOPER, *Senator U. S.*

The undersigned cheerfully concur in the foregoing testimonial.

Millard Fillmore, *Vice President, U. S.*

John A. King, Representative 1st. Congressional District, N. Y.

J. Phillips Phoenix, Representative 3rd. Congressional District, N. Y.

Walter Underhill, Representative 4th. Congressional District, N. Y.

Geo. Briggs, Representative 5th. Congressional District, N. Y.

James Brooks, Representative 6th. Congressional District, N. Y.


*From Joseph M. Graham.*                                    U.

Little Bay, Ark.,

Nov. 9th., 1850.

I wrote you some three months since, and have not as yet received a reply, and presume that you did not receive it, or that your duties have been so pressing that you have not had leisure. I have been here a little more than twelve months, and we have (both black and white) generally enjoyed fine health, and have gotten along quite well. We settled, as you know, in the wild woods, and had to cut the first stick. We have now our negro houses built, Corn Crib, Barn, Black Smith Shop, Kitchen, Smoke house, and will commence our dwelling next week. My buildings are all neat and substantial, and are much better than those I had in Carolina.

I have cleared and have in cultivation one hundred and fifty acres of land, and have gathered from it Twenty two hundred bushels of Corn; eight hundred bushels of Sweet Potatoes, Twenty Bales of Cotton, Seventy five bushels of Rice, besides peas, & pumpkins in abundance. We have had quite a fine garden for a new place. Mary has gathered and put in pickle two barrels of Cucumbers, which she says she intends to sell to the Steamboats this Winter. We are only a mile and a half from navigation, and can easily dispose of every article we have to sell, and at a good price.

The range for stock of all kinds is particularly fine, and particularly hogs, I have about one hundred and sixty head, and we never think of feeding them more than to give them a little Bran and salt occasionally, to keep them gentle.

Our Country is rapidly settling up by an intelligent population; a good many of whom are from Carolina. There are quite a host of Smiths from Granville, and Caswell, also the Eatons, and Mr. Somerville, all good farmers and very well off. Mr. Warren, who married a Sister of Uncle Jo's wife lives not far from me. He is quite an estimable man, and a fine neighbor. He tells me George Graham and his eldest sister intend visiting him this winter, and George thinks of settleing a farm in this section of country.

Henry and Mr. Rounsaville are both living in Camden, Twenty five miles above me on the river. They are both getting a good practice, and I have no doubt will do well, as Camden is destined to be a considerable place, being the head of navigation on the Ouchita River.

Mr. R., Henry and Martha are all quite well, Henry will leave in a few days for New York for the purpose of laying in a new stock of drugs. He will stop for a short time in Carolina, on business.

The legislature of this State has just met. They are bitterly opposed to some of the recent acts of Congress, with regard to the Slavery question, and there is strong talk of disunion here. Graham Witherspoon is a representative from Jackson County on White River. Sidney W., I understand, is practising medicine on the Arkansas River.

\* \* \* \* \*

Please let me hear from you when you have leisure. And I would be obliged if you would occasionally send me some public documents. Direct to "Camden."

### From Daniel Webster. U.

*Private & Confidential.*

Boston,

Nov'r 13th., 1850.

The Whigs of this State owe their recent misfortunes, especially the re-election of Mr. Horace Mann,[147] very much to the support given to him by certain Whig papers, at the head of which is the Boston Atlas. Other causes concurred, and, among these other

---

[147] Horace Mann (1796-1859), of Massachusetts, a graduate of Brown University, lawyer, state legislator, who reorganized and revolutionized the public school system of Massachusetts, while secretary of the board of education, 1837-1848. He was a Democratic member of congress, 1848-1853, and president of Antioch College, 1853-1859.

causes, one is, the favor shown towards Mr. Mann's election by certain Officers of the Custom House. This last subject may be attended to hereafter, but my present purpose is to request that the patronage of your Department may be altogether withdrawn from the Boston Atlas.

The reliable Whig papers in this City are; the Boston Daily Advertisers; and the Boston Courier. These are large Daily Papers, ably conducted and entirely sound. The Bee is a penny paper of great circulation, and of good principles.

About the Country papers I will enquire, and give you information hereafter. Meantime, it is safe to say that the Springfield Republican is a highly respectable and thorough Union paper.

Yours with true regard

*From Haywood W. Guion.*                              U.

Lincolnton,

Nov'r 14th., 1850.

I have just returned from Mecklenburg Court, where I saw and conferred with Messrs. Osborne, Boyden, and your brother James, in relation to the subject matter of your letter, and now, as I promised, send you the result of our conference. Your letter to me was exhibited to them severally, and received from each of them, I know, full consideration. The result was, that each heartily agreed to recommend Gen'l S. F. Patterson as the most suitable person for the office of Assistant Post Master [General.] and of course for the Chief Clerkship, if he would consent to accept it; and we further joined in the opinion, that it is all important to know whether he will consent to accept it, or either of the offices, provided a tender should be made to him. I have accordingly addressed him a letter, stating to him that we have been requested to recommend some suitable person from this part of the State to fill the offices, according to the tenor of your letter, and that, if he would accept, we should join in forwarding his name; and I further requested him without delay to signify to me by letter, whether he will accept or not. His answer, when received, shall be immediately forwarded, and if he refuses, I will confer with Mr. Sumner upon the subject of his accepting the same, and send you his answer also.

The truth is, there is a great dearth of the *proper material* in this part of the State, and to answer your request and furnish proper persons, is sufficient to satisfy any one of the futility of Mr. Clingman's labored complaints that the West has always been neglected in the distribution of offices. We all concur in opinion that Gen'l Patterson's appointment will give credit to the Administration, be of service to the department, and prove highly acceptable to the Whigs of this section, and the whole State. Mr. Boyden spoke highly of Mr. John B. Lord, of Salisbury, as also did your brother, but Gen'l Patterson was preferred to him.

When I last wrote to you, and partially agreed to accept the office of Ass't P. M., I had not then received any intimation whatever that my brother-in-law, Mr. Waddell, was receiving favors at the hands of the administration. The appointment that he gets is a rich one, and is highly approved by all persons, and you receive the credit of it, and were I now to obtain another, it might, in the eyes of many, narrow your motives to the limits of a family circle. I therefore claim the priviledge of withdrawing the assent I gave you in my last, to present my name; and I do so without reluctance under all the circumstances of the case, trusting that, in a short time, I shall be able to forward to you the assent of Gen'l Patterson, or Mr. Sumner.

*From Robert B. Gilliam.* U.

Oxford, N. C.,

Nov. 21st., 1850.

I fear you will think my chief employment is to besiege you with applications for favors. I am sensible that I have already trespassed on your kindness, and after this, I shall endeavour to make my practice conform a little better to my notions of propriety and fitness. Instead of assailing you *once a week,* with these paper missiles, the intervals of attack shall be extended to the term of a calendar month, at the least.

A friend of yours and mine, a good Whig, and a capital good fellow, Mr. Leonidas C. Edwards,[148] is anxious to be employed by the government. He, as you know, is well educated, and is decidedly above the average order of intelligence in his profes-

---

[148] Leonidas Compton Edwards (1825-1907), of Oxford, a native of Person County, a graduate of the university, lawyer, assistant clerk of the convention of 1861, state senator, 1870-1872.

sion. Being threatened with a disease of the lungs, he would be glad to remove for a year or two to a warm, dry climate, in the hope of finding improvement, and perhaps permanent relief. He does not care about the *profits* of the station,—provided he could get one which would furnish a decent support, during his residence abroad. If any of the West India, or S. American consulships are vacant, of the kind I have alluded to, he would willingly, and indeed gladly, accept one.

However desirable it might be, he does not ask for an office of the first grade, or one that would be sought after for it's profits. His main object being the pursuit of health, he would be content to take one that would barely pay expenses. With these very moderate views, he would, I suppose, scarcely come in competition with strong claims from any quarter.

I should be greatly rejoiced if he could be gratified. Having suffered with the same kind of apprehensions under which Mr. Edwards labors, though probably with less occasion, I know how anxious he must be to get to some place where the sudden alterations of heat and cold are not keeping him in perpetual dread.

Mr. Edwards has a small property, enough, possibly, with great care and economy, to support him at home, but totally insufficient to maintain him in a residence abroad.

Having laid his case before you, I am content to leave it in your hands; being entirely satisfied, that if consistent with other duties and obligations, it will receive a favorable consideration.

You have doubtless heard of the discussion in Oxford between Venable[149] and Miller.[150] My engagements in Court prevented me from hearing it, but there is no mistake about its being an utter demolition of Venable. He survives, and that is all. I understand that Venable pronounced the present administration to be "a free soil, abolition administration." I have no doubt of his having so said, for I heard Miller's reply to that part of his speech. Miller denounced the charge as *"a gross calumny and slander, come from what quarter it might,"* and said many other things of and to Mr. V., which induced a gentleman standing by me to ask "if Venable was a fighting man."

---

[149] Abraham Watkins Venable (1799-1876), of Granville County, a native of Virginia, a graduate of Hampden-Sidney College and of Princeton, lawyer, who came to North Carolina in 1829, Democratic member of congress, 1847-1853, member of the Confederate congress, 1861-1864.

[150] Henry W. Miller.

*From James E. Harvey.*[151]                    U.

North American Office,

Philadelphia.

November 25th., 1850.

Since my return from Washington, I have inquired more particularly into the facts regarding the alleged obstructions in the
Delaware, which were assigned to you by the proper bureau, as
reason for removing the Susquehanna to some other port for
completion. I am informed by our Commercial houses, engaged
in foreign Commerce, and by Officers of the Navy, who have been
on this station for years, that no difficulty or danger in regard
to ice in the river, such as has been ascribed, exists. In severe
Seasons the river is kept always open by the means of Steam tugs,
which are constantly in use, but for several years past, they have
been only occasionally necessary. The Susquehanna now lies in a
place of perfect safety, protected, even if ice should appear, in
extraordinary quantities, against all apprehension of injury.

I mention these facts for no purpose, but to enable you to have
a correct comprehension of the case. The opposition press,—
Pennsylvanian, & Spirit of the Times,—have already assailed you
for the proposed change of the Steamer, on the ground of opposition to Philadelphia, and it does not become us, who are friends
of the Administration, to sit by and see you, as one of it's able and
efficient members, charged with responsibility which, we understand, belongs to the head of a bureau, holding the same political
faith as your assailants. To us, personally, this is a matter of indifference, & I speak of it in behalf of myself & my colleagues on
our paper, as a subject affecting yourself, & the party, and as one
exhibiting in its external aspect, a spirit of great illiberality towards the Mechanics of this City.

P. S. If the order to remove the Steamer was countermanded, and
we were authorized to announce it officially, it would produce a
favorable reaction.

---

[151] James E. Harvey, journalist, a native of Charleston, South Carolina, who
was Washington correspondent for the Philadelphia *North American*. Later he
provoked a storm by notifying the South Carolina authorities in 1861 of the
expedition for the relief of Fort Sumter, but was supported by William H. Seward,
who had authorized it. Lincoln made him minister to Portugal.

*From Thomas J. Lemay & Son.*[152]          U.

Raleigh,

November 29th, [1850.]

Report says President's message will be delivered to Editors in principle Cities on Telegraph announcement of presentation by taking such steps as are in your power to have us or our post master furnished with a copy of same. You will oblige our citizens, the Legislature, & especially yours.

*From James P. McRee.*[153]          A.

Sommerville,

Decm. 2nd, 1850.

You may think it somewhat Strang to receive a letter from me, no doubt you have almost fagoten me

I married the daughter of Adam Brevard *Rebecca* who no doubt you remember better than me, I have herd her say she has nussed you when you were a child. My object in writing to you is to know whether she is intitled to bounty land her father having served in the Revolutionary War as a Malishey Man he served at one time nine months he was out at an othra time, but we know nothing of his discharge nor who he served under. I think if the children of any man that don servise in any of the Wars in the U. S. is entitled to bounty Land his should be, in view of the fact that he wrote the first declaration of Independence that was wrote in America, to wit, the Mecklenburg Dec'n. Some may say he did not do it that Ephram Brevard wrote it, its true that E. Brevard was a delegate in the Convention and one of the commitee that was appointed to write it but Adam Brevard being then a student at Law living with his brother Ephram in Charlotte wrote it, and Ephram being the Chairman of the Commtee laid it before the Convention.

The above facts I have heard Adam Brevard speak of a great many times he lived with me for 8 or 10 years before his death. We would like to have some of the great quantity of land that is held by the U. S. there is but two of his children alive now your

---

[152] Telegram. Thomas J. Lemay was editor of the Raleigh *Star* and the *North Carolina Farmer.*

[153] James Polk McRee (1778-1873), a jeweler, whose mother was a Polk.

Aunt Davidson and my wife. I have writen to our representative
F. P. Stanton[154] he may speak to you on the subject.

You will discover that I am not in the habbit of writing

Very respectfully your &c

*From Samuel F. Patterson to Haywood W. Guion.*

Palmyra,

December 4th., 1850.

Your kind letter dated at Charlotte the 14th. ultimo, but postmarked Lincolnton the 21st. reached me only by the last mail,
and I embrace the earliest opportunity to reply.

The Salary of Chief Clerk of the P. O. Department would not
justify me in abandoning my present pursuits to accept such a
situation. Were there any patronage attached to the office, whereby
I might be instrumental in promoting our political party, it
might compensate to some extent the want of pecuniary inducement, as I have always been willing to make any reasonable sacrifice for such a purpose, but of this there is none.

With regard to the office of Assistant P. M. General, I confess
that I hardly know what to say. You are aware that there are three
assistants, and to each, I presume, is assigned specific duties. You
do not state, and perhaps you are not informed, which one of the
three offices is expected shortly to be made vacant. I cannot therefore tell whether or not the duties would be agreeable to my taste,
or within my competency to perform. Should the expected vacancy
occur *very shortly*, and the appointment be tendered to me, it
would not be in my power to accept it, owing to existing engagements, but, should it be deferred, until after the close of the present Session of Congress, and I can in the mean time obtain satisfactory information on the points above indicated, I should then
be prepared to give a definite answer. I wish it, however, to be
distinctly understood that no consideration of me either now or
hereafter is to interfere in the least with the selection of any other
individual who might perhaps prove both more competent and
worthy than myself.

---

[154] Frederick Perry Stanton (1814-1894), of Tennessee, a native of Virginia, grad-
uate of Columbian College (now George Washington University), lawyer in
Memphis, Democratic member of congress, 1845-1855, territorial governor of Kansas.
Later he returned to Virginia, and then moved to Florida.

Thanking you, and the other friends with whom you have conferred, most cordially for the interest you have manifested in my behalf.

*From Charles L. Hinton.*                    A.

Raleigh

Dec. 6th. 1850.

\* \* \* \* \*

The papers give you such a full account of the proceedings of the Legislature that there is but little of the under current worth naming.

Mine is the only election to come off. Courts[155] is the Caucus candidate and I suppose will get the party vote.

I fear there is more of the ultra feeling on the Southern questions than I expected, but as yet there has been no test question.

*From William Hogan Jones.*[156]                 U.

Raleigh,

December 9th., 1850.

I will be as breaf as possible, hoping to be one of many that will address you in Major W. F. Collins' behalf, is my apology for troubling you. You know Major C. to have been an entirely competent officer, was a Whig and for this alone has been turned out of office.

You *know* the incumbent of the P. Office here, the history of his "Whig Recommendation," and the value to place of such papers, and the manuvers to get it up. The P. O. here is the best Office in the State, Salary $3000. It ought not to be in the hands of a Loco, and such a Loco,[157] we get no credit for retaining him, and it being a Distributing Office, ought to be in the hands of a Whig, the Whigs of the State have an interest in the matter, and

---

[155] Daniel William Courts (1800-1884), of Rockingham County, a native of Virginia, a graduate of the university. He represented Surry County in the commons, 1831-1833, 1836-1837, and was state treasurer, 1852-1862. In 1839 he was appointed consul at Matanzas, and upon his return moved to Rockingham County, which he represented in the state senate, 1850-1852, and 1864-1865.

[156] William Hogan Jones of Chatham County, a graduate of the university, banker, later a Confederate major.

[157] William White.

its astonishing *our* Senator allows such an appointment, some unaccountable influence, somewhere.

We get no credit for retaining the present incumbent, Loco *Slander* is not to be appeased by such acts of liberality, or I would not say a word, but seeing *you* weekly slandered by implication, insinuation, & directly by name, and a Whig Administration daily vilafied by an unscrupulus press, & Less Scrupuluss politicians, and Whigs proscribed for simply being Whigs, I cannot longer hold my peace.

I would have written to others in y'r City, but fear some undue influence operates—or courage is lacking to make an effort.

Major W. F. Collins ought to be appointed P. M. here, forthwith, it would be acceptable and agreeable to the Community, and highly gratafing to all Whigs.

*From Dorothea L. Dix.*[158]     U.

Trenton,
New Jersey,
December 11th., [1850.]

*Private*

I wish to ask counsel of you—if you can spare a few moments admidst the onerous duties which crowd y'r time. I have much confidence in y'r clear and calm judgment, and I shall be much obliged if you can offer me any guiding suggestions in regard to the best mode of introducing the *ten million Land Bill* for reconsideration. I would wish to see this so carefully managed as to assure thereby consideration and successful action. My own idea as to *time* was, that the middle of January or February would be early enough, and possibly a later period would well serve. At present it has seemed to me nothing important could be accomplished: perhaps you will judge differently.

My health, as yet not re-established, is subject to serious attacks upon even slight exposures, and I am now under treatment for an obstinate cough, and symptomatic inflamation of the throat. My medical advisers wish me to suspend, as far as is practicable,

[158] Dorothea Lynde Dix (1802-1887), humanitarian. Born in Maine, she became a teacher, was an invalid always, but devoted her life to the betterment of the insane, working all over the United States and also in England. She was largely responsible for the establishment of the state mental hospital which is called by her name. She was made superintendent of women army nurses in the Civil War, but was greatly hampered in her work by Surgeon General Hammond.

the use of my voice, and fatiguing exertions for several weeks, believing that rest, and an equal, carefully regulated temperature, will accomplish a complete cure—which they will not promise so long as exciting causes conflict with curative treatment. I am really anxious concerning the modes by which the Land Bill may best be placed before Congress. Is it too much to ask and expect of that body a prompt and efficient attention to what so much concerns all parties, as does its successful passage?

With cordial and sincere friendly regards, I am,

respectfully yours,

*From Basil Manly.*[159]                    U.

University of Alabama,

December 11th., 1850.

I write to introduce to your acquaintance Lieut. Handy, of the U. S. Navy. Not enjoying that honor myself, an apology for this apparent intrusion might seem to be necessary, but for the assurance that your generous appreciation of the services and privations of those brave and hardy fellows who constitute the main arm of our National defence, and who have shed imperishable renown on our Country, will lead you spontaneously to greet each one of them, on his return to our shores, with almost parental cordiality and kindness.

Lieut Handy[160] has been absent from the Country for several years, on duty, in California, and other seas and shores South and West of us. His Sister, being the wife of our Prof. Tuomey,[161] his visit to her for a day or two has given me the opportunity of a short but pleasant acquaintance with him.

---

[159] Basil Manly (1798-1868), of Alabama, Baptist minister, educator, a native of Chatham County, North Carolina, the brother of Matthias and Charles Manly. He was educated at the Bingham School and entered the ministry. Later he was graduated from South Carolina College. He was one of the founders of Furman University, declined the presidency of South Carolina College, was president of the University of Alabama, 1837-1855. He was instrumental in the founding of Judson, Howard, and Central colleges, and the Southern Baptist Theological Seminary.

[160] Probably Edward Handy, who entered the navy in 1826. He was promoted to commander in 1855, and resigned in 1861, and consequently marked in the naval register as dismissed.

[161] Michael Tuomey (1808-1857), of Alabama, a native of Ireland, a graduate of Rensselaer Polytechnic Institute, state geologist of Maryland, South Carolina, and, later, of Alabama. He was also a professor in the University of Alabama and the author of important geological reports.

From Prof. Tuomey and myself please accept a copy of a Report on the Geology of Alabama, with the accompanying map; which will be delivered to you by Lieut. Handy.

Claiming the right to rejoice in every honor and success gained by a son of my native State, I tender to you the assurance of my respect.

P. S. May I ask to be presented, in much Christian affection, to your pious and excellent Lady; with whose character my own venerable Mother has made me acquainted?


*From Nathan K. Hall.*                                U.

Washington,

December 12th., 1850.


Mr. Webster's house being still in the hands of the painters, I have his permission to invite you to meet the other members of the Cabinet at my house, tomorrow evening, at 7 o'clock, for the purpose of discussing such political, social, and ceremonial matters as are thought to require an early consideration.


*From Rufus Haywood.*                                U.

Tuscaloosa,

Dec. 12th, 1850.

* * * * *

We have but little of public interest in Alabama. Dissolution of the Union for a time seemed to have many advocates, and amongst them some of our most sober minded and reflecting Citizens. But little is said now on the subject. The excitement, I think, has passed off, And a more general confidence established that Congress will have wisdom enough to pass no act that will again disturb the conflicting sections of the Union.

* * * * *

*From Edward G. Benners.*[162]                                  U.

Marshall, Texas,

December 13th., 1850.

Though many years have elapsed since I have had the pleasure of seeing you, and you may have lost all recollection of me since my residence in the South West. Yet, as an old North Carolinian, I doubt not you will excuse the liberty I take in addressing you to ask a favour.

An effort will be made at the present session of Congress to establish a Federal District Court at some point in Eastern Texas, for which a separate Judge will be appointed. The object of this letter is to interest you in my behalf, and solicit the aid of your influence to procure the appointment for me. I am not acquainted with either of the members [illegible] distinguished Gentlemen in my native State [illegible] particularly mention the names of Mr. Badger, Gov. Manly, Judge Manly, Edw'd Stanly, W. H. Haywood, Gov. Swain, Bishop Ives, et. cet. A number of years past, my residence has been in Mobile, where also, as well as elsewhere in Ala. I am favourably known. I have made Texas my home but recently, and have located at Jefferson, in Cass County, engaged in the practice of my profession. Having been now fifteen years actively engaged in the practice of the Law, I do not hesitate to prefer my claims with any who may apply for this appointment.

As regards my political predilections, in the last Presidential Canvass, I was a warm and zealous supporter of Gen. Taylor, and in Texas, on the exciting question of Pierce's Boundary Bill, which but recently was submitted to the People, I warmly advocated the adoption of that measure, and though, like every true Southerner, I am opposed to the aggressions that are being made upon our peculiar institution by the Fanatics of the North, yet I desire to see the South, while they maintain a firm and united stand upon their rights, pursue a direct course, and not hazard the continuance of our national existence by hasty and precipitate action.

If, then, I can be favoured with your valuable aid and influence with the President, and your influential friends in and out of Congress, I doubt not the accomplishment of my wishes,

---

[162] Edward Graham Benners was one of a North Carolina family that removed to Alabama. Descendants of his still live in Texas. He was a nephew of Edward Graham of New Bern, an eminent lawyer.

and I assure you, my dear Sir, your kind attention will ever be most gratefully remembered.

*From Edward Stanly.*                    U.

December 17th., 1850.

*Private.*

I called on Mr. Owen, of Georgia: & he says the following are Whig papers, sound, conservative, etc.

| | |
|---|---|
| Georgia Journal & Messenger,<br>Macon, Geo:<br>American Whig.<br>Griffin, Geo: | In Mr. Owen's[163] district. |
| The Recorder,<br>Milledgeville, Geo: | A. H. Stephen's[164] district. |
| Chronicle & Sentinel,<br>Augusta, Geo: | Toomb's[165] district. |
| Savannah Republican,<br>Savannah, Geo: | Jackson's[166] district. |

Mr. O. says the first named has an extensive circulation, & is very true to the Country. Owen himself, in the midst of all the excitement last Session, though acting with his colleagues, always talked like a patriot, & was a Union man.

Cabell[167] is out of the City.

---

[163] Allen Ferdinand Owen (1816-1865), of Georgia, a native of North Carolina, a graduate of Franklin College (now the University of Georgia), of Yale, and of the Harvard Law School, state legislator, Whig member of congress, 1849-1851, consul to Havana.

[164] Alexander Hamilton Stephens (1812-1883), of Georgia, a graduate of the University of Georgia, lawyer, state legislator, Whig member of congress, 1843-1859, delegate to the secession convention, member of the Confederate provisional congress, and Confederate vice president, 1861-1865. He was a member of the Hampton Roads conference, was imprisoned at Fort Warren, but, released, was elected United States senator in 1866. He was not seated. He was a Democratic member of congress, 1873-1882, and governor, 1882-1883.

[165] Robert Toombs (1810-1885), of Georgia, graduate of Union College after being a student at the University of Georgia, where he later studied law. He was a captain in the Creek War, 1838, state legislator, Democratic member of congress, 1845-1852, United States senator, 1853-1861, delegate to the Confederate provisional congress, secretary of state, and brigadier general.

[166] Joseph Webber Jackson (1796-1854), of Georgia, state legislator, Democratic member of congress, 1850-1853, state judge.

[167] Edward Carrington Cabell (1817-1896), of Florida, a native of Virginia, and a graduate of the University of Virginia, planter, member of congress, 1847-1853.

Mr. Holmes[168] I could not see, the House adjourned, after the announcement was made of the death of Mr. Harmanson[169] of La.

[Notation in William A. Graham's handwriting.]
+The Sentinel, Tallahassee.
+Pensacola Gazette, Pensacola.
Florida Whig, Mariana.
+Jacksonville Republican at Jacksonville.

*From Bartholomew F. Moore.*                                    A.

Raleigh,

Decr. 18th, 1850.

I have recd your very excellent letter and have used it amongst some of our conservative friends. I have been confined at home for fifteen days with an inflamed foot caused by the merest trifle. I shall be able to go out in a day or two, & will endeavor to impress your views (for they are mine) on such as I may approach. I sent for Miller the other evening, and he came and brought with him—which he read to me—a most capital article intended as an editorial for the Register. I was exceedingly pleased with it; and it puts forth your views in regard to secession, and the extreme impolicy, at this time, of avowing the doctrine, with extraordinary power & vigor.

I read your letter to Col. Joyner, Washington, Gilmer & Woodfin, and they all concurred in the views.

I, too, have sent an article to the Register, written with some inconvenience during my confinement, reprobating any State action by taxes & retaliations signed "A Constituent" addressed to "the members of the Legislature" urging many of your views in opposition to the policy.

There is a madness among our members concerning *Resolutions*. A large number of them seem to think that they are either the high road to political renown, or will serve as alarm guns on the North. Their great number and the marked and irreconcileable differences in their suggestions and recommendations, will, however, in my opinion serve to disperse any united bad action.

---

[168] Isaac Edward Holmes (1796-1867), of South Carolina, graduate of Yale, lawyer, state legislator, Democratic member of congress, 1839-1851. He twice moved to California and then back to South Carolina.

[169] John Henry Harmanson (1803-1850), of Louisiana, a native of Virginia, lawyer, state legislator, Democratic member of congress, 1845-1850.

I do not believe that any of the movers think there is any great and pressing necessity for action or any likelihood of real utility to the repose of the Country springing out of the movements. They are easy methods of getting notice abroad, and fulfilling the expectations that they are to do *something*.

I think the shower will end in sunshine, that moderate Resolutions will pass, and that no tag bill will be enacted. Certainly, if no untoward event shall occur at the North, and no agitation of a serious character spring up at Washington, the Union will lose no friends here.

Shepards Resolutions[170] are debating in the Senate, and I am told he gets no quarter, & will have none shewn to him. His speech, especially the part proving the *"right"* of secession, is very important; and, in my view, the very best text that could be offered to shew its absurdity & destitution of authority to support it.

I read with surprise his quotation of Mr. Fox's remark that "the people of England have the *right* to dethrone their King" to prove *the right* of secession. Truly Mr. Fox spoke and most clearly (& not more clearly could he) spoke of *Revolution*—A right begun in force & supported by arms. Twice the British Monarch has been dethroned under the sanction of this *right*, from *all* his dominions, & each time it is called Revolution. Once (in the War of '76) dethroned from a part of his dominions, and this too was a bloody and forcible revolution. Really I had supposed that he was not quite so shallow.

I shall watch events at Washington with great anxiety. There, I think, for the next two years, will be the battle ground that is to decide our fate.

I have been a very warm admirer of Mr. Winthrop,[171] until just before he left the House of Representatives. When transferred to the Senate, I looked to him to rise with his position, and reach the topmost fame of his great family name; I have been sadly mortified. And still I hope that he will, now that the measures are passed, once more step out of New England and plant himself on broad American Ground. Would to God that Daniel Webster was forty five, with all his present name & wisdom, I should yet look on that sun, he so eloquently describes

---

[170] William B. Shepard, who represented Pasquotank County in the state senate at this session, offered a series of resolutions, asserting the right of secession and demanding proper protection for property in slaves. They were not passed.

[171] Robert C. Winthrop.

in the peroration of his great speech, as in the heavens, high full & bright.

When I get out and look around me a little, I will give you the time O'night.

*From C. K. Smith.*                                              U.

St. Paul,

Territory of Minnesota.,

December 19th., 1850.

Sir:

I have the agreeable duty of informing you of your election as a member of the "Minnesota Historical Society."

A primary object of this Association is the collection and preservation of a Library; Mineralogical and Geological specimens; Indian curiosities, and every matter and thing connected with, and calculated to illustrate and perpetuate the history and settlement of the Territory of Minnesota; and to publish in book form the most valuable manuscripts that may come into the possession of the Society. I need not advise you, that it is the earnest wish of the Society, that you will cheerfully act in a capacity of so great importance to the honor of the present, and the benefit of the future age.

Accompanying this, you will receive a pamphlet published by the Society, that more fully explains its objects.

I avail myself of the opportunity which the occasion presents, of expressing to you the great pleasure with which I subscribe myself,

Your obedient servant,

Sec'y of the Minnesota Hist'l Society.

*To C. N. Stetson.*                                              U.

Washington City,

Dec. 21st, 1850.

Your polite invitation, on behalf of the New England Society, in the City of New York, to their Anniversary dinner at the Astor House on the 23rd. instant, has been received.

The history of the New England colonies and States, which date their origin from the landing of the pilgrims on the day you celebrate, especially in the great contest for American Independence, records a most important part of the history of our race on this Continent, and contains much for the admiration of every true patriot.

The people of the State and section of my birth, though many hundred miles distant, participated early in this admiration, and became united to their brethren of New England in the strongest bonds of sympathy. When Boston was beleaguered by a hostile army, they made her cause their own, and tendered assistance, and declared absolute independence of the British crown at Mecklenburg upon the first information of the shedding of American blood at Lexington. When a new seat of justice was established in consequence of the division of this territory, it was honored with the name of Concord. When in process of time a new village sprung up, in the neighboring country, they called it Lexington. And scarcely had the struggle of the Revolution terminated, when the County in which I first saw the light, exchanged the name of Tryon, one of the last of the royal Governors, for that of Lincoln.

In this feeling of respect and attachment, the people of North Carolina entered into the Federal Union, and in this feeling they have kept the covenants of the Constitution; not with a grudging and reluctant obedience, to any of its stipulations, but with a loyal and hearty good will.

If in the oath of allegience, to that Constitution, as a whole, they have "sworn to their own hurt," in the operation of any of its parts; they have been ever mindful of their obligations, of duty, and honor, "change not," except in the modes appointed and authorized. That faith, which in the expressive language of Burke "binds the worst elements of the world together" requires a no less scrupulous observance, so long as the Government endures, of that which we would have rejected, had we been consulted in its formation, as of that which we approve.

It cannot and should not, be disguised, that this long cherished affection for New England has been materially abated, and even loyalty to the Constitution has become less ardent, at the South, by reason of the disposition, openly manifested in some quarters at the North, and entertained, it is apprehended, more extensively than it has been manifested, to evade and oppose the requirements of the Constitution, in regard to African slavery, as it existed in nearly all the States at the time of its adoption, and as it still exists in our section of the Union.

The adjustment of the strife arising out of this, and kindred causes, made with much labor, sacrifice & difficulty, by the united efforts of patriots of all parties, at the last Session of Congress, will I feel assured, if adhered to, and fulfilled, in the spirit of fidelity, in which it was adopted, prove eventually acceptable, to reasonable men, in all parts of the Country. But if crimination, shall continue, and the laws of Congress made in the disposition, and for the purpose of reconcilement, shall be evaded or defied, I more than fear, that the recollection of the virtues of our ancestors, their self sacrificing devotion, and noble cooperation, in the great cause of republican liberty, will be the only bond of Union left to us.

I am gratified however in believing that the stand taken by the friends of the Constitution and the Union, in your great City, in Philadelphia, and more recently in Boston, following the lead of that son of New England, in the Senate of the United States, in March last, whose fame has become the common property of the Nation, will give pause to agitation, on this vital subject, bring the minds of honest and patriotic men everywhere, to view it in its true light, and lead to the restoration, of harmony and cordiality between the elements which now threaten our peace and Union.

Regretting that my official engagements deny me the pleasure of being present at your festival, I beg the New England Society of New York to be assured of the admiration I entertain for the historical personages, whose characters they design to commemorate, and of my high respect for their Institution and members.

I am Sir very Respectfully

Your Obedt, Servt.

*From Jackson Morton.*[172]                              U.

Washington,

Dec. 23rd., 1850.

Sir

Fearing I may not, in the hurry of the moment, have given you correctly the names of the Whig papers in Florida, I here repeat them, viz:

> "Pensacola Gazette"—Pensacola
> "Florida Sentinel"—Tallahassee
> "Florida Whig"—Marianna
> "Florida Republican"—Jacksonville
> "Apalachicola Gazette"—Apalachicola

> Very Respectfully your
> Ob't Serv't.


*From Edmund Strudwick.*                              U.

Hillsboro',

Dec. 24th., 1850.

Allow me to trouble you with a word about our Rail Road. Some of us are scared, & I am among the number. Our Directors met recently in Raleigh, as you know, & we are not satisfied exactly with the action or rather, non-action, of the Board. Inasmuch as the Stock was taken in consequence of pledges made by the gentlemen who interested themselves by making public addresses in its behalf, & as the Stock would not have been taken without the expectation on the part of the subscribers that a large portion of their Stock should be worked off, & furthermore, as the State (the larger interest or Stockholder) had no agency in making these pledges, we thought the Board of Directors should have informed the present legislature of all these circumstances, & called upon it to sanction the principle of working off the Stock, or of allowing the Stockholders to abandon the enterprise, by receiving from them the charter.

---

[172] Jackson Morton (1794-1874), of Florida, a native of Virginia, graduate of Washington College (now Washington and Lee University), who moved to Florida and engaged in the lumber business. He served in the territorial legislative council, as a delegate to the convention of 1837, as navy agent at Pensacola, and as Whig United States senator, 1849-1855. He was a delegate to the Confederate provisional congress, 1861-1862, and a member of the lower house, 1862-1865.

We also thought it would have [been] proper to ask for an amendment to the charter, permitting the Stockholders to pay the half million in work and not in money, & upon the execution of this amount of work, the State to pay its half million in money, & elect her directors, and come regularly into the Company. Now we fear that if the work is commenced, without consulting the legislature, the Company will be involved in many difficulties, & will be utterly unable to accomplish the transfer of Stock from the Stockholders to Contractors, & bring the whole road into disrepute, and cast odium upon all who are concerned in it.

I propose, in conjunction with several Stockholders, to call upon the directors to consult the legislature, & let every thing be understood & fairly agreed upon by the State, and the private S. holders, & if we fail in this to get a meeting of the S. holders, to memorialize the Legislature, & if we fail in this, that as many of the S. holders as possible will address a memorial to the legislature, asking it to confer upon this present Board of Directors the right & power to work off the stock, and if the legislature is unwilling to do this, to instruct the Directors to insist upon the payment of the half million by the private S. holders, in money, before a blow is struck upon the road, & that, without this strict compliance with the charter, the State will not pay its half million, or any portion of its Stock, if the Leg. is unwilling to sanction the work-off principle, & shall insist on the payment of the half million by the private S. H. the charter w'd be tendered to the Leg. unanimously. I want the whole scheme to fail, to go down, if I am not to receive the relief and advantage of having my stock worked off. I am unwilling to be the victim of trimmers & speculators, & from the silence of the B. of directors, I think their plan and purpose is to work off the stock if they can, but if they find it necessary to the success of the road, in whole or in part, as suits their taste or interest, they will require the payment of every dollar of Stock in money, if it consigns to ruin many of the Stockholders, who confided in the public pledges as a sure protection to their interest.

Now I have hurriedly, after a long, cold ride, given you the above statement. I beg your counsel and advice, as well of the morality, as of the propriety of the course I design to take.

. . . Your black family are all well, I have not felt the pulse of a single servant of yours since you left.

My Bro. William, of Ala, has written to you to know if you can send any dispatches by him any where, so that he may find his way to the World's Fair, on the public expense. If any arrangement of this kind, consistently with your public duty, can be made, you would be conferring a great favor on one of the worthiest and best of men.

*From John W. Norwood.* U.

Hillsborough,

Dec. 27th, 1850.

\* \* \* \* \*

With regard to our Rail Road. I think the determination of the Directors is to build it at all hazards, and if the *working off* principle is abandoned, as I think it will be, I with many others who put their whole trust in that scheme, will be nearly ruined. The Road located from Goldsborough to Waynesboro' to within 9 miles of Raleigh & from Lexington to Charlotte. And as soon as the Legislature adjourns it will be located through Raleigh. It is conditionally located from Raleigh via Hillsborough to the Guilford line. The condition being, that if the Chief Engineer, after examination, shall think a route by Chapel Hill practicable at all, he shall survey it, & then if in his judgment it will at all compare with the Hillsborough line, the matter is again to be submitted to the Directors, otherwise the present line stands.

The Legislature will be applied to for the purpose of sanctioning the working off principle, etc., but not by the Directors, I think.

Public affairs seem to be wearing a more threatening aspect again, and it will require all the patriotism and wisdom of the Nation, I fear, to save us from trouble.

I would be much pleased to hear from you. All friends here will. I expect to go down to Raleigh to attend the Supreme Court, and look after the Rail Road, & on Friday next. In haste.

*From William W. Kirkland.*          U.

Hillsboro',

December 28th., 1850.

I have again taken the liberty of trespassing upon your time, but I trust you will excuse. I have written to the Pres. to grant me an appointment to West Point in his next annual app'ts, and humbly beg your influence in my behalf. Please answer my letter as soon as convenient. My Parent's respects to you and yours.

Your People are all well and I hope that these few lines will find you in the enjoyment of the same blessing.

*From John M. Morehead.*          A.

Greensboro,

Dec. 28th, 1850.

Doubtless you are kept fully advised of the proceedings of our Legislature & the moves that are made hostile to our Road. I spent about a fortnight at Raleigh & think the resolutions of Sherrard[173] & Bridges[174] had a decided tendency to strengthen our Road. I think there is a decidedly kind feeling towards it, & shall not be at all surprised to find the State coming in pari passu in payments. We tell the Legislature we do not wish to have the money *piled up* on us at the rate of ½ million every six months; we had rather receive it in smaller doses.

You have noticed the project of the Deep River Company to extend their improvement higher up Deep River, thence by a Portage Rail Road to Yadkin, and then lock & Dam that River & have sectional Boats transported from one river to the other by the Railway as at Phila. and Pittsburg. I have suggested to that Company it will be much better to improve the Haw River to our Road and we can bring their boats for them, using ours as their portage Road, and then they need only improve the Yadkin from our Road upwards. This idea seems to be taking generally, & if this lock & Dam improvement shall succeed as well

---

[173] W. R. W. Sherrod who represented Martin County in the state senate. I have been unable to find any mention in the journal of his introduction of resolutions.

[174] Josiah Bridgers, who represented Edgecombe County in the commons, introduced a resolution declaring it inexpedient to construct the North Carolina Railroad which had been chartered by the previous legislature. It was quickly postponed indefinitely.

as its friends seem to think it will, an extension of our road 20 or 25 miles more will reach the Catawba which may be improved in like manner & thus our Road become the Portage Road for both Rivers. This I think it can do, & not interfere with the ordinary business, and it will certainly be much better than to have two roads running parallel not more than from 20 to 40 miles apart.

We shall be prepared to let our contracts by April, our rout is good, but not quite as good as we expected. Gov. Swain & Chapel Hill insist that a reconnaisance by Chapel Hill should be made, the result of which I have not yet heard—a tolerable fair rout by Hillsboro can be got.

Major Hinton shewed me your letter. I think Secession will not flourish in our Legislature yet I found more than I expected.

President Fillmore's course I think has been worthy of all commendation, and is very generally approved.

What do you think of taking a little respite and going over to the World's Fair, to see what scale John Bull does things? If the Legislature would just hand me over the first million, I should be pleased to go now and secure the iron when so very low. In that event I should want the Secretary of the Navy along to keep old Neptune on his behavior, while I was afloat; for I always felt as if I had a great alacrity at sinking

By the bye—you must keep a look out for our approaching Tariff upon iron, that we may secure ours before it is imposed.

Madame Perly of N. Y. desires me to recommend her son Edward to you for a place in the Naval School at Annapolis, I believe it is. Of course you know I must comply with her request.

Our friend Collins, who has lately been proscribed, desires the post office at Raleigh in the event of White's removal.

I shall be glad to receive any suggestions relative to our great enterprise, which may occur to you.

## List of Whig Newspapers in N. York.

| County | Name of paper | Place of Publication | Character |
| --- | --- | --- | --- |
| Albany | State Register* | Albany | Right |
| " | Evening Journal* | " | Abolition |
| " | Morning Express* | " | Right |
| Allegany | Advocate | Angelica | Abolition |
| Broome | Republican* | Binghampton | " |
| Cattaraugus | Whig | Ellicottville | " |
| Cayuga | Advertiser* | Auburn | " |
| Chatauque | Messenger | Westfield | " |
| " | Censor | Fredonia | Fairish |
| " | Journal | Jamestown | Fair |
| " | Journal | Dunkirk | Very fair |
| Chemung | Republican | Elmira | Abolition |
| Journal | Journal | Havanna | " |
| Chenango | Telegraph | Norwich | " |
| " | Times | Oxford | " |
| Clinton | Whig | Plattsburg | " |
| Columbia | Republican | Hudson | " |
| Cortland | Whig | Homer | " |
| Delaware | Express | Delhi | Fair and about right |

*Daily papers

| | | | |
|---|---|---|---|
| Dutchess | Standard | Fishkill | Right |
| " | Journal & Eagle | Poughkeepsie | Non committal |
| Erie | Com. Advertiser* | Buffalo | Right |
| " | Express | " | Abolition |
| " | Herald | Springville | " |
| Essex | Republican | Keeseville | Right |
| Franklin | Palladium | Malone | Abolition |
| Fulton | Republican | Johnstown | " |
| Genesee | Genesee Courier | LeRoy | Right |
| Genesee | Republican Advocate | Batavia | Right |
| " | Gazette (Editor Abolition) | LeRoy | (paper Fairish) |
| Greene | Whig | Catskill | Fair |
| Herkimer | Journal | Little Falls | Abolition |
| Jefferson | Northern State Journal | Watertown | " |
| " | Sackets Harbor Observer | Sackets Harbor | Was right, but fell off after Syracuse Con. |

*Daily papers

| County | Paper | Place | Character |
|---|---|---|---|
| Kings | Advertiser* | Brooklyn | Abolition |
| " | Star* | " | Fairish |
| " | Gazette* | Williamsburgh | Abolition |
| Lewis | Northern Journal | Lowville | " |
| Livingston | Republican | Genesee | Abolition |
| " | Union | Mount Morris | Was right, but fell off |
| " | Herald | Dansville | Abolition |
| " | Telegraph | Nunda | " |
| Madison | Whig | Cazenovia | Fairish |
| " | Journal | Hamilton | Abolition |
| Monroe | American* | Rochester | Right |
| " | Democrat* | " | Abolition |
| " | Watchmen | Brockport | " |
| Montgomery | Intelligencer | Amsterdam | Fair |
| " | Phoenix | Fort Plain | Right |
| " | Whig | Fultonville | Abolition |
| " | Mohawk Valley Gazette | Canajoharie | Fair |
| Niagara | Courier* | Lockport | Abolition (but is sold out, & will be right after 1st July.) |
| New York | Express* | New York | Right |
| " | Mirror* | " | Venal, & admits ugly articles. |

*Daily papers

| County | Paper | City | Opinion |
|---|---|---|---|
| " | Day Book* | " | Right |
| " | Com. Advertiser* | " | Rightish |
| " | Courier & Enquirer* | " | Abolition should be cultivated. |
|  | Tribune* | " | Abolition |
| Oneida | Gazette* | Utica | Right |
| Oneida | Herald* | Utica | Abolition |
| " | Citizen* | Rome | " |
| Onondaga | Star* | Syracuse | Right |
| " | Journal* | " | Abolition |
| " | Columbian | Skaneateles | Fairish |
| Ontario | Repository | Canandaigua | Right |
| " | Courier | Geneva | Was right, but has been sold to Aboli. |
| Orange | Gazette | Newburgh | Right |
| " | Democrat & Whig | Goshen | Abolition |
| Orleans | American | Albion | Right |
| Oswego | Advertiser* | Oswego | " |
| " | Journal* |  | Abolition |
| Otsego | Republican | Cooperstown | " |
| Queens | Long Island Farmer | Jamaica | Fairish |

*Daily papers

| County | Paper | Place | |
|---|---|---|---|
| Rensselear | Whig* | Troy | Right |
| " | Post* | " | Abolition |
| St. Lawrence | Gazette | Lansingburgh | Fair |
| " | Sentinel | Ogdensburgh | Abolition |
| | Forum | " | " |
| Saratoga | Whig | Saratoga | " |
| " | Journal | Balston | " |
| Schenectady | Cabinet | Schenectady | Right, but softly. |
| Schoharie | Patriot | Schoharie | Abolition |
| Seneca | Courier | Seneca Falls | Was fair, but sold to Abolitionists. |
| Suffolk | Gazette | River Head | Right |
| " | Correctoo | Sag Harbor | Abolition |
| Sullivan | Whig | Bloomingburgh | " |
| Steuben | Courier | Bath | " |
| " | Journal | Corning | Right |
| Tioga | Advertiser | Oswego | " |
| Tompkins | Chronicle | Ithaca | " |
| Ulster | Dem. Journal | Kingston | Abolition |
| Warren | Clarion | Glens Falls | " |
| Washington | Post | Salem | Abolition |
| " | Press | " | " |
| " | Journal | Greenwich | Fair |

*Daily papers

| County | Newspaper | Town | |
|---|---|---|---|
| " | Chronicle | White Hall | " |
| Wayne | Whig | Lyons | Was fair, but now leans towards Abolition. |
| " | Courier | Palmyra | Abolition |
| Westchester | Hudson River Chronicle | Sing Sing | Abolition |
| | Republican | Peekskill | Right |
| " | Western New Yorker | Warsaw | Abolition |
| Wyoming | Whig | Pen Yan | " |
| Yates | | | " |

*Memorandum on Presidential Elections.*[175]    A.

Should amendment be proposed to Constitution,
as to mode of electing a President, as a
means of destroying the asperity of party
feeling and restoring harmony?

As to dissolution, on account of election of objectionable President. This implies that the Govt. is a monarchy and the President a Sovereign, with all power concentrated in himself. Whereas the different departments of Govt. are distinct and separate, and he is under limitations, which if respected will deprive him of mischievous power—this—not the democratic idea.

If his powers are so great, & the election of an adverse candidate so dangerous, it is an argument for abridging his powers by law, or a change of the Constitution; all other remedies are to be resorted to, before amputation.

If these fail, then change the mode of appointment, do anything in the way of change, before resorting to dismemberment.

Disunion implies ever a dishonor to the seceding State. To say nothing of questions of right, and the duty of the Federal Government to compel obedience of a recusant State, let us suppose a single State to have withdrawn leaving the Federal Constitution in full force among the other States, her whole frontiers become foreign frontiers, to be dotted with custom houses and military stations, No Post offices, forts, Army Navy dockyards et cet. except what she might provide for herself. Such State would illustrate the Eastern custom among barbarous Indian nations of a

The question on this subject has always been raised in regard to some Agricultural State of the South, and it has been vehemently insisted that her right to withdraw is perfect, and that such secession would be no cause of offence.

If the right exists at all, it belongs alike to every State. Let us suppose that New York determines to secede—New York whose harbors have been dredged, improved and fortified, by contributions from the Federal treasury of thirty three States, within whose borders, but not upon her soil, (that has been ceded to the Federal Govt) rests the Navy Yard of the Union, with its magnificent stone docks & appliances for building and arming ships of war—whose streets are adorned with marble palaces designated Custom houses, Post offices etc. all the purchase of the

---

[175] A fragment in Graham's writing.

National Treasury, untill she has become the pride of the American Continent. Suppose that New York should, in a fit of excitement, or upon a sordid calculation of advantages to be derived from exactions on the Commerce of the other States, to secede from the Union, and to hold all the public establishments within her limits, although erected and sustained out of the treasure of all the States, would the most zealous defender of State rights allow her to do so, without full equivalents & compensations for all she had received from the Nation?

Imagine, that the seceding State should be California, with all her mines of gold, that we have recently purchased at a great price in treasure and some effusion of the common blood of the Union, would she be allowed to go in peace, and transfer perchance, her golden sands and rich placers, with the predominating influence, if not the sovereignty of Eastern shores of the Pacific to Great Britain or France?

But suppose, the slave holding states in a body, should have declared their independence and determined to secede, would they be content to relinquish all claim to a share in the armaments, arms, Navy yards, docks, arsenals, public structures, and establishments which are ten to one in the Northern States as compared with the Southern, in the hundred Ships of War and their armaments and furniture, which all have contributed the means of acquiring—and the immense domain of the public lands, the common property of all, but situated chiefly in the non slave holding States. Would they be satisfied to relinquish all these national properties and necessities, the fruits of seventy five years of common levies and contributions to their late associates and partners, now rivals and enemies, and begin the world in national destitution, with the prospect in something less than a Century of building up for themselves a fortune in National goods and lands, such as they had contributed to prepare for the Northern confederacy. I say would they consent to a dissolution on these unequal terms? Public sense as well as the most obvious dictates of self defence and protection would forbid it. They would require an equal division in specie of all this public property where it is capable of being reduced to their possession and use, and a full equivalent for what from its nature could not be transferred within their boundaries: and they would be the veriest cravens if they did not exact it. It is thus that a contest of arms would become inevitable. Granting that the Federal Government remained in operation in the adhering States, and that the authorities of that Government should use no effort to enforce the laws against their seceding brethren—the seceding States would be necessitated to make war, for their just share in the present National inheritance, and to take the initiative in that war, or submit to ignominy, poverty and a denial of what they would deem to be the simplest justice. A proposition therefore for secession is a proposition for War, not necessarily by the Government against the seceders, but by the seceders of necessity, against those retaining possession of the Government, and of the public property —A war embittered

# INDEX

## A

Abolitionism, discussed, 204-206.
Abolitionists, mentioned, 359, 369, 371.
Act of Congress, authorizing President to call for volunteers, provisions of, discussed, 149-151.
Adams, James H., on committee desiring to establish newspaper, 207.
Adams, Jesse, identified, 135n.
Adams, John, autograph of, presenting views on form of government, 47; Legislature seeks advice of, 66, 68; letters and correspondence of, mentioned, 65-66.
Adams, John Quincy, proposed to give notice to Great Britain, 106; views of, 90.
Adelphian Society, problems concerning library of at Caldwell Institute, 50-52.
Agricultural Society, Mecklenburg, Constitution and rules of, mentioned, 86, 93.
Albright, William R., mentioned, 272, 273.
Alexander, "Aunt Suzy," mentioned, 58, 61.
Alexander, B., mentioned, 82.
Alexander, H. P., mentioned, 396.
Alexander, J. F., suitable for minor clerkship, 471.
Alexander, John McNitt, copy of document of, mentioned, 220; descendent of, has paper, 93; identified, 82n; mentioned, 83; mentioned as preserver of original Mecklenburg document, 148; paper of, mentioned, 87; reproduced from memory resolutions adopted in Mecklenburg, 82n.
Alexander, Joseph McKnitt, identified, 87n; original papers returned to, 170.
Alexander, Junius, identified, 182n.
Alexander, M. R., has Constitution and rules of the Agricultural Society, 86.
Alexander, Moses Winslow, brother-in-law of Graham, death of, mentioned, 37.
Alexander, Nathaniel, mentioned, 406.
Alexander, Robert, mentioned, 82.
Allen, William, mentioned, 29, 109.
Allison, Dick, mentioned, 173.
Allison, Joseph, letter from, 214-216; makes suggestions for Judge of Supreme Court, 214-216.
Allison, Richard Monroe, identified, 471n.
Allison, Thomas, identified, 471n.
Allston, R. F. W., on committee desiring to establish newspaper, 207.
Alston, Geo. L., mentioned, 339.
Alston, W. F. S., identified, 339n; letter from, 339; seeks public office, 339; unsuccessful concerning *Goldsborough Telegraph*, 339.
Amazon River trip, object of, 434-435.
*American Whig*, mentioned, 493.
Amis, James Sanders, identified, 327n; on commencement program, 129.
Anderson, Walker, identified, 260n; threatened with removal as Navy Agent, 285-286.
Anderson, William E., letter from, 260-261; requests Graham to recommend brother, 260-261.
André, Major (John), trial of, mentioned, 226n.
Andrews, S. A., identified, 164n; letter from, 164-165; recommends Gatlin for appointment, 165; requests delay of appointment in favor of Gatlin, 164-165.
Antitariff movement, only friends of Calhoun interested in, 104.
*Apalachicola Gazette*, mentioned, 499.
Archdale, John, mentioned, 3.
Archer's Resolutions, identified, 64n.
Arnold, Benedict, mentioned, 17n.
Ashe, John S., on committee desiring to establish newspaper, 207.
Ashe, Richard, arrives in Raleigh, 259.
Ashe, Samuel, mentioned, 406.
Ashe, William Shepperd, identified, 267n; re-elected, 242n.
Ashley, Lord, appointed to prepare form of government, 3.
Ashmore, Geo., mentioned, 396.
Attmore, advised Hunter to apply to Bryan for Notary Public, 105; mentioned, 102-103.
Avery, Isaac Thomas, identified, 470n.
Avery, Waightstill, identified, 225n; mentioned, 470.
Avery, William Waightstill, elected

by Burke County, 354; identified, 354n.

Axley, Felix, identified, 141n; letter from, 141-142; relates plans for convention, 141-142; reports on election, 141; requests Graham's views on Cherokee problem, 142.

## B

Badger, George E., aid of, sought, 274, 280, 285; concerned over possible loss of legislature, 236; co-operation of, sought, 265; letter from, 173, 236; letter of David W. Siler sent to, 376; letter of introduction to, sought, 281; letter to, from James Graham, 390-391; may have copy of speech, 113; mentioned, 44, 50, 78, 167, 173, 217-218, 249, 254, 262, 283-284, 313, 319, 348, 355, 356, 389-390, 400, 455, 492; mentioned as secretary of navy, 261; nominated by Whigs, 158; recommends Simonton and his undertaking, 479; relates proceedings of Court of Enquiry in Mexico, 236; requested to see post master general regarding improving mail facilities, 391; sends report on lighthouses, 173; speech of, mentioned, 174n.

Badger, Mrs. George E., mentioned, 455.

Bailey, Henry, on committee desiring to establish newspaper, 207.

Baker, Daniel B., solicits aid in grape enterprise, 396.

Baker, Simmons Jones, identified, 34n.

Ballard, Henry E., identified, 455n.

Ballard, Mrs. Henry E., mentioned, 455.

Ballew, L., mentioned, 138.

Banks, discussed, 112-114; mentioned, 172.

Barnard, John, mentioned, 242n.

Barnwell, Robert W., on committee desiring to establish newspaper, 207.

Barringer, Daniel M., chances of, in the ascendant, 284; letter from, 29, 164, 177-178; mentioned, 133, 178; mentions discontent among volunteers, 177-178; opinion on Oregon question, 29; opinion on Texas question, 29; suggests volunteers to rendezvous at Charlotte, 164.

Barringer, Rufus, elected, 241; identified, 241n.

Bates, Edward, appointed secretary of war, 332, 336; declination of, 369; identified, 332n.

Battle of Brandywine, detailed account of, found, 73.

Battle, Turner W., on commencement program, 129.

Battle, William H., appointed Judge of Supreme Court, 218n; letter for, written by Charles L. Hinton, 401; letter from, 259; letter to, from Samuel F. Phillips, 259-260; mentioned, 16, 108, 215, 260; presides in Superior Court, 227; seeks advice of Graham, 259; votes of, 262.

Battley, John, mentioned, 352.

Battley, Joseph F., congratulates Graham on accession to navy department, 352; expresses satisfaction in Virginia with Graham's appointment, 352; letter from, 352.

Bee, penny paper of Boston, 384, 482.

Benners, Edward Graham, identified, 492n; letter from, 492-493; seeks aid in securing appointment, 492-493.

Benton, Thomas Hart, declares himself candidate for House, 371; mentioned, 23, 29, 173, 174n.

Berkely, William, instructed to organize government in Carolina, 3.

Berrien, John MacPherson, calls to Graham's attention cases of two midshipmen, 403; letter from, 403.

Berry, John, identified, 243n; mentioned, 253, 260, 263-264, 268, 272.

Bettner, George S., mentioned, 21.

Bey, Amin, identified, 402n; Lion of the Day in Washington, 402; to visit with Webster, 456.

Bill, to admit California, to pass without amendment, 370.

Bills, for establishments of territorial governments in New Mexico and Utah, to pass without amendment, 370.

Bittinger, B. F., mentioned, 473.

Bittinger, Edmund Coskery, identified, 473n; letter from, 473-474; offers services, 474; thanks Graham for appointment, 473.

Blake, B. T., mentioned, 341.

Blake, William Kennedy, identified, 74n; on commencement program, 129.

Bloodworthy, Timothy, mentioned, 406.

Davis, Jefferson, gives Kirkland army commission, 375n.

Davis, John, mentioned, 370.

Davis, Oroondates, identified, 28n.

Deaf and Dumb School, opens, 45.

Deberry, Edmund, may be elected, 310; mentioned, 355, 452.

Deems, Charles Force, on committee to arrange program for Polk, 187.

DeHaven, Edward Jesse, commands vessels searching for Sir John Franklin, 363; identified, 363n.

Democratic party, differences of, 113-114; intentions of, 110.

Democrats, mentioned, 106-107, 136.

Desaussure, W. F., on committee desiring to establish newspaper, 207.

Dickinson, P. K., solicits aid in grape enterprise, 396.

Dickson, James Henderson, identified, 394n; letter from, 394-395; solicits aid in behalf of Togno, 394-395.

Dickson, John, Norfolk citizen, makes request, 398.

Dix, Dorothea Lynde, efforts of, for insane asylum, 270; health of, 489-490; identified, 489n; letter from, 489-490; seeks suggestions for introducing bill for reconsideration, 489-490.

Dix, John Adams, identified, 29n.

Dobbin, James Cochran, identified, 98n; may be candidate for governor, 318, 320; plank road of, 267-268; sends letter directed to Taylor in behalf of P. M. Henry, 281.

Dobbs, Arthur, appointed governor, 4; consents to law re-establishing the counties, 5; dies, 2, 5; mentioned, 406.

Dockery, Alfred, accepts offer of Commandant, 160; canvasses for Congress, 80; expresses views on appointment of field officers, 174-175; identified, 116n; letter from, 160, 174-175.

Donoho, Monroe, mentioned, 349.

Douglas, Stephen A., goes to Mississippi to look after estate, 230.

Douglas, Mrs. Stephen A., mentioned, 230.

Downey, James W., describes excursion, 85; identified, 84n; letter from, 84-85; seeks opinion of Whitney's scheme, 85.

Dromgoole, George Coke, identified, 63n; resolution of, 63.

Drummond, William, appointed governor, 3; dies, 3.

Duane, William J., mentioned, 250.

Dudley, E. B., solicits aid in grape enterprise, 396.

Duke, William James, identified, 74n.

Dusenbery, Henry McRorie, identified, 243n; on committee of Dialectic Society, 243.

Duties on Indian Corn and Pork, mentioned, 107.

### E

East Tennessee Historical and Antiquarian Society, objects and intentions of, 220-221.

Eaton, George, elected representative of county in Arkansas, 361.

Eden, Charles, arrives, 3-4; dies, 4.

Edney, Bayles M., may be appointed consul at Glasgow, 319.

Edwards, James G., identified, 141n.

Edwards, Leonidas Compton, identified, 483n; seeks government employment abroad, 483-484.

Ehringhaus, John Christoph Blucher, identified 139n; mentioned, 135.

Eliot, Samuel Atkins, elected, 370; identified, 370n.

Ellis, John Willis, identified, 241n; re-elected, 241.

Episcopal Church, provided for, 5.

Erwin, Adolphus Lorenzo, identified, 470n; mentioned, 471.

Erwin, Bulow, mentioned, 471.

Erwin, Edward Jones, identified, 470n.

Erwin, Joseph J., identified, 470n.

Estill, Benjamin, identified, 352n.

Eustis, George, identified, 351n; letter of, recommending Robert Ogden, mentioned, 351.

Evans, Charles N. B., explains advertising account, 132-133; identified, 132n; letter from, 132-133; solicits appointment of W. A. Whitfield, 132.

Evans, Frederic W., mentioned, 56.

Everard, Richard, appointed governor, 4; mentioned, 406; removed, 4.

F

Fagg, John A., identified, 161n; letter to, 183-184; mentioned, 178, 179, 181; recommended as Lieutenant Colonel, 161.

Fairfield, John, identified, 29n.

Fanning, Edmund, identified, 28n.

Fayetteville Arsenal, mentioned, 152.

*Fayetteville Observer*, comments of, 97n; mentioned, 313-314.

Fearn, Richard Lee, letter from, 304-305; suggests usefulness of his son, 304-305.

Ferrand, William Pugh, identified, 140n.

Ficklin, Orlando Bell, identified, 171n.

Fillmore, Millard, administration of, mentioned, 392, 401, 458; appoints Graham acting Secretary of Interior, 453; appoints Graham acting Secretary of War, 447; cabinet of, mentioned, 326-327, 329, 333, 348, 353, 359; concurs in testimonial of Simonton, 480; confidence in, expressed, 387; congratulated as president, 338; course of, commended, 503; determines to tender an appointment to North Carolina, 327; Graham sends acceptance to, 337-338; hopes Graham will accept secretary of navy office, 333; insists Graham take the Interior office, 369; instructions of, regarding use of marines in civil matters, 468-469; letter from, 333, 348; letter to, 337-338, 396, 398-399; mentioned, 326, 330, 331, 332n, 334, 351, 362, 369, 371, 377, 388, 402, 403, 405, 450, 456, 459, 462, 464, 492; message of, delivered, 486; nominations of, 336; note from, 447, 453; reply of, sent for publication, 237; requested dispatches be sent to Graham, 336; requested to make changes in offices, 396; requested to remove navy agent, 398; requests cabinet members to remain one month, 331; returns "heir loom" to Graham, 348; thanks Graham for books on navy, 348; written to regarding West Point appointment, 502.

First steam vessel, mentioned, 431.

Fisher, Charles, arrives in Washington, 90; conduct of, mentioned, 116; mentioned as candidate for governor, 88, 90.

Fitzpatrick, Benjamin, identified, 111n.

Fleming, Samuel, identified, 193n; mentioned, 193-194.

Florian, identified, 226n.

*Florida Republican*, mentioned, 499.

*Florida Sentinel*, mentioned, 499.

*Florida Whig*, mentioned, 494, 499.

Foltz, Jonathan M., desires to be surgeon on "Susquehanna," 385; identified, 384n.

Foote, William Henry, attempts to set up school, 94; desires corrected copy of original papers, 93; enclosure of, to Swain, 93-94; his history of the Presbyterian church, 83; his *Sketches of North Carolina*, ready for perusal, 152; identified, 82n; letter from, 82-83, 85-86, 152; letter to, 86-87; mentioned, 83; thanks Graham for assistance, 152.

Forbes, Richard N., on commencement program, 129.

Foster, Ephraim, identified, 64n.

Foy, William, identified, 140n.

Francis, Michael, letter to, 134; mentioned, 194.

Franklin, Jesse, identified, 224n; mentioned, 406.

Franklin, Sir John, search for, mentioned, 363.

Fraser, P. W., on committee desiring to establish newspaper, 207.

Freeman, William G., discusses instructions for inspecting and mustering volunteers, 153-156; identified, 153n; letter from, to R. D. A. Wade, 153-156.

Free trade, mentioned, 172.

Fremont, Sewall L., identified, 180n; mentioned, 184.

French, David, letter from, 55-56; sends and discusses Shaker book, 55-57.

Fugitive Slave Bill, passes Senate, 369; to pass without amendment, 370.

G

Gadsden, James, on committee desiring to establish newspaper, 207.

Gaines, Edmund Pendleton, identified, 17n; letter from, 17-20; views on defense of sea port towns, 17-20.

Gaither, Burgess S., hopes Graham will visit western counties, 133-134; letter from, 133-134; men-

## P

Paine, Robert Treat, acquittal of, 236; commands regiment, 212n; discussed, 216-217; identified, 139n; letter from, 287-288, 289, 305-306, 460; mutiny of troops of, 212n, possible resignation of, 212-217; regrets Graham's declination of appointment to Spain, 305; requests Graham to promote Dr. Warren's wishes, 460; sends letter directed to Taylor in behalf of Patrick M. Henry, 281; suggests that Graham prevail on Senator Mangum to return home, 306; urges Graham to accept appointment to Spain, 287-288, 289; vindication of, 236.

Parsley, O. G., solicits aid in grape enterprise, 396.

Patillo, Henry, seeks appointment, 14.

Patterson, Mann, son of, mentioned, 263.

Patterson, Samuel F., declines appointment, 137; elected senator, 138; letter from, 136-138; letter from, to Haywood W. Guion, 487-488; recommended as Assistant Post Master General and chief clerkship, 482-483; recommends W. F. Jones for appointment, 137; sends copy of election returns, 137; would decline appointment, 487.

Pearce, James Alfred, appointed Secretary of Interior, 331, 336; identified, 331n.

Pearson, Richmond M., favor of, expressed, 215, 219; mentioned, 241n, 260, 313; suggested for appointment as Judge of Supreme Court, 213-214, 214-216.

Peel, Robert, mentioned, 107.

Pender, Josiah S., conduct of, investigated, 217; identified, 212n; suggests Paine's resignation, 212n.

Pendleton, Edward, mentioned, 28n.

Pendleton, John Strother, identified, 465n; letter from, 465-467; relates cases of political disappointment, 465-467.

Penitentiary, question of, identified, 109n.

Penn, John, descendants having papers of, sought, 359; identified, 28n; mentioned, 406.

*Pennsylvanian,* assails Graham regarding removal of "Susquehanna," 485.

*Pensacola Gazette,* mentioned, 494, 499.

Perkins, J. Q., letter from, 158; seeks appointment as chief surgeon, 158.

Perkins, Thomas Handasyd, identified, 21n.

Perly, Edward, desires place at Annapolis, 503.

Peronneau, H. W., on committee desiring to establish newspaper, 207.

Perry, Matthew Calbraith, identified, 474n; mentioned as commander of Gosport Navy Yard, 474-476.

Peyton, Balie, letter to, mentioned, 237; requested to send letter, 236.

Phelps, Samuel Shethar, identified, 35n; letter from, 35-36; letter to, 39; requests Graham's recollection on charges against him, 35-36.

Phillips, James, mentioned, 324n.

Phillips, Samuel Field, identified, 324n; letter from, 324; letter to William H. Battle, 259-260; requests Graham's advice, 324.

Phillips, Tutor, on committee to arrange program for Polk, 187.

Phoenix, J. Phillips, concurs in Simonton testimonial, 480.

Pickens, Israel, identified, 226n.

Pierce's Boundary Bill, mentioned, 492.

Piggott, Jennings, identified, 140n.

Pitkin, Timothy, identified, 148n.

Plank road bill, passes, 273.

Plympton, G. M., identified, 355n; seeks appointment as midshipman, 355.

Plympton, Joseph, identified, 355n; son of, seeks appointment as midshipman, 355.

Poindexter, John F., senator from Stokes, 139.

Polk, Ezekiel, mentioned in connection with Mecklenburg Declaration; 92; identified, 92n; name of, found on Constitution and rules of an Agricultural Society, 93.

Polk, James K., administration of, mentioned, 223n, 344, 345, 381; choice paper of, 344; communicates proceedings of Court of Enquiry, 236; course of, in relation to Texas, mentioned, 113; identified, 185n; illness of, 209; killed by having filled the Presidential chair, 353; mail facilities during misrule of, 390; mentioned, 79, 250; message of, 90; opinion on, 246; physical condition of, 109; plans to visit University, 185; receives L.L.D. degree, 47; visit of, to University, 187, 188, 192.

Polk, Leonidas, mentioned 346.

Polk, Lucius Junius, identified, 22n; mentioned, 346.

Polk, William, mentioned, 22n.

Pollock, Thomas, dies, 4.

Pope, William, on committee desiring to establish newspaper, 207.

Porter, William David, identified, 403n; letter from, 403; sends pipe and sample of tobacco, 403.

Potter, George W., commission requested for, 159.

Presidents of the United States, list of and information about the first 11, 49-50.

Preston, John S., on committee desiring to establish newspaper, 207.

Preston, William Ballard, administration of, refused printing to Syme, 350; identified, 350n.

Pringle, William Bull, on committee desiring to establish newspaper, 207.

Puett, William, mentioned, 138.

Putnam, H., mentioned, 396.

### Q

Quincy, Joseph, plans resistance to mother country policy, 226n.

Quincy, Josiah, heads agitation of Fugitive Slave law, 453; identified, 453n.

Quitman, John Anthony, identified, 240n.

### R

Railroad, bill, discussed, 267n; convention, to be held in Salisbury, 278, 282, 284; mentioned, 108, 116, 321; project, favor shown for, 262; stock, all subscribed, 318.

Raleigh and Gaston Railroad, liabilities for, mentioned, 110.

*Raleigh Register*, copy of charter published in, 277; Manly to reply in, 365; mentioned, 68, 181, 192, 247, 494; quotation from, 119n.

Raleigh *Sentinel*, mentioned, 314n.

Raleigh, Sir Walter, mentioned, 2.

Raleigh *Star*, mentioned, 486n.

Ramsey, James Gettys McGready, identified, 219n; letter from, 219-220; seeks information on early history of Tennessee from North Carolina archives, 219-220.

Rankin, Robert G., identified, 159n.

Ransom, Chandler R., supports administration, 384.

Rayner, Kenneth, declination of candidacy for governor, mentioned, 212; letter from, 23, 461-462; letter to, from Charles Lee Jones, 157; seeks continuance of mail service to Winton, 461-462; sends letter directed to Taylor in behalf of Patrick M. Henry, 281.

Read, George Campbell, identified, 468n; letter to, 468-470.

Read, J. Harleston, on committee desiring to establish newspaper, 207.

Recommendation, in favor of grape enterprise, 395-396.

Reed, Robert Rantoul, identified, 341n; mentioned, 396.

Reed, William, succeeds Pollock as president of council, 4.

Reid, David Settle, addresses people in Raleigh, 230; beats Manly, 354; demagoguical doctrine of free suffrage of, mentioned, 238; furnishes issue of equal suffrage, 230; Manly's majority over, 343; may run against Manly, 318; not as strong electionally as before, 337; proposition of, 232-235; sends letter directed to Taylor in behalf of Patrick M. Henry, 281; votes of, 240-241, 242.

Reid, James, affirms to defend and preserve Constitution, 387; expresses desire that Union be upheld, 387-388; letter from, 387-388; seeks job as agent in Post Office Department, 388.

Reid, Rufus, mentioned, 471.

Reinhardt, David, letter from, 196-199; views and suggestions on railroads, 196-199.

*Republic*, had government advertisements by choice of the President, 345.

*Republican*, rumor of Knox's drowning made appearance in, 458.

Rice, Nathaniel, dies, 4; succeeds Johnston as governor, 4.

Richards, Willard, identified, 43n.

Richardson, John P., on committee desiring to establish newspaper, 207.

Riddle, Charles, member of invitation committee for ball honoring Henry Clay, 315.

communication to, 237; death of, 326, 347-349; desired Pendleton to go on mission, 467; discussed as military man president, 249-250; fear of, 283; in conversation with Johnston, 211-212; letter to, feared lost, 236; may be rejected by Alabama, 245; mentioned, 171, 173, 222, 240, 245, 249, 251, 255, 261, 274, 281, 342, 350, 353, 371, 397, 401, 466, 492; nominated, 230; popularity of, destroyed by Clayton, 398; promise of, sought, regarding Gatlin's appointment, 356; support of, 246, 248; to be nominee, 229; votes of, 252, 255.

Tazewell, Littleton Waller, identified, 38n.

Temple, Robert Emmet, identified, 274n.

Templeton, Rufus R., mentioned, 471.

Tennessee, legislature of, list of members of, seeking government patronage for *True Whig*, 367-368.

*Ten* Regiment Bill, mentioned, 178-179.

Texas, annexation, 33, 63-65, 89, 457; boundary bill, 370, 392; question, 29; resolution, 23.

Thomas, John W., identified, 311n.

Thomas, William H., elected, 242n.

Thompson, Lewis, identified, 272n.

Thompson, Waddy, mentioned, 371.

Thurman, John R., mentioned, 396.

Tibbalt, John Williston, identified, 274n.

Togno, Joseph, at University commencement states wishes to introduce culture of grape in North Carolina, 393-394, 399; desires aid of consuls in securing grapevine cuttings, 394-395; establishes vineyard near Wilmington, 393; gives directions for packing cuttings, 400; identified, 393n; letter from, 399-400; seeks Graham's aid in his behalf, 394-395, 400.

Tomlinson, Theodore E., identified, 315n; member of invitation committee for ball honoring Henry Clay, 315.

Toombs, Robert, identified, 493n.

Trapier, W. H., on committee desiring to establish newspaper, 207.

Treaty of 1818, provisions of, mentioned, 90.

Trenholm, George A., on committee desiring to establish newspaper, 207.

Trousdale, William, elected governor of Tennessee, 309.

Tryon, William, army of, mentioned, 225; expedition of, 224n; liberal towards dissenters, 5; mentioned, 406; succeeds Dobbs as governor, 5.

Tuomey, Michael, identified, 490n; sends copy of Report of Geology of Alabama to Graham, 491.

Turnbull, Andrew, on committee desiring to establish newspaper, 207.

Turner, James, mentioned, 406.

Turner, Josiah, identified, 312n.

Turnpike Road, discussed, 33-34.

### U

Underhill, Walter, concurs in Simonton testimonial, 480; mentioned, 396.

*Union*, had government advertisements by law, 345; mentioned, 206.

University of North Carolina, enrollment of, 377.

### V

Van Buren, Martin, mentioned, 33, 208, 248.

Venable, Abraham Watkins, discussion with Miller, 484; identified, 484n.

Venable, Samuel Frederick, identified, 184n.

Vesuvius Furnace, gold and limestone found near, 227.

Virginia, boundary line of, run, 4.

*Volksblatt*, mentioned, 345.

Volunteers, discontent of, 177-178.

### W

Waddell, Hugh, agrees to be presented for consulate at Havana, 462; appointed to treat with Indians, 4; appointment as minister abroad, 283-284; appointment of, 288, 483; believed entitled to seat, 268; compliments Graham, 338; disturbed concerning premature publicity of appointment as consulate, 472-473; elected, 241, 242, 248; expresses gratitude to Graham, 463-464; expresses thoughts on position of consul, 462-463; informs Graham of Central Railroad Bill passage in Senate, 271; letter from, 175-176, 252-255, 263-264, 271-272, 338, 462-463, 463-464, 472-473; letter of, to University Board of Trustees, mentioned, 52-53; may not obtain seat, 272; mentioned, 78, 139, 213, 243, 249, 259, 260,